A·N·N·U·A·L E·D·I·T·I·O·N·S

Anthropology

Twenty-Sixth Edition

03/04

EDITOR

Elvio Angeloni

Pasadena City College

Elvio Angeloni received his B.A. from UCLA in 1963, his M.A. in anthropology from UCLA in 1965, and his M.A. in communication arts from Loyola Marymount University in 1976. He has produced several films, including *Little Warrior,* winner of the Cinemedia VI Best Bicentennial Theme, and *Broken Bottles*, shown on PBS. He most recently served as an academic adviser on the instructional television series *Faces of Culture*.

McGraw-Hill/Dushkin

530 Old Whitfield Street, Guilford, Connecticut 06437

Visit us on the Internet
http://www.dushkin.com

Credits

1. **Anthropological Perspectives**
   Unit photo—United Nations photo by Doranne Jacobson.
2. **Culture and Communication**
   Unit photo—United Nations photo
3. **The Organization of Society and Culture**
   Unit photo—United Nations photo.
4. **Other Families, Other Ways**
   Unit photo—United Nations photo
5. **Gender and Status**
   Unit photo—United Nations photo by A. Hollmann.
6. **Religion, Belief, and Ritual**
   Unit photo—© 2003 by PhotoDisc, Inc.
7. **Sociocultural Change: The Impact of the West**
   Unit photo—© Robert Azzi/Woodfin Camp.

Copyright

Cataloging in Publication Data
Main entry under title: Annual Editions: Anthropology. 2003/2004.
1. Anthropology—Periodicals. I. Angeloni, Elvio II. Title: Anthropology.
ISBN 0–07–254851–7   658'.05   ISSN 1091–613X

Twenty-Sixth Edition

Cover image © 2003 PhotoDisc, Inc.
Printed in the United States of America   1234567890BAHBAH543   Printed on Recycled Paper

Editors/Advisory Board

Members of the Advisory Board are instrumental in the final selection of articles for each edition of ANNUAL EDITIONS. Their review of articles for content, level, currentness, and appropriateness provides critical direction to the editor and staff. We think that you will find their careful consideration well reflected in this volume.

To the Reader

In publishing ANNUAL EDITIONS we recognize the enormous role played by the magazines, newspapers, and journals of the public press in providing current, first-rate educational information in a broad spectrum of interest areas. Many of these articles are appropriate for students, researchers, and professionals seeking accurate, current material to help bridge the gap between principles and theories and the real world. These articles, however, become more useful for study when those of lasting value are carefully collected, organized, indexed, and reproduced in a low-cost format, which provides easy and permanent access when the material is needed. That is the role played by ANNUAL EDITIONS.

This twenty-sixth edition of *Annual Editions: Anthropology* contains a variety of articles on contemporary issues in social and cultural anthropology. In contrast to the broad range of topics and minimum depth typical of standard textbooks, this anthology provides an opportunity to read firsthand accounts by anthropologists of their own research. In allowing scholars to speak for themselves about the issues on which they are expert, we are better able to understand the kind of questions anthropologists ask, the ways in which they ask them, and how they go about searching for answers. Indeed, where there is disagreement among anthropologists, this format allows the readers to draw their own conclusions.

Given the very broad scope of anthropology—in time, space, and subject matter—the present collection of highly readable articles has been selected according to certain criteria. The articles have been chosen from both professional and nonprofessional publications for the purpose of supplementing the standard textbook in cultural anthropology that is used in introductory courses. Some of the articles are considered classics in the field, while others have been selected for their timely relevance.

Included in this volume are a number of features designed to make it useful for students, researchers, and professionals in the field of anthropology. While the articles are arranged along the lines of broadly unifying themes, the *topic guide* can be used to establish specific reading assignments tailored to the needs of a particular course of study. Other useful features include the *table of contents* abstracts, which summarize each article and present key concepts in italics, and a comprehensive *index*. In addition, each unit is preceded by an overview, which provides a background for informed reading of the articles, emphasizes critical issues, and presents *key points to consider*.

Finally, there are *World Wide Web* sites that can be used to further explore the topics.

Annual Editions: Anthropology 03/04 will continue to be updated annually. Those involved in producing the volume wish to make the next one as useful and effective as possible. Your criticism and advice always are welcome. Please fill out the postage-paid article rating form on the last page of the book and let us know your opinions. Any anthology can be improved. This continues to be—annually.

Elvio Angeloni
Editor
evangeloni@paccd.cc.ca.us

Contents

UNIT 1
Anthropological Perspectives

Five selections examine the role of anthropologists in studying different cultures. The innate problems in developing productive relationships between anthropologists and exotic cultures are considered by reviewing a number of fieldwork experiences.

The concepts in bold italics are developed in the article. For further expansion, please refer to the Topic Guide and the Index.

UNIT 2
Culture and Communication

Four selections discuss communication as an element of culture. Ingrained social and cultural values have a tremendous effect on an individual's perception or interpretation of both verbal and nonverbal communication.

UNIT 3
The Organization of Society and Culture

The four selections in this unit discuss the influence of the environment and culture on the organization of the social structures of groups.

The concepts in bold italics are developed in the article. For further expansion, please refer to the Topic Guide and the Index.

UNIT 4
Other Families, Other Ways

Eight selections examine some of the influences on the family structure of different cultures. The strength of the family unit is affected by both economic and social pressures.

The concepts in bold italics are developed in the article. For further expansion, please refer to the Topic Guide and the Index.

UNIT 5
Gender and Status

The six selections in this unit discuss some of the sex roles prescribed by the social, economic, and political forces of a culture.

The concepts in bold italics are developed in the article. For further expansion, please refer to the Topic Guide and the Index.

UNIT 6
Religion, Belief, and Ritual

Five selections examine the roles of religion, ritual, and magic in a culture. The need to develop a religion is universal among societies.

UNIT 7
Sociocultural Change: The Impact of the West

Eight articles examine the influence that the developed world has had on primitive cultures. Exposure to the industrial West often has disastrous effects on the delicate balance of primitive society.

The concepts in bold italics are developed in the article. For further expansion, please refer to the Topic Guide and the Index.

The concepts in bold italics are developed in the article. For further expansion, please refer to the Topic Guide and the Index.

Topic Guide

This topic guide suggests how the selections in this book relate to the subjects covered in your course. You may want to use the topics listed on these pages to search the Web more easily.

On the following pages a number of Web sites have been gathered specifically for this book. They are arranged to reflect the units of this *Annual Edition.* You can link to these sites by going to the DUSHKIN ONLINE support site at *http://www.dushkin.com/online/.*

ALL THE ARTICLES THAT RELATE TO EACH TOPIC ARE LISTED BELOW THE BOLD-FACED TERM.

Acculturation
20. Dowry Deaths in India: 'Let Only Your Corpse Come Out of That House'
21. Who Needs Love! In Japan, Many Couples Don't
28. It Takes a Village Healer
34. The Arrow of Disease
35. "Drought Follows the Plow"
36. The Price of Progress
37. A Pacific Haze: Alcohol and Drugs in Oceania
38. A Plunge Into the Present
39. Underground Potlatch

Aggression
20. Dowry Deaths in India: 'Let Only Your Corpse Come Out of That House'
34. The Arrow of Disease

Altruism
4. Eating Christmas in the Kalahari
12. Too Many Bananas, Not Enough Pineapples, and No Watermelon at All: Three Object Lessons in Living With Reciprocity

Child care
16. Death Without Weeping
17. Our Babies, Ourselves
26. Where Fat Is a Mark of Beauty

Children
16. Death Without Weeping
17. Our Babies, Ourselves
26. Where Fat Is a Mark of Beauty

Communication
6. Language, Appearance, and Reality: Doublespeak in 1984
7. Why Don't You Say What You Mean?
8. "I Can't Even Open My Mouth"
9. Shakespeare in the Bush

Cooperation
4. Eating Christmas in the Kalahari
12. Too Many Bananas, Not Enough Pineapples, and No Watermelon at All: Three Object Lessons in Living With Reciprocity

Cross-cultural experience
1. Doing Fieldwork Among the Yanomamö
2. Spin-Doctoring the Yanomamö
3. Doctor, Lawyer, Indian Chief
4. Eating Christmas in the Kalahari
7. Why Don't You Say What You Mean?
9. Shakespeare in the Bush
10. Understanding Eskimo Science
12. Too Many Bananas, Not Enough Pineapples, and No Watermelon at All: Three Object Lessons in Living With Reciprocity
16. Death Without Weeping
17. Our Babies, Ourselves
19. Arranging a Marriage in India

Cultural change
28. It Takes a Village Healer
40. What Americans Don't Know About Indians

2. Spin-Doctoring the Yanomamö
13. Life Without Chiefs
17. Our Babies, Ourselves
20. Dowry Deaths in India: 'Let Only Your Corpse Come Out of That House'
21. Who Needs Love! In Japan, Many Couples Don't
28. It Takes a Village Healer
33. Why Can't People Feed Themselves?
34. The Arrow of Disease
35. "Drought Follows the Plow"
36. The Price of Progress
37. A Pacific Haze: Alcohol and Drugs in Oceania
38. A Plunge Into the Present
39. Underground Potlatch

Cultural diversity
7. Why Don't You Say What You Mean?
13. Life Without Chiefs
17. Our Babies, Ourselves
19. Arranging a Marriage in India
23. The Berdache Tradition
25. What About "Female Genital Mutilation"?
28. It Takes a Village Healer
35. "Drought Follows the Plow"
39. Underground Potlatch
40. What Americans Don't Know About Indians

Cultural identity
5. Battle of the Bones
17. Our Babies, Ourselves
25. What About "Female Genital Mutilation"?
26. Where Fat Is a Mark of Beauty
38. A Plunge Into the Present
39. Underground Potlatch

Cultural relativity
1. Doing Fieldwork Among the Yanomamö
4. Eating Christmas in the Kalahari
7. Why Don't You Say What You Mean?
17. Our Babies, Ourselves
19. Arranging a Marriage in India
25. What About "Female Genital Mutilation"?
28. It Takes a Village Healer
31. Body Ritual Among the Nacirema
40. What Americans Don't Know About Indians

Culture shock
1. Doing Fieldwork Among the Yanomamö

Ecology and society
10. Understanding Eskimo Science
11. Mystique of the Masai
14. When Brothers Share a Wife
22. Society and Sex Roles
33. Why Can't People Feed Themselves?
34. The Arrow of Disease

World Wide Web Sites

The following World Wide Web sites have been carefully researched and selected to support the articles found in this reader. The easiest way to access these selected sites is to go to our DUSHKIN ONLINE support site at *http://www.dushkin.com/online/*.

AE: Anthropology 03/04

The following sites were available at the time of publication. Visit our Web site—we update DUSHKIN ONLINE regularly to reflect any changes.

General Sources

American Anthropologist

http://www.aaanet.org

Check out this site—the home page of the American Anthropology Association—for general information about the field of anthropology as well as access to a wide variety of articles.

Anthropology Links

http://www.gmu.edu/departments/anthro/links.htm

George Mason University's Department of Anthropology Web site provides a number of interesting links.

Latin American Studies

http://www.library.arizona.edu/research.htm

Click on Latin American Studies to access an extensive list of resources—links to encyclopedias, journals, indexes, almanacs, and handbooks, and to the Latin American Network Information Center and Internet Resources for Latin American Studies.

Web Resources for Visual Anthropology

http://www.usc.edu/dept/elab/urlist/index.html

This UR-List offers a mouse-click selection of Web resources by cross-indexing 375 anthropological sites according to 22 subject categories.

UNIT 1: Anthropological Perspectives

American Indian Sites on the Internet

http://www.library.arizona.edu/library/teams/sst/anthro/web/indians.html

This Web page points out a number of Internet sites of interest to different kinds of anthropologists.

Anthropology Fieldstudy

http://www.truman.edu/academics/ss/faculty/tamakoshil/index.html

This site gives a detailed report on how to prepare for and conduct fieldwork. Laura Zimmer Tamakoshi's experience in Papua New Guinea is must reading for any anthropologist planning to do research in the field.

Archaeology and Anthropology Computing and Study Skills

http://www.bodley.ox.ac.uk/isca/CASShome.html

Consult this site of the Institute of Social and Cultural Anthropology to learn about ways to use the computer as an aid in conducting fieldwork, methodology, and analysis.

The Crisis in Anthropology

http://www.comma2000.com/max-gluckman/index.html

The differences between anthropologists' perspectives are made clear in this First Max Gluckman Memorial Lecture, delivered by Professor Bruce Kapferer on May 17, 1997.

Introduction to Anthropological Fieldwork and Ethnography

http://web.mit.edu/dumit/www/syl-anth.html

This class outline can serve as an invaluable resource for conducting anthropological fieldwork. Addressing such topics as The Interview and Power Relations in the Field, the site identifies many important books and articles for further reading.

Theory in Anthropology

http://www.indiana.edu/~wanthro/theory.htm

These Web pages cover subdisciplines within anthropology, changes in perspectives over time, and prominent theorists, reflecting 30 years of dramatic changes in the field.

UNIT 2: Culture and Communication

Exploratorium Magazine: "The Evolution of Languages"

http://www.exploratorium.edu/exploring/language

Where did languages come from and how did they evolve? This educational site explains the history and origin of language. You can also investigate words, word stems, and the similarities between different languages.

Hypertext and Ethnography

http://www.umanitoba.ca/anthropology/tutor/aaa_presentation.html

Presented by Brian Schwimmer of the University of Manitoba, this site will be of great value to people who are interested in culture and communication. Schwimmer addresses such topics as multivocality and complex symbolization.

Language Extinction

http://www.colorado.edu/iec/alis/articles/langext.htm

"An often overlooked fact in the ecological race against environmental extinction is that many of the world's languages are disappearing at an alarming rate." This article investigates language extinction and its possible consequences.

Showcase Anthropology

http://www.usc.edu/dept/education/mascha/showcase.html

Examples of documents that make innovative use of the Web as a tool for "an anthropology of the future"—one consisting of multimedia representations in a nonlinear and interactive form—are provided on this Web site.

UNIT 3: The Organization of Society and Culture

Huarochirì, a Peruvian Culture in Time

http://wiscinfo.doit.wisc.edu/chaysimire/

Take a tour of this Andean province, visit Tupicocha (a modern village), and learn about the ancient Quechua Book and Khipus, a unique legacy.

Smithsonian Institution Web Site

http://www.si.edu

Looking through this site, which provides access to many of the enormous resources of the Smithsonian, will give a sense of the scope of anthropological inquiry today.

www.dushkin.com/online/

Sociology Guy's Anthropology Links

http://www.trinity.edu/~mkearl/anthro.html

This list of anthropology resources on the Web is suggested by a sociology professor at Trinity University and includes cultures of Asia, Africa, the Middle East; Aztecan, Mayan, and aboriginal cultures; sections on Mythology, Folklore, Legends, and Archeology; plus much more.

What Is Culture?

http://www.wsu.edu:8001/vcwsu/commons/topics/culture/culture-index.html

Here is a source for everything you might want to know about "culture," starting with a baseline definition.

UNIT 4: Other Families, Other Ways

Dowry Death

http://www.indianwomenonline.com/womenhome/Serious/law/dowry/dowrybot.asp

This article from Indian Women Online describes the legal actions that can be taken to help put a stop to dowry death.

"Here, No Stigma Is Attached to Polyandry"

http://www.hindustantimes.com/nonfram/260600/detNAT05.htm

This essay describes polyandry—an age-old custom that allows a woman to keep more than one husband—and why this is normal practice in the Himalayan region.

Kinship and Social Organization

http://www.umanitoba.ca/anthropology/tutor/kinmenu.html

Kinship, marriage systems, residence rules, incest taboos, and cousin marriages are explored in this kinship tutorial.

UNIT 5: Gender and Status

Arranged Marriages

http://women3rdworld.miningco.com/cs/arrangedmarriage/

This site, provided by ABOUT, contains a number of papers on arranged marriages. It also has links to other related women's issues subjects and forums.

Bonobo Sex and Society

http://songweaver.com/info/bonobos.html

This site includes a *Scientific American* article discussing a primate's behavior that challenges traditional assumptions about male supremacy in human evolution.

FGM Research

http://www.fgm.com

Dedicated to research pertaining to Female Genital Mutilation (FGM), this site presents a variety of perspectives: psychological, cultural, sexual, human rights, and so on.

OMIM Home Page-Online Mendelian Inheritance in Man

http://www3.ncbi.nlm.nih.gov/omim/

This National Center for Biotechnology Information database is a catalog of human genes and genetic disorders. It contains text, pictures, and reference information.

Reflections on Sinai Bedouin Women

http://www.sherryart.com/women/bedouin.html

Social anthropologist Ann Gardner tells something of her culture shock while first living with a Sinai Bedouin family as a teenager. She provides links to sites about organization of society and culture, particularly with regard to women.

UNIT 6: Religion, Belief, and Ritual

Anthropology Resources Page

http://www.usd.edu/anth/

Many topics can be accessed from this University of South Dakota Web site. Repatriation and reburial are just two.

Masks.org

http://www.masks.org

Masks have been an important part of many cultures' burial and death rituals. Visit this site to look at an exhibition center showing the work of maskmakers from around the world.

Philosophy of Religion: Magic, Ritual, and Symbolism

http://www.kcmetro.cc.mo.us/longview/socsci/philosophy/religion/magic.htm

This site presents course notes for a Philosophy of Religion class in which the roles of magic, ritual, and symbolism are examined. Links to many helpful reading options are provided.

Yahoo: Society and Culture: Death

http://dir.yahoo.com/Society_and_Culture/Death_and_Dying/

This Yahoo site has an extensive index to diverse issues related how different people approach death, such as beliefs about euthanasia, reincarnation, and burial.

UNIT 7: Sociocultural Change: The Impact of the West

Human Rights and Humanitarian Assistance

http://www.etown.edu/vl/humrts.html

Through this site you can conduct research into a number of human rights topics and issues affecting indigenous peoples in the modern era.

The Indigenous Rights Movement in the Pacific

http://www.inmotionmagazine.com/pacific.html

This article addresses issues that pertain to the problems of the Pacific Island peoples as a result of U.S. colonial expansion in the Pacific and Caribbean 100 years ago.

RomNews Network—Online

http://www.romnews.com/community/index.php

This is a Web site dedicated to news and information for and about the Roma (European Gypsies). Visit here to learn more about their culture and the discrimation they constantly face.

WWW Virtual Library: Indigenous Studies

http://www.cwis.org/wwwvl/indig-vl.html

This site presents resources collected by the Center for World Indigenous Studies (CWIS) in Africa, Asia and the Middle East, Central and South America, Europe, and the Pacific.

World Map

Scale: 1 to 125,000,000

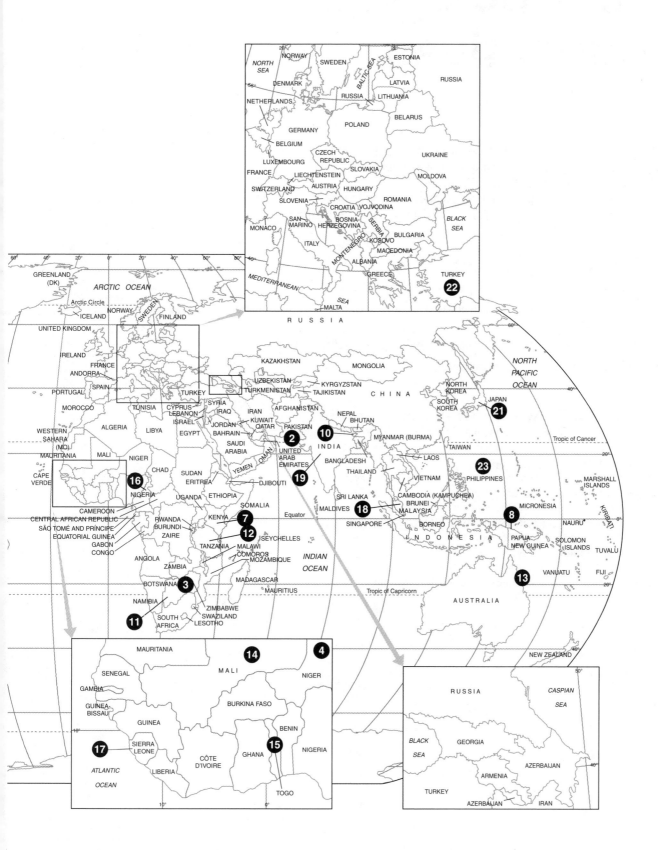

UNIT 1
Anthropological Perspectives

Unit Selections

1. **Doing Fieldwork Among the Yanomamö**, Napoleon A. Chagnon
2. **Spin-Doctoring the Yanomamö**, Michael Shermer
3. **Doctor, Lawyer, Indian Chief**, Richard Kurin
4. **Eating Christmas in the Kalahari**, Richard Borshay Lee
5. **Battle of the Bones**, Robson Bonnichsen and Alan L. Schneider

Key Points to Consider

- What is culture shock?

- How can anthropologists who become personally involved with a community through participant observation maintain their objectivity as scientists?

- In what ways do the results of fieldwork depend on the kinds of questions asked?

- In what sense is sharing intrinsic to egalitarianism?

 **Links: www.dushkin.com/online/**
These sites are annotated in the World Wide Web pages.

American Indian Sites on the Internet
http://www.library.arizona.edu/library/teams/sst/anthro/web/indians.html

Anthropology Fieldstudy
http://www.truman.edu/academics/ss/faculty/tamakoshil/index.html

Archaeology and Anthropology Computing and Study Skills
http://www.bodley.ox.ac.uk/isca/CASShome.html

The Crisis in Anthropology
http://www.comma2000.com/max-gluckman/index.html

Introduction to Anthropological Fieldwork and Ethnography
http://web.mit.edu/dumit/www/syl-anth.html

Theory in Anthropology
http://www.indiana.edu/~wanthro/theory.htm

For at least a century, the goals of anthropology have been to describe societies and cultures throughout the world and to compare the differences and similarities among them. Anthropologists study in a variety of settings and situations, ranging from small hamlets and villages to neighborhoods and corporate offices of major urban centers throughout the world. They study hunters and gatherers, peasants, farmers, labor leaders, politicians, and bureaucrats. They examine religious life in Latin America as well as revolutionary movements.

Wherever practicable, anthropologists take on the role of "participant observer." Through active involvement in the lifeways of people, they hope to gain an insider's perspective without sacrificing the objectivity of the trained scientist. Sometimes the conditions for achieving such a goal seem to form an almost insurmountable barrier, but anthropologists call on persistence, adaptability, and imagination to overcome the odds against them.

The diversity of focus in anthropology means that it is earmarked less by its particular subject matter than by its perspective. Although the discipline relates to both the biological and social sciences, anthropologists know that the boundaries drawn between disciplines are highly artificial. For example, while in theory it is possible to examine only the social organization of a family unit or the organization of political power in a nation-state, in reality it is impossible to separate the biological from the social, from the economic, from the political. The explanatory perspective of anthropology, as the articles in this unit demonstrate, is to seek out interrelationships among all these factors. The first four articles in this section illustrate varying degrees of difficulty that an anthropologist may encounter in taking on the role of the participant observer. Napoleon Chagnon's essay, "Doing Fieldwork Among the Yanomamö," shows the hardships imposed by certain physical conditions and the vast differences in values and attitudes to be bridged by the anthropologist just to get along. In "Spin-Doctoring the Yanomamö," we see how Chagnon's problems have escalated into conflicts with his academic peers and some powerful Roman Catholic missionaries as well.

Richard Kurin, in "Doctor, Lawyer, Indian Chief," and Richard Lee, in "Eating Christmas in the Kalahari," apparently had few problems with the physical conditions and the personalities of the people they were studying. However, they were not completely accepted by the communities until they modified their behavior to conform to the expectations of their hosts and found ways to participate as equals in the socioeconomic exchange systems.

Much is at stake in these discussions as we attempt to achieve a more objective understanding of the diversity of peoples' ways. After all, the purpose of anthropology is not only to describe and explain, but also to develop a special vision of the world in which cultural alternatives (past, present, and future) can be measured against one another and used as guides for human action.

Doing Fieldwork among the Yąnomamö[1]

Napoleon A. Chagnon

VIGNETTE

The Yąnomamö are thinly scattered over a vast and verdant tropical forest, living in small villages that are separated by many miles of unoccupied land. They have no writing, but they have a rich and complex language. Their clothing is more decorative than protective. Well-dressed men sport nothing more than a few cotton strings around their wrists, ankles, and waists. They tie the foreskins of their penises to the waist string. Women dress about the same. Much of their daily life revolves around gardening, hunting, collecting wild foods, collecting firewood, fetching water, visiting with each other, gossiping, and making the few material possessions they own: baskets, hammocks, bows, arrows, and colorful pigments with which they paint their bodies. Life is relatively easy in the sense that they can 'earn a living' with about three hours' work per day. Most of what they eat they cultivate in their gardens, and most of that is plantains—a kind of cooking banana that is usually eaten green, either roasted on the coals or boiled in pots. Their meat comes from a large variety of game animals, hunted daily by the men. It is usually roasted on coals or smoked, and is always well done. Their villages are round and open—and very public. One can hear, see, and smell almost everything that goes on anywhere in the village. Privacy is rare, but sexual discreetness is possible in the garden or at night while others sleep. The villages can be as small as 40 to 50 people or as large as 300 people, but in all cases there are many more children and babies than there are adults. This is true of most primitive populations and of our own demographic past. Life expectancy is short.

The Yąnomamö fall into the category of Tropical Forest Indians called 'foot people.' They avoid large rivers and live in interfluvial plains of the major rivers. They have neighbors to the north, Carib-speaking Ye'kwana, who are true 'river people': They make elegant, large dug-out canoes and travel extensively along the major waterways. For the Yąnomamö, a large stream is an obstacle and can be crossed only in the dry season. Thus, they have traditionally avoided larger rivers and, because of this, contact with outsiders who usually come by river.

They enjoy taking trips when the jungle abounds with seasonally ripe wild fruits and vegetables. Then, the large village—the *shabono*—is abandoned for a few weeks and everyone camps out for from one to several days away from the village and garden. On these trips, they make temporary huts from poles, vines, and leaves, each family making a separate hut.

Two major seasons dominate their annual cycle: the wet season, which inundates the low-lying jungle, making travel difficult, and the dry season—the time of visiting other villages to feast, trade, and politic with allies. The dry season is also the time when raiders can travel and strike silently at their unsuspecting enemies. The Yąnomamö are still conducting intervillage warfare, a phenomenon that affects all aspects of their social organization, settlement pattern, and daily routines. It is not simply 'ritualistic' war: At least one-fourth of all adult males die violently in the area I lived in.

Social life is organized around those same principles utilized by all tribesmen: kinship relationships, descent from ancestors, marriage exchanges between kinship/descent groups, and the transient charisma of distinguished headmen who attempt to keep order in the village and whose responsibility it is to determine the village's relationships with those in other villages. Their positions are largely the result of kinship and marriage patterns; they come from the largest kinship groups within the village. They can, by their personal wit, wisdom, and charisma, become autocrats, but most of them are largely 'greaters' among equals. They, too, must clear gardens, plant crops, collect wild foods, and hunt. They are simultaneously peacemakers and valiant warriors. Peacemaking often requires the threat or actual use of force, and most headmen have an acquired reputation for being *waiteri*: fierce.

The social dynamics within villages are involved with giving and receiving marriageable girls. Marriages are arranged by older kin, usually men, who are brothers, uncles, and the father. It is a political process, for girls are promised in marriage while they are young, and the men who do this attempt to create alliances with other men via marriage exchanges. There is a shortage of women due in part to a sex-ratio imbalance in the younger age categories, but also complicated by the fact that some men have multiple wives. Most fighting within the village stems from sexual affairs or failure to deliver a promised woman—or out-and-out seizure of a married woman by some other man. This can lead to internal fighting and conflict of such an intensity that villages split up and fission, each group then becoming a new village and, often, enemies to each other.

But their conflicts are not blind, uncontrolled violence. They have a series of graded forms of violence that ranges from chest-pounding and club-fighting duels to out-and-out shooting to kill. This gives them a good deal of flexibility in settling disputes without immediate resort to lethal violence. In addition, they have developed patterns of alliance and friendship that serve to limit violence—trading and feasting with others in order to become friends. These alliances can, and often do, result in intervillage exchanges of marriageable women, which leads to additional amity between villages. No good thing lasts forever, and most alliances crumble. Old friends become hostile and, occasionally, treacherous. Each village must therefore be keenly aware that its neighbors are fickle and must behave accordingly. The thin line between friendship and animosity must be traversed by the village leaders, whose political acumen and strategies are both admirable and complex.

Each village, then, is a replica of all others in a broad sense. But each village is part of a larger political, demographic, and ecological process, and it is difficult to attempt to understand the village without knowing something of the larger forces that affect it and its particular history with all its neighbors.

COLLECTING THE DATA IN THE FIELD

I have now spent over 60 months with Yąnomamö, during which time I gradually learned their language and, up to a point, submerged myself in their culture and way of life.[2] As my research progressed, the thing that impressed me most was the importance that aggression played in shaping their culture. I had the opportunity to witness a good many incidents that expressed individual vindictiveness on the one hand and collective bellicosity on the other hand. These

ranged in seriousness from the ordinary incidents of wife beating and chest pounding to dueling and organized raids by parties that set out with the intention of ambushing and killing men from enemy villages. One of the villages was raided approximately twenty-five times during my first 15 months of fieldwork—six times by the group among whom I was living. And, the history of every village I investigated, from 1964 to 1991, was intimately bound up in patterns of warfare with neighbors that shaped its politics and determined where it was found at any point in time and how it dealt with its current neighbors.

The fact that the Yąnomamö have lived in a chronic state of warfare is reflected in their mythology, ceremonies, settlement pattern, political behavior, and marriage practices. Accordingly, I have organized this case study in such a way that students can appreciate the effects of warfare on Yąnomamö culture in general and on their social organization and political relationships in particular.

I collected the data under somewhat trying circumstances, some of which I will describe to give a rough idea of what is generally meant when anthropologists speak of 'culture shock' and 'fieldwork.' It should be borne in mind, however, that each field situation is in many respects unique, so that the problems I encountered do not necessarily exhaust the range of possible problems other anthropologists have confronted in other areas. There are a few problems, however, that seem to be nearly universal among anthropological fieldworkers, particularly those having to do with eating, bathing, sleeping, lack of privacy, loneliness, or discovering that the people you are living with have a lower opinion of you than you have of them or you yourself are not as culturally or emotionally 'flexible' as you assumed.

The Yąnomamö can be difficult people to live with at times, but I have spoken to colleagues who have had difficulties living in the communities they studied. These things vary from society to society, and probably from one anthropologist to the next. I have also done limited fieldwork among the Yąnomamö's northern neighbors, the Carib-speaking Ye'kwana Indians. By contrast to many

experiences I had among the Yąnomamö, the Ye'kwana were very pleasant and charming, all of them anxious to help me and honor bound to show any visitor the numerous courtesies of their system of etiquette. In short, they approached the image of 'primitive man' that I had conjured up in my mind before doing fieldwork, a kind of 'Rousseauian' view, and it was sheer pleasure to work with them. Other anthropologists have also noted sharp contrasts in the people they study from one field situation to another. One of the most startling examples of this is in the work of Colin Turnbull, who first studied the Ituri Pygmies (1965, 1983) and found them delightful to live with, but then studied the Ik (1972) of the desolate outcroppings of the Kenya/Uganda/Sudan border region, a people he had difficulty coping with intellectually, emotionally, and physically. While it is possible that the anthropologist's reactions to a particular people are personal and idiosyncratic, it nevertheless remains true that there are enormous differences between whole peoples, differences that affect the anthropologist in often dramatic ways.

Hence, what I say about some of my experiences is probably equally true of the experiences of many other fieldworkers. I describe some of them here for the benefit of future anthropologists—because I think I could have profited by reading about the pitfalls and field problems of my own teachers. At the very least I might have been able to avoid some of my more stupid errors. In this regard there is a growing body of excellent descriptive work on field research. Students who plan to make a career in anthropology should consult these works, which cover a wide range of field situations in the ethnographic present.[3]

The Longest Day: The First One
My first day in the field illustrated to me what my teachers meant when they spoke of 'culture shock.' I had traveled in a small, aluminum rowboat propelled by a large outboard motor for two and a half days. This took me from the territorial capital, a small town on the Orinoco River, deep into Yąnomamö country. On the morning of the third day we reached

a small mission settlement, the field 'headquarters' of a group of Americans who were working in two Yąnomamö villages. The missionaries had come out of these villages to hold their annual conference on the progress of their mission work and were conducting their meetings when I arrived. We picked up a passenger at the mission station, James P. Barker, the first non-Yąnomamö to make a sustained, permanent contact with the tribe (in 1950). He had just returned from a year's furlough in the United States, where I had earlier visited him before leaving for Venezuela. He agreed to accompany me to the village I had selected for my base of operations to introduce me to the Indians. This village was also his own home base, but he had not been there for over a year and did not plan to join me for another three months. Mr. Barker had been living with this particular group about five years.

We arrived at the village, Bisaasi-teri, about 2:00 P.M. and docked the boat along the muddy bank at the terminus of the path used by Yąnomamö to fetch their drinking water. It was hot and muggy, and my clothing was soaked with perspiration. It clung uncomfortably to my body, as it did thereafter for the remainder of the work. The small biting gnats, *bareto*, were out in astronomical numbers, for it was the beginning of the dry season. My face and hands were swollen from the venom of their numerous stings. In just a few moments I was to meet my first Yąnomamö, my first primitive man. What would he be like? I had visions of entering the village and seeing 125 social facts running about altruistically calling each other kinship terms and sharing food, each waiting and anxious to have me collect his genealogy. I would wear them out in turn. Would they like me? This was important to me; I wanted them to be so fond of me that they would adopt me into their kinship system and way of life. I had heard that successful anthropologists always get adopted by their people. I had learned during my seven years of anthropological training at the University of Michigan that kinship was equivalent to society in primitive tribes and that it was a moral way of life, 'moral' being something 'good' and 'desirable.' I was determined to work my way into their moral system of kinship and become a member of their society—to be 'accepted' by them.

How Did They Accept You?

My heart began to pound as we approached the village and heard the buzz of activity within the circular compound. Mr. Barker commented that he was anxious to see if any changes had taken place while he was away and wondered how many of them had died during his absence. I nervously felt my back pocket to make sure that my notebook was still there and felt personally more secure when I touched it.

The entrance to the village was covered over with brush and dry palm leaves. We pushed them aside to expose the low opening to the village. The excitement of meeting my first Yąnomamö was almost unbearable as I duck-waddled through the low passage into the village clearing.

I looked up and gasped when I saw a dozen burly, naked, sweaty, hideous men staring at us down the shafts of their drawn arrows! Immense wads of green tobacco were stuck between their lower teeth and lips making them look even more hideous, and strands of dark-green slime dripped or hung from their nostrils—strands so long that they clung to their pectoral muscles or drizzled down their chins. We arrived at the village while the men were blowing a hallucinogenic drug up their noses. One of the side effects of the drug is a runny nose. The mucus is always saturated with the green powder and they usually let it run freely from their nostrils. My next discovery was that there were a dozen or so vicious, underfed dogs snapping at my legs, circling me as if I were to be their next meal. I just stood there holding my notebook, helpless and pathetic. Then the stench of the decaying vegetation and filth hit me and I almost got sick. I was horrified. What kind of welcome was this for the person who came here to live with you and learn your way of life, to become friends with you? They put their weapons down when they recognized Barker and returned to their chanting, keeping a nervous eye on the village entrances.

We had arrived just after a serious fight. Seven women had been abducted the day before by a neighboring group, and the local men and their guests had just that morning recovered five of them in a brutal club fight that nearly ended in a shooting war. The abductors, angry because they had lost five of their seven new captives, vowed to raid the Bisaasi-teri. When we arrived and entered the village unexpectedly, the Indians feared that we were the raiders. On several occasions during the next two hours the men in the village jumped to their feet, armed themselves, nocked their arrows and waited nervously for the noise outside the village to be identified. My enthusiasm for collecting ethnographic facts diminished in proportion to the number of times such an alarm was raised. In fact, I was relieved when Barker suggested that we sleep across the river for the evening. It would be safer over there.

As we walked down the path to the boat, I pondered the wisdom of having decided to spend a year and a half with these people before I had even seen what they were like. I am not ashamed to admit that had there been a diplomatic way out, I would have ended my fieldwork then and there. I did not look forward to the next day—and months—when I would be left alone with the Yąnomamö; I did not speak a word of their language, and they were decidedly different from what I had imagined them to be. The whole situation was depressing, and I wondered why I ever decided to switch from physics and engineering in the first place. I had not eaten all day, I was soaking wet from perspiration, the *bareto* were biting me, and I was covered with red pigment, the result of a dozen or so complete examinations I had been given by as many very pushy Yąnomamö men. These examinations capped an otherwise grim day. The men would blow their noses into their hands, flick as much of the mucus off that would separate in a snap of the wrist, wipe the residue into their hair, and then carefully examine my face, arms, legs, hair, and the contents of my pockets. I asked Barker how to say, 'Your hands are dirty'; my comments were met by the Yąnomamö in the following way: They would 'clean' their hands by spitting a quantity of slimy tobacco juice into them, rub them together, grin, and then proceed with the examination.

Mr. Barker and I crossed the river and slung our hammocks. When he pulled his hammock out of a rubber bag, a heavy disagreeable odor of mildewed cotton and stale wood smoke came with it. 'Even the missionaries are filthy,' I thought to myself. Within two weeks, everything I owned smelled the same way, and I lived with that odor for the remainder of the fieldwork. My own habits of personal cleanliness declined to such levels that I didn't even mind being examined by the Yąnomamö, as I was not much cleaner than they were after I had adjusted to the circumstances. It is difficult to blow your nose gracefully when you are stark naked and the invention of handkerchiefs is millenia away.

Life in the Jungle: Oatmeal, Peanut Butter, and Bugs

It isn't easy to plop down in the Amazon Basin for a year and get immediately into the anthropological swing of things. You have been told about horrible diseases, snakes, jaguars, electric eels, little spiny fish that will swim up your urine into your penis, quicksand, and getting lost. Some of the dangers are real, but your imagination makes them more real and threatening than many of them really are. What my teachers never bothered to advise me about, however, was the mundane, nonexciting, and trivial stuff—like eating, defecating, sleeping, or keeping clean. These turned out to be the bane of my existence during the first several months of field research. I set up my household in Barker's abandoned mud hut, a few yards from the village of Bisaasi-teri, and immediately set to work building my own mud/thatch hut with the help of the Yąnomamö. Meanwhile, I had to eat and try to do my 'field research.' I soon discovered that it was an enormously time-consuming task to maintain my own body in the manner to which it had grown accustomed in the relatively antiseptic environment of the northern United States. Either I could be relatively well fed and relatively comfortable in a fresh change of clothes and do very little fieldwork, or I

could do considerably more fieldwork and be less well fed and less comfortable.

It is appalling how complicated it can be to make oatmeal in the jungle. First, I had to make two trips to the river to haul the water. Next, I had to prime my kerosene stove with alcohol to get it burning, a tricky procedure when you are trying to mix powdered milk and fill a coffee pot at the same time. The alcohol prime always burned out before I could turn the kerosene on, and I would have to start all over. Or, I would turn the kerosene on, optimistically hoping that the Coleman element was still hot enough to vaporize the fuel, and start a small fire in my palm-thatched hut as the liquid kerosene squirted all over the table and walls and then ignited. Many amused Yąnomamö onlookers quickly learned the English phrase 'Oh, Shit!' and, once they discovered that the phrase offended and irritated the missionaries, they used it as often as they could in their presence. I usually had to start over with the alcohol. Then I had to boil the oatmeal and pick the bugs out of it. All my supplies, of course, were carefully stored in rat-proof, moisture-proof, and insect-proof containers, not one of which ever served its purpose adequately. Just taking things out of the multiplicity of containers and repacking them afterward was a minor project in itself. By the time I had hauled the water to cook with, unpacked my food, prepared the oatmeal, milk, and coffee, heated water for dishes, washed and dried the dishes, repacked the food in the containers, stored the containers in locked trunks, and cleaned up my mess, the ceremony of preparing breakfast had brought me almost up to lunch time!

Eating three meals a day was simply out of the question. I solved the problem by eating a single meal that could be prepared in a single container, or, at most, in two containers, washed my dishes only when there were no clean ones left, using cold river water, and wore each change of clothing at least a week to cut down on my laundry problem—a courageous undertaking in the tropics. I reeked like a jockstrap that had been left to mildew in the bottom of some dark gym locker. I also became less concerned about sharing my provisions with the rats, insects,

Yąnomamö, and the elements, thereby eliminating the need for my complicated storage process. I was able to last most of the day on *café con leche*, heavily sugared espresso coffee diluted about five to one with hot milk. I would prepare this in the evening and store it in a large thermos. Frequently, my single meal was no more complicated than a can of sardines and a package of soggy crackers. But at least two or three times a week I would do something 'special' and sophisticated, like make a batch of oatmeal or boil rice and add a can of tuna fish or tomato paste to it. I even saved time by devising a water system that obviated the trips to the river. I had a few sheets of tin roofing brought in and made a rain water trap; I caught the water on the tin surface, funneled it into an empty gasoline drum, and then ran a plastic hose from the drum to my hut. When the drum was exhausted in the dry season, I would get a few Yąnomamö boys to fill it with buckets of water from the river, 'paying' them with crackers, of which they grew all too fond all too soon.

I ate much less when I traveled with the Yąnomamö to visit other villages. Most of the time my travel diet consisted of roasted or boiled green plantains (cooking bananas) that I obtained from the Yąnomamö, but I always carried a few cans of sardines with me in case I got lost or stayed away longer than I had planned. I found peanut butter and crackers a very nourishing 'trail' meal, and a simple one to prepare. It was nutritious and portable, and only one tool was required to make the meal: a hunting knife that could be cleaned by wiping the blade on a convenient leaf. More importantly, it was one of the few foods the Yąnomamö would let me eat in relative peace. It looked suspiciously like animal feces to them, an impression I encouraged. I referred to the peanut butter as the feces of babies or 'cattle.' They found this disgusting and repugnant. They did not know what 'cattle' were, but were increasingly aware that I ate several canned products of such an animal. Tin cans were thought of as containers made of 'machete skins,' but how the cows got inside was always a mystery to them. I went out of my way to describe my foods in such a way as to make them sound unpalatable to them, for it gave me some peace of mind while I ate: They wouldn't beg for a share of something that was too horrible to contemplate. Fieldworkers develop strange defense mechanisms and strategies, and this was one of my own forms of adaptation to the fieldwork. On another occasion I was eating a can of frankfurters and growing very weary of the demands from one of the onlookers for a share in my meal. When he finally asked what I was eating, I replied: 'Beef.' He then asked: 'Shaki!⁴ What part of the animal are you eating?' To which I replied, 'Guess.' He muttered a contemptuous epithet, but stopped asking for a share. He got back at me later, as we shall see.

Meals were a problem in a way that had nothing to do with the inconvenience of preparing them. Food sharing is important to the Yąnomamö in the context of displaying friendship. 'I am hungry!' is almost a form of greeting with them. I could not possibly have brought enough food with me to feed the entire village, yet they seemed to overlook this logistic fact as they begged for my food. What became fixed in their minds was the fact that I did not share my food with whomsoever was present—usually a small crowd—at each and every meal. Nor could I easily enter their system of reciprocity with respect to food. Every time one of them 'gave' me something 'freely,' he would dog me for months to 'pay him back,' not necessarily with food but with knives, fishhooks, axes, and so on. Thus, if I accepted a plantain from someone in a different village while I was on a visit, he would most likely visit me in the future and demand a machete as payment for the time that he 'fed' me. I usually reacted to these kinds of demands by giving a banana, the customary reciprocity in their culture—food for food—but this would be a disappointment for the individual who had nursed visions of that single plantain growing into a machete over time. Many years after beginning my fieldwork, I was approached by one of the prominent men who demanded a machete for a piece of meat he claimed he had given me five or six years earlier.

Despite the fact that most of them knew I would not share my food with

them at their request, some of them always showed up at my hut during mealtime. I gradually resigned myself to this and learned to ignore their persistent demands while I ate. Some of them would get angry because I failed to give in, but most of them accepted it as just a peculiarity of the subhuman foreigner who had come to live among them. If or when I did accede to a request for a share of my food, my hut quickly filled with Yąnomamö, each demanding their share of the food that I had just given to one of them. Their begging for food was not provoked by hunger, but by a desire to try something new and to attempt to establish a coercive relationship in which I would accede to a demand. If one received something, all others would immediately have to test the system to see if they, too, could coerce me.

A few of them went out of their way to make my meals downright unpleasant—to spite me for not sharing, especially if it was a food that they had tried before and liked, or a food that was part of their own cuisine. For example, I was eating a cracker with peanut butter and honey one day. The Yąnomamö will do almost anything for honey, one of the most prized delicacies in their own diet. One of my cynical onlookers—the fellow who had earlier watched me eating frankfurters—immediately recognized the honey and knew that I would not share the tiny precious bottle. It would be futile to even ask. Instead, he glared at me and queried icily, 'Shaki! What kind of animal semen are you pouring onto your food and eating?' His question had the desired effect and my meal ended.

Finally, there was the problem of being lonely and separated from your own kind, especially your family. I tried to overcome this by seeking personal friendships among the Yąnomamö. This usually complicated the matter because all my 'friends' simply used my confidence to gain privileged access to my hut and my cache of steel tools and trade goods—and looted me when I wasn't looking. I would be bitterly disappointed that my erstwhile friend thought no more of me than to finesse our personal relationship exclusively with the intention of getting at my locked up possessions, and my depression would hit new lows every

time I discovered this. The loss of the possessions bothered me much less than the shock that I was, as far as most of them were concerned, nothing more than a source of desirable items. No holds were barred in relieving me of these, since I was considered something subhuman, a non-Yąnomamö.

The hardest thing to learn to live with was the incessant, passioned, and often aggressive demands they would make. It would become so unbearable at times that I would have to lock myself in my hut periodically just to escape from it. Privacy is one of our culture's most satisfying achievements, one you never think about until you suddenly have none. It is like not appreciating how good your left thumb feels until someone hits it with a hammer. But I did not want privacy for its own sake; rather, I simply had to get away from the begging. Day and night for almost the entire time I lived with the Yąnomamö, I was plagued by such demands as: 'Give me a knife, I am poor!'; 'If you don't take me with you on your next trip to Widokaiyateri, I'll chop a hole in your canoe!'; 'Take us hunting up the Mavaca River with your shotgun or we won't help you!'; 'Give me some matches so I can trade with the Reyaboböwei-teri, and be quick about it or I'll hit you!'; 'Share your food with me, or I'll burn your hut!'; 'Give me a flashlight so I can hunt at night!'; 'Give me all your medicine, I itch all over!'; 'Give me an ax or I'll break into your hut when you are away and steal all of them!' And so I was bombarded by such demands day after day, month after month, until I could not bear to see a Yąnomamö at times.

It was not as difficult to become calloused to the incessant begging as it was to ignore the sense of urgency, the impassioned tone of voice and whining, or the intimidation and aggression with which many of the demands were made. It was likewise difficult to adjust to the fact that the Yąnomamö refused to accept 'No' for an answer until or unless it seethed with passion and intimidation—which it did after a few months. So persistent and characteristic is the begging that the early 'semiofficial' maps made by the Venezuelan Malaria Control Service (Malarialogía) designated the site of their first permanent field station, next to the village of Bisaasi-teri, as *Yababuhii:* 'Gimme.' I had to become like the Yąnomamö to be able to get along with them on their terms: somewhat sly, aggressive, intimidating, and pushy.

It became indelibly clear to me shortly after I arrived there that had I failed to adjust in this fashion I would have lost six months of supplies to them in a single day or would have spent most of my time ferrying them around in my canoe or taking them on long hunting trips. As it was, I did spend a considerable amount of time doing these things and did succumb often to their outrageous demands for axes and machetes, at least at first, for things changed as I became more fluent in their language and learned how to defend myself socially as well as verbally. More importantly, had I failed to demonstrate that I could not be pushed around beyond a certain point, I would have been the subject of far more ridicule, theft, and practical jokes than was the actual case. In short, I had to acquire a certain proficiency in their style of interpersonal politics and to learn how to imply subtly that certain potentially undesirable, but unspecified, consequences might follow if they did such and such to me. They do this to each other incessantly in order to establish precisely the point at which they cannot goad or intimidate an individual any further without precipitating some kind of retaliation. As soon as I realized this and gradually acquired the self-confidence to adopt this strategy, it became clear that much of the intimidation was calculated to determine my flash point or my 'last ditch' position—and I got along much better with them. Indeed, I even regained some lost ground. It was sort of like a political, interpersonal game that everyone had to play, but one in which each individual sooner or later had to give evidence that his bluffs and implied threats could be backed up with a sanction. I suspect that the frequency of wife beating is a component in this syndrome, since men can display their *waiteri* (ferocity) and 'show' others that they are capable of great violence. Beating a wife with a club is one way of displaying ferocity, one that does not expose the man

to much danger—unless the wife has concerned, aggressive brothers in the village who will come to her aid. Apparently an important thing in wife beating is that the man has displayed his presumed potential for violence and the intended message is that other men ought to treat him with circumspection, caution, and even deference.

After six months, the level of Yąnomamö demand was tolerable in Bisaasi-teri, the village I used for my base of operations. We had adjusted somewhat to each other and knew what to expect with regard to demands for food, trade goods, and favors. Had I elected to remain in just one Yąnomamö village for the entire duration of my first 15 months of fieldwork, the experience would have been far more enjoyable than it actually was. However, as I began to understand the social and political dynamics of this village, it became patently obvious that I would have to travel to many other villages to determine the demographic bases and political histories that lay behind what I could understand in the village of Bisaasi-teri. I began making regular trips to some dozen neighboring Yąnomamö villages as my language fluency improved. I collected local genealogies there, or rechecked and cross-checked those I had collected elsewhere. Hence, the intensity of begging was relatively constant and relatively high for the duration of my fieldwork, for I had to establish my personal position in each village I visited and revisited.

For the most part, my own 'fierceness' took the form of shouting back at the Yąnomamö as loudly and as passionately as they shouted at me, especially at first, when I did not know much of the language. As I became more fluent and learned more about their political tactics, I became more sophisticated in the art of bluffing and brinksmanship. For example, I paid one young man a machete (then worth about $2.50) to cut a palm tree and help me make boards from the wood. I used these to fashion a flooring in the bottom of my dugout canoe to keep my possessions out of the water that always seeped into the canoe and sloshed around. That afternoon I was working with one of my informants in the village.

The long-awaited mission supply boat arrived and most of the Yąnomamö ran out of the village to see the supplies and try to beg items from the crew. I continued to work in the village for another hour or so and then went down to the river to visit with the men on the supply boat. When I reached the river I noticed, with anger and frustration, that the Yąnomamö had chopped up all my new floor boards to use as crude paddles to get their own canoes across the river to the supply boat.[5] I knew that if I ignored this abuse I would have invited the Yąnomamö to take even greater liberties with my possessions in the future. I got into my canoe, crossed the river, and docked amidst their flimsy, leaky craft. I shouted loudly to them, attracting their attention. They were somewhat sheepish, but all had mischievous grins on their impish faces. A few of them came down to the canoe, where I proceeded with a spirited lecture that revealed my anger at their audacity and license. I explained that I had just that morning paid one of them a machete for bringing me the palmwood, how hard I had worked to shape each board and place it in the canoe, how carefully and painstakingly I had tied each one in with vines, how much I had perspired, how many *bareto* bites I had suffered, and so on. Then, with exaggerated drama and finality, I withdrew my hunting knife as their grins disappeared and cut each one of their canoes loose and set it into the strong current of the Orinoco River where it was immediately swept up and carried downstream. I left without looking back and huffed over to the other side of the river to resume my work.

They managed to borrow another canoe and, after some effort, recovered their dugouts. Later, the headman of the village told me, with an approving chuckle, that I had done the correct thing. Everyone in the village, except, of course, the culprits, supported and defended my actions—and my status increased as a consequence.

Whenever I defended myself in such ways I got along much better with the Yąnomamö and gradually acquired the respect of many of them. A good deal of their demeanor toward me was directed with the forethought of establishing the point at which I would draw the line and react defensively. Many of them, years later, reminisced about the early days of my fieldwork when I was timid and *mohode* ("stupid") and a little afraid of them, those golden days when it was easy to bully me into giving my goods away for almost nothing.

Theft was the most persistent situation that required some sort of defensive action. I simply could not keep everything I owned locked in trunks, and the Yąnomamö came into my hut and left at will. I eventually developed a very effective strategy for recovering almost all the stolen items: I would simply ask a child who took the item and then I would confiscate that person's hammock when he was not around, giving a spirited lecture to all who could hear on the antisociality of thievery as I stalked off in a faked rage with the thief's hammock slung over my shoulder. Nobody ever attempted to stop me from doing this, and almost all of them told me that my technique for recovering my possessions was ingenious. By nightfall the thief would appear at my hut with the stolen item or send it over with someone else to make an exchange to recover his hammock. He would be heckled by his covillagers for having got caught and for being embarrassed into returning my item for his hammock. The explanation was usually, 'I just borrowed your ax! I wouldn't think of stealing it!'

Collecting Yąnomamö Genealogies and Reproductive Histories

My purpose for living among Yąnomamö was to systematically collect certain kinds of information on genealogy, reproduction, marriage practices, kinship, settlement patterns, migrations, and politics. Much of the fundamental data was genealogical—who was the parent of whom, tracing these connections as far back in time as Yąnomamö knowledge and memory permitted. Since 'primitive' society is organized largely by kinship relationships, figuring out the social organization of the Yąnomamö essentially meant collecting extensive data on genealogies, marriage, and reproduction. This turned out to be a staggering and very frustrating problem. I could not have deliberately picked a more difficult

people to work with in this regard. They have very stringent name taboos and eschew mentioning the names of prominent living people as well as all deceased friends and relatives. They attempt to name people in such a way that when the person dies and they can no longer use his or her name, the loss of the word in their language is not inconvenient. Hence, they name people for specific and minute parts of things, such as 'toenail of sloth,' 'whisker of howler monkey,' and so on, thereby being able to retain the words 'toenail' or 'whisker' but somewhat handicapped in referring to these anatomical parts of sloths and monkeys respectively. The taboo is maintained even for the living, for one mark of prestige is the courtesy others show you by not using your name publicly. This is particularly true for men, who are much more competitive for status than women in this culture, and it is fascinating to watch boys grow into young men, demanding to be called either by a kinship term in public, or by a teknonymous reference such as 'brother of Himotoma.' The more effective they are at getting others to avoid using their names, the more public acknowledgment there is that they are of high esteem and social standing. Helena Valero, a Brazilian woman who was captured as a child by a Yąnomamö raiding party, was married for many years to a Yąnomamö headman before she discovered what his name was (Biocca, 1970; Valero, 1984). The sanctions behind the taboo are more complex than just this, for they involve a combination of fear, respect, admiration, political deference, and honor.

At first I tried to use kinship terms alone to collect genealogies, but Yąnomamö kinship terms, like the kinship terms in all systems, are ambiguous at some point because they include so many possible relatives (as the term 'uncle' does in our own kinship system). Again, their system of kin classification merges many relatives that we 'separate' by using different terms: They call both their actual father and their father's brother by a single term, whereas we call one 'father' and the other 'uncle.' I was forced, therefore, to resort to personal names to collect unambiguous genealogies or 'pedigrees.' They quickly grasped what I was up to and that I was

determined to learn everyone's 'true name,' which amounted to an invasion of their system of prestige and etiquette, if not a flagrant violation of it. They reacted to this in a brilliant but devastating manner: They invented false names for everybody in the village and systematically learned them, freely revealing to me the 'true' identities of everyone. I smugly thought I had cracked the system and enthusiastically constructed elaborate genealogies over a period of some five months. They enjoyed watching me learn their names and kinship relationships. I naively assumed that I would get the 'truth' to each question and the best information by working in public. This set the stage for converting my serious project into an amusing hoax of the grandest proportions. Each 'informant' would try to outdo his peers by inventing a name even more preposterous or ridiculous than what I had been given by someone earlier, the explanations for discrepancies being 'Well, he has two names and this is the other one.' They even fabricated devilishly improbable genealogical relationships, such as someone being married to his grandmother, or worse yet, to his mother-in-law, a grotesque and horrifying prospect to the Yąnomamö. I would collect the desired names and relationships by having my informant whisper the name of the person softly into my ear, noting that he or she was the parent of such and such or the child of such and such, and so on. Everyone who was observing my work would then insist that I repeat the name aloud, roaring in hysterical laughter as I clumsily pronounced the name, sometimes laughing until tears streamed down their faces. The 'named' person would usually react with annoyance and hiss some untranslatable epithet at me, which served to reassure me that I had the 'true' name. I conscientiously checked and rechecked the names and relationships with multiple informants, pleased to see the inconsistencies disappear as my genealogy sheets filled with those desirable little triangles and circles, thousands of them.

My anthropological bubble was burst when I visited a village about 10 hours' walk to the southwest of Bisaasi-teri some five months after I had begun collecting genealogies on the Bisaasi-teri. I was chatting with the local headman of this village and happened to casually drop the name of the wife of the Bisaasi-teri headman. A stunned silence followed, and then a villagewide roar of uncontrollable laughter, choking, gasping, and howling followed. It seems that I thought the Bisaasi-teri headman was married to a woman named "hairy cunt." It also seems that the Bisaasi-teri headman was called 'long dong' and his brother 'eagle shit.' The Bisaasi-teri headman had a son called "asshole" and a daughter called 'fart breath.' And so on. Blood welled up my temples as I realized that I had nothing but nonsense to show for my five months' of dedicated genealogical effort, and I had to throw away almost all the information I had collected on this the most basic set of data I had come there to get. I understood at that point why the Bisaasi-teri laughed so hard when they made me repeat the names of their covillagers, and why the 'named' person would react with anger and annoyance as I pronounced his 'name' aloud.

I was forced to change research strategy—to make an understatement to describe this serious situation. The first thing I did was to begin working in private with my informants to eliminate the horseplay and distraction that attended public sessions. Once I did this, my informants, who did not know what others were telling me, began to agree with each other and I managed to begin learning the 'real' names, starting first with children and gradually moving to adult women and then, cautiously, adult men, a sequence that reflected the relative degree of intransigence at revealing names of people. As I built up a core of accurate genealogies and relationships—a core that all independent informants had verified repetitiously—I could 'test' any new informant by soliciting his or her opinion and knowledge about these 'core' people whose names and relationships I was confident were accurate. I was, in this fashion, able to immediately weed out the mischievous informants who persisted in trying to deceive me. Still, I had great difficulty getting the names of dead kinsmen, the only accurate way to extend genealogies back in

time. Even my best informants continued to falsify names of the deceased, especially closely related deceased. The falsifications at this point were not serious and turned out to be readily corrected as my interviewing methods improved (see below). Most of the deceptions were of the sort where the informant would give me the name of a living man as the father of some child whose actual father was dead, a response that enabled the informant to avoid using the name of a deceased kinsman or friend.

The quality of a genealogy depends in part on the number of generations it embraces, and the name taboo prevented me from making any substantial progress in learning about the deceased ancestors of the present population. Without this information, I could not, for example, document marriage patterns and interfamilial alliances through time. I had to rely on older informants for this information, but these were the most reluctant informants of all for this data. As I became more proficient in the language and more skilled at detecting fabrications, any informants became better at deception. One old man was particularly cunning and persuasive, following a sort of Mark Twain policy that the most effective lie is a sincere lie. He specialized in making a ceremony out of false names for dead ancestors. He would look around nervously to make sure nobody was listening outside my hut, enjoin me never to mention the name again, become very anxious and spooky, and grab me by the head to whisper a secret name into my ear. I was always elated after a session with him, because I managed to add several generations of ancestors for particular members of the village. Others steadfastly refused to give me such information. To show my gratitude, I paid him quadruple the rate that I had been paying the others. When word got around that I had increased the pay for genealogical and demographic information, volunteers began pouring into my hut to 'work' for me, assuring me of their changed ways and keen desire to divest themselves of the 'truth.'

Enter Rerebawä: Inmarried Tough Guy

I discovered that the old man was lying quite by accident. A club fight broke out in the village one day, the result of a dispute over the possession of a woman.

She had been promised to a young man in the village, a man named Rerebawä, who was particularly aggressive. He had married into Bisaasi-teri and was doing his 'bride service'—a period of several years during which he had to provide game for his wife's father and mother, provide them with wild foods he might collect, and help them in certain gardening and other tasks. Rerebawä had already been given one of the daughters in marriage and was promised her younger sister as his second wife. He was enraged when the younger sister, then about 16 years old, began having an affair with another young man in the village, Bäkotawä, making no attempt to conceal it. Rerebawä challenged Bäkotawä to a club fight. He swaggered boisterously out to the duel with his 10-foot-long club, a roof-pole he had cut from the house on the spur of the moment, as is the usual procedure. He hurled insult after insult at both Bäkotawä and his father, trying to goad them into a fight. His insults were bitter and nasty. They tolerated them for a few moments, but Rerebawä's biting insults provoked them to rage. Finally, they stormed angrily out of their hammocks and ripped out roof-poles, now returning the insults verbally, and rushed to the village clearing. Rerebawä continued to insult them, goading them into striking him on the head with their equally long clubs. Had either of them struck his head—which he held out conspicuously for them to swing at—he would then have the right to take his turn on their heads with his club. His opponents were intimidated by his fury, and simply backed down, refusing to strike him, and the argument ended. He had intimidated them into submission. All three retired pompously to their respective hammocks, exchanging nasty insults as they departed. But Rerebawä had won the showdown and thereafter swaggered around the village, insulting the two men behind their backs at every opportunity. He was genuinely angry with them, to the point of calling the older man by the name of his long-deceased father. I quickly seized on this incident as an opportunity to collect an accurate genealogy and confidentially asked Rerebawä about his adversary's ancestors. Rerebawä had been particularly 'pushy' with me up to this point, but we soon became warm friends and staunch allies: We were both 'outsiders' in Bisaasi-teri and, although he was a Yąnomamö, he nevertheless had to put up with some considerable amount of pointed teasing and scorn from the locals, as all inmarried 'sons-in-law' must. He gave me the information I requested of his adversary's deceased ancestors, almost with devilish glee. I asked about dead ancestors of other people in the village and got prompt, unequivocal answers: He was angry with everyone in the village. When I compared his answers to those of the old man, it was obvious that one of them was lying. I then challenged his answers. He explained, in a sort of 'you damned fool, don't you know better?' tone of voice that everyone in the village knew the old man was lying to me and gloating over it when I was out of earshot. The names the old man had given to me were names of dead ancestors of the members of a village so far away that he thought I would never have occasion to check them out authoritatively. As it turned out, Rerebawä knew most of the people in that distant village and recognized the names given by the old man.

I then went over all my Bisaasi-teri genealogies with Rerebawä, genealogies I had presumed to be close to their final form. I had to revise them all because of the numerous lies and falsifications they contained, much of it provided by the sly old man. Once again, after months of work, I had to recheck everything with Rerebawä's aid. Only the living members of the nuclear families turned out to be accurate; the deceased ancestors were mostly fabrications.

Discouraging as it was to have to recheck everything all over again, it was a major turning point in my fieldwork. Thereafter, I began taking advantage of local arguments and animosities in selecting my informants, and used more extensively informants who had married into the village in the recent past. I also began traveling more regularly to other villages at this time to check on genealogies, seeking out villages whose members were on strained terms with the people about whom I wanted information. I would then return to my base in

the village of Bisaasi-teri and check with local informants the accuracy of the new information. I had to be careful in this work and scrupulously select my local informants in such a way that I would not be inquiring about *their* closely related kin. Thus, for each of my local informants, I had to make lists of names of certain deceased people that I dared not mention in their presence. But despite this precaution, I would occasionally hit a new name that would put some informants into a rage, or into a surly mood, such as that of a dead 'brother' or 'sister'[6] whose existence had not been indicated to me by other informants. This usually terminated my day's work with that informant, for he or she would be too touchy or upset to continue any further, and I would be reluctant to take a chance on accidentally discovering another dead close kinsman soon after discovering the first.

These were unpleasant experiences, and occasionally dangerous as well, depending on the temperament of my informant. On one occasion I was planning to visit a village that had been raided recently by one of their enemies. A woman, whose name I had on my census list for that village, had been killed by the raiders. Killing women is considered to be bad form in Yąnomamö warfare, but this woman was deliberately killed for revenge. The raiders were unable to bushwhack some man who stepped out of the village at dawn to urinate, so they shot a volley of arrows over the roof into the village and beat a hasty retreat. Unfortunately, one of the arrows struck and killed a woman, an accident. For that reason, her village's raiders *deliberately* sought out and killed a woman in retaliation—whose name was on my list. My reason for going to the village was to update my census data on a name-by-name basis and estimate the ages of all the residents. I knew I had the name of the dead woman in my list, but nobody would dare to utter her name so I could remove it. I knew that I would be in very serious trouble if I got to the village and said her name aloud, and I desperately wanted to remove it from my list. I called on one of my regular and usually cooperative informants and asked him to tell me the woman's name. He refused ada-

mantly, explaining that she was a close relative—and was angry that I even raised the topic with him. I then asked him if he would let me whisper the names of *all* the women of that village in his ear, and he would simply have to nod when I hit the right name. We had been 'friends' for some time, and I thought I was able to predict his reaction, and thought that our friendship was good enough to use this procedure. He agreed to the procedure, and I began whispering the names of the women, one by one. We were alone in my hut so that nobody would know what we were doing and nobody could hear us. I read the names softly, continuing to the next when his response was a negative. When I ultimately hit the dead woman's name, he flew out of his chair, enraged and trembling violently, his arm raised to strike me: 'You son-of-a-bitch!' he screamed. 'If you say her name in my presence again, I'll kill you in an instant!' I sat there, bewildered, shocked, and confused. And frightened, as much because of his reaction, but also because I could imagine what might happen to me should I unknowingly visit a village to check genealogy accuracy without knowing that someone had just died there or had been shot by raiders since my last visit. I reflected on the several articles I had read as a graduate student that explained the 'genealogical method,' but could not recall anything about its being a potentially lethal undertaking. My furious informant left my hut, never again to be invited back to be an informant. I had other similar experiences in different villages, but I was always fortunate in that the dead person had been dead for some time, or was not very closely related to the individual into whose ear I whispered the forbidden name. I was usually cautioned by one of the men to desist from saying any more names lest I get people 'angry.'[7]

Kaobawä: The Bisaasi-teri Headman Volunteers to Help Me

I had been working on the genealogies for nearly a year when another individual came to my aid. It was Kaobawä, the headman of Upper Bisaasi-teri. The village of Bisaasi-teri was split into two components, each with its own garden and own circular house. Both were in sight of each other. However, the intensity and frequency of internal bickering and argumentation was so high that they decided to split into two separate groups but remain close to each other for protection in case they were raided. One group was downstream from the other; I refer to that group as the 'Lower' Bisaasi-teri and call Kaobawä's group 'Upper' (upstream) Bisaasi-teri, a convenience they themselves adopted after separating from each other. I spent most of my time with the members of Kaobawä's group, some 200 people when I first arrived there. I did not have much contact with Kaobawä during the early months of my work. He was a somewhat retiring, quiet man, and among the Yąnomamö, the outsider has little time to notice the rare quiet ones when most everyone else is in the front row, pushing and demanding attention. He showed up at my hut one day after all the others had left. He had come to volunteer to help me with the genealogies. He was 'poor,' he explained, and needed a machete. He would work only on the condition that I did not ask him about his own parents and other very close kinsmen who had died. He also added that he would not lie to me as the others had done in the past.

This was perhaps the single most important event in my first 15 months of field research, for out of this fortuitous circumstance evolved a very warm friendship, and among the many things following from it was a wealth of accurate information on the political history of Kaobawä's village and related villages, highly detailed genealogical information, sincere and useful advice to me, and hundreds of valuable insights into the Yąnomamö way of life. Kaobawä's familiarity with his group's history and his candidness were remarkable. His knowledge of details was almost encyclopedic, his memory almost photographic. More than that, he was enthusiastic about making sure I learned the truth, and he encouraged me, indeed, *demanded that* I learn all details I might otherwise have ignored. If there were subtle details he could not recite on the spot, he would advise me to wait until he could check things out with someone else in the village. He would often do this

clandestinely, giving me a report the next day, telling me who revealed the new information and whether or not he thought they were in a position to know it. With the information provided by Kaobawä and Rerebawä, I made enormous gains in understanding village interrelationships based on common ancestors and political histories and became lifelong friends with both. And both men knew that I had to learn about his recently deceased kin from the other one. It was one of those quiet understandings we all had but none of us could mention.

Once again I went over the genealogies with Kaobawä to recheck them, a considerable task by this time. They included about two thousand names, representing several generations of individuals from four different villages. Rerebawä's information was very accurate, and Kaobawä's contribution enabled me to trace the genealogies further back in time. Thus, after nearly a year of intensive effort on genealogies, Yąnomamö demographic patterns and social organization began to make a good deal of sense to me. Only at this point did the patterns through time begin to emerge in the data, and I could begin to understand how kinship groups took form, exchanged women in marriage over several generations, and only then did the fissioning of larger villages into smaller ones emerge as a chronic and important feature of Yąnomamö social, political, demographic, economic, and ecological adaptation. At this point I was able to begin formulating more sophisticated questions, for there was now a pattern to work from and one to flesh out. Without the help of Rerebawä and Kaobawä it would have taken much longer to make sense of the plethora of details I had collected from not only them, but dozens of other informants as well.

I spent a good deal of time with these two men and their families, and got to know them much better than I knew most Yąnomamö. They frequently gave their information in a way which related themselves to the topic under discussion. We became warm friends as time passed, and the formal 'informant/anthropologist' relationship faded into the background. Eventually, we simply stopped

'keeping track' of work and pay. They would both spend hours talking with me, leaving without asking for anything. When they wanted something, they would ask for it no matter what the relative balance of reciprocity between us might have been at that point....

For many of the customary things that anthropologists try to communicate about another culture, these two men and their families might be considered to be 'exemplary' or 'typical.' For other things, they are exceptional in many regards, but the reader will, even knowing some of the exceptions, understand Yąnomamö culture more intimately by being familiar with a few examples.

Kaobawä was about 40 years old when I first came to his village in 1964. I say "about 40" because the Yąnomamö numeration system has only three numbers: one, two, and more-than-two. It is hard to give accurate ages or dates for events when the informants have no means in their language to reveal such detail. Kaobawä is the headman of his village, meaning that he has somewhat more responsibility in political dealings with other Yąnomamö groups, and very little control over those who live in his group except when the village is being raided by enemies. We will learn more about political leadership and warfare in a later chapter, but most of the time men like Kaobawä are like the North American Indian 'chief' whose authority was characterized in the following fashion: "One word from the chief, and each man does as he pleases." There are different 'styles' of political leadership among the Yąnomamö. Some leaders are mild, quiet, inconspicuous most of the time, but intensely competent. They act parsimoniously, but when they do, people listen and conform. Other men are more tyrannical, despotic, pushy, flamboyant, and unpleasant to all around them. They shout orders frequently, are prone to beat their wives, or pick on weaker men. Some are very violent. I have met headmen who run the entire spectrum between these polar types, for I have visited some 60 Yąnomamö villages. Kaobawä stands at the mild, quietly competent end of the spectrum. He has had six wives thus far—and temporary affairs with as many more, at least one of which resulted in a child that is publicly acknowledged as his child. When I first met him he had just two wives: Bahimi and Koamashima. Bahimi had two living children when I first met her; many others had died. She was the older and enduring wife, as much a friend to him as a mate. Their relationship was as close to what we think of as 'love' in our culture as I have seen among the Yąnomamö. His second wife was a girl of about 20 years, Koamashima. She had a new baby boy when I first met her, her first child. There was speculation that Kaobawä was planning to give Koamashima to one of his younger brothers who had no wife; he occasionally allows his younger brother to have sex with Koamashima, but only if he asks in advance. Kaobawä gave another wife to one of his other brothers because she was *beshi* ("horny"). In fact, this earlier wife had been married to two other men, both of whom discarded her because of her infidelity. Kaobawä had one daughter by her. However, the girl is being raised by Kaobawä's brother, though acknowledged to be Kaobawä's child.

Bahimi, his oldest wife, is about five years younger than he. She is his cross-cousin—his mother's brother's daughter. Ideally, all Yąnomamö men should marry a cross-cousin.... Bahimi was pregnant when I began my field work, but she destroyed the infant when it was born—a boy in this case—explaining tearfully that she had no choice. The new baby would have competed for milk with Ariwari, her youngest child, who was still nursing. Rather than expose Ariwari to the dangers and uncertainty of an early weaning, she chose to terminate the newborn instead. By Yąnomamö standards, this has been a very warm, enduring marriage. Kaobawä claims he beats Bahimi only 'once in a while, and only lightly' and she, for her part, never has affairs with other men.

Kaobawä is a quiet, intense, wise, and unobtrusive man. It came as something of a surprise to me when I learned that he was the headman of his village, for he stayed at the sidelines while others would surround me and press their demands on me. He leads more by example than by coercion. He can afford to be this

way at his age, for he established his reputation for being forthright and as fierce as the situation required when he was younger, and the other men respect him. He also has five mature brothers or half-brothers in his village, men he can count on for support. He also has several other mature 'brothers' (parallel cousins, whom he must refer to as 'brothers' in his kinship system) in the village who frequently come to his aid, but not as often as his 'real' brothers do. Kaobawä has also given a number of his sisters to other men in the village and has promised his young (8-year-old) daughter in marriage to a young man who, for that reason, is obliged to help him. In short, his 'natural' or 'kinship' following is large, and partially because of this support, he does not have to display his aggressiveness to remind his peers of his position.

Rerebawä is a very different kind of person. He is much younger—perhaps in his early twenties. He has just one wife, but they have already had three children. He is from a village called Karohi-teri, located about five hours' walk up the Orinoco, slightly inland off to the east of the river itself. Kaobawä's village enjoys amicable relationships with Rerebawä's, and it is for this reason that marriage alliances of the kind represented by Rerebawä's marriage into Kaobawä's village occur between the two groups. Rerebawä told me that he came to Bisaasi-teri because there were no eligible women from him to marry in his own village, a fact that I later was able to document when I did a census of his village and a preliminary analysis of its social organization. Rerebawä is perhaps more typical than Kaobawä in the sense that he is chronically concerned about his personal reputation for aggressiveness and goes out of his way to be noticed, even if he has to act tough. He gave me a hard time during my early months of fieldwork, intimidating, teasing, and insulting me frequently. He is, however, much braver than the other men his age and is quite prepared to back up his threats with immediate action—as in the club fight incident just described above. Moreover, he is fascinated with political relationships and knows the details of intervillage relationships over a large area of the tribe. In this respect he shows all the attributes of being a headman, although

he has too many competent brothers in his own village to expect to move easily into the leadership position there.

He does not intend to stay in Kaobawä's group and refuses to make his own garden—a commitment that would reveal something of an intended long-term residence. He feels that he has adequately discharged his obligations to his wife's parents by providing them with fresh game, which he has done for several years. They should let him take his wife and return to his own village with her, but they refuse and try to entice him to remain permanently in Bisaasi-teri to continue to provide them with game when they are old. It is for this reason that they promised to give him their second daughter, their only other child, in marriage. Unfortunately, the girl was opposed to the marriage and ultimately married another man, a rare instance where the woman in the marriage had this much influence on the choice of her husband.

Although Rerebawä has displayed his ferocity in many ways, one incident in particular illustrates what his character can be like. Before he left his own village to take his new wife in Bisaasi-teri, he had an affair with the wife of an older brother. When it was discovered, his brother attacked him with a club. Rerebawä responded furiously: He grabbed an ax and drove his brother out of the village after soundly beating him with the blunt side of the single-bit ax. His brother was so intimidated by the thrashing and promise of more to come that he did not return to the village for several days. I visited this village with Kabawä shortly after this event had taken place; Rerebawä was with me as my guide. He made it a point to introduce me to this man. He approached his hammock, grabbed him by the wrist, and dragged him out on the ground: 'This is the brother whose wife I screwed when he wasn't around!' A deadly insult, one that would usually provoke a bloody club fight among more valiant Yąnomamö. The man did nothing. He slunk sheepishly back into his hammock, shamed, but relieved to have Rerebawä release his grip.

Even though Rerebawä is fierce and capable of considerable nastiness, he has a charming, witty side as well. He has a biting sense of humor and can entertain the group for hours with jokes and clever manipulations of language. And, he is one of few Yąnomamö that I feel I can trust. I recall indelibly my return to Bisaasi-teri after being away a year—the occasion of my second field trip to the Yąnomamö. When I reached Bisaasi-teri, Rerebawä was in his own village visiting his kinsmen. Word reached him that I had returned, and he paddled downstream immediately to see me. He greeted me with an immense bear hug and exclaimed, with tears welling up in his eyes, 'Shaki! Why did you stay away so long? Did you not know that my will was so cold while you were gone that I could not at times eat for want of seeing you again?' I, too, felt the same way about him—then, and now.

Of all the Yąnomamö I know, he is the most genuine and the most devoted to his culture's ways and values. I admire him for that, although I cannot say that I subscribe to or endorse some of these values. By contrast, Kaobawä is older and wiser, a polished diplomat. He sees his own culture in a slightly different light and seems even to question aspects of it. Thus, while many of his peers enthusiastically accept the 'explanations' of things given in myths, he occasionally reflects on them—even laughing at some of the most preposterous of them.... Probably more of the Yąnomamö are like Rerebawä than like Kaobawä , or at least try to be. ....

NOTES

1. The word Yąnomamö is nasalized through its entire length, indicated by the diacritical mark ','. When this mark appears on any Yąnomamö word, the whole word is nasalized. The vowel 'ö' represents a sound that does not occur in the English language. It is similar to the umlaut 'ö' in the German language or the 'oe' equivalent, as in the poet Goethe's name. Unfortunately, many presses and typesetters simply eliminate diacritical marks, and this has led to multiple spellings of the word Yąnomamö—and multiple mispronunciations. Some anthropologists have chosen to introduce a slightly different spelling of the word Yąnomamö since I began writing about them, such as Yąnomami, leading to additional misspellings as their diacritics are characteristically eliminated by presses, and to the *incorrect* pronunciation 'Yąnoma-meee.' Vowels indicated as 'ä' are pronounced as the 'uh' sound in the word 'duck'. Thus, the name Kaobawä would be pronounced 'cow-ba-wuh,' but entirely nasalized.

2. I spent a total of 60 months among the Yąnomamö between 1964 and 1991. The first edition of this case study was based on the first 15 months I spent among them in Venezuela. I have, at the time of this writing, made 20 field trips to the Yąnomamö and this edition reflects the new information and understandings I have acquired over the years. I plan to return regularly to continue what has now turned into a lifelong study.

3. See Spindler (1970) for a general discussion of field research by anthropologists who have worked in other cultures. Nancy Howell has recently written a very useful book (1990) on some of the medical, personal, and environmental hazards of doing field research, which includes a selected bibliography on other fieldwork programs.

4. They could not pronounce "Chagnon." It sounded to them like their name for a pesky bee, shaki, and that is what they called me: pesky, noisome bee.

5. The Yąnomamö in this region acquired canoes very recently. The missionaries would purchase them from the Ye'kwana Indians to the north for money, and then trade them to the Yąnomamö in exchange for labor, produce, or 'informant' work in translating. It should be emphasized that those Yąnomamö who lived on navigable portions of the Upper Orinoco River moved there recently from the deep forest in order to have contact with the missionaries and acquire the trade goods the missionaries (and their supply system) brought.

6. Rarely were there actual brothers or sisters. In Yąnomamö kinship classifications, certain kinds of cousins are classified as siblings. See Chapter 4.

7. Over time, as I became more and more 'accepted' by the Yąnomamö, they became less and less concerned about my genealogical inquiries and now, provide me with this information quite willingly because I have been very discrete with it. Now, when I revisit familiar villages I am called aside by someone who whispers to me things like, "Don't ask about so-and-so's father."

Spin-Doctoring the Yanomamö

Science as a Candle in the Darkness of the Anthropology Wars

Michael Shermer

THERE IS A MAXIM ANTHROPOLOGISTS OFTEN CITE about the geopolitics of diplomacy and warfare among indigenous peoples: *The enemy of my enemy is my friend.* In reality, of course, the maxim applies to virtually all groups, from tribes and villages to city-states and nation-states—recall the temporary friendship between the US and USSR from 1941–1945 that promptly dissolved into the Cold War upon the defeat of their common enemy.

I thought of this maxim on Monday, November 20, 2000, when I interviewed journalist Patrick Tierney for the science edition of NPR affiliate KPCC's *Airtalk*, when he was in Los Angeles on tour for his just published book *Darkness in El Dorado: How Scientists and Journalists Devastated the Amazon.*[1] Tierney had just flown down from San Francisco where, the previous day, he was pummeled by a panel of experts in front of a thousand scientists gathered at the annual meeting of the American Anthropological Association.

Among the many scientists that Tierney goes after none take more hits than the anthropologist Napoleon Chagnon, whose study of the Yanomamö people of Amazonia is arguably the most famous ethnography since Margaret Mead's Samoan classics. Since I knew of Chagnon's reputation as an intellectual pugilist who has accumulated a score of enemies over the decades, I fully expected that, in obedience to the maxim they would have rallied around Tierney in a provisional alliance. With a couple of minor exceptions, however, there was almost universal condemnation of the book. A British science writer told SKEPTIC Senior Editor Frank Miele, who was in attendance: "If I had taken such a beating as Tierney I would have crawled out of the room and cut my throat."[2]

Tierney did seem shell-shocked, as he timorously tiptoed into the studio with a subdued countenance. On the air he seemed almost apologetic for his book, emphasizing that he was not presenting the final word on the subject of the mistreatment of the Yanomamö but, rather, he was merely suggesting the need to investigate the scandalous charges against Chagnon and others that he had gathered in his decade of research.

A wispy thin man with an edge of wilderness about him, left over from a waif-like nomadic lifestyle spent chasing down what he thought might be (and his publisher trumpeted as) the anthropological scandal of all time, Tierney struck me as a conciliatory man ill-suited for the fight he had instigated. Indeed, he seemed the very embodiment of the type of man Rush Limbaugh would call a bleeding-heart, tree-hugging liberal, and someone environmentalists would call a friend. His publicist at W. W. Norton told me that he was flat broke from years of grant-less, salary-less research and that his very survival hinged on the success of this book. Her interpretation of the AAA meeting, which she attended in hopes of this being a coming out celebration for a potentially bestselling book, was that Tierney had few friends there because he was an outsider, a mere journalist at play in the field of the scientists.[3] Who was he to stick his nose in the private business of professionals whose union card—the Ph.D.—was hard earned through the centuries-long system of mentorship and hoop-jumping, not unlike the rites of passage young men endure in many indigenous cultures? Had Tierney simply not paid his scientific dues, or was there something else going on that turned Chagnon's erstwhile enemies into new found friends?

Despite his lack of scientific training Tierney did spend 11 years researching his book, and since outsiders occasionally do make important contributions to science, I wanted to give him a chance. His on-air stories were eye-popping, and his book is filled with so many stories and anecdotes, charges and accusa-

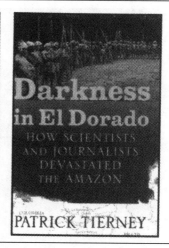

Figure 1. Judging the Yanomamö by their covers. The book jackets of Napoleon Chagnon's *Yanomamö*, Kenneth Good's *Into the Heart*, and Patrick Tierney's *Darkness in El Dorado*. Although all three show the Yanomamö in ceremonial feathers and spears as part of a formal feast, Tierney claims that Chagnon depicts the Yanomamö as violent and aggressive while Good portrays them as peaceful and loving. This is spin-doctoring science. In reality, Good's narrative account supports Chagnon's scientific treatise.

tions, backed by interviews, documents, and 70 pages of endnotes and bibliography, that at first blush one is left thinking that if only half, or even a tenth of them are true, there is darkness in anthropology, indeed, in all of science.

DARWIN'S DICTUM AND DAMAGED DATA

Humans are storytelling animals.[4] Thus, following what I call Darwin's Dictum—"all observation must be for or against some view if it is to be of any service"[5]—we begin by recognizing that Tierney is telling a story against a view he believes has been put forth by certain anthropologists about the Yanomamö and, by implication, about all humanity. Chagnon, he points out, subtitled his best-selling ethnographic monograph on the Yanomamö "The Fierce People." The French anthropologist Jacques Lizot, Tierney notes, calls the Yanomamö "the erotic people."[6] Chagnon and Lizot, of course, are not immune from the human tendency to dichotomize and pigeonhole, but in telling a story—especially one for or against some view—one is obligated to be fair in properly contextualizing observations and conclusions because the data never just speak for themselves. Thus, the substrate of this essay is the relationship between data and theory, and how journalists and scientists differ in their treatment of that relationship.

For example, Tierney spares no ink in presenting a picture of Chagnon as a fierce anthropologist who sees in the Yanomamö nothing more than a reflection of himself. Chagnon's sociobiological theories of the most violent and aggressive males winning the most copulations and thus passing on their genes for "fierceness," says Tierney, is a Rorschachian window into Chagnon's own libidinous impulses. Chagnon is the *bête noire of Darkness in El Dorado*. In Tierney's pantheon of anti-heroes, Chagnon is the anti-Christ of the Yanomamö. The gold miners who kill Yanomamö and destroy their land, and the missionaries who want to "civilize" the Yanomamö by replacing their animistic superstition with a monotheistic one, by comparison, are let off easy. Indeed, Chagnon is well-known in anthropological circles for being tough-minded and occasionally abrasive, and Tierney seemed to encounter no shortage of stories of brag-

gadocio and bellicosity peppered throughout descriptions of a man who himself might best be described as "fierce," both in the jungles of Amazonia and the halls of academia. In a letter to the *Santa Barbara News Press*, for example, Chagnon called his critics "so much skunk in the elephant soup":

> I used a metaphor to try to put the nature of academic things into perspective: a soup comprised of one elephant and one skunk. The vast majority of my professional colleagues regard my work with esteem—the elephant part of the soup.... But, a highly vocal minority persists in denigrating me and my research in nonacademic ways for a variety of reasons, most notably professional jealousy. These represent the acrid flavor that a skunk, even in a very large elephant soup, imparts to it.[7]

"In Tierney's pantheon of anti-heroes, Chagnon is the anti-Christ of the Yanomamö. Gold miners who kill Yanomamö and destroy their land, and missionaries who want to "civilize" the Yanomamö by replacing their animistic superstition with a monotheistic one... are let off easy."

In a private e-mail that was forwarded to and published in *Newsweek* (without Chagnon's permission), the embattled anthropologist expressed himself like a true alpha male: "I am encouraged to believe that *The New Yorker* and W.W. Norton [Tierney's excerpter and publisher] are sticking their peckers into a very powerful pickle slicer."[8]

In a two-page account designed to arouse emotion in the reader (it does), Tierney recounts a story told to him by the anthropologist Kenneth Good, who spent 12 years among the Ya-

Figure 2. The man behind the controversy: anthropologist Napoleon Chagnon accompanies two Yanomamö men on a 1995 field study. From Darkness in El Dorado, 2000.

nomamö (first as a graduate student of Chagnon, then with the German ethologist Irenäus Eib-Eibesfeldt, and finally with the cultural anthropologist Marvin Harris). Good recalled in a 1995 interview with Tierney that he and Chagnon "used to go down to bars and drink together. It was an embarrassment, but I did it because he was going to be my chair. He was the type of guy who had German shepherd attack dogs, and he'd have people come over to his house in the afternoon and he'd have the students dress up in padded suits and have the dogs attack them. Oh, yes. They'd have to put out an arm or a leg and the dog would attack. Students could get injured."[9] Tierney then turns to Good's book, *Into the Heart*, to retell the story of a violent outburst by Chagnon. Here is how Tierney describes it:

> During his first, nervous night in the jungle, Good was terrified when two screaming men burst inside, pushed him into a table, and ripped his mosquito netting. In the ensuing tussle, all three men wound up sprawling on the ground, bruised and covered with mud, but not before Good recognized his assailants as Chagnon and another anthropologist, both drunk. Good, a tall, husky man, was so angry he threw Chagnon, who is much smaller, over an embankment.

"*Tranquilo*, Ken," Lizot said, as he helped bring peace. Fortunately, Chagnon could not remember what had happened to him when he woke up, rather bruised and muddy, the next day. Good never forgot the experience, however. It was the only time anyone ever attacked him in Yanomamiland. "In my twelve years, I witnessed only one raid."[10]

Attack dogs and drunken brawls—it would appear from this narrative that Chagnon is the fierce one, not the Yanomamö. Perhaps, as Tierney argues, even the occasional acts of violence committed by the Yanomamö were nothing more than Chagnon-stimulated outbursts, like something out of *The Gods Must be Crazy*, where the mere introduction of a Coke bottle disrupts the entire !Kung culture (this analogy is not mine—Chagnon's critics began making it soon after the film's release).[11] As the jacket flap for *Darkness in El Dorado* dramatically concludes: "Tierney explores the hypocrisy, distortions, and humanitarian crimes committed in the name of research, and reveals how the Yanomami's internecine warfare was, in fact, triggered by the repeated visits of outsiders who went looking for a 'fierce' people whose existence lay primarily in the imagination of the West."

Tierney's tale about Chagnon was so inflammatory that I read it aloud to my associates at SKEPTIC, exclaiming "Can you believe this guy?" I privately wondered whether we all [had] been duped by Chagnon. In fact, *Darkness in El Dorado* is filled with such stories, typically told mostly in Tierney's words with snippets of partial quotes from his various sources. This literary style always makes me uneasy, so when I interviewed Good I asked him about this incident. He indicated that it happened pretty much as Tierney summarized it, adding that it was more than a little irritating that his mosquito net was torn (malaria-carrying mosquitoes infest the Amazon), and that he was not at all amused by his mentor's inappropriate behavior.[12]

It was with much interest, then, when Good kindly sent me a copy of *Into the Heart* that I read the original account. Here is Good's rather different description of the event Tierney portrayed as an act of inebriated violence:

> Chagnon, Lizot, and the French anthropologist all knew the Yanomami, and of course their reputation for violence, and having had more than a little to drink, they figured it would be a lot of fun to scare the pants off us. It was, after all, the first night Ray, Eric, and I were spending in a Yanomami village, and who knew what kinds of fears might be racing through our heads. So they decided they would initiate us....
>
> As Eric and I were busy working with our hammocks and nets, all of a sudden out of the night two big figures burst into the hut screaming, "Aaaaaaaaaaahhhhhhhh!" grabbing us, and shoving us toward our hammocks, ripping the mosquito netting. My heart skipped a beat. I heard Eric gasp. Bracing myself against a table to keep from falling, I twisted around and saw in the glow of the Coleman Chagnon and the French anthropologist, both of them completely drunk....
>
> Still screaming, I grabbed Chagnon with one arm and the Frenchman with the other and went stampeding out

Figure 3. Anthropologist Kenneth Good studied the dietary habits of the Yanomamö. Here he weighs a peccary to document hunting fields. From *Into the Heart*, 1991.

the door with them. There something tripped me up, and I sprawled on the ground, watching as Chagnon and his friend rolled into the eight-foot-deep pit from which the Indians had excavated clay for the hut. Lying there panting, I looked up and saw Lizot emerge from the darkness. "*Tranquilo*, Ken, *tranquilo*," he said. "Take it easy, they were just joking."[13]

Note that Tierney leaves off Lizot's qualifier "they were just joking." It was a prank! Tierney turned horseplay into horror. Sure, Good was not amused by the caper, and no doubt alcohol enhanced the pranksters' enthusiasm for playing a practical joke before the long grind of fieldwork was to begin. But regardless of how it is received, a prank is not an "attack" or a "raid."

In my interview with Chagnon he initially called Tierney a "disgusting, slippery, conniving guy," but later reflected that perhaps Tierney's book was simply a case of self-deception, where the author's political agenda of protecting the Yanomamö forced him to misread the data and ethnographies of those he perceived as harming his self-proclaimed charges.[14] At first I went along with Chagnon in his assessment, as I have witnessed first hand how powerful self-deception can be among such ideologues as creationists and Holocaust deniers. The more you believe in your own cause, the easier it is to get others to go along. While there may be some self-deception at work

here, I fail to see how it can account for the butchering Tierney made of this humorously intended escapade.

Finally, what of Chagnon's "attack dogs"? It turns out that Chagnon is a serious dog trainer; so serious, in fact, that he wrote a book on the subject entitled *Toward the Ph.D. for Dogs: Obedience Training from Novice Through Utility*, published by Harcourt in 1974. Chagnon was merely demonstrating to his students his highly trained dogs.

THE ANTHROPOLOGY WARS

Tierney's book is only the latest in a long line of skirmishes and battles that have erupted in the century-long anthropology wars. The reason such controversies draw so much public attention is that what's at stake is nothing less than the true nature of human nature, and how that nature can most profitably be studied—through rigorous quantitative science or through some other set of methods.

Derek Freeman's life-long battle with the legacy of Margaret Mead, for example, was not really about whether Samoan girls are promiscuous or prudish. Mead's philosophy (which she inherited from her mentor Franz Boas) that human nature is primarily shaped by the environment was apparently supported by her "discovery" that Samoan girls are promiscuous (because in other cultures promiscuity is taboo and therefore sexual behavior—and by implication all behavior—is culturally malleable). Freeman says Mead was duped by a couple of Samoan hoaxers and had she been more rigorous and quantitative in her research she would have discovered this fact before going to press with what became the all-time anthropological bestseller—*Coming of Age in Samoa*. But, says Freeman, Mead's ideology trumped her science and anthropology lost.[15]

So heated can these debates become that in at least one instance it has led to the complete fissioning of an academic department. Stanford University now houses the Department of Anthropological Sciences and the Department of Cultural Anthropology. The chairman of the former, Bill Durham, explained to me that the split was not simply between physical and cultural anthropologists, nor is it between those who prefer biological theories of human nature versus those who favor cultural theories. "The split is really between those who use and stand behind scientific methods in field and lab work, and those who think science is just another way of knowing, just another paradigm among others. It just so happens that anthropologists often divide on this issue between physical and cultural anthropologists, but not always. There are plenty of cultural anthropologists who conduct rigorous quantitative research. But many others are steeped in postmodernism."[16] Interestingly, Chagnon's ethnography, *Yanomamö* the epicenter of this whole affair, was published as part of an academic series on "Case Studies in Cultural Anthropology" whose series editors are at Stanford University!

Another venomous snake in the viper pit of the anthropology wars is the question of research ethics. It is simply impossible for anthropologists to observe anything remotely resembling *Star Trek's* "prime directive," where one never interferes with

17

Figure 4. *Into the Heart* is a moving love story between anthropologist Kenneth Good and a young Yanomamö woman named Yarima. They eventually married, had children, and returned to the United States. Yarima grew bored with American life and returned to the more stimulating environment of Amazonia. From *Into the Heart*, 1991.

the subject of one's study. To get to know the people you have to interface with them on numerous levels and no one has ever gotten around the problem of the "observer effect" and still had anything worth saying about a people. That's a given, and the *Code of Ethics* published by the American Anthropological Association is correspondingly vague, offering such "ethical obligations" as:

> To avoid harm or wrong, understanding that the development of knowledge can lead to change which may be positive or negative for the people or animals worked with or studied.
>
> To respect the well-being of humans and nonhuman primates.
>
> To work for the long-term conservation of the archaeological, fossil, and historical records.
>
> To consult actively with the affected individuals or group(s), with the goal of establishing a working relationship that can be beneficial to all parties involved.

Can you have sexual relations with the natives? The *Code of Ethics* is no help. Point 5 under Section A states: "Anthropological researchers who have developed close and enduring relationships (i.e., covenantal relationships) with either individual persons providing information or with hosts must adhere to the obligations of openness and informed consent, while carefully

and respectfully negotiating the limits of the relationship."[17] That's as clear as Amazonian mud during the rainy season. Thus, it is hard to say whether the scientists Tierney says were unethical were, in fact, in violation of their professional standards and obligations.

Tierney's strongest case may be against Jacques Lizot who, he documents, engaged in homosexual activities for years with so many young Yanomamö men, and so frequently, that he became known in Yanomamöspeak as "Bosinawarewa," which translates politely as "Ass Handler" and not so politely as "anus devourer."[18] In response to these claims not only did Lizot not deny the basic charges (that also included exchanging goods for sex), but he admitted to *Time* magazine: "I am a homosexual, but my house is not a brothel. I gave gifts because it is part of the Yanomamö culture. I was single. Is it forbidden to have sexual relations with consenting adults?"[19] No, but Tierney disputes both the age of Lizot's partners and whether or not they consented, and suggests that even if it were both legal and moral this is hardly the standard of objectivity one might have hoped for in scientific research, and that it is Lizot who best deserves the descriptive adjective "erotic."

I asked Ken Good about the charges against Lizot. Good said he never once witnessed homosexual behavior in any Yanomamö village and that, in his opinion, it was obvious that the Yanomamö young men were involved with Lizot for one reason only—to obtain machetes and trade goods. I have been unable to resolve any more on the Lizot affair and, in any case, he seems to be a secondary player in this anthropological drama. Despite Tierney's characterization of the Chagnon-Lizot relationship as hostile, Chagnon had no comment at all on Lizot's sexual behavior, and instead told me that "Lizot is a quite capable and thorough scientist, but he's not a particularly good synthetic thinker. He does not always see the bigger picture in his research."[20]

Chagnon, by contrast, is a synthetic, big picture thinker, and thus it is that the ethics of his research have come under closer scrutiny. Anthropologist Kim Hill from the University of New Mexico, for example, was strongly critical of *Darkness in El Dorado*, yet he expressed his concern about many of the ethical issues the book raises:

> I was concerned about the negative attitude that many Yanomamö I have met seem to have towards Chagnon, and despite the fact that much of this attitude is clearly due to coaching by Chagnon enemies, I do believe that some Yanomamö have sincere and legitimate grievances against Chagnon that should be addressed by him. The strongest complaints that I heard were about his lack of material support for the tribe despite having made an entire career (and a good deal of money) from working with them, and his lack of sensitivity concerning some cultural issues and the use of film portrayals. However, I think most of Chagnon's shortcomings amount to little more than bad judgment and an occasional unwise penchant for self promotion (something which seems to infuriate Yanomamö specialists who are less well known than Chagnon).[21]

Figure 5. Despite Tierney's claim that Chagnon exaggerated the level of aggression and rape among the Yanomamö, Kenneth Good documented both. Top photo: "two men duel over the infidelity of one of their wives." From *Into the Heart*, 1991. Bottom photo: many Yanomamö men have masses of scar tissue on their heads from such battles, as shown by Chagnon in *Yanomamö*, 1992.

Since evolutionary psychologist Steven Pinker co-authored a letter in defense of Chagnon in the *New York Times Book Review* (in response to John Horgan's surprisingly uncritical review of Tierney's book there), I queried him about some of the specific charges. He replied, "the idea that Chagnon caused the Yanomamö to fight is preposterous and contradicted by every account of the Yanomamö and other nonstate societies. Tierney is a zealot and a character assassin, and all his serious claims crumble upon scrutiny." What about the charge of ethical breaches? "There are, of course, serious issues about ethics in ethnography, and I don't doubt that some of Chagnon's practices, especially in the 1960s, were questionable (as were the practices in most fields, such as my own—for example, the Milgram studies). But the idea that the problems of Native Americans are caused by anthropologists is crazy. In the issues that matter to us—skepticism, scientific objectivity, classic liberalism. etc.—Chagnon is on the right side."[22]

The carping over minutiae in Chagnon's research methods and ethics that has dogged him throughout his career, however, is secondary to the deeper underlying issue in the anthropology wars. What Chagnon is really being accused of is biological determinism. To postmodernists and cultural determinists in calling the Yanomamö "fierce" and explaining their fierceness through a Darwinian model of competition and sexual selection,

Chagnon appears to be indicting all of humanity as innately evil and condemning us to a future of ineradicable violence, rape, and war. Are we really this bad? Are the Yanomamö?

EROTIC OR FIERCE?

Anthropology is a sublime science because it deals with such profoundly deep questions as the nature of human nature. This whole "fierce people" business is really tapping into the question of the nature of human good and evil. But to even ask such questions as "Are we by nature good or evil?" misses the complexity of human affairs and falsely simplifies the science behind the study of human diversity. (The propensity to do so is very probably grounded in the tendency of humans to dichotomize the world into unambiguous categories.)

Thus, the failure of Tierney's book has less to do with getting the story straight and more to do with a fundamental misunderstanding of the plasticity and diversity of human behavior and a lack of understanding of how science properly proceeds in its attempt to catalogue such variation and to generalize from behavioral particulars to categorical universals. Upon finishing the book I let it sit for a couple of days and then plowed through the 147-page rebuttal published on the Internet by the University of Michigan, as well as the many other responses by Chagnon and his colleagues at the University of California, Santa Barbara.[23] I also reread Chagnon's classic work *Yanomamö*. Tellingly, the fourth edition dropped the subtitle *The Fierce People* (although Tierney, characteristically, refers to the book *only* by the old *subtitle*). Had Chagnon determined that the Yanomamö were not "the fierce people" after all? No. He realized that too many people were unable to move past the moniker to grasp the complex and subtle variations contained in all human populations, and he became concerned that they "might get the impression that being 'fierce' is incompatible with having other sentiments or personal characteristics like compassion, fairness, valor, etc."[24]

In fact, the Yanomamö call themselves "waiteri" ("fierce") and Chagnon's attribution of them as such was merely attempting "to represent valor, honor, and independence" that the Yanomamö saw in themselves. As he notes in his opening chapter, the Yanomamö "are simultaneously peacemakers and valiant warriors." Like all people, the Yanomamö have a deep repertoire of responses for varying social interactions and differing contexts, even those that are potentially violent: "They have a series of graded forms of violence that ranges from chest-pounding and club-fighting duels to out-and-out shooting to kill. This gives them a good deal of flexibility in settling disputes without immediate resort to lethal violence."[25]

Chagnon has often been accused of using the Yanomamö to support a sociobiological model of an aggressive human nature. Even here, returning to the primary sources in question shows that Chagnon's deductions from the data are not so crude, as when he notes that the Yanomamö's northern neighbors, the Ye'Kwana Indians—in contrast to the Yanomamö's initial reaction to him—"were very pleasant and charming, all of them anxious to help me and honor bound to show any visitor the nu-

Figure 6. The realities of Yanomamö life, and of human life, is nuanced in all its richness by Chagnon in his ethnography entitled simply *Yanomamö*. Earlier editions included the subtitle "The Fierce People," but readers missed the multi-layered meaning of courage, valor, and compassion. But warfare among the Yanomamö is a reality, as it is for all of humanity. Armed visitors to a village feast (top) adorned with buzzard feathers and red paint, pause after dancing. The Yanomamö dress differently for war (bottom), without feathers and their faces painted black with masticated charcoal. From *Yanomamö*, 1992.

"We have the evolved capacity to adopt either strategy."[27] These are hardly the words of a hidebound ideologue. In fact, in 1995 Chagnon told *Scientific American* editor John Horgan that because male aggression is esteemed in Yanomamö culture, aggression as a human trait is highly malleable and culturally influenced—an observation that might have been made by Stephen Jay Gould, considered by most sociobiologists to be Satan incarnate. "Steve Gould and I probably agree on a lot of things," Chagnon surprisingly concluded.[28]

"To post-modernists and cultural determinists, calling the Yanomamö "fierce" and explaining their fierceness through a Darwinian model competition and sexual selection, Chagnon appears to be indicting all of humanity as innately evil and condemning us to a future of ineradicable violence, rape, and war."

Even when he is talking about the Yanomamö casually and not for publication, Chagnon carefully nuances and contextualizes everything he says. For example, at the Skeptics Society 1996 Caltech conference on evolutionary psychology Chagnon delivered a fact-packed lecture mixing anecdotes and data, including the graphs from his now-famous *Science* article revealing the positive correlation between levels of violence among Yanomamö men and their corresponding number of wives and offspring. "Here are the Satanic Verses' that I committed in anthropology," Chagnon joked, as he reviewed his data:

> I didn't intend for this correlation to pop out, but when I discovered it, it did not surprise me. If you take men who are in the same age category and divide them by those who have killed other men (*unokais*) and those who have not killed other men (non-*unokais*), in every age category *unokais* had more offspring. In fact, *unokais* averaged 4.91 children versus 1.59 for non-*unokais*. The reason is clear in the data on the number of wives: *unokais* averaged 1.63 wives versus 0.63 for non-*unokais*. This was an unacceptable finding for those who hold the ideal view of the Noble Savage. 'Here's Chagnon saying that war has something good in it.' I never said any such thing. I merely pointed out that in the Yanomamö society, just like in our own and other societies, people who are successful and good warriors, who defend the folks back home, are showered with praise and rewards. In our own culture, for example, draft dodgers are considered a shame. Being a successful warrior has social rewards in all cultures.

merous courtesies of their system of etiquette," and therefore that it "remains true that there are enormous differences between whole peoples."[26] Even on the final page of his chapter on Yanomamö warfare, Chagnon inquires about "the likelihood that people, throughout history, have based their political relationships with other groups on predatory versus religious or altruistic strategies and the cost-benefit dimensions of what the response should be if they do one or the other." He concludes:

The Yanomamö warriors do not get medals and media. They get more wives.[29]

And despite the mountains of data Chagnon has accumulated on Yanomamö aggression, he was careful to note throughout his lecture the many other behaviors and emotions expressed by the Yanomamö: "When I called the Yanomamö the 'fierce people,' I did not mean they were fierce all the time. Their family life is very tranquil. Even though they have high mortality rates due to violence and aggression and competition is very high, they are not sweating fiercely, eating fiercely, belching fiercely, etc. They do kiss their kids and are quite pleasant people."[30]

Even in the question and answer period, when given the opportunity to make his case for an extreme sociobiological view of humans to an obviously receptive audience dominated by older males who encouraged such answers with leading questions, Chagnon gently but firmly demurred. One gentleman inquired whether Chagnon thought that his data implied there might be genes for violence that are passed down to future generations by the *unokais*, and whether this implied that perhaps all human violence is innate. Chagnon unhesitatingly answered in the negative: "No, I do not think violence is that directly connected to specific genes, although there is undoubtedly a biological substrate underlying violence. Violence is a facultative trait. You have to look at the environmental cues to see what touches it off. Because they are an inbred population we can expect that Yanomamö genes are different from other populations, but I do not think that they are any different genetically from other populations in terms of violence."[31]

In light of his data on warriors who are rewarded with more wives, one questioner wondered what happens to the men who get no wives, and if this means that the Yanomamö are polygamous. Chagnon explained that, indeed, some Yanomamö men have no wives and that it is often they who are the causes of violence as they either resort to rape or they stir up trouble with men who have more than one wife. But he added an important proviso that indicates, once again, Chagnon's sensitivity to the nuances and complexities within all cultures, and the danger of gross generalizations: "Anthropologists tend to pigeonhole societies as monogamous or polygamous or polyandrous, as if these are three different kinds of societies. In fact, you have to look at marriage as a life-historical process in all societies. There are, for example, cases of monogamy in Yanomamö society. In fact, monogamy is the most common type of marriage. But there are also polyandrous families where one woman marries two men, who tend to be brothers. There are, in fact, examples of all three types of marriage arrangements in Yanomamö culture."[32]

Even at work Chagnon refrains from oversimplifying his research. I asked anthropologist Donald Symons, Chagnon's colleague from the University of California, Santa Barbara, about the accusations that Chagnon is a sociobiological ideologue bent on painting a portrait of humanity as self-centered, competitive, and violent. Symons replied: "You know, it's interesting that people make such charges against Nap, because when you ask him about this or that aspect of the Yanomamö he never just offers some simple opinion. He'll says things like 'I think I can

get that data for you,' or 'let me check that and get back to you.'" So then why does Chagnon seem to have so many enemies, I inquired? "Well, sometimes he responds to his critics in a belligerent manner that is off-putting to many people. His initial defense is typically *ad hominem*, where he will call his critics Marxists or Rousseauian idealists. That's not the way to defend against charges, which should be answered point by point."[33]

"While spin-doctoring has gone on and does go on in science... we hope that peer-review and other checks and balances that are part of the self-correcting nature of science keep it at a tolerable minimum. What we are witnessing in this latest battle in the anthropology wars is journalistic spin-doctoring of what is, for the most part, solid science."

That is, in fact, what is being done by a cadre of Chagnon defenders, who have compiled an impressive literature of point by point refutations of Tierney's accusations. Even Chagnon was taken by surprise. "I've received a number of e-mails from people identifying themselves on the academic left, who made it clear they while they disagree with me on a number of theoretical points they do not want anything to do with Tierney or his book."[34]

SPIN-DOCTORING SCIENCE

In politics, spin-doctoring is the art of interpreting words and actions in the light most favorable to one's position or cause. Spin-doctoring is openly practiced in politics and spin doctors have become star players on politician's teams (there is even a television show called *Spin City* that revolves around a spin doctor played by Michael J. Fox). While spin-doctoring has gone on and does go on in science, ideally we strive for objectivity and we hope that peer-review and the other checks and balances that are part of the self-correcting nature of science keep it at a tolerable minimum.

What we are witnessing in this latest battle in the anthropology wars is journalistic spin-doctoring of what is, for the most part, solid science. In carefully reading Good's *Into the Heart* and Chagnon's *Yanomamö* back to back over the course of several days of intense study, I found myself continually wondering how Tierney could possibly have read both books and come away with the impressions he did, unless this was a clear-cut case of spin-doctoring. The same descriptions of violence, aggression, and especially rape are present in both books; it all depends on the "spin" one puts on the data. For example, Good writes:

> I got increasingly upset about Chagnon's "Fierce People" portrayal. The man had clearly taken one aspect of Yanomamö behavior out of context and in so doing had sensationalized it. In the process he had stigmatized these remarkable people as brutish and hateful. I wasn't fooling myself into thinking that the Yanomami were some kind of Shangri-la race, all peace and light. Far, far from it. They were a volatile, emotional people, capable of behavior we would consider barbaric.[35]

Well, if the Yanomamö are really "barbaric," then why is it sensationalistic to call them "brutish"? It all depends on the spin.

Into the Heart is a page-turner because the very features of Yanomamö culture that Chagnon's critics claim he overemphasizes are, in fact, present in spades in every chapter of Good's gripping tale. As Chagnon's graduate student Good immersed himself in Yanomamöland, and in time he found himself falling in love with a beautiful young Yanomamö girl named Yarima. (Columbia Pictures bought the rights to produce a dramatic film based on the book, and Good even received a phone call from the actor Richard Gere, who was interested in playing him. That deal has since fallen through and others have shown interest in a film deal, but nothing has come of it to date. Good has avoided commenting publicly about the Tierney-Chagnon controversy, he said, because he doesn't want his half-Yanomamö children to become the focus of media attention.[36])

As the years passed and he had a falling out first with Chagnon and then with the world-renowned ethologist Irenäus Eibl-Eibesfeldt, Good became emotionally distraught over leaving Yarima alone when he was forced to return to Caracas to renew his permit, or when he was to return to the U.S. or Germany to attend conferences or work on his doctoral dissertation. Why? When Yarima came of age (defined as first menses in Yanomamöland), she and Good began living together and consummated their "marriage" (Yanomamö do not have a marriage ceremony per se; instead a couple, usually the man, declares that they are married and the two begin living together). Good's problem was that he was all too aware of what Yanomamö men are really like:

> They will grab a woman while she is out gathering and rape her. They don't consider it a crime or a horrendously antisocial thing to do. It is simply what happens. It's standard behavior. In such a small, enclosed community this (together with affairs) is the only way unmarried men have of getting sex.[37]

Good's worries were justified and the universal emotion of jealousy was no more attenuated in this highly civilized, educated man than it was in any of the people he was studying to earn his Ph.D. In short, Good was on an emotional roller coaster and couldn't get off.

> I felt the tension, and I tried to deal with it. I wanted to think that Yarima would be faithful to me. But I knew the limits of any woman's faithfulness here. Fidelity in Yanomami land is not considered a standard of any sort, let alone a

moral principle. Here it is every man for himself. Stealing, rape, even killing—these acts aren't measured by some moral standard. They aren't thought of in terms of proper or improper social behavior. Here everyone does what he can and everyone defends his own rights. A man gets up and screams and berates someone for stealing plantains from his section of the garden, then he'll go and do exactly the same thing. I protect myself, you protect yourself. You try something and I catch you, I'll stop you.[38]

Many antisocial behaviors, such as theft, are kept at a minimum through such social constraints as shunning, or personal constraints as fear of violence and retaliation. But, as Good explains, "sex is a different story":

> The sex drive demands an outlet, especially with the young men. It cannot be stopped. Thus the personal and social constraints have less force, they're more readily disregarded. As a result, a woman often has no choice. And if a woman is raped, she will not tell her husband, because she knows that her husband will beat her, or worse. In most cases the husband will become extremely angry, at both his wife and at the man who has raped her. But his anger will most likely not have the intensity or duration to provoke a village-shattering conflict, unless perhaps his wife is young and has not had a child yet. In that case the husband might find he cannot tolerate it; he might lose control utterly and embark on violent action. He badly wants to at least get his family started himself, rather than have someone else make her pregnant.[39]

How different is Good's analysis from Chagnon's description of a raid triggered by a desire to seek revenge for an earlier killing, that also included the abduction of women:

> Generally, however, the desire to abduct women does not lead to the initiation of hostilities between groups that have had no history of mutual raiding in the past. New wars usually develop when charges of sorcery are leveled against the members of a different group. Once raiding has begun between two villages, however, the raiders all hope to acquire women if the circumstances are such that they can flee without being discovered. If they catch a man and his wife at some distance from the village, they will more than likely take the woman after they kill her husband. A captured woman is raped by all the men in the raiding party and, later, by the men in the village who wish to do so but did not participate in the raid. She is then given to one of the men as a wife.[40]

It's all in how one spin-doctors the data. Chagnon carefully parcels it into contextualized units as quantitative data. Good uses it anecdotally as part of a literary narrative, and Tierney uses Good to weave it into an indictment. For example, Tierney accuses Chagnon of acting "fiercely" around the Yanomamö, dressing up like them, using their drugs, pounding his chest, and screaming. Tierney gleefully explains how "Chagnon suddenly went from being an impoverished Ph.D. student at the bottom of the totem pole to being a figure of preternatural power," then quotes Chagnon's own description of how he immersed himself into the Yanomamö culture:

> The village I'm living in really thinks I am the be-all and the end-all. I broke the final ice with them by participating in their dancing and singing one night. That really impressed them. They want to take me all over Waicaland to show me off. Their whole attitude toward me changed dramatically. Unfortunately, they want me to dance all the time now. You should have seen me in my feathers and loincloth![41]

"Who is the Hobbesian anthropologist? ... I fail to see any difference between Chagnon's and Good's description of the Yanomamö. Tierney has merely spin-doctored them to support his cause."

Contrast this passage, quoted by Tierney to incriminate Chagnon, with Good's explanation of why he did nearly the same thing as Chagnon did in order to be accepted into Yanomamö culture:

> What people, even some anthropologists, do not understand is how truly different it is to live with people whose conception of morality, laws, restrictions, controls differs so radically from ours. If you don't protect yourself, if you don't defend yourself, if you don't demand respect—you don't survive. It's as simple as that. If you act down here as you would up there, you'll be so intimidated, so worked over, you'll be running out of here. And lots of guys have been.[42]

Despite these rather brutish descriptions of the Yanomamö, Good concludes: "The point is that it's what you want to see, it's what you are drawn to write about. And that's supposedly anthropology. Chagnon made them out to be waning, fighting, belligerent people, confrontations, showdowns, stealing women, raping them, cutting off their ears. That may be his image of the Yanomami; it's certainly not mine."[43]

This is what I mean by spin-doctoring. The entire second half of Good's book is a spellbinding narrative about how Good spent most of his time warding off men from his wife who, despite his best efforts, was gang-raped, beaten, had an earlobe torn off, and was stolen by a man while Good was away renewing his permit. And Good admits that this "was more or less standard conduct. Men will threaten, and they'll carry out their threats, too. They'll shoot a woman for not going with them. I know of more than one woman who has been killed for rejecting advances made under threat. What usually happens is that she goes along with it. There isn't any choice. You go and make the best of it."[44]

Who is the Hobbesian anthropologist? As an outsider with no relationship to any of the players in this anthropological drama, and no commitment to any theoretical position within the science, I fail to see any difference between Chagnon's description of the Yanomamö and Good's. Tierney has merely spin-doctored them to support his cause.

SCIENCE AS A CANDLE IN THE DARK

The psychology and sociology of science is interesting and important in understanding the history and development of scientific theories and ideas, but the bottom-line question here is this: did Chagnon get the science right? Some anthropologists question the *level* of violence reported by Chagnon, claiming that they have recorded different (and often lower) rates in other areas of Yanomamöland. Good, for example, is quoted by Tierney as saying: "In my opinion, the Fierce People is the biggest misnomer in the history of anthropology." Did he mean that, I asked him?

> All along I have felt that Chagnon has not represented the Yanomamö accurately. I feel he might have slanted, or even cooked, some of his data. In over a dozen villages in the course of a dozen years of research, I never saw what Chagnon reported that he saw in terms of the violence both within and between villages. I have said from the beginning that (1) Chagnon did bad field work, or (2) there was something wrong with the villages Chagnon studies, or (3) Chagnon was in a "hot" area with a lot of activity whose disruptive forces led to higher levels of violence.[45]

What about Chagnon's data, I wondered? It strikes me as heavily quantitative and easily checkable. "Yeah, well, let me tell you about anthropological 'data'," Good retorted. "An anthropologist goes into the field for 15 months, comes out and tells the world what the people he has studied are like. No one was there with him. How can those observations be checked? This is a serious problem in anthropology. I'm sure that 90 percent of anthropologists are doing good field work, but in my opinion there are problems with both Chagnon's and Lizot's data." Perhaps he and Chagnon had studied different Yanomamö villages and this might account for their differing conclusions? "I went to several of the same villages as Chagnon, and I just didn't see what he saw."[46]

Considering his reputation I half expected Chagnon to explode over the phone when I queried him about these charges. Not only did he respond with dispassionate coolness, he had nothing critical at all to say about Good, commenting only that it is entirely possible that he and his former student did see different behaviors: "Good spent much of his time trekking with the Yanomamö, going on hunting trips outside of the village. If a village contains, say, 150 people in a complex web of relations, but you are spending most of your time with just a dozen or so away from the village, of course you are going to make different observations."[47]

In *Yanomamö* Chagnon notes that such variation in violence observed by different scientists can be accounted for by a concatenation of intervening variables, such as geography, ecology, population size, resources, and especially the contingent history of each group where "the lesson is that past events and history must be understood to comprehend the current observable patterns. As the Roman poet Lucretius mused, "nothing yet from nothing ever came."[48]

After reading through the literature and interviewing many on all sides of this issue, my conclusion is that Chagnon's view of the Yanomamö—while in the service of some view (a Darwinian one)—is fundamentally supported by the available evidence. His data and interpretations are corroborated by many other anthropologists who have studied the Yanomamö. Even at their "fiercest," however, the Yanomamö are not so different from many other peoples around the globe (recall Captain Bligh's numerous violent encounters with Polynesians, and Captain Cook's murder at the hands of Hawaiian natives), even when studied by tender-minded, non-fierce scientists. (I do find it ironic, however, that in their attempts to portray the Yanomamö as Rousseauian noble savages—in defense of a view of human nature as basically benign and infinitely flexible—a few anthropologists have proven *themselves* to be fierce and persistent warriors in their battles with Chagnon.)

Evolutionary biologist Jared Diamond, for example, told me that he found the role of warfare among the peoples of New Guinea that he has studied over the past 30 years quite similar to Chagnon's depiction of the role of warfare among the Yanomamö.[49] And, judging by the latest archaeological research presented in such books as Arthur Ferrill's *The Origins of War* and Lawrence Keeley's *War Before Civilization*, Yanomamö violence and warfare is no more extreme than that of our paleolithic ancestors who, around the world and throughout the past 20,000 years, appear to have brutally butchered one another with all too frequent abandon.[50] Finally, if the last five thousand years of recorded human history is any measure of a species' "fierceness," the Yanomamö have got nothing on either Western or Eastern "civilization," whose record includes the murder of hundreds of millions of people.

Homo sapiens in general, like the Yanomamö in particular, are the erotic-fierce people, making love and war far too frequently for our own good as both overpopulation and war threaten our very existence. Just as science has been our candle in the dark illuminating our path into the heart of human nature, science is our greatest hope for the future, showing us how best we can utilize our natures to insure our survival.

References

1. Tierney, P. 2000. *Darkness in El Dorado: How Scientists and Journalists Devastated the Amazon.* New York: W. W. Norton.

2. Personal correspondence with Frank Miele, November 29, 2000.

3. Personal correspondence with Louise Brocket from W. W. Norton, November 20, 2000.

4. In defense of this statement see Shermer, M. 1999. *How We Believe: The Search for God in an Age of Science.* New York: W. H. Freeman, Chapter 7.

5. I coined "Darwin's Dictum" in my inaugural column for *Scientific American*, May, 2001, from a letter Darwin wrote to a friend on December 18, 1861. The full quote reads: "About thirty years ago there was much talk that geologists ought only to observe and not theorize; and I well remember someone saying that at this rate a man might as well go into a gravel-pit and count the pebbles and describe the colours. How odd it is that anyone should not see that all observation must be for or against some view if it is to be of any service!"

6. Tierney, 2000, 15. See also Lizot, J. 1985. *Tales of the Yanomami: Daily Life in the Venezuelan Forest.* New York: Cambridge University Press.

7. See: http://www.anth.ucsb.edu/chagnon.html

8. Begley, Sharon, 2000. "Into the Heart of Darkness." *Newsweek.* November 27, 70-75.

9. Tierney, 2000, 130.

10. Ibid., 131. Different authors use different spellings of the people's name, the two most common being Yanomamö and Yanomami. According to Chagnon, the "ö" is similar to the German ö, rendered "oe" in English transliteration and pronounced as it is in the German poet "Goethe."

11. Chagnon joked about the analogy with the film *The Gods Must Be Crazy* when he spoke at the Skeptics Society 1996 Caltech conference.

12. Interview with Kenneth Good, December 5, 2000.

13. Good, K. 1991. *Into the Heart: One Man's Pursuit of Love and Knowledge Among the Yanomami.* New York: HarperCollins, 5.

14. Interview with Napoleon Chagnon, December 12, 2000.

15. Freeman, D. 1997. "Paradigms in Collision: Margaret Mead's Mistake and What it Has Done to Anthropology." *Skeptic*, Vol. 5, No. 3: 66–73. This entire issue of *Skeptic* is devoted to anthropological controversies.

16. Interview with Bill Durham, December 1, 2000.

17. American Anthropological Association, *Code of Ethics*, from "Section A. Responsibility to people and animals with whom anthropological researchers work and whose lives and cultures they study."

18. Tierney, 2000, 132–133.

19. Roosevelt, M. 2000. "Yanomami: What Have We Done to Them?" *Time.* October 2: 77–78.

20. Interview with Napoleon Chagnon, December 12, 2000.

21. Statement by Kim Hill is at http://www.anth.ucsb.edu/chagnon.html

22. Personal correspondence with Steven Pinker, December 1, 2000.

23. Go to http://www.anth.ucsb.edu to begin searching. Links and search engine scans under the names of the various anthropologists will net hundreds of pages of relevant documents.

24. Chagnon, N. 1992. *Yanomamö.* New York: Harcourt Brace College Publishers, xii–xiii.

25. Ibid., 7.

26. Ibid., 10.

27. Ibid., 206.

28. Horgan, J. 1995. "The New Social Darwinists." *Scientific American.* October: 150–157.

29. Chagnon, N. 1996. "The Myth of the Noble Savage: Lessons From the Yanomamö People of the Amazon." *Skeptics Society Conference on Evolutionary Psychology and Humanistic Ethics*, March 30.

30. Ibid.

31. Ibid.

32. Ibid.

33. Interview with Donald Symons, November 28, 2000.

34. Interview with Napoleon Chagnon, December 12, 2000.

35. Good, 1991, 42.

36. Interview with Kenneth Good, December 5, 2000.

37. Ibid., 115.

38. Ibid., 116.

39. Ibid.
40. Chagnon, 1992, 190.
41. Tierney, 2000, 31.
42. Good, 1991, 128.
43. Ibid., 129.
44. Ibid., 185.
45. Interview with Kenneth Good, December 5, 2000.
46. Ibid.
47. Interview with Napoleon Chagnon, December 12, 2000.
48. Chagnon, 1992, 1.
49. Interview with Jared Diamond, November 27, 2000.
50. Keeley, L. H. 1996. *War Before Civilization: The Myth of the Peaceful Savage*. New York: Oxford University Press. Ferrill, A. 1988. *The Origins of War From the Stoneage to Alexander the Great*. London: Thames and Hudson.

Dr. Michael Shermer is Publisher of Skeptic, Director of the Skeptics Society, host of *Science Talk* on KPCC radio, (the NPR affiliate for Southern California), columnist for *Scientific American*, and the Consulting Producer and co-host of the Fox Family television series *Exploring the Unknown*. He Is the author of *The Borderlands Of Science*, *How We Believe: The Search for God in an Age of Science*, *Denying History*, and *Why People Believe Weird Things*. His next book is a biography of Alfred Russel Wallace. He is also the author of *Teach Your Child Science* and co-author of *Teach Your Child Math* and *Mathemagics* (with Dr. Arthur Benjamin). For 16 years he taught psychology, the history of science, and the history of ideas at Occidental College, California State University, Los Angeles, and Glendale College.

From *Skeptic*, Vol. 9, No. 1, 2001, pp. 36-47. © 2001 by Skeptic Magazine www.skeptic.com. Reprinted by permission.

Doctor, Lawyer, Indian Chief

As Punjabi villagers say, "You never really know who a man is until you know who his grandfather and his ancestors were"

Richard Kurin

I was full of confidence when—equipped with a scholarly proposal, blessings from my advisers, and generous research grants—I set out to study village social structure in the Punjab province of Pakistan. But after looking for an appropriate fieldwork site for several weeks without success, I began to think that my research project would never get off the ground. Daily I would seek out villages aboard my puttering motor scooter, traversing the dusty dirt roads, footpaths, and irrigation ditches that crisscross the Punjab. But I couldn't seem to find a village amenable to study. The major problem was that the villagers I did approach were baffled by my presence. They could not understand why anyone would travel ten thousand miles from home to a foreign country in order to live in a poor village, interview illiterate peasants, and then write a book about it. Life, they were sure, was to be lived, not written about. Besides, they thought, what of any importance could they possibly tell me? Committed as I was to ethnographic research, I readily understood their viewpoint. I was a *babu log*—literally, a noble; figuratively, a clerk; and simply, a person of the city. I rode a motor scooter, wore tight-fitting clothing, and spoke Urdu, a language associated with the urban literary elite. Obviously, I

did not belong, and the villagers simply did not see me fitting into their society.

The Punjab, a region about the size of Colorado, straddles the northern border of India and Pakistan. Partitioned between the two countries in 1947, the Punjab now consists of a western province, inhabited by Muslims, and an eastern one, populated in the main by Sikhs and Hindus. As its name implies—*punj* meaning "five" and *ab* meaning "rivers"—the region is endowed with plentiful resources to support widespread agriculture and a large rural population. The Punjab has traditionally supplied grains, produce, and dairy products to the peoples of neighboring and considerably more arid states, earning it a reputation as the breadbasket of southern Asia.

Given this predilection for agriculture, Punjabis like to emphasize that they are earthy people, having values they see as consonant with rural life. These values include an appreciation of, and trust in, nature; simplicity and directness of expression; an awareness of the basic drives and desires that motivate men (namely, *zan, zar, zamin*—"women, wealth, land"); a concern with honor and shame as abiding principles of social organization; and for Muslims, a deep faith in Allah and the teachings of his prophet Mohammed.

Besides being known for its fertile soils, life-giving rivers, and superlative agriculturists, the Punjab is also perceived as a zone of transitional culture, a region that has experienced repeated invasions of people from western and central Asia into the Indian subcontinent. Over the last four thousand years, numerous groups, among them Scythians, Parthians, Huns, Greeks, Moguls, Persians, Afghans, and Turks, have entered the subcontinent through the Punjab in search of bountiful land, riches, or power. Although Punjabis—notably Rajputs, Sikhs, and Jats—have a reputation for courage and fortitude on the battlefield, their primary, self-professed strength has been their ability to incorporate new, exogenous elements into their society with a minimum of conflict. Punjabis are proud that theirs is a multiethnic society in which diverse groups have been largely unified by a common language and by common customs and traditions.

Given this background, I had not expected much difficulty in locating a village in which to settle and conduct my research. As an anthropologist, I viewed myself as an "earthy" social scientist who, being concerned with basics, would have a good deal in common with rural Punjabis. True, I might be looked on as an invader of a sort; but I was benevolent, and sensing this, villagers were sure to incorporate me into their society with even greater ease than was the case for the would-be conquering armies that had preceded me. Indeed, they would welcome me with open arms.

I was wrong. The villages whom I approached attributed my desire to live with them either to neurotic delusions or nefarious ulterior motives. Perhaps, so the arguments went, I was really after women, land, or wealth.

On the day I had decided would be my last in search of a village, I was driving along a road when I saw a farmer running through a rice field waving me down. I stopped and he climbed on the scooter. Figuring I had nothing to lose, I began to explain why I wanted to live in a village. To my surprise and delight, he was very receptive, and after sharing a pomegranate milkshake at a roadside shop, he invited me to his home. His name was Allah Ditta, which means "God given," and I took this as a sign that I had indeed found my village.

"My" village turned out to be a settlement of about fifteen hundred people, mostly of the Nunari *qaum*, or "tribe." The Nunaris engage primarily in agriculture (wheat, rice, sugar cane, and cotton), and most families own small plots of land. Members of the Bhatti tribe constitute the largest minority in the village. Although traditionally a warrior tribe, the Bhattis serve in the main as the village artisans and craftsmen.

On my first day in the village I tried explaining in great detail the purposes of my study to the village elders and clan leaders. Despite my efforts, most of the elders were perplexed about why I wanted to live in their village. As a guest, I was entitled to the hospitality traditionally bestowed by Muslim peoples of Asia, and during the first evening I was assigned a place to stay. But I was an enigma, for guests leave, and I wanted to remain. I was also perceived as being strange, for I was both a non-Muslim and a non-Punjabi, a type of person not heretofore encountered by most of the villagers. Although I tried to temper my behavior, there was little I could say or do to dissuade my hosts from the view that I embodied the antithesis of Punjabi

values. While I was able to converse in their language, Jatki, a dialect of western Punjabi, I was only able to do so with the ability of a four-year-old. This achievement fell far short of speaking the *t'et'*, or "genuine form," of the villagers. Their idiom is rich with the terminology of agricultural operations and rural life. It is unpretentious, uninflected, and direct, and villagers hold high opinions of those who are good with words, who can speak to a point and be convincing. Needless to say, my infantile babble realized none of these characteristics and evoked no such respect.

Similarly, even though I wore indigenous dress, I was inept at tying my *lungi*, or pant cloth. The fact that my *lungi* occasionally fell off and revealed what was underneath gave my neighbors reason to believe that I indeed had no shame and could not control the passions of my *nafs*, or "libidinous nature."

This image of a doltish, shameless infidel barely capable of caring for himself lasted for the first week of my residence in the village. My inability to distinguish among the five varieties of rice and four varieties of lentil grown in the village illustrated that I knew or cared little about nature and agricultural enterprise. This display of ignorance only served to confirm the general consensus that the mysterious morsels I ate from tin cans labeled "Chef Boy-ar-Dee" were not really food at all. Additionally, I did not oil and henna my hair, shave my armpits, or perform ablutions, thereby convincing some commentators that I was a member of a species of subhuman beings, possessing little in the form of either common or moral sense. That the villagers did not quite grant me the status of a person was reflected by their not according me a proper name. In the Punjab, a person's name is equated with honor and respect and is symbolized by his turban. A man who does not have a name, or whose name is not recognized by his neighbors, is unworthy of respect. For such a man, his turban is said to be either nonexistent or to lie in the dust at the feet of others. To be given a name is to have one's head crowned by a turban, an acknowledgment that one leads a responsible and respectable life. Although I repeatedly introduced myself as "Rashid Karim," a

fairly decent Pakistani rendering of Richard Kurin, just about all the villagers insisted on calling me *Angrez* ("Englishman"), thus denying me full personhood and implicitly refusing to grant me the right to wear a turban.

As I began to pick up the vernacular, to question villagers about their clan and kinship structure and trace out relationships between different families, my image began to change. My drawings of kinship diagrams and preliminary census mappings were looked upon not only with wonder but also suspicion. My neighbors now began to think there might be a method to my madness. And so there was. Now I had become a spy. Of course it took a week for people to figure out whom I was supposedly spying for. Located as they were at a crossroads of Asia, at a nexus of conflicting geopolitical interests, they had many possibilities to consider. There was a good deal of disagreement on the issue, with the vast majority maintaining that I was either an American, Russian, or Indian spy. A small, but nonetheless vocal, minority held steadfastly to the belief that I was a Chinese spy. I thought it all rather humorous until one day a group confronted me in the main square in front of the nine-by-nine-foot mud hut that I had rented. The leader spoke up and accused me of spying. The remainder of the group grumbled *jahsus! jahsus!* ("spy! spy!"), and I realized that this ad hoc committee of inquiry had the potential of becoming a mob.

To be sure, the villagers had good reason to be suspicious. For one, the times were tense in Pakistan—a national political crisis gripped the country and the populace had been anxious for months over the uncertainty of elections and effective governmental functions. Second, keenly aware of their history, some of the villagers did not have to go too far to imagine that I was at the vanguard of some invading group that had designs upon their land. Such intrigues, with far greater sophistication, had been played out before by nations seeking to expand their power into the Punjab. That I possessed a gold seal letter (which no one save myself could read) from the University of Chicago to the effect that I was pursuing legitimate studies was not enough to convince the crowd that I was indeed an innocent scholar.

I repeatedly denied the charge, but to no avail. The shouts of *jahsus! jahsus!* prevailed. Confronted with this I had no choice.

"Okay," I said. "I admit it. I am a spy!"

The crowd quieted for my long-awaited confession.

"I am a spy and am here to study this village, so that when my country attacks you we will be prepared. You see, we will not bomb Lahore or Karachi or Islamabad. Why should we waste our bombs on millions of people, on factories, dams, airports, and harbors? No, it is far more advantageous to bomb this strategic small village replete with its mud huts, livestock, Persian wheels, and one light bulb. And when we bomb this village, it is imperative that we know how Allah Ditta is related to Abdullah, and who owns the land near the well, and what your marriage customs are."

Silence hung over the crowd, and then one by one the assemblage began to disperse. My sarcasm had worked. The spy charges were defused. But I was no hero in light of my performance, and so I was once again relegated to the status of a nonperson without an identity in the village.

I remained in limbo for the next week, and although I continued my attempts to collect information about village life, I had my doubts as to whether I would ever be accepted by the villagers. And then, through no effort of my own, there was a breakthrough, this time due to another Allah Ditta, a relative of the village headman and one of my leading accusers during my spying days.

I was sitting on my woven string bed on my porch when Allah Ditta approached, leading his son by the neck. "Oh, *Angrez!*" he yelled, "this worthless son of mine is doing poorly in school. He is supposed to be learning English, but he is failing. He has a good mind, but he's lazy. And his teacher is no help, being more intent upon drinking tea and singing film songs than upon teaching English. Oh son of an Englishman, do you know English?"

"Yes, I know English," I replied, "after all, I am an *Angrez.*"

"Teach him," Allah Ditta blurted out, without any sense of making a tactful request.

And so, I spent the next hour with the boy, reviewing his lessons and correcting his pronunciation and grammar. As I did so, villagers stopped to watch and listen, and by the end of the hour, nearly one hundred people had gathered around, engrossed by this tutoring session. They were stupefied. I was an effective teacher, and I actually seemed to know English. The boy responded well, and the crowd reached a new consensus. I had a brain. And in recognition of this achievement I was given a name—"Ustad Rashid," or Richard the Teacher.

Achieving the status of a teacher was only the beginning of my success. The next morning I awoke to find the village sugar vendor at my door. He had a headache and wanted to know if I could cure him.

"Why do you think I can help you?" I asked.

Bhai Khan answered, "Because you are a *ustad*, you have a great deal of knowledge."

The logic was certainly compelling. If I could teach English, I should be able to cure a headache. I gave him two aspirins.

An hour later, my fame had spread. Bhai Khan had been cured, and he did not hesitate to let others know that it was the *ustad* who had been responsible. By the next day, and in fact for the remainder of my stay, I was to see an average of twenty-five to thirty patients a day. I was asked to cure everything from coughs and colds to typhoid, elephantiasis, and impotency. Upon establishing a flourishing and free medical practice, I received another title, *hakim*, or "physician." I was not yet an anthropologist, but I was on my way.

A few days later I took on yet another role. One of my research interests involved tracing out patterns of land ownership and inheritance. While working on the problem of figuring out who owned what, I was approached by the village watchman. He claimed he had been swindled in a land deal and requested my help. As the accused was not another villager, I agreed to present the watchman's case to the local authorities.

Somehow, my efforts managed to achieve results. The plaintiff's grievance was redressed, and I was given yet another title in the village—*wakil*, or "lawyer." And in the weeks that followed, I was steadily called upon to read, translate, and advise upon various court orders that affected the lives of the villagers.

My roles as teacher, doctor, and lawyer not only provided me with an identity but also facilitated my integration into the economic structure of the community. As my imputed skills offered my neighbors services not readily available in the village, I was drawn into exchange relationships known as *seipi*. *Seipi* refers to the barter system of goods and services among village farmers, craftsmen, artisans, and other specialists. Every morning Roshan the milkman would deliver fresh milk to my hut. Every other day Hajam Ali the barber would stop by and give me a shave. My next-door neighbor, Nura the cobbler, would repair my sandals when required. Ghulam the horse-cart driver would transport me to town when my motor scooter was in disrepair. The parents of my students would send me sweets and sometimes delicious meals. In return, none of my neighbors asked for direct payment for the specific actions performed. Rather, as they told me, they would call upon me when they had need of my services. And they did. Nura needed cough syrup for his children, the milkman's brother needed a job contact in the city, students wanted to continue their lessons, and so on. Through *seipi* relations, various neighbors gave goods and services to me, and I to them.

Even so, I knew that by Punjabi standards I could never be truly accepted into village life because I was not a member of either the Nunari or Bhatti tribe. As the villagers would say, "You never really know who a man is until you know who his grandfather and his ancestors were." And to know a person's grandfather or ancestors properly, you had to be a member of the same or a closely allied tribe.

The Nunari tribe is composed of a number of groups. The nucleus consists of four clans—Naul, Vadel, Sadan, and More—each named for one of four brothers thought to have originally founded the tribe. Clan members are said to be related by blood ties, also called *pag da sak*, or "ties of the turban." In sharing the turban, members of each clan share the same name. Other clans, unrelated by ties of blood to these four, have become attached to this nucleus through a history of marital relations or of continuous political and economic interdependence. Marital relations, called *gag da sak*, or "ties of the skirt," are conceived of as relations in which alienable turbans (skirts) in the form of women are exchanged with other, non-turban-sharing groups. Similarly, ties of political and economic domination and subordination are thought of as relations in which the turban of the client is given to that of the patron. A major part of my research work was concerned with reconstructing how the four brothers formed the Nunari tribe, how additional clans became associated with it, and how clan and tribal identity were defined by nomenclature, codes of honor, and the symbols of sharing and exchanging turbans.

To approach these issues I set out to reconstruct the genealogical relationships within the tribe and between the various clans. I elicited genealogies from many of the villagers and questioned older informants about the history of the Nunari tribe. Most knew only bits and pieces of this history, and after several months of interviews and research, I was directed to the tribal genealogists. These people, usually not Nunaris themselves, perform the service of memorizing and then orally relating the history of the tribe and the relationships among its members. The genealogist in the village was an aged and arthritic man named Hedayat, who in his later years was engaged in teaching the Nunari genealogy to his son, who would then carry out the traditional and hereditary duties of his position.

The villagers claimed that Hedayat knew every generation of the Nunari from the present to the founding brothers and even beyond. So I invited Hedayat to my hut and explained my purpose.

"Do you know Allah Ditta son of Rohm?" I asked.

"Yes, of course," he replied.

"Who was Rohm's father?" I continued.

"Shahadat Mohammad," he answered.

"And his father?"

"Hamid."

"And his?"

"Chigatah," he snapped without hesitation.

I was now quite excited, for no one else in the village had been able to recall an ancestor of this generation. My estimate was that Chigatah had been born sometime between 1850 and 1870. But Hedayat went on.

"Chigatah's father was Kamal. And Kamal's father was Nanak. And Nanak's father was Sikhu. And before him was Dargai, and before him Maiy. And before him was Siddiq. And Siddiq's father was Nur. And Nur's Asmat. And Asmat was of Channa. And Channa of Nau. And Nau of Bhatta. And Bhatta was the son of Koduk."

Hedayat had now recounted sixteen generations of lineal ascendants related through the turban. Koduk was probably born in the sixteenth century. But still Hedayat continued.

"Sigun was the father of Koduk. And Man the father of Sigun. And before Man was his father Maneswar. And Maneswar's father was the founder of the clan, Naul."

This then was a line of the Naul clan of the Nunari tribe, ascending twenty-one generations from the present descendants (Allah Ditta's son) to the founder, one of four brothers who lived perhaps in the fifteenth century. I asked Hedayat to recite genealogies of the other Nunari clans, and he did, with some blanks here and there, ending with Vadel, More, and Saddan, the other three brothers who formed the tribal nucleus. I then asked the obvious question, "Hedayat, who was the father of these four brothers? Who is the founding ancestor of the Nunari tribe?"

"The father of these brothers was not a Muslim. He was an Indian rajput [chief]. The tribe actually begins with the conversion of the four brothers," Hedayat explained.

"Well then," I replied, "who was this Indian chief?"

"He was a famous and noble chief who fought against the Moguls. His name was Raja Kurin, who lived in a massive fort in Kurinnagar, about twenty-seven miles from Delhi."

"What!" I asked, both startled and unsure of what I had heard.

"Raja Kurin is the father of the brothers who make up—"

"But his name! It's the same as mine," I stammered. "Hedayat, my name is Richard Kurin. What a coincidence! Here I am living with your tribe thousands of miles from my home and it turns out that I have the same name as the founder of the tribe! Do you think I might be related to Raja Kurin and the Nunaris?"

Hedayat looked at me, but only for an instant. Redoing his turban, he tilted his head skyward, smiled, and asked, "What is the name of your father?"

I had come a long way. I now had a name that could be recognized and respected, and as I answered Hedayat, I knew that I had finally and irrevocably fit into "my" village. Whether by fortuitous circumstances or by careful manipulation, my neighbors had found a way to take an invading city person intent on studying their life and transform him into one of their own, a full person entitled to wear a turban for participating in, and being identified with, that life. As has gone on for centuries in the region, once again the new and exogenous had been recast into something Punjabi.

Epilogue: There is no positive evidence linking the Nunaris to a historical Raja Kurin, although there are several famous personages identified by that name (also transcribed as Karan and Kurran). Estimated from the genealogy recited by Hedayat, the founding of the tribe by four brothers appears to have occurred sometime between 440 and 640 years ago, depending on the interval assumed for each generation. On that basis, the most likely candidate for Nunari progenitor (actual or imputed) is Raja Karan, ruler of Anhilvara (Gujerat), who was defeated by the Khilji Ala-ud-Din in 1297 and again in 1307. Although this is slightly earlier than suggested by the genealogical data, such genealogies are often telescoped or otherwise unreliable.

Nevertheless, several aspects of Hedayat's account make this association doubtful. Hedayat clearly identifies Raja Kurin's conquerors as Moguls, whereas the Gujerati Raja Karan was defeated by the Khiljis. Second, Hedayat places the Nunari ancestor's kingdom only twenty-seven miles from Delhi. The Gujerati Raja Karan ruled several kingdoms, none closer than several hundred miles to Delhi.

Other circumstances, however, offer support for this identification of the Nunari ancestor. According to Hedayat, Raja Kurin's father was named Kam Deo. Although the historical figure was the son of Serung Deo, the use of "Deo," a popular title for the rajas of the Vaghela and Solonki dynasties, does seem to place the Nunari fonder in the context of medieval Gujerat. Furthermore, Hedayat clearly identifies the saint (*pir*) said to have initiated the conversion of the Nunaris to Islam. This saint, Mukhdum-i-Jehaniyan, was a contemporary of the historical Raja Karan.

Also of interest, but as yet unexplained, is that several other groups living in Nunari settlement areas specifically claim to be descended from Raja Karan of Gujerat, who is said to have migrated northward into the Punjab after his defeat. Controverting this theory, the available evidence indicates that Raja Karan fled, not toward the Punjab, but rather southward to the Deccan, and that his patriline ended with him. It is his daughter, Deval Devi who is remembered: she is the celebrated heroine of "Ashiqa," a famous Urdu poem written by Amir Khusrau in 1316. She was married to Khizr Khan, the son of Karan's conqueror; nothing is known of her progeny.

Richard Kurin is the Deputy Director of Folklife Programs at the Smithsonian Institution.

Eating Christmas in the Kalahari

Richard Borshay Lee

The !Kung Bushmen's knowledge of Christmas is thirdhand. The London Missionary Society brought the holiday to the southern Tswana tribes in the early nineteenth century. Later, native cate-chists spread the idea far and wide among the Bantu-speaking pastoralists, even in the remotest corners of the Kala-hari Desert. The Bushmen's idea of the Christmas story, stripped to its essen-tials, is "praise the birth of white man's god-chief"; what keeps their interest in the holiday high is the Tswana-Herero custom of slaughtering an ox for his Bushmen neighbors as an annual good-will gesture. Since the 1930's, part of the Bushmen's annual round of activities has included a December congregation at the cattle posts for trading, marriage brokering, and several days of trance-dance feasting at which the local Tswana headman is host.

As a social anthropologist working with !Kung Bushmen, I found that the Christmas ox custom suited my pur-poses. I had come to the Kalahari to study the hunting and gathering subsis-tence economy of the !Kung, and to ac-complish this it was essential not to provide them with food, share my own food, or interfere in any way with their food-gathering activities. While liberal handouts of tobacco and medical sup-plies were appreciated, they were scarcely adequate to erase the glaring disparity in wealth between the anthro-pologist, who maintained a two-month inventory of canned goods, and the Bushmen, who rarely had a day's supply

of food on hand. My approach, while paying off in terms of data, left me open to frequent accusations of stinginess and hard-heartedness. By their lights, I was a miser.

The Christmas ox was to be my way of saying thank you for the cooperation of the past year; and since it was to be our last Christmas in the field, I determined to slaughter the largest, meatiest ox that money could buy, insuring that the feast and trance-dance would be a success.

Through December I kept my eyes open at the wells as the cattle were brought down for watering. Several ani-mals were offered, but none had quite the grossness that I had in mind. Then, ten days before the holiday, a Herero friend led an ox of astonishing size and mass up to our camp. It was solid black, stood five feet high at the shoulder, had a five-foot span of horns, and must have weighed 1,200 pounds on the hoof. Food consumption calculations are my spe-cialty, and I quickly figured that bones and viscera aside, there was enough meat—at least four pounds—for every man, woman, and child of the 150 Bush-men in the vicinity of /ai/ai who were ex-pected at the feast.

Having found the right animal at last, I paid the Herero £20 ($56) and asked him to keep the beast with his herd until Christmas day. The next morning word spread among the people that the big solid black one was the ox chosen by / ontah (my Bushman name; it means, roughly, "whitey") for the Christmas feast. That afternoon I received the first

delegation. Ben!a, an outspoken sixty-year-old mother of five, came to the point slowly.

"Where were you planning to eat Christmas?"

"Right here at /ai/ai," I replied.

"Alone or with others?"

"I expect to invite all the people to eat Christmas with me."

"Eat what?"

"I have purchased Yehave's black ox, and I am going to slaughter and cook it."

"That's what we were told at the well but refused to believe it until we heard it from yourself."

"Well, it's the black one," I replied expansively, although wondering what she was driving at.

"Oh, no!" Ben!a groaned, turning to her group. "They were right." Turning back to me she asked, "Do you expect us to eat that bag of bones?"

"Bag of bones! It's the biggest ox at / ai/ai."

"Big, yes, but old. And thin. Every-body knows there's no meat on that old ox. What did you expect us to eat off it, the horns?"

Everybody chuckled at Ben!a's one-liner as they walked away, but all I could manage was a weak grin.

That evening it was the turn of the young men. They came to sit at our evening fire. /gaugo, about my age, spoke to me man-to-man.

"/ontah, you have always been square with us," he lied. "What has happened to change your heart? That sack of guts and bones of Yehave's will hardly feed one camp, let alone all the Bushmen around ai/ai." And he proceeded to enumerate the seven camps in the /ai/ai vicinity, family by family. "Perhaps you have forgotten that we are not few, but many. Or are you too blind to tell the difference between a proper cow and an old wreck? That ox is thin to the point of death."

"Look, you guys," I retorted, "that is a beautiful animal, and I'm sure you will eat it with pleasure at Christmas."

"Of course we will eat it; it's food. But it won't fill us up to the point where we will have enough strength to dance. We will eat and go home to bed with stomachs rumbling."

That night as we turned in, I asked my wife, Nancy: "What did you think of the black ox?"

"It looked enormous to me. Why?"

"Well, about eight different people have told me I got gypped; that the ox is nothing but bones."

"What's the angle?" Nancy asked. "Did they have a better one to sell?"

"No, they just said that it was going to be a grim Christmas because there won't be enough meat to go around. Maybe I'll get an independent judge to look at the beast in the morning."

Bright and early, Halingisi, a Tswana cattle owner, appeared at our camp. But before I could ask him to give me his opinion on Yehave's black ox, he gave me the eye signal that indicated a confidential chat. We left the camp and sat down.

"/ontah, I'm surprised at you: you've lived here for three years and still haven't learned anything about cattle."

"But what else can a person do but choose the biggest, strongest animal one can find?" I retorted.

"Look, just because an animal is big doesn't mean that it has plenty of meat on it. The black one was a beauty when it was younger, but now it is thin to the point of death."

"Well I've already bought it. What can I do at this stage?"

"Bought it already? I thought you were just considering it. Well, you'll have to kill it and serve it, I suppose. But don't expect much of a dance to follow."

My spirits dropped rapidly. I could believe that Ben!a and /gaugo just might be putting me on about the black ox, but

Halingisi seemed to be an impartial critic. I went around that day feeling as though I had bought a lemon of a used car.

In the afternoon it was Tomazo's turn. Tomazo is a fine hunter, a top trance performer... and one of my most reliable informants. He approached the subject of the Christmas cow as part of my continuing Bushman education.

"My friend, the way it is with us Bushmen," he began, "is that we love meat. And even more than that, we love fat. When we hunt we always search for the fat ones, the ones dripping with layers of white fat: fat that turns into a clear, thick oil in the cooking pot, fat that slides down your gullet, fills your stomach and gives you a roaring diarrhea," he rhapsodized.

"So, feeling as we do," he continued, "it gives us pain to be served such a scrawny thing as Yehave's black ox. It is big, yes, and no doubt its giant bones are good for soup, but fat is what we really crave and so we will eat Christmas this year with a heavy heart."

The prospect of a gloomy Christmas now had me worried, so I asked Tomazo what I could do about it.

"Look for a fat one, a young one... smaller, but fat. Fat enough to make us //gom ('evacuate the bowels'), then we will be happy."

My suspicions were aroused when Tomazo said that he happened to know of a young, fat, barren cow that the owner was willing to part with. Was Tomazo working on commission, I wondered? But I dispelled this unworthy thought when we approached the Herero owner of the cow in question and found that he had decided not to sell.

The scrawny wreck of a Christmas ox now became the talk of the /ai/ai water hole and was the first news told to the outlying groups as they began to come in from the bush for the feast. What finally convinced me that real trouble might be brewing was the visit from u!au, an old conservative with a reputation for fierceness. His nickname meant spear and referred to an incident thirty years ago in which he had speared a man to death. He had an intense manner; fixing me with his eyes, he said in clipped tones:

"I have only just heard about the black ox today, or else I would have come here earlier. /ontah, do you honestly think you can serve meat like that to people and avoid a fight?" He paused, letting the implications sink in. "I don't mean fight you, /ontah; you are a white man. I mean a fight between Bushmen. There are many fierce ones here, and with such a small quantity of meat to distribute, how can you give everybody a fair share? Someone is sure to accuse another of taking too much or hogging all the choice pieces. Then you will see what happens when some go hungry while others eat."

The possibility of at least a serious argument struck me as all too real. I had witnessed the tension that surrounds the distribution of meat from a kudu or gemsbok kill, and had documented many arguments that sprang up from a real or imagined slight in meat distribution. The owners of a kill may spend up to two hours arranging and rearranging the piles of meat under the gaze of a circle of recipients before handing them out. And I also knew that the Christmas feast at /ai/ai would be bringing together groups that had feuded in the past.

Convinced now of the gravity of the situation, I went in earnest to search for a second cow; but all my inquiries failed to turn one up.

The Christmas feast was evidently going to be a disaster, and the incessant complaints about the meagerness of the ox had already taken the fun out of it for me. Moreover, I was getting bored with the wisecracks, and after losing my temper a few times, I resolved to serve the beast anyway. If the meat fell short, the hell with it. In the Bushmen idiom, I announced to all who would listen:

"I am a poor man and blind. If I have chosen one that is too old and too thin, we will eat it anyway and see if there is enough meat there to quiet the rumbling of our stomachs."

On hearing this speech, Ben!a offered me a rare word of comfort. "It's thin," she said philosophically, "but the bones will make a good soup."

At dawn Christmas morning, instinct told me to turn over the butchering and cooking to a friend and take off with Nancy to spend Christmas alone in the bush. But curiosity kept me from retreating. I wanted to see what such a scrawny ox looked like on butchering and if there *was* going to be a fight, I wanted to catch every word of it. Anthropologists are incurable that way.

The great beast was driven up to our dancing ground, and a shot in the forehead dropped it in its tracks. Then, freshly cut branches were heaped around the fallen carcass to receive the meat. Ten men volunteered to help with the cutting. I asked /gaugo to make the breast bone cut. This cut, which begins the butchering process for most large game, offers easy access for removal of the viscera. But it also allows the hunter to spot-check the amount of fat on the animal. A fat game animal carries a white layer up to an inch thick on the chest, while in a thin one, the knife will quickly cut to bone. All eyes fixed on his hand as /gaugo, dwarfed by the great carcass, knelt to the breast. The first cut opened a pool of solid white in the black skin. The second and third cut widened and deepened the creamy white. Still no bone. It was pure fat; it must have been two inches thick.

"Hey /gau," I burst out, "that ox is loaded with fat. What's this about the ox being too thin to bother eating? Are you out of your mind?"

"Fat?" /gau shot back, "You call that fat? This wreck is thin, sick, dead!" And he broke out laughing. So did everyone else. They rolled on the ground, paralyzed with laughter. Everybody laughed except me; I was thinking.

I ran back to the tent and burst in just as Nancy was getting up. "Hey, the black ox. It's fat as hell! They were kidding about it being too thin to eat. It was a joke or something. A put-on. Everyone is really delighted with it!"

"Some joke," my wife replied. "It was so funny that you were ready to pack up and leave /ai/ai."

If it had indeed been a joke, it had been an extraordinarily convincing one, and tinged, I thought, with more than a touch of malice as many jokes are. Nevertheless, that it was a joke lifted my spirits considerably, and I returned to the butchering site where the shape of the ox was rapidly disappearing under the axes and knives of the butchers. The atmo-

sphere had become festive. Grinning broadly, their arms covered with blood well past the elbow, men packed chunks of meat into the big cast-iron cooking pots, fifty pounds to the load, and muttered and chuckled all the while about the thinness and worthlessness of the animal and /ontah's poor judgment.

We danced and ate that ox two days and two nights; we cooked and distributed fourteen potfuls of meat and no one went home hungry and no fights broke out.

But the "joke" stayed in my mind. I had a growing feeling that something important had happened in my relationship with the Bushmen and that the clue lay in the meaning of the joke. Several days later, when most of the people had dispersed back to the bush camps, I raised the question with Hakekgose, a Tswana man who had grown up among the !Kung, married a !Kung girl, and who probably knew their culture better than any other non-Bushman.

"With us whites," I began, "Christmas is supposed to be the day of friendship and brotherly love. What I can't figure out is why the Bushmen went to such lengths to criticize and belittle the ox I had bought for the feast. The animal was perfectly good and their jokes and wisecracks practically ruined the holiday for me."

"So it really did bother you," said Hakekgose. "Well, that's the way they always talk. When I take my rifle and go hunting with them, if I miss, they laugh at me for the rest of the day. But even if I hit and bring one down, it's no better. To them, the kill is always too small or too old or too thin; and as we sit down on the kill site to cook and eat the liver, they keep grumbling, even with their mouths full of meat. They say things like, 'Oh this is awful! What a worthless animal! Whatever made me think that this Tswana rascal could hunt!'"

"Is this the way outsiders are treated?" I asked.

"No, it is their custom; they talk that way to each other too. Go and ask them."

/gaugo had been one of the most enthusiastic in making me feel bad about the merit of the Christmas ox. I sought him out first.

"Why did you tell me the black ox was worthless, when you could see that it was loaded with fat and meat?"

"It is our way," he said smiling. "We always like to fool people about that. Say there is a Bushman who has been hunting. He must not come home and announce like a braggard, 'I have killed a big one in the bush!' He must first sit down in silence until I or someone else comes up to his fire and asks, 'What did you see today?' He replies quietly, 'Ah, I'm no good for hunting. I saw nothing at all [pause] just a little tiny one.' Then I smile to myself," /gaugo continued, "because I know he has killed something big."

"In the morning we make up a party of four or five people to cut up and carry the meat back to the camp. When we arrive at the kill we examine it and cry out, 'You mean to say you have dragged us all the way out here in order to make us cart home your pile of bones? Oh, if I had known it was this thin I wouldn't have come.' Another one pipes up, 'People, to think I gave up a nice day in the shade for this. At home we may be hungry but at least we have nice cool water to drink.' If the horns are big, someone says, 'Did you think that somehow you were going to boil down the horns for soup?'

"To all this you must respond in kind. 'I agree,' you say, 'this one is not worth the effort; let's just cook the liver for strength and leave the rest for the hyenas. It is not too late to hunt today and even a duiker or a steenbok would be better than this mess.'

"Then you set to work nevertheless; butcher the animal, carry the meat back to the camp and everyone eats," /gaugo concluded.

Things were beginning to make sense. Next, I went to Tomazo. He corroborated /gaugo's story of the obligatory insults over a kill and added a few details of his own.

"But," I asked, "why insult a man after he has gone to all that trouble to track and kill an animal and when he is going to share the meat with you so that your children will have something to eat?"

"Arrogance," was his cryptic answer.

"Arrogance?"

"Yes, when a young man kills much meat he comes to think of himself as a chief or a big man, and he thinks of the rest of us as his servants or inferiors. We can't accept this. We refuse one who boasts, for someday his pride will make him kill somebody. So we always speak of his meat as worthless. This way we cool his heart and make him gentle."

"But why didn't you tell me this before?" I asked Tomazo with some heat.

"Because you never asked me," said Tomazo, echoing the refrain that has come to haunt every field ethnographer.

The pieces now fell into place. I had known for a long time that in situations of social conflict with Bushmen I held all the cards. I was the only source of tobacco in a thousand square miles, and I was not incapable of cutting an individual off for non-cooperation. Though my boycott never lasted longer than a few days, it was an indication of my strength. People resented my presence at the water hole, yet simultaneously dreaded my leaving. In short I was a perfect target for the charge of arrogance and for the Bushmen tactic of enforcing humility.

I had been taught an object lesson by the Bushmen; it had come from an unexpected corner and had hurt me in a vulnerable area. For the big black ox was to be the one totally generous, unstinting act of my year at /ai/ai, and I was quite unprepared for the reaction I received.

As I read it, their message was this: There are no totally generous acts. All "acts" have an element of calculation. One black ox slaughtered at Christmas does not wipe out a year of careful manipulation of gifts given to serve your own ends. After all, to kill an animal and share the meat with people is really no more than Bushmen do for each other every day and with far less fanfare.

In the end, I had to admire how the Bushmen had played out the farce—collectively straight-faced to the end. Curiously, the episode reminded me of the *Good Soldier Schweik* and his marvelous encounters with authority. Like Schweik, the Bushmen had retained a thorough-going skepticism of good intentions. Was it this independence of spirit, I wondered, that had kept them culturally viable in the face of generations of contact with more powerful societies, both black and white? The thought that the Bushmen were alive and well in the Kalahari was strangely comforting. Perhaps, armed with that independence and with their superb knowledge of their environment, they might yet survive the future.

Richard Borshay Lee is a full professor of anthropology at the University of Toronto. He has done extensive fieldwork in southern Africa, is coeditor of Man the Hunter *(1968) and* Kalahari Hunter-Gatherers *(1976), and author of* The !Kung San: Men, Women, and Work in a Foraging Society.

Battle of the Bones

Recent archaeological findings have led to revolutionary new theories about the first Americans—and to a tug-of-war between scientists and contemporary Native Americans

By Robson Bonnichsen and Alan L. Schneider

Some Crow traditionalists believe that the world, the animals and all humans were created by a wise and powerful being named Old Man Coyote. The Brule Sioux have a different tradition: after a great flood, the only survivor was a beautiful girl, who was rescued by an eagle. She married the eagle, and their children became the Sioux people. Where did the native people of the Americas really come from? When did they first appear in those lands, and how? Just as the Judeo-Christian tradition teaches that human beings originated when God created Adam and Eve in the Garden of Eden, so every Native American tribe has at least one creation story.

Archaeologists, meanwhile, take a different view of how people first appeared in the Americas. Although they are sharply divided about the details, they are convinced by the archaeological record that the original peoples of the Americas migrated there from elsewhere. Where they came from and when they arrived are questions that remain to be resolved. Some answers, however, are beginning to emerge, and they indicate a process that was far more complicated than was ever imagined.

In one sense, both scientific theories about human origins and nonscientific traditions about the genesis of a particular tribe have something in common. All people and all cultures strive to understand the world and their place in it. Origin stories—whether traditional accounts or scientific theories—help satisfy those yearnings. They describe how and when people came to be on the earth, and they explain how people survived and prospered in their surroundings. But there are key differences as well. Scientific origin theories are subject to reevaluation as new evidence emerges: indeed, in the past several years the prevailing scientific view about the origins of the first Americans has shifted dramatically. Nonscientific origin theories, by contrast, derive from supernatural or mystical revelation; they tolerate neither doubt nor revision, and must be accepted on faith.

Until recently, archaeologists were able to pin only a few firm dates on the ancient human remains that had been discovered in the Americas. Part of the reason was that the existing dating technology required that large samples— sometimes an entire bone—be destroyed, and so the process was infrequently applied. But in the past decade several new analytical methods have emerged: DNA typing of ancient biological material, comparative skull measurements and accelerator mass spectrometry, a radiocarbon-dating technique that requires only minuscule amounts of bone. Those new techniques have made it possible to accurately determine the ages of skeletal remains, as well as to classify the various human ethnic groups far more precisely than ever before. Moreover, in recent years a few very ancient and well-preserved new skeletons have been unearthed. Those discoveries, combined with the new analyses, have led archaeologists to some startling conclusions—including the possibility that modern-day Native Americans are not descended from the earliest people who colonized the Americas.

Thus the past few years have been an exciting time in the field of Paleo-American prehistory (also known as First Americans studies). And yet, ironically, the period has also been one of disappointment and uncertainty, as government and museum officials are being asked to curtail and even prohibit archaeological research. The reason for the political ferment is that Native American origin theories, which had long been relegated to the realm of personal religious beliefs, are suddenly being thrust into the domain of public policy. That clash between science and religion has commanded the attention of the media, and a surge of new books and articles about the first Americans has been released in recent months. The subject is of more than topical interest: the outcome of the debate could determine the course of American archaeology for decades to come.

The shifts in public policy stem largely from a ten-year-old federal law, the Native American Graves Protection and Repatriation Act (NAGPRA). Bolstered by that law, some Native American activists are demanding possession of all prehistoric human remains found on federal or tribal lands in the United States and a halt to all study of those remains. In most cases, their intent is to rebury the ancient bones. Native American activists maintain that they already know where they come from, and see no need for further inquiry. They say their oral traditions report that their ancestors have lived in the Americas since the beginning of time. To them, the bones and skulls of ancient people are family members to be put to rest with dignity. Not all Native Americans share those views; many want to learn more about American prehistory and support the scientific study of all relevant remains, artifacts and associated information. Unfortunately, though, many government decision makers seem disposed to side with the anti-science advocates, assigning more legitimacy to Native American religious traditions than to scientific investigation and discourse.

Kennewick Man, a 9,200-year-old skeleton that was discovered on federal land in eastern Washington State on July 28, 1996, has become an important test case. Four weeks after it was found, preliminary radiocarbon-dating results were released, indicating that the skeleton was among the oldest ever unearthed in North America. Within a few days, however, federal officials decided to give the remains to a coalition of five local tribes—despite the fact that the bones had received only a preliminary examination. To forestall what would have been a tragic loss for science, one of us (Bonnichsen) and seven other experts in Paleo-American studies filed a federal lawsuit in Portland, Oregon, to prevent transfer of the skeleton. (The other author, Schneider, is an attorney in the case.) We requested, successfully, that the skeleton be kept in federal custody until our lawsuit was resolved. Today the bones remain in limbo as the dispute drags on.

Native American beliefs about the past and the dead certainly deserve respect, but they should not be allowed to dictate government policy on the investigation and interpretation of early American prehistory. If a choice must be made among competing theories of human origins, primacy should be given to theories based on the scientific method. Only scientific theories are built on empirical evidence; only scientific theories can be adjusted or overturned. True, influential scientists have sometimes been able to temporarily smother scholarly debate on views they opposed. But as recent developments in First Americans studies demonstrate, science is an inherently flexible, self-correcting endeavor. Even long-accepted scientific views can be challenged, and truth eventually wins out.

Ever since Thomas Jefferson began collecting Native American artifacts and displaying them in his foyer, many theories have been proposed to explain how people first came to North and South America. The most widely accepted was the Clovis-first theory, named for the elegant, fluted spear points found in association with the remains of mammoths, bison and other animals near Clovis, New Mexico, in 1932. In subsequent years many similar stone spearheads were found throughout the Great Plains, and eventually in much of the United States and Central and South America. By the late 1960s radiocarbon dating had confirmed that the Clovis artifacts were between 10,800 and 11,500 years old.

In the 1960s and early 1970s the ecologist Paul S. Martin and the geoarchaeologist C. Vance Haynes Jr., both of the University of Arizona in Tucson, together with James E. Mossiman of the National Institutes of Health in Bethesda, Maryland, began to develop a dramatic theory about how the Americas were settled. They hypothesized that about 11,500 years ago, at the end of the most recent Ice Age, a single band of mammoth hunters from Siberia crossed the Bering land bridge into Alaska, and from there began spreading across North America. According to the theory of Martin and his colleagues, there were no people in the New World, as the Americas are sometimes called, until that time. The new arrivals and their descendants prospered and, in just a few centuries, purportedly settled two continents.

The Clovis-first model gained enormous scientific prominence—in fact, to question it was to risk virtual professional suicide. Implicit in the theory is the premise that a single biological population, with a single culture and language, spawned the enormously diverse array of peoples—with their widely divergent cultures and languages—who were living in the New World at the time of European contact. Now, however, thanks to the new archaeological finds and analytical advances, the Clovis-first model has been refuted.

In 1977 Thomas D. Dillehay—an anthropologist at the University of Kentucky in Lexington and the author of one of the books under review, *The Settlement of the Americas*—began excavations at the Monte Verde site in southern Chile. Dillehay's work showed Monte Verde to be at least 12,500 years old, and he was widely criticized for challenging the validity of the Clovis-first theory [see "The Battle of Monte Verde," by Thomas D. Dillehay, January/February 1997]. Dillehay, however, did not back down, and three years ago a special team of archaeologists, including avowed skeptics, inspected Monte Verde. The result was vindication: the experts confirmed that Monte Verde was a legitimate pre-Clovis site. Acceptance of Dillehay's site broke a logjam in First Americans studies. Other sites—and there were many—that had been in limbo because they seemed to predate Clovis could now be acknowledged, too.

Some of those potential pre-Clovis sites include several in southeastern Wisconsin, where the archaeologist David F. Overstreet of Marquette University in Milwaukee has found 12,250-year-old stone tools and mammoth bones with cut marks. And at the Meadowcroft Rockshelter near Pittsburgh, Pennsylvania, the archaeologist James M. Adovasio of Mercyhurst College in Erie, Pennsylvania, has discovered tapered points and bladelike flakes dated to between 12,000 and 16,000 years ago. Similar artifacts have been excavated at the Cactus Hill site near Richmond, Virginia; investigators have dated that site to between 12,000 and 17,000 years old.

And in the oldest archaeological deposits at Monte Verde, Dillehay himself has uncovered flaked stone tools that are apparently about 33,000 years old.

In *The Settlement of the Americas*, Dillehay provides a well-organized synthesis of early Paleo-American archaeological findings. But the book falters in an important way. Dillehay is reluctant to recognize human presence in the Americas prior to 15,000 to 20,000 years ago, despite the older artifacts found at his own site. Although Dillehay assures the reader that his research at Monte Verde is sound, he will not accept the 33,000-year-old radiocarbon dates associated with the stone tools, he writes, until additional artifacts of such antiquity are confirmed at other sites. We find it disappointing that Dillehay, who has done so much to push back the date for the peopling of the Americas, is hesitant to confront the implications of his own data for early human presence in the New World.

In *Bones, Boats, and Bison*, E. James Dixon does for North America what Dillehay did for South America, providing a useful, up-to-date overview of the complex and scattered archaeological literature. Dixon is even more conservative than Dillehay: he favors the idea that the first Americans arrived only about 13,500 years ago. Around that time, he theorizes, people from the Pacific Rim of Asia traveled in small boats to North and South America and settled on the western shores of both continents. But like Dillehay, Dixon is resolute that the Americas were inhabited long before the Clovis artifacts were deposited.

Not only has the idea that the Americas were devoid of people until 11,500 years ago been disproved, but a second important tenet of the Clovis-first theory has also crumbled: the assertion that the Americas were colonized only once. The latest research shows that the New World probably underwent multiple colonizations: instead of originating in a small area of northeast Siberia, as predicted by the Clovis-first model, the first Americans probably came from many parts of Eurasia.

Perhaps the nail in the coffin for the Clovis-first theory is that no Clovis-style artifacts have ever been retrieved from archaeological sites in Siberia. Furthermore, the variety of the artifacts discovered in the rain forests, deserts and coastal areas of South America indicate that early New World people were not members of one homogeneous clan of big-game hunters, as the Clovis-first theory proposed. Depending on their environments, some survived by hunting small game, some by fishing and some by general foraging. As a result, investigators have concluded that, rather than signaling a distinct migration, the Clovis spear points that appear in the archaeological record beginning around 11,500 years ago may simply be the evidence of a technological innovation that took place at that time within groups of people who already lived in the Americas.

Thousands of years before Columbus and the Vikings made their forays, people from Europe may have come to the Americas.

The idea that the Americas were settled more than once and by different groups of people is supported by evidence from ancient skeletons that have been examined with new techniques, such as the study of the DNA in the mitochondria of cells. Mitochondrial DNA is a more stable source of information about genetic lineages than is the DNA in the nucleus of a cell because, rather than representing a melding of maternal and paternal genes, mitochondrial DNA is almost always passed on by the mother alone.

The molecular anthropologist Theodore Schurr of the Southwest Foundation for Biomedical Research in San Antonio, Texas, and other investigators have identified five distinct mitochondrial lineages, or haplogroups, as they are called, in modern Native Americans. Four of the haplogroups—A, B, C and D—are also found in varying frequencies in different Asian populations, which suggest that early immigrants to the Americas may have come from more than one region of Asia. The fifth haplogroup, known as X, is much rarer than the other four haplogroups, and its origin is not clear. It occurs among certain European populations but is absent in contemporary Asian populations, which suggests that it may record another discrete migration to the Americas, possibly from western Eurasia.

In fact, there is growing speculation that Europeans may have traveled to the Americas thousands of years before Columbus and the Vikings made their westward forays. The archaeologists Dennis J. Stanford of the Smithsonian Institution in Washington, D.C., and Bruce A. Bradley of Primitive Tech Enterprises, Inc., in Cortez, Colorado, have noted distinct similarities between the stone tools of the Clovis people and the ones made in France and Spain by members of the Solutrean culture, which flourished between 16,500 and 21,000 years ago. (The theory, only recently proposed, is highly controversial and has yet to be explored in depth.)

The advent of the personal computer has enabled Paleo-American investigators to apply powerful statistical techniques to multiple sets of data. As a result, teams of physical anthropologists have been able to perform comparative analyses of skeletal remains from Asia, North America and South America, based on extensive measurements of skulls, limb bones and teeth, and on dates derived from accelerator mass spectrometry.

The work has yielded some tantalizing results that corroborate much of the DNA evidence. For example, the physical anthropologist C. Loring Brace and his research team from the University of Michigan in Ann Arbor have concluded that the modern native peoples of North America are the descendants of at least four different colonizing populations from two different parts of Asia. Furthermore, Brace argues, those populations probably arrived in the New World at different times and by various routes.

Likewise, the physical anthropologists D. Gentry Steele of Texas A&M University in College Station, Douglas Owsley of the Smithsonian Institution, Richard L. Jantz of the University of

Tennessee in Knoxville and Walter Neves of the University of São Paulo in Brazil have compiled and analyzed measurements from the earliest known North and South American skeletons. Their research has demonstrated that early New World skulls are quite distinct from the skulls of modern Native Americans. Many of the early skulls display relatively narrow faces, long crania, and oval-shaped eye sockets—characteristics that are more typical of skulls from the Pacific Islands and southern Asia than they are of skulls from modern Native Americans.

The reasons for the difference between early and later New World skulls have yet to be fully explained. The discrepancies may be the result of gradual evolutionary changes that took place over time. On the other hand, the differences may indicate that the early skeletons are unrelated to those of modern Native Americans.

Thus a radical new idea has emerged: the people who inhabited the Americas when Columbus arrived—the tribes referred to today as Native Americans—may not be descended from the earliest Americans. There is no reason to assume that the first immigrants to the Americas took hold and prospered. Perhaps some of the early colonizing groups died out before later groups arrived. Or it may be that later colonizing groups replaced earlier groups as a result of warfare, the introduction of new diseases, or higher birth or survival rates. If so, the question then becomes not which tribe does Kennewick Man belong to, but whether the skeleton belongs to any existing tribe at all.

Two new books—*Riddle of the Bones*, by the freelance writer Roger Downey, and *Skull Wars*, by David Hurst Thomas, an anthropologist at the American Museum of Natural History in New York City—present the Native American perspective on the argument. We must concede up front that we are far from impartial reviewers. Both of those books discuss the lawsuit that we initiated, and both seem to support the position of our adversaries: that tribal permission is needed before the Kennewick skeleton can be studied.

Downey attempts to relate the Kennewick Man controversy to the more fundamental question of the peopling of the Americas, but his analysis lacks depth and understanding. He presents a misleading view of the scientists involved in the lawsuit, often resorting to simplistic characterizations and innuendos to attack their motives and research goals. Moreover, he implies that science is not a credible method for explaining the past. From Downey's perspective, Native American origin theories are as legitimate as the scientific ones; in his view, both are only theories, and it is impossible to choose between them.

In *Skull Wars* Thomas attempts to provide the historical context that led to the passage of NAGPRA. He describes, for instance, the so-called skull science of the nineteenth century, which was pioneered by the American physician Samuel George Morton. Morton asserted that the variation in skull size among various ethnic groups proved the intellectual superiority of people of white European stock. Thomas writes that Morton's ideas led to a disregard for the rights of Native Americans, and provided a justification for the looting and robbing of Native American graves.

Thomas's treatment of the past, however, is selective and largely one-sided. He seems to delight in pointing out the failings and racial biases of early investigators, as if to convince the reader that modern science is fatally tainted by past wrongdoing. Meanwhile, he pays little attention to investigators who championed the cause of Native Americans, dedicating their lives to the preservation of knowledge about those vanishing cultures.

Thomas argues that traditional Native American view about the past should be accommodated in decisions concerning the investigation and interpretation of American prehistory. He makes no attempt, however, to explain how belief systems that reject the need for research and critical analysis can provide a workable basis for scientific programs or for setting public policy. Given Thomas's scholarly stature and professional credentials, his failure to address the fundamental differences that separate supernatural origin theories from scientific explanations may confuse both the public and scientists who are not familiar with the subject.

Downey's outlook—that scientific ideas about the settling of the Americas are only theories, and thus no more reliable than any other account—evokes a familiar precedent. Fundamentalist Christians, who maintain that people were created by the God of the Bible, often assert that evolution deserves little respect because it is only a theory. Indeed, the controversy about the first Americans is similar to the dispute about whether children should be taught evolution or creationism in public schools. In both cases, what is at stake is the role of religion in public institutions. One debate threatens educational standards; the other, the future of American archaeology.

Until a decade ago, government intervention in archaeology was limited to the protection and preservation of archaeological sites and resources. Knowledge of American prehistory was considered the common heritage of all Americans, and investigators were free to explore new theories, regardless of their perspectives or research objectives. But now, even though biological knowledge of the earliest humans in the Americas is amazingly thin—fewer than ten relatively complete, securely dated skeletons more than 8,000 years old have been unearthed in North America—government decision makers are bowing to tribal demands for the control of ancient human skeletal remains and artifacts.

For example, the 10,600-year-old Buhl Woman, discovered in Idaho in 1989, was turned over by Idaho state officials to the Shoshone-Bannock tribes, even though scientific evidence indicates that the Shoshone-Bannock have resided in the area for less than 2,000 years. Before its reburial the Buhl skeleton was examined by only one physical anthropologist. Likewise, just a few years later, the 7,800-year-old Hourglass Cave skeleton from Colorado was reburied after limited study. Recently, a 7,800-year-old human skull known as Pelican Rapids

Woman, along with the 8,700-year-old so-called Browns Valley Man, both from Minnesota, were repatriated to a coalition of Sioux tribes and subsequently reburied in South Dakota.

In addition, the study of key archaeological materials and sites is becoming increasingly difficult. In deference to tribal religious beliefs, the government prohibited independent scientists from studying the Kennewick Man discovery site, then buried the site under 600 tons of rock and fill. Genetic analysis of a 9,400-year-old skeleton that was discovered in Nevada, known as the Spirit Cave Mummy, has yet to be allowed because of objections from the Paiute. And several years ago, a team led by one of us (Bonnichsen) was prevented from conducting DNA tests on ancient human hair from the Mammoth Meadow site in Montana, because several tribes claimed possession of the hair [see "Roots," by Robson Bonnichsen and Alan L. Schneider, May/June 1995].

Those decisions by the government to hand over key archaeological evidence and to restrict scientific work are dictated by misguided public policy. Congress did not anticipate that NAGPRA would be applied to very early human remains that might have no direct relation to modern Native Americans. The purpose of NAGPRA was to reunite Native American skeletal remains, funerary items and ceremonial objects with living members of the culture that had produced them. Yet in many cases the tribes invoking NAGPRA to block scientific study have no known cultural or biological connection with the remains or artifacts in question.

Traditional stories about supernatural origins may provide a workable structure for ordering human affairs when all the people affected share the same belief system. They do not, however, provide a satisfactory mechanism for setting government policy in a pluralistic, multicultural society such as the United States. If Native American origin theories are accepted as a basis for determining the ownership and study of archaeological resources uncovered on public land, a dangerous precedent will have been set. What will stop the government from in-

corporating other religious beliefs into its policies?

Scientific theories often offend one or more segments of society because the conclusions of science may differ from those expected by people seeking spiritual answers. Such conflicts are to be expected. But when the government attempts to mediate disputes of that kind, it inevitably ends up censoring the open dissemination of information and ideas. In the quest to understand the history of our species, we need more information, not less. Respect for Native Americans should not cause us to abandon science in favor of politically expedient compromises.

ROBSON BONNICHSEN, an archaeologist at Oregon State University in Corvallis, is the director of the university's Center for the Study of the First Americans. ALAN L. SCHNEIDER is an expert in cultural resources law and an attorney for the scientists in Bonnichsen et al. v. United States of America, *a lawsuit regarding access to the ancient skeletal remains known as Kennewick Man. Bonnichsen is participating in the lawsuit as a private citizen.*

UNIT 2

Culture and Communication

Unit Selections

Key Points to Consider

- What common strategies are used throughout the world to overcome linguistic barriers?

- How can language restrict our thought processes?

- In what ways is communication difficult in a cross-cultural situation?

- How has this section enhanced your ability to communicate more effectively?

 **Links: www.dushkin.com/online/**
These sites are annotated in the World Wide Web pages.

Exploratorium Magazine: "The Evolution of Languages"
http://www.exploratorium.edu/exploring/language

Hypertext and Ethnography
http://www.umanitoba.ca/anthropology/tutor/aaa_presentation.html

Language Extinction
http://www.colorado.edu/iec/alis/articles/langext.htm

Showcase Anthropology
http://www.usc.edu/dept/education/mascha/showcase.html

Anthropologists are interested in all aspects of human behavior and how they interrelate with each other. Language is a form of such behavior (albeit primarily verbal behavior) and, therefore, worthy of study. Although it changes over time, language is patterned and passed down from one generation to the next through learning, not instinct. In keeping with the idea that language is integral to human social interaction, it has long been recognized that human communication through language is by its nature different from the kind of communication found among other animals. Central to this difference is the fact that humans communicate abstractly, with symbols that have meaning independent of the immediate sensory experiences of either the sender or the receiver of messages. Thus, for instance, humans are able to refer to the future and the past instead of just the here and now.

Recent experiments have shown that anthropoid apes can be taught a small portion of Ameslan or American Sign Language. It must be remembered, however, that their very rudimentary ability has to be tapped by painstaking human effort, and that the degree of difference between apes and humans serves only to emphasize the peculiarly human need for and development of language.

Just as the abstract quality of symbols lifts our thoughts beyond immediate sense perception, it also inhibits our ability to think about and convey the full meaning of our personal experience. No categorical term can do justice to its referents—the variety of forms to which the term refers. The degree to which this is an obstacle to clarity of thought and communication relates to the degree of abstraction in the symbols involved. The word "chair," for instance, would not present much difficulty, since it has objective referents. However, consider the trouble we have in thinking and communicating with words whose referents are not tied to immediate sense perception—words such as "freedom," "democracy," and "justice." At best, the likely result is symbolic confusion: an inability to think or communicate in objectively definable symbols. At worst, language may be used to purposefully obfuscate, as William Lutz shows in "Language, Appearance, and Reality: Doublespeak in 1984."

A related issue has to do with the fact that languages differ as to what is relatively easy to express within the restrictions of their particular vocabularies. Thus, although a given language may not have enough words to cope with a new situation or a new field of activity, the typical solution is to invent words or to

41

borrow them. In this way, it may be said that any language can be used to teach anything. This point is illustrated by Laura Bohannan's attempt to convey the "true" meaning of Shakespeare's *Hamlet* to the West African Tiv (see "Shakespeare in the Bush"). Much of her task was devoted to finding the most appropriate words in the Tiv language to convey her Western thoughts. At least part of her failure was due to the fact that some of the words are just not there, and her inventions were unacceptable to the Tiv.

In a somewhat different manner, Deborah Tannen, in "I Can't Even Open My Mouth" and "Why Don't You Say What You Mean?" points out that there are subtleties to language that cannot be found in a dictionary and whose meaning can only be interpreted in the context of the social situation.

Taken collectively, the articles in this unit show how symbolic confusion may occur between individuals or groups. In addition, they demonstrate the tremendous potential of recent research to enhance effective communication among all of us.

Language, Appearance, and Reality: Doublespeak in 1984

William D. Lutz

There are at least four kinds of doublespeak. The first kind is the euphemism, a word or phrase that is designed to avoid a harsh or distasteful reality. When a euphemism is used out of sensitivity for the feelings of someone or out of concern for a social or cultural taboo, it is not doublespeak. For example, we express grief that someone has *passed away* because we do not want to say to a grieving person, "I'm sorry your father is dead." The euphemism *passed away* functions here not just to protect the feelings of another person but also to communicate our concern over that person's feelings during a period of mourning.

However, when a euphemism is used to mislead or deceive, it becomes doublespeak. For example, the U.S. State Department decided in 1984 that in its annual reports on the status of human rights in countries around the world it would no longer use the word *killing*. Instead, it used the phrase *unlawful or arbitrary deprivation of life*. Thus the State Department avoids discussing the embarrassing situation of the government-sanctioned killings in countries that are supported by the United States. This use of language constitutes doublespeak because it is designed to mislead, to cover up the unpleasant. Its real intent is at variance with its apparent intent. It is language designed to alter our perception of reality.

A second kind of doublespeak is jargon, the specialized language of a trade, profession, or similar group. It is the specialized language of doctors, lawyers, engineers, educators, or car mechanics. Jargon can serve an important and useful function. Within a group, jargon allows members of the group to communicate with each other clearly, efficiently, and quickly. Indeed, it is a mark of membership in the group to be able to use and understand the group's jargon. For example, lawyers speak of an *involuntary conversion* of property when discussing the loss or destruction of property through theft, accident, or condemnation When used by lawyers in a legal situation, such jargon is a legitimate use of language, since all members of the group can be expected to understand the term.

However, when a member of the group uses jargon to communicate with a person outside the group, and uses it knowing that the nonmember does not understand such language, then there is doublespeak. For example, a number of years ago a commercial airliner crashed on takeoff, killing three passengers, injuring twenty-one others, and destroying the airplane, a 727. The insured value of the airplane was greater than its book value, so the airline made a profit of three million dollars on the destroyed airplane. But the airline had two problems: it did not want to talk about one of its airplanes crashing and it had to account for the three million dollars when it issued its annual report to its stockholders. The airline solved these problems by inserting a footnote in its annual report explaining that this three million dollars was due to "the involuntary conversion of a 727." Note that airline officials could thus claim to have explained the crash of the airplane and the subsequent three million dollars in profit. However, since most stockholders in the company, and indeed most of the general public, are not familiar with legal jargon, the use of such jargon constitutes doublespeak.

A third kind of doublespeak is gobbledygook or bureaucratese. Basically, such doublespeak is simply a matter of piling on words, of overwhelming the audience with words, the bigger the better. For example, when Alan Greenspan was chairman of the President's Council of Economic Advisors, he made this statement when testifying before a Senate committee:

It is a tricky problem to find the particular calibration in timing that would be appropriate to stem the acceleration in risk premiums created by falling incomes without prematurely aborting the decline in the inflation-generated risk premiums.

Did Alan Greenspan's audience really understand what he was saying? Did he believe his statement really explained anything? Perhaps there is some meaning beneath all those words, but it would take some time to search it out. This seems to be language that pretends to communicate but does not.

The fourth kind of doublespeak is inflated language. Inflated language designed to make the ordinary seem extraordinary, the common, uncommon; to make everyday things seem impressive; to give an air of importance to people, situations, or things that would not normally be considered important; to make the simple seem complex. With this kind of language, car mechanics become *automotive internists*, elevator operators become members of the *vertical transportation corps*, used cars become not just *pre-owned* but *experienced cars*. When the Pentagon uses the phrase *preemptive counterattack* to mean that American forces attacked first, or when it uses the phrase *engage the enemy on all sides* to describe an ambush of American troops, or when it uses the phrase *tactical redeployment* to describe a retreat by American troops, it is using doublespeak. The electronics company that sells the television set with *nonmulticolor capability* is also using the doublespeak of inflated language.

Doublespeak is not a new use of language peculiar to the politics or economics of the twentieth century. Thucydides in *The Peloponnesian War* wrote that

revolution thus ran its course from city to city.... Words had to change their ordinary meanings and to take those which were now given them. Reckless audacity came to be considered the courage of a loyal ally; prudent hesitation, specious cowardice; moderation was held to be a cloak for unmanliness; ability to see all sides of a question, inaptness to act on any. Frantic violence become the attribute of manliness; cautious plotting, a justifiable means of self-defense. The advocate of extreme measures was always trustworthy; his opponent, a man to be suspected.[1]

Caesar in his account of the Gallic Wars described his brutal conquest as "pacifying" Gaul. Doublespeak has a long history.

Military doublespeak seems always to have been with us. In 1947 the name of the War Department was changed to the more pleasing if misleading *Defense Department*. During the Vietnam War the American public learned that it was an *incursion*, not an invasion; a *protective reaction strike* or a *limited duration protective reaction strike* or *air support*, not bombing; and *incontinent ordinance*, not bombs and artillery shells, fell on civilians. This use of language continued with the invasion of Grenada, which was conducted not by the United States Army, Navy, or Air Force, but by the Caribbean Peace Keeping Forces. Indeed, according to the Pentagon, it was not an invasion of Grenada, but a *predawn, vertical insertion*. And it wasn't that the armed forces lacked intelligence data on Grenada before the invasion, it was just that "we were not micromanaging Grenada intelligencewise until about that time frame." In today's army forces, it's not a shovel but a *combat emplacement evacuator*, not a toothpick but a *wood interdental stimulator*, not a pencil but a *portable, handheld communications inscriber*, not a bullet hole but a *ballistically induced aperture in the subcutaneous environment*.

Members of the military and politicians are not the only ones who use doublespeak. People in all parts of society use it. Take educators, for example. On some college campuses what was once the Department of Physical Education is now the *Department of Human Kinetics* or the *College of Applied Life Studies*. Home Economics is now the *School of Human Resources and Family Studies*. College campuses no longer have libraries but *learning resource centers*. Those are not desks in the classroom, they are *pupil stations*. Teachers—*classroom managers* who apply an *action plan* to a *knowledge base*—are concerned with the *basic fundamentals*, which are *inexorably linked to the education user's* (not student's) *time-on-task*. Students don't take tests; now it is *criterion referencing testing* which measures whether a student has achieved the *operational cur-*

ricular objectives. A school system in Pennsylvania uses the following grading system on report cards: "no effort, less than minimal effort, minimal effort, more than minimal effort, less than full effort, full effort, better than full effort, effort increasing, effort decreasing." Some college students in New York come from *economically nonaffluent* families, while the coach at a Southern university wasn't fired, "he just won't be asked to continue in that job." An article in a scholarly journal suggests teaching students three approaches to writing to help them become better writers: "concretization of goals, procedural facilitation, and modeling planning." An article on family relationships entitled "Familial Love and Intertemporal Optimality" observes that "an altruistic utility function promotes intertemporal efficiency. However, altruism creates an externality that implies that satisfying the condition for efficiency does not insure intertemporal optimality." A research report issued by the U.S. Office of Education contains this sentence: "In other words, feediness is the shared information between toputness, where toputness is at a time just prior to the inputness." Education contributes more than its share to current doublespeak.

The world of business has produced large amounts of doublespeak. If an airplane crash is one of the worst things that can happen to an airline company, a recall of automobiles because of a safety defect is one of the worst things that can happen to an automobile company. So a few years ago, when one of the three largest car companies in America had to recall two of its models to correct mechanical defects, the company sent a letter to all those who had bought those models. In its letter, the company said that the rear axle bearings of the cars "can deteriorate" and that "continued driving with a failed bearing could result in disengagement of the axle shaft and adversely affect vehicle control." This is the language of nonresponsibility. What are "mechanical deficiencies"—poor design, bad workmanship? If they do, what causes the deterioration? Note that "continued driving" is the subject of the sentence and suggests that it is not the company's poor manufacturing which is at fault but the driver who persists in driving. Note, too, "failed bearing," which implies that the bearing failed, not the company. Finally, "adversely affect vehicle control" means nothing more than that the driver could lose control of the car and get killed.

If we apply Hugh Rank's criteria for examining such language, we quickly discover the doublespeak here. What the car company should be saying to its customers is that the car the company sold them has a serious defect which should be corrected immediately—otherwise the customer runs the risk of being killed. But the reader of the letter must find this message beneath the doublespeak the company has used to disguise the harshness of its message. We will probably never know how many of the customers never brought their cars in for the necessary repairs because they did not think the problem serious enough to warrant the inconvenience involved.

When it comes time to fire employees, business has produced more than enough doublespeak to deal with the unpleasant situation. Employees are, of course, never fired. They are *selected out, placed out, non-retained, released, dehired, non-renewed*. A corporation will *eliminate the redundancies in the human resources area*, assign *candidates for derecruitment* to a *mobility pool, revitalize the department* by placing executives on *special assignment, enhance the efficiency of operations, streamline the field sales organization*, or *further rationalize marketing efforts*. The reality behind all this doublespeak is that companies are firing employees, but no one wants the stockholders, public, or competition to know that times are tough and people have to go.

Recently the oil industry has been hard hit by declining sales and a surplus of oil. Because of *reduced demand for product*, which results in *spare refining capacity* and problems in *down-stream operations*, oil companies have been forced to *re-evaluate and consolidate their operations* and take *appropriate cost reduction actions*, in order to *enhance the efficiency of operations*, which has meant the *elimination of marginal outlets, accelerating the divestment program*, and the *disposition of low*

throughput marketing units. What this doublespeak really means is that oil companies have fired employees, cut back on expenses, and closed gas stations and oil refineries because there's surplus of oil and people are not buying as much gas and oil as in the past.

One corporation faced with declining business sent a memorandum to its employees advising them that the company's "business plans are under revision and now reflect a more moderate approach toward our operating and capital programs." The result of this "more moderate approach" is a "surplus of professional/technical employees." To "assist in alleviating the surplus, selected professional and technical employees" have been "selected to participate" in a "Voluntary Program." Note that individuals were selected to "resign voluntarily." What this memorandum means, of course, is that expenses must be cut because of declining business, so employees will have to be fired.

It is rare to read that the stock market *fell*. Members of the financial community prefer to say that the stock market *retreated, eased, made a technical adjustment* or a *technical correction*, or perhaps that *prices were off due to profit taking*, or *off in light trading*, or *lost ground*. But the stock market never falls, not if stockbrokers have their say. As a side note, it is interesting to observe that the stock market never rises because of a *technical adjustment* or *correction*, nor does it ever *ease* upwards.

The business sections of newspapers, business magazines, corporate reports, and executive speeches are filled with words and phrases such as *marginal rates of substitution, equilibrium price, getting off margin, distribution coalition, non-performing assets*, and *encompassing organizations*. Much of this is jargon or inflated language designed to make the simple seem complex, but there are other examples of business doublespeak that mislead, that are designed to avoid a harsh reality. What should we make of such expressions as *negative deficit* or *revenue excesses* for profit, *invest in* for buy, *price enhancement* or *price adjustment* for price increase, *shortfall* for a mistake in planning or *period of acceler-*

ated negative growth or *negative economic growth* for recession?

Business doublespeak often attempts to give substance to wind, to make ordinary actions seem complex. Executives *operate* in *timeframes* within the *context* of which a *task force* will serve as the proper *conduit* for all the necessary *input* to *program a scenario* that, within acceptable *parameters*, and with the proper *throughput*, will *generate* the *maximum output* for a *print out* of *zero defect terminal objectives* that will *enhance the bottom line*.

There are instances, however, where doublespeak becomes more than amusing, more than a cause for a weary shake of the head. When the anesthetist turned the wrong knob during a Caesarean delivery and killed the mother and unborn child, the hospital called it a *therapeutic misadventure*. The Pentagon calls the neutron bomb "an efficient nuclear weapon that eliminates an enemy with a minimum degree of damage to friendly territory." The Pentagon also calls expected civilian casualties in a nuclear war *collateral damage*. And it was the Central Intelligence Agency which during the Vietnam War created the phrase *eliminate with extreme prejudice* to replace the more direct verb *kill*.

Identifying doublespeak can at times be difficult. For example, on July 27, 1981, President Ronald Reagan said in a speech televised to the American public: "I will not stand by and see those of you who are dependent on Social Security deprived of the benefits you've worked so hard to earn. You will continue to receive your checks in the full amount due you." This speech had been billed as President Reagan's position on Social Security, a subject of much debate at the time. After the speech, public opinion polls revealed that the great majority of the public believed that President Reagan had affirmed his support for Social Security and that he would not support cuts in benefits. However, five days after the speech, on July 31, 1981, an article in the *Philadelphia Inquirer* quoted White House spokesman David Gergen as saying that President Reagan's words had been "carefully chosen." What President Reagan did mean, according to Gergen, was that he was reserving the right to decide who was "dependent" on those benefits, who had "earned" them, and who, therefore, was "due" them.[2]

The subsequent remarks of David Gergen reveal the real intent of President Reagan as opposed to his apparent intent. Thus Hugh Rank's criteria for analyzing language to determine whether it is doublespeak, when applied in light of David Gergen's remarks, reveal the doublespeak of President Reagan. Here indeed is the insincerity of which Orwell wrote. Here, too, is the gap between the speaker's real and declared aim.

In 1982 the Republican National Committee sponsored a television advertisement which pictured an elderly, folksy postman delivering Social Security checks "with the 7.4% cost-of-living raise that President Reagan promised." The postman then added that "he promised that raise and he kept his promise, in spite of those sticks-in-the-mud who tried to keep him from doing what we elected him to do." The commercial was, in fact, deliberately misleading. The cost-of-living increases had been provided automatically by law since 1975, and President Reagan tried three times to roll them back or delay them but was overruled by congressional opposition. When these discrepancies were pointed out to an official of the Republican National Committee, he called the commercial "inoffensive" and added, "Since when is a commercial supposed to be accurate? Do women really smile when they clean their ovens?"

Again, applying Hugh Rank's criteria to this advertisement reveals the doublespeak in it once we know the facts of past actions by President Reagan. Moreover, the official for the Republican National Committee assumes that all advertisements, whether for political candidates or commercial products, are lies, or in his doublespeak term, *inaccurate*. Thus, the real intent of the advertisement was to mislead while the apparent purpose was to inform the public of President Reagan's position on possible cuts in Social Security benefits. Again their is insincerity, and again there is a gap between the speaker's real and declared aims.

In 1981 Secretary of State Alexander Haig testified before congressional com-

mittees about the murder of three American nuns and a Catholic lay worker in El Salvador. The four women had been raped and shot at close range, and there was clear evidence that the crime had been committed by soldiers of the Salvadoran government. Before the House Foreign Affairs Committee, Secretary Haig said,

> I'd like to suggest to you that some of the investigations would lead one to believe that perhaps the vehicle the nuns were riding in may have tried to run a roadblock, or may accidentally have been perceived to have been doing so, and there'd been an exchange of fire and then perhaps those who inflicted the casualties sought to cover it up. And this could have been at a very low level of both competence and motivation in the context of the issue itself. But the facts on this are not clear enough for anyone to draw a definitive conclusion.

The next day, before the Senate Foreign Relations Committee, Secretary Haig claimed that press reports on his previous testimony were inaccurate. When Senator Claiborne Pell asked whether Secretary Haig was suggesting the possibility that "the nuns may have run through a roadblock." Secretary Haig replied, "You mean that they tried to violate…? Not at all, no, not at all. My heavens! The dear nuns who raised me in my parochial schooling would forever isolate me from their affections and respect." When Senator Pell asked Secretary Haig, "Did you mean that the nuns were firing at the people, or what did 'exchange of fire' mean?" Secretary Haig replied, "I haven't met any pistol-packing nuns in my day, Senator. What I meant was that if one fellow starts shooting, then the next thing you know they all panic." Thus did the secretary of state of the United States explain official government policy on the murder of four American citizens in a foreign land.

Secretary Haig's testimony implies that the women were in some way responsible for their own fate. By using such vague wording as "would lead one

to believe" and "may accidentally have been perceived to have been," he avoids any direct assertion. The use of "inflicted the casualties" not only avoids using the word *kill* but also implies that at the worst the killings were accidental or justifiable. The result of this testimony is that the secretary of state has become an apologist for murder. This is indeed language in defense of the indefensible; language designed to make lies sound truthful and murder respectable; language designed to give an appearance of solidity to pure wind.

These last three examples of doublespeak should make it clear that doublespeak is not the product of careless language or sloppy thinking. Indeed, most doublespeak is the product of clear thinking and is language carefully designed and constructed to appear to communicate when in fact it does not. It is language designed not to lead but to mislead. It is language designed to distort reality and corrupt the mind. It is not a tax increase but *revenue enhancement* or *tax base broadening*, so how can you complain about higher taxes? It is not acid rain, but *poorly buffered precipitation*, so don't worry about all those dead trees. That is not the Mafia in Atlantic City, New Jersey, those are *members of a career offender cartel*, so don't worry about the influence of organized crime in the city. The judge was not addicted to the pain-killing drug he was taking, it was just that the drug had "established an interrelationship with the body, such that if the drug is removed precipitously, there is a reaction," so don't worry that his decisions might have been influenced by his drug addiction. It's not a Titan II nuclear-armed, intercontinental ballistic missile with a warhead 630 times more powerful than the atomic bomb dropped on Hiroshima, it is just a *very large, potentially disruptive re-entry system*, so don't worry about the threat of nuclear destruction. It is not a neutron bomb but a *radiation enhancement device*, so don't worry about escalating the arms race. It is not an invasion but a *rescue mission*, or a *predawn vertical insertion*, so don't worry about any violations of United States or international law.

Doublespeak has become so common in our everyday lives that we fail to notice it. We do not protest when we are asked to check our packages at the desk "for our convenience" when it is not for our convenience at all but for someone else's convenience. We see advertisements for *genuine imitation leather, virgin vinyl,* or *real counterfeit diamonds* and do not question the language or the supposed quality of the product. We do not speak of slums or ghettos but of the *inner city* or *substandard housing where the disadvantaged* live and thus avoid talking about the poor who have to live in filthy, poorly heated, ramshackle apartments or houses. Patients do not die in the hospital; it is just *negative patient care outcome.*

Doublespeak which calls cab drivers *urban transportation specialists,* elevator operators *members of the vertical transportation corps,* and automobile mechanics *automotive internists* can be considered humorous and relatively harmless. However, doublespeak which calls a fire in a nuclear reactor building *rapid oxidation,* an explosion in a nuclear power plant an *energetic disassembly,* the illegal overthrow of a legitimate administration *destabilizing a government,* and lies *inoperative statements* is language which attempts to avoid responsibility, which attempts to make the bad seem good, the negative appear positive, something unpleasant appear attractive, and which seems to communicate but does not. It is language designed to alter our perception of reality and corrupt our minds. Such language does not provide us with the tools needed to develop and preserve civilization. Such language breeds suspicion, cynicism, distrust, and, ultimately, hostility.

Doublespeak is insidious because it can infect and ultimately destroy the function of language, which is communication between people and social groups. If this corrupting process does occur, it can have serious consequences in a country that depends upon an informed electorate to make decisions in selecting candidates for office and deciding issues of public policy. After a while we may really believe that politicians don't lie but only *misspeak,* that illegal acts are merely *inappropriate actions,* that fraud and criminal conspiracy are just *miscertification.* And if we really believe that we understand such language, then the world of *Nineteen Eighty-four* with its control of reality through language is not far away.

The consistent use of doublespeak can have serious and far-reaching consequences beyond the obvious ones. The pervasive use of doublespeak can spread so that doublespeak becomes the coin of the political realm with speakers and listeners convinced that they really understand such language. President Jimmy Carter could call the aborted raid to free the hostages in Tehran in 1980 an "incomplete success" and really believe that he had made a statement that clearly communicated with the American public. So, too, President Ronald Reagan could say in 1985 that "ultimately our security and our hopes for success at the arms reduction talks hinge on the determination that we show here to continue our program to rebuild and refortify our defenses" and really believe that greatly increasing the amount of money spent building new weapons will lead to a reduction in the number of weapons in the world.

The task of English teachers is to teach not just the effective use of language but respect for language as well. Those who use language to conceal or prevent or corrupt thought must be called to account. Only by teaching respect for and love of language can teachers of English instill in students the sense of outrage they should experience when they encounter doublespeak. But before students can experience that outrage, they must first learn to use language effectively, to understand its beauty and power. Only then will we begin to make headway in the fight against doublespeak, for only by using language well will we come to appreciate the perversion inherent in doublespeak.

In his book *The Miracle of Language,* Charlton Laird notes that

> language is… the most important tool man ever devised.… Language is [man's] basic tool. It is the tool more than any other with which he makes his living, makes his home, makes his life. As man becomes more and more a social being, as the world becomes more and more a social community, communication grows ever more imperative. And language is the basis of communication. Language is also the instrument with which we think, and thinking is the rarest and most needed commodity in the world.[3]

In this opinion Laird echoes Orwell's comment that "if thought corrupts language, language can also corrupt thought."[4] Both men have given us a legacy of respect for language, a respect that should prompt us to cry "Enough!" when we encounter doublespeak. The greatest honor we can do Charlton Laird is to continue to have the greatest respect of language in all its manifestations, for, as Laird taught us, language is a miracle.

NOTES AND REFERENCES

1. Thucydides, *The Peloponnesian War,* 3.82.
2. David Hess, "Reagan's Language on Benefits Confused, Angered Many," *Philadelphia Inquirer,* July 31, 1981, p. 6-A.
3. Charlton Laird, *The Miracle of Language* (New York: Fawcett, Premier Books, 1953), p. 224.
4. Orwell, *The Collected Essays,* 4:137.

William D. Lutz, chair of the Department of English at Rutgers University, is also chair of the National Council of Teachers of English (NCTE) Committee on Public Doublespeak and editor of the Quarterly Review of Doublespeak.

From *Et Cetera (ETC),* Winter 1987, pp. 383–391. Excerpted from *The Legacy of Language: A Tribute to Charlton Laird,* edited by Phillip C. Boardman. © 1987 by the University of Nevada Press. Reprinted by permission.

Why Don't You Say What You Mean?

Directness is not necessarily logical or effective. Indirectness is not necessarily manipulative or insecure.

Deborah Tannen

A university president was expecting a visit from a member of the board of trustees. When her secretary buzzed to tell her that the board member had arrived, she left her office and entered the reception area to greet him. Before ushering him into her office, she handed her secretary a sheet of paper and said: "I've just finished drafting this letter. Do you think you could type it right away? I'd like to get it out before lunch. And would you please do me a favor and hold all calls while I'm meeting with Mr. Smith?"

When they sat down behind the closed door of her office, Mr. Smith began by telling her that he thought she had spoken inappropriately to her secretary. "Don't forget," he said. "*You're* the president!"

Putting aside the question of the appropriateness of his admonishing the president on her way of speaking, it is revealing—and representative of many Americans' assumptions—that the indirect way in which the university president told her secretary what to do struck him as self-deprecating. He took it as evidence that she didn't think she had the right to make demands of her secretary. He probably thought he was giving her a needed pep talk, bolstering her self-confidence.

I challenge the assumption that talking in an indirect way necessarily reveals powerlessness, lack of self-confidence or anything else about the character of the speaker. Indirectness is a fundamental element in human communication. It is also one of the elements that varies most from one culture to another, and one that can cause confusion and misunderstanding when speakers have different habits with regard to using it. I also want to dispel the assumption that American women tend to be more indirect than American men. Women and men are both indirect, but in addition to differences associated with their backgrounds—regional, ethnic and class—they tend to be indirect in different situations and in different ways.

At work, we need to get others to do things, and we all have different ways of accomplishing this. Any individual's ways will vary depending on who is being addressed—a boss, a peer or a subordinate. At one extreme are bald commands. At the other are requests so indirect that they don't sound like requests at all, but are just a statement of need or a description of a situation. People with direct styles of asking others to do things perceive indirect requests—if they perceive them as requests at all—as manipulative. But this is often just a way of blaming others for our discomfort with their styles.

The indirect style is no more manipulative than making a telephone call, asking "Is Rachel there?" and expecting whoever answers the phone to put Rachel on. Only a child is likely to answer "Yes" and continue holding the phone—not out of orneriness but because of inexperience with the conventional meaning of the questions. (A mischievous adult might do it to tease.) Those who feel that indirect orders are illogical or manipulative do not recognize the conventional nature of indirect requests.

Issuing orders indirectly can be the prerogative of those in power. Imagine, for example, a master who says "It's cold in here" and expects a servant to make a move to close a window, while a servant who says the same thing is not likely to see his employer rise to correct the situation and make him more comfortable. Indeed, a Frenchman raised in Brittany tells me that his family never gave bald commands to their servants but always communicated orders in indirect and highly polite ways. This pattern renders less surprising the finding of David Bellinger and Jean Berko Gleason that fathers' speech to their young children had a higher incidence than mothers' of both direct imperatives like "Turn the bolt with the wrench" *and* indirect orders like "The wheel is going to fall off."

The use of indirectness can hardly be understood without the cross-cultural perspective. Many Americans find it self-evident that directness is logical and aligned with power while indirectness is akin to dishonesty and reflects subservience. But for speakers raised in most of the world's cultures, varieties of indirectness are the norm in communication. This is the pattern found by a Japanese sociolinguist, Kunihiko Harada, in his analysis of a conversation he recorded between a Japanese boss and a subordinate.

The markers of superior status were clear. One speaker was a Japanese man in his late 40's who managed the local branch of a Japanese private school in the United States. His conversational partner was Japanese-American woman in her early 20's who worked at the school. By virtue of his job, his age and his native fluency in the language being taught, the man was in the superior position. Yet when he addressed the woman, he frequently used polite language and almost always used indirectness. For example, he had tried and failed to find a photography store that would make a black-and-white print from a color negative for a brochure they were producing. He let her know that he wanted her to take over the task by stating the situation and allowed her to volunteer to do it: (This is a translation of the Japanese conversation.)

On this matter, that, that, on the leaflet? This photo, I'm thinking of changing it to black-and-white and making it clearer.... I went to a photo shop and asked them. They said they didn't do black-and-white. I asked if they knew any place that did. They said they didn't know. They weren't very helpful, but anyway, a place must be found, the negative brought to it, the picture developed.

Harada observes, "Given the fact that there are some duties to be performed and that there are two parties present, the subordinate is supposed to assume that those are his or her obligation." It was precisely because of his higher status that the boss was free to choose whether to speak formally or informally, to assert his power or to play it down and build rapport—an option not available to the subordinate, who would have seemed cheeky if she had chosen a style that enhanced friendliness and closeness.

The same pattern was found by a Chinese sociolinguist, Yuling Pan, in a meeting of officials involved in a neighborhood youth program. All spoke in ways that reflected their place in the hierarchy. A subordinate addressing a superior always spoke in a deferential way, but a superior addressing a subordinate could either be authoritarian, demonstrating his power, or friendly, establishing rapport. The ones in power had the option of choosing which style to use. In this spirit, I have been told by people who prefer their bosses to give orders indirectly that those who issue bald commands must be pretty insecure; otherwise why would they have to bolster their egos by throwing their weight around?

I am not inclined to accept that those who give orders directly are really insecure and powerless, any more than I want to accept that judgment of those who give indirect orders. The conclusion to be drawn is that ways of talking should not be taken as obvious evidence of inner psychological states like insecurity or lack of confidence. Considering the many influences on conversational style, individuals have a wide range of ways of getting things done and expressing their emotional states. Personality characteristics like insecurity cannot be linked to ways of speaking in an automatic, self-evident way.

Those who expect orders to be given indirectly are offended when they come unadorned. One woman said that when her boss gives her instructions, she feels she should click her heels, salute, and say "Yes, Boss!" His directions strike her as so imperious as to border on the militaristic. Yet I received a letter from a man telling me that indirect orders were a fundamental part of his military training: He wrote:

Many years ago, when I was in the Navy, I was training to be a radio technician. One class I was in was taught by a chief radioman, a regular Navy man who had been to sea, and who was then in his third hitch. The students, about 20 of us, were fresh out of boot camp, with no sea duty and little knowledge of real Navy life. One day in class the chief said it was hot in the room. The student didn't react, except to

nod in agreement. The chief repeated himself: "It's hot in this room." Again there was no reaction from the students.

Then the chief explained. He wasn't looking for agreement or discussion from us. When he said that the room was hot, he expected us to do something about it—like opening the window. He tried it one more time, and this time all of us left our workbenches and headed for the windows. We had learned. And we had many opportunities to apply what we had learned.

This letter especially intrigued me because "It's cold in here" is the standard sentence used by linguists to illustrate an indirect way of getting someone to do something—as I used it earlier. In this example, it is the very obviousness and rigidity of the military hierarchy that makes the statement of a problem sufficient to trigger corrective action on the part of subordinates.

A man who had worked at the Pentagon reinforced the view that the burden of interpretation is on subordinates in the military—and he noticed the difference when he moved to a position in the private sector. He was frustrated when he'd say to his new secretary, for example, "Do we have a list of invitees?" and be told, "I don't know; we probably do" rather than "I'll get it for you." Indeed, he explained, at the Pentagon, such a question would likely be heard as a reproach that the list was not already on his desk.

The suggestion that indirectness is associated with the military must come as a surprise to many. But everyone is indirect, meaning more than is put into words and deriving meaning from words that are never actually said. It's a matter of where, when and how we each tend to be indirect and look for hidden meanings. But indirectness has a built-in liability. There is a risk that the other will either miss or choose to ignore your meaning.

On Jan. 13, 1982, a freezing cold, snowy day in Washington, Air Florida Flight 90 took off from National Airport, but could not get the lift it needed to keep climbing. It crashed into a bridge linking Washington to the state of Virginia and plunged into the Potomac. Of the 79 people on board all but 5 perished, many floundering and drowning in the icy water while horror-stricken by-standers watched helplessly from the river's edge and millions more watched, aghast, on their television screens. Experts later concluded that the plane had waited too long after de-icing to take off. Fresh buildup of ice on the wings and engine brought the plane down. How could the pilot and co-pilot have made such a blunder? Didn't at least one of them realize it was dangerous to take off under these conditions?

> *The co-pilot repeatedly called attention to dangerous conditions, but the captain didn't get the message.*

Charlotte Linde, a linguist at the Institute for Research on Learning in Palo Alto, Calif., has studied the "black box" recordings of cockpit conversations that preceded crashes as well as tape recordings of conversations that took place among crews during flight simulations in which problems were presented. Among the black box conversations she studied was the one between the pilot and co-pilot just before the Air Florida crash. The pilot, it turned out, had little experience flying in icy weather. The co-pilot had a bit more, and it became heartbreakingly clear on analysis that he had tried to warn the pilot, but he did so indirectly.

The co-pilot repeatedly called attention to the bad weather and to ice building up on other planes:

Co-pilot: Look how the ice is just hanging on his, ah, back, back there, see that?…

Co-pilot: See all those icicles on the back there and everything?

Captain: Yeah.

He expressed concern early on about the long waiting time between de-icing:

Co-pilot: Boy, this is a, this is a losing battle here on trying to de-ice those

things, it [gives] you a false feeling of security, that's all that does.

Shortly after they were given clearance to take off, he again expressed concern:

Co-pilot: Let's check these tops again since we been setting here awhile.

Captain: I think we get to go here in a minute.

When they were about to take off, the co-pilot called attention to the engine instrument readings, which were not normal:

Co-pilot: That don't seem right, does it? [three-second pause] Ah, that's not right….

Captain: Yes, it is, there's 80.

Co-pilot: Naw, I don't think that's right. [seven-second pause] Ah, maybe it is.

Captain: Hundred and twenty.

Co-pilot: I don't know.

The takeoff proceeded, and 37 seconds later the pilot and co-pilot exchanged their last words.

The co-pilot had repeatedly called the pilot's attention to dangerous conditions but did not directly suggest they abort the takeoff. In Linde's judgment, he was expressing his concern indirectly, and the captain didn't pick up on it—with tragic results.

That the co-pilot was trying to warn the captain indirectly is supported by evidence from another airline accident—a relatively minor one—investigated by Linde that also involved the unsuccessful use of indirectness.

On July 9, 1978, Allegheny Airlines Flight 453 was landing at Monroe County Airport in Rochester, when it overran the runway by 728 feet. Everyone survived. This meant that the captain and co-pilot could be interviewed. It turned out that the plane had been flying too fast for a safe landing. The captain should have realized this and flown around a second time, decreasing his speed before trying to land. The captain said he simply had not been aware that he was going too fast. But the co-pilot told interviewers that he "tried to warn the captain in subtle ways, like mentioning the possibility of a tail wind and the slowness of flap extension." His exact words were recorded in the black box. The cross-hatches indicate words deleted

by the National Transportation Safety Board and were probably expletives:

Co-pilot: Yeah, it looks like you got a tail wind here.

Yeah.

[?]: Yeah [it] moves awfully # slow.

Co-pilot: Yeah the # flaps are slower than a #.

Captain: We'll make it, gonna have to add power.

Co-pilot: I know.

The co-pilot thought the captain would understand that if there was a tail wind, it would result in the plane going too fast, and if the flaps were slow, they would be inadequate to break the speed sufficiently for a safe landing. He thought the captain would then correct for the error by not trying to land. But the captain said he didn't interpret the co-pilot's remarks to mean they were going too fast.

Linde believes it is not a coincidence that the people being indirect in these conversations were the co-pilots. In her analyses of flight-crew conversations she found it was typical for the speech of subordinates to be more mitigated—polite, tentative or indirect. She also found that topics broached in a mitigated way were more likely to fail, and that captains were more likely to ignore hints from their crew members than the other way around. These findings are evidence that not only can indirectness and other forms of mitigation be misunderstood, but they are also easier to ignore.

In the Air Florida case, it is doubtful that the captain did not realize what the co-pilot was suggesting when he said, "Let's check these tops again since we been setting here awhile" (though it seems safe to assume he did not realize the gravity of the co-pilot's concern). But the indirectness of the co-pilot's phrasing certainly made it easier for the pilot to ignore it. In this sense, the captain's response, "I think we get to go here in a minute," was an indirect way of saying, "I'd rather not." In view of these patterns, the flight crews of some airlines are now given training to express their concerns, even to superiors, in more direct ways.

The conclusion that people should learn to express themselves more directly has a ring of truth to it—especially for Americans. But direct communication is not necessarily always preferable. If more direct expression is better communication, then the most direct-speaking crews should be the best ones. Linde was surprised to find in her research that crews that used the most mitigated speech were often judged the best crews. As part of the study of talk among cockpit crews in flight simulations, the trainers observed and rated the performances of the simulation crews. The crews they rated top in performance had a higher rate of mitigation than crews they judged to be poor.

This finding seems at odds with the role played by indirectness in the examples of crashes that we just saw. Linde concluded that since every utterance functions on two levels—the referential (what is says) and the relational (what it implies about the speaker's relationships), crews that attend to the relational level will be better crews. A similar explanation was suggested by Kunihiko Harada. He believes that the secret of successful communication lies not in teaching subordinates to be more direct, but in teaching higher-ups to be more sensitive to indirect meaning. In other words, the crashes resulted not only because the co-pilots tried to alert the captains to danger indirectly but also because the captains were not attuned to the co-pilots' hints. What made for successful performance among the best crews might have been the ability—or willingness—of listeners to pick up on hints, just as members of families or longstanding couples come to understand each other's meaning without anyone being particularly explicit.

It is not surprising that a Japanese sociolinguist came up with this explanation; what he described is the Japanese system, by which good communication is believed to take place when meaning is gleaned without being stated directly—or at all.

While Americans believe that "the squeaky wheel gets the grease" (so it's best to speak up), the Japanese say, "The nail that sticks out gets hammered back in" (so it's best to remain silent if you don't want to be hit on the head). Many Japanese scholars writing in English have tried to explain to bewildered Americans the ethics of a culture in which silence is often given greater value than speech, and ideas are believed to be best communicated without being explicitly stated. Key concepts in Japanese give a flavor of the attitudes toward language that they reveal—and set in relief the strategies that Americans encounter at work when talking to other Americans.

Takie Sugiyama Lebra, a Japanese-born anthropologist, explains that one of the most basic values in Japanese culture is *omoiyari*, which she translates as "empathy." Because of *omoiyari*, it should not be necessary to state one's meaning explicitly; people should be able to sense each other's meaning intuitively. Lebra explains that it is typical for a Japanese speaker to let sentences trail off rather than complete them because expressing ideas before knowing how they will be received seems intrusive. "Only an insensitive, uncouth person needs a direct, verbal, complete message," Lebra says.

Sasshi, the anticipation of another's message through insightful guesswork, is considered an indication of maturity.

Considering the value placed on direct communication by Americans in general, and especially by American business people, it is easy to imagine that many American readers may scoff at such conversational habits. But the success of Japanese businesses makes it impossible to continue to maintain that there is anything inherently inefficient about such conversational conventions. With indirectness, as with all aspects of conversational style, our own habitual style seems to make sense—seems polite, right and good. The light cast by the habits and assumptions of another culture can help us see our way to the flexibility and respect for other styles that is the only best way of speaking.

Deborah Tannen is University Professor of Linguistics at Georgetown University.

From *The New York Times Magazine*, August 28, 1994, pp. 46–49. Adapted from *Talking 9 to 5: How Women's and Men's Conversational Styles Affect Who Gets Heard, Who Gets Credit, and What Gets Done at Work* by Deborah Tannen, Ph.D. © 1994 by Deborah Tannen, Ph.D. Reprinted by permission of William Morrow & Company, Inc.

"I Can't Even Open My Mouth"

Separating Messages from Metamessages in Family Talk

"DO YOU REALLY need another piece of cake?" Donna asks George.

"You bet I do," he replies, with that edge to his voice that implies, "If I wasn't sure I needed it before, I am darned sure now."

Donna feels hamstrung. She knows that George is going to say later that he wished he hadn't had that second piece of cake.

"Why are you always watching what I eat?" George asks.

"I was just watching out for you," Donna replies. "I only say it because I love you."

Elizabeth, in her late twenties, is happy to be making Thanksgiving dinner for her extended family in her own home. Her mother, who is visiting, is helping out in the kitchen. As Elizabeth prepares the stuffing for the turkey, her mother remarks, "Oh, you put onions in the stuffing?"

Feeling suddenly as if she were sixteen years old again, Elizabeth turns on her mother and says, "*I'm* making the stuffing, Mom. Why do you have to criticize everything I do?"

"I didn't criticize," her mother replies. "I just asked a question. What's got into you? I can't even open my mouth."

The allure of family—which is, at heart, the allure of love—is to have someone who knows you so well that you don't have to explain yourself. It is the promise of someone who cares enough about you to protect you against the world of strangers who do not wish you well. Yet, by an odd and cruel twist, it is the family itself that often causes pain. Those we love are looking at us so close-up that they see all our blemishes—see them as if through a magnifying glass. Family members have innumerable opportunities to witness our faults and feel they have a right to point them out. Often their intention is to help us improve. They feel, as Donna did, "I only say it because I love you."

Family members also have a long shared history, so everything we say in a conversation today echoes with meanings from the past. If you have a tendency to be late, your parent, sibling, or spouse may say, "We have to leave at eight"—and then add, "It's really important. Don't be late. Please start your shower at seven, not seven-thirty!" These extra injunctions are demeaning and interfering, but they are based on experience. At the same time, having experienced negative judgments in the past, we develop a sixth sense to sniff out criticism in almost anything a loved one says—even an innocent question about ingredients in the stuffing. That's why Elizabeth's mother ends up feeling as if she can't even open her mouth—and Elizabeth ends up feeling criticized.

When we are children our family constitutes the world. When we grow up, family members—not only our spouses but also our grown-up children and adult sisters and brothers—keep this larger-than-life aura. We overreact to their judgments because it feels as if they were handed down by the Supreme Court and are unassailable assessments of our value as human beings. We bristle because these judgments seem unjust; or because we sense a kernel of truth we would rather not face; or because we fear that if someone who knows us so well judges us harshly we must really be guilty, so we risk losing not only that person's love but everyone else's, too. Along with this heavy load of implications comes a dark resentment that a loved one is judging us at all—and has such power to wound.

"I still fight with my father," a man who had reached a high position in journalism said to me. "He's been dead twenty-one years." I asked for an example. "He'd tell me that I had to comb my hair and dress better, that I'd learn when I grew up that appearance is important." When he said this I noticed that his hair was uncombed, and the tails of his faded shirt were creeping out from the waist of his pants. He went on, "I told him I'd ignore that. And now sometimes when I'm going somewhere important, I'll look in the mirror and think—I'll say to him in my mind, 'See? I *am* a success and it didn't matter.'"

This man's "fights" with his father are about approval. No matter what age we've reached, no matter whether our parents are alive or dead, whether we were close to them or not, there are times when theirs are the eyes through which we view ourselves, theirs the standards against which we measure ourselves when we wonder whether we have measured up. The criticism of parents carries extra weight, even when children are adults.

I CARE, THEREFORE I CRITICIZE

Some family members feel they have not only a right but an obligation to tell you when they think you're doing something wrong. A woman from Thailand recalls that when she was in her late teens and early twenties, her mother frequently had talks with her in which she tried to set her daughter straight. "At the end of each lecture," the woman says, "my mother would always tell me, 'I have to complain about you because I am your mother and I love you. Nobody else will talk to you the way I do because they don't care.'"

It sometimes seems that family members operate under the tenet "I care, therefore I criticize." To the one who is being told to do things differently, what comes through loudest and clearest is the criticism. But the one offering suggestions and judgments is usually focused on the caring. A mother, for example, was expressing concern about her daughter's boyfriend: He didn't have a serious job, he didn't seem to want one, and she didn't think he was a good prospect for marriage. The daughter protested that her mother disapproved of everyone she dated. Her mother responded indignantly, "Would you rather I didn't care?"

As family members we wonder why our parents, children, siblings, and spouses are so critical of us. But as family members we also feel frustrated because comments we make in the spirit of caring are taken as criticizing.

Both sentiments are explained by the double meaning of giving advice: a loving sign of caring, a hurtful sign of criticizing. It's impossible to say which is right; both meanings are there. Sorting out the ambiguous meanings of caring and criticizing is difficult because language works on two levels: the message and the metamessage. Separating these levels—and being aware of both—is crucial to improving communication in the family.

THE INTIMATE CRITIC: WHEN METAMESSAGES HURT

Because those closest to us have front-row seats to view our faults, we quickly react—sometimes overreact—to any hint of criticism. The result can be downright comic, as in Phyllis Richman's novel *Who's Afraid of Virginia Ham?* One scene, a conversation between the narrator and her adult daughter, Lily, shows how criticism can be the metronome providing the beat for the family theme song. The dialogue goes like this:

LILY: Am I too critical of people?
MOTHER: What people? Me?
LILY: Mamma, don't be so self-centered.
MOTHER: Lily, don't be so critical.
LILY: I knew it. You do think I'm critical. Mamma, why do you always have to find something wrong with me?

The mother then protests that it was Lily who asked if she was too critical, and now she's criticizing her mother for answering. Lily responds, "I can't follow this. Sometimes you're impossibly hard to talk to."

It turns out that Lily is upset because her boyfriend, Brian, told her she is too critical of him. She made a great effort to stop criticizing, but now she's having a hard time keeping her resolve. He gave her a sexy outfit for her birthday—it's expensive and beautiful—but the generous gift made her angry because she took it as criticism of the way she usually dresses.

In this brief exchange Richman captures the layers of meaning that can make the most well-intentioned comment or action a source of conflict and hurt among family members. Key to understanding why Lily finds the conversation so hard to follow—and her mother so hard to talk to—is separating messages from metamessages. The *message* is the meaning of the words and sentences spoken, what anyone with a dictionary and a grammar book could figure out. Two people in a conversation usually agree on what the message is. The *metamessage* is meaning that is not said—at least not in so many words—but that we glean from every aspect of context: the way something is said, who is saying it, or the fact that it is said at all.

Because they do not reside in the words themselves, metamessages are hard to deal with. Yet they are often the source of both comfort and hurt. The message (as I've said) is the word meaning while the metamessage is the heart meaning—the meaning that we react to most strongly, that triggers emotion.

When Lily asked her mother if she was too critical of people, the message was a question about Lily's own personality. But her mother responded to what she perceived as the metamessage: that Lily was feeling critical of *her*. This was probably based on experience: Her daughter had been critical of her in the past. If Lily had responded to the message alone, she would have answered, "No, not you. I was thinking of Brian." But she, too, is reacting to a metamessage—that her mother had made herself the point of a comment that was not about her mother at all. Perhaps Lily's resentment was also triggered because her mother still looms so large in her life.

The mixing up of message and metamessage also explains Lily's confused response to the gift of sexy clothing from her boyfriend. The message is the gift. But what made Lily angry was what she thought the gift implied: that Brian finds the way she usually dresses not sexy enough—and unattractive. This implication is the metamessage, and it is what made Lily critical of the gift, of Brian, and of herself. Metamessages speak louder than messages, so this is what Lily reacted to most strongly.

It's impossible to know whether Brian intended this metamessage. It's possible that he wishes Lily would dress differently; it's also possible that he likes the way she dresses just fine but simply thought this particular outfit would look good on her. That's what makes metamessages so difficult to pinpoint and talk about: They're implicit, not explicit.

When we talk about messages, we are talking about the meanings of words. But when we talk about metamessages, we are talking about relationships. And when family members react to each other's comments, it's metamessages they are usually responding to. Richman's dialogue is funny because it shows how we all get confused between messages and metamessages when we talk to those we are close to. But when it happens in the context of a relationship we care about, our reactions often lead to hurt rather than to humor.

In all the conversations that follow, both in this chapter and throughout the book, a key to improving relationships within the family is distinguishing the message from the metamessage, and being clear about which one you are reacting to. One way you can do this is *metacommunicating*—talking about communication.

"WHAT'S WRONG WITH FRENCH BREAD?" TRY METACOMMUNICATING

The movie *Divorce American Style* begins with Debbie Reynolds and Dick Van Dyke preparing for dinner guests—and arguing. She lodges a complaint: that all he does is criticize. He protests that he doesn't. She says she can't discuss it right then because she has to take the French bread out of the oven. He asks, "French bread?"

A simple question, right? Not even a question, just an observation. But on hearing it Debbie Reynolds turns on him, hands on hips, ready for battle: "What's wrong with French bread?" she asks, her voice full of challenge.

"Nothing," he says, all innocence. "It's just that I really like those little dinner rolls you usually make." This is like the bell that sets in motion a boxing match, which is stopped by another bell—the one at the front door announcing their guests have arrived.

Did he criticize or didn't he? On the message level, no. He simply asked a question to confirm what type of bread she was preparing. But on the metamessage level, yes. If he were satisfied with her choice of bread, he would not comment, except perhaps to compliment. Still, you might ask, So what? So what if he prefers the dinner rolls she usually makes to French bread? Why is it such a big deal? The big deal is explained by her original complaint: She feels that he is *always* criticizing—always telling her to do things differently than she chose to do them.

The big deal, in a larger sense, is a paradox of family: We depend on those closest to us to see our best side, and often they do. But because they are so close, they also see our worst side. You want the one you love to be an intimate ally who reassures you that you're doing things right, but sometimes you find instead an intimate critic who implies, time and again, that you're doing things

wrong. It's the cumulative effect of minor, innocent suggestions that creates major problems. You will never work things out if you continue to talk about the message—about French bread versus dinner rolls—rather than the metamessage—the implication that your partner is dissatisfied with everything you do. (*Divorce American Style* was made in 1967; that it still rings true today is evidence of how common—and how recalcitrant—such conversational quagmires are.)

One way to approach a dilemma like this is to *metacommunicate*—to talk about ways of talking. He might *say* that he feels he can't open his mouth to make a suggestion or comment because she takes everything as criticism. She might *say* that she feels he's always dissatisfied with what she does, rather than turn on him in a challenging way. Once they both understand this dynamic, they will come up with their own ideas about how to address it. For example, he might decide to preface his question with a disclaimer: "I'm not criticizing the French bread." Or maybe he *does* want to make a request—a direct one—that she please make dinner rolls because he likes them. They might also set a limit on how many actions of hers he can question in a day. The important thing is to talk about the metamessage she is reacting to: that having too many of her actions questioned makes her feel that her partner in life has changed into an in-house inspection agent, on the lookout for wrong moves.

LIVING WITH THE RECYCLING POLICE

"This is recyclable," Helen exclaims, brandishing a small gray cylinder that was once at the center of a roll of toilet paper. There she stops, as if the damning evidence is sufficient to rest her case.

"I know it's recyclable," says Samuel. "You don't have to tell me." He approves of recycling and generally practices it, if not quite as enthusiastically (he would say obsessively) as Helen. But this time he slipped: In a moment of haste he tossed the cardboard toilet paper tube into the wastebasket. Now Helen has found it and wants to know why it was there. "You can't go through the

garbage looking for things I threw away," Samuel protests. "Our relationship is more important than a toilet paper carcass."

"I'm not talking about our relationship," Helen protests. "I'm talking about recycling."

Helen was right: She *was* talking about recycling. But Samuel was right, too. If you feel like you're living with the recycling police—or the diet police, or the neatness police—someone who assumes the role of judge of your actions and repeatedly finds you guilty—it takes the joy out of living together. Sometimes it even makes you wish, for a fleeting moment, that you lived alone, in peace. In that sense, Samuel was talking about the relationship.

Helen was focusing on the message: the benefits of recycling. Samuel was focusing on the metamessage: the implication he perceives that Helen is enforcing rules and telling him he broke one. Perhaps, too, he is reacting to the metamessage of moral superiority in Helen's being the more fervent recycler. Because messages lie in words, Helen's position is more obviously defensible. But it's metamessages that have clout, because they stir emotions, and emotions are the currency of relationships.

In understanding Samuel's reaction, it's also crucial to bear in mind that the meaning of Helen's remark resides not just in the conversation of the moment but in the resonance of all the conversations on the subject they've had in their years together—as well as the conversations Samuel had before that, especially while growing up in his own family. Furthermore, it's her *repeatedly* remarking on what he does or does not recycle that gives Samuel the impression that living with Helen is like living with the recycling police.

GIVE ME CONNECTION, GIVE ME CONTROL

There is another dimension to this argument—another aspect of communication that complicates everything we say to each other but that is especially powerful in families. That is our simultaneous but conflicting desires for connection and for control.

In her view Helen is simply calling her husband's attention to a small oversight in their mutual pursuit of a moral good—an expression of their connection. Their shared policy on recycling reflects their shared life: his trash is her trash. But Samuel feels that by installing herself as the judge of his actions, she is placing herself one-up. In protest he accuses, "You're trying to control me."

Both connection and control are at the heart of family. There is no relationship as close—and none as deeply hierarchical—as the relationship between parent and child, or between older and younger sibling. To understand what goes on when family members talk to each other, you have to understand how the forces of connection and control reflect both closeness and hierarchy in a family.

"He's like family," my mother says of someone she likes. Underlying this remark is the assumption that *family* connotes closeness, being connected to each other. We all seek connection: It makes us feel safe; it makes us feel loved. But being close means you care about what those you are close to think. Whatever you do has an impact on them, so you have to take their needs and preferences into account. This gives them power to control your actions, limiting your independence and making you feel hemmed in.

Parents and older siblings have power over children and younger siblings as a result of their age and their roles in the family. At the same time, *ways of talking create power.* Younger siblings or children can make life wonderful or miserable for older siblings or parents by what they say—or refuse to say. Some family members increase their chances of getting their way by frequently speaking up, or by speaking more loudly and more forcefully. Some increase their influence by holding their tongues, so others become more and more concerned about winning them over.

"Don't tell me what to do. Don't try to control me" are frequent protests within families. It is automatic for many of us to think in terms of power relations and to see others' incursions on our freedom as control maneuvers. We are less likely to think of them as connection maneuvers, but they often are that, too. At every mo-

ment we're struggling not only for control but also for love, approval, and involvement. What's tough is that the *same* actions and comments can be either control maneuvers or connection maneuvers—or, as in most cases, both at once.

CONTROL MANEUVER OR CONNECTION MANEUVER?

"Don't start eating yet," Louis says to Claudia as he walks out of the kitchen. "I'll be right there."

Famished, Claudia eyes the pizza before her. The aroma of tomato sauce and melted cheese is so sweet, her mouth thinks she has taken a bite. But Louis, always slow-moving, does not return, and the pizza is cooling. Claudia feels a bit like their dog Muffin when she was being trained: "Wait!" the instructor told Muffin, as the hungry dog poised pitifully beside her bowl of food. After pausing long enough to be convinced Muffin would wait forever, the trainer would say, "Okay!" Only then would Muffin fall into the food.

Was Louis intentionally taking his time in order to prove he could make Claudia wait no matter how hungry she was? Or was he just eager for them to sit down to dinner together? In other words, when he said, "Don't start eating yet," was it a control maneuver, to make her adjust to his pace and timing, or a connection maneuver, to preserve their evening ritual of sharing food? The answer is, it was both. Eating together is one of the most evocative rituals that bond individuals as a family. At the same time, the requirement that they sit down to dinner together gave Louis the power to make Claudia wait. So the need for connection entailed control, and controlling each other is in itself a kind of connection.

Control and connection are intertwined, often conflicting forces that thread through everything said in a family. These dual forces explain the double meaning of caring and criticizing. Giving advice, suggesting changes, and making observations are signs of caring when looked at through the lens of connection. But looked at through the lens of control, they are put-downs, interfering with our desire to manage our own lives

and actions, telling us to do things differently than we choose to do them. That's why caring and criticizing are tied up like a knot.

The drives toward connection and toward control are the forces that underlie our reactions to metamessages. So the second step in improving communication in the family—after distinguishing between message and metamessage—is understanding the double meaning of control and connection. Once these multiple layers are sorted out and brought into focus, talking about ways of talking—metacommunicating—can help solve family problems rather than making them worse.

SMALL SPARK, BIG EXPLOSION

Given the intricacies of messages and metamessages, and of connection and control, the tiniest suggestion or correction can spark an explosion fueled by the stored energy of a history of criticism. One day, for example, Vivian was washing dishes. She tried to fix the drain cup in an open position so it would catch debris and still allow water to drain, but it kept falling into the closed position. With a mental shrug of her shoulders, she decided to leave it, since she didn't have many dishes to wash and the amount of water that would fill the sink wouldn't be that great. But a moment later her husband, Mel, happened by and glanced at the sink. "You should keep the drain open," he said, "so the water can drain."

This sounds innocent enough in the telling. Vivian could have said, "I tried, but it kept slipping in, so I figured it didn't matter that much." Or she could have said, "It's irritating to feel that you're looking over my shoulder all the time, telling me to do things differently from the way I'm doing them." This was, in fact, what she was feeling—and why she experienced, in reaction to Mel's suggestion, a small eruption of anger that she had to expend effort to suppress.

Vivian was surprised at what she did say. She made up a reason and implied she had acted on purpose: "I figured it would be easier to clean the strainer if I let it drain all at once." This thought *had* occurred to her when she decided not to struggle any longer to balance the drain cup in an open position, though it wasn't true that she did it on purpose for that reason. But by justifying her actions, Vivian gave Mel the opening to argue for his method, which he did.

"The whole sink gets dirty if you let it fill up with water," Mel said. Vivian decided to let it drop and remained silent. Had she spoken up, the result would probably have been an argument.

Throughout this interchange Vivian and Mel focused on the message: When you wash the dishes, should the drain cup be open or closed? Just laying out the dilemma in these terms shows how ridiculous it is to argue about. Wars are being fought; people are dying; accident or illness could throw this family into turmoil at any moment. The position of the drain cup in the sink is not a major factor in their lives. But the conversation wasn't really about the message—the drain cup—at least not for Vivian.

Mel probably thought he was just making a suggestion about the drain cup, and in the immediate context he was. But messages always bring metamessages in tow: In the context of the history of their relationship, Mel's comment was not so much about a drain cup as it was about Vivian's ability to do things right and Mel's role as judge of her actions.

This was clear to Vivian, which is why she bristled at his comment, but it was less clear to Mel. Our field of vision is different depending on whether we're criticizing or being criticized. The critic tends to focus on the message: "I just made a suggestion. Why are you so touchy?" The one who feels criticized, however, is responding to the metamessage, which is harder to explain. If Vivian had complained, "You're always telling me how to do things," Mel would surely have felt, and might well have said, "I can't even open my mouth."

At the same time, connection and control are in play. Mel's assumption that he and Vivian are on the same team makes him feel comfortable giving her pointers. Furthermore, if a problem develops with the sink's drainage, he's the one who will have to fix it. Their lives are intertwined; that's where the connec-

tion lies. But if Vivian feels she can't even wash dishes without Mel telling her to do it differently, then it seems to her that he is trying to control her. It's as if she has a boss to answer to in her own kitchen.

Vivian might explain her reaction in terms of metamessages. Understanding and respecting her perspective, Mel might decide to limit his suggestions and corrections. Or Vivian might decide that she is overinterpreting the metamessage and make an effort to focus more on the message, taking some of Mel's suggestions and ignoring others. Once they both understand the metamessages as well as the messages they are communicating and reacting to, they can metacommunicate: talk about each other's ways of talking and how they might talk differently to avoid hurt and recriminations.

"WOULDN'T YOU RATHER HAVE SALMON?"

Irene and David are looking over their menus in a restaurant. David says he will order a steak. Irene says, "Did you notice they also have salmon?"

This question exasperates David; he protests, "Will you please stop criticizing what I eat?"

Irene feels unfairly accused: "I didn't criticize. I just pointed out something on the menu I thought you might like."

The question "Did you notice they also have salmon?" is not, on the message level, a criticism. It could easily be friendly and helpful, calling attention to a menu item her husband might have missed. But, again, conversations between spouses—or between any two people who have a history—are always part of an ongoing relationship. David knows that Irene thinks he eats too much red meat, too much dessert, and, generally speaking, too much.

Against the background of this aspect of their relationship, any indication that Irene is noticing what he is eating is a reminder to David that she disapproves of his eating habits. That's why the question "Do you really want to have dessert?" will be heard as "You shouldn't have dessert," and the observation "That's a big piece of cake" will commu-

nicate "That piece of cake is too big," regardless of how they're intended. The impression of disapproval comes not from the message—the words spoken—but from the metamessage, which grows out of their shared history.

It's possible that Irene really was not feeling disapproval when she pointed out the salmon on the menu, but it's also possible that she was and preferred not to admit it. Asking a question is a handy way of expressing disapproval without seeming to. But to the extent that the disapproval comes through, such indirect means of communicating can make for more arguments, and more hurt feelings on both sides. Irene sees David overreacting to an innocent, even helpful, remark, and he sees her hounding him about what he eats and then denying having done so. Suppose he had announced he was going to order salmon. Would she have said, "Did you notice they also have steak?" Not likely. It is reasonable, in this context, to interpret any alternative suggestion to an announced decision as dissatisfaction with that decision.

Though Irene and David's argument has much in common with the previous examples, the salmon versus steak decision is weightier than French bread versus dinner rolls, recycling, or drain cups. Irene feels that David's health—maybe even his life—is at stake. He has high cholesterol, and his father died young of a heart attack. Irene has good reason to want David to eat less red meat. She loves him, and his health and life are irrevocably intertwined with hers. Here is another paradox of family: A blessing of being close is knowing that someone cares about you: cares what you do and what happens to you. But caring also means interference and disapproval.

In other words, here again is the paradox of connection and control. From the perspective of control, Irene is judging and interfering; from the perspective of connection, she is simply recognizing that her life and David's are intertwined. This potent brew is family: Just knowing that someone has the closeness to care and the right to pass judgment—and that you care so much about that judgment—creates resentment that can turn into anger.

CRYING LITERAL MEANING: HOW NOT TO RESOLVE ARGUMENTS

When Irene protested, "I didn't criticize," she was crying literal meaning: taking refuge in the message level of talk, ducking the metamessage. All of us do that when we want to avoid a fight but still get our point across. In many cases this defense is sincere, though it does not justify ignoring or denying the metamessage someone else may have perceived. If the person we're talking to believes it wasn't "just a suggestion," keeping the conversation focused on the message can result in interchanges that sound like a tape loop playing over and over. Let's look more closely at an actual conversation in which this happened—one that was taped by the people who had it.

Sitting at the dining room table, Evelyn is filling out an application. Because Joel is the one who has access to a copy machine at work, the last step of the process will rest on his shoulders. Evelyn explains, "Okay, so you'll have to attach the voided check here, after you make the Xerox copy. Okay?" Joel takes the papers, but Evelyn goes on: "Okay just—Please get that out tomorrow. I'm counting on you, hon. I'm counting on you, love."

Joel reacts with annoyance: "Oh, for Pete's sake."

Evelyn is miffed in turn: "What do you mean by that?"

Joel turns her words back on her: "What do *you* mean by that?"

The question "What do you mean by that?" is a challenge. When communication runs smoothly, the meanings of words are self-evident, or at least we assume they are. (We may discover later that we misinterpreted them.) Although "What do you mean?" might be an innocent request for clarification, adding "by that" usually signals not so much that you didn't understand what the other person meant but that you understood—all too well—the *implication* of the words, and you didn't like it.

Evelyn cries literal meaning. She sticks to the message: "Oh, honey, I just mean I'm *counting* on you."

Joel calls attention to the metamessage: "Yes, but you say it in a way that suggests I can't be counted on."

Evelyn protests, accurately, "I never said that."

But Joel points to evidence of the metamessage: "I'm talking about your *tone*."

I suspect Joel was using *tone* as a catchall way of describing the metamessage level of talk. Moreover, it probably wasn't only the way Evelyn spoke—her tone—that he was reacting to but the fact that Evelyn said it at all. If she really felt she could count on him, she would just hand over the task. "I'm counting on you" is what people say to reinforce the importance of doing something when they believe extra reinforcement is needed. Here, the shared history of the relationship adds meaning to the metamessage as well. Joel has reason to believe that Evelyn feels she can't count on him.

Later in the same conversation, Joel takes a turn crying literal meaning. He unplugs the radio from the wall in the kitchen and brings it into the dining room so they can listen to the news. He sets it on the table and turns it on.

"Why aren't you using the plug?" Evelyn asks. "Why waste the batteries?" This sparks a heated discussion about the relative importance of saving batteries. Evelyn then suggests, "Well, we could plug it in right here," and offers Joel the wire.

Joel shoots her a look.

Evelyn protests, "Why are you giving me a dirty look?"

And Joel cries literal meaning: "I'm not!" After all, you can't prove a facial expression; it's not in the message.

"You are!" Evelyn insists, reacting to the metamessage: "Just because I'm handing this to you to plug in."

I have no doubt that Joel did look at Evelyn with annoyance or worse, but not because she handed him a plug—that would be literal meaning, too. He was surely reacting to the metamessage of being corrected, of her judging his actions. For her part, Evelyn probably felt Joel was irrationally refusing to plug in the radio when an electrical outlet was staring them in the face.

How to sort through this jumble of messages and metamessages? The message level is a draw. Some people prefer the convenience of letting the radio run on batteries when it's moved from its normal

perch to a temporary one. Others find it obviously reasonable to plug the radio in when there's an outlet handy, to save batteries. Convenience or frugality, take your pick. We all do. But when you live with someone else—caution! It may seem natural to suggest that others do things the way you would do them, but that is taking account only of the message. Giving the metamessage its due, the expense in spirit and goodwill is more costly than batteries. Being corrected all the time is wearying. And it's even more frustrating when you try to talk about what you believe they implied and they cry literal meaning—denying having "said" what you know they communicated.

Consider, too, the role of connection and control. Telling someone what to do is a control maneuver. But it is also a connection maneuver: Your lives are intertwined, and anything one person does has an impact on the other. In the earlier example, when Evelyn said, "I'm counting on you," I suspect some readers sympathized with Joel and others with Evelyn, depending on their own experience with people they've lived with. Does it affect your reaction to learn that Joel forgot to mail the application? Evelyn had good reason, based on years of living with Joel, to have doubts about whether he would remember to do what he said he would do.

Given this shared history, it might have been more constructive for Evelyn to admit that she did not feel she could completely count on Joel, rather than cry literal meaning and deny the metamessage of her words. Taking into account Joel's forgetfulness—or maybe his being overburdened at work—they could devise a plan: Joel might write himself a reminder and place it strategically in his briefcase. Or Evelyn might consider mailing the form herself, even though that would mean a trip to make copies. Whatever they decide, they stand a better chance of avoiding arguments—and getting the application mailed on time—if they acknowledge their metamessages and the reasons motivating them.

WHO BURNED THE POPCORN?

Living together means coordinating so many tasks, it's inevitable that family members will have different ideas of how to perform those tasks. In addition, everyone makes mistakes; sometimes the dish breaks, you forget to mail the application, the drain cup falls into the closed position. At work, lines of responsibility and authority are clear (at least in principle). But in a family—especially when adults are trying to share responsibilities and authority—there are fewer and fewer domains that belong solely to one person. As couples share responsibility for more and more tasks, they also develop unique and firm opinions about how those tasks should be done—and a belief in their right to express their opinions.

Even the most mundane activity, such as making popcorn (unless you buy the microwave type or an electric popper), can spark conflict. First, it takes a little going, and people have their own ideas of how to do it best. Second, popcorn is often made in the evening, when everyone's tired. Add to that the paradox of connection and control—wanting the person you love to approve of what you do, yet having someone right there to witness and judge mistakes—and you have a potful of kernels sizzling in oil, ready to pop right out of the pot.

More than one couple have told me of arguments about how to make popcorn. One such argument broke out between another couple who were taping their conversations. Since their words were recorded, we have a rare opportunity to listen in on a conversation very much like innumerable ones that vanish into air in homes all around the country. And we have the chance to think about how it could have been handled differently.

The seed of trouble is planted when Molly is in the kitchen and Kevin is watching their four-year-old son, Benny. Kevin calls out, "Molly! Mol! Let's switch. You take care of him. I'll do whatever you're doing."

"I'm making popcorn," Molly calls back. "You always burn it."

Molly's reply is, first and foremost, a sign of resistance. She doesn't want to switch jobs with Kevin. Maybe she's had enough of a four-year-old's company and is looking forward to being on her own in the kitchen. Maybe she is enjoying making popcorn. And maybe her reason is truly the one she gives: She

doesn't want Kevin to make the popcorn because he always burns it. Whatever her motivation, Molly resists the switch Kevin proposes by impugning his ability to make popcorn. And this comes across as a call to arms.

Kevin protests, "No I don't! I never burn it. I make it perfect." He joins Molly in the kitchen and peers over her shoulder. "You making popcorn? In the big pot?" (Remember this line; it will become important later.)

"Yes," Molly says, "but you're going to ruin it."

"No I won't," Kevin says. "I'll get it just right." With that they make the switch. Kevin becomes the popcorn chef, Molly the caretaker. But she is not a happy caretaker.

Seeing a way she can be both caretaker and popcorn chef, Molly asks Benny, "You want to help Mommy make popcorn? Let's not let Daddy do it. Come on."

Hearing this, Kevin insists, "I know how to make popcorn!" Then he ups the ante: "I can make popcorn better than you can!" After that the argument heats up faster than the popcorn. "I cook every kernel!" Kevin says.

"No you won't," says Molly.

"I will too! It's never burned!" Kevin defends himself. And he adds, "It always burns when you do it!"

"Don't make excuses!"

"There's a trick to it," he says.

And she says, "I know the trick!"

"No you don't," he retorts, "'cause you always burn it."

"I do not!" she says. "What are you, crazy?"

It is possible that Kevin is right—that Molly, not he, is the one who always burns the popcorn. It is also possible that Molly is right—that he always burns the popcorn, that she doesn't, and that he has turned the accusation back onto her as a self-defense strategy. Move 1: I am not guilty. Move 2: You are guilty.

In any case, Kevin continues as popcorn chef. After a while Molly returns to the kitchen. "Just heat it!" she tells Kevin. "Heat it! No, I don't want you—"

"It's going, it's going," Kevin assures her. "Hear it?"

Molly is not reassured, because she does not like what she hears. "It's too

slow," she says. "It's all soaking in. You hear that little—"

"It's not soaking in," Kevin insists. "It's fine."

"It's just a few kernels," Molly disagrees.

But Kevin is adamant: "All the popcorn is being popped!"

Acting on her mounting unease about the sounds coming from the popping corn, Molly makes another suggestion. She reminds Kevin, "You gotta take the trash outside."

But Kevin isn't buying. "I can't," he says. "I'm doing the popcorn." And he declines Molly's offer to watch it while he takes out the trash.

In the end Molly gets to say, "See, what'd I tell you?" But Kevin doesn't see the burned popcorn as a reason to admit fault. Remember his earlier question, "In the big pot?" Now he protests, "Well, I never *use* this pot, I use the other pot."

Molly comes back, "It's not the pot! It's you!"

"It's the pot," Kevin persists. "It doesn't heat up properly. If it did, then it would get hot." But pots can't really be at fault; those who choose pots can. So Kevin accuses, "You should have let me do it from the start."

"You *did* it from the start!" Molly says.

"No, I didn't," says Kevin. "You chose this pan. I would've chosen a different pan." So it's the pot's fault, and Molly's fault for choosing the pot.

This interchange is almost funny, especially for those of us—most of us, I'd bet—who have found ourselves in similar clashes.

How could Kevin and Molly have avoided this argument? Things might have turned out better if they had talked about their motivations: Is either one of them eager to get a brief respite from caring for Benny? If so, is there another way they can accomplish that goal? (Perhaps they could set Benny up with a task he enjoys on his own.) With this motivation out in the open, Molly might have declined to switch places when Kevin proposed it, saying something like, "I'm making popcorn. I'm enjoying making it. I'd rather not switch." The justification Molly used, "You always burn it," may have seemed to her a better tactic because it claims her right to keep making popcorn on the basis of the family good rather than her own preference. But the metamessage of incompetence can come across as provocative, in addition to being hurtful.

It's understandable that Kevin would be offended to have his popcorn-making skills impugned, but he would have done better to avoid the temptation to counter-attack by insisting he does it better, that it's Molly who burns it. He could have prevented the argument rather than esca-late it if he had metacommunicated: "You can make the popcorn if you want," he might have said, "but you don't have to say I can't do it." For both Molly and Kevin—as for any two people negotiating who's going to do what—metacommuni-cating is a way to avoid the flying metamessages of incompetence.

"I KNOW A THING OR TWO"

One of the most hurtful metamessages, and one of the most frequent, that family talk entails is the implication of incom-petence—even (if not especially) when children grow up. Now that we're adults we feel we should be entitled to make our own decisions, lead our own lives, imperfect though they may be. But we still want to feel that our parents are proud of us, that they believe in our com-petence. That's the metamessage we yearn for. Indeed, it's because we want their approval so much that we find the opposite metamessage—that they don't trust our competence—so distressing.

Martin and Gail knew that Gail's mother tended to be critical of whatever they did, so they put off letting her see their new home until the purchase was fi-nal. Once the deal was sealed they showed her, with pride, the home they had chosen while the previous owner's furni-ture was still in it. They were sure she would be impressed by the house they were now able to afford, as well as its spotless condition. But she managed to find something to criticize—even if it was invisible: "They may've told you it's in move-in condition," she said with author-ity, "but I know a thing or two, and when they take those pictures off the wall, there will be holes!" Even though they were fa-miliar with her tendency to find fault, Gail and Martin were flummoxed.

The aspect of the house Gail's mother found to criticize was profoundly insig-nificant: Every home has pictures on the wall, every picture taken down leaves holes, and holes are easily spackled in and painted over. It seems that Gail's mother was really reaching to find *some-thing* about their new home to criticize. From the perspective of control, it would be easy to conclude that Gail's mother was trying to take the role of expert in or-der to put them down, or even to spoil the joy of their momentous purchase. But consider the perspective of connection. Pointing out a problem that her children might not have noticed shows that she can still be of use, even though they are grown and have found this wonderful house without her help. She was being protective, watching out for them, mak-ing sure no one pulled the wool over their eyes.

Because control and connection are inextricably intertwined, protection im-plies incompetence. If Gail and Martin need her mother's guidance, they are in-capable of taking care of themselves. Though Gail's mother may well have been reacting to—and trying to over-come—the metamessage that they don't need her anymore, the metamessage they heard is that she can't approve whole-heartedly of anything they do.

"SHE KNEW WHAT WAS RIGHT"

In addition to concern about their chil-dren's choice of home, parents often have strong opinions about adult children's partners, jobs, and—especially—how they treat their own children. Raising chil-dren is something at which parents self-evidently have more experience, but metamessages of criticism in this area, though particularly common, are also par-ticularly hurtful, because young parents want so much to be good parents.

A woman of seventy still recalls the pain she felt when her children were small and her mother-in-law regarded her as an incompetent parent. It started in the first week of her first child's life. Her mother-in-law had come to help—and didn't want to go home. Finally, her fa-ther-in-law told his wife it was time to leave the young couple on their own. Un-convinced, she said outright—in front of her son and his wife—"I can't trust them with the baby."

Usually signs of distrust are more subtle. For example, during a dinner con-versation among three sisters and their mother, the sisters were discussing what the toddlers like to eat. When one said that her two-year-old liked fish, their mother cautioned, "Watch the bones." How easy it would be to take offense (though there was no indication this woman did): "You think I'm such an in-competent mother that I'm going to let my child swallow fish bones?" Yet the grandmother's comment was her way of making a contribution to the conversa-tion—one that exercises her lifelong re-sponsibility of protecting children.

It is easy to scoff at the mother-in-law who did not want to leave her son and his wife alone with their own baby. But con-sider the predicament of parents who be-come grandparents and see (or believe they see) their beloved grandchildren treated in ways they feel are hurtful. One woman told me that she loves being a grandmother—but the hardest part is having to bite her tongue when her daughter-in-law treats her child in a way the grandmother feels is misguided, un-fair, or even harmful. "You see your chil-dren doing things you think aren't right," she commented, "but at least they're adults; they'll suffer the consequences. But a child is so defenseless."

In some cases grandparents really do know best. My parents recall with linger-ing guilt a time they refused to take a grandparent's advice—and later wished they had. When their first child, my sister Naomi, was born, my parents, like many of their generation, relied on expert ad-vice for guidance in what was best for their child. At the time, the experts coun-seled that, once bedtime comes, a child who cries should not be picked up. After all, the reasoning went, that would sim-ply encourage the baby to cry rather than go to sleep.

One night when she was about a year old, Naomi was crying after being put to sleep in her crib. My mother's mother, who lived with my parents, wanted to go in and pick her up, but my parents wouldn't let her. "It tore us apart to hear her cry," my father recalls, "but we wanted to do what was best for her." It later turned out that Naomi was crying because she was sick. My parents cringe when they tell this story. "My mother pleaded with us to pick her up," my mother says. "She knew what was right."

I'M GROWN UP NOW

Often a parent's criticism is hurtful—or makes us angry—even when we know it is right, maybe especially if we sense it is right. That comes clear in the following example.

Two couples were having dinner together. One husband, Barry, was telling about how he had finally—at the age of forty-five—learned to ignore his mother's criticism. His mother, he said, had commented that he is too invested in wanting the latest computer gizmo, the most up-to-date laptop, regardless of whether he needs it. At that point his wife interrupted. "It's true, you are," she said—and laughed. He laughed, too: "I know it's true." Then he went back to his story and continued, unfazed, about how in the past he would have been hurt by his mother's comment and would have tried to justify himself to her, but this time he just let it pass. How easily Barry acknowledged the validity of his mother's criticism—when it was his wife making it. Yet acknowledging that the criticism was valid didn't change his view of his mother's comment one whit: He still thought she was wrong to criticize him.

When we grow up we feel we should be free from our parents' judgment (even though we still want their approval). Ironically, there is often extra urgency in parents' tendency to judge children's behavior when children are adults, because parents have a lot riding on how their children turn out. If the results are good, everything they did as parents gets a seal of approval. My father, for example, recalls that as a young married man he visited an older cousin, a woman he did not know well. After a short time the cousin remarked, "Your mother did a good job." Apparently, my father had favorably impressed her, but instead of complimenting him, she credited his mother.

By the same token, if their adult children have problems—if they seem irresponsible or make wrong decisions—parents feel their life's work of child rearing has been a failure, and those around them feel that way, too. This gives extra intensity to parents' desire to set their children straight. But it also can blind them to the impact of their corrections and suggestions, just as those in power often underestimate the power they wield.

When adult children move into their own homes, the lid is lifted off the pressure cooker of family interaction, though the pot may still be simmering on the range. If they move far away—as more and more do—visits turn into intense interactions during which the pressure cooker lid is clicked back in place and the steam builds up once again. Many adult children feel like they're kids again when they stay with their parents. And parents often feel the same way: that their adult children are acting like kids. Visits become immersion courses in return-to-family.

Parents with children living at home have the ultimate power—asking their children to move out. But visiting adult children have a new power of their own: They can threaten not to return, or to stay somewhere else. Margaret was thrilled that her daughter Amanda, who lives in Oregon, would be coming home for a visit to the family farm in Minnesota. It had been nearly a year since Margaret had seen her grandchildren, and she was eager to get reacquainted with them. But near the end of the visit, there was a flare-up. Margaret questioned whether Amanda's children should be allowed to run outside barefoot. Margaret thought it was dangerous; Amanda thought it was harmless. And Amanda unsheathed her sword: "This isn't working," she said. "Next time I won't stay at the farm. I'll find somewhere else to stay." Because Margaret wants connection—time with her daughter and grandchildren—the ability to dole out that connection gives her daughter power that used to be in Margaret's hands.

THE PARADOX OF FAMILY

When I was a child I walked to elementary school along Coney Island Avenue in Brooklyn, praying that if a war came I'd be home with my family when it happened. During my childhood in the 1950s my teachers periodically surprised the class by calling out, "Take cover!" At that cry we all ducked under our desks and curled up in the way we had been taught: elbows and knees tucked in, heads down, hands clasped over our necks. With the possibility of a nuclear attack made vivid by these exercises, I walked to school in dread—not of war but of the possibility that it might strike when I was away from my family.

But there is another side to family, the one I have been exploring in this chapter. My nephew Joshua Marx, at thirteen, pointed out this paradox: "If you live with someone for too long, you notice things about them," he said. "That's the reason you don't like your parents, your brother. There's a kid I know who said about his friend, 'Wouldn't it be cool if we were brothers?' and I said, 'Then you'd hate him.'"

We look to communication as a way through the minefield of this paradox. And often talking helps. But communication itself is a minefield because of the complex workings of message and metamessage. Distinguishing messages from metamessages, and taking into account the underlying needs for connection and control, provides a basis for metacommunicating. With these insights as foundation, we can delve further into the intricacies of family talk. Given our shared and individual histories of talk in relationships, and the enormous promise of love, understanding, and listening that family holds out, it's worth the struggle to continue juggling—and talking.

From *I Only Say This Because I Love You*, by Deborah Tannen, © 2001, pp. 3–28 by Deborah Tannen. Used by permission of Random House, Inc.

Shakespeare in the Bush

Laura Bohannan

Just before I left Oxford for the Tiv in West Africa, conversation turned to the season at Stratford. "You Americans," said a friend, "often have difficulty with Shakespeare. He was, after all, a very English poet, and one can easily misinterpret the universal by misunderstanding the particular."

I protested that human nature is pretty much the same the whole world over; at least the general plot and motivation of the greater tragedies would always be clear—everywhere—although some details of custom might have to be explained and difficulties of translation might produce other slight changes. To end an argument we could not conclude, my friend gave me a copy of *Hamlet* to study in the African bush: it would, he hoped, lift my mind above its primitive surroundings, and possibly I might, by prolonged meditation, achieve the grace of correct interpretation.

It was my second field trip to that African tribe, and I thought myself ready to live in one of its remote sections—an area difficult to cross even on foot. I eventually settled on the hillock of a very knowledgeable old man, the head of a homestead of some hundred and forty people, all of whom were either his close relatives or their wives and children. Like the other elders of the vicinity, the old man spent most of his time performing ceremonies seldom seen these days in the more accessible parts of the tribe. I was delighted. Soon there would be three months of enforced isolation and leisure, between the harvest that takes place just before the rising of the swamps and the clearing of new farms when the water goes down. Then, I thought, they would have even more time to perform ceremonies and explain them to me.

I was quite mistaken. Most of the ceremonies demanded the presence of elders from several homesteads. As the swamps rose, the old men found it too difficult to walk from one homestead to the next, and the ceremonies gradually ceased. As the swamps rose even higher, all activities but one came to an end. The women brewed beer from maize and millet. Men, women, and children sat on their hillocks and drank it.

People began to drink at dawn. By midmorning the whole homestead was singing, dancing, and drumming. When it rained, people had to sit inside their huts: there they drank and sang or they drank and told stories. In any case, by noon or before, I either had to join the party or retire to my own hut and my books. "One does not discuss serious matters when there is beer. Come, drink with us." Since I lacked their capacity for the thick native beer, I spent more and more time with *Hamlet*. Before the end of the second month, grace descended on me. I was quite sure that *Hamlet* had only one possible interpretation, and that one universally obvious.

Early every morning, in the hope of having some serious talk before the beer party, I used to call on the old man at his reception hut—a circle of posts supporting a thatched roof above a low mud wall to keep out wind and rain. One day I crawled through the low doorway and found most of the men of the homestead sitting huddled in their ragged cloths on stools, low plank beds, and reclining chairs, warming themselves against the chill of the rain around a smoky fire. In the center were three pots of beer. The party had started.

The old man greeted me cordially. "Sit down and drink." I accepted a large calabash full of beer, poured some into a small drinking gourd, and tossed it down. Then I poured some more into the same gourd for the man second in seniority to my host before I handed my calabash over to a young man for further distribution. Important people shouldn't ladle beer themselves.

"It is better like this," the old man said, looking at me approvingly and plucking at the thatch that had caught in my hair. "You should sit and drink with us more often. Your servants tell me that when you are not with us, you sit inside your hut looking at a paper."

The old man was acquainted with four kinds of "papers": tax receipts, bride price receipts, court fee receipts, and letters. The messenger who brought him letters from the chief used them mainly as a badge of office, for he always knew what was in them and told the old man. Personal letters for the few who had relatives in the government or mission stations were kept until someone went to a large market where there was a letter writer and reader. Since my arrival, letters were brought to me to be read. A few men also brought me bride price receipts, privately, with requests to change the figures to a higher sum. I found moral arguments were of no avail, since in-laws are fair game, and the technical hazards of forgery difficult to explain to an illiterate people. I did not wish them to think me silly enough to look at any such papers for days on end, and I hastily explained that my "paper" was one of the "things of long ago" of my country.

"Ah," said the old man. "Tell us."

I protested that I was not a storyteller. Story telling is a skilled art among them; their standards are high, and the audiences critical—and vocal in their criticism. I protested in vain. This morning they wanted to hear a story while they drank. They threatened to tell me no more stories until I told them one of mine. Finally, the old man promised that no one would criticize my style "for we know you are struggling with our language." "But," put in one of the elders, "you must explain what we do not understand, as we do when we tell you our stories." Realizing that here was my chance to prove *Hamlet* universally intelligible, I agreed.

The old man handed me some more beer to help me on with my storytelling. Men filled their long wooden pipes and knocked coals from the fire to place in the pipe bowls; then, puffing contentedly, they sat back to listen. I began in the proper style, "Not yesterday, not yesterday, but long ago, a thing occurred. One night three men were keeping watch outside the homestead of the great chief, when suddenly they saw the former chief approach them."

"Why was he no longer their chief?"

"He was dead," I explained. "That is why they were troubled and afraid when they saw him."

"Impossible," began one of the elders, handing his pipe on to his neighbor, who interrupted, "Of course it wasn't the dead chief. It was an omen sent by a witch. Go on."

Slightly shaken, I continued. "One of these three was a man who knew things"—the closest translation for scholar, but unfortunately it also meant witch. The second elder looked triumphantly at the first. "So he spoke to the dead chief saying, 'Tell us what we must do so you may rest in your grave,' but the dead chief did not answer. He vanished, and they could see him no more. Then the man who knew things—his name was Horatio—said this event was the affair of the dead chief's son, Hamlet."

There was a general shaking of heads round the circle. "Had the dead chief no living brothers? Or was this son the chief?"

"No," I replied. "That is, he had one living brother who became the chief when the elder brother died."

The old men muttered: such omens were matters for chiefs and elders, not for youngsters; no good could come of going behind a chief's back; clearly Horatio was not a man who knew things.

"Yes, he was," I insisted, shooing a chicken away from my beer. "In our country the son is next to the father. The dead chief's younger brother had become the great chief. He had also married his elder brother's widow only about a month after the funeral."

"He did well," the old man beamed and announced to the others, "I told you that if we knew more about Europeans, we would find they really were very like us. In our country also," he added to me, "the younger brother marries the elder brother's widow and becomes the father of his children. Now, if your uncle, who married your widowed mother, is your father's full brother, then he will be a real father to you. Did Hamlet's father and uncle have one mother?"

His question barely penetrated my mind; I was too upset and thrown too far off balance by having one of the most important elements of *Hamlet* knocked straight out of the picture. Rather uncertainly I said that I thought they had the same mother, but I wasn't sure—the story didn't say. The old man told me severely that these genealogical details made all the difference and that when I got home I must ask the elders about it. He shouted out the door to one of his younger wives to bring his goatskin bag.

Determined to save what I could of the mother motif, I took a deep breath and began again. "The son Hamlet was very sad because his mother had married again so quickly. There was no need for her to do so, and it is our custom for a widow not to go to her next husband until she has mourned for two years."

"Two years is too long," objected the wife, who had appeared with the old man's battered goatskin bag. "Who will hoe your farms for you while you have no husband?"

"Hamlet," I retorted without thinking, "was old enough to hoe his mother's farms himself. There was no need for her to remarry." No one looked convinced. I gave up. "His mother and the great chief told Hamlet not to be sad, for the great chief himself would be a father to Hamlet. Furthermore, Hamlet would be the next chief: therefore he must stay to learn the things of a chief. Hamlet agreed to remain, and all the rest went off to drink beer."

While I paused, perplexed at how to render Hamlet's disgusted soliloquy to an audience convinced that Claudius and Gertrude had behaved in the best possible manner, one of the younger men asked me who had married the other wives of the dead chief.

"He had no other wives," I told him.

"But a chief must have many wives! How else can he brew beer and prepare food for all his guests?"

I said firmly that in our country even chiefs had only one wife, that they had servants to do their work, and that they paid them from tax money.

It was better, they returned, for a chief to have many wives and sons who would help him hoe his farms and feed his people; then everyone loved the chief who gave much and took nothing—taxes were a bad thing.

I agreed with the last comment, but for the rest fell back on their favorite way of fobbing off my questions: "That is the way it is done, so that is how we do it."

I decided to skip the soliloquy. Even if Claudius was here thought quite right to marry his brother's widow, there remained the poison motif, and I knew they would disapprove of fratricide. More hopefully I resumed, "That night Hamlet kept watch with the three who had seen his dead father. The dead chief again appeared, and although the others were afraid, Hamlet followed his dead father off to one side. When they were alone, Hamlet's dead father spoke."

"Omens can't talk!" The old man was emphatic.

"Hamlet's dead father wasn't an omen. Seeing him might have been an omen, but he was not." My audience looked as confused as I sounded. "It *was* Hamlet's dead father. It was a thing we call a 'ghost.'" I had to use the English word, for unlike many of the neighboring tribes, these people didn't believe in the survival after death of any individuating part of the personality.

"What is a 'ghost?' An omen?"

"No, a 'ghost' is someone who is dead but who walks around and can talk, and people can hear him and see him but not touch him."

They objected. "One can touch zombis."

"No, no! It was not a dead body the witches had animated to sacrifice and eat. No one else made Hamlet's dead father walk. He did it himself."

"Dead men can't walk," protested my audience as one man.

I was quite willing to compromise. "A 'ghost' is the dead man's shadow."

But again they objected. "Dead men cast no shadows."

"They do in my country," I snapped.

The old man quelled the babble of disbelief that arose immediately and told me with that insincere, but courteous, agreement one extends to the fancies of the young, ignorant, and superstitious, "No doubt in your country the dead can also walk without being zombis." From the depths of his bag he produced a withered fragment of kola nut, bit off one end to show it wasn't poisoned, and handed me the rest as a peace offering.

"Anyhow," I resumed, "Hamlet's dead father said that his own brother, the one who became chief, had poisoned him. He wanted Hamlet to avenge him. Hamlet believed this in his heart, for he did not like his father's brother." I took another swallow of beer. "In the country of the great chief, living in the same homestead, for it was a very large one, was an important elder who was often with the chief to advise and help him. His name was Polonius. Hamlet was courting his daughter, but her father and her brother… [I cast hastily about for some tribal analogy] warned her not to let Hamlet visit her when she was alone on her farm, for he would be a great chief and so could not marry her."

"Why not?" asked the wife, who had settled down on the edge of the old man's chair. He frowned at her for asking stupid questions and growled, "They lived in the same homestead."

"That was not the reason," I informed them. "Polonius was a stranger who lived in the homestead because he helped the chief, not because he was a relative."

"Then why couldn't Hamlet marry her?"

"He could have," I explained, "but Polonius didn't think he would. After all, Hamlet was a man of great importance who ought to marry a chief's daughter, for in his country a man could have only one wife. Polonius was afraid that if Hamlet made love to his daughter, then no one else would give a high price for her."

"That might be true," remarked one of the shrewder elders, "but a chief's son would give his mistress's father enough presents and patronage to more than make up the difference. Polonius sounds like a fool to me."

"Many people think he was," I agreed. "Meanwhile Polonius sent his son Laertes off to Paris to learn the things of that country, for it was the homestead of a very great chief indeed. Because he was afraid that Laertes might waste a lot of money on beer and women and gambling, or get into trouble by fighting, he sent one of his servants to Paris secretly, to spy out what Laertes was doing. One day Hamlet came upon Polonius's daughter Ophelia. He behaved so oddly he frightened her. Indeed"—I was fumbling for words to express the dubious quality of Hamlet's madness—"the chief and many others had also noticed that when Hamlet talked one could understand the words but not what they meant. Many people thought that he had become mad." My audience suddenly became much more attentive. "The great chief wanted to know what was wrong with Hamlet, so he sent for two of Hamlet's age mates [school friends would have taken long explanation] to talk to Hamlet and find out what troubled his heart. Hamlet, seeing that they had been bribed by the chief to betray him, told them nothing. Polonius, however, insisted that Hamlet was mad because he had been forbidden to see Ophelia, whom he loved."

"Why," inquired a bewildered voice, "should anyone bewitch Hamlet on that account?"

"Bewitch him?"

"Yes, only witchcraft can make anyone mad, unless, of course, one sees the beings that lurk in the forest."

I stopped being a storyteller, took out my notebook and demanded to be told more about these two causes of madness. Even while they spoke and I jotted notes, I tried to calculate the effect of this new factor on the plot. Hamlet had not been exposed to the beings that lurk in the forests. Only his relatives in the male line could bewitch him. Barring relatives not mentioned by Shakespeare, it had to be Claudius who was attempting to harm him. And, of course, it was.

For the moment I staved off questions by saying that the great chief also refused to believe that Hamlet was mad for the love of Ophelia and nothing else. "He was sure that something much more important was troubling Hamlet's heart."

"Now Hamlet's age mates," I continued, "had brought with them a famous storyteller. Hamlet decided to have this man tell the chief and all his homestead a story about a man who had poisoned his brother because he desired his brother's wife and wished to be chief himself. Hamlet was sure the great chief could not hear the story without making a sign if he was indeed guilty, and then he would discover whether his dead father had told him the truth."

The old man interrupted, with deep cunning, "Why should a father lie to his son?" he asked.

I hedged: "Hamlet wasn't sure that it really was his dead father." It was impossible to say anything, in that language, about devil-inspired visions.

"You mean," he said, "it actually was an omen, and he knew witches sometimes send false ones. Hamlet was a fool not to go to one skilled in reading omens and divining the truth in the first place. A man-who-sees-the-truth could have told him how his father died, if he really had been poisoned, and if there was witchcraft in it; then Hamlet could have called the elders to settle the matter."

The shrewd elder ventured to disagree. "Because his father's brother was a great chief, one-who-sees-the-truth might therefore have been afraid to tell it. I think it was for that reason that a friend of Hamlet's father—a witch and an elder—sent an omen so his friend's son would know. Was the omen true?"

"Yes," I said, abandoning ghosts and the devil; a witch-sent omen it would have to be. "It was true, for when the storyteller was telling his tale before all the homestead, the great chief rose in fear. Afraid that Hamlet knew his secret he planned to have him killed."

The stage set of the next bit presented some difficulties of translation. I began cautiously. "The great chief told Hamlet's mother to find out from her son what he knew. But because a woman's children are always first in her heart, he had the important elder Polonius hide behind a cloth that hung against the wall of Hamlet's mother's sleeping hut. Hamlet started to scold his mother for what she had done."

There was a shocked murmur from everyone. A man should never scold his mother.

"She called out in fear, and Polonius moved behind the cloth. Shouting, 'A rat!' Hamlet took his machete and slashed through the cloth." I paused for dramatic effect. "He had killed Polonius!"

The old men looked at each other in supreme disgust. "That Polonius truly was a fool and a man who knew nothing! What child would not know enough to shout, 'It's me!'" With a pang, I remembered that these people are ardent hunters, always armed with bow, arrow, and machete; at the first rustle in the grass an arrow is aimed and ready, and the hunter shouts "Game!" If no human voice answers immediately, the arrow speeds on its way. Like a good hunter Hamlet had shouted, "A rat!"

I rushed in to save Polonius's reputation. "Polonius did speak. Hamlet heard him. But he thought it was the chief and wished to kill him earlier that evening...." I broke down, unable to describe to these pagans, who had no belief in individual afterlife, the difference between dying at one's prayers and dying "unhousell'd, disappointed, unaneled."

This time I had shocked my audience seriously. "For a man to raise his hand against his father's brother and the one who has become his father—that is a terrible thing. The elders ought to let such a man be bewitched."

I nibbled at my kola nut in some perplexity, then pointed out that after all the man had killed Hamlet's father.

"No," pronounced the old man, speaking less to me than to the young men sitting behind the elders. "If your father's brother has killed your father, you must appeal to your father's age mates; *they* may avenge him. No man may use violence against his senior relatives." Another thought struck him. "But if his father's brother had indeed been wicked enough to bewitch Hamlet and make him mad that would be a good story indeed, for it would be his fault that Hamlet, being mad, no longer had any sense and thus was ready to kill his father's brother."

There was a murmur of applause. *Hamlet* was again a good story to them, but it no longer seemed quite the same story to me. As I thought over the coming complications of plot and motive, I lost courage and decided to skim over dangerous ground quickly.

"The great chief," I went on, "was not sorry that Hamlet had killed Polonius. It gave him a reason to send Hamlet away, with his two treacherous mates, with letters to a chief of a far country, saying that Hamlet should be killed. But Hamlet changed the writing on their papers, so that the chief killed his age mates instead." I encountered a reproachful glare from one of the men whom I had told undetectable forgery was not merely immoral but beyond human skill. I looked the other way.

"Before Hamlet could return, Laertes came back for his father's funeral. The great chief told him Hamlet had killed Polonius. Laertes swore to kill Hamlet because of this, and because his sister Ophelia, hearing her father had been killed by the man she loved, went mad and drowned in the river."

"Have you already forgotten what we told you?" The old man was reproachful. "One cannot take vengeance on a madman; Hamlet killed Polonius in his madness. As for the girl, she not only went mad, she was drowned. Only witches can make people drown. Water itself can't hurt anything. It is merely something one drinks and bathes in."

I began to get cross. "If you don't like the story, I'll stop."

The old man made soothing noises and himself poured me some more beer. "You tell the story well, and we are lis-

tening. But it is clear that the elders of your country have never told you what the story really means. No, don't interrupt! We believe you when you say your marriage customs are different, or your clothes and weapons. But people are the same everywhere; therefore, there are always witches and it is we, the elders, who know how witches work. We told you it was the great chief who wished to kill Hamlet, and now your own words have proved us right. Who were Ophelia's male relatives?"

"There were only her father and her brother." *Hamlet* was clearly out of my hands.

"There must have been many more; this also you must ask of your elders when you get back to your country. From what you tell us, since Polonius was dead, it must have been Laertes who killed Ophelia, although I do not see the reason for it."

We had emptied one pot of beer, and the old men argued the point with slightly tipsy interest. Finally one of them demanded of me, "What did the servant of Polonius say on his return?"

With difficulty I recollected Reynaldo and his mission. "I don't think he did return before Polonius was killed."

"Listen," said the elder, "and I will tell you how it was and how your story will go, then you may tell me if I am right. Polonius knew his son would get into trouble, and so he did. He had many fines to pay for fighting, and debts from gambling. But he had only two ways of getting money quickly. One was to marry off his sister at once, but it is difficult to find a man who will marry a woman desired by the son of a chief. For if the chief's heir commits adultery with your wife, what can you do? Only a fool calls a case against a man who will someday be his judge. Therefore Laertes had to take the second way: he killed his sister by witchcraft, drowning her so he could secretly sell her body to the witches."

I raised an objection. "They found her body and buried it. Indeed Laertes jumped into the grave to see his sister once more—so, you see, the body was truly there. Hamlet, who had just come back, jumped in after him."

"What did I tell you?" The elder appealed to the others. "Laertes was up to no good with his sister's body. Hamlet prevented him, because the chief's heir, like a chief, does not wish any other man to grow rich and powerful. Laertes would be angry, because he would have killed his sister without benefit to himself. In our country he would try to kill Hamlet for that reason. Is this not what happened?"

"More or less," I admitted. "When the great chief found Hamlet was still alive, he encouraged Laertes to try to kill Hamlet and arranged a fight with machetes between them. In the fight both the young men were wounded to death. Hamlet's mother drank the poisoned beer that the chief meant for Hamlet in case he won the fight. When he saw his mother die of poison, Hamlet, dying, managed to kill his father's brother with his machete."

"You see, I was right!" exclaimed the elder.

"That was a very good story," added the old man, "and you told it with very few mistakes. There was just one more error, at the very end. The poison Hamlet's mother drank was obviously meant for the survivor of the fight, whichever it was. If Laertes had won, the great chief would have poisoned him, for no one would know that he arranged Hamlet's death. Then, too, he need not fear Laertes' witchcraft; it takes a strong heart to kill one's only sister by witchcraft.

"Sometime," concluded the old man, gathering his ragged toga about him, "you must tell us some more stories of your country. We, who are elders, will instruct you in their true meaning, so that when you return to your own land your elders will see that you have not been sitting in the bush, but among those who know things and who have taught you wisdom."

Laura Bohannan is a former professor of anthropology at the University of Illinois, at Chicago.

From *Natural History,* August/September 1966. © 1966 by Laura Bohannan. Reprinted by permission.

UNIT 3

The Organization of Society and Culture

Unit Selections

Key Points to Consider

- What traditional Inuit (Eskimo) practices do you find contrary to values professed in your society but important to Eskimo survival under certain circumstances?

- What can contemporary hunter-collector societies tell us about the quality of life in the prehistoric past?

- Under what circumstances do social stratification and centralization of power appear in human societies?

- What are the rules of reciprocity?

 **Links: www.dushkin.com/online/**
These sites are annotated in the World Wide Web pages.

Huarochirì, a Peruvian Culture in Time
http://wiscinfo.doit.wisc.edu/chaysimire/

Smithsonian Institution Web Site
http://www.si.edu

Sociology Guy's Anthropology Links
http://www.trinity.edu/~mkearl/anthro.html

What Is Culture?
http://www.wsu.edu:8001/vcwsu/commons/topics/culture/culture-index.html

Human beings do not interact with one another or think about their world in random fashion. Instead, they engage in both structured and recurrent physical and mental activities. In this section, such patterns of behavior and thought—referred to here as the organization of society and culture—may be seen in a number of different contexts, from the hunting tactics of the Inupiaq Eskimos of the Arctic (see "Understanding Eskimo Science") to the cattle-herding Masai of East Africa (in "Mystique of the Masai").

Of special importance are the ways in which people make a living—in other words, the production, distribution, and consumption of goods and services. It is only by knowing the basic subsistence systems that we can hope to gain insight into the other levels of social and cultural phenomena, for, as anthropologists have found, they are all inextricably bound together.

Noting the various aspects of a sociocultural system in harmonious balance, however, does not imply an anthropological seal of approval. To understand infanticide (killing of the newborn) in the manner that it is practiced among some peoples is neither to condone nor condemn it. The adaptive patterns that have been in existence for a great length of time, such as many of the patterns of hunters and gatherers, probably owe their existence to their contributions to long-term human survival. Anthropologists, however, are not content with the data derived from individual experience. On the contrary, personal descriptions must become the basis for sound anthropological theory. Otherwise, they remain meaningless, isolated relics of culture in the manner of museum pieces. Thus, in "Too Many Bananas, Not Enough Pineapples, and No Watermelon at All: Three Object Lessons in Living With Reciprocity," David Counts provides us with ground rules for reciprocity that were derived from his own particular field experience and yet are cross-culturally applicable. Finally, "Life Without Chiefs" by Marvin Harris expresses that constant striving in anthropology to develop a general perspective from particular events by showing how environmental circumstances and shifts in technology may result in marked changes in lifestyle and centralization of political power.

While the articles in this unit are to some extent descriptive, they also serve to challenge both academic and commonsense notions about why people behave and think as they do. They remind us that assumptions are never really safe. Anytime anthropologists can be kept on their toes, their field as a whole is the better for it.

Understanding Eskimo Science

Traditional hunters' insights into the natural world are worth rediscovering.

Richard Nelson

Just below the Arctic Circle in the boreal forest of interior Alaska; an amber afternoon in mid-November; the temperature -20°; the air adrift with frost crystals, presaging the onset of deeper cold.

Five men—Koyukon Indians—lean over the carcass of an exceptionally large black bear. For two days they've traversed the Koyukuk River valley, searching for bears that have recently entered hibernation dens. The animals are in prime condition at this season but extremely hard to find. Den entrances, hidden beneath 18 inches of powdery snow, are betrayed only by the subtlest of clues—patches where no grass protrudes from the surface because it's been clawed away for insulation, faint concavities hinting of footprint depressions in the moss below.

Earlier this morning the hunters took a yearling bear. In accordance with Koyukon tradition, they followed elaborate rules for the proper treatment of killed animals. For example, the bear's feet were removed first, to keep its spirit from wandering. Also, certain parts were to be eaten away from the village, at a kind of funeral feast. All the rest would be eaten either at home or at community events, as people here have done for countless generations.

Koyukon hunters know that an animal's life ebbs slowly, that it remains aware and sensitive to how people treat its body. This is especially true for the potent and demanding spirit of the bear.

The leader of the hunting group is Moses Sam, a man in his 60s who has trapped in this territory since childhood. He is known for his detailed knowledge of the land and for his extraordinary success as a bear hunter. "No one else has that kind of luck with bears," I've been told. "Some people are born with it. He always takes good care of his animals—respects them. That's how he keeps his luck."

Moses pulls a small knife from his pocket, kneels beside the bear's head, and carefully slits the clear domes of its eyes. "Now," he explains softly, "the bear won't see if one of us makes a mistake or does something wrong."

Contemporary Americans are likely to find this story exotic, but over the course of time episodes like this have been utterly commonplace, the essence of people's relationship to the natural world. After all, for 99 percent of human history we lived exclusively as hunter-gatherers; by comparison, agriculture has existed only for a moment and urban societies scarcely more than a blink.

From this perspective, much of human experience over the past several million years lies beyond our grasp. Probably no society has been so deeply alienated as ours from the community of nature, has viewed the natural world from a greater distance of mind, has lapsed into a murkier comprehension of its connections with the sustaining environment. Because of this, we have great difficulty understanding our rootedness to earth, our affinities with nonhuman life.

I believe it's essential that we learn from traditional societies, especially those whose livelihood depends on the harvest of a wild environment—hunters, fishers, trappers, and gatherers. These people have accumulated bodies of knowledge much like our own sciences. And they can give us vital insights about responsible membership in the community of life, insights founded on a wisdom we'd long forgotten and now are beginning to rediscover.

Since the mid-1960s I have worked as an ethnographer in Alaska, living intermittently in remote northern communities and recording native traditions centered around the natural world. I spent about two years in Koyukon Indian villages and just over a year with Inupiaq Eskimos on the Arctic coast—traveling by dog team and snowmobile, recording traditional knowledge, and learning the hunter's way.

Eskimos have long inhabited some of the harshest environments on earth, and they are among the most exquisitely adapted of all human groups. Because plant life is so scarce in their northern terrain, Eskimos depend more than any other people on hunting.

Eskimos are famous for the cleverness of their technology—kayaks, harpoons, skin clothing, snow houses, dog teams. But I believe their greatest genius, and the basis of their success, lies in the less tangible realm of the intellect—the nexus of mind and nature. For what repeatedly struck me above all else was their profound knowledge of the environment.

Several times, when my Inupiaq hunting companion did something especially clever, he'd point to his head and declare: "You see—Eskimo scientist!" At first I took it as hyperbole, but as time went by I realized he was speaking the truth. Scientists had often come to his village, and he saw in them a familiar commitment to the empirical method.

Traditional Inupiaq hunters spend a lifetime acquiring knowledge—from others in the community and from their own observations. If they are to survive, they must have absolutely reliable information. When I first went to live with Inupiaq people, I doubted many things they told me. But the longer I stayed, the more I trusted their teachings.

For example, hunters say that ringed seals surfacing in open leads—wide cracks in the sea ice—can reliably forecast the weather. Because an unexpected gale might set people adrift on the pack ice, accurate prediction is a matter of life and death. When seals rise chest-high in the water, snout pointed skyward, not going anywhere in particular, it indicates stable weather, the Inupiaq say. But if they surface briefly, head low, snout parallel to the water, and show themselves only once or twice, watch for a sudden storm. And take special heed if you've also noticed the sled dogs howling incessantly, stars twinkling erratically, or the current running strong from the south. As time passed, my own experiences with seals and winter storms affirmed what the Eskimos said.

Like a young Inupiaq in training, I gradually grew less skeptical and started to apply what I was told. For example, had I ever been rushed by a polar bear, I would have jumped away to the animal's *right* side. Inupiaq elders say polar bears are left-handed, so you have a slightly better chance to avoid their right paw, which is slower and less accurate. I'm pleased to say I never had the chance for a field test. But in judging assertions like this, remember that Eskimos have had close contact with polar bears for several thousand years.

The Inupiaq hunter possesses as much knowledge as a highly trained scientist in our own society

During winter, ringed and bearded seals maintain tunnel-like breathing holes in ice that is many feet thick. These holes are often capped with an igloo-shaped dome created by water sloshing onto the surface when the animal enters from below. Inupiaq elders told me that polar bears are clever enough to excavate around the base of this dome, leaving it perfectly intact but weak enough that a hard swat will shatter the ice and smash the seal's skull. I couldn't help wondering if this were really true; but then a younger man told me he'd recently followed the tracks of a bear that had excavated one seal hole after another, exactly as the elders had described.

In the village where I lived, the most respected hunter was Igruk, a man in his 70s. He had an extraordinary sense of animals—a gift for understanding and predicting their behavior. Although he was no longer quick and strong, he joined a crew hunting bowhead whales during the spring migration, his main role being that of adviser. Each time Igruk spotted a whale coming from the south, he counted the number of blows, timed how long it stayed down, and noted the distance it traveled along the open lead, until it vanished toward the north. This way he learned to predict, with uncanny accuracy, where hunters could expect the whale to resurface.

I believe the expert Inupiaq hunter possesses as much knowledge as a highly trained scientist in our own society, although the information may be of a different sort. Volumes could be written on the behavior, ecology, and utilization of Arctic animals—polar bear, walrus, bowhead whale, beluga, bearded seal, ringed seal, caribou, musk ox, and others—based entirely on Eskimo knowledge.

Comparable bodies of knowledge existed in every Native American culture

before the time of Columbus. Since then, even in the far north, Western education and cultural change have steadily eroded these traditions. Reflecting on a time before Europeans arrived, we can imagine the whole array of North American animal species—deer, elk, black bear, wolf, mountain lion, beaver, coyote, Canada goose, ruffed grouse, passenger pigeon, northern pike—each known in hundreds of different ways by tribal communities; the entire continent, sheathed in intricate webs of knowledge. Taken as a whole, this composed a vast intellectual legacy, born of intimacy with the natural world. Sadly, not more than a hint of it has ever been recorded.

Like other Native Americans, the Inupiaq acquired their knowledge through gradual accretion of naturalistic observations—year after year, lifetime after lifetime, generation after generation, century after century. Modern science often relies on other techniques—specialized full-time observation, controlled experiments, captive-animal studies, technological devices like radio collars—which can provide similar information much more quickly.

Yet Eskimo people have learned not only *about* animals but also *from* them. Polar bears hunt seals not only by waiting at their winter breathing holes, but also by stalking seals that crawl up on the ice to bask in the spring warmth. Both methods depend on being silent, staying downwind, keeping out of sight, and moving only when the seal is asleep or distracted. According to the elders, a stalking bear will even use one paw to cover its conspicuous black nose.

Inupiaq methods for hunting seals, both at breathing holes and atop the spring ice, are nearly identical to those of the polar bear. Is this a case of independent invention? Or did ancestral Eskimos learn the techniques by watching polar bears, who had perfected an adaptation to the sea-ice-environment long before humans arrived in the Arctic?

The hunter's genius centers on knowing an animal's behavior so well he can turn it to his advantage. For instance, Igruk once saw a polar bear far off across flat ice, where he couldn't stalk it without being seen. But he knew an old technique of mimicking a seal. He lay down in plain sight, conspicuous in his dark parka and pants, then lifted and dropped his head like a seal, scratched the ice, and imitated flippers with his hands. The bear mistook his pursuer for prey. Each time Igruk lifted his head the animal kept still; whenever Igruk "slept" the bear crept closer. When it came near enough, a gunshot pierced the snowy silence. That night, polar bear meat was shared among the villagers.

A traditional hunter like Igruk plumbs the depths of his intellect—his capacity to manipulate complex knowledge. But he also delves into his animal nature, drawing from intuitions of sense and body and heart: feeling the wind's touch, listening for the tick of moving ice, peering from crannies, hiding as if he himself were the hunted. He moves in a world of eyes, where everything watches—the bear, the seal, the wind, the moon and stars, the drifting ice, the silent waters below. He is beholden to powers we have long forgotten or ignored.

In Western society we rest comfortably on our own accepted truths about the nature of nature. We treat the environment as if it were numb to our presence and blind to our behavior. Yet despite our certainty on this matter, accounts of traditional people throughout the world reveal that most of humankind has concluded otherwise. Perhaps our scientific method really does follow the path to a single, absolute truth. But there may be wisdom in accepting other possibilities and opening ourselves to different views of the world.

I remember asking a Koyukon man about the behavior and temperament of the Canada goose. He described it as a gentle and good-natured animal, then added: "Even if [a goose] had the power to knock you over, I don't think it would do it."

For me, his words carried a deep metaphorical wisdom. They exemplified the Koyukon people's own restraint toward the world around them. And they offered a contrast to our culture, in which possessing the power to overwhelm the en-vironment has long been sufficient justification for its use.

"Each animal knows way more than you do," a Koyukon Indian elder was fond of telling me.

We often think of this continent as having been a pristine wilderness when the first Europeans arrived. Yet for at least 12,000 years, and possibly twice that long, Native American people had inhabited and intensively utilized the land; had gathered, hunted, fished, settled, and cultivated; had learned the terrain in all its details, infusing it with meaning and memory; and had shaped every aspect of their life around it. That humans could sustain membership in a natural community for such an enormous span of time without profoundly degrading it fairly staggers the imagination. And it gives strong testimony to the adaptation of mind—the braiding together of knowledge and ideology—that linked North America's indigenous people with their environment.

A Koyukon elder, who took it upon himself to be my teacher, was fond of telling me: "Each animal knows way more than you do." He spoke as if it summarized all that he understood and believed.

This statement epitomizes relationships to the natural world among many Native American people. And it goes far in explaining the diversity and fecundity of life on our continent when the first sailing ship approached these shores.

There's been much discussion in recent years about what biologist E. O. Wilson has termed "biophilia"—a deep, pervasive, ubiquitous, all-embracing affinity for nonhuman life. Evidence for this "instinct" may be elusive in Western cultures, but not among traditional societies. People like the Koyukon manifest biophilia in virtually all dimensions of their existence. Connectedness with non-human life infuses the whole spectrum of their thought, behavior, and belief.

It's often said that a fish might have no concept of water, never having left it. In the same way, traditional peoples might never stand far enough outside themselves to imagine a generalized concept of biophilia. Perhaps it would be impossible for people to intimately bound with the natural world, people who recognize that all nature is our own embracing community. Perhaps, to bring a word like *biophilia* into their language, they would first need to separate themselves from nature.

In April 1971 I was in a whaling camp several miles off the Arctic coast with a group of Inupiaq hunters, including Igruk, who understood animals so well he almost seemed to enter their minds.

Onshore winds had closed the lead that migrating whales usually follow, but one large opening remained, and here the Inupiaq men placed their camp. For a couple of days there had been no whales, so everyone stayed inside the warm tent, talking and relaxing. The old man rested on a soft bed of caribou skins with his eyes closed. Then, suddenly, he interrupted the conversation: "I think a whale is coming, and perhaps it will surface very close...."

To my amazement everyone jumped into action, although none had seen or heard anything except Igruk's words. Only he stayed behind, while the others rushed for the water's edge. I was last to leave the tent. Seconds after I stepped outside, a broad, shining back cleaved the still water near the opposite side of the opening, accompanied by the burst of a whale's blow.

Later, when I asked how he'd known, Igruk said, "There was a ringing inside my ears." I have no explanation other than his; I can only report what I saw. None of the Inupiaq crew members even commented afterward, as if nothing out of the ordinary had happened.

This article originally appeared in *Audubon* magazine, September/October 1993, pp. 102–109. Adapted from *Biophilia* by Richard Nelson, 1993. Published by Island Press. © 1993 by Richard Nelson. Reprinted by permission of Susan Bergholz Literary Services, New York. All rights reserved.

Mystique of the Masai

Pastoral as well as warlike, they have persisted in maintaining their unique way of life

Ettagale Blauer

The noble bearing, self-assurance, and great beauty of the Masai of East Africa have been remarked upon from the time the first Europeans encountered them on the plains of what are now Kenya and Tanzania. (The word 'Masai' derives from their spoken language, Maa.) Historically, the Masai have lived among the wild animals on the rolling plains of the Rift Valley, one of the most beautiful parts of Africa. Here, the last great herds still roam freely across the plains in their semiannual migrations.

Although the appearance of people usually marks the decline of the game, it is precisely the presence of the Masai that has guaranteed the existence of these vast herds. Elsewhere in Kenya and Tanzania, and certainly throughout the rest of Africa, the herds that once roamed the lands have been decimated. But the Masai are not hunters, whom they call *iltorrobo*—poor men—because they don't have cattle. The Masai do not crave animal trophies, they do not value rhinoceros horns for aphrodisiacs, meat is not part of their usual diet, and they don't farm the land, believing it to be a sacrilege to break the earth. Traditionally, where Masai live, the game is unmolested.

In contrast to their peaceful and harmonious relationship to the wildlife, however, the Masai are warlike in relationship to the neighboring tribes, conducting cattle raids where they take women as well as cattle for their prizes, and they have been fiercely independent in resisting the attempts of colonial governments to change or subdue them. Although less numerous than the neighboring Kikuyu, the Masai have a strong feeling of being "chosen" people, and have been stubborn in maintaining their tribal identity.

However, that traditional tribal way of life is threatened by the exploding populations of Kenya and Tanzania (41 million people), who covet the vast open spaces of Masai Mara, Masai Amboseli, and the Serengeti Plain. Today, more than half of the Masai live in Kenya, with a style of life that requires extensive territory for cattle herds to roam in search of water and pastureland, and the freedom to hold ceremonies that mark the passage from one stage of life to the next. The Masai's need for land for their huge herds of cattle is not appreciated by people who value the land more for agriculture than for pasturage and for herds of wild animals.

The Masai live in countries that are attractive to tourists and whose leaders have embraced the values and life-style of the Western world. These two facts make it increasingly difficult for the Masai to live according to traditional patterns. The pressure to change in Kenya comes in part from their proximity to urban centers, especially the capital city of Nairobi, whose name is a Masai word meaning cool water.

Still, many Masai live in traditional homes and dress in wraps of bright cloth or leather, decorated with beaded jewelry, their cattle nearby. But the essence of the Masai culture—the creation of age-sets whose roles in life are clearly delineated—is under constant attack. In both Kenya and Tanzania, the governments continually try to "civilize" the Masai, to stop cattle raiding, and especially to put an end to the *morani*—the warriors—who are seen as the most disruptive of the age-sets.

TRADITIONAL LIFE

Masai legends trace the culture back some 300 years, and are recited according to age-groups, allowing fifteen years for each group. But anthropologists believe they arrived in the region some 1,000 years ago, having migrated from southern Ethiopia. As a racial group, they are considered a Nilo-Hamitic mix. Although deep brown in color, their features are not negroid. (Their extensive use of ochre may give their skin the look of American Indians but that is purely cosmetic.)

Traditional Masai people are governed by one guiding principle: that all the cattle on earth are theirs, that they were put there for them by *Ngai*, who is the god of both heaven and earth, existing also in the rains which bring the precious grass to feed the cattle. Any cattle they do not presently own are only temporarily out of their care, and must be recaptured. The Masai do not steal material objects; theft for them is a separate matter from raiding cattle, which is seen as the *return* of cattle to their rightful owners. From this basic belief, an entire culture has grown. The grass that feeds the cattle and the ground on which it grows are sacred; to the Masai, it is sacrilege to break the ground for any reason, whether

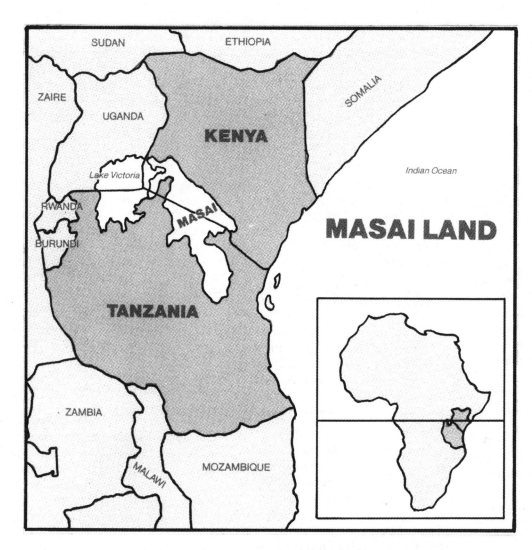

EMIKO OZAKI/THE WORLD & I

A map of Masai Land. The Masai's traditional territory exists within the two countries of Kenya and Tanzania.

to grow food or to dig for water, or even to bury the dead.

Cattle provide their sole sustenance: milk and blood to drink, and the meat feast when permitted. Meat eating is restricted to ceremonial occasions, or when it is needed for gaining strength, such as when a woman gives birth or someone is recovering from an illness. When they do eat meat at a ceremony they consume their own oxen, which are sacrificed for a particular reason and in the approved way. Hunting and killing for meat are not Masai activities. It is this total dependence on their cattle, and their disdain for the meat of game animals, that permits them to coexist with the game, and which, in turn, has kept intact the great herds of the Masai Mara and the Serengeti Plain. Their extraordinary diet of milk, blood, and occasionally, meat,

keeps them sleek and fit, and Westerners have often noted their physical condition with admiration.

In 1925 Norman Leys wrote, "Physically they are among the handsomest of mankind, with slender bones, narrow hips and shoulders and most beautifully rounded muscles and limbs." That same description holds today. The Masai live on about 1,300 calories a day, as opposed to our consumption of nearly 3,000. They are invariably lean.

Traditional nomadic life of the Masai, however, was ferocious and warlike in relation to other tribes. The warriors *(morani)* built *manyattas*, a type of shelter, throughout the lands and used each for a few months at a time, then moved to another area when the grazing was used up. As the seasons changed, they would return to those manyattas. They often

went out raiding cattle from neighboring tribes whom they terrorized with their great ferocity.

A large part of that aggressiveness is now attributed to drugs; the morani worked themselves into a frenzy as they prepared for a raid, using the leaves and barks of certain trees known to create such moods. A soup was made of fat, water, and the bark of two trees, *il kitosloswa* and *il kiluretti*. From the description, these seem to act as hallucinogens. As early as the 1840s, Europeans understood that the morani's extremely aggressive behavior derived from drug use. Drugs were used for endurance and for strength throughout warriorhood. During a meat feast, which could last a month, they took stimulants throughout, raising them to a virtual frenzy. This, combined with the natural excitement attendant to crowd behavior, made them formidable foes.

Having gained this supernatural energy and courage, they were ready to go cattle raiding among other tribes. To capture the cattle, the men of the other tribe had to be killed. Women were never touched in battle, but were taken to Masailand to become Masai wives. The rate of intermarriage was great during these years. Today, intermarriage is less frequent and the result mostly of chance meetings with other people. It is likely that intermarriage has actually prolonged the life of the Masai as a people; many observers from the early 1900s remarked upon the high rate of syphilis among the Masai, attributable to their habit of taking multiple sexual partners. Their birthrate is notably lower than the explosive population growth of the other peoples of Kenya and Tanzania. Still, they have increased from about 25,000 people at the turn of the century to the estimated 300,000–400,000 they are said to number today.

While the ceaseless cycle of their nomadic life has been sharply curtailed, many still cross the border between the two countries as they have for hundreds of years, leading their cattle to water and grazing lands according to the demands of the wet and dry seasons. They are in tune with the animals that migrate from the Serengeti Plain in Tanzania to Masai Mara in Kenya, and back again.

MALE AGE-SETS

The life of a traditional Masai male follows a well-ordered progression through a series of life stages.

Masai children enjoy their early years as coddled and adored love objects. They are raised communally, with great affection. Children are a great blessing in Africa. Among the Masai, with the lack of emphasis on paternity, and with a woman's prestige tied to her children, natural love for children is enhanced by their desirability in the society. Children are also desired because they bring additional cattle to a family, either as bride-price in the case of girls or by raiding in the case of boys.

During their early years, children play and imitate the actions of the elders, a natural school in which they learn the rituals and daily life practices of their people. Learning how to be a Masai is the lifework of every one in the community. Infant mortality in Africa remains high; catastrophic diseases introduced by Europeans, such as smallpox, nearly wiped them out. That memory is alive in their oral traditions; having children is a protection against the loss of the entire culture, which they know from experience could easily happen. Africans believe that you must live to see your face reflected in that of a child; given the high infant mortality rate, the only way to protect that human chain is by having as many children as possible.

For boys, each stage of life embraces an age-group created at an elaborate ceremony, the highlight of their lives being the elevation to moran. Once initiated, they learn their age-group's specific duties and privileges. Males pass through four stages: childhood, boyhood, warriorhood, and elderhood. Warriors, divided into junior and senior, form one generation, or age-set.

Four major ceremonies mark the passage from one group to another: boys who are going to be circumcised participate in the *Alamal Lenkapaata* ceremony, preparation for circumcision; *Emorata* is followed by initiation into warriorhood—status of moran; the passage from warrior to elderhood is marked by the *Eunoto* ceremony; and total elderhood is confirmed by the *Olngesherr*. All ceremonies have in common ritual head shaving, continual blessings, slaughter of an animal, ceremonial painting of face or body, singing, dancing, and feasting. *Laibons*—spiritual advisers—must be present at all ceremonies, and the entire tribe devotes itself to these preparations.

Circumcision is a rite of passage and more for teenage boys. It determines the role the boy will play throughout his life, as leader or follower. How he conducts himself during circumcision is keenly observed by all; a boy who cries out during the painful operation is branded a coward and shunned for a long time; his mother is disgraced. A boy who is brave, and who had led an exemplary life, becomes the leader of his age-group.

It takes months of work to prepare for these ceremonies so the exact date of such an event is rarely known until the last minute. Westerners, with contacts into the Masai community, often stay ready for weeks, hoping to be on hand when such a ceremony is about to take place. Each such ceremony may well be the last, it is thought.

Before they can be circumcised, boys must prove themselves ready. They tend the cattle—the Masai's only wealth—and guard them from predators whose tracks they learn to recognize. They know their cattle individually, the way we know people. Each animal has a name and is treated as a personality. When they feel they are ready, the boys approach the junior elders and ask them to open a new circumcision period. If this is approved, they begin a series of rituals, among them the Alamal Lenkapaata, the last step before the formal initiation. The boys must have a liabon, a leader with the power to predict the future, to guide them in their decisions. He creates a name for this new generation. The boys decorate themselves with chalky paint, and spend the night out in the open. The elders sing and celebrate and dance through the night to honor the boys.

An Alamal Lenkapaata held in 1983 was probably the most recent to mark the opening of a new age-set. Ceremonies were held in Ewaso Ngiro, in the Rift Valley. As boys joined into groups and danced, they raised a cloud of dust around themselves. All day long, groups would form and dance, then break apart and later start again.

Under a tree, elders from many areas gathered together and their discussion was very intense. John Galaty, professor of anthropology from McGill University in Montreal, who has studied the Masai extensively, flew in specifically to attend this ceremony. He is fluent in Masai and translated the elders' talk. "We are lucky," they said, "to be able to have this ceremony. The government does not want us to have it. We have to be very careful. The young men have to be warned that there should be no cattle raiding." And there wasn't any.

An ox was slaughtered, for meat eating is a vital element of this ceremony.

The boys who were taking part cut off hunks of meat which they cooked over an open fire. Though there was a hut set aside for them, the boys spent little time sleeping. The next day, all the elders gathered to receive gifts of sugar and salt from John Keen, a member of Kenya's parliament, and himself a Masai. (Kenya has many Masai in government, including the Minister of Finance, George Saitoti.) The dancing, the meat eating, all the elements of the ceremony continued for several days. If this had been a wealthy group, they might have kept up the celebration for as long as a month.

Once this ceremony is concluded, the boys are allowed to hold councils and to discuss important matters. They choose one from their own group to be their representative. The Alamal Lenkapaata ceremony includes every boy of suitable age, preparing him for circumcision and then warriorhood. The circumcisions will take place over the next few years, beginning with the older boys in this group. The age difference may be considerable in any age-group since these ceremonies are held infrequently; once a circumcision period ends, though, it may not be opened again for many years.

THE MORAN

The Masai who exemplifies his tribe is the moran. This is the time of life that expresses the essence of the Masai—bravery, willingness to defend their people and their cattle against all threats, confidence to go out on cattle raids to increase their own herds, and ability to stand up to threats even from Europeans, whose superior weapons subdued the Masai but never subjugated them. The Masai moran is the essence of that almost mythical being, the noble savage, a description invented by Europeans but here actually lived out. With his spear, his elaborately braided and reddened hair, his bountiful beaded jewelry, his beautiful body and proud bearing, the moran is the symbol of everything that is attractive about the Masai. When a young man becomes a moran, his entire culture looks upon him with reverence.

The life a moran enjoys as his birthright is centered on cattle raiding, enhancing his appearance, and sex. The need to perform actual work, such as building fences, rescuing a cow that has gone astray, and standing ready to defend their homeland—Masailand—is only occasionally required. Much of his time is devoted to the glorification of his appearance. His body is a living showcase of Masai art.

From the moment a boy undergoes the circumcision ceremony, he looks ahead to the time when he will be a moran. He grows his hair long so it can be braided into myriad tiny plaits, thickened with ochre and lat. The age-mates spend hours at this, the whole outdoors being their salon. As they work, they chat, always building the bonds between them. Their beaded jewelry is made by their girlfriends. Their bare legs are ever-changing canvases on which they trace patterns, using white chalk and ochre. Though nearly naked, they are a medley of patterns and colors.

After being circumcised, the young men "float" in society for up to two years, traveling in loose groups and living in temporary shelters called *inkangitie*. After that time they can build a manyatta. Before fully becoming a moran, however, they must enter a "holy house" at a special ceremony. Only a young man who has not slept with a circumcised woman can enter the holy house. The fear of violating this taboo is very strong, and young men who do not enter the house are beaten by their parents and carry the disrespect of the tribe all their lives.

The dancing of the morani celebrates everything that they consider beautiful and strong: morani dance competitively by jumping straight into the air, knees straight, over and over again, each leap trying to go higher than the last, as they sing and chant and encourage each other. The morani also dance with their young girlfriends. Each couple performs sinuous motions repeatedly, then breaks off and another couple takes their place. A hypnotic rhythm develops as they follow the chanting and hand clapping of their mates.

Although they are now forbidden by the governments of Kenya and Tanzania to kill a lion—a traditional test of manhood—or to go cattle raiding, they retain all the trappings of a warrior, without the possibility of practicing their skill. They occasionally manage a cattle raid, but even without it, they still live with pride and dignity. Masai remain morani for about fifteen years, building up unusually strong relationships among their age-mates with whom they live during that time. Hundreds of boys may become morani at one time.

Traditionally, every fifteen years saw the advent of a new generation of warriors. Now, both colonial governments and independent black-ruled governments have tampered with this social process, and have been successful in reducing the time men spend as warriors. By forcing this change, the governments hope to mold the Masai male into a more tractable citizen, especially by forbidding such disruptive activities as lion killing and cattle raiding. But tinkering with the Masai system can have unforeseen and undesirable consequences. It takes a certain number of years before a moran is ready to take on the duties of that age-group. They need time to build up herds of cattle to be used for bride-price and to learn to perform the decision-making tasks expected. This change also leaves the younger boys without warriors to keep them in check, and to guide them through the years leading up to the circumcision ceremony.

More significantly, since 1978 it has been illegal to build a manyatta, and warriors from that time have been left with no place to live. Their mothers cannot live with them, they cannot tend their cattle or increase their herds, they have no wives or jobs. Since, once they become warriors, they are not allowed to enter another person's house to eat, they are forced to steal other peoples' cattle and live off the land.

Circumcision exists for women as well as for men. From the age of nine until puberty, young girls live with the morani as sexual partners; it is an accepted part of Masai life that girls do not reach puberty as virgins. It is because of this practice that syphilis causes the most serious problems for the Masai. The girls, unfamiliar with their bodies, contract the disease and leave it untreated until sterility results. This sexual activity changes dramatically when a girl reaches puberty. At that time, she is circumcised and forbidden to stay with the warriors. This is to prevent her from becoming pregnant before she is married. As soon as she recovers from the circumcision, or clitoridectomy, an operation that destroys her ability to experience orgasm, she is considered ready for marriage. Circumcision is seen as a means of equalizing men and women. By removing any vestige of the appearance of the organs of the opposite sex, it purifies the gender. Although female circumcision has long been banned by the Kenyan government, few girls manage to escape the operation.

While the entire tribe devotes itself to the rituals that perpetuate the male age-set system, girls travel individually through life in their roles as lovers, wives, and child bearers, in all instances subservient to the boys and men. They have no comparable age-set system and hence do not develop the intensely felt friendships of the men who move through life together in groups, and who, during the period of senior warriorhood live together, away from their families.

It is during this period that the mothers move away from their homes. They build manyattas in which they live with their sons who have achieved the status of senior morani, along with their sons' girlfriends, and away from their own small children. The husbands, other wives, and the other women of the tribe, take care of these children.

The male-female relationship is dictated according to the male age-sets. When a newly circumcised girl marries, she joins the household of her husband's family, and likely will be one among several of his wives. Her role is to milk the cows, to build the house, and to bear children, especially male children. Only through childbirth can she achieve high status; all men, on the other hand, achieve status simply by graduating from one age-set to the next.

A childless Masai woman is virtually without a role in her society. One of the rarest ceremonies among the Masai is a blessing for women who have not given birth and for women who want more children. While the women play a peripheral role in the men's ceremonies, the men are vital to the women's, for it is a man who blesses the women. To pre-

pare for the ritual, the women brew great quantities of beer and offer beer and lambs to the men who are to bless them.

In their preparation for this ceremony, and in conducting matters that pertain to their lives, the women talk things out democratically, as do the men. They gather in the fields and each woman presents her views. Not until all who want to speak have done so does the group move toward a consensus. As with the men, a good speaker is highly valued and her views are listened to attentively. But these sessions are restricted to women's issues; the men have the final say over all matters relating to the tribe. Boys may gather in councils as soon as they have completed the Alamal Lenkapaata; girls don't have similar opportunities. They follow their lovers, the morani, devotedly, yet as soon as they reach the age when they can marry, they are wrenched out of this love relationship and given in marriage to much older men, men who have cattle for bride-price.

Because morani do not marry until they are elevated to elderhood, girls must accept husbands who are easily twice their age. But just as the husband has more than one wife, she will have lovers, who are permitted as long as they are members of her husband's circumcision group, not the age group for whom she was a girlfriend. This is often the cause of tension among the Masai. All the children she bears are considered to be her husband's even though they may not be his biologically. While incest taboos are clearly observed and various other taboos also pertain, multiple partners are expected. Polygamy in Masailand (and anywhere it prevails) dictates that some men will not marry at all. These men are likely to be those without cattle, men who cannot bring bride-price. For the less traditional, the payment of bride-price is sometimes made in cash, rather than in cattle, and to earn money, men go to the cities to seek work. Masai tend to find jobs that permit them to be outside and free; for this reason, many of the night watchmen in the capital city of Nairobi are Masai. They sit around fires at night, chatting, in an urban version of their life in the countryside....

RAIDING, THEFT, AND THE LAW

Though now subject to national laws, the Masai do not turn to official bodies or courts for redress. They settle their own disputes democratically, each man giving his opinion until the matter at hand is settled. Men decide all matters for the tribe (women do not take part in these discussions), and they operate virtually without chiefs. The overriding concern is to be fair in the resolution of problems because kinship ties the Masai together in every aspect of their lives. Once a decision is made, punishment is always levied in the form of a fine. The Masai have no jails, nor do they inflict physical punishment. For a people who value cattle as much as they do, there is no greater sacrifice than to give up some of their animals.

The introduction of schools is another encroachment upon traditional life which was opposed by the Masai. While most African societies resisted sending their children to school, the Masai reacted with particular intensity. They compared school to death or enslavement; if children did go to school, they would be lost to the Masai community. They would forget how to survive on the land, how to identify animals by their tracks, and how to protect the cattle. All of these things are learned by example and by experience.

David Read is a white Kenyan, fluent in Masai who said that, as a boy: "I may not have been able to read or write, but I knew how to live in the bush. I could hunt my dinner if I had to."

The first school in their territory was opened in 1919 at Narok but few children attended. The Masai scorned the other tribes, such as the Kikuyu, who later embraced Western culture and soon filled the offices of the government's bureaucracies. The distance between the Masai and the other tribes became even greater. The Masai were seen as a painful reminder of the primitivism that Europeans as well as Africans had worked so hard to erase. Today, however, many Masai families will keep one son at home to maintain traditional life, and send another one to school. In this way, they experience the benefits of literacy, opportunities for employment, money, connections to the government, and new knowledge, especially veterinary practices, while keeping their traditions intact. Masai who go to school tend to succeed, many of them graduating from college with science degrees. Some take up the study of animal diseases, and bring this knowledge back to help their communities improve the health of their cattle. The entire Masai herd was once nearly wiped out during the rinderpest epidemic in the late nineteenth century. Today, the cattle are threatened by tsetse flies. But where the Masai were able to rebuild their herds in the past, today, they would face tremendous pressure to give up cattle raising entirely.

LIVING CONDITIONS

While the Masai are admired for their great beauty, their living conditions are breeding grounds for disease. Since they keep their small livestock (sheep and goats) in the huts where they live, they are continually exposed to the animals' excrement. The cattle are just outside, in an open enclosure, and their excrement is added to the mix. Flies abound wherever cattle are kept, but with the animals living right next to the huts, they are ever-present. Like many tribal groups living in relative isolation, the Masai are highly vulnerable to diseases brought in by others. In the 1890s, when the rinderpest hit their cattle, the Masai were attacked by smallpox which, coupled with drought, reduced their numbers almost to the vanishing point.

For the most part, the Masai rely on the remedies of their traditional medicine and are renowned for their extensive knowledge and use of natural plants to treat illnesses and diseases of both people and cattle. Since they live in an area that had hardly any permanent sources of water, the Masai have learned to live without washing. They are said to have one bath at birth, another at marriage. Flies are pervasive; there is scarcely a picture of a Masai taken in their home environment that does not show flies alit on them.

Their rounded huts, looking like mushrooms growing from the ground, are built by the women. On a frame of wooden twigs, they begin to plaster mud and cow dung. Layers and layers of this are added until the roof reaches the desired thickness. Each day, cracks and holes are repaired, especially after the rains, using the readily available dung. Within the homes, they use animal hides. Everything they need can be made from the materials at hand. There are a few items such as sugar, tea, and cloth that they buy from the *dukas*, or Indian shops, in Narok, Kajiado, and other nearby towns, but money is readily obtained by selling beaded jewelry, or simply one's own image. Long ago, the Masai discovered their photogenic qualities. If they cannot survive as warriors by raiding, they will survive as icons of warriors, permitting tourists to take their pictures for a fee, and that fee is determined by hard bargaining. One does not simply take a picture of a Masai without payment; that is theft.

Their nomadic patterns have been greatly reduced; now they move only the cattle as the seasons change. During the dry season, the Masai stay on the higher parts of the escarpment and use the pastures there which they call *osukupo*. This offers a richer savannah with more trees. When the rains come, they move down to the pastures of the Rift Valley to the plains called *okpurkel*.

Their kraals are built a few miles from the water supply. The cattle drink on one day only, then are grazed the next, so they can conserve the grazing by using a larger area than they would be able to if they watered the cattle every day. But their great love of cattle has inevitably brought them to the point of overstocking. As the cattle trample their way to and from the waterhole, they destroy all vegetation near it, and the soil washes away. Scientists studying Masai land use have concluded that with the change from a totally nomadic way of life, the natural environmental resistance of this system was destroyed; there is no self-regulating mechanism left. Some Masai have permitted wheat farming on their land for the exploding Kenyan population, taking away the marginal lands that traditionally provided further grazing for their cattle.

PRESSURE TO CHANGE

In June 1901, Sir Charles Eliot, colonial governor of Kenya, said, "I regard the Masai as the most important and dangerous of the tribes with whom we have to deal in East Africa and I think it will be long necessary to maintain an adequate military force in the districts which they inhabit."

The traditional Masai way of life has been under attack ever since. The colonial British governments of Kenya and Tanzania (then Tanganyika) outlawed Masai cattle raiding and tried to stifle the initiation ceremony; the black governments that took over upon independence in the 1960s continued the process. The Masai resisted these edicts, ignored them, and did their best to circumvent them throughout the century. In some areas, they gave in entirely—cattle raiding, the principal activity of the morani—rarely occurs, but their ceremonies, the vital processes by which a boy becomes a moran and a moran becomes an elder, remain intact, although they have been banned over and over again. Stopping these ceremonies is more difficult than just proclaiming them to be over, as the Kenyan government did in 1985.

Some laws restrict the very essence of a Masai's readiness to assume the position of moran. Hunting was banned entirely in Kenya and nearly so in Tanzania (except for expensive permits issued to tourists, and restricted to designated hunting blocks), making it illegal for a moran to kill a lion to demonstrate his bravery and hunting skills. Although the Masai ignore the government whenever possible, at times such as this, conflict is unavoidable. Lions are killed occasionally, but stealthily; some modern Masai boys say, "Who needs to kill a lion? It doesn't prove anything."

The Kenyan governments requirement that Masai children go to school has also affected the traditional roles of girls and women, who traditionally married at age twelve or thirteen and left school. Now the government will send fathers and husbands to jail for taking these girls out of school. There was a case in Kenya in 1986 of a girl who wrote to the government protesting the fact that her father had removed her from school to prepare for marriage. Her mother carried the letter to the appropriate government officials, the father was tried, and the girl was allowed to return to school.

Sometimes there is cooperation between governmental policy and traditional life-style. Ceremonies are scheduled to take place in school holidays, and while government policies continue to erode traditional customs, the educated and traditional groups within the Masai community try to support each other.

TRADITION IN THE FACE OF CHANGE

Although the Masai in both countries are descended from the same people, national policies have pushed the Kenyan Masai further away from their traditions. The Tanzanian Masai, for example, still dress occasionally in animal skins, decorated with beading. The Kenyan Masai dress almost entirely in cloth, reserving skins for ceremonial occasions.

In 1977, Kenya and Tanzania closed their common border, greatly isolating the Tanzanian Masai from Western contact. Though the border has been reopened, the impact on the Masai is clear. The Kenyan Masai became one of the sights of the tourist route while the Tanzanian Masai were kept from such interaction. This has further accelerated change among the Kenyan Masai. Tepilit Ole Saitoti sees a real difference in character between the Masai of Kenya and Tanzania. "Temperamentally" he says, "the Tanzanian Masai tend to be calmer and slower than those in Kenya."

Tribal people throughout Africa are in a constant state of change, some totally urbanized, their traditions nearly forgotten; others are caught in the middle, part of the tribe living traditionally, some moving to the city and adopting Western ways. The Masai have retained their culture, their unique and distinctive way of life, longer than virtually all the other tribes of East Africa, and they have done so while living in the very middle of the tourist traffic. Rather than disappear into the bush, the Masai use their attractiveness and mystique to their own benefit. Masai Mara and Amboseli, two reserves set aside for them, are run by them for their own profit.

Few tribes in Africa still put such a clear cultural stamp on an area; few have so successfully resisted enormous efforts to change them, to modernize and "civilize" them, to make them fit into the larger society. We leave it to Tepilit Ole Saitoti to predict the future of his own people: "Through their long and difficult history, the Masai have fought to maintain their traditional way of life. Today, however, they can no longer resist the pressures of the modern world. The survival of Masai culture has ceased to be a question; in truth, it is rapidly disappearing."

BIBLIOGRAPHY

Bleeker, Sonia, *The Masai, Herders of East Africa*, 1963.

Fedders, Andrew, *Peoples and Cultures of Kenya*, TransAfrica Books, Nairobi, 1979.

Fisher, Angela, *Africa Adorned*, Harry N. Abrams Inc., New York, 1984.

Kinde, S. H., *Last of the Masai*, London, 1901.

Kipkorir, B., *Kenya's People, People of the Rift Valley*, Evans Bros. Ltd., London, 1978.

Lamb, David, *The Africans*, Vintage Books, New York, 1984.

Moravia, Alberto, *Which Tribe Do You Belong To?*, Farrar, Straus & Giroux, Inc., New York, 1974.

Ole Saitoti, Tepilit, *Masai*, Harry N. Abrams, Inc., New York, 1980.

Ricciardi, Mirella, *Vanishing Africa*, Holt, Rinehart & Winston, 1971.

Sankan, S. S., *The Masai*, Kenya Literature Bureau, Nairobi, 1971.

Thomson, Joseph, *Through Masai Land*, Sampson Low, Marstan & Co., London, 1885.

Tignor, Robert, *The Colonial Transformation of Kenya, The Kamba, Kikuyu and Masai from 1900 to 1939*, Princeton, NJ, 1976.

Ettagale Blauer is a New York-based writer who has studied the Masai culture extensively in numerous trips to Africa and who specializes in writing about Africa and jewelry.

This article originally appeared in *The World & I,* March 1987, pp. 497–513. © 1987 by Ettagale Blauer. Reprinted by permission.

Too Many Bananas, Not Enough Pineapples, and No Watermelon at All: Three Object Lessons in Living with Reciprocity

David Counts
McMaster University

NO WATERMELON AT ALL

The woman came all the way through the village, walking between the two rows of houses facing each other between the beach and the bush, to the very last house standing on a little spit of land at the mouth of the Kaini River. She was carrying a watermelon on her head, and the house she came to was the government "rest house," maintained by the villagers for the occasional use of visiting officials. Though my wife and I were graduate students, not officials, and had asked for permission to stay in the village for the coming year, we were living in the rest house while the debate went on about where a house would be built for us. When the woman offered to sell us the watermelon for two shillings, we happily agreed, and the kids were delighted at the prospect of watermelon after yet another meal of rice and bully beef. The money changed hands and the seller left to return to her village, a couple of miles along the coast to the east.

It seemed only seconds later that the woman was back, reluctantly accompanying Kolia, the man who had already made it clear to us that he was the leader of the village. Kolia had no English, and at that time, three or four days into our first stay in Kandoka Village on the island of New Britain in Papua New Guinea, we had very little Tok Pisin. Language difficulties notwithstanding, Kolia managed to make his message clear: The woman had been outrageously wrong to sell us the watermelon for two shillings and we were to return it to her and reclaim our money immediately. When we tried to explain that we thought the price to be fair and were happy with the bargain, Kolia explained again and finally made it clear that we had missed the point. The problem wasn't that we had paid too much; it was that we had paid at all. Here he was, a leader, responsible for us while we were living in his village, and we had shamed him. How would it look if he let guests in his village *buy* food? If we wanted watermelons, or bananas, or anything else, all that was necessary was to let him know. He told us that it would be all right for us to give little gifts to people who brought food to us (and they surely would), but *no one* was to sell food to us. If anyone

were to try—like this woman from Lauvore—then we should refuse. There would be plenty of watermelons without us buying them.

The woman left with her watermelon, disgruntled, and we were left with our two shillings. But we had learned the first lesson of many about living in Kandoka. We didn't pay money for food again that whole year, and we did get lots of food brought to us... but we never got another watermelon. That one was the last of the season.

LESSON 1: *In a society where food is shared or gifted as part of social life, you may not buy it with money.*

TOO MANY BANANAS

In the couple of months that followed the watermelon incident, we managed to become at least marginally competent in Tok Pisin, to negotiate the construction of a house on what we hoped was neutral ground, and to settle into the routine of our fieldwork. As our village leader had predicted, plenty of food was brought to us. Indeed, seldom did a day pass without something coming in—some sweet potatoes, a few taro, a papaya, the occasional pineapple, or some bananas—lots of bananas.

We had learned our lesson about the money, though, so we never even offered to buy the things that were brought, but instead made gifts, usually of tobacco to the adults or chewing gum to the children. Nor were we so gauche as to haggle with a giver over how much of a return gift was appropriate, though the two of us sometimes conferred as to whether what had been brought was a "two-stick" or a "three-stick" stalk, bundle, or whatever. A "stick" of tobacco was a single large leaf, soaked in rum and then twisted into a ropelike form. This, wrapped in half a sheet of newsprint (torn for use as cigarette paper), sold in the local trade stores for a shilling. Nearly all of the adults in the village smoked a great deal, and they seldom had much cash, so our stocks of twist tobacco and stacks of the Sydney *Morning Herald* (all, unfortunately, the same day's issue) were seen as a real boon to those who preferred "stick" to the locally grown product.

We had established a pattern with respect to the gifts of food. When a donor appeared at our veranda we would offer our thanks and talk with them for a few minutes (usually about our children, who seemed to hold a real fascination for the villagers and for whom most of the gifts were intended) and then we would inquire whether they could use some tobacco. It was almost never refused, though occasionally a small bottle of kerosene, a box of matches, some laundry soap, a cup of rice, or a tin of meat would be requested instead of (or even in addition to) the tobacco. Everyone, even Kolia, seemed to think this arrangement had worked out well.

Now, what must be kept in mind is that while we were following their rules—or seemed to be—we were *really still buying food*. In fact we kept a running account of what came in and what we "paid" for it. Tobacco as currency got a little complicated, but since the exchange rate was one stick to one shilling, it was not too much trouble as long as everyone was happy, and meanwhile we could account for the expenditure of "in-

formant fees" and "household expenses." Another thing to keep in mind is that not only did we continue to think in terms of our buying the food that was brought, we thought of them as *selling it*. While it was true they never quoted us a price, they also never asked us if we needed or wanted whatever they had brought. It seemed clear to us that when an adult needed a stick of tobacco, or a child wanted some chewing gum (we had enormous quantities of small packets of Wrigley's for just such eventualities) they would find something surplus to their own needs and bring it along to our "store" and get what they wanted.

By late November 1966, just before the rainy season set in, the bananas were coming into flush, and whereas earlier we had received banana gifts by the "hand" (six or eight bananas in a cluster cut from the stalk), donors now began to bring bananas, "for the children," by the *stalk!* The Kaliai among whom we were living are not exactly specialists in banana cultivation—they only recognize about thirty varieties, while some of their neighbors have more than twice that many—but the kinds they produce differ considerably from each other in size, shape, and taste, so we were not dismayed when we had more than one stalk hanging on our veranda. The stalks ripen a bit at the time, and having some variety was nice. Still, by the time our accumulation had reached *four* complete stalks, the delights of variety had begun to pale a bit. The fruits were ripening progressively and it was clear that even if we and the kids ate nothing but bananas for the next week, some would still fall from the stalk onto the floor in a state of gross overripeness. This was the situation as, late one afternoon, a woman came bringing yet another stalk of bananas up the steps of the house.

Several factors determined our reaction to her approach: one was that there was literally no way we could possibly use the bananas. We hadn't quite reached the point of being crowded off our veranda by the stalks of fruit, but it was close. Another factor was that we were tired of playing the gift game. We had acquiesced in playing it—no one was permitted to sell us anything, and in turn we only gave things away, refusing un-

der any circumstances to sell tobacco (or anything else) for money. But there had to be a limit. From our perspective what was at issue was that the woman wanted something and she had come to trade for it. Further, what she had brought to trade was something we neither wanted nor could use, and it should have been obvious to her. So we decided to bite the bullet.

The woman, Rogi, climbed the stairs to the veranda, took the stalk from where it was balanced on top of her head, and laid it on the floor with the words, "Here are some bananas for the children." Dorothy and I sat near her on the floor and thanked her for her thought but explained, "You know, we really have too many bananas—we can't use these; maybe you ought to give them to someone else...." The woman looked mystified, then brightened and explained that she didn't want anything for them, she wasn't short of tobacco or anything. They were just a gift for the kids. Then she just sat there, and we sat there, and the bananas sat there, and we tried again. "Look," I said, pointing up to them and counting, "we've got four stalks already hanging here on the veranda—there are too many for us to eat now. Some are rotting already. Even if we eat only bananas, we can't keep up with what's here!"

Rogi's only response was to insist that these were a gift, and that she didn't want anything for them, so we tried yet another tack: "Don't *your* children like bananas?" When she admitted that they did, and that she had none at her house, we suggested that she should take them there. Finally, still puzzled, but convinced we weren't going to keep the bananas, she replaced them on her head, went down the stairs, and made her way back through the village toward her house.

As before, it seemed only moments before Kolia was making his way up the stairs, but this time he hadn't brought the woman in tow. "What was wrong with those bananas? Were they no good?" he demanded. We explained that there was nothing wrong with the bananas at all, but that we simply couldn't use them and it seemed foolish to take them when we had so many and Rogi's own children had none. We obviously didn't make ourselves clear because Kolia then took up the same refrain that Rogi had—he insisted that we shouldn't be worried about taking the bananas, because they were a gift for the children and Rogi hadn't wanted anything for them. There was no reason, he added, to send her away with them—she would be ashamed. I'm afraid we must have seemed as if we were hard of hearing or thought he was, for our only response was to repeat our reasons. We went through it again—there they hung, one, two, three, *four* stalks of bananas, rapidly ripening and already far beyond our capacity to eat—we just weren't ready to accept any more and let them rot (and, we added to ourselves, pay for them with tobacco, to boot).

Kolia finally realized that we were neither hard of hearing nor intentionally offensive, but merely ignorant. He stared at us for a few minutes, thinking, and then asked: "Don't you frequently have visitors during the day and evening?" We nodded. Then he asked, "Don't you usually offer them cigarettes and coffee or milo?" Again, we nodded. "Did it ever occur to you to suppose," he said, "that your visitors might be hungry?" It was at this point in the conversation, as we recall, that we began to see the depth of the pit we had dug for ourselves. We nodded, hesitantly. His last words to us before he went down the stairs and stalked away were just what we were by that time afraid they might be. "When your guests are hungry, *feed them bananas!*"

LESSON 2: *Never refuse a gift, and never fail to return a gift. If you cannot use it, you can always give it away to someone else—there is no such thing as too much—there are never too many bananas.*

NOT ENOUGH PINEAPPLES

During the fifteen years between that first visit in 1966 and our residence there in 1981 we had returned to live in Kandoka village twice during the 1970s, and though there were a great many changes in the village, and indeed for all of Papua New Guinea during that time, we continued to live according to the lessons of

reciprocity learned during those first months in the field. We bought no food for money and refused no gifts, but shared our surplus. As our family grew, we continued to be accompanied by our younger children. Our place in the village came to be something like that of educated Kaliai who worked far away in New Guinea. Our friends expected us to come "home" when we had leave, but knew that our work kept us away for long periods of time. They also credited us with knowing much more about the rules of their way of life than was our due. And we sometimes shared the delusion that we understood life in the village, but even fifteen years was not long enough to relieve the need for lessons in learning to live within the rules of gift exchange.

In the last paragraph I used the word *friends* to describe the villagers intentionally, but of course they were not all our friends. Over the years some really had become friends, others were acquaintances, others remained consultants or informants to whom we turned when we needed information. Still others, unfortunately, we did not like at all. We tried never to make an issue of these distinctions, of course, and to be even-handed and generous to all, as they were to us. Although we almost never actually refused requests that were made of us, over the long term our reciprocity in the village was balanced. More was given to those who helped us the most, while we gave assistance or donations of small items even to those who were not close or helpful.

One elderly woman in particular was a trial for us. Sara was the eldest of a group of siblings and her younger brother and sister were both generous, informative, and delightful persons. Her younger sister, Makila, was a particularly close friend and consultant, and in deference to that friendship we felt awkward in dealing with the elder sister.

Sara was neither a friend nor an informant, but she had been, since she returned to live in the village at the time of our second trip in 1971, a constant (if minor) drain on our resources. She never asked for much at a time. A bar of soap, a box of matches, a bottle of kerosene, a cup of rice, some onions, a stick or two

of tobacco, or some other small item was usually all that was at issue, but whenever she came around it was always to ask for something—or to let us know that when we left, we should give her some of the furnishings from the house. Too, unlike almost everyone else in the village, when she came, she was always empty-handed. We ate no taro from her gardens, and the kids chewed none of her sugarcane. In short, she was, as far as we could tell, a really grasping, selfish old woman—and we were not the only victims of her greed.

Having long before learned the lesson of the bananas, one day we had a stalk that was ripening so fast we couldn't keep up with it, so I pulled a few for our own use (we only had one stalk at the time) and walked down through the village to Ben's house, where his five children were playing. I sat down on his steps to talk, telling him that I intended to give the fruit to his kids. They never got them. Sara saw us from across the open plaza of the village and came rushing over, shouting, "My bananas!" Then she grabbed the stalk and went off gorging herself with them. Ben and I just looked at each other.

Finally it got to the point where it seemed to us that we had to do something. Ten years of being used was long enough. So there came the afternoon when Sara showed up to get some tobacco—again. But this time, when we gave her the two sticks she had demanded, we confronted her.

First, we noted the many times she had come to get things. We didn't mind sharing things, we explained. After all, we had plenty of tobacco and soap and rice and such, and most of it was there so that we could help our friends as they helped us, with folktales, information, or even gifts of food. The problem was that she kept coming to get things, but never came to talk, or to tell stories, or to bring some little something that the kids might like. Sara didn't argue—she agreed. "Look," we suggested, "it doesn't have to be much, and we don't mind giving you things—but you can help us. The kids like pineapples, and we don't have any—the next time you need something, bring something—like maybe a pineapple." Obviously somewhat embarrassed, she took her tobacco and left, saying that she would bring something soon. We were really pleased with ourselves. It had been a very difficult thing to do, but it was done, and we were convinced that either she would start bringing things or not come. It was as if a burden had lifted from our shoulders.

It worked. Only a couple of days passed before Sara was back, bringing her bottle to get it filled with kerosene. But this time, she came carrying the biggest, most beautiful pineapple we had seen the entire time we had been there. We had a friendly talk, filled her kerosene container, and hung the pineapple up on the veranda to ripen just a little further. A few days later we cut and ate it, and whether the satisfaction it gave came from the fruit or from its source would be hard to say, but it was delicious. That, we assumed, was the end of that irritant.

We were wrong, of course. The next afternoon, Mary, one of our best friends for years (and no relation to Sara), dropped by for a visit. As we talked, her eyes scanned the veranda. Finally she asked whether we hadn't had a pineapple there yesterday. We said we had, but that we had already eaten it. She commented that it had been a really nice-looking one, and we told her that it had been the best we had eaten in months. Then, after a pause, she asked, "Who brought it to you?" We smiled as we said, "Sara!" because Mary would appreciate our coup—she had commented many times in the past on the fact that Sara only *got* from us and never gave. She was silent for a moment, and then she said, "Well,

I'm glad you enjoyed it—my father was waiting until it was fully ripe to harvest it for you, but when it went missing I thought maybe it was the one you had here. I'm glad to see you got it. I thought maybe a thief had eaten it in the bush."

LESSON 3: *Where reciprocity is the rule and gifts are the idiom, you cannot demand a gift, just as you cannot refuse a request.*

It says a great deal about the kindness and patience of the Kaliai people that they have been willing to be our hosts for all these years despite our blunders and lack of good manners. They have taught us a lot, and these three lessons are certainly not the least important things we learned.

From *The Humbled Anthropologist: Tales from the Pacific* by David Counts, 1990, pp. 18–24. Published by Wadsworth Publishing Company. © 1990 by David Counts. Reprinted by permission.

Life Without Chiefs

Are we forever condemned to a world of haves and have-nots, rulers and ruled? Maybe not, argues a noted anthropologist—if we can relearn some ancient lessons.

Marvin Harris

Can humans exist without some people ruling and others being ruled? To look at the modern world, you wouldn't think so. Democratic states may have done away with emperors and kings, but they have hardly dispensed with gross inequalities in wealth, rank, and power.

However, humanity hasn't always lived this way. For about 98 percent of our existence as a species (and for four million years before then), our ancestors lived in small, largely nomadic hunting-and-gathering bands containing about 30 to 50 people apiece. It was in this social context that human nature evolved. It has been only about ten thousand years since people began to settle down into villages, some of which eventually grew into cities. And it has been only in the last two thousand years that the majority of people in the world have not lived in hunting-and-gathering societies. This brief period of time is not nearly sufficient for noticeable evolution to have taken place. Thus, the few remaining foraging societies are the closest analogues we have to the "natural" state of humanity.

To judge from surviving examples of hunting-and-gathering bands and villages, our kind got along quite well for the greater part of prehistory without so much as a paramount chief. In fact, for tens of thousands of years, life went on without kings, queens, prime ministers, presidents, parliaments, congresses, cabinets, governors, and mayors—not to mention the police officers, sheriffs, marshals, generals, lawyers, bailiffs, judges, district attorneys, court clerks, patrol cars, paddy wagons, jails, and penitentiaries that help keep them in power. How in the world did our ancestors ever manage to leave home without them?

Small populations provide part of the answer. With 50 people per band or 150 per village, everybody knew everybody else intimately. People gave with the expectation of taking and took with the expectation of giving. Because chance played a great role in the capture of animals, collection of wild foodstuffs, and success of rudimentary forms of agriculture, the individuals who had the luck of the catch on one day needed a handout on the next. So the best way for them to provide for their inevitable rainy day was to be generous. As expressed by anthropologist Richard Gould, "The greater the amount of risk, the greater the extent of sharing." Reciprocity is a small society's bank.

In reciprocal exchange, people do not specify how much or exactly what they expect to get back or when they expect to get it. That would besmirch the quality of that transaction and make it similar to mere barter or to buying and selling. The distinction lingers on in societies dominated by other forms of exchange, even capitalist ones. For we do carry out a give-and-take among close kin and friends that is informal, uncalculating, and imbued with a spirit of generosity. Teen-agers do not pay cash for their meals at home or for the use of the family car, wives do not bill their husbands for cooking a meal, and friends give each other birthday gifts and Christmas presents. But much of this is marred by the expectation that our generosity will be acknowledged with expression of thanks.

Where reciprocity really prevails in daily life, etiquette requires that generosity be taken for granted. As Robert Dentan discovered during his fieldwork among the Semai of Central Malaysia, no one ever says "thank you" for the meat received from another hunter. Having struggled all day to lug the carcass of a pig home through the jungle heat, the hunter allows his prize to be cut up into exactly equal portions, which he then gives away to the entire group. Dentan explains that to express gratitude for the portion received indicates that you are the kind of ungenerous person who calculates how much you give and take: "In this context, saying 'thank you' is very rude, for it suggests, first, that one has calculated the amount of a gift and, second, that one did not expect the donor to be so generous." To call attention to one's generosity is to indicate that others are in debt to you and that you expect them to repay you. It is repugnant to egalitarian peoples even to suggest that they have been treated generously.

Canadian anthropologist Richard Lee tells how, through a revealing incident, he learned about this aspect of reciprocity. To please the !Kung, the "bushmen" of the Kalahari desert, he decided to buy a large ox and have it slaughtered as a present. After days of searching Bantu agricultural villages for the largest and fattest ox in the region, he acquired what appeared to be a perfect specimen. But his friends took him aside and assured him that he had been duped into buying an absolutely worthless animal. "Of course, we will eat it," they said, "but it won't fill us up—we will eat and go home to bed with stomachs rumbling." Yet, when Lee's ox was slaughtered, it turned out to be covered with a thick layer of fat. Later, his friends explained why they had said his gift was valueless, even though they knew better than he what lay under the animal's skin:

"Yes, when a young man kills much meat he comes to think of himself as a chief or a big man, and he thinks of the rest of us as his servants or inferiors. We can't accept this, we refuse one who boasts, for someday his pride will make him kill somebody. So we always speak of his meat as worthless. This way we cool his heart and make him gentle."

Lee watched small groups of men and women returning home every evening with the animals and wild fruits and plants that they had killed or collected. They shared everything equally, even with campmates who had stayed behind and spent the day sleeping or taking care of their tools and weapons.

"Not only do families pool that day's production, but the entire camp—residents and visitors alike—shares equally in the total quantity of food available," Lee observed. "The evening meal of any one family is made up of portions of food from each of the other families resident. There is a constant flow of nuts, berries, roots, and melons from one family fireplace to another, until each person has received an equitable portion. The fol-

lowing morning a different combination of foragers moves out of camp, and when they return late in the day, the distribution of foodstuffs is repeated."

In small, prestate societies, it was in everybody's best interest to maintain each other's freedom of access to the natural habitat. Suppose a !Kung with a lust for power were to get up and tell his campmates, "From now on, all this land and everything on it belongs to me. I'll let you use it but only with my permission and on the condition that I get first choice of anything you capture, collect, or grow." His campmates, thinking that he had certainly gone crazy, would pack up their few belongings, take a long walk, make a new camp, and resume their usual life of egalitarian reciprocity. The man who would be king would be left by himself to exercise a useless sovereignty.

THE HEADMAN: LEADERSHIP, NOT POWER

To the extent that political leadership exists at all among band-and-village societies, it is exercised by individuals called headmen. These headmen, however, lack the power to compel others to obey their orders. How can a leader be powerful and still lead?

The political power of genuine rulers depends on their ability to expel or exterminate disobedient individuals and groups. When a headman gives a command, however, he has no certain physical means of punishing those who disobey. So, if he wants to stay in "office," he gives few commands. Among the Eskimo, for instance, a group will follow an outstanding hunter and defer to his opinion with respect to choice of hunting spots. But in all other matters, the leader's opinion carries no more weight than any other man's. Similarly, among the !Kung, each band has its recognized leaders, most of whom are males. These men speak out more than others and are listened to with a bit more deference. But they have no formal authority and can only persuade, never command. When Lee asked the !Kung whether they had headmen—meaning powerful chiefs—they told him, "Of course we have headmen! In fact, we are

all headmen. Each one of us is headman over himself."

Headmanship can be a frustrating and irksome job. Among Indian groups such as the Mehinacu of Brazil's Zingu National Park, headmen behave something like zealous scoutmasters on overnight cookouts. The first one up in the morning, the headman tries to rouse his companions by standing in the middle of the village plaza and shouting to them. If something needs to be done, it is the headman who starts doing it, and it is the headman who works harder than anyone else. He sets an example not only for hard work but also for generosity: After a fishing or hunting expedition, he gives away more of his catch than anyone else does. In trading with other groups, he must be careful not to keep the best items for himself.

In the evening, the headman stands in the center of the plaza and exhorts his people to be good. He calls upon them to control their sexual appetites, work hard in their gardens, and take frequent baths in the river. He tells them not to sleep during the day or bear grudges against each other.

COPING WITH FREELOADERS

During the reign of reciprocal exchange and egalitarian headmen, no individual, family, or group smaller than the band or village itself could control access to natural resources. Rivers, lakes, beaches, oceans, plants and animals, the soil and subsoil were all communal property.

Among the !Kung, a core of people born in a particular territory say that they "own" the water holes and hunting rights, but this has no effect on the people who happen to be visiting and living with them at any given time. Since !Kung from neighboring bands are related through marriage, they often visit each other for months at a time and have free use of whatever resources they need without having to ask permission. Though people from distant bands must make a request to use another band's territory, the "owners" seldom refuse them.

The absence of private possession in land and other vital resources means that a form of communism probably existed among prehistoric hunting and collecting bands and small villages. Perhaps I should emphasize that this did not rule out the existence of private property. People in simple band-and-village societies own personal effects such as weapons, clothing, containers, ornaments, and tools. But why should anyone want to steal such objects? People who have a bush camp and move about a lot have no use for extra possessions. And since the group is small enough that everybody knows everybody else, stolen items cannot be used anonymously. If you want something, better to ask for it openly, since by the rules of reciprocity such requests cannot be denied.

I don't want to create the impression that life within egalitarian band-and-village societies unfolded entirely without disputes over possessions. As in every social group, nonconformists and malcontents tried to use the system for their own advantage. Inevitably there were freeloaders, individuals who consistently took more than they gave and lay back in their hammocks while others did the work. Despite the absence of a criminal justice system, such behavior eventually was punished. A widespread belief among band-and-village peoples attributes death and misfortune to the malevolent conspiracy of sorcerers. The task of identifying these evildoers falls to a group's shamans, who remain responsive to public opinion during their divinatory trances. Well-liked individuals who enjoy strong support from their families need not fear the shaman. But quarrelsome, stingy people who do not give as well as take had better watch out.

FROM HEADMAN TO BIG MAN

Reciprocity was not the only form of exchange practiced by egalitarian band-and-village peoples. Our kind long ago found other ways to give and take. Among them the form of exchange known as redistribution played a crucial role in creating distinctions of rank during the evolution of chiefdoms and states.

Redistribution occurs when people turn over food and other valuables to a prestigious figure such as a headman, to be pooled, divided into separate portions, and given out again. The primordial form of redistribution was probably keyed to seasonal hunts and harvests, when more food than usual became available.

True to their calling, headmen-redistributors not only work harder than their followers but also give more generously and reserve smaller and less desirable portions for themselves than for anyone else. Initially, therefore, redistribution strictly reinforced the political and economic equality associated with reciprocal exchange. The redistributors were compensated purely with admiration and in proportion to their success in giving bigger feasts, in personally contributing more than anybody else, and in asking little or nothing for their effort, all of which initially seemed an innocent extension of the basic principle of reciprocity.

But how little our ancestors understood what they were getting themselves into! For if it is a good thing to have a headman give feasts, why not have several headmen give feasts? Or, better yet, why not let success in organizing and giving feasts be the measure of one's legitimacy as a headman? Soon, where conditions permit, there are several would-be headmen vying with each other to hold the most lavish feasts and redistribute the most food and other valuables. In this fashion there evolved the nemesis that Richard Lee's !Kung informants had warned about: the youth who wants to be a "big man."

A classic anthropological study of big men was carried out by Douglas Oliver among the Siuai, a village people who live on the South Pacific island of Bougainville, in the Solomon Islands. In the Siuai language, big men were known as *mumis*. Every Siuai boy's highest ambition was to become a mumi. He began by getting married, working hard, and restricting his own consumption of meats and coconuts. His wife and parents, impressed with the seriousness of his intentions, vowed to help him prepare for his first feast. Soon his circle of supporters widened and he began to construct a

clubhouse in which his male followers could lounge about and guests could be entertained and fed. He gave a feast at the consecration of the clubhouse; if this was a success, the circle of people willing to work for him grew larger still, and he began to hear himself spoken of as a mumi. Larger and larger feasts meant that the mumi's demands on his supporters became more irksome. Although they grumbled about how hard they had to work, they remained loyal as long as their mumi continued to maintain and increase his renown as a "great provider."

Finally the time came for the new mumi to challenge the older ones. He did this at a *muminai* feast, where both sides kept a tally of all the pigs, coconut pies, and sago-almond puddings given away by the host mumi and his followers to the guest mumi and his followers. If the guests could not reciprocate with a feast as lavish as that of the challengers, their mumi suffered a great social humiliation, and his fall from mumihood was immediate.

At the end of a successful feast, the greatest of mumis still faced a lifetime of personal toil and dependence on the moods and inclinations of his followers. Mumihood did not confer the power to coerce others into doing one's bidding, nor did it elevate one's standard of living above anyone else's. In fact, because giving things away was the essence of mumihood, great mumis consumed less meat and other delicacies than ordinary men. Among the Kaoka, another Solomon Islands group, there is the saying, "The giver of the feast takes the bones and the stale cakes; the meat and the fat go to the others." At one great feast attended by 1,100 people, the host mumi, whose name was Soni, gave away thirty-two pigs and a large quantity of sago-almond puddings. Soni himself and some of his closest followers went hungry. "We shall eat Soni's renown," they said.

FROM BIG MAN TO CHIEF

The slide (or ascent?) toward social stratification gained momentum wherever extra food produced by the inspired diligence of redistributors could be stored while awaiting muminai feasts, potlatches, and other occasions of redistribution. The more concentrated and abundant the harvest and the less perishable the crop, the greater its potential for endowing the big man with power. Though others would possess some stored-up foods of their own, the redistributor's stores would be the largest. In times of scarcity, people would come to him, expecting to be fed; in return, he could call upon those who had special skills to make cloth, pots, canoes, or a fine house for his own use. Eventually, the redistributor no longer needed to work in the fields to gain and surpass big-man status. Management of the harvest surpluses, a portion of which continued to be given to him for use in communal feasts and other communal projects (such as trading expeditions and warfare), was sufficient to validate his status. And, increasingly, people viewed this status as an office, a sacred trust, passed on from one generation to the next according to the rules of hereditary succession. His dominion was no longer a small, autonomous village but a large political community. The big man had become a chief.

Returning to the South Pacific and the Trobriand Islands, one can catch a glimpse of how these pieces of encroaching stratification fell into place. The Trobrianders had hereditary chiefs who held sway over more than a dozen villages containing several thousand people. Only chiefs could wear certain shell ornaments as the insignia of high rank, and it was forbidden for commoners to stand or sit in a position that put a chief's head at a lower elevation. British anthropologist Bronislaw Malinowski tells of seeing all the people present in the village of Bwoytalu drop from their verandas "as if blown down by a hurricane" at the sound of a drawn-out cry warning that an important chief was approaching.

Yams were the Trobrianders' staff of life; the chiefs validated their status by storing and redistributing copious quantities of them acquired through donations from their brothers-in-law at harvest time. Similar "gifts" were received by husbands who were commoners, but chiefs were polygymous and, having as many as a dozen wives, received many

more yams than anyone else. Chiefs placed their yam supply on display racks specifically built for this purpose next to their houses. Commoners did the same, but a chief's yam racks towered over all the others.

This same pattern recurs, with minor variations, on several continents. Striking parallels were seen, for example, twelve thousand miles away from the Trobrianders, among chiefdoms that flourished throughout the southeastern region of the United States—specifically among the Cherokee, former inhabitants of Tennessee, as described by the eighteenth-century naturalist William Bartram.

At the center of the principal Cherokee settlements stood a large circular house where a council of chiefs discussed issues involving their villages and where redistributive feasts were held. The council of chiefs had a paramount who was the principal figure in the Cherokee redistributive network. At the harvest time a large crib, identified as the "chief's granary," was erected in each field. "To this," explained Bartram, "each family carries and deposits a certain quantity according to his ability or inclination, or none at all if he so chooses." The chief's granaries functioned as a public treasury in case of crop failure, a source of food for strangers or travelers, and as military store. Although every citizen enjoyed free access to the store, commoners had to acknowledge that it really belonged to the supreme chief, who had "an exclusive right and ability… to distribute comfort and blessings to the necessitous."

Supported by voluntary donations, chiefs could now enjoy lifestyles that set them increasingly apart from their followers. They could build bigger and finer houses for themselves, eat and dress more sumptuously, and enjoy the sexual favors and personal services of several wives. Despite these harbingers, people in chiefdoms voluntarily invested unprecedented amounts of labor on behalf of communal projects. They dug moats, threw up defensive earthen embankments, and erected great log palisades around their villages. They heaped up small mountains of rubble and soil to form platforms and mounds on top of

which they built temples and big houses for their chief. Working in teams and using nothing but levers and rollers, they moved rocks weighing fifty tons or more and set them in precise lines and perfect circles, forming sacred precincts for communal rituals marking the change of seasons.

If this seems remarkable, remember that donated labor created the megalithic alignments of Stonehenge and Carnac, put up the great statues on Easter Island, shaped the huge stone heads of the Olmec in Vera Cruz, dotted Polynesia with ritual precincts set on great stone platforms, and filled the Ohio, Tennessee, and Mississippi valleys with hundreds of large mounds. Not until it was too late did people realize that their beautiful chiefs were about to keep the meat and fat for themselves while giving nothing but bones and stale cakes to their followers.

IN THE END

As we know, chiefdoms would eventually evolve into states, states into empires. From peaceful origins, humans created and mounted a wild beast that ate continents. Now that beast has taken us to the brink of global annihilation.

Will nature's experiment with mind and culture end in nuclear war? No one knows the answer. But I believe it is essential that we understand our past before we can create the best possible future. Once we are clear about the roots of human nature, for example, we can refute, once and for all, the notion that it is a biological imperative for our kind to form hierarchical groups. An observer viewing human life shortly after cultural takeoff would easily have concluded that our species was destined to be irredeemably egalitarian except for distinctions of sex and age. That someday the world would be divided into aristocrats and commoners, masters and slaves, billionaires and homeless beggars would have seemed wholly contrary to human nature as evidenced in the affairs of every human society then on Earth.

Of course, we can no more reverse the course of thousands of years of cultural evolution than our egalitarian ancestors could have designed and built the space shuttle. Yet, in striving for the preservation of mind and culture on Earth, it is vital that we recognize the significance of cultural takeoff and the great difference between biological and cultural evolution. We must rid ourselves of the notion that we are an innately aggressive species for whom war is inevitable. We must reject as unscientific claims that there are superior and inferior races and that the hierarchical divisions within and between societies are the consequences of natural selection rather than of a long process of cultural evolution. We must struggle to gain control over cultural selection through objective studies of the human condition and the recurrent process of history. Not only a more just society, but our very survival as a species may depend on it.

Marvin Harris is a graduate research professor of anthropology at the University of Florida and chair of the general anthropology division of the American Anthropological Association. His seventeen books include Cows, Pigs, Wars and Witches *and* Cannibals and Kings.

From *New Age Journal,* November/December 1989, pp. 42–45, 205–209. Excerpted from *Our Kind* by Marvin Harris. © 1989 by Marvin Harris. Reprinted by permission of HarperCollins Publishers, Inc.

UNIT 4
Other Families, Other Ways

Unit Selections

Key Points to Consider

- Why do you think "fraternal polyandry" is socially acceptable in Tibet but not in our society?

- How do differences in child care relate to economic circumstances?

- How have dietary changes affected birth rates and women's health?

- Why do child care practices vary from culture to culture?

- What are the pros and cons of arranged marriages versus freedom of choice?

- Under what circumstances do "dowry deaths" occur?

- Is the institution of marriage necessary for family stability?

 **Links: www.dushkin.com/online/**
These sites are annotated in the World Wide Web pages.

Dowry Death
   http://www.indianwomenonline.com/womenhome/Serious/law/dowry/dowrybot.asp
"Here, No Stigma Is Attached to Polyandry"
   http://www.hindustantimes.com/nonfram/260600/detNAT05.htm
Kinship and Social Organization
   http://www.umanitoba.ca/anthropology/tutor/kinmenu.html

Since most people in small-scale societies of the past spent their whole lives within a local area, it is understandable that their primary interactions—economic, religious, and otherwise—were with their relatives. It also makes sense that through marriage customs, they strengthened those kinship relationships that clearly defined their mutual rights and obligations. Indeed, the resulting family structure may be surprisingly flexible and adaptive, as witnessed in the essays "When Brothers Share a Wife" by Melvyn Goldstein, "Parallel Brides" by Mustafa Turker Ersen, and "Arranging a Marriage in India" by Serena Nanda. Even where there is no apparent need for marriage, as revealed in "The Visit," the family is still of paramount importance.

For these reasons, anthropologists have looked upon family and kinship as the key mechanisms for transmitting culture from one generation to the next. (See "Our Babies, Ourselves" by Meredith Small.) Social changes may have been slow to take place throughout the world, but as social horizons have widened, family relationships and community alliances are increasingly based upon new principles. Even as birth rates have increased, kinship networks have diminished in size and strength. As people have increasingly become involved with others as co-workers in a market economy, our associations depend more and more upon factors such as personal aptitudes, educational backgrounds, and job opportunities. Yet the family is still there. Except for some rather unusual exceptions, such as depicted in "Dowry Deaths in India:, 'Let Only Your Corpse Come Out of That House'" the family is smaller, but still functions in its age-old nurturing and protective role, even under conditions where there is little affection (see "Who Needs Love! In Japan, Many Couples Don't" by Nicholas Kristof) or under conditions of extreme poverty and a high infant mortality rate (see "Death Without Weeping" by Nancy Scheper-Hughes). Beyond the immediate family, the situation is in a state of flux. Certain ethnic groups, especially those in poverty, still have a need for the broader network and in some ways seem to be reformulating those ties.

We do not know where the changes described in this section will lead us and which ones will ultimately prevail. One thing is certain: anthropologists will be there to document the trends, for the discipline of anthropology has had to change as well. One important feature of the essays in this section is the growing interest of anthropologists in the study of complex societies where old theoretical perspectives are increasingly inadequate.

Current trends, however, do not necessarily mean the eclipse of the kinship unit. The large family network is still the best guarantee of individual survival and well-being in an urban setting.

When Brothers Share a Wife

Among Tibetans, the good life relegates many women to spinsterhood

Melvyn C. Goldstein

Eager to reach home, Dorje drives his yaks hard over the 17,000-foot mountain pass, stopping only once to rest. He and his two older brothers, Pema and Sonam, are jointly marrying a woman from the next village in a few weeks, and he has to help with the preparations.

Dorje, Pema, and Sonam are Tibetans living in Limi, a 200-square-mile area in the northwest corner of Nepal, across the border from Tibet. The form of marriage they are about to enter—fraternal polyandry in anthropological parlance—is one of the world's rarest forms of marriage but is not uncommon in Tibetan society, where it has been practiced from time immemorial. For many Tibetan social strata, it traditionally represented the ideal form of marriage and family.

The mechanics of fraternal polyandry are simple. Two, three, four, or more brothers jointly take a wife, who leaves her home to come and live with them. Traditionally, marriage was arranged by parents, with children, particularly females, having little or no say. This is changing somewhat nowadays, but it is still unusual for children to marry without their parents' consent. Marriage ceremonies vary by income and region and range from all the brothers sitting together as grooms to only the eldest one formally doing so. The age of the brothers plays an important role in determining this: very young brothers almost never participate in actual marriage ceremonies, although they typically join the marriage when they reach their mid-teens.

The eldest brother is normally dominant in terms of authority, that is, in managing the household, but all the brothers share the work and participate as sexual partners. Tibetan males and females do not find the sexual aspect of sharing a spouse the least bit unusual, repulsive, or scandalous, and the norm is for the wife to treat all the brothers the same.

Offspring are treated similarly. There is no attempt to link children biologically to particular brothers, and a brother shows no favoritism toward his child even if he knows he is the real father because, for example, his other brothers were away at the time the wife became pregnant. The children, in turn, consider all of the brothers as their fathers and treat them equally, even if they also know who is their real father. In some regions children use the term "father" for the eldest brother and "father's brother" for the others, while in other areas they call all the brothers by one term, modifying this by the use of "elder" and "younger."

Unlike our own society, where monogamy is the only form of marriage permitted, Tibetan society allows a variety of marriage types, including monogamy, fraternal polyandry, and polygyny. Fraternal polyandry and monogamy are the most common forms of marriage, while polygyny typically occurs in cases where the first wife is barren. The widespread practice of fraternal polyandry, therefore, is not the outcome of a law requiring brothers to marry jointly. There is choice, and in fact, divorce traditionally was relatively simple in Tibetan society.

If a brother in a polyandrous marriage became dissatisfied and wanted to separate, he simply left the main house and set up his own household. In such cases, all the children stayed in the main household with the remaining brother(s), even if the departing brother was known to be the real father of one or more of the children.

The Tibetans' own explanation for choosing fraternal polyandry is materialistic. For example, when I asked Dorje why he decided to marry with his two brothers rather than take his own wife, he thought for a moment, then said it prevented the division of his family's farm (and animals) and thus facilitated all of them achieving a higher standard of living. And when I later asked Dorje's bride whether it wasn't difficult for her to cope with three brothers as husbands, she laughed and echoed the rationale of avoiding fragmentation of the family and land, adding that she expected to be better off economically, since she would have three husbands working for her and her children.

Exotic as it may seem to Westerners, Tibetan fraternal polyandry is thus in many ways analogous to the way primogeniture functioned in nineteenth-century England. Primogeniture dictated that the eldest son inherited the family estate, while younger sons had to leave home and seek their own employment—for example, in the military or the clergy. Primogeniture maintained family estates intact over generations by permitting only one heir per generation. Fraternal

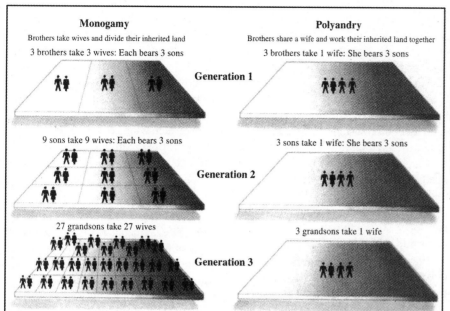

Monogamy	Polyandry
Brothers take wives and divide their inherited land	Brothers share a wife and work their inherited land together

3 brothers take 3 wives: Each bears 3 sons

3 brothers take 1 wife: She bears 3 sons

Generation 1

9 sons take 9 wives: Each bears 3 sons

3 sons take 1 wife: She bears 3 sons

Generation 2

27 grandsons take 27 wives

3 grandsons take 1 wife

Generation 3

Family Planning in Tibet

An economic rationale for fraternal polyandry is outlined in the diagram below, which emphasizes only the male offspring in each generation. If every wife is assumed to bear three sons, a family splitting up into monogamous households would rapidly multiply and fragment the family land. In this case, a rule of inheritance, such as primogeniture, could retain the family land intact, but only at the cost of creating many landless male offspring. In contrast, the family practicing fraternal polyandry maintains a steady ratio of persons to land.

Joe LeMonnier

polyandry also accomplishes this but does so by keeping all the brothers together with just one wife so that there is only one *set* of heirs per generation.

While Tibetans believe that in this way fraternal polyandry reduces the risk of family fission, monogamous marriages among brothers need not necessarily precipitate the division of the family estate: brothers could continue to live together, and the family land could continue to be worked jointly. When I asked Tibetans about this, however, they invariably responded that such joint families are unstable because each wife is primarily oriented to her own children and interested in their success and well-being over that of the children of the other wives. For example, if the youngest brother's wife had three sons while the eldest brother's wife had only one daughter, the wife of the youngest brother might begin to demand more resources for her children since, as males, they represent the future of the family. Thus, the children from different wives in the same generation are competing sets of heirs, and this makes such families inherently unstable. Tibetans perceive that conflict will spread from the wives to their husbands and consider this likely to cause family fission. Consequently, it is almost never done.

Although Tibetans see an economic advantage to fraternal polyandry, they do not value the sharing of a wife as an end in itself. On the contrary, they articulate a number of problems inherent in the practice. For example, because authority is customarily exercised by the eldest brother, his younger male siblings have to subordinate themselves with little hope of changing their status within the family. When these younger brothers are aggressive and individualistic, tensions and difficulties often occur despite there being only one set of heirs.

In addition, tension and conflict may arise in polyandrous families because of sexual favoritism. The bride normally sleeps with the eldest brother, and the two have the responsibility to see to it that the other males have opportunities for sexual access. Since the Tibetan subsistence economy requires males to travel a lot, the temporary absence of one or more brothers facilitates this, but there are also other rotation practices. The cultural ideal unambiguously calls for the wife to show equal affection and sexuality to each of the brothers (and vice versa), but deviations from this ideal occur, especially when there is a sizable difference in age between the partners in the marriage.

Dorje's family represents just such a potential situation. He is fifteen years old and his two older brothers are twenty-five and twenty-two years old. The new bride is twenty-three years old, eight

years Dorje's senior. Sometimes such a bride finds the youngest husband immature and adolescent and does not treat him with equal affection; alternatively, she may find his youth attractive and lavish special attention on him. Apart from that consideration, when a younger male like Dorje grows up, he may consider his wife "ancient" and prefer the company of a woman his own age or younger. Consequently, although men and women do not find the idea of sharing a bride or bridegroom repulsive, individual likes and dislikes can cause familial discord.

Two reasons have commonly been offered for the perpetuation of fraternal polyandry in Tibet: that Tibetans practice female infanticide and therefore have to marry polyandrously, owing to a shortage of females; and that Tibet, lying at extremely high altitudes, is so barren and bleak that Tibetans would starve without resort to this mechanism. A Jesuit who lived in Tibet during the eighteenth century articulated this second view: "One reason for this most odious custom is the sterility of the soil, and the small amount of land that can be cultivated owing to the lack of water. The crops may suffice if the brothers all live together, but if they form separate families they would be reduced to beggary."

Both explanations are wrong, however. Not only has there never been institutionalized female infanticide in Tibet, but Tibetan society gives females considerable rights, including inheriting the family estate in the absence of brothers. In such cases, the woman takes a bridegroom who comes to live in her family and adopts her family's name and identity. Moreover, there is no demographic evidence of a shortage of females. In Limi, for example, there were (in 1974) sixty females and fifty-three males in the fifteen- to thirty-five-year age category, and many adult females were unmarried.

The second reason is also incorrect. The climate in Tibet is extremely harsh, and ecological factors do play a major role perpetuating polyandry, but polyandry is not a means of preventing starvation. It is characteristic, not of the poorest segments of the society, but rather of the peasant landowning families.

In the old society, the landless poor could not realistically aspire to prosperity, but they did not fear starvation. There was a persistent labor shortage throughout Tibet, and very poor families with little or no land and few animals could subsist through agricultural labor, tenant farming, craft occupations such as carpentry, or by working as servants. Although the per person family income could increase somewhat if brothers married polyandrously and pooled their wages, in the absence of inheritable land, the advantage of fraternal polyandry was not generally sufficient to prevent them from setting up their own households. A more skilled or energetic younger brother could do as well or better alone, since he would completely control his income and would not have to share it with his siblings. Consequently, while there was and is some polyandry among the poor, it is much less frequent and more prone to result in divorce and family fission.

An alternative reason for the persistence of fraternal polyandry is that it reduces population growth (and thereby reduces the pressure on resources) by relegating some females to lifetime spinsterhood. Fraternal polyandrous marriages in Limi (in 1974) averaged 2.35 men per woman, and not surprisingly, 31 percent of the females of child-bearing age (twenty to forty-nine) were unmarried. These spinsters either continued to live at home, set up their own households, or worked as servants for other families. They could also become Buddhist nuns. Being unmarried is not synonymous with exclusion from the reproductive pool. Discreet extramarital relationships are tolerated, and actually half of the adult unmarried women in Limi had one or more children. They raised these children as single mothers, working for wages or weaving cloth and blankets for sale. As a group, however, the unmarried woman had far fewer offspring than the married women, averaging only 0.7 children per woman, compared with 3.3 for married women, whether polyandrous, monogamous, or polygynous. While polyandry helps regulate population, this function of polyandry is not consciously perceived by Tibetans and is not the reason they consistently choose it.

If neither a shortage of females nor the fear of starvation perpetuates fraternal polyandry, what motivates brothers, particularly younger brothers, to opt for this system of marriage? From the perspective of the younger brother in a landholding family, the main incentive is the attainment or maintenance of the good life. With polyandry, he can expect a more secure and higher standard of living, with access not only to this family's land and animals but also to its inherited collection of clothes, jewelry, rugs, saddles, and horses. In addition, he will experience less work pressure and much greater security because all responsibility does not fall on one "father." For Tibetan brothers, the question is whether to trade off the greater personal freedom inherent in monogamy for the real or potential economic security, affluence, and social prestige associated with life in a larger, labor-rich polyandrous family.

A brother thinking of separating from his polyandrous marriage and taking his own wife would face various disadvantages. Although in the majority of Tibetan regions all brothers theoretically have rights to their family's estate, in reality Tibetans are reluctant to divide their land into small fragments. Generally, a younger brother who insists on leaving the family will receive only a small plot of land, if that. Because of its power and wealth, the rest of the family usually can block any attempt of the younger brother to increase his share of land through litigation. Moreover, a younger brother may not even get a house and cannot expect to receive much above the minimum in terms of movable possessions, such as furniture, pots, and pans. Thus, a brother contemplating going it on his own must plan on achieving economic security and the good life not through inheritance but through his own work.

The obvious solution for younger brothers—creating new fields from virgin land—is generally not a feasible option. Most Tibetan populations live at high altitudes (above 12,000 feet), where arable land is extremely scarce. For example, in Dorje's village, agriculture ranges only from about 12,900 feet, the lowest point in the area, to 13,300 feet. Above that altitude, early frost and snow destroy the staple barley crop. Furthermore, because of the low rainfall caused by the Himalayan rain shadow, many areas in Tibet and northern Nepal that are within the appropriate altitude range for agriculture have no reliable sources of irrigation. In the end, although there is plenty of unused land in such areas, most of it is either too high or too arid.

Even where unused land capable of being farmed exists, clearing the land and building the substantial terraces necessary for irrigation constitute a great undertaking. Each plot has to be completely dug out to a depth of two to two and half feet so that the large rocks and boulders can be removed. At best, a man might be able to bring a few new fields under cultivation in the first years after separating from his brothers, but he could not expect to acquire substantial amounts of arable land this way.

In addition, because of the limited farmland, the Tibetan subsistence economy characteristically includes a strong emphasis on animal husbandry. Tibetan farmers regularly maintain cattle, yaks, goats, and sheep, grazing them in the areas too high for agriculture. These herds produce wool, milk, cheese, butter, meat, and skins. To obtain these resources, however, shepherds must accompany the animals on a daily basis. When first setting up a monogamous household, a younger brother like Dorje would find it difficult to both farm and manage animals.

In traditional Tibetan society, there was an even more critical factor that operated to perpetuate fraternal polyandry—a form of hereditary servitude somewhat analogous to serfdom in Europe. Peasants were tied to large estates held by aristocrats, monasteries, and the Lhasa government. They were allowed the use of some farmland to produce their own subsistence but were required to provide taxes in kind and corvée (free labor) to their lords. The corvée was a substantial hardship, since a peasant household was in many cases required to furnish the lord with one laborer daily for most of the year and more on specific occasions such as the harvest. This en-

forced labor, along with the lack of new land and ecological pressure to pursue both agriculture and animal husbandry, made polyandrous families particularly beneficial. The polyandrous family allowed an internal division of adult labor, maximizing economic advantage. For example, while the wife worked the family fields, one brother could perform the lord's corvée, another could look after the animals, and a third could engage in trade.

Although social scientists often discount other people's explanations of why they do things, in the case of Tibetan fraternal polyandry, such explanations are very close to the truth. The custom, however, is very sensitive to changes in its political and economic mi-

lieu and, not surprisingly, is in decline in most Tibetan areas. Made less important by the elimination of the traditional serf-based economy, it is disparaged by the dominant non-Tibetan leaders of India, China, and Nepal. New opportunities for economic and social mobility in these countries, such as the tourist trade and government employment, are also eroding the rationale for polyandry, and so it may vanish within the next generation.

Melvyn C. Goldstein, now a professor of anthropology at Case Western Reserve University in Cleveland, has been interested in the Tibetan practice of fraternal polyandry (several brothers marrying one wife) since he was a graduate student in the 1960s.

Reprinted with permission from *Natural History,* March 1987, pp. 39–48. © 1987 by the American Museum of Natural History.

The Visit

Clifford Geertz

A Society Without Fathers or Husbands: The Na of China by Cai Hua, translated from the French by Asti Hustvedt. Zone books, 505 pp., $33.00

> *Love and marriage, love and*
> *marriage*
> *Go together like a horse and*
> *carriage*
> *Dad was told by mother*
> *You can't have one without the*
> *other*
>
> —"Love and Marriage,"
> Sammy Cahn and
> Jimmy van Heusen

Not everywhere.

Among the Na, a tribal people hidden away in the Yongning hills of Yunnan province in southern China and the subject of the French-trained Chinese anthropologist Cai Hua's provocative new monograph, there is no marriage, in fact or word. Mothers exist, as do children, but there are no dads. Sexual intercourse takes place between casual, opportunistic lovers, who develop no broader, more enduring relations to one another. The man "visits," usually furtively, the woman at her home in the middle of the night as impulse and opportunity appear, which they do with great regularity. Almost everyone of either sex has multiple partners, serially or simultaneously; simultaneously usually two or three, serially as many as a hundred or two. There are no nuclear families, no in-laws, no stepchildren. Brothers and sisters, usually several of each, reside together, along with perhaps a half-dozen of their

nearer maternal relatives, from birth to death under one roof—making a living, keeping a household, and raising the sisters' children.

The incest taboo is of such intensity that not only may one not sleep with opposite sex members of one's own household, one cannot even allude to sexual matters in their presence. One may not curse where they can hear, or sit with them in the same row at the movies, lest an emotional scene appear on the screen. As paternity is socially unrecognized, and for the most part uncertain, fathers may happen, now and again, to sleep with daughters. A man is free to sleep with his mother's brother's daughter, who is not considered any kind of relative, not even a "cousin." There is no word for bastard, none for promiscuity, none for infidelity; none, for that matter, for incest, so unthinkable is it. Jealousy is infra dig:

"You know, Luzo [who is nineteen] has not had a lot of [lovers], but he has made many visits [his friend said]. This is because he only goes to the homes of beauties. In particular, he goes to visit Seno, a pretty girl in our village. Do you want to go [visit her] at her house?" he asked me.

"No! If I go there, Luzo will be jealous," I answered.

"How could I be jealous!" [Luzo] responded. "You can ask whomever you want. You will see that… we don't know how to be jealous."

"He's right!" his friend interjected. And to explain himself he added: "Girls [are available] to everyone. Whoever wants to can visit them. There is nothing to be jealous about."

Obviously, this is an interesting place for an anthropologist—especially for an anthropologist brought up on that King Charles's head of his profession, "kinship theory."

1.

There are two major variants of such theory, "descent theory" and "alliance theory," and the Na, Hua says, fit neither of them. In the first, associated with the name of the British anthropologist A.R. Radcliffe-Brown and his followers, the "nuclear," "basic," or "elementary" family—a man, his wife, and their children—"founded as it is on natural requirements," is universal, and "forms the hard core around which any social organization revolves." The relationship between parents and children, "filiation," is critical, and out of it are developed various "jural," that is, normative, rules of descent which group certain sets of relatives together against others: lineages, clans, kindreds, and the like. "Families can be compared to threads which it is the task of nature to warp in order that the social fabric can develop."

In the alliance model, deriving in the main from the French anthropologist, and Hua's mentor, Claude Lévi-Strauss, "the institutionalized exchange of women" between families "by the alliance of marriage [is taken] to be the central point of kinship." The universality of the incest taboo, "a natural phenomenon," necessitates marriage and the creation of the "transversal [that is, affinal or 'in-law'] networks of alliances [that] engender all social organization."

Since the Na have no matrimonial relationship they falsify both theories. They neither form elementary families out of which a filiative social fabric can be spun, nor, though they have a variety of the incest taboo (an odd variety, in that with its father-daughter twist it does not exclude all primary relatives), do they form twined and expandable affinal networks, or indeed any networks of "in-laws" at all. "From now on," Hua proclaims at the end of his book, "marriage can no longer be considered the only possible institutionalized mode of sexual behavior." The Na "visit" demonstrates that

> Marriage, affinity, alliance of marriage, family, [usually considered] essential to anthropology,... seem absent from this culture. The Na case attests to the fact that marriage and the family (as well as the Oedipus complex) can no longer be considered universal, neither logically nor historically.

This is a little grand, for there are other "institutionalized modes of sexual behavior"—concubinage, prostitution, wife-borrowing—just about everywhere, and whether the Oedipus complex is universal or not, or even whether it exists at all, is not dependent upon marital arrangements. But clearly, "the visit" is an unusual, perhaps—though one never knows what is coming next out of Papua, the Amazon, or Central Asia—a unique institution sustaining a most unusual "kinship system," its existence often regarded as impossible. It is a system in which the facts of reproduction (though recognized—the Na know where babies come from) are incidental and all ties are (conceived to be) "blood ties"—the entire house can be called consanguineous.[1]

The Na "visit," for all its fluidity, opportunism, and apparent freedom from moral or religious anxiety, is as well out-

lined a social institution, as deeply embedded in a wider social structure, as marriage is elsewhere. (The Na are Tibetan-style Buddhists, nearly a third of the adult men being monks, whose sexual practices, a handful of Lhasa-bound celibates aside, are the same as those of laymen.) This is clear from the exact and explicit terminology that marks it out:

> Society calls a man and a woman who set up this kind of sexual relationship *nana sésé hing*, which means people in a relationship of furtive meetings; the man and the woman discreetly call each other *açia* ["discreetly" because of the "incest" taboo against public references to sexuality where opposite sex consanguines may hear them]. The term *açia* is made up of the diminutive prefix *a* and the root *çia*. The Na add *a* to names and proper nouns to indicate intimacy, affection, friendship, and respect; *çia*, when used as a noun, means lover. The same word is used for both sexes, and as a verb it means literally to lie down and figuratively to mate, to sleep and to tempt. *Açia* means lover.
>
> A Na saying depicts those who are *açia* very well:... It is not enough to say that we are *çia* for it to be so, sleeping together once makes (us) *çia*.

The enactment of such a relationship shows the same detailed cultural patterning: it is not a matter of brute and unfettered physical desire, but of a modeled, almost balletic self-control. The rendezvous takes place in the bedroom of the woman around midnight. (A bit earlier in the winter, Hua says, a bit later in the summer.) The man comes in near-perfect quietness, does what he does (Hua is wholly silent about what that might be and about how the cries of love are muffled), and leaves at cockcrow, creeping as stealthily back to his own house. As men and women enjoy "complete equality" and are "in daily contact, in town, in the workplace, and elsewhere," either can make the first advance and either may accept or refuse:

A girl might say to a boy, "Come stay at my house tonight." The boy might then respond, "Your mother is not easygoing." And then the girl might say, "She won't scold you. Come secretly in the middle of the night." If the boy accepts, he says, "Okay." If the boy refuses, he says, "I don't want to come. I'm not going to come over to sleep." In this case, no matter what the girl says, nothing will change his mind.

When the man takes the initiative... he often uses the expression "I'll come to your house tonight, okay?," to which the woman responds with a smile or by saying, "Okay." Some come straight out and ask "Do you want to be my *açia*?" If a woman refuses..., she can use a ready-made formula: "No, it is not possible. I already have one for tonight." In that case, the man will not insist.[2]

There are other, more oblique ways of making one's wishes known. One can snatch away some personal object—a scarf, a pack of cigarettes—from the desired partner. If he or she does not protest, the tryst is on. One can shout from a distance, "Hey, hey, do you want to trade something?" If you get a "hey, hey" back, you exchange belts and fix an appointment. These days, Chinese movies—shown virtually every night, though they are imperfectly understood by the Tibeto-Burmese-speaking Na—are a particularly favored setting for putting things in motion:

> The young men and women purchase tickets and wait in front of the theater, getting to know each other.... One man can offer several women a ticket, just as one woman can offer a ticket to more than one man. Once a ticket is handed over, the man and woman move away from each other and only get back together inside the theater. During the film, the viewers talk loudly, often drowning out the sound from the speakers. If they have had a good time during the movie and reached an agreement, they leave

discreetly to spend an amorous night together.

The "amorous night" itself may be a one-time thing. Or it may be repeated at shorter or longer intervals over the course of months or years. It may be begun, broken off for awhile, then begun again. It may be stopped altogether at any time by either party, usually without prior notice or much in the way of explanation. It does not, in short, involve any sort of exclusive and permanent "horse and carriage" commitment. But it, too, is, for all its fluidity and seeming negligence, carefully patterned—framed and hemmed in by an elaborate collection of cultural routines, a love-nest ethic.

When the *amant* arrives at the *amante*'s house, usually after having climbed over a fence or two and thrown a bone to the guard dog, he will give some sort of signal of his presence—toss pebbles on the roof, crouch at the woman's bedroom window (Hua says that every man in a village complex—four or five hundred people—knows the location of every woman's bedroom), or, if he is confident of being received or has been there often, simply knock on the front door. "In a household where there are women of the age to receive visitors [there may be several such on one night, and even a woman may have, in turn, more than one visitor], every evening after nightfall, the men of the house will not open the front door."

Usually, the woman who is waiting will herself open the door and the two will creep wordlessly off to her bedroom. If the wrong woman opens the door—a sister or a cousin, or perhaps even one of those "not easygoing" mothers—this causes little embarrassment: the man simply proceeds to the right woman's bedroom. During the encounter, the lovers must whisper "so that nothing will reach the ears of the woman's relatives, above all the men (especially uncles and great-uncles)."

No one can force anyone else in these matters. The woman can always, and at any time, refuse the man's entreaties and send him packing. A woman may never, in any case, visit a man; so if she is scorned she is just out of luck. A legend accounts for this virtually unique exception to rigorous symmetry of the system:

When humanity originated, no one knew how to regulate visits. Abaodgu, the god in charge of setting all the rules, proposed the following test: he ordered that a man be shut up in a house and that a woman be sent to join him. To reach the man, the woman had to pass through nine doors. At dawn, she had reached the seventh door. Then Abaodgu tested the man, who succeeded in passing through three doors.... Abaodgu [concluded] that women were too passionate [to do] the visiting.... The men [would have to] visit the women.

Hua goes on to trace out, methodically and in remorseless detail, the variations, the social ramifications, and the ethnographical specifics of all this, worried, not without reason, that if he does not make his arguments over and over again and retail every last fact he has gathered in four periods of fieldwork (1985, 1986, 1988–1989, 1992) his account will not be believed.

He describes two other, special and infrequent "modalities" of sexual encounter—"the conspicuous visit" and "cohabitation." In the conspicuous visit, which always follows upon a series of furtive visits, the effort to conceal the relationship is abandoned ("vomited up," as the idiom has it), mainly because the principals have grown older, perhaps tired of the pretense and folderol, and everyone knows about them anyway.

In cohabitation, an even rarer variant, a household that is short of women by means of which to produce children or of men to labor for it in its fields will adopt a man or woman from a household with a surplus to maintain its reproductive or economic viability, the adopted one becoming a sort of permanent conspicuous visitor (more or less: these arrangements often break up too). Among chiefly families, called *zhifu*, a Chinese word for "regional governor," successive relationships are established over several generations, leading to a peculiar household

alternation of chiefship and a greater restriction on who may mate with whom.

Hua describes, analyzes, and redescribes larger matrilineal groupings, which are mere notational devices to keep descent straight, as well as the internal structure of the household—a matter of careful seating arrangements, ritual obligations, and double, male-female headship. He gives accounts of the physical construction of the house, of various kin-related feasts and gift exchanges, and of beliefs about procreation (the man "waters" the woman as rain waters the grass, an act of "charity" to the woman's household which needs children to perpetuate itself).

But in the end, "The visit... is essential and basic; it is the preeminent modality of sexual life in this society.... Everyone is forced to follow it, its practice being determined not just by individual will but... [by] societal coercion."

2.

As one prepares to book passage for Yunnan, however, a troubling thought arises: Can all this really be true? No-fault sexuality? Multiple partners? No jealousy, no recriminations, no in-laws? Gender equality? A life full of assignations? It sounds like a hippie dream or a Falwell nightmare. We have learned recently, if we did not know already, to be wary of anthropological stories about obscure and distant people whose thoughts and behaviors are not just different than our own, but are some sort of neatly inversive, fun-mirror mockery of them: clockwork Hawaiian ritualists, murderous Amazonian hunters, immoralist Iks, "never-in-anger" Eskimos, selfless Hopi, complaisant Samoan maidens. Such stories may or may not be true, and argument, in most cases, continues. But if even the most famous bearer of tales out of China, Marco Polo (he has a passage in his *Travels* of 1298 vaguely alluding to Na promiscuity), is now accused of having never set foot in the place, can this bit of the world turned upside-down exotica escape suspicion?

So far as the harder facts of the matter are concerned, there would seem to be little room for doubt. Hua, now professor of social anthropology at the University of Beijing, was trained at the Laboratory of Social Anthropology at the Collège de France, and his book comes recommended by Lévi-Strauss, the founder of the Laboratory ("Dr. Cai Hua has done Western Anthropology a great service.... The Na now have their place in the anthropological literature") as well as by the former professor of anthropology at Oxford, Rodney Needham ("The ethnography is thorough and patently reliable, replete with valuable findings... ").

Hua spent about two years among the Na, and, though himself a Han Chinese, he appears to have gained a good command of the Na language. He conducted systematic interviews in five villages (sixty-five households, 474 people—the total Na population is about thirty thousand), patiently constructing genealogies and tabulating *açia* relationships. (The female champion claimed 150 lovers, the male, 200—perhaps Abaodgu was, after all, mistaken.) He read through the extensive Chinese annals on the group, running back through the Qing (1644–1911) and Ming (1368–1644) dynasties to the, in this part of China, barely visible Yuan (1279–1368), as well as through mountains of more recent government reports and surveys. He traveled through the region, reviewed the (somewhat confused) anthropological literature on matrilineal systems, and looked at least briefly into all sorts of collateral matters: land tenure, migration, trade, ethnic connections, folk healing, chiefship, and the local penetration of national politics. There can be little doubt that he walked the walk.

And yet, something large, hard to define, and overwhelmingly important is missing from Na's brisk, professional, conceptually self-sealing account: there is an aching hole at its very center, an oppressive absence. A few hurried and abbreviated passing remarks aside, an anecdote here, an incident there, we hear little of the tone and temper of Na life, of the color of their disposition, the curve of their experience. There is nothing, or almost nothing, of individual feelings and personal judgments, of hopes, fears, dissents, and resistances, of fantasy, remorse, pride, humor, loss, or dis-

appointment. The question that in the end we most want answered and the one most insistently raised by the very circumstantiality of Hua's ethnography— "What is it like to be a Na?"—goes largely unattended. We are left with a compact, well-arranged world of rules, institutions, customs, and practices: a "kinship system."

Can this be enough? "Na-ness" as a form-of-life, a way-of-being-in-the-world, is, whatever it is, a much wider, more ragged, unsettled, less articulated, and less articulable thing. It is a mood and an atmosphere, a suffusing gloss on things, and it is hard to describe or systematize, impossible to contain in summary categories. How are children, raised by those life-partner sister-brother pairs in those tight little consanguineous households thick with erotic pretense and incest worry, brought around to seeing themselves as tireless sexual conspirators— waiting bedside if they are women, stumbling through the dark if they are men? What does that do to their overall sense of agency? of identity? of authority? of pleasure? of trust? What does "gender equality" mean, what can it mean, in such a context?

What, really, does *çia*, which Hua so nonchalantly renders as "love" while never giving us even reported or second-hand descriptions of what goes on erotically, in beds or out of them, mean? No performance failure? no carnal inventiveness? no *folie*? no frigidity? no deviance? And what is all that business about "vomiting up" secret affairs and about mothers not being "easygoing"? The emotional and moral topography of Na life must be, surely, at least as unusual as their mating conventions and their adoptive practices. But of it we are afforded only the most general of senses; hints and glimpses, nervously brushed by en route to "findings."

Some of this inability—or unwillingness, it is hard to be certain which—to face up to the less edged and outlined dimensions of Na life may be due to what we have come these days to call Hua's "subject position." As a Han Chinese, brought up in what must be one of the most family-minded, most explicitly moralized, least unbuttoned societies in the world, studying as non-Han a society as it seems possible to imagine (and one located in "China" to boot) by using the

concerns and preconceptions of Western-phrased "science," Hua has his work cut out for him. In itself, this predicament is common to all field anthropologists, even ones working in less dramatic circumstances, and there is no genuine escape from it. The problem is that Hua seems unaware that the predicament exists—that the passing of "Na institutions" through Chinese perceptions on the way to "doing the West a service" by placing them "in the anthropological literature" raises questions not just about the institutions, but about the perceptions and the literature as well.

In particular, the very idea of a "kinship system," a culture-bound notion if there ever was one, may be a large part of the problem. It may flatten our perceptions of a people such as the Na, whose world is centered more around the figuration of sexuality and the symmetries of gender than around the ordering of genealogical connection or the stabilization of descent, and turn us, as it does Hua, toward such worn and academical questions as the naturalness of the nuclear family, the function of residence rules, or the proper definition of marriage.

The "symbolic anthropologist" the late David Schneider (who, after a lifetime working on the subject, came to believe that his profession's obsession with "kinship," "the idiom of kinship," and "the kin-based society" was some sort of primal mistake brought on by biologism, a tin ear, and a fear of difference) said that "the first task of anthropology, *prerequisite to all others*, is to understand and formulate the symbols and meanings and their configurations that a particular culture consists of."[3] If he was right, then it may be that Hua's exact and careful account of the Na will be remembered less for the institutional oddities it assembles and celebrates than for the half-glimpsed cosmos it lets escape.

This is all the more saddening because, after centuries of resistance to efforts to bring it into line with what is around it—that is, Han propriety—that cosmos is now apparently at last dissolving. The pressures on the Na to shape up and mate morally like normal human beings have been persistent and unremitting. As early as 1656, the Manchurian Qing, troubled by succession problems among "barbarian" tribes, decreed that the chiefs of such tribes, including the Na, must marry in the standard way and produce standard sons, grandsons, and cousins to follow them legitimately into office.

The extent to which this rule was enforced varied over time with the strengths and interests of the various dynasties. But the intrusion of Han practices—virilocality (by which married couples live near the husband's parents), patrifiliation (making kinship through fathers central), polygynous marriage (i.e., involving several wives), written genealogies, and "ancestor worship" (the Na cast the ashes of their dead unceremoniously across the hillsides)—into the higher reaches of Na society provided an alternative cultural model, a model that the Na, for the most part, contrived to keep at bay. Members of chiefly families, and some of the wealthy commoners and resident immigrants, began to marry to preserve their estates and to secure a place in the larger Chinese society. But most of the population proceeded as before, despite being continuously reviled as "primitive," "depraved," "backward," "licentious," "unclean," and ridden with sexual disease. (The last was, and is, more or less true. "More than 50 percent of Na adults have syphilis… a significant percentage of the women are sterile… people are deformed…. The… population is stagnating.")

This cultural guerrilla war, with edicts from the center and evasions from the periphery, continued fitfully for nearly three hundred years, until the arrival of the Communists in the 1950s rendered matters more immediate.[4] The Party considered the tradition of the visit "a 'backward and primitive custom'… contraven[ing] the matrimonial legislation of the People's Republic of China… [and disrupting] productiveness at work because the men think of nothing but running off to visit someone." The Party's first move against the tradition was a regulation designed to encourage nuclear family formation by distributing land to men who would set up and maintain such a family. When this failed to have any effect at all ("the government

could not understand how it was possible that Na men did not want to have their own land"), it moved on, during the Great Leap Forward, to a full press effort to "encourage monogamy" through a licensing system, an effort "guided" by the recommendation of two groups of ethnologists, who insisted that, "with planning," Na men and women could be led toward setting up families as economic units and raising their children together. Though this was a bit more successful—in Hua's "sample" seven couples officially married—it too soon ran out of steam in the face of Na indifference to the sanctions involved.

The small carrot and the little stick having failed to produce results, the Party proceeded in the period of the Cultural Revolution (1966–1969) to get real about the problem. Dedicated to the national project of "sweeping out the four ancients" (customs, habits, morality, culture), the People's Commune of Yongning pronounced it "shameful not to know who one's genitor is" and imposed marriage by simple decree on any villager involved in a conspicuous visit relationship. But this too failed. As soon as the cadres departed, the couples broke up.

Finally, in 1974, the provincial governor of Yunnan, declaring that "the reformation of this ancient matrimonial system comes under the framework of the class struggle in the ideological domain and therefore constitutes a revolution in the domain of the superstructure" (one can almost hear the collective Na, "*Huh?*"), made it the law that: (1) everyone under fifty in a relationship "that has lasted for a long time" must officially marry forthwith at commune headquarters; (2) every woman who has children must publically state who their genitor is, cart him off to headquarters, and marry him; (3) those who divorce without official sanction will have their annual grain ration suspended; (4) any child born out of wedlock will also not get a ration and must be supported by his genitor until age eighteen; and, (5) visiting, furtive or conspicuous, was forbidden.

This, supported by nightly meetings of the local military brigade and some

collusive informing, seemed finally to work—after a fashion, and for a while:

[The] District government sent a Jeep filled with marriage licenses to the People's Commune of Yongning. Ten and twenty at a time, couples were rounded up in the villages… and a leader would take their fingerprints on the marriage form and hand them each a marriage license.… [When] the day [for the ceremony] came, horse-drawn carriages were sent into the villages to provide transportation for the "newlyweds" to [Party] headquarters…They each received a cup of tea, a cigarette, and several pieces of candy, and then everybody participated in a traditional dance. The government called this "the new way of getting married."

It was new enough, but for the Na it was ruinous. "No other ethnic group in China underwent as deep a disruption as the Na did during the Cultural Revolution," Hua writes in a rare show of feeling. "To understand the trouble this reform caused in Na society, it is enough to imagine a reform in our society, but with the reverse logic":

During that period [one of Hua's informants said], the tension was so high that our thoughts never strayed from this subject. No one dared to make a furtive visit. Before, we were like roosters. We took any woman we could catch. We went to a woman's house at least once a night. But, with that campaign, we got scared. We did not want to get married and move into someone else's house, and as a result, we no longer dared to visit anyone. Because of this, we took a rest for a few years.

After the accession of Deng Xiaoping in 1981, the more draconian of these measures—the denial of rations, the exposure of genitors—were softened or suspended, and emphasis shifted toward "educational," that is, assimilationist, approaches. In particular, the expansion of the state school system, where "all the textbooks are impregnated with Han ideas and values," is leading to rapid and thorough Sinicization of the Na. Today—or, anyway, in 1992—the school, assisted by movies and other "modern" imports, is accomplishing what political pressure could not: the withering away of "Na-ism":

> When students graduate from middle school, they must complete a form that includes a column requesting information on their civil status. Unable to fill in the blank asking for the name of their father, they suddenly become aware they do not have a father, while their classmates from other ethnic backgrounds do. Some of the Na students, usually the most brilliant ones, find a quiet spot where they can cry in private.... The message [of the school] is clear.... There is only one culture that is legitimate, and that is Han culture.

In China, as elsewhere, it is not licentiousness that powers most fear. Nor even immorality. It is difference.

NOTES

1. For the supposed impossibility of purely "consanguineous" (here, purely matrilineal) kinship systems, see G.P. Murdock, *Social Structure* (Free Press, 1996), pp. 41ff.; cf. D.M. Schneider and K. Gough, *Matrilineal Kinship* (University of California Press, 1961). Of course, "consanguineous" ties are not always phrased in terms of "blood," as they are with us. Among the Na, the idiom is "bone": matrilineally connected individuals are said to be "of one bone.'

2. Hua includes the Na vernacular for these various phrases in his text; I have removed them and repunctuated accordingly.

3. David M. Schneider, *A Critique of the Study of Kinship* (University of Michigan Press, 1984), p. 196. Italics original.

4. The Communists of course came to power in 1949, but the Na area remained essentially Kuomintang country until 1956, when the Party installed its own local government, placing Han commissars in the region and effectively ending the traditional chiefship system.

Death Without Weeping

Has poverty ravaged mother love in the shantytowns of Brazil?

Nancy Scheper-Hughes

I have seen death without weeping,
The destiny of the Northeast is death,
Cattle they kill,
To the people they do
   something worse
—Anonymous Brazilian singer
   (1965)

"WHY DO THE CHURCH BELLS RING SO often?" I asked Nailza de Arruda soon after I moved into a corner of her tiny mud-walled hut near the top of the shantytown called the Alto do Cruzeiro (Crucifix Hill). I was then a Peace Corps volunteer and community development/health worker. It was the dry and blazing hot summer of 1965, the months following the military coup in Brazil, and save for the rusty, clanging bells of N. S. das Dores Church, an eerie quiet had settled over the market town that I call Bom Jesus da Mata. Beneath the quiet, however, there was chaos and panic. "It's nothing," replied Nailza, "just another little angel gone to heaven."

Nailza had sent more than her share of little angels to heaven, and sometimes at night I could hear her engaged in a muffled but passionate discourse with one of them, two-year-old Joana. Joana's photograph, taken as she lay propped up in her tiny cardboard coffin, her eyes open, hung on a wall next to one of Nailza and Ze Antonio taken on the day they eloped.

Nailza could barely remember the other infants and babies who came and went in close succession. Most had died unnamed and were hastily baptized in their coffins. Few lived more than a month or two. Only Joana, properly bap-

tized in church at the close of her first year and placed under the protection of a powerful saint, Joan of Arc, had been expected to live. And Nailza had dangerously allowed herself to love the little girl.

In addressing the dead child, Nailza's voice would range from tearful imploring to angry recrimination: "Why did you leave me? Was your patron saint so greedy that she could not allow me one child on this earth?" Ze Antonio advised me to ignore Nailza's odd behavior, which he understood as a kind of madness that, like the birth and death of children, came and went. Indeed, the premature birth of a stillborn son some months later "cured" Nailza of her "inappropriate" grief, and the day came when she removed Joana's photo and carefully packed it away.

More than fifteen years elapsed before I returned to the Alto do Cruzeiro, and it was anthropology that provided the vehicle of my return. Since 1982 I have returned several times in order to pursue a problem that first attracted my attention in the 1960s. My involvement with the people of the Alto do Cruzeiro now spans a quarter of a century and three generations of parenting in a community where mothers and daughters are often simultaneously pregnant.

The Alto do Cruzeiro is one of three shantytowns surrounding the large market town of Bom Jesus in the sugar plantation zone of Pernambuco in Northeast Brazil, one of the many zones of neglect that have emerged in the shadow of the now tarnished economic miracle of Bra-

zil. For the women and children of the Alto do Cruzeiro the only miracle is that some of them have managed to stay alive at all.

The Northeast is a region of vast proportions (approximately twice the size of Texas) and of equally vast social and developmental problems. The nine states that make up the region are the poorest in the country and are representative of the Third World within a dynamic and rapidly industrializing nation. Despite waves of migrations from the interior to the teeming shantytowns of coastal cities, the majority still live in rural areas on farms and ranches, sugar plantations and mills.

Life expectancy in the Northeast is only forty years, largely because of the appallingly high rate of infant and child mortality. Approximately one million children in Brazil under the age of five die each year. The children of the Northeast, especially those born in shantytowns on the periphery of urban life, are at a very high risk of death. In these areas, children are born without the traditional protection of breast-feeding, subsistence gardens, stable marriages, and multiple adult caretakers that exists in the interior. In the hillside shantytowns that spring up around cities or, in this case, interior market towns, marriages are brittle, single parenting is the norm, and women are frequently forced into the shadow economy of domestic work in the homes of the rich or into unprotected and oftentimes "scab" wage labor on the surrounding sugar plantations, where they clear land for planting and weed for a pittance, sometimes less than a dollar a day. The women of the Alto may not bring their babies with them into the homes of the wealthy, where the often-sick infants are considered sources of contamination, and they cannot carry the little ones to the riverbanks where they wash clothes because the river is heavily infested with schistosomes and other deadly parasites. Nor can they carry their young children to the plantations, which are often several miles away. At wages of a dollar a day, the women of the Alto cannot hire baby sitters. Older children who are not in school will sometimes serve as somewhat indifferent caretakers. But any child not in school is also expected to find wage work. In most cases, babies are simply left at home alone, the door securely fastened. And so many also die alone and unattended.

Bom Jesus da Mata, centrally located in the plantation zone of Pernambuco, is within commuting distance of several sugar plantations and mills. Consequently, Bom Jesus has been a magnet for rural workers forced off their small subsistence plots by large landowners wanting to use every available piece of land for sugar cultivation. Initially, the rural migrants to Bom Jesus were squatters who were given tacit approval by the mayor to put up temporary straw huts on each of the three hills overlooking the town. The Alto do Cruzeiro is the oldest, the largest, and the poorest of the shantytowns. Over the past three decades many of the original migrants have become permanent residents, and the primitive and temporary straw huts have been replaced by small homes (usually of two rooms) made of wattle and daub, sometimes covered with plaster. The more affluent residents use bricks and tiles. In most Alto homes, dangerous kerosene lamps have been replaced by light bulbs. The once tattered rural garb, often fashioned from used sugar sacking, has likewise been replaced by store-brought clothes, often castoffs from a wealthy *patrão* (boss). The trappings are modern, but the hunger, sickness, and death that they conceal are traditional, deeply rooted in a history of feudalism, exploitation, and institutionalized dependency.

My research agenda never wavered. The questions I addressed first crystallized during a veritable "die-off" of Alto babies during a severe drought in 1965. The food and water shortages and the political and economic chaos occasioned by the military coup were reflected in the handwritten entries of births and deaths in the dusty, yellowed pages of the ledger books kept at the public registry office in Bom Jesus. More than 350 babies died in the Alto during 1965 alone—this from a shantytown population of little more than 5,000. But that wasn't what surprised me. There were reasons enough for the deaths in the miserable conditions of shantytown life. What puzzled me was the seeming indifference of Alto women to the death of their infants, and their willingness to attribute to their own tiny offspring an aversion to life that made their death seem wholly natural, indeed all but anticipated.

Although I found that it was possible, and hardly difficult, to rescue infants and toddlers from death by diarrhea and dehydration with a simple sugar, salt, and water solution (even bottled Coca-Cola worked fine), it was more difficult to enlist a mother herself in the rescue of a child she perceived as ill-fated for life or better off dead, or to convince her to take back into her threatened and besieged home a baby she had already come to think of as an angel rather than as a son or daughter.

I learned that the high expectancy of death, and the ability to face child death with stoicism and equanimity, produced patterns of nurturing that differentiated between those infants thought of as thrivers and survivors and those thought of as born already "wanting to die." The survivors were nurtured, while stigmatized, doomed infants were left to die, as mothers say, *a mingua*, "of neglect." Mothers stepped back and allowed nature to take its course. This pattern, which I call mortal selective neglect, is called passive infanticide by anthropologist Marvin Harris. The Alto situation, although culturally specific in the form that it takes, is not unique to Third World shantytown communities and may have its correlates in our own impoverished urban communities in some cases of "failure to thrive" infants.

I use as an example the story of Zezinho, the thirteen-month-old toddler of one of my neighbors, Lourdes. I became involved with Zezinho when I was called in to help Lourdes in the delivery of another child, this one a fair and robust little tyke with a lusty cry. I noted that while Lourdes showed great interest in the newborn, she totally ignored Zezinho who, wasted and severely malnourished, was curled up in a fetal position on a piece of urine- and feces-soaked cardboard placed under his mother's hammock. Eyes open and vacant, mouth slack, the little boy seemed doomed.

When I carried Zezinho up to the community day-care center at the top of the hill, the Alto women who took turns caring for one another's children (in order to free themselves for part-time work in the cane fields or washing clothes) laughed at my efforts to save Ze, agreeing with Lourdes that here was a baby without a ghost of a chance. Leave him alone, they cautioned. It makes no sense to fight with death. But I did do battle with Ze, and after several weeks of force-feeding (malnourished babies lose their interest in food), Ze began to succumb to my ministrations. He acquired some flesh across his taut chest bones, learned to sit up, and even tried to smile. When he seemed well enough, I returned him to Lourdes in her miserable scrap-material lean-to, but not without guilt about what I had done. I wondered whether returning Ze was at all fair to Lourdes and to his little brother. But I was busy and washed my hands of the matter. And Lourdes did seem more interested in Ze now that he was looking more human.

When I returned in 1982, there was Lourdes among the women who formed my sample of Alto mothers—still struggling to put together some semblance of life for a now grown Ze and her five other surviving children. Much was made of my reunion with Ze in 1982, and everyone enjoyed retelling the story of Ze's rescue and of how his mother had given him up for dead. Ze would laugh the loudest when told how I had had to force-feed him like a fiesta turkey. There was no hint of guilt on the part of Lourdes and no resentment on the part of Ze. In fact, when questioned in private as to who was the best friend he ever had in life, Ze took a long drag on his cigarette and answered without a trace of irony, "Why my mother, of course." "But of course," I replied.

Part of learning how to mother in the Alto do Cruzeiro is learning when to let go of a child who shows that it "wants" to die or that it has no "knack" or no "taste" for life. Another part is learning when it is safe to let oneself love a child. Frequent child death remains a powerful shaper of maternal thinking and practice. In the absence of firm expectation that a child will survive, mother love as we conceptualize it (whether in popular terms or in the psychobiological notion of maternal bonding) is attenuated and delayed with consequences for infant survival. In an environment already precarious to young life, the emotional detachment of mothers toward some of their babies contributes even further to the spiral of high mortality—high fertility in a kind of macabre lock-step dance of death.

The average woman of the Alto experiences 9.5 pregnancies, 3.5 child deaths, and 1.5 stillbirths. Seventy percent of all child deaths in the Alto occur in the first six months of life, and 82 percent by the end of the first year. Of all deaths in the community each year, about 45 percent are of children under the age of five.

Women of the Alto distinguish between child deaths understood as natural (caused by diarrhea and communicable diseases) and those resulting from sorcery, the evil eye, or other magical or supernatural afflictions. They also recognize a large category of infant deaths seen as fated and inevitable. These hopeless cases are classified by mothers under the folk terminology "child sickness" or "child attack." Women say that there are at least fourteen different types of hopeless child sickness, but most can be subsumed under two categories—chronic and acute. The chronic cases refer to infants who are born small and wasted. They are deathly pale, mothers say, as well as weak and passive. They demonstrate no vital force, no liveliness. They do not suck vigorously; they hardly cry. Such babies can be this way at birth or they can be born sound but soon show no re-

sistance, no "fight" against the common crises of infancy: diarrhea, respiratory infections, tropical fevers.

The acute cases are those doomed infants who die suddenly and violently. They are taken by stealth overnight, often following convulsions that bring on head banging, shaking, grimacing, and shrieking. Women say it is horrible to look at such a baby. If the infant begins to foam at the mouth or gnash its teeth or go rigid with its eyes turned back inside its head, there is absolutely no hope. The infant is "put aside"—left alone—often on the floor in a back room, and allowed to die. These symptoms (which accompany high fevers, dehydration, third-stage malnutrition, and encephalitis) are equated by Alto women with madness, epilepsy, and worst of all, rabies, which is greatly feared and highly stigmatized.

Most of the infants presented to me as suffering from chronic child sickness were tiny, wasted famine victims, while those labeled as victims of acute child attack seemed to be infants suffering from the deliriums of high fever or the convulsions that can accompany electrolyte imbalance in dehydrated babies.

Local midwives and traditional healers, praying women, as they are called, advise Alto women on when to allow a baby to die. One midwife explained: "If I can see that a baby was born unfortuitously, I tell the mother that she need not wash the infant or give it a cleansing tea. I tell her just to dust the infant with baby powder and wait for it to die." Allowing nature to take its course is not seen as sinful by these often very devout Catholic women. Rather, it is understood as co-operating with God's plan.

Often I have been asked how consciously women of the Alto behave in this regard. I would have to say that consciousness is always shifting between allowed and disallowed levels of awareness. For example, I was awakened early one morning in 1987 by two neighborhood children who had been sent to fetch me to a hastily organized wake for a two-month-old infant whose mother I had unsuccessfully urged to breast-feed. The infant was being sustained on sugar water, which the mother referred to as *soro* (serum), using a medical term for the infant's starvation re-

gime in light of his chronic diarrhea. I had cautioned the mother that an infant could not live on *soro* forever.

The two girls urged me to console the young mother by telling her that it was "too bad" that her infant was so weak that Jesus had to take him. They were coaching me in proper Alto etiquette. I agreed, of course, but asked, "And what do *you* think?" Xoxa, the eleven-year-old, looked down at her dusty flip-flops and blurted out, "Oh, Dona Nanci, that baby never got enough to eat, but you must never say that!" And so the death of hungry babies remains one of the best kept secrets of life in Bom Jesus da Mata.

Most victims are waked quickly and with a minimum of ceremony. No tears are shed, and the neighborhood children form a tiny procession, carrying the baby to the town graveyard where it will join a multitude of others. Although a few fresh flowers may be scattered over the tiny grave, no stone or wooden cross will mark the place, and the same spot will be reused within a few months' time. The mother will never visit the grave, which soon becomes an anonymous one.

What, then, can be said of these women? What emotions, what sentiments motivate them? How are they able to do what, in fact, must be done? What does mother love mean in this inhospitable context? Are grief, mourning, and melancholia present, although deeply repressed? If so, where shall we look for them? And if not, how are we to understand the moral visions and moral sensibilities that guide their actions?

I have been criticized more than once for presenting an unflattering portrait of poor Brazilian women, women who are, after all, themselves the victims of severe social and institutional neglect. I have described these women as allowing some of their children to die, as if this were an unnatural and inhuman act rather than, as I would assert, the way any one of us might act, reasonably and rationally, under similarly desperate conditions. Perhaps I have not emphasized enough the real pathogens in this environment of high risk: poverty, deprivation, sexism, chronic hunger, and economic exploitation. If mother love is, as many psychologists and some feminists believe, a seemingly natural and universal maternal script, what does it mean to women for whom scarcity, loss, sickness, and deprivation have made that love frantic and robbed them of their grief, seeming to turn their hearts to stone?

Throughout much of human history—as in a great deal of the impoverished Third World today—women have had to give birth and to nurture children under ecological conditions and social arrangements hostile to child survival, as well as to their own well-being. Under circumstances of high childhood mortality, patterns of selective neglect and passive infanticide may be seen as active survival strategies.

They also seem to be fairly common practices historically and across cultures. In societies characterized by high childhood mortality and by a correspondingly high (replacement) fertility, cultural practices of infant and child care tend to be organized primarily around survival goals. But what this means is a pragmatic recognition that not all of one's children can be expected to live. The nervousness about child survival in areas of northeast Brazil, northern India, or Bangladesh, where a 30 percent or 40 percent mortality rate in the first years of life is common, can lead to forms of delayed attachment and a casual or benign neglect that serves to weed out the worst bets so as to enhance the life chances of healthier siblings, including those yet to be born. Practices similar to those that I am describing have been recorded for parts of Africa, India, and Central America.

Life in the Alto do Cruzeiro resembles nothing so much as a battlefield or an emergency room in an overcrowded inner-city public hospital. Consequently, mortality is guided by a kind of "lifeboat ethics," the morality of triage. The seemingly studied indifference toward the suffering of some of their infants, conveyed in such sayings as "little critters have no feelings," is understandable in light of these women's obligation to carry on with their reproductive and nurturing lives.

In their slowness to anthropomorphize and personalize their infants, everything is mobilized so as to prevent maternal overattachment and, therefore, grief at death. The bereaved mother is told not to cry, that her tears will dampen the wings of her little angel so that she cannot fly up to her heavenly home. Grief at the death of an angel is not only inappropriate, it is a symptom of madness and of a profound lack of faith.

Infant death becomes routine in an environment in which death is anticipated and bets are hedged. While the routinization of death in the context of shantytown life is not hard to understand, and quite possible to empathize with, its routinization in the formal institutions of public life in Bom Jesus is not as easy to accept uncritically. Here the social production of indifference takes on a different, even a malevolent, cast.

In a society where triplicates of every form are required for the most banal events (registering a car, for example), the registration of infant and child death is informal, incomplete, and rapid. It requires no documentation, takes less than five minutes, and demands no witnesses other than office clerks. No questions are asked concerning the circumstances of the death, and the cause of death is left blank, unquestioned and unexamined. A neighbor, grandmother, older sibling, or common-law husband may register the death. Since most infants die at home, there is no question of a medical record.

From the registry office, the parent proceeds to the town hall, where the mayor will give him or her a voucher for a free baby coffin. The full-time municipal coffinmaker cannot tell you exactly how many baby coffins are dispatched each week. It varies, he says, with the seasons. There are more needed during the drought months and during the big festivals of Carnaval and Christmas and São Joao's Day because people are too busy, he supposes, to take their babies to the clinic. Record keeping is sloppy.

Similarly, there is a failure on the part of city-employed doctors working at two free clinics to recognize the malnutrition of babies who are weighed, measured, and immunized without comment and as if they were not, in fact, anemic, stunted, fussy, and irritated starvation babies. At best the mothers are told to pick up free vitamins or a health "tonic" at the municipal chambers. At worst, clinic personnel will give tranquilizers and sleeping pills to quiet the hungry cries of "sick-to-death" Alto babies.

The church, too, contributes to the routinization of, and indifference toward, child death. Traditionally, the local Catholic church taught patience and resignation to domestic tragedies that were said to reveal the imponderable workings of God's will. If an infant died suddenly, it was because a particular saint had claimed the child. The infant would be an angel in the service of his or her heavenly patron. It would be wrong, a sign of a lack of faith, to weep for a child with such good fortune. The infant funeral was, in the past, an event celebrated with joy. Today, however, under the new regime of "liberation theology," the bells of N. S. das Dores parish church no longer peal for the death of Alto babies, and no priest accompanies the procession of angels to the cemetery where their bodies are disposed of casually and without ceremony. Children bury children in Bom Jesus da Mata. In this most Catholic of communities, the coffin is handed to the disabled and irritable municipal gravedigger, who often chides the children for one reason or another. It may be that the coffin is larger than expected and the gravedigger can find no appropriate space. The children do not wait for the gravedigger to complete his task. No prayers are recited and no sign of the cross made as the tiny coffin goes into its shallow grave.

When I asked the local priest, Padre Marcos, about the lack of church ceremony surrounding infant and childhood death today in Bom Jesus, he replied; "In the old days, child death was richly celebrated. But those were the baroque customs of a conservative church that wallowed in death and misery. The new church is a church of hope and joy. We no longer celebrate the death of child angels. We try to tell mothers that Jesus doesn't want all the dead babies they send him." Similarly, the new church has changed its baptismal customs, now often refusing to baptize dying babies brought to the back door of a church or rectory. The mothers are scolded by the church attendants and told to go home and take care of their sick babies. Baptism, they are told, is for the living; it is not to be confused with the sacrament of extreme unction, which is the anointing of the dying. And so it appears to the women of the Alto that even the church has turned away from them, denying the traditional comfort of folk Catholicism.

The contemporary Catholic church is caught in the clutches of a double bind. The new theology of liberation imagines a kingdom of God on earth based on justice and equality, a world without hunger, sickness, or childhood mortality. At the same time, the church has not changed its official position on sexuality and reproduction, including its sanctions against birth control, abortion, and sterilization. The padre of Bom Jesus da Mata recognizes this contradiction intuitively, although he shies away from discussions on the topic, saying that he prefers to leave questions of family planning to the discretion and the "good consciences" of his impoverished parishioners. But this, of course, sidesteps the extent to which those good consciences have been shaped by traditional church teachings in Bom Jesus, especially by his recent predeces-

sors. Hence, we can begin to see that the seeming indifference of Alto mothers toward the death of some of their infants is but a pale reflection of the official indifference of church and state to the plight of poor women and children.

Nonetheless, the women of Bom Jesus are survivors. One woman, Biu, told me her life history, returning again and again to the themes of child death, her first husband's suicide, abandonment by her father and later by her second husband, and all the other losses and disappointments she had suffered in her long forty-five years. She concluded with great force, reflecting on the days of Carnaval '88 that were fast approaching:

No, Dona Nanci, I won't cry, and I won't waste my life thinking about it from morning to night.... Can I argue with God for the state that I'm in? No! And so I'll dance and I'll jump and I'll play Carnaval! And yes, I'll laugh and people will wonder at a *pobre* like me who can have such a good time.

And no one did blame Biu for dancing in the streets during the four days of Carnaval—not even on Ash Wednesday, the day following Carnaval '88 when we all assembled hurriedly to assist in the burial of Mercea, Biu's beloved *casula*, her last-born daughter who had died at home of pneumonia during the festivities. The rest of the family barely had time to change out of their costumes. Severino, the child's uncle and godfather, sprinkled holy water over the little angel while he prayed: "Mercea, I don't know whether you were called, taken, or thrown out of this world. But look down at us from your heavenly home with tenderness, with pity, and with mercy." So be it.

Nancy Scheper-Hughes is a professor in the Department of Anthropology at the University of California, Berkeley. She has written Death Without Weeping: Violence of Everyday Life in Brazil *(1992).*

Our Babies, Ourselves

By Meredith F. Small

During one of his many trips to Gusii-land in southwestern Kenya, anthropologist Robert LeVine tried an experiment: he showed a group of Gusii mothers a videotape of middle-class American women tending their babies. The Gusii mothers were appalled. Why does that mother ignore the cries of her unhappy baby during a simple diaper change? And how come that grandmother does nothing to soothe the screaming baby in her lap? These American women, the Gusii concluded, are clearly incompetent

mothers. In response, the same charge might be leveled at the Gusii by American mothers. What mother hands over her tiny infant to a six-year-old sister and expects the older child to provide adequate care? And why don't those Gusii women spend more time talking to their babies, so that they will grow up smart?

Both culture—the traditional way of doing things in a particular society—and individual experience guide parents in their tasks. When a father chooses to pick up his newborn and not let it cry,

when a mother decides to bottle-feed on a schedule rather than breast-feed on demand, when a couple bring the newborn into their bed at night, they are prompted by what they believe to be the best methods of caregiving.

For decades, anthropologists have been recording how children are raised in different societies. At first, the major goals were to describe parental roles and understand how child-rearing practices and rituals helped to generate adult per-

---

Gusii Survival Skills

By Robert A. LeVine

Farming peoples of subSaharan Africa have long faced the grim reality that many babies fail to survive, often succumbing to gastrointestinal diseases, malaria, or other infections. In the 1970s, when I lived among the Gusii in a small town in southwestern Kenya, infant mortality in that nation was on the decline but was still high—about eighty deaths per thousand live births during the first years, compared with about ten in the United States at that time and six to eight in Western Europe.

The Gusii grew corn, millet, and cash crops such as coffee and tea. Women handled the more routine tasks of cultivation, food processing, and trading, while men were supervisors or entrepreneurs. Many men worked at jobs outside the village, in urban centers or on plantations. The society was

polygamous, with perhaps 10 percent of the men having two or more wives. A woman was expected to give birth every two years, from marriage to menopause, and the average married women bore about ten live children— one of the highest fertility rates in the world.

Nursing mothers slept alone with a new infant for fifteen months to insure its health. For the first three to six months, the Gusii mothers were especially vigilant for signs of ill health or slow growth, and they were quick to nurture unusually small or sick infants by feeding and holding them more often. Mothers whose newborns were deemed particularly at risk—including twins and those born prematurely—entered a ritual seclusion for several weeks, staying with their infants in a hut with a constant fire.

Mothers kept infants from crying in the early months by holding them constantly and being quick to comfort them. After three to six months—if the baby was growing normally—mothers began to entrust the baby to the care of other children (usually six to twelve years old) in order to pursue tasks that helped support the family. Fathers did not take care of infants, for this was not a traditional male activity.

Because they were so worried about their children's survival, Gusii parents did not explicitly strive to foster cognitive, social, and emotional development. These needs were not neglected, however, because from birth Gusii babies entered an active and responsive interpersonal environment, first with their mothers and young caregivers, and later as part of a group of children.

An Infant's Three Rs

By Sara Harkness and Charles M. Super

You are an American visitor spending a morning in a pleasant middle-class Dutch home to observe the normal routine of a mother and her six-month-old baby. The mother made sure you got there by 8:30 to witness the morning bath, an opportunity for playful interaction with the baby. The baby was then dressed in cozy warm clothes, her hair brushed and styled with a tiny curlicue atop her head. The mother gave her the midmorning bottle, then sang to her and played patty-cake for a few minutes before placing her in the playpen to entertain herself with a mobile while the mother attended to other things nearby. Now, about half an hour later, the baby is beginning to get fussy.

The mother watches for a minute, then offers a toy and turns away. The baby again begins to fuss. "Seems bored and in need of attention," you think. But the mother looks at the baby sympathetically and in a soothing voice says, "Oh, are you tired?" Without further ado she picks up the baby, carries her upstairs, tucks her into her crib, and pulls down the shades. To your surprise, the baby fusses for only a few more moments, then is quiet. The mother returns looking serene. "She needs plenty of sleep in order to grow," she explains. "When she doesn't have her nap or go to bed on time, we can always tell the difference—she's not so happy and playful."

Different patterns in infant sleep can be found in Western societies that seem quite similar to those of the United States. We discovered the "three R's" of Dutch child rearing—*rust* (rest), *regelmaat* (regularity) and *reinheid* (cleanliness)—while doing research on a

sample of sixty families with infants or young children in a middle-class community near Leiden and Amsterdam, the sort of community typical of Dutch life styles in all but the big cities nowadays. At six months, the Dutch babies were sleeping more than a comparison group of American babies—a total of fifteen hours per day compared with thirteen hours for the Americans. While awake at home, the Dutch babies were more often left to play quietly in their playpens or infant seats. A daily ride in the baby carriage provided time for the baby to look around at the passing scene or to doze peacefully. If the mother needed to go out for a while without the baby, she could leave it alone in bed for a short period or time her outing with the baby's nap time and ask a neighbor to monitor with a "baby phone."

To understand how Dutch families manage to establish such a restful routine by the time their babies are six months old, we made a second research visit to the same community. We found that by two weeks of age, the Dutch babies were already sleeping more than same-age American babies. In fact, a dilemma for some Dutch parents was whether to wake the baby after eight hours, as instructed by the local health care providers, or let them sleep longer. The main method for establishing and maintaining this pattern was to create a calm, regular, and restful environment for the infant throughout the day.

Far from worrying about providing "adequate stimulation," these mothers were conscientious about avoiding overstimulation in the form of late family outings, disruptions in the regularity

of eating and sleeping, or too many things to look at or listen to. Few parents were troubled by their babies' nighttime sleep routines. Babies's feeding schedules were structured following the guidelines of the local baby clinic (a national service). If a baby continued to wake up at night when feeding was no longer considered necessary, the mother (or father) would most commonly give it a pacifier and a little back rub to help it get back to sleep. Only in rare instances did parents find themselves forced to choose between letting the baby scream and allowing too much night waking.

Many aspects of Dutch society support the three Rs throughout infancy and childhood—for example, shopping is close to home, and families usually have neighbors and relatives nearby who are available to help out with child care. The small scale of neighborhoods and a network of bicycle paths provide local play sites and a safe way for children to get around easily on their own (no "soccer moms" are needed for daily transportation!). Work sites for both fathers and mothers are also generally close to home, and there are many flexible or part-time job arrangements.

National policies for health and other social benefits insure universal coverage regardless of one's employment status, and the principle of the "family wage" has prevailed in labor relations so that mothers of infants and young children rarely work more than part-time, if at all. In many ways, the three Rs of Dutch child rearing are just one aspect of a calm and unhurried life style for the whole family.

sonality. In the 1950s, for example, John and Beatrice Whiting, and their colleagues at Harvard, Yale, and Cornell Universities, launched a major comparative study of childhood, looking at six varied communities in different regions: Okinawa, the Philippines, northern India, Kenya, Mexico, and New

England. They showed that communal expectations play a major role in setting parenting styles, which in turn play a part in shaping children to become accepted adults.

More recent work by anthropologists and child-development researchers has shown that parents readily accept their

society's prevailing ideology on how babies should be treated, usually because it makes sense in their environmental or social circumstances. In the United States, for example, where individualism is valued, parents do not hold babies as much as in other cultures, and they place them in rooms of their own to

Doctor's Orders

By Edward Z. Tronick

In Boston, a pediatric resident is experiencing a vague sense of disquiet as she interviews a Puerto Rican mother who has brought her baby in for a checkup. When she is at work, the mother explains, the two older children, ages six and nine, take care of the two younger ones, a two-year-old and the three-month-old baby. Warning bells go off for the resident: young children cannot possibly be sensitive to the needs of babies and toddlers. And yet the baby is thriving; he is well over the ninetieth percentile in weight and height and is full of smiles.

The resident questions the mother in detail: How is the baby fed? Is the apartment safe for a two-year-old? The responses are all reassuring, but the resident nonetheless launches into a lecture on the importance of the mother to normal infant development. The mother falls silent, and the resident is now convinced that something is seriously wrong. And something is—the resident's model of child care.

The resident subscribes to what I call the "continuous care and contact" model of parenting, which demands a high level of contact, frequent feeding, and constant supervision, with almost all care provided by the mother. According to this model, a mother should

also enhance cognitive development with play and verbal engagement. The pediatric resident is comfortable with this formula—she is not even conscious of it—because she was raised this way and treats her own child in the same manner. But at the Child Development Unit of Children's Hospital in Boston, which I direct, I want residents to abandon the idea that there is only one way to raise a child. Not to do so may interfere with patient care.

Many models of parenting are valid. Among Efe foragers of Congo's Ituri Forest, for example, a newborn is routinely cared for by several people. Babies are even nursed by many women. But few individuals ever play with the infant; as far as the Efe are concerned, the baby's job is to sleep.

In Peru, the Quechua swaddle their infants in a pouch of blankets that the mother, or a child caretaker, carries on her back. Inside the pouch, the infant cannot move, and its eyes are covered. Quechua babies are nursed in a perfunctory fashion, with three or four hours between feedings.

As I explain to novice pediatricians, such practices do not fit the continuous care and contact model; yet these babies grow up just fine. But my residents see these cultures as exotic,

not relevant to the industrialized world. And so I follow up with examples closer to home: Dutch parents who leave an infant alone in order to go shopping, sometimes pinning the child's shirt to the bed to keep the baby on its back; or Japanese mothers who periodically wake a sleeping infant to teach the child who is in charge. The questions soon follow. "How could a mother leave her infant alone?" "Why would a parent ever want to wake up a sleeping baby?"

The data from cross-cultural studies indicate that child-care practices vary, and that these styles aim to make the child into a culturally appropriate adult. The Efe make future Efe. The resident makes future residents. A doctor who has a vague sense that something is wrong with how someone cares for a baby may first need to explore his or her own assumptions, the hidden "shoulds" that are based solely on tradition. Of course, pediatric residents must make sure children are cared for responsibly. I know I have helped residents broaden their views when their lectures on good mothering are replaced by such comments as "What a gorgeous baby! I can't imagine how you manage both work and three others at home!"

sleep. Pediatricians and parents alike often say this fosters independence and self-reliance. Japanese parents, in contrast, believe that individuals should be well integrated into society, and so they "indulge" their babies: Japanese infants are held more often, not left to cry, and sleep with their parents. Efe parents in Congo believe even more in a communal life, and their infants are regularly nursed, held, and comforted by any number of group members, not just parents. Whether such practices

help form the anticipated adult personality traits remains to be shown, however.

Recently, a group of anthropologists, child-development experts, and pediatricians have taken the cross-cultural approach in a new direction by investigating how differing parenting styles affect infant health and growth. Instead of emphasizing the development of adult personality, these researchers, who call themselves ethnopediatricians, focus on the child as an organism. Ethnopediatricians see the human infant as a product of evolution,

geared to enter a particular environment of care. What an infant actually gets is a compromise, as parents are pulled by their offspring's needs and pushed by social and personal expectations.

Compared with offspring of many other mammals, primate infants are dependent and vulnerable. Baby monkeys and apes stay close to the mother's body, clinging to her stomach or riding on her back, and nursing at will. They are protected in this way for many months, until they develop enough motor and cogni-

The Crying Game

By Ronald G. Barr

All normal human infants cry, although they vary a great deal in how much. A mysterious and still unexplained phenomenon is that crying tends to increase in the first few weeks of life, peaks in the second or third month, and then decreases. Some babies in the United States cry so much during the peak period—often in excess of three hours a day—and seem so difficult to soothe that parents come to doubt their nurturing skills or begin to fear that their offspring is suffering from a painful disease. Some mothers discontinue nursing and switch to bottle-feeding because they believe their breast milk is insufficiently nutritious and that their infants are always hungry. In extreme cases, the crying may provoke physical abuse, sometimes even precipitating the infant's death.

A look at another culture, the !Kung San hunter-gatherers of southern Africa, provides us with an opportunity to see whether caregiving strategies have any effect on infant crying. Both the !Kung San and Western infants escalate their crying during the early weeks of life, with a similar peak at two or three months. A comparison of Dutch, American, and !Kung San infants shows that the number of individual crying episodes are virtually identical. What differs is their length: !Kung San infants cry about half as long as Western babies. This implies that caregiving can influence only some aspects of crying, such as duration.

What is particularly striking about child-rearing among the !Kung San is that infants are in constant contact with a caregiver; they are carried or held most of the time, are usually in an upright position, and are breast-fed about four times an hour for one to two minutes at a time. Furthermore, the mother almost always responds to the smallest cry or fret within ten seconds.

I believe that crying was adaptive for our ancestors. As seen in the contemporary !Kung San, crying probably elicited a quick response, and thus consisted of frequent but relatively short episodes. This pattern helped keep an adult close by to provide adequate nutrition as well as protection from predators. I have also argued that crying helped an infant forge a strong attachment with the mother and—because new pregnancies are delayed by the prolongation of frequent nursing—secure more of her caregiving resources.

In the United States, where the threat of predation has receded and adequate nutrition is usually available even without breast-feeding, crying may be less adaptive. In any case, caregiving in the United States may be viewed as a cultural experiment in which the infant is relatively more separated—and separable—from the mother, both in terms of frequency of contact and actual distance.

The Western strategy is advantageous when the mother's employment outside of the home and away from the baby is necessary to sustain family resources. But the trade-off seems to be an increase in the length of crying bouts.

tive skills to move about. Human infants are at the extreme: virtually helpless as newborns, they need twelve months just to learn to walk and years of social learning before they can function on their own.

Dependence during infancy is the price we pay for being hominids, members of the group of upright-walking primates that includes humans and their extinct relatives. Four million years ago, when our ancestors became bipedal, the hominid pelvis underwent a necessary renovation. At first, this new pelvic architecture presented no problem during birth because the early hominids, known as australopithecines, still had rather small brains, one-third the present size. But starting about 1.5 million years ago, human brain size ballooned. Hominid babies now had to twist and bend to pass through the birth canal, and more impor-

tant, birth had to be triggered before the skull grew too big.

As a result, the human infant is born neurologically unfinished and unable to coordinate muscle movement. Natural selection has compensated for this by favoring a close adult-infant tie that lasts years and goes beyond meeting the needs of food and shelter. In a sense, the human baby is not isolated but is part of a physiologically and emotionally entwined dyad of infant and caregiver. The adult might be male or female, a birth or adoptive parent, as long as at least one person is attuned to the infant's needs.

The signs of this interrelationship are many. Through conditioning, a mother's breast milk often begins to flow at the sound of her own infant's cries, even before the nipple is stimulated. New mothers also easily recognize the cries (and smells) of their infants over those of

other babies. For their part, newborns recognize their own mother's voice and prefer it over others. One experiment showed that a baby's heart rate quickly synchronizes with Mom's or Dad's, but not with that of a friendly stranger. Babies are also predisposed to be socially engaged with caregivers. From birth, infants move their bodies in synchrony with adult speech and the general nature of language. Babies quickly recognize the arrangement of a human face—two eyes, a nose, and a mouth in the right place—over other more Picasso-like rearrangements. And mothers and infants will position themselves face-to-face when they lie down to sleep.

Babies and mothers seem to follow a typical pattern of play, a coordinated waltz that moves from attention to inattention and back again. This innate social connection was tested experimentally by

When to Wean

By Katherine A. Dettwyler

Breast-feeding in humans is a biological process grounded in our mammalian ancestry. It is also an activity modified by social and cultural constraints, including a mother's everyday work schedule and a variety of beliefs about personal autonomy, the proper relationship between mother and child (or between mother and father), and infant health and nutrition. The same may be said of the termination of breast-feeding, or weaning.

In the United States, children are commonly bottle-fed from birth or weaned within a few months. But in some societies, children as old as four or five years may still be nursed. The American Academy of Pediatrics currently advises breast-feeding for a minimum of one year (this may be revised upward), and the World Health Organization recommends two years or more. Amid conflicting advice, many wonder how long breast-feeding should last to provide an infant with optimal nutrition and health.

Nonhuman primates and other mammals give us some clues as to what the "natural" age of weaning would be if humans were less bound by cultural norms. Compared with most other orders of placental mammals, primates (including humans) have longer life spans and spend more time at each life stage, such as gestation, infant dependency, and puberty. Within the primate order itself, the trend in longevity increases from smaller-bodied, smaller-brained, often solitary prosimians through the larger-bodied, larger-brained, and usually social apes and humans. Gestation, for instance, is eighteen weeks in lemurs, twenty-four weeks in macaques, thirty-three weeks in chimpanzees, and thirty-eight weeks in humans.

Studies of nonhuman primates offer a number of different means of estimating the natural time for human weaning. First, large-bodied primates wean their offspring some months after the young have quadrupled their birth weight. In modern humans, this weight milestone is passed at about two and a half to three years of age. Second, like many other mammals, primate offspring tend to be weaned when they have attained about one third of their adult weight; humans reach this level between four and seven years of age. Third, in all species studied so far, primates also wean their offspring at the time the first permanent molars erupt; this occurs at five and a half to six years in modern humans. Fourth, in chimpanzees and gorillas, breast-feeding usually lasts about six times the duration of gestation. On this basis, a human breast-feeding would be projected to continue for four and a half years.

Taken together, these and other projections suggest that somewhat more than two and a half years is the natural minimum age of weaning for humans and seven years the maximum age, well into childhood. The high end of this range, six to seven years, closely matches both the completion of human brain growth and the maturation of the child's immune system.

In many non-Western cultures, children are routinely nursed for three to five years. Incidentally, this practice inhibits ovulation in the mother, providing a natural mechanism of family planning. Even in the United States, a significant number of children are breast-fed beyond three years of age. While not all women are able or willing to nurse each of their children for many years, those who do should be encouraged and supported. Health care professionals, family, friends, and nosy neighbors should be reassured that "extended" breast-feeding, for as long as seven years, appears physiologically normal and natural.

Substantial evidence is already available to suggest that curtailing the duration of breast-feeding far below two and a half years—when the human child has evolved to expect more—can be deleterious. Every study that includes the duration of breast-feeding as a variable shows that, on average, the longer a baby is nursed, the better its health and cognitive development. For example, breast-fed children have fewer allergies, fewer ear infections, and less diarrhea, and their risk for sudden infant death syndrome (a rare but devastating occurrence) is lower. Breast-fed children also have higher cognitive test scores and lower incidence of attention deficit hyperactivity disorder.

In many cases, specific biochemical constituents of breast milk have been identified that either protect directly against disease or help the child's body develop its own defense system. For example, in the case of many viral diseases, the baby brings the virus to the mother, and her gut-wall cells manufacture specific antibodies against the virus, which then travel to the mammary glands and go back to the baby. The docosahesanoic acid in breast milk may be responsible for improved cognitive and attention functions. And the infant's exposure to the hormones and cholesterol in the milk appears to condition the body, reducing the risk of heart disease and breast cancer in later years. These and other discoveries show that breast-feeding serves functions for which no simple substitute is available.

Jeffrey Cohn and Edward Tronick in a series of three-minute laboratory experiments at the University of Massachu- setts, in which they asked mothers to act depressed and not respond to baby's cues. When faced with a suddenly unre- sponsive mother, a baby repeatedly reaches out and flaps around, trying to catch her eye. When this tactic does not

Bedtime Story

By James J. McKenna

For as far back as you care to go, mothers have followed the protective and convenient practice of sleeping with their infants. Even now, for the vast majority of people across the globe, "co-sleeping" and nighttime breast-feeding remain inseparable practices. Only in the past 200 years, and mostly in Western industrialized societies, have parents considered it normal and biologically appropriate for a mother and infant to sleep apart.

In the sleep laboratory at the University of California's Irvine School of Medicine, my colleagues and I observed mother-infant pairs as they slept both apart and together over three consecutive nights. Using a polygraph, we recorded the mother's and infant's heart rates, brain waves (EEGs), breathing, body temperature, and episodes of nursing. Infrared video photography simultaneously monitored their behavior.

We found that bed-sharing infants face their mothers for most of the night and that both mother and infants are highly responsive to each other's movements, wake more frequently, and spend more time in lighter stages of sleep than they do while sleeping alone. Bed-sharing infants nurse almost twice as often, and three times as long per bout, than they do when sleeping alone. But they rarely cry. Mothers who routinely sleep with their infants get at least as much sleep as mothers who sleep without them.

In addition to providing more nighttime nourishment and greater protection, sleeping with the mother supplies the infant with a steady stream of sensations of the mother's presence, including touch, smell, movement, and warmth. These stimuli can perhaps even compensate for the human infant's extreme neurological immaturity at birth.

Cosleeping might also turn out to give some babies protection from sudden infant death syndrome (SIDS), a heartbreaking and enigmatic killer. Cosleeping infants nurse more often, sleep more lightly, and have practice responding to maternal arousals. Arousal deficiencies are suspected in some SIDS deaths, and long periods in deep sleep may exacerbate this problem. Perhaps the physiological changes induced by cosleeping, especially when combined with nighttime breast-feeding, can benefit some infants by helping them sleep more lightly. At the same time, cosleeping makes it easier for a mother to detect and respond to an infant in crisis. Rethinking another sleeping practice has already shown a dramatic effect: In the United States, SIDS rates fell at least 30 percent after 1992, when the American Academy of Pediatrics recommended placing sleeping babies on their backs, rather than face down.

The effect of cosleeping on SIDS remains to be proved, so it would be premature to recommend it as the best arrangement for all families. The possible hazards of cosleeping must also be assessed. Is the environment otherwise safe, with appropriate bedding materials? Do the parents smoke? Do they use drugs or alcohol? (These appear to be the main factors in those rare cases in which a mother inadvertently smothers her child.) Since cosleeping was the ancestral condition, the future for our infants may well entail a borrowing back from ancient ways.

---

work, the baby gives up, turning away and going limp. And when the mother begins to respond again, it takes thirty seconds for the baby to reengage.

Given that human infants arrive in a state of dependency, ethnopediatricians have sought to define the care required to meet their physical, cognitive, and emotional needs. They assume there must be ways to treat babies that have proved adaptive over time and are therefore likely to be most appropriate. Surveys of parenting in different societies reveal broad patterns. In almost all cultures, infants sleep with their parents in the same room and most often in the same bed. At all other times, infants are usually carried. Caregivers also usually respond quickly to infant cries; mothers most often by offering the breast. Since most hunter-gatherer groups also follow this overall style, this is probably the ancestral pattern. If there is an exception to these generalizations, it is the industrialized West.

Nuances of caretaking, however, do vary with particular social situations. !Kung San mothers of Botswana usually carry their infants on gathering expeditions, while the forest-living Ache of Paraguay, also hunters and gatherers, usually leave infants in camp while they gather. Gusii mothers working in garden plots leave their babies in the care of older children, while working mothers in the West may turn to unrelated adults. Such choices have physiological or behavioral consequences for the infant. As parents navigate between infant needs and the constraints of making a life, they may face a series of trade-offs that set the caregiver-infant dyad at odds. The areas of greatest controversy are breast-feeding, crying, and sleep—the major preoccupations of babies and their parents.

Strapped to their mothers' sides or backs in traditional fashion, human infants have quick access to the breast. Easy access makes sense because of the nature of human milk. Compared with that of other mammals, primate milk is relatively low in fat and protein but high in carbohydrates. Such milk is biologically suitable if the infant can nurse on a frequent basis. Most Western babies are fed in a somewhat different way. At least half are bottle-fed from birth, while others are weaned from breast to bottle after only a few months. And most—whether nursed or bottle-fed—are fed at scheduled times, waiting hours between feedings. Long intervals in nursing disrupt the manufacture of breast milk, making it still lower in fat and thus less satisfying the next time the nipple is offered. And so crying over food and even the struggles of weaning result from the infant's unfulfilled expectations.

Sleep is also a major issue for new parents. In the West, babies are encouraged to sleep all through the night as soon as possible. And when infants do not do so, they merit the label "sleep problem" from both parents and pediatricians. But infants seem predisposed to sleep rather lightly, waking many times during the night. And while sleeping close to an adult allows infants to nurse more often and may have other beneficial effects, Westerners usually expect babies to sleep alone. This practice has roots in ecclesiastical laws enacted to protect against the smothering of infants by "lying over"—often a thinly disguised cover for infanticide—which was a concern in Europe beginning in the Middle Ages. Solitary sleep is reinforced by the rather recent notion of parental privacy. Western parents are also often convinced that solitary sleep will mold strong character.

Infants' care is shaped by tradition, fads, science, and folk wisdom. Cross-cultural and evolutionary studies provide a useful perspective for parents and pediatricians as they sift through the alternatives. Where these insights fail to guide us, however, important clues are provided by the floppy but interactive babies themselves. Grinning when we talk to them, crying in distress when left alone, sleeping best when close at heart, they teach us that growth is a cooperative venture.

RECOMMENDED READING

Parents' Cultural Belief Systems: Their Origins, Expressions, and Consequences, by Sara Harkness and Charles M. Super (Guilford Press, 1996)
Child Care and Culture: Lessons from Africa, by Robert A. LeVine et al. (Cambridge University Press, 1994)
Our Babies, Ourselves, by Meredith F. Small (Anchor Books/Doubleday, 1998)
Breastfeeding: Biocultural Perspectives, edited by Patricia Stuart-Macadam and Katherine A. Dettwyler (Aldine de Gruyler, 1995)
The Family Bed: An Age Old Concept in Childrearing, by Tine Thevenin (Avery Publishing Group, 1987)
Human Birth: An Evolutionary Perspective, by Wenda R. Trevathan (Aldine de Gruyter, 1987)
Six Cultures: Studies of Child Rearing, edited by Beatrice B. Whiting (John Wiley, 1963)

A professor of anthropology at Cornell University, **Meredith F. Small** became interested in "ethnopediatrics" in 1995, after interviewing anthropologist James J. McKenna on the subject of infant sleep. Trained as a primate behaviorist, Small has observed female mating behavior in three species of macaque monkeys. She now writes about science for a general audience; her book *Our Babies, Ourselves* is published by Anchor Books/Doubleday (1998). Her previous contributions to *Natural History* include "These Animals Think, Therefore…" (August 1996) and "Read in the Bone" (June 1997).

Parallel Brides

For some families in Turkey, matchmaking is an intricate dance.

Story by Mustafa Türker Ersen

It is a bright Sunday in the tiny Arab village of Lower Arbit in southeastern Turkey. Cheerful melodies issue from a cassette player powered by a tractor battery. I watch as Nuri and Türkân, brother and sister, join the snaking line of the *halay* dance in front of their house, over which flies a Turkish flag. Meanwhile, a few miles away, in the village of Mengalan, a similar scene must be unfolding for Mehmet and Feride, who are also brother and sister. All four are to be wed today: Nuri to Feride, and Mehmet to Türkân.

Such a double wedding is known as a *berdel*, which in Kurdish means "in place of the one." Instead of paying the required bride-price to another family so that his son may have a bride, a father arranges to offer a bride from his own family in compensation. In Nuri's and Mehmet's cases, both fathers have a daughter of their own to offer, but if they didn't, they might have drawn upon a niece or other eligible female in the extended family. Whatever the arrangement, the actual exchange of brides is the most critical part of the process—as tricky as dropping off a ransom payment in return for a kidnap victim.

Around noontime, two dust clouds appear on the horizon, both heading toward the designated rendezvous point midway between the two villages. The cars carrying the brides are approaching. Timing, as well as having an equal number of attendees, is crucial; the possibility that some slipup will cause one of the parties to cancel the deal inevitably creates a stressful atmosphere. There is only one way to overcome the tension—to be

quick. The vehicles park side by side, the brides are hastily exchanged, and the cars head home to the waiting grooms. In both villages the women shout and pray when the bride arrives at her new home; that same day, an imam joins the couple in matrimony.

On maps of Turkey, the zone where Lower Arbit is located appears empty of inhabitants; it is a "government productivity farm," off-limits to settlement. Nevertheless, a few tiny villages cling to the rocky terrain. Electricity, schools, and other facilities are lacking, and the village residents, forbidden to grow crops on government property, must depend for their livelihood on herding sheep and other livestock. In this setting, where raising enough money for a bride-price can be difficult, a *berdel* can have practical advantages. But it is much more than an economic convenience. According to Serpil Altuntek, an anthropologist at Hacettepe University in Ankara, "*Berdel*, cousin marriage, and similar arrangements are better viewed as part of a family's strategy to forge and maintain favorable political and economic alliances." The choice of spouse also contributes to the solidarity of the encompassing kin groups—lineage, clan, and tribe—which are the backbone of social life.

Berdel marriage is found primarily among Kurdish, Arabic, and Turkic peoples in what is now southern and southeastern Turkey. Altuntek points out that before the establishment of the Turkish republic in 1923, when new borders were drawn with Syria, Iraq, and other neighboring countries, these groups led a pas-

toral life that involved nomadic movements and social ties over a much wider region. Under the new national arrangements, most of the people who remained within Turkey's borders were obliged to take up a sedentary way of life, and many of their ties with distant allies were weakened or severed. "Nowadays," says Altuntek, "*berdel* and other close-kin marriages function as a means to re-create strong group ties." (Haci Halef Varli, a villager in Lower Arbit, tells me about his experience in the 1960s: It had been arranged for him to marry his mother's brother's daughter, who had emigrated to Syria. "We smuggled the brides over the border, to the east of Ceylanpinar," he recalls.)

The tradition of *berdel* crosses not only ethnic lines but also the urban-rural divide. When Ahmet Börek got married recently in the city of Sanliurfa, sixty miles west of Lower Arbit, his sister married his wife's brother. "Through a *berdel* deal," I ask, "you had to marry a girl you only saw once before the wedding. Are you happy?" The twenty-three-year-old groom doesn't hesitate for a moment: "Yes," he answers. "I saw her. I liked her. In the old days, you did not even have the chance to see her." Ahmet also observes that he had no realistic opportunity "to meet someone in a pastry shop," and adds, "If I had not accepted, my father would not have forced me to."

A go-between helped Ahmet Börek's family arrange the deal with a family from another clan, but this is not typical in *berdel* exchanges. Usually marriages are arranged within a clan, and the right to ask for a young woman as a bride traditionally goes first to the son of a brother of her father and then to the sons of other close relatives. Thus, the families are relieved of the burden of choosing. Pairings are sometimes made in childhood, so everybody knows who will be marrying whom. In any case, the elders have the final word.

From the point of view of the two couples, however, the social arrangement can entail its own special pain. In theory and sometimes in practice, if one of the exchanged brides is divorced and sent back to her family, the other marriage will be undone. This possibility may act as a deterrent to divorce, especially as time goes by and children are born. Nevertheless, I hear stories of returned brides who subsequently wed other men but who still keep their ex-husbands' prayer beads as souvenirs, despite fearing the wrath of their new husbands should they be found out.

"Is it fair," I ask Ahmet, "to force a happy couple to break up their marriage because of an unhappy one?" But this is not uppermost in his mind. No matter how much he loves his wife, he tells me, he wouldn't think of letting a sister suffer in an alien home. "The brother is his sister's shadow," he says. "If not, who else does the sister have to depend upon?"

Still, there is a traditional way to keep the happy bride at home. The bridegroom may be willing to pay a bride-price to the bride's family in order to retain the right to keep her. (Even so, his own family may question this solution: "Those people did not want your sister," they might say, "so why should we keep their girl in our family?")

Most arrangements for bride-price or *berdel* bride exchange do not involve official contracts, and, particularly in rural areas, marriages may not be officially registered with the civil authorities. Under these circumstances, divorces and divorce settlements are usually a private matter. But if a dispute erupts into violence or a man is accused of harboring an underage bride (men and women may not legally marry before the age of eighteen), a case may wind up in court.

Aslan Veyseloglu, a lawyer from Viransehir, a small city north of Lower Arbit, gives me an example: A young couple eloped to get married. As a compensation for the loss, the young woman's family claimed a bride from the young man's family. Eventually, however, disagreements arose between the two families, and both brides were sent back. The case was taken to court. Finally, through the lawyers' assistance, the families reconciled and the brides were returned to their husbands.

The custom of *berdel* still seems secure in a vast region of Turkey. But this land—incessantly fought over in the past by Arabs, Safavids, Christian crusaders, people of all nations—is poised for change. Dams have had a positive impact on agriculture, industry, and trade. Labor is being redefined through the diversification of crops and the creation of more stable jobs. This economic awakening, in conjunction with new means of communication, is affecting education and values. Thousands of migrants from rural areas are now trying to create new lives in Sanliurfa, which is becoming increasingly cosmopolitan. Still, even in Sanliurfa, bride-price payments are not a thing of the past. Indeed, they start at nearly $2,000 and soar to $7,000 or more.

A pink flag flies over a house in one of Sanliurfa's new districts, signaling that a wedding is taking place. The house belongs to sixty-year-old Kadir Yön, whose son Ahmet and daughter Veze will be part of a *berdel* marriage. Kadir, one of two chiefs of the Abuhamdan clan, sold his ancestral land about a decade ago and moved to the city. I wonder why he frets so much, why his eyes are misty. Is this simply a father's excitement, or could Kadir be feeling that the city wedding will lack the joy of a rural one? No black tents for feasts, no galloping horses in clouds of dust—not any longer.

The beat of the *dabla* drum may sound weaker in the urban setting, yet the celebration still has its special aura. Women dressed in festive outfits of velvet and silk, men in their everyday clothes and head scarves, and hundreds of children float through the streets from one wedding house to the other. In the house of the Ögüs family, with whom the *berdel* exchange is taking place, the noisy celebrants crowd into the courtyard. Both parties are close to the climax; the trousseau was sent long before, and the "henna night"—the women's evening of entertainment before the day of the wedding, when the bride has her fingers and toes freshly tinged with henna—has been celebrated already.

In the street where the Yön family lives, a long chain of men and women move to the rhythm of the *halay* dance. The dancers' faces do not reflect great joy; they look as if they are only doing their duty. Suddenly the double-reed *zurna* and the *dabla* drum stop playing, and a wave of excitement surges through the crowd. Veze, Kadir Yön's daughter, comes out of the house and steps into the waiting car. An older brother will take her to the appointed place of exchange, where her brother Ahmet's bride, Dürsün, will be waiting.

We reach the site of the rendezvous, but there is no sign of Dürsün's car. Nobody looks worried about the delay, however, because the brides' families are close relatives. Then a convoy of several pink-flagged cars nears us, horns sounding. All of a sudden, the mood changes. The brother accompanying Veze shouts, "Back to the car! I am not giving the bride!" He is angry because it was agreed that each party would come in only one car, but here they are with a convoy! As the menfolk beg Veze's brother to keep calm, the convoy of cars passes us by, ignoring us. In a moment, everything is clear: the convoy belongs to another wedding. Soon we hear celebratory gunshots in the next neighborhood.

At last, Dürsün arrives. The two brides get out of their cars at precisely the same moment, and the exchange is made. Finally, everybody can take a deep breath and relax. And now comes the shooting of guns in the air for celebration, with a few shell cases spurting out toward me. I pick one up to keep as a souvenir.

Arranging a Marriage in India

Serena Nanda

John Jay College of Criminal Justice

Sister and doctor brother-in-law invite correspondence from North Indian professionals only, for a beautiful, talented, sophisticated, intelligent sister, 5'3", slim, M.A. in textile design, father a senior civil officer. Would prefer immigrant doctors, between 26–29 years. Reply with full details and returnable photo. A well-settled uncle invites matrimonial correspondence from slim, fair, educated South Indian girl, for his nephew, 25 years, smart, M.B.A., green card holder, 5'6". Full particulars with returnable photo appreciated.

Matrimonial Advertisements,
India Abroad

IN INDIA, ALMOST ALL MARRIAGES ARE arranged. Even among the educated middle classes in modern, urban India, marriage is as much a concern of the families as it is of the individuals. So customary is the practice of arranged marriage that there is a special name for a marriage which is not arranged: It is called a "love match."

On my first field trip to India, I met many young men and women whose parents were in the process of "getting them married." In many cases, the bride and groom would not meet each other before the marriage. At most they might meet for a brief conversation, and this meeting would take place only after their parents had decided that the match was suitable. Parents do not compel their children to marry a person who either marriage partner finds objectionable. But only after one match is refused will another be sought.

As a young American woman in India for the first time, I found this custom of arranged marriage oppressive. How could any intelligent young person agree to such a marriage without great reluctance? It was contrary to everything I believed about the importance of romantic love as the only basis of a happy marriage. It also clashed with my strongly held notions that the choice of such an intimate and permanent relationship could be made only by the individuals involved. Had anyone tried to arrange my marriage, I would have been defiant and rebellious!

> *Young men and women do not date and have very little social life involving members of the opposite sex.*

At the first opportunity, I began, with more curiosity than tact, to question the young people I met on how they felt about this practice. Sita, one of my young informants, was a college graduate with a degree in political science. She had been waiting for over a year while her parents were arranging a match for her. I found it difficult to accept the docile manner in which this well-educated young woman awaited the outcome of a process that would result in her spending the rest of her life with a man she hardly knew, a virtual stranger, picked out by her parents.

"How can you go along with this?" I asked her, in frustration and distress. "Don't you care who you marry?"

"Of course I care," she answered." This is why I must let my parents choose a boy for me. My marriage is too important to be arranged by such an inexperienced person as myself. In such matters, it is better to have my parents' guidance."

I had learned that young men and women in India do not date and have very little social life involving members of the opposite sex. Although I could not disagree with Sita's reasoning, I continued to pursue the subject.

"But how can you marry the first man you have ever met? Not only have you missed the fun of meeting a lot of different people, but you have not given yourself the chance to know who is the right man for you."

"Meeting with a lot of different people doesn't sound like any fun at all," Sita answered. "One hears that in America the girls are spending all their time worrying about whether they will meet a man and get married. Here we have the chance to enjoy our life and let our parents do this work and worrying for us."

She had me there. The high anxiety of the competition to "be popular" with the opposite sex certainly was the most prominent feature of life as an American teenager in the late fifties. The endless worrying about the rules that governed our behavior and about our popularity ratings sapped both our self-esteem and our enjoyment of adolescence. I reflected that absence of this competition in India most certainly may have contributed to the self-confidence and natural charm of so many of the young women I met.

And yet, the idea of marrying a perfect stranger, whom one did not know and did not "love," so offended my American ideas of individualism and romanticism, that I persisted with my objections.

"I still can't imagine it," I said. "How can you agree to marry a man you hardly know?"

"But of course he will be known. My parents would never arrange a marriage for me without knowing all about the boy's family background. Naturally we will not rely only on what the family tells us. We will check the particulars out ourselves. No one will want their daughter to marry into a family that is not good. All these things we will know beforehand."

Impatiently, I responded, "Sita, I don't mean know the family, I mean, know the man. How can you marry someone you don't know personally and don't love? How can you think of spending your life with someone you may not even like?"

"If he is a good man, why should I not like him?" she said. "With you people, you know the boy so well before you marry, where will be the fun to get married? There will be no mystery and no romance. Here we have the whole of our married life to get to know and love our husband. "This way is better, is it not?"

Her response made further sense, and I began to have second thoughts on the matter. Indeed, during months of meeting many intelligent young Indian people, both male and female, who had the same ideas as Sita, I saw arranged marriages in a different light. I also saw the importance of the family in Indian life and realized that a couple who took their marriage into their own hands was taking a big risk, particularly if their families were irreconcilably opposed to the match. In a country where every important resource in life—a job, a house, a social circle—is gained through family connections, it seemed foolhardy to cut oneself off from a supportive social network and depend solely on one person for happiness and success.

Six years later I returned to India to again do fieldwork, this time among the middle class in Bombay, a modern, sophisticated city. From the experience of my earlier visit, I decided to include a study of arranged marriages in my

project. By this time I had met many Indian couples whose marriages had been arranged and who seemed very happy. Particularly in contrast to the fate of many of my married friends in the United States who were already in the process of divorce, the positive aspects of arranged marriages appeared to me to outweigh the negatives. In fact, I thought I might even participate in arranging a marriage myself. I had been fairly successful in the United States in "fixing up" many of my friends, and I was confident that my matchmaking skills could be easily applied to this new situation, once I learned the basic rules. "After all," I thought, "how complicated can it be? People want pretty much the same things in a marriage whether it is in India or America."

In a society where divorce is still a scandal and where, in fact, the divorce rate is exceedingly low, an arranged marriage is the beginning of a lifetime relationship not just between the bride and groom but between their families as well.

An opportunity presented itself almost immediately. A friend from my previous Indian trip was in the process of arranging for the marriage of her eldest son. In India there is a perceived shortage of "good boys," and since my friend's family was eminently respectable and the boy himself personable, well educated, and nice looking, I was sure that by the end of my year's fieldwork, we would have found a match.

The basic rule seems to be that a family's reputation is most important. It is understood that matches would be arranged only within the same caste and general social class, although some crossing of subcastes is permissible if the class positions of the bride's and groom's families are similar. Although dowry is now prohibited by law in India, extensive gift exchanges took place with

every marriage. Even when the boy's family do not "make demands," every girl's family nevertheless feels the obligation to give the traditional gifts, to the girl, to the boy, and to the boy's family. Particularly when the couple would be living in the joint family—that is, with the boy's parents and his married brothers and their families, as well as with unmarried siblings—which is still very common even among the urban, upper-middle class in India, the girls' parents are anxious to establish smooth relations between their family and that of the boy. Offering the proper gifts, even when not called "dowry," is often an important factor in influencing the relationship between the bride's and groom's families and perhaps, also, the treatment of the bride in her new home.

In a society where divorce is still a scandal and where, in fact, the divorce rate is exceedingly low, an arranged marriage is the beginning of a lifetime relationship not just between the bride and groom but between their families as well. Thus, while a girl's looks are important, her character is even more so, for she is being judged as a prospective daughter-in-law as much as a prospective bride. Where she would be living in a joint family, as was the case with my friend, the girls's ability to get along harmoniously in a family is perhaps the single most important quality in assessing her suitability.

My friend is a highly esteemed wife, mother, and daughter-in-law. She is religious, soft-spoken, modest, and deferential. She rarely gossips and never quarrels, two qualities highly desirable in a woman. A family that has the reputation for gossip and conflict among its womenfolk will not find it easy to get good wives for their sons. Parents will not want to send their daughter to a house in which there is conflict.

My friend's family were originally from North India. They had lived in Bombay, where her husband owned a business, for forty years. The family had delayed in seeking a match for their eldest son because he had been an Air Force pilot for several years, stationed in such remote places that it had seemed fruitless to try to find a girl who would be willing to accompany him. In their social

Even today, almost all marriages in India are arranged. It is believed that parents are much more effective at deciding whom their daughters should marry.

class, a military career, despite its economic security, has little prestige and is considered a drawback in finding a suitable bride. Many families would not allow their daughters to marry a man in an occupation so potentially dangerous and which requires so much moving around.

The son had recently left the military and joined his father's business. Since he was a college graduate, modern, and well traveled, from such a good family, and, I thought, quite handsome, it seemed to me that he, or rather his family, was in a position to pick and choose. I said as much to my friend.

While she agreed that there were many advantages on their side, she also said, "We must keep in mind that my son is both short and dark; these are drawbacks in finding the right match." While the boy's height had not escaped my notice, "dark" seemed to me inaccurate; I would have called him "wheat" colored perhaps, and in any case, I did not realize that color would be a consideration. I discovered, however, that while a boy's

skin color is a less important consideration than a girl's, it is still a factor.

An important source of contacts in trying to arrange her son's marriage was my friend's social club in Bombay. Many of the women had daughters of the right age, and some had already expressed an interest in my friend's son. I was most enthusiastic about the possibilities of one particular family who had five daughters, all of whom were pretty, demure, and well educated. Their mother had told my friend, "You can have your pick for your son, whichever one of my daughters appeals to you most."

I saw a match in sight. "Surely," I said to my friend, "we will find one there. Let's go visit and make our choice." But my friend held back; she did not seem to share my enthusiasm, for reasons I could not then fathom.

When I kept pressing for an explanation of her reluctance, she admitted, "See, Serena, here is the problem. The family has so many daughters, how will they be able to provide nicely for any of them? We are not making any demands,

but still, with so many daughters to marry off, one wonders whether she will even be able to make a proper wedding. Since this is our eldest son, it's best if we marry him to a girl who is the only daughter, then the wedding will truly be a gala affair." I argued that surely the quality of the girls themselves made up for any deficiency in the elaborateness of the wedding. My friend admitted this point but still seemed reluctant to proceed.

"Is there something else," I asked her, "some factor I have missed?" "Well," she finally said, "there is one other thing. They have one daughter already married and living in Bombay. The mother is always complaining to me that the girl's in-laws don't let her visit her own family often enough. So it makes me wonder, will she be that kind of mother who always wants her daughter at her own home? This will prevent the girl from adjusting to our house. It is not a good thing." And so, this family of five daughters was dropped as a possibility.

Somewhat disappointed, I nevertheless respected my friend's reasoning and geared up for the next prospect. This was also the daughter of a woman in my friend's social club. There was clear interest in this family and I could see why. The family's reputation was excellent; in fact, they came from a subcaste slightly higher than my friend's own. The girl, who was an only daughter, was pretty and well educated and had a brother studying in the United States. Yet, after expressing an interest to me in this family, all talk of them suddenly died down and the search began elsewhere.

"What happened to that girl as a prospect?" I asked one day. "You never mention her any more. She is so pretty and so educated, what did you find wrong?"

"She is too educated. We've decided against it. My husband's father saw the girl on the bus the other day and thought her forward. A girl who 'roams about' the city by herself is not the girl for our family." My disappointment this time was even greater, as I thought the son would have liked the girl very much. But then I thought, my friend is right, a girl who is going to live in a joint family cannot be too independent or she will make life miserable for everyone. I also learned that if the family of the girl has even a slightly higher social status than the family of the boy, the bride may think herself too good for them, and this too will cause problems. Later my friend admitted to me that this had been an important factor in her decision not to pursue the match.

The next candidate was the daughter of a client of my friend's husband. When the client learned that the family was looking for a match for their son, he said, "Look no further, we have a daughter." This man then invited my friends to dinner to see the girl. He had already seen their son at the office and decided that "he liked the boy." We all went together for tea, rather than dinner—it was less of a commitment—and while we were there, the girl's mother showed us around the house. The girl was studying for her exams and was briefly introduced to us.

After we left, I was anxious to hear my friend's opinion. While her husband liked the family very much and was impressed with his client's business accomplishments and reputation, the wife didn't like the girl's looks. "She is short, no doubt, which is an important plus point, but she is also fat and wears glasses." My friend obviously thought she could do better for her son and asked her husband to make his excuses to his client by saying that they had decided to postpone the boy's marriage indefinitely.

> *"If a mistake is made we have not only ruined the life of our son or daughter, but we have spoiled the reputation of our family as well."*

By this time almost six months had passed and I was becoming impatient. What I had thought would be an easy matter to arrange was turning out to be quite complicated. I began to believe that between my friend's desire for a girl who was modest enough to fit into her joint family, yet attractive and educated enough to be an acceptable partner for her son, she would not find anyone suitable. My friend laughed at my impatience: "Don't be so much in a hurry," she said. "You Americans want everything done so quickly. You get married quickly and then just as quickly get divorced. Here we take marriage more seriously. We must take all the factors into account. It is not enough for us to learn by our mistakes. This is too serious a business. If a mistake is made we have not only ruined the life of our son or daughter, but we have spoiled the reputation of our family as well. And that will make it much harder for their brothers and sisters to get married. So we must be very careful."

What she said was true and I promised myself to be more patient, though it was not easy. I had really hoped and expected that the match would be made before my year in India was up. But it was not to be. When I left India my friend seemed no further along in finding a suitable match for her son than when I had arrived.

Two years later, I returned to India and still my friend had not found a girl for her son. By this time, he was close to thirty, and I think she was a little worried. Since she knew I had friends all over India, and I was going to be there for a year, she asked me to "help her in this work" and keep an eye out for someone suitable. I was flattered that my judgment was respected, but knowing now how complicated the process was, I had lost my earlier confidence as a matchmaker. Nevertheless, I promised that I would try.

It was almost at the end of my year's stay in India that I met a family with a marriageable daughter whom I felt might be a good possibility for my friend's son. The girl's father was related to a good friend of mine and by coincidence came from the same village as my friend's husband. This new family had a successful business in a medium-sized city in central India and were from the same subcaste as my friend. The daughter was pretty and chic; in fact, she had studied fashion design in college. Her parents would not allow her to go off by herself to any of the major cities in India where she could make a career, but they had compromised with her wish to work by allowing her to run a small dress-making boutique from their home. In spite of her desire to have a career, the daughter was both modest and home-loving and had had a traditional, sheltered upbringing. She had only one other sister, already married, and a brother who was in his father's business.

I mentioned the possibility of a match with my friend's son. The girl's parents were most interested. Although their daughter was not eager to marry just yet, the idea of living in Bombay—a sophisticated, extremely fashion-conscious city where she could continue her education in clothing design—was a great inducement. I gave the girl's father my friend's address and suggested that when they went to Bombay on some business or whatever, they look up the boy's family.

Returning to Bombay on my way to New York, I told my friend of this newly discovered possibility. She seemed to feel there was potential but, in spite of my urging, would not make any moves

Appendix

Further Reflections on Arranged Marriage...

This essay was written from the point of view of a family seeking a daughter-in-law. Arranged marriage looks somewhat different from the point of view of the bride and her family. Arranged marriage continues to be preferred, even among the more educated, Westernized sections of the Indian population. Many young women from these families still go along, more or less willingly, with the practice, and also with the specific choices of their families. Young women do get excited about the prospects of their marriage, but there is also ambivalence and increasing uncertainty, as the bride contemplates leaving the comfort and familiarity of her own home, where as a "temporary guest" she had often been indulged, to live among strangers. Even in the best situation she will now come under the close scrutiny of her husband's family. How she dresses, how she behaves, how she gets along with others, where she goes, how she spends her time, her domestic abilities—all of this and much more—will be observed and commented on by a whole new set of relations. Her interaction with her family of birth will be monitored and curtailed

considerably. Not only will she leave their home, but with increasing geographic mobility, she may also live very far from them, perhaps even on another continent. Too much expression of her fondness for her own family, or her desire to visit them, may be interpreted as an inability to adjust to her new family, and may become a source of conflict. In an arranged marriage the burden of adjustment is clearly heavier for a woman than for a man. And that is in the best of situations.

In less happy circumstances, the bride may be a target of resentment and hostility from her husband's family, particularly her mother-in-law or her husband's unmarried sisters, for whom she is now a source of competition for the affection, loyalty, and economic resources of their son or brother. If she is psychologically, or even physically abused, her options are limited, as returning to her parents' home, or divorce, are still very stigmatized. For most Indians, marriage and motherhood are still considered the only suitable roles for a woman, even for those who have careers, and few women can comfortably contemplate remaining

unmarried. Most families still consider "marrying off" their daughters as a compelling religious duty and social necessity. This increases a bride's sense of obligation to make the marriage a success, at whatever cost to her own personal happiness.

The vulnerability of a new bride may also be intensified by the issue of dowry, which although illegal, has become a more pressing issue in the consumer conscious society of contemporary urban India. In many cases, where a groom's family is not satisfied with the amount of dowry a bride brings to her marriage, the young bride will be constantly harassed to get her parents to give more. In extreme cases, the bride may even be murdered, and the murder disguised as an accident or suicide. This also offers the husband's family an opportunity to arrange another match for him, thus bringing in another dowry. This phenomena, called dowry death, calls attention not just to the "evils of dowry" but also to larger issues of the powerlessness of women as well.

Serena Nanda
March 1998

herself. She rather preferred to wait for the girl's family to call upon them. I hoped something would come of this introduction, though by now I had learned to rein in my optimism.

A year later I received a letter from my friend. The family had indeed come to visit Bombay, and their daughter and

my friend's daughter, who were near in age, had become very good friends. During that year, the two girls had frequently visited each other. I thought things looked promising.

Last week I received an invitation to a wedding: My friend's son and the girl were getting married. Since I had found

the match, my presence was particularly requested at the wedding. I was thrilled. Success at last! As I prepared to leave for India, I began thinking, "Now, my friend's younger son, who do I know who has a nice girl for him...?"

From *Stumbling Toward Truth: Anthropologists at Work,* edited by Philip R. Devita, 2000, pp. 196–204. Published by Waveland Press. © 2000 by Serena Nanda. Reprinted by permission.

Dowry Deaths In India

'Let only your corpse come out of that house'

Paul Mandelbaum

On the outskirts of Delhi, in the shadow of the famed Qutab Minar tower, lies the village of Saidulajab. Through its narrow rutted dirt alleyways, a local resident takes me to the home of his one-time neighbor, Manju Singh. It is there that he heard her cries of agony on July 10, 1996.

Enacting an elaborate pantomime, Manju's neighbor indicates, by pointing to the browned leaves of a backyard plant, the spot where he found her and from which he took her, in the back of his bicycle rickshaw, to a local clinic.

The next day, lying in South Delhi's Safdarjung Hospital with burns covering nearly her entire body, the twenty-seven-year-old regained consciousness long enough to tell a local police officer that her husband and in-laws had threatened to beat her the previous afternoon, haranguing her yet again over the inadequacy of her dowry. As she tried to escape—so alleges the police report—her husband and brother-in-law caught hold of her while her mother-in-law doused her with kerosene; then Manju's husband struck the match that would eventually kill her.

Manju's case is one of an alleged six thousand "dowry deaths" a year in India. The term typically refers to a newly-wed bride who, upon moving into her husband's family home, is harassed over the goods and cash she brought to the marriage, leading to her murder or suicide. Antidowry activists claim the actual death toll is much higher, and the British journal *Orbit* recently put the annual figure at fifteen thousand.

Twenty years ago, India's feminist leadership began sounding the alarm. Responding to a groundswell of pressure from women's groups and the media, in the mid-1980s India's Parliament passed sweeping amendments to the largely moribund Dowry Prohibition Act of 1961, as well as the Indian Evidence Act and the penal code. The new laws acknowledged a quasi-manslaughter crime called "dowry death," and placed the burden of proof on the accused in any situation where a bride dies unnaturally during the first seven years of marriage, if a history of dowry harassment can be shown. In the ensuing years, the violence seems only to have escalated.

As late as 1987, high concentrations of dowry-death cases were mostly confined to the corridor connecting Punjab, traditionally a very patriarchal and violent part of northwest India, to Delhi and, further east, Uttar Pradesh. But by the mid-1990s, significant per-capita concentrations of dowry death had infested half of India's thirty-two states and union territories.

Often the conflicts are not so much about material goods *per se* as about the family status such items represent. Sometimes, dowry conflicts may mask other underlying problems—infidelity, sexual incompatibility, for example—that are unthinkably intimate for many families to acknowledge and discuss.

In most cases of dowry death, the physical evidence is murky. Often a bride's death is staged to look like an accident—hence the popularity of burning.

Fire can obscure a variety of incriminating details, and the cheap kerosene stoves to which many Indian wives are virtually chained often do explode, providing offenders with a plausible scenario.

In the days before kerosene stoves, writes historian Veena Talwar Oldenburg, Indian brides fell down wells with suspicious regularity. Oldenburg has traced some of the roots of India's dowry problems to the British Raj and the economic pressures imposed by its agricultural tax system, which in turn pitted Indian farmers against one another. The parents of sons, according to Oldenburg, capitalized on the urgency felt by the parents of daughters to arrange a marriage by an acceptably early age. This urgency fueled a climate of extortion. Other cultural observers speculate that such a climate may have arrived earlier, when Hindu parents felt anxiety about protecting their daughters' honor from Muslim invaders.

In any case, modern-day dowry came to corrupt two ancient Hindu customs associated with arranged marriage. The first, *kanyadan*, called for enhancing the virgin bride with an array of jewels. The second, *stridhan*, provided the bride with a premortem inheritance from her parents. These two concepts merged and have mutated into a type of groom-price, now practiced not only by Hindus but also by some of their Muslim neighbors. Even some tribal groups who until recently preferred the inverse custom of bride-price have switched.

Today, Indian brides and their families feel compelled to buy their way into a marriage alliance with "gifts" of cash, jewels, and consumer goods for the in-laws' pleasure. This "marriage settlement" is often calculated in direct relationship to a groom's prospects. Grooms working for the elite Indian Administrative Service can sometimes command dowries equivalent to $100,000 or more. Indian grooms living in the United States seek compensation not only for their own self-perceived worth but for providing access to the American dream. In many cases, dowry is seen by both parties as an acknowledgment of the groom's desirability.

Manju Singh's parents felt obliged to present a significant endowment, even though she held a bachelor's degree from Delhi University while her fiancé was a village shopkeeper. Her father, Nawab Singh, has a thirty-one-item list of the bounty he gave, including 70,000 rupees (close to one year's salary), a scooter, a color TV, 224 grams of gold jewelry, 2 kilograms of silver, bedroom furnishings, and thirty-five suits of clothes for the groom's side. Several months after the wedding, he says, Manju's in-laws demanded a washing machine, a refrigerator, and 50,000 rupees. "So many things," the school teacher recalls for me harriedly over his lunch break. "I tried to give as much as I could." Nonetheless, he alleges, Manju's in-laws began to harass and beat her in a spiral of domestic violence leading to her death. "She was burned by them purposely for dowry," says Nawab Singh.

Even if the last quarter of the twentieth century did not create dowry death, several intersecting social and economic trends seem to have escalated the problem. For one, availability of a host of household appliances, as well as their increasing promotion on television have created a hunger among the lower-middle class and others who lack the purchasing power to afford what they are being encouraged to desire. The families of grooms have seized an opportunity, through negotiation of the customary premarital settlements, to acquire some of these items through dowry, leaving it to the bride's family to worry about the bills. At the same time, some brides' families have been doing quite well, so

well that they might wish to hide surpluses of hard currency from the tax authorities. They have seen dowry as a means to invest that money under the table and to secure their daughters a place in higher-status families. Ultimately, these two forms of dowry inflation have increased the likelihood that more and more brides' families will have a harder time fulfilling the terms of the marriage settlements they feel obliged to enter into, setting the stage for dire consequences.

The transience of the modern world has also put other pressures on arranged marriage. In the small southern town of Bangarapet, a village elder recalls for me the dowry negotiation he mediated on behalf of a local family. The prospective groom's father, visiting from New York, objected strenuously to the offer of three *lakhs*, or roughly $8,500, on the following grounds: "What do you think of me? What do you know about my status? I know the president of America. I know the president of India. What will be the state of my prestige if I collect three *lakhs* from you?"

While most Indian marriages are still made by parents as a way of ensuring a suitable match within an appropriate range of subcastes, as more Indians move from the countryside to teeming cities or abroad in pursuit of opportunity, chances have grown that a bride would marry into a family geographically removed from and previously unknown to her own parents.

Increasingly, today's marriage alliances are made blindly through brokers, classified ads, and Internet services. When it was time to marry off his twenty-nine-year-old daughter Sangeeta, who had completed her Ph.D. in solid-state physics, Bimal Agarwal of Kanpur started replying to ads in the *Sunday Times of India*. Turning to the June 27, 1993, classified section, he found one looking for a "beautiful educated match" for a "Kanpur-based handsome boy 29/173/5000 employed leading industrial house only son of senior business executive with own residence...."

Agarwal telephoned the father of this twenty-nine-year-old businessman earning 5,000 rupees per month, and over the next four days the families met several

times to negotiate marriage expenditures. On July 1, Sangeeta was engaged.

As her father and I converse on his apartment balcony, I am distracted by the anachronism of a laser eye-surgery center located across a narrow dirt street crowded with sleeping pigs. A passing woman carries atop her head the dried cow chips commonly used for cooking fires. When I get around to asking Mr. Agarwal if his daughter's engagement was decided hastily, he assures me it was quite typical.

Problems, however, began at the wedding itself, when, alleges Agarwal, the groom's family demanded a car. He adds that the ensuing pressure became a nightmare for Sangeeta. One day, roughly five months after her wedding, she and her father met for lunch. "She was weeping," he recalls. "She said, 'Father, go and talk to those people.'" But he had recently tried that, he says, and was reluctant to intervene again so soon.

Two days later, Sangeeta was found dead from "asphyxiation as a result of hanging," according to a postmortem report.

Her husband, Sanjay Goel, points out for me the ceiling fan in his family's middle-class living room. He maintains that Sangeeta committed suicide not because of any dowry demands but possibly because she had no desire to marry him in the first place.

Sangeeta's father, however, alleges that not only did dowry play a role in her death, but that she was murdered. The courts have yet to settle the case. Whatever the outcome, it seems fair to say that Sangeeta Goel, like many Indian women today, was burdened with the worst of two worlds: the marriage mandate of tradition combined with the compassionless anonymity of modern-day life.

Meanwhile, the day-to-day struggles fall to a handful of privately run women's shelters. One of the best known, Shakti Shalini, was formed thirteen years ago by mothers who were grieving for their lost daughters and who wanted to offer a haven to endangered brides. Shakti Shalini also gives counseling sessions designed to restore such troubled marriages, a service not appreciated by everyone.

"They're taking too much of a chance with somebody's life," charges Himendra Thakur, who heads the International Society against Dowry and Bride-Burning in India, an organization he runs from his home in Salem, Massachusetts. "They feel very good when they send somebody back. They think they're saving a home," says Thakur, who maintains that at the first sign of dowry harassment, "the marriage should be dissolved."

But this stance has met great resistance in India. Speaking before a Kanpur civic organization in order to pitch his dream of building a series of "residential training centers" for abused brides, Thakur is confronted by an elderly man in the front row, who stands up and demands, "What about divorce?" This strikes me as an absurd question: How could divorce conceivably approach the tragedy of dowry death? But in the mind of this gentleman and many others in India, divorce is viewed with an alarm difficult to appreciate in the United States.

In general, Hindus face a spiritual imperative to marry and remain married, with nothing less than the salvation of their forebears at stake. Furthermore, the ancient Laws of Manu enjoin a wife to suffer her husband's trespasses (thus, most marital breakdowns are viewed as the wife's fault). Such traditions serve to keep many Indian wives married, even when their safety is in danger.

As indicated by the traditional Hindu parting to a newly wed daughter ("We are sending your bridal palanquin today. Let only your corpse come out of that house."), Hindu parents have long stressed that a married daughter should refrain from returning home. A bride's parents may be especially reluctant to allow her back if there are still maiden sisters whose chances of marrying might be hurt by the reputation of coming from a "difficult" family. Sadly, this reluctance has hardened in recent years, according to Delhi University sociology professor Veena Das. "There is something that has become pathological in India," she asserts. Typically in the case of dowry death, one thing is very shocking: "The girl has gone to her parents repeatedly and says she wants to come back, but the parents refuse to take responsibility for her."

Paul Mandelbaum's journalism has appeared in the New York Times Magazine *and elsewhere. He is currently completing a novel about marriage set partly in India, for which he has received a 1999 James Michener/Copernicus Society of America fellowship.*

Who Needs Love! In Japan, Many Couples Don't

Nicholas D. Kristof

OMIYA, Japan—Yuri Uemura sat on the straw tatami mat of her living room and chatted cheerfully about her 40-year marriage to a man whom, she mused, she never particularly liked.

"There was never any love between me and my husband," she said blithely, recalling how he used to beat her. "But, well, we survived."

A 72-year-old midwife, her face as weathered as an old baseball and etched with a thousand seams, Mrs. Uemura said that her husband had never told her that he liked her, never complimented her on a meal, never told her "thank you," never held her hand, never given her a present, never shown her affection in any way. He never calls her by her name, but summons her with the equivalent of a grunt or a "Hey, you."

"Even with animals, the males cooperate to bring the females some food," Mrs. Uemura said sadly, noting the contrast to her own marriage. "When I see that, it brings tears to my eyes."

In short, the Uemuras have a marriage that is as durable as it is unhappy, one couple's tribute to the Japanese sanctity of family.

The divorce rate in Japan is at a record high but still less than half that of the United States, and Japan arguably has one of the strongest family structures in the industrialized world. As the United States and Europe fret about the disintegration of the traditional family, most Japanese families remain as solid as the small red table on which Mrs. Uemura rested her tea.

A study published last year by the Population Council, an international nonprofit group based in New York, suggested that the traditional two-parent household is on the wane not only in America but throughout most of the world. There was one prominent exception: Japan.

It does not seem that Japanese families survive because husbands and wives love each other more than American couples, but rather because they perhaps love each other less

---

In Japan, for example, only 1.1 percent of births are to unwed mothers—virtually unchanged from 25 years ago. In the United States, the figure is 30.1 percent and rising rapidly.

Yet if one comes to a little Japanese town like Omiya to learn the secrets of the Japanese family, the people are not as happy as the statistics.

"I haven't lived for myself," Mrs. Uemura said, with a touch of melancholy, "but for my kids, and for my family, and for society."

Mrs. Uemura's marriage does not seem exceptional in Japan, whether in the big cities or here in Omiya. The people of Omiya, a community of 5,700 nestled in the rain-drenched hills of the Kii Peninsula in Mie Prefecture, nearly 200 miles southwest of Tokyo, have spoken periodically to a reporter about various aspects of their daily lives. On this visit they talked about their families.

SURVIVAL SECRETS OFTEN, THE COUPLES EXPECT LITTLE

Osamums Torida furrowed his brow and looked perplexed when he was asked if he loved his wife of 33 years.

"Yeah, so-so, I guess," said Mr. Torida, a cattle farmer. "She's like air or water. You couldn't live without it, but most of the time, you're not conscious of its existence."

The secret to the survival of the marriage, Mr. Torida acknowledged, was not mutual passion.

"Sure, we had fights about our work," he explained as he stood beside his barn. "But we were preoccupied by work and our debts, so we had no time to fool around."

That is a common theme in Omiya. It does not seem that Japanese families survive because husbands and wives love each other more than American couples, but rather because they perhaps love each other less.

"I think love marriages are more fragile than arranged marriages," said Tomika Kusukawa, 49, who married her high-school sweetheart and now runs a car repair shop with him. "In love marriages, when something happens or if the couple falls out of love, they split up."

If there is a secret to the strength of the Japanese family it consists of three ingredients: low expectations, patience, and shame.

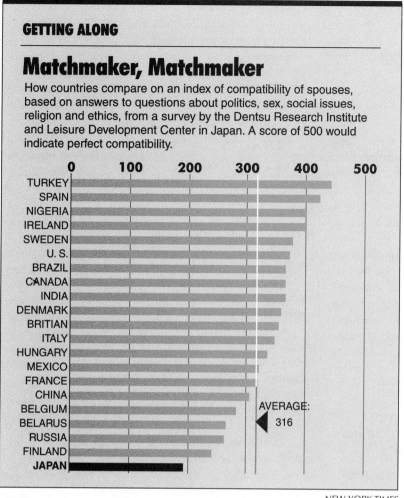

The advantage of marriages based on low expectations is that they have built in shock absorbers. If the couple discover that they have nothing in common, that they do not even like each other, then that is not so much a reason for divorce as it is par for the course.

Even the discovery that one's spouse is having an affair is often not as traumatic in a Japanese marriage as it is in the West. A little sexual infidelity on the part of a man (though not on the part of his wife) was traditionally tolerated, so long as he did not become so besotted as to pay his mistress more than he could afford.

Tsuzuya Fukuyama, who runs a convenience store and will mark her 50th wedding anniversary this year, toasted her hands on an electric heater in the front of the store and declared that a woman would be wrong to get angry if her husband had an affair.

> *The durability of the Japanese family is particularly wondrous because couples are, by international standards, exceptionally incompatible*

"It's never just one side that's at fault," Mrs. Fukuyama said sternly. "Maybe the husband had an affair because his wife wasn't so hot herself. So she should look at her own faults."

Mrs. Fukuyama's daughter came to her a few years ago, suspecting that her husband was having an affair and asking what to do.

"I told her, 'Once you left this house, you can only come back if you divorce; if you're not prepared to get a divorce, then you'd better be patient,'" Mrs. Fukuyama recalled. "And so she was patient. And then she got pregnant and had a kid, and now they're close again."

The word that Mrs. Fukuyama used for patience is "gaman," a term that comes up whenever marriage is discussed in Japan. It means toughing it out, enduring hardship, and many Japanese regard gaman with pride as a national trait.

Many people complain that younger folks divorce because they do not have enough gaman, and the frequency with which the term is used suggests a rather bleak understanding of marriage.

"I didn't know my husband very well when we married, and afterward we used to get into bitter fights," said Yoshiko Hirowaki, 56, a store owner. "But then we had children, and I got very busy with the kids and with this shop. Time passed."

Now Mrs. Hirowaki has been married 34 years, and she complains about young people who do not stick to their vows.

"In the old days, wives had more gaman," she said. "Now kids just don't have enough gaman."

The durability of the Japanese family is particularly wondrous because couples are, by international standards, exceptionally incompatible.

One survey asked married men and their wives in 37 countries how they felt about politics, sex, religion, ethics and social issues. Japanese couples ranked dead last in compatibility of views, by a huge margin. Indeed, another survey found that if they were doing it over again, only about one-third of Japanese would marry the same person.

A national survey found that 30 percent of fathers spend less than 15 minutes a day on weekends talking with or playing with their children

Incompatibility might not matter so much, however, because Japanese husbands and wives spend very little time talking to each other.

"I kind of feel there's nothing new to say to her," said Masayuki Ogita, an egg farmer, explaining his reticence.

In a small town like Omiya, couples usually have dinner together, but in Japanese cities there are many "7-11 husbands," so called because they leave at 7 A.M. and return after 11 P.M.

Masahiko Kondo now lives in Omiya, working in the chamber of commerce, but he used to be a salesman in several big cities. He would leave work each morning at 7, and about four nights a week would go out for after-work drinking or mah-jongg sessions with buddies.

"I only saw my baby on Saturdays or Sundays," said Mr. Kondo, a lanky good-natured man of 37. "But in fact, I really enjoyed that life. It didn't bother me that I never spent time with my kid on weekdays."

Traditionally, many companies were reluctant to promote employees who had divorced or who had major problems at home

Mr. Kondo's wife, Keiko, had her own life, spent with her child and the wives of other workaholic husbands.

"We had birthday parties, but they were with the kids and the mothers," she remembers. "No fathers ever came."

A national survey found that 30 percent of fathers spend less than 15 minutes a day on weekdays talking with or playing with their children. Among eighth graders, 51 percent reported that they never spoke with their fathers on weekdays.

As a result, the figures in Japan for single-parent households can be deceptive. The father is often more a theoretical presence than a homework-helping reality.

Still, younger people sometimes want to see the spouses in daylight, and a result is a gradual change in focus of lives from work to family. Two decades ago, nearly half of young people said in surveys that they wanted their fathers to put priority on work rather than family. Now only one-quarter say that.

SOCIAL PRESSURES
SHAME IS KEEPING BONDS IN PLACE

For those who find themselves desperately unhappy, one source of pressure to keep plugging is shame.

"If you divorce, you lose face in society," said Tatsumi Kinoshita, a tea farmer." People say, 'His wife escaped.' So folks remain married because they hate to be gossiped about."

Shame is a powerful social sanction in Japan, and it is not just a matter of gos-

sip. Traditionally, many companies were reluctant to promote employees who had divorced or who had major problems at home.

"If you divorce, it weakens your position at work," said Akihiko Kanda, 27, who works in a local government office. "Your bosses won't give you such good ratings, and it'll always be a negative factor."

The idea, Mr. Kanda noted, is that if an employee cannot manage his own life properly, he should not be entrusted with important corporate matters.

Financial sanctions are also a major disincentive for divorce. The mother gets the children in three-quarters of divorces, but most mothers in Japan do not have careers and have few financial resources. Fathers pay child support in only 15 percent of all divorces with children, partly because women often hesitate to go to court to demand payments and partly because men often fail to pay even when the court orders it.

"The main reason for lack of divorce is that women can't support themselves," said Mizuko Kanda, a 51-year-old housewife. "My friends complain about their husbands and say that they'd divorce if they could, but they can't afford to."

The result of these social and economic pressures is clear.

Even in Japan, there are about 24 divorces for every 100 marriages, but that compares with 32 in France, and 42 in England, and 55 in the United States.

THE OUTLOOK
CHANGE CREEPS IN, IMPERILING FAMILY

But society is changing in Japan, and it is an open question whether these changes will undermine the traditional family as they have elsewhere around the globe.

The nuclear family has already largely replaced the extended family in Japan, and shame is eroding as a sanction. Haruko Okumura, for example, runs a kindergarten and speaks openly about her divorce.

"My Mom was uneasy about it, but I never had an inferiority complex about being divorced," said Mrs. Okumura, as dozens of children played in the next room. "And people accepted me easily."

Mrs. Okumura sees evidence of the changes in family patterns every day: fathers are playing more of a role in the kindergarten. At Christmas parties and sports contests, fathers have started to show up along with mothers. And Mrs. Okumura believes that divorce is on the upswing.

"If there's a weakening of the economic and social pressures to stay married," she said, "surely divorce rates will soar."

Already divorce rates are rising, approximately doubling over the last 25 years. But couples are very reluctant to divorce when they have children, and so single-parent households account for exactly the same proportion today as in 1965.

Shinsuke Kawaguchi, a young tea farmer, is one of the men for whom life is changing. Americans are not likely to be impressed by Mr. Kawaguchi's openmindedness, but he is.

"I take good care of my wife," he said. "I may not say 'I love you,' but I do hold her hand. And I might say, after she makes dinner, 'This tastes good.'"

"Of course," Mr. Kawaguchi quickly added, "I wouldn't say that unless I'd just done something really bad."

Even Mrs. Uemura, the elderly woman whose husband used to beat her, said that her husband was treating her better.

"The other day, he tried to pour me a cup of tea," Mrs. Uemura recalled excitedly. "It was a big change. I told all my friends."

UNIT 5
Gender and Status

Unit Selections

Key Points to Consider

- What is it about foraging societies that encourages an egalitarian relationship between the sexes? Why are the Eskimo (Inuit) an exception?

- What kinds of shifts in the social relations of production are necessary for women to achieve equality with men?

- Why do many cultures the world over treat menstruating women as taboo?

- How does female circumcision differ from male circumcision in terms of its social functions?

- How and why do perceptions of feminine beauty vary from culture to culture?

 **Links: www.dushkin.com/online/**
These sites are annotated in the World Wide Web pages.

Arranged Marriages
http://women3rdworld.miningco.com/cs/arrangedmarriage/

Bonobo Sex and Society
http://songweaver.com/info/bonobos.html

FGM Research
http://www.fgm.com

OMIM Home Page-Online Mendelian Inheritance in Man
http://www3.ncbi.nlm.nih.gov/omim/

Reflections on Sinai Bedouin Women
http://www.sherryart.com/women/bedouin.html

The feminist movement in the United States has had a significant impact upon the development of anthropology. Feminists have rightly charged that anthropologists have tended to gloss over the lives of women in studies of society and culture. In part this is because, until recent times, most anthropologists have been men. The result has been an undue emphasis upon male activities as well as male perspectives in descriptions of particular societies.

These charges, however, have proven to be a firm corrective. In the last few years, anthropologists have begun to study women and, more particularly, the sexual division of labor and its relation to biology as well as to social and political status. In addition, these changes in emphasis have been accompanied by an increase in the number of women in the field. (See "A Woman's Curse?" by Meredith Small.)

Feminist anthropologists have begun to attack critically many of the established anthropological beliefs. They have shown, for example, that field studies of nonhuman primates, which were often used to demonstrate the evolutionary basis of male dominance, distorted the actual evolutionary record by focusing primarily on baboons. (Male baboons are especially dominant and aggressive.) Other, less-quoted primate studies show how dominance and aggression are highly situational phenomena, sensitive to ecological variation. Feminist anthropologists have also shown that the subsistence contribution of women has likewise been ignored by anthropologists. A classic case is that of the !Kung, a hunting and gathering people in southern Africa, where women provide the bulk of the foodstuffs, including most of the available protein, and who, not coincidentally, enjoy a more egalitarian relationship than usual with men.

The most common occurrence has been male domination over women. Recent studies have concerned themselves with why there has been such gender inequality. Although the subordination of women is widespread, Ernestine Friedl, in "Society and Sex Roles," explains that the sex that controls the valued goods of exchange in a society is the dominant one. Thus, since this control is a matter of cultural variation, male authority is not biologically predetermined. In fact, women have played visibly prominent roles in many cultures. And, there are many cultures in which some men may play a more feminine or, at least, asexual role, as described in "The Berdache Tradition." As we see in "The Initiation of a Maasai Warrior," "What About 'Female Genital Mutilation'?" and "Where Fat Is a Mark of Beauty," gender relationships are deeply embedded in social experience.

Society and Sex Roles

Ernestine Friedl

"Women must respond quickly to the demands of their husbands," says anthropologist Napoleon Chagnon describing the horticultural Yanomano Indians of Venezuela. When a man returns from a hunting trip, "the woman, no matter what she is doing, hurries home and quietly but rapidly prepares a meal for her husband. Should the wife be slow in doing this, the husband is within his rights to beat her. Most reprimands... take the form of blows with the hand or with a piece of firewood.... Some of them chop their wives with the sharp edge of a machete or axe, or shoot them with a barbed arrow in some nonvital area, such as the buttocks or leg."

Among the Semai agriculturalists of central Malaya, when one person refuses the request of another, the offended party suffers *punan*, a mixture of emotional pain and frustration. "Enduring *punan* is commonest when a girl has refused the victim her sexual favors," reports Robert Dentan. "The jilted man's 'heart becomes sad.' He loses his energy and his appetite. Much of the time he sleeps, dreaming of his lost love. In this state, he is in fact very likely to injure himself 'accidentally.'" The Semai are afraid of violence; a man would never strike a woman.

The social relationship between men and women has emerged as one of the principal disputes occupying the attention of scholars and the public in recent years. Although the discord is sharpest in the United States, the controversy has

spread throughout the world. Numerous national and international conferences, including one in Mexico sponsored by the United Nations, have drawn together delegates from all walks of life to discuss such questions as the social and political rights of each sex, and even the basic nature of males and females.

As Western history and the anthropological record have told us, equality between the sexes is rare; in most known societies females are subordinate.

Whatever their position, partisans often invoke examples from other cultures to support their ideas about the proper role of each sex. Because women are clearly subservient to men in many societies, like the Yanomamo, some experts conclude that the natural pattern is for men to dominate. But among the Semai no one has the right to command others, and in West Africa women are often chiefs. The place of women in these societies supports the argument of those who believe that sex roles are not fixed, that if there is a natural order, it allows for many different arrangements.

The argument will never be settled as long as the opposing sides toss examples from the world's cultures at each other like intellectual stones. But the effect of

biological differences on male and female behavior can be clarified by looking at known examples of the earliest forms of human society and examining the relationship between technology, social organization, environment, and sex roles. The problem is to determine the conditions in which different degrees of male dominance are found, to try to discover the social and cultural arrangements that give rise to equality or inequality between the sexes, and to attempt to apply this knowledge to our understanding of the changes taking place in modern industrial society.

As Western history and the anthropological record have told us, equality between the sexes is rare; in most known societies females are subordinate. Male dominance is so widespread that it is virtually a human universal; societies in which women are consistently dominant do not exist and have never existed.

Evidence of a society in which women control all strategic resources like food and water, and in which women's activities are the most prestigious has never been found. The Iroquois of North America and the Lovedu of Africa came closest. Among the Iroquois, women raised food, controlled its distribution, and helped to choose male political leaders. Lovedu women ruled as queens, exchanged valuable cattle, led ceremonies, and controlled their own sex lives. But among both the Iroquois and the Lovedu, men owned the land and held other positions of power and prestige. Women were equal to men; they did not have ultimate authority over them. Neither culture was a true matriarchy.

The source of male power among hunter-gatherers lies in their control of a scarce, hard to acquire, but necessary nutrient— animal protein.

Patriarchies are prevalent, and they appear to be strongest in societies in which men control significant goods that are exchanged with people outside the family. Regardless of who produces food, the person who gives it to others creates the obligations and alliances that are at the center of all political relations. The greater the male monopoly on the distribution of scarce items, the stronger their control of women seems to be. This is most obvious in relatively simple hunter-gatherer societies.

Hunter-gatherers, or foragers, subsist on wild plants, small land animals, and small river or sea creatures gathered by hand; large land animals and sea mammals hunted with spears, bows and arrows, and blow guns; and fish caught with hooks and nets. The 300,000 hunter-gatherers alive in the world today include the Eskimos, the Australian aborigines, and the Pygmies of Central Africa.

Foraging has endured for two million years and was replaced by farming and animal husbandry only 10,000 years ago; it covers more than 99 percent of human history. Our foraging ancestry is not far behind us and provides a clue to our understanding of the human condition.

Hunter-gatherers are people whose ways of life are technologically simple and socially and politically egalitarian. They live in small groups of 50 to 200 and have neither kings, nor priests, nor social classes. These conditions permit anthropologists to observe the essential bases for inequalities between the sexes without the distortions induced by the complexities of contemporary industrial society.

The source of male power among hunter-gatherers lies in their control of a scarce, hard to acquire, but necessary nutrient—animal protein. When men in a hunter-gatherer society return to camp with game, they divide the meat in some customary way. Among the !Kung San of Africa, certain parts of the animal are given to the owner of the arrow that killed the beast, to the first hunter to sight the game, to the one who threw the first spear and to all men in the hunting party. After the meat has been divided, each hunter distributes his share to his blood relatives and his in-laws, who in turn share it with others. If an animal is large enough, every member of the band will receive some meat.

Vegetable foods, in contrast, are not distributed beyond the immediate household. Women give food to their children, to their husbands, to other members of the household, and rarely, to the occasional visitor. No one outside the family regularly eats any of the wild fruit and vegetables that are gathered by the women.

The meat distributed by the men is a public gift. Its source is widely known, and the donor expects a reciprocal gift when other men return from a successful hunt. He gains honor as a supplier of a scarce item and simultaneously obligates others to him.

These obligations constitute a form of power or control over others, both men and women. The opinions of hunters play an important part in decisions to move the village; good hunters attract the most desirable women; people in other groups join camps with good hunters; and hunters, because they already participate in an internal system of exchange, control exchange with other groups for flint, salt, and steel axes. The male monopoly on hunting unites men in a system of exchange and gives them power; gathering vegetable food does not give women equal power even among foragers who live in the tropics, where the food collected by women provides more than half the hunter-gatherer diet.

If dominance arises from a monopoly on big-game hunting, why has the male monopoly remained unchallenged? Some women are strong enough to par-

ticipate in the hunt and their endurance is certainly equal to that of men. Dobe San women of the Kalahari Desert in Africa walk an average of 10 miles a day carrying from 15 to 33 pounds of food plus a baby.

Women do not hunt, I believe, because of four interrelated factors: variability in the supply of game; the different skills required for hunting and gathering; the incompatibility between carrying burdens and hunting; and the small size of semi-nomadic foraging populations.

Because the meat supply is unstable, foragers must make frequent expeditions to provide the band with gathered food. Environmental factors such as seasonal and annual variation in rainfall often affect the size of the wildlife population. Hunters cannot always find game, and when they do encounter animals, they are not always successful in killing their prey. In northern latitudes, where meat is the primary food, periods of starvation are known in every generation. The irregularity of the game supply leads hunter-gatherers in areas where plant foods are available to depend on these predictable foods a good part of the time. Someone must gather the fruits, nuts, and roots and carry them back to camp to feed unsuccessful hunters, children, the elderly, and anyone who might not have gone foraging that day.

Foraging falls to the women because hunting and gathering cannot be combined on the same expedition. Although gatherers sometimes notice signs of game as they work, the skills required to track game are not the same as those required to find edible roots or plants. Hunters scan the horizon and the land for traces of large game; gatherers keep their eyes to the ground, studying the distribution of plants and the texture of the soil for hidden roots and animal holes. Even if a woman who was collecting plants came across the track of an antelope, she could not follow it; it is impossible to carry a load and hunt at the same time. Running with a heavy load is difficult, and should the animal be sighted, the hunter would be off balance and could neither shoot an arrow nor throw a spear accurately.

Photo credit: American Museum of Natural History–Dr. F. Rainey

In the maritime Inuit (Eskimo) societies, inequality between the sexes is matched by the ability to supply food for the group. The men hunt for meat and control the economy. Women perform all the other duties that support life in the community, and are virtually treated as objects.

Pregnancy and child care would also present difficulties for a hunter. An unborn child affects a woman's body balance, as does a child in her arms, on her back, or slung at her side. Until they are two years old, many hunter-gatherer children are carried at all times, and until they are four, they are carried some of the time.

An observer might wonder why young women do not hunt until they become pregnant, or why mature women and men do not hunt and gather on alternate days, with some women staying in camp to act as wet nurses for the young. Apart from the effects hunting might have on a mother's milk production, there are two reasons. First, young girls begin to bear children as soon as they are physically mature and strong enough to hunt, and second, hunter-gatherer bands are so small that there are

unlikely to be enough lactating women to serve as wet nurses. No hunter-gatherer group could afford to maintain a specialized female hunting force.

Because game is not always available, because hunting and gathering are specialized skills, because women carrying heavy loads cannot hunt, and because women in hunter-gatherer societies are usually either pregnant or caring for young children, for most of the last two million years of human history men have hunted and women have gathered.

If male dominance depends on controlling the supply of meat, then the degree of male dominance in a society should vary with the amount of meat available and the amount supplied by the men. Some regions, like the East African grasslands and the North American woodlands, abounded

with species of large mammals; other zones, like tropical forests and semi-deserts, are thinly populated with prey. Many elements affect the supply of game, but theoretically, the less meat provided exclusively by the men, the more egalitarian the society.

All known hunter-gatherer societies fit into four basic types; those in which men and women work together in communal hunts and as teams gathering edible plants, as did the Washo Indians of North America; those in which men and women each collect their own plant foods although the men supply some meat to the group, as do the Hadza of Tanzania; those in which male hunters and female gatherers work apart but return to camp each evening to share their acquisitions, as do the Tiwi of North Australia; and those in which the men provide all the food by hunting large game, as do the Eskimo. In each case the extent of male dominance increases directly with the proportion of meat supplied by individual men and small hunting parties.

Among the most egalitarian of hunter-gatherer societies are the Washo Indians... Since everyone participated in most food-gathering activities, there w[as] relatively little difference in male and female rights

---

Among the most egalitarian of hunter-gatherer societies are the Washo Indians, who inhabited the valleys of the Sierra Nevada in what is now southern California and Nevada. In the spring they moved north to Lake Tahoe for the large fish runs of sucker and native trout. Everyone—men, women, and children—participated in the fishing. Women spent the summer gathering edible berries and seeds while the men continued to fish. In the fall some men hunted deer but the most important source of animal protein was the jack rabbit, which was captured in communal hunts. Men and women together drove the rabbits into nets tied end to end. To provide food for the winter, husbands and wives worked as teams in the late fall to collect pine nuts.

Since everyone participated in most food-gathering activities, there were no individual distributions of food and relatively little difference in male and female rights. Men and women were not segregated from each other in daily activities; both were free to take lovers after marriage; both had the right to separate whenever they chose; menstruating women were not isolated from the rest of the group; and one of the two major Washo rituals celebrated hunting while the other celebrated gathering. Men were accorded more prestige if they had killed a deer, and men directed decisions about the seasonal movement of the group. But if no male leader stepped forward,

women were permitted to lead. The distinctive feature of groups such as the Washo is the relative equality of the sexes.

The sexes are also relatively equal among the Hadza of Tanzania but this near-equality arises because men and women tend to work alone to feed themselves. They exchange little food. The Hadza lead a leisurely life in the seemingly barren environment of the East African Rift Gorge that is, in fact, rich in edible berries, roots, and small game. As a result of this abundance, from the time they are 10 years old, Hadza men and women gather much of their own food. Women take their young children with them into the bush, eating as they forage, and collect only enough food for a light family meal in the evening. The men eat berries and roots as they hunt for small game, and should they bring down a rabbit or a hyrax, they eat the meat on the spot. Meat is carried back to the camp and shared with the rest of the group only on those rare occasions when a poisoned arrow brings down a large animal—an impala, a zebra, an eland, or a giraffe.

Because Hadza men distribute little meat, their status is only slightly higher than that of the women. People flock to the camp of a good hunter and the camp might take on his name because of his popularity, but he is in no sense a leader of the group. A Hadza man and a woman have an equal right to divorce and each can repudiate a marriage simply by living apart for a few weeks. Couples tend to live in the same camp as the wife's mother but they sometimes make long visits to the camp of the husband's mother. Although a man may take more than one wife, most Hadza males cannot afford to indulge in this luxury. In order to maintain a marriage, a man must supply both his wife and his mother-in-law with some meat and trade goods, such as beads and cloth, and the Hadza economy gives few men the wealth to provide for more than one wife and mother-in-law. Washo equality is based on cooperation; Hadza equality is based on independence.

In contrast to both these groups, among the Tiwi of Melville and Bathurst Islands off the northern coast of Australia, male hunters dominate female gath-

erers. The Tiwi are representative of the most common form of foraging society, in which the men supply large quantities of meat, although less than half the food consumed by the group. Each morning Tiwi women, most with babies on their backs, scatter in different directions in search of vegetables, grubs, worms, and small game such as bandicoots, lizards, and opossums. To track the game, they use hunting dogs. On most days women return to camp with some meat and with baskets full of *korka*, the nut of a native palm, which is soaked and mashed to make a porridge-like dish. The Tiwi men do not hunt small game and do not hunt every day, but when they do they often return with kangaroo, large lizards, fish, and game birds.

The porridge is cooked separately by each household and rarely shared outside the family, but the meat is prepared by a volunteer cook, who can be male or female. After the cook takes one of the parts of the animal traditionally reserved for him or her, the animal's "boss," the one who caught it, distributes the rest to all near kin and then to all others residing with the band. Although the small game supplied by the women is distributed in the same way as the big game supplied by the men, Tiwi men are dominant because the game they kill provides most of the meat.

The power of the Tiwi men is clearest in their betrothal practices. Among the Tiwi, a woman must always be married. To ensure this, female infants are betrothed at birth and widows are remarried at the gravesides of their late husbands. Men form alliances by exchanging daughters, sisters, and mothers in marriage and some collect as many as 25 wives. Tiwi men value the quantity and quality of the food many wives can collect and the many children they can produce.

The dominance of the men is offset somewhat by the influence of adult women in selecting their next husbands. Many women are active strategists in the political careers of their male relatives, but to the exasperation of some sons attempting to promote their own futures, widowed mothers sometimes insist on selecting their own partners. Women also influence the marriages of their daughters and granddaughters, especially when the selected husband dies before the bestowed child moves to his camp.

Among the Eskimos, representative of the rarest type of forager society, inequality between the sexes is matched by inequality in supplying the group with food. Inland Eskimo men hunt caribou throughout the year to provision the entire society, and maritime Eskimo men depend on whaling, fishing, and some hunting to feed their extended families. The women process the carcasses, cut and sew skins to make clothing, cook, and care for the young; but they collect no food of their own and depend on the men to supply all the raw materials for their work. Since men provide all the meat, they also control the trade in hides, whale oil, seal oil, and other items that move between the maritime and inland Eskimos.

Eskimo women are treated almost exclusively as objects to be used, abused, and traded by men. After puberty all Eskimo girls are fair game for any interested male. A man shows his intentions by grabbing the belt of a woman and if she protests, he cuts off her trousers and forces himself upon her. These encounters are considered unimportant by the rest of the group. Men offer their wives' sexual services to establish alliances with trading partners and members of hunting and whaling parties.

Despite the consistent pattern of some degree of male dominance among foragers, most of these societies are egalitarian compared with agricultural and industrial societies. No forager has any significant opportunity for political leadership. Foragers, as a rule, do not like to give or take orders, and assume leadership only with reluctance. Shamans (those who are thought to be possessed by spirits) may be either male or female. Public rituals conducted by women in order to celebrate the first menstruation of girls are common, and the symbolism in these rituals is similar to that in the ceremonies that follow a boy's first kill.

In any society, status goes to those who control the distribution of valued goods and services outside the family. Equality arises when both sexes work side by side in food production, as do the Washo, and the products are simply distributed among the workers. In such circumstances, no person or sex has greater access to valued items than do others. But when women make no contribution to the food supply, as in the case of the Eskimo, they are completely subordinate.

As women gain access to positions that control the exchange of resources, male dominance may become archaic, and industrials societies may one day become as egalitarian as the Washo

---

When we attempt to apply these generalizations to contemporary industrial society, we can predict that as long as women spend their discretionary income from jobs on domestic needs, they will gain little social recognition and power. To be an effective source of power, money must be exchanged in ways that require returns and create obligations. In other words, it must be invested.

Jobs that do not give women control over valued resources will do little to advance their general status. Only as managers, executives, and professionals are women in a position to trade goods and services, to do others favors, and therefore to obligate others to them. Only as controllers of valued resources can women achieve prestige, power, and equality.

Within the household, women who bring in income from jobs are able to function on a more nearly equal basis with their husbands. Women who contribute services to their husbands and children without pay, as do some middle-class Western housewives, are especially vulnerable to dominance. Like Eskimo women, as long as their services are limited to domestic distribution they have little power relative to their husbands and none with respect to the outside world.

As for the limits imposed on women by their procreative functions in hunter-gatherer societies, child-bearing and child care are organized around work as much as work is organized around repro-duction. Some foraging groups space their children three to four years apart and have an average of only four to six children, far fewer than many women in other cultures. Hunter-gatherers nurse their infants for extended periods, sometimes for as long as four years. This custom suppresses ovulation and limits the size of their families. Sometimes, although rarely, they practice infanticide. By limiting reproduction, a woman who is gathering food has only one child to carry.

Different societies can and do adjust the frequency of birth and the care of children to accommodate whatever productive activities women customarily engage in. In horticultural societies, where women work long hours in gardens that may be far from home, infants get food to supplement their mothers' milk, older children take care of younger children, and pregnancies are widely spaced. Throughout the world, if a society requires a woman's labor, it finds ways to care for her children.

In the United States, as in some other industrial societies, the accelerated entry of women with preschool children into the labor force has resulted in the development of a variety of child-care arrangements. Individual women have called on friends, relatives, and neighbors. Public and private child-care centers are growing. We should realize that the declining birth rate, the increasing acceptance of childless or single-child families, and a de-emphasis on motherhood are adaptations to a sexual division of labor reminiscent of the system of production found in hunter-gatherer societies.

In many countries where women no longer devote most of their productive years to childbearing, they are beginning to demand a change in the social relationship of the sexes. As women gain access to positions that control the exchange of resources, male dominance may become archaic, and industrial societies may one day become as egalitarian as the Washo.

REFERENCES

Friedl, Ernestine, *Women and Men: An Anthropologist's View*, Holt, Rinehart and Winston, 1975.

Martin, M. Kay, and Barbara Voorhies, eds., *Female of the Species*, Columbia University Press, 1977.

Murphy, Yolanda, and Robert Murphy, *Women of the Forest*, Columbia University Press, 1974.

Reiter, Rayna, ed., *Toward an Anthropology of Women*, Monthly Review Press, 1975.

Rosaldo, M. Z., and Louise Lamphere, eds., *Women, Culture, and Society*, Stanford University Press, 1974.

Schlegel, Alice, ed., *Sexual Stratification; A Cross-Cultural View*, Columbia University Press, 1977.

Strathern, Marilyn, *Women in Between: Female Roles in a Male World*, Academic Press, 1972.

Ernestine Friedl is a professor of anthropology at Duke University; a former president of the American Anthropological Association, a fellow of the American Academy of Arts and Sciences, and an advisory editor to Human Nature. *She received her Ph.D. from Columbia University in 1950. Until recently, Friedl was a firm believer in the relative equality of women in the field of anthropology and had little interest in the anthropological study of women. None of her field work among the Pomo and Chippewa Indians of North America, or in rural and urban Greece was concerned with women's issues.*

In the early 1970s, while serving on the American Anthropological Association Committee on the Status of Women, Friedl became convinced that women were discriminated against as much in anthropology as in the other academic disciplines. Since that time, she has devoted her efforts to the cross-cultural study of sex roles and has written one book on the topic, Women and Men: An Anthropologist's View. *Friedl now accounts for her own success in part by the fact that she attended an all-women's college and taught for many years at the City University of New York, a university system that included a women's college.*

The Berdache Tradition

Walter L. Williams

Because it is such a powerful force in the world today, the Western Judeo-Christian tradition is often accepted as the arbiter of "natural" behavior of humans. If Europeans and their descendant nations of North America accept something as normal, then anything different is seen as abnormal. Such a view ignores the great diversity of human existence.

This is the case of the study of gender. How many genders are there? To a modern Anglo-American, nothing might seem more definite than the answer that there are two: men and women. But not all societies around the world agree with Western culture's view that all humans are either women or men. The commonly accepted notion of "the opposite sex," based on anatomy, is itself an artifact of our society's rigid sex roles.

Among many cultures, there have existed different alternatives to "man" or "woman." An alternative role in many American Indian societies is referred to by anthropologists as *berdache*.... The role varied from one Native American culture to another, which is a reflection of the vast diversity of aboriginal New World societies. Small bands of hunter-gatherers existed in some areas, with advanced civilizations of farming peoples in other areas. With hundreds of different languages, economies, religions, and social patterns existing in North America alone, every generalization about a cultural tradition must acknowledge many exceptions.

This diversity is true for the berdache tradition as well, and must be kept in mind. My statements should be read as being specific to a particular culture, with generalizations being treated as loose patterns that might not apply to peoples even in nearby areas.

Briefly, a berdache can be defined as a morphological male who does not fill a society's standard man's role, who has a nonmasculine character. This type of person is often stereotyped as effeminate, but a more accurate characterization is androgyny. Such a person has a clearly recognized and accepted social status, often based on a secure place in the tribal mythology. Berdaches have special ceremonial roles in many Native American religions, and important economic roles in their families. They will do at least some women's work, and mix together much of the behavior, dress, and social roles of women and men. Berdaches gain social prestige by their spiritual, intel-lectual, or craftwork/artistic contributions, and by their reputation for hard work and generosity. They serve a mediating function between women and men, precisely because their character is seen as distinct from either sex. They are not seen as men, yet they are not seen as women either. They occupy an alternative gender role that is a mixture of diverse elements.

In their erotic behavior berdaches also generally (but not always) take a nonmasculine role, either being asexual or becoming the passive partner in sex with men. In some cultures the berdache might become a wife to a man. This male-male sexual behavior became the focus of an attack on berdaches as "sodomites" by the Europeans who, early on, came into contact with them. From the first Spanish conquistadors to the Western frontiersmen and the Christian missionaries and government officials, Western culture has had a considerable impact on the berdache tradition. In the last two decades, the most recent impact on the tradition is the adaptation of a modern Western gay identity.

To Western eyes berdachism is a complex and puzzling phenomenon, mixing and redefining the very concepts of what is considered male and female. In a culture with only two recognized genders, such individuals are gender nonconformist, abnormal, deviant. But to American Indians, the institution of another gender role means that berdaches are not deviant—indeed, they do conform to the requirements of a custom in which their culture tells them they fit. Berdachism is a way for society to recognize and assimilate some atypical individuals without imposing a change on them or stigmatizing them as deviant. This cultural institution confirms their legitimacy for what they are.

Societies often bestow power upon that which does not neatly fit into the usual. Since no cultural system can explain everything, a common way that many cultures deal with these inconsistencies is to imbue them with negative power, as taboo, pollution, witchcraft, or sin. That which is not understood is seen as a threat. But an alternative method of dealing with such things, or people, is to take them out of the realm of threat and to sanctify them.[1] The berdaches' role as mediator is thus not just between women and men, but also between the physical and the spiritual. American Indian cultures have taken what Western culture calls negative, and made it a positive; they have successfully utilized the different skills and insights of a class of people that Western culture has stigmatized and whose spiritual powers have been wasted.

Many Native Americans also understood that gender roles have to do with more than just biological sex. The standard Western view that one's sex is always a certainty, and that one's gender identity and sex role always conform to one's morphological sex is a view that dies hard. Western thought is typified by such dichotomies of groups perceived to be mutually exclusive: male and female, black and white, right and wrong, good and evil. Clearly, the world is not so simple; such clear divisions are not always realistic. Most American Indian worldviews generally are much more accepting of the ambiguities of life. Acceptance of gender variation in the berdache tradition is typical of many native cultures' approach to life in general.

Overall, these are generalizations based on those Native American societies that had an accepted role for berdaches. Not all cultures recognized such a respected status. Berdachism in aboriginal North America was most established among tribes in four areas: first, the Prairie and western Great Lakes, the northern and central Great Plains, and the lower Mississippi Valley; second, Florida and the Caribbean; third, the Southwest, the Great Basin, and California; and fourth, scattered areas of the Northwest, western Canada, and Alaska. For some reason it is not noticeable in eastern North America, with the exception of its southern rim....

AMERICAN INDIAN RELIGIONS

Native American religions offered an explanation for human diversity by their creation stories. In some tribal religions, the Great Spiritual Being is conceived as neither male nor female but as a combination of both. Among the Kamia of the Southwest, for example, the bearer of plant seeds and the introducer of Kamia culture was a man-woman spirit named Warharmi.[2] A key episode of the Zuni creation story involves a battle between the kachina spirits of the agricultural Zunis and the enemy hunter spirits. Every four years an elaborate ceremony commemorates this myth. In the story a kachina spirit called *ko'lhamana* was captured by the enemy spirits and transformed in the process. This transformed spirit became a mediator between the two sides, using his peacemaking skills to merge the differing lifestyles of hunters and farmers. In the ceremony, a dramatic reenactment of the myth, the part of the transformed *ko'lhamana* spirit, is performed by a berdache.[3] The Zuni word for berdache is *lhamana*, denoting its closeness to the spiritual mediator who brought hunting and farming together.[4] The moral of this story is that the berdache was created by the deities for a special purpose, and that this creation led to the improvement of society. The continual reenactment of this story provides a justification for the Zuni berdache in each generation.

In contrast to this, the lack of spiritual justification in a creation myth could denote a lack of tolerance for gender variation. The Pimas, unlike most of their Southwestern neighbors, did not respect a berdache status. *Wi-kovat*, their derogatory word, means "like a girl," but it does not signify a recognized social role. Pima mythology reflects this lack of acceptance, in a folk tale that explains male androgyny as due to Papago witchcraft. Knowing that the Papagos respected berdaches, the Pimas blamed such an occurrence on an alien influence.[5] While the Pimas' condemnatory attitude is unusual, it does point out the importance of spiritual explanations for the acceptance of gender variance in a culture.

Other Native American creation stories stand in sharp contrast to the Pima explanation. A good example is the account of the Navajos, which presents women and men as equals. The Navajo origin tale is told as a story of five worlds. The first people were First Man and First Woman, who were created equally and at the same time. The first two worlds that they lived in were bleak and unhappy, so they escaped to the third world. In the third world lived two twins, Turquoise Boy and White Shell Girl, who were the first berdaches. In the Navajo language the world for berdache is *nadle*, which means "changing one" or "one who is transformed." It is applied to hermaphrodites—those who are born with the genitals of both male and female—and also to "those who pretend to be *nadle*," who take on a social role that is distinct from either men or women.[6]

In the third world, First Man and First Woman began farming, with the help of the changing twins. One of the twins noticed some clay and, holding it in the palm of his/her hand, shaped it into the first pottery bowl. Then he/she formed a plate, a water dipper, and a pipe. The second twin observed some reeds and began to weave them, making the first basket. Together they shaped axes and grinding stones from rocks, and hoes from bone. All these new inventions made the people very happy.[7]

The message of this story is that humans are dependent for many good things on the inventiveness of *nadle*. Such individuals were present from the earliest eras of human existence, and their presence was never questioned. They were part of the natural order of the universe, with a special contribution to make.

Later on in the Navajo creation story, White Shell Girl entered the moon and became the Moon Bearer. Turquoise Boy, however, remained with the people. When First Man realized that Turquoise Boy could do all manner of women's work as well as women, all the men left the women and crossed a big river. The men hunted and planted crops. Turquoise Boy ground the corn, cooked the food, and weaved cloth for the men. Four years passed with the women and men separated, and the men were happy with the *nadle*. Later, however the women wanted to learn how to grind corn from the *nadle*, and both the men and women had decided that it was not good to continue living separately. So the women crossed the river and the people were reunited.[8]

They continued living happily in the third world, until one day a great flood began. The people ran to the highest mountaintop, but the water kept rising and they all feared they would be drowned. But just in time, the ever-inventive Turquoise Boy found a large reed. They climbed upward inside the tall hollow reed, and came out at the top into the fourth world. From there, White Shell Girl brought another reed, and the climbed again to the fifth world, which is the present world of the Navajos.[9]

These stories suggest that the very survival of humanity is dependent on the inventiveness of berdaches. With such a mythological belief system, it is no wonder that the Navajos held *nadle* in high regard. The concept of the *nadle* is well formulated in the creation story. As children were educated by these stories, and all Navajos believed in them, the high status accorded to gender variation was passed down from generation to generation. Such stories also provided instruction for *nadle* themselves to live by. A spiritual explanation guaranteed a special place for a person who was considered different but not deviant.

For American Indians, the important explanations of the world are spiritual ones. In their view, there is a deeper reality than the here-and-now. The real essence or wisdom occurs when one finally gives up trying to explain events in terms of "logic" and "reality." Many confusing aspects of existence can better be explained by actions of a multiplicity of spirits. Instead of a concept of a single god, there is an awareness of "that which we do not understand." In Lakota religion, for example, the term *Wakan Tanka* is often translated as "god." But a more proper translation, according to the medicine people who taught me, is "The Great Mystery."[10]

While rationality can explain much, there are limits to human capabilities of understanding. The English language is structured to account for cause and effect. For example, English speakers say, "It is raining," with the implication that there is a cause "it" that leads to rain. Many Indian languages, on the other hand, merely note what is most accurately translated as "raining" as an observable fact. Such an approach brings a freedom to stop worrying about causes of things, and merely to relax and accept that our human insights can go only so far. By not taking ourselves too seriously, or overinflating human importance, we can get beyond the logical world.

The emphasis of American Indian religions, then, is on the spiritual nature of all things. To understand the physical world, one must appreciate the underlying spiritual essence. Then one can begin to see that the physical is only a faint shadow, a partial reflection, of a supernatural and extrarational world. By the Indian view, everything that exists is spiritual. Every object—plants, rocks, water, air, the moon, animals, humans, the earth itself—has a spirit. The spirit of one thing (including a human) is not superior to the spirit of any other. Such a view promotes a sophisticated ecological awareness of the place that humans have in the larger environment. The function of religion is not to try to condemn or to change what exists, but to accept the realities of the world and to appreciate their contributions to life. Everything that exists has a purpose.[11]

One of the basic tenets of American Indian religion is the notion that everything in the universe is related. Nevertheless, things that exist are often seen as having a counterpart: sky and earth, plant and animal, water and fire. In all of these polarities, there exist mediators. The role of the mediator is to hold the polarities together, to keep the world from disintegrating. Polarities exist within human society also. The most important category within Indian society is gender. The notions of Woman and Man underlie much of social interaction and are comparable to the other major polarities. Women, with their nurtural qualities, are associated with the earth, while men are associated

with the sky. Women gatherers and farmers deal with plants (of the earth), while men hunters deal with animals.

The mediator between the polarities of woman and man, in the American Indian religious explanation, is a being that combines the elements of both genders. This might be a combination in a physical sense, as in the case of hermaphrodites. Many Native American religions accept this phenomenon in the same way that they accept other variations from the norm. But more important is their acceptance of the idea that gender can be combined in ways other than physical hermaphroditism. The physical aspects of a thing or a person, after all, are not nearly as important as its spirit. American Indians use the concept of a person's *spirit* in the way that other Americans use the concept of a person's *character*. Consequently, physical hermaphroditism is not necessary for the idea of gender mixing. A person's character, their spiritual essence, is the crucial thing.

THE BERDACHE'S SPIRIT

Individuals who are physically normal might have the spirit of the other sex, might range somewhere between the two sexes, or might have a spirit that is distinct from either women or men. Whatever category they fall into, they are seen as being different from men. They are accepted spiritually as "Not Man." Whichever option is chosen, Indian religions offer spiritual explanations. Among the Arapahos of the Plains, berdaches are called *haxu'xan* and are seen to be that way as a result of a supernatural gift from birds or animals. Arapaho mythology recounts the story of Nih'a'ca, the first *haxu'xan*. He pretended to be a woman and married the mountain lion, a symbol for masculinity. The myth, as recorded by ethnographer Alfred Kroeber about 1900, recounted that "These people had the natural desire to become women, and as they grew up gradually became women. They gave up the desires of men. They were married to men. They had miraculous power and could do supernatural things. For instance, it was one of them that first made an intoxicant from rainwater."[12] Besides the theme of inventiveness, similar to the Navajo creation story, the berdache role is seen as a product of a "natural desire." Berdaches "gradually became women," which underscores the notion of woman as a social category rather than as a fixed biological entity. Physical biological sex is less important in gender classification than a person's desire—one's spirit.

They myths contain no prescriptions for trying to change berdaches who are acting out their desires of the heart. Like many other cultures' myths, the Zuni origin myths simply sanction the idea that gender can be transformed independently of biological sex.[13] Indeed, myths warn of dire consequences when interference with such a transformation is attempted. Prince Alexander Maximilian of the German state of Wied, traveling in the northern Plains in the 1830s, heard a myth about a warrior who once tried to force a berdache to avoid women's clothing. The berdache resisted, and the warrior shot him with an arrow. Immediately the berdache disappeared, and the warrior saw only a pile of stones with his arrow in them. Since then, the story concluded, no intelligent person would try to coerce a berdache.[14] Making the point even more directly, a Mandan myth told of an Indian who tried to force *mihdake* (berdaches) to give up their distinctive dress and status, which led the spirits to punish many people with death. After that, no Mandans interfered with berdaches.[15]

With this kind of attitude, reinforced by myth and history, the aboriginal view accepts human diversity. The creation story of the Mohave of the Colorado River Valley speaks of a time when people were not sexually differentiated. From this perspective, it is easy to accept that certain individuals might combine elements of masculinity and femininity.[16] A respected Mohave elder, speaking in the 1930s, stated this viewpoint simply: "From the very beginning of the world it was meant that there should be [berdaches], just as it was instituted that there should be shamans. They were intended for that purpose."[17]

This elder also explained that a child's tendencies to become a berdache are apparent early, by about age nine to twelve, before the child reaches puberty: "That is the time when young persons become initiated into the functions of their sex.... None but young people will become berdaches as a rule."[18] Many tribes have a public ceremony that acknowledges the acceptance of berdache status. A Mohave shaman related the ceremony for his tribe: "When the child was about ten years old his relatives would begin discussing his strange ways. Some of them disliked it, but the more intelligent began envisaging an initiation ceremony." The relatives prepare for the ceremony without letting the boy know if it. It is meant to take him by surprise, to be both an initiation and a test of his true inclinations. People from various settlements are invited to attend. The family wants the community to see it and become accustomed to accepting the boy as an *alyha*.

On the day of the ceremony, the shaman explained, the boy is led into a circle: "If the boy showed a willingness to remain standing in the circle, exposed to the public eye, it was almost certain that he would go through with the ceremony. The singer, hidden behind the crowd, began singing the songs. As soon as the sound reached the boy he began to dance as women do." If the boy is unwilling to assume *alyha* status, he would refuse to dance. But if his character—his spirit—is *alyha*, "the song goes right to his heart and he will dance with much intensity. He cannot help it. After the fourth song he is proclaimed." After the ceremony, the boy is carefully bathed and receives a woman's skirt. He is then led back to the dance ground, dressed as an *alyha*, and announces his new feminine name to the crowd. After that he would resent being called by his old male name.[19]

Among the Yuman tribes of the Southwest, the transformation is marked by a social gathering, in which the berdache prepares a meal for the friends of the family.[20] Ethnographer Ruth Underhill, doing fieldwork among the Papago Indians in the early 1930s, wrote that berdaches were common among the Papago Indians, and were usually publicly acknowledged in childhood. She recounted that a boy's parents would test him if they noticed that he preferred female pursuits. The regular pattern, mentioned by many of Underhill's Papago informants, was to build a small brush enclosure. Inside the enclosure they placed a man's bow and arrows, and also a woman's basket. At the appointed time the boy was brought to the enclosure as the

adults watched from outside. The boy was told to go inside the circle of brush. Once he was inside, the adults "set fire to the enclosure. They watched what he took with him as he ran out and if it was the basketry materials, they reconciled themselves to his being a berdache."[21]

What is important to recognize in all of these practices is that the assumption of a berdache role was not forced on the boy by others. While adults might have their suspicions, it was only when the child made the proper move that he was considered a berdache. By doing woman's dancing, preparing a meal, or taking the woman's basket he was making an important symbolic gesture. Indian children were not stupid, and they knew the implications of these ceremonies beforehand. A boy in the enclosure could have left without taking anything, or could have taken both the man's and the woman's tools. With the community standing by watching, he was well aware that his choice would mark his assumption of berdache status. Rather than being seen as an involuntary test of his reflexes, this ceremony may be interpreted as a definite statement by the child to take on the berdache role.

Indians do not see the assumption of berdache status, however, as a free will choice on the part of the boy. People felt that the boy was acting out his basic character. The Lakota shaman Lame Deer explained:

> They were not like other men, but the Great Spirit made them *winktes* and we accepted them as such.... We think that if a woman has two little ones growing inside her, if she is going to have twins, sometimes instead of giving birth to two babies they have formed up in her womb into just one, into a half-man/half-woman kind of being.... To us a man is what nature, or his dreams, make him. We accept him for what he wants to be. That's up to him.[22]

While most of the sources indicate that once a person becomes a berdache it is a lifelong status, directions from the spirits determine everything. In at least one documented case, concerning a nineteenth-century Klamath berdache named Lele'ks, he later had a supernatural experience that led him to leave the berdache role. At that time Lele'ks began dressing and acting like a man, then married women, and eventually became one of the most famous Klamath chiefs.[23] What is important is that both in assuming berdache status and in leaving it, supernatural dictate is the determining factor.

DREAMS AND VISIONS

Many tribes see the berdache role as signifying an individual's proclivities as a dreamer and a visionary....

Among the northern Plains and related Great Lakes tribes, the idea of supernatural dictate through dreaming—the vision quest—had its highest development. The goal of the vision quest is to try to get beyond the rational world by sensory deprivation and fasting. By depriving one's body of nourishment, the brain could escape from logical thought and connect with the higher reality of the supernatural. The person doing the quest simply sits and waits for a vision. But a vision might not come easily; the person might have to wait for days.

The best way that I can describe the process is to refer to my own vision quest, which I experienced when I was living on a Lakota reservation in 1982. After a long series of prayers and blessings, the shaman who had prepared me for the ceremony took me out to an isolated area where a sweat lodge had been set up for my quest. As I walked to the spot, I worried that I might not be able to stand it. Would I be overcome by hunger? Could I tolerate the thirst? What would I do if I had to go to the toilet? The shaman told me not to worry, that a whole group of holy people would be praying and singing for me while I was on my quest.

He had me remove my clothes, symbolizing my disconnection from the material would, and crawl into the sweat lodge. Before he left me I asked him, "What do I think about?" He said, "Do not think. Just pray for spiritual guidance." After a prayer he closed the flap tightly and I was left in total darkness. I still do not understand what happened to me during my vision quest, but during the day and a half that I was out there, I never once felt hungry or thirsty or the need to go to the toilet. What happened was an intensely personal experience that I cannot and do not wish to explain, a process of being that cannot be described in rational terms.

When the shaman came to get me at the end of my time, I actually resented having to end it. He did not need to ask if my vision quest were successful. He knew that it was even before seeing me, he explained, because he saw an eagle circling over me while I underwent the quest. He helped interpret the signs I had seen, then after more prayers and singing he led me back to the others. I felt relieved, cleansed, joyful, and serene. I had been through an experience that will be a part of my memories always.

If a vision quest could have such an effect on a person not even raised in Indian society, imagine its impact on a boy who from his earliest years had been waiting for the day when he could seek his vision. Gaining his spiritual power from his first vision, it would tell him what role to take in adult life. The vision might instruct him that he is going to be a great hunter, a craftsman, a warrior, or a shaman. Or it might tell him that he will be a berdache. Among the Lakotas, or Sioux, there are several symbols for various types of visions. A person becomes *wakan* (a sacred person) if she or he dreams of a bear, a wolf, thunder, a buffalo, a white buffalo calf, or Double Woman. Each dream results in a different gift, whether it is the power to cure illness or wounds, a promise of good hunting, or the exalted role of a *heyoka* (doing things backward).

A white buffalo calf is believed to be a berdache. If a person has a dream of the sacred Double Woman, this means that she or he will have the power to seduce men. Males who have a vision of Double Woman are presented with female tools. Taking such tools means that the male will become a berdache. The Lakota word *winkte* is composed of *win*, "woman," and *kte*, "would become."[24] A contemporary Lakota berdache explains, "To become a *winkte*, you have a medicine man put you up on the hill, to search for your vision. "You can become a *winkte* if you truly are by nature. You see a vision of the White Buffalo Calf Pipe. Sometimes it varies. A vision is like a scene in a movie."[25] Another way to become a *winkte* is to have a vision given by a *winkte* from the past.[26]…

By interpreting the result of the vision as being the work of a spirit, the vision quest frees the person from feeling responsible for his transformation. The person might even claim that the change was done against his will and without his control. Such a claim does not suggest a negative attitude about berdache status, because it is common for people to claim reluctance to fulfill their spiritual duty no matter what vision appears to them. Becoming any kind of sacred person involves taking on various social responsibilities and burdens.[27]…

A story was told among the Lakotas in the 1880s of a boy who tried to resist following his vision from Double Woman. But according to Lakota informants "few men succeed in this effort after having taken the strap in the dream." Having rebelled against the instructions given him by the Moon Being, he committed suicide.[28] The moral of that story is that one should not resist spiritual guidance, because it will lead only to grief. In another case, an Omaha young man told of being addressed by a spirit as "daughter," whereupon he discovered that he was unconsciously using feminine styles of speech. He tried to use male speech patterns, but could not. As a result of this vision, when he returned to his people he resolved himself to dress as a woman.[29] Such stories function to justify personal peculiarities as due to a fate over which the individual has no control.

Despite the usual pattern in Indian societies of using ridicule to enforce conformity, receiving instructions from a vision inhibits others from trying to change the berdache. Ritual explanation provides a way out. It also excuses the community from worrying about the cause of that person's difference, or the feeling that it is society's duty to try to change him.[30] Native American religions, above all else, encourage a basic respect for nature. If nature makes a person different, many Indians conclude, a mere human should not undertake to counter this spiritual dictate. Someone who is "unusual" can be accommodated without being stigmatized as "abnormal." Berdachism is thus not alien or threatening; it is a reflection of spirituality.

NOTES

1. Mary Douglas, *Purity and Danger* (Baltimore: Penguin, 1966), p. 52. I am grateful to Theda Perdue for convincing me that Douglas's ideas apply to berdachism. For an application of Douglas's thesis to berdaches, see James Thayer, "The Berdache of the Northern Plains: A Socioreligious Perspective," *Journal of Anthropological Research 36* (1980): 292–93.

2. E. W. Gifford, "The Kamia of Imperial Valley," *Bureau of American Ethnology Bulletin 97* (1931): 12.

3. By using present tense verbs in this text, I am not implying that such activities are necessarily continuing today. I sometimes use the present tense in the "ethnographic present," unless I use the past tense when I am referring to something that has not continued. Past tense implies that all such prac-

tices have disappeared. In the absence of fieldwork to prove such disappearance, I am not prepared to make that assumption, on the historic changes in the berdache tradition.

4. Elsie Clews Parsons, "The Zuni La' Mana," *American Anthropologist* 18 (1916): 521; Matilda Coxe Stevenson, "Zuni Indians," *Bureau of American Ethnology Annual Report 23* (1903): 37; Franklin Cushing, "Zuni Creation Myths," *Bureau of American Ethnology Annual Report 13* (1894): 401–3. Will Roscoe clarified this origin story for me.

5. W. W. Hill, "Note on the Pima Berdache," *American Anthropologist 40* (1938): 339.

6. Aileen O'Bryan, "The Dine': Origin Myths of the Navaho Indians," *Bureau of American Ethnology Bulletin 163* (1956): 5; W. W. Hill, "The Status of the Hermaphrodite and Transvestite in Navaho Culture," *American Anthropologist 37* (1935): 273.

7. Martha S. Link, *The Pollen Path: A Collection of Navajo Myths* (Stanford: Stanford University Press, 1956).

8. O'Bryan, "Dine'," pp. 5, 7, 9–10.

9. Ibid.

10. Lakota informants, July 1982. See also William Powers, *Oglala Religion* (Lincoln: University of Nebraska Press, 1977).

11. For this admittedly generalized overview of American Indian religious values, I am indebted to traditionalist informants of many tribes, but especially those of the Lakotas. For a discussion of native religions see Dennis Tedlock, *Finding the Center* (New York: Dial Press, 1972); Ruth Underhill, *Red Man's Religion* (Chicago: University of Chicago Press, 1965); and Elsi Clews Parsons, *Pueblo Indian Religion* (Chicago: University of Chicago Press, 1939).

12. lfred Kroeber, "The Arapaho," *Bulletin of the American Museum of Natural History 18* (1902–7): 19.

13. Parsons, "Zuni La' Mana," p. 525.

14. Alexander Maximilian, *Travels in the interior of North America, 1832–1834*, vol. 22 of *Early Western Travels,* ed. Reuben Gold Thwaites, 32 vols. (Cleveland: A. H. Clark, 1906), pp. 283–84, 354. Maximilian was quoted in German in the early homosexual rights book by Ferdinand Karsch-Haack, *Das Gleichgeschlechtliche Leben der Naturvölker* (The same-sex life of nature peoples) (Munich: Verlag von Ernst Reinhardt, 1911; reprinted New York: Arno Press, 1975), pp. 314, 564.

15. Oscar Koch, *Der Indianishe Eros* (Berlin: Verlag Continent, 1925), p. 61.

16. George Devereux, "Institutionalized Homosexuality of the Mohave Indians," *Human Biology 9* (1937): 509.

17. Ibid., p. 501

18. Ibid.

19. Ibid., pp. 508–9.

20. C. Daryll Forde, "Ethnography of the Yuma Indians," *University of California Publications in American Archaeology and Ethnology 28* (1931): 157.

21. Ruth Underhill, *Social Organization of the Papago Indians* (New York: Columbia University Press, 1938), p. 186. This story is also mentioned in Ruth Underhill, ed., *The Autobiography of a Papago Woman* (Menasha, Wisc.: American Anthropological Association, 1936), p. 39.

22. John Fire and Richard Erdoes, *Lame Deer, Seeker of Visions* (New York: Simon and Schuster, 1972), pp. 117, 149.

23. Theodore Stern, *The Klamath Tribe: A People and Their Reservation* (Seattle: University of Washington Press, 1965), pp. 20, 24; Theodore Stern, "Some Sources of Variability in Klamath Mythology," *Journal of American Folklore 69* (1956): 242ff; Leshe Spier, *Klamath Ethnography* (Berkeley: University of California Press, 1930), p. 52.

24. Clark Wissler, "Societies and Ceremonial Associations in the Oglala Division of the Teton Dakota," *Anthoropological Papers of the american Museum of Natural History 11*, pt. 1 (1916): 92; Powers, *Oglala Religion*, pp. 57–59.

25. Ronnie Loud Hawk, Lakota informant 4, July 1982.

26. Terry Calling Eagle, Lakota informant 5, July 1982.

27. James S. Thayer, "The Berdache of the Northern Plains: A Socioreligious Perspective," *Journal of Anthropological Research 36* (1980): 289.

28. Fletcher, "Elk Mystery," p. 281.

29. Alice Fletcher and Francis La Flesche, "The Omaha Tribe," *Bureau of American Ethnology Annual Report 27* (1905–6): 132.

30. Harriet Whitehead offers a valuable discussion of this element of the vision quest in "The Bow and the Burden Strap: A New Look at Institutionalized Homosexuality in Native North America," in *Sexual Meanings,* ed. Sherry Ortner and Harriet Whitehead (Cambridge: Cambridge University Press, 1981), pp. 99–102. See also Erikson, "Childhood," p. 329.

From *The Meaning of Difference*, 2000, pp. 92-99. © 2000 by Beacon Press.

A Woman's Curse?

*Why do cultures the world over treat menstruating women as taboo?
An anthropologist offers a new answer—and a challenge to Western
ideas about contraception*

By Meredith F. Small

THE PASSAGE FROM GIRLHOOD TO womanhood is marked by a flow of blood from the uterus. Without elaborate ceremony, often without discussion, girls know that when they begin to menstruate, their world is changed forever. For the next thirty years or so, they will spend much energy having babies, or trying not to, reminded at each menstruation that either way, the biology of reproduction has a major impact on their lives.

Anthropologists have underscored the universal importance of menstruation by documenting how the event is interwoven into the ideology as well as the daily activities of cultures around the world. The customs attached to menstruation take peculiarly negative forms: the so-called menstrual taboos. Those taboos may prohibit a woman from having sex with her husband or from cooking for him. They may bar her from visiting sacred places or taking part in sacred activities. They may forbid her to touch certain items used by men, such as hunting gear or weapons, or to eat certain foods or to wash at certain times. They may also require that a woman paint her face red or wear a red hip cord, or that she segregate herself in a special hut while she is menstruating. In short, the taboos set menstruating women apart from the rest of their society, marking them as impure and polluting.

Anthropologists have studied menstrual taboos for decades, focusing on the negative symbolism of the rituals as a cultural phenomenon. Perhaps, suggested one investigator, taking a Freudian perspective, such taboos reflect the anxiety that men feel about castration, an anxiety that would be prompted by women's genital bleeding. Others have suggested that the taboos serve to prevent menstrual odor from interfering with hunting, or that they protect men from microorganisms that might otherwise be transferred during sexual intercourse with a menstruating woman. Until recently, few investigators had considered the possibility that the taboos—and the very fact of menstruation—might instead exist because they conferred an evolutionary advantage.

In the mid-1980s the anthropologist Beverly I. Strassmann of the University of Michigan in Ann Arbor began to study the ways men and women have evolved to accomplish (and regulate) reproduction. Unlike traditional anthropologists, who focus on how culture affects human behavior, Strassmann was convinced that the important role played by biology was being neglected. Menstruation, she suspected, would be a key for observing and understanding the interplay of biology and culture in human reproductive behavior.

To address the issue, Strassmann decided to seek a culture in which making babies was an ongoing part of adult life. For that she had to get away from industrialized countries, with their bias toward contraception and low birthrates. In a "natural-fertility population," she rea-soned, she could more clearly see the connection between the physiology of women and the strategies men and women use to exploit that physiology for their own reproductive ends.

Strassmann ended up in a remote corner of West Africa, living in close quarters with the Dogon, a traditional society whose indigenous religion of ancestor worship requires that menstruating women spend their nights at a small hut. For more than two years Strassmann kept track of the women staying at the hut, and she confirmed the menstruations by testing urine samples for the appropriate hormonal changes. In so doing, she amassed the first long-term data describing how a traditional society appropriates a physiological event—menstruation—and refracts that event through a prism of behaviors and beliefs.

What she found explicitly challenges the conclusions of earlier investigators about the cultural function of menstrual taboos. For the Dogon men, she discovered, enforcing visits to the menstrual hut serves to channel parental resources into the upbringing of their own children. But more, Strassmann, who also had training as a reproductive physiologist, proposed a new theory of why menstruation itself evolved as it did—and again, the answer is essentially a story of conserving resources. Finally, her observations pose provocative questions about women's health in industrialized societies, raising serious doubts about the tactics favored by Western medicine for developing contraceptive technology.

Menstruation is the visible stage of the ovarian cycle, orchestrated primarily by hormones secreted by the ovaries: progesterone and a family of hormones called estrogens. At the beginning of each cycle (by convention, the first day of a woman's period) the levels of the estrogens begin to rise. After about five days, as their concentrations increase, they cause the blood- and nutrient-rich inner lining of the uterus, called the endometrium, to thicken and acquire a densely branching network of blood vessels. At about the middle of the cycle, ovulation takes place, and an egg makes its way from one of the two ovaries down one of the paired fallopian tubes to the uterus. The follicle from which the egg was released in the ovary now begins to secrete progesterone as well as estrogens, and the progesterone causes the endometrium to swell and become even richer with blood vessels—in short, fully ready for a pregnancy, should conception take place and the fertilized egg become implanted.

If conception does take place, the levels of estrogens and progesterone continue to rise throughout the pregnancy. That keeps the endometrium thick enough to support the quickening life inside the uterus. When the baby is born and the new mother begins nursing, the estrogens and progesterone fall to their initial levels, and lactation hormones keep them suppressed. The uterus thus lies quiescent until frequent lactation ends, which triggers the return to ovulation.

If conception does not take place after ovulation, all the ovarian hormones also drop to their initial levels, and menstruation—the shedding of part of the uterine lining—begins. The lining is divided into three layers: a basal layer that is constantly maintained, and two superficial layers, which shed and regrow with each menstrual cycle. All mammals undergo cyclical changes in the state of the endometrium. In most mammals the sloughed-off layers are resorbed into the body if fertilization does not take place. But in some higher primates, including

humans, some of the shed endometrium is not resorbed. The shed lining, along with some blood, flows from the body through the vaginal opening, a process that in humans typically lasts from three to five days.

Of course, physiological facts alone do not explain why so many human groups have infused a bodily function with symbolic meaning. And so in 1986 Strassmann found herself driving through the Sahel region of West Africa at the peak of the hot season, heading for a sandstone cliff called the Bandiagara Escarpment, in Mali. There, permanent Dogon villages of mud or stone houses dotted the rocky plateau. The menstrual huts were obvious: round, low-roofed buildings set apart from the rectangular dwellings of the rest of the village.

The Dogon are a society of millet and onion farmers who endorse polygyny, and they maintain their traditional culture despite the occasional visits of outsiders. In a few Dogon villages, in fact, tourists are fairly common, and ethnographers had frequently studied the Dogon language, religion and social structure before Strassmann's arrival. But her visit was the first time someone from the outside wanted to delve into an intimate issue in such detail.

It took Strassmann a series of hikes among villages, and long talks with male elders under the thatched-roof shelters where they typically gather, to find the appropriate sites for her research. She gained permission for her study in fourteen villages, eventually choosing two. That exceptional welcome, she thinks, emphasized the universality of her interests. "I'm working on all the things that really matter to [the Dogon]—fertility, economics—so they never questioned my motives or wondered why I would be interested in these things," she says. "It seemed obvious to them." She set up shop for the next two and a half years in a stone house in the village, with no running water or electricity. Eating the daily fare of the Dogon, millet porridge, she and a research assistant began to integrate themselves into village life, learning the language, getting to know people and tracking visits to the menstrual huts.

Following the movements of menstruating women was surprisingly easy. The menstrual huts are situated outside the walled compounds of the village, but in full view of the men's thatched-roof shelters. As the men relax under their shelters, they can readily see who leaves the huts in the morning and returns to them in the evening. And as nonmenstruating women pass the huts on their way to and from the fields or to other compounds, they too can see who is spending the night there. Strassmann found that when she left her house in the evening to take data, any of the villagers could accurately predict whom she would find in the menstrual huts.

The huts themselves are cramped, dark buildings—hardly places where a woman might go to escape the drudgery of work or to avoid an argument with her husband or a co-wife. The huts sometimes become so crowded that some occupants are forced outside—making the women even more conspicuous. Although babies and toddlers can go with their mothers to the huts, the women consigned there are not allowed to spend time with the rest of their families. They must cook with special pots, not their usual household possessions. Yet they are still expected to do their usual jobs, such as working in the fields.

Why, Strassmann wondered, would anyone put up with such conditions?

The answer, for the Dogon, is that a menstruating woman is a threat to the sanctity of religious altars, where men pray and make sacrifices for the protection of their fields, their families and their village. If menstruating women come near the altars, which are situated both indoors and outdoors, the Dogon believe that their aura of pollution will ruin the altars and bring calamities upon the village. The belief is so ingrained that the women themselves have internalized it, feeling its burden of responsibility and potential guilt. Thus violations of the taboo are rare, because a menstruating woman who breaks the rules knows that she is personally responsible if calamities occur.

NEVERTHELESS, STRASSMANN STILL thought a more functional explanation for menstrual taboos might also exist, one closely related to reproduction. As she was well aware, even before her studies among the Dogon, people around the world have a fairly sophisticated view of how reproduction works. In general, people everywhere know full well that menstruation signals the absence of a pregnancy and the possibility of another one. More precisely, Strassmann could frame her hypothesis by reasoning as follows: Across cultures, men and women recognize that a lack of menstrual cycling in a woman implies she is either pregnant, lactating or menopausal. Moreover, at least among natural-fertility cultures that do not practice birth control, continual cycles during peak reproductive years imply to people in those cultures that a woman is sterile. Thus, even though people might not be able to pinpoint ovulation, they can easily identify whether a woman will soon be ready to conceive on the basis of whether she is menstruating. And that leads straight to Strassmann's insightful hypothesis about the role of menstrual taboos: information about menstruation can be a means of tracking paternity.

"There are two important pieces of information for assessing paternity," Strassmann notes: timing of intercourse and timing of menstruation. "By forcing women to signal menstruation, men are trying to gain equal access to one part of that critical information." Such information, she explains, is crucial to Dogon men, because they invest so many resources in their own offspring. Descent is marked through the male line; land and the food that comes from the land is passed down from fathers to sons. Information about paternity is thus crucial to a man's entire lineage. And because each man has as many as four wives, he cannot possibly track them all. So forcing women to signal their menstrual periods, or lack thereof, helps men avoid cuckoldry.

TO TEST HER HYPOTHESIS, STRASS-mann tracked residence in the menstrual huts for 736 consecutive days, collecting data on 477 complete cycles. She noted who was at each hut and how long each woman stayed. She also collected urine from ninety-three women over a ten-week period, to check the correlation between residence in the menstrual hut and the fact of menstruation.

The combination of ethnographic records and urinalyses showed that the Dogon women mostly play by the rules. In 86 percent of the hormonally detected menstruations, women went to the hut. Moreover, none of the tested women went to the hut when they were not menstruating. In the remaining 14 percent of the tested menstruations, women stayed home from the hut, in violation of the taboo, but some were near menopause and so not at high risk for pregnancy. More important, none of the women who violated the taboo did it twice in a row. Even they were largely willing to comply.

Thus, Strassmann concluded, the huts do indeed convey a fairly reliable signal, to men and to everyone else, about the status of a woman's fertility. When she leaves the hut, she is considered ready to conceive. When she stops going to the hut, she is evidently pregnant or menopausal. And women of prime reproductive age who visit the hut on a regular basis are clearly infertile.

It also became clear to Strassmann that the Dogon do indeed use that information to make paternity decisions. In several cases a man was forced to marry a pregnant woman, simply because everyone knew that the man had been the woman's first sexual partner after her last visit to the menstrual hut. Strassmann followed one case in which a child was being brought up by a man because he was the mother's first sexual partner after a hut visit, even though the woman soon married a different man. (The woman already knew she was pregnant by the first man at the time of her marriage, and she did not visit the menstrual hut before she married. Thus the truth was obvious to everyone, and the real father took the child.)

In general, women are cooperative players in the game because without a man, a woman has no way to support herself or her children. But women follow the taboo reluctantly. They complain about going to the hut. And if their husbands convert from the traditional religion of the Dogon to a religion that does not impose menstrual taboos, such as Is-lam or Christianity, the women quickly cease visiting the hut. Not that such a religious conversion quells a man's interest in his wife's fidelity: far from it. But the rules change. Perhaps the sanctions of the new religion against infidelity help keep women faithful, so the men can relax their guard. Or perhaps the men are willing to trade the reproductive advantages of the menstrual taboo for the economic benefits gained by converting to the new religion. Whatever the case, Strassmann found an almost perfect correlation between a husband's religion and his wives' attendance at the hut. In sum, the taboo is established by men, backed by supernatural forces, and internalized and accepted by women until the men release them from the belief.

BUT BEYOND THE CULTURAL MACHI-nations of men and women that Strassmann expected to find, her data show something even more fundamental—and surprising—about female biology. On average, she calculates, a woman in a natural-fertility population such as the Dogon has only about 110 menstrual periods in her lifetime. The rest of the time she will be prepubescent, pregnant, lactating or menopausal. Women in industrialized cultures, by contrast, have more than three times as many cycles: 350 to 400, on average, in a lifetime. They reach menarche (their first menstruation) earlier—at age twelve and a half, compared with the onset age of sixteen in natural-fertility cultures. They have fewer babies, and they lactate hardly at all. All those factors lead women in the industrialized world to a lifetime of nearly continuous menstrual cycling.

The big contrast in cycling profiles during the reproductive years can be traced specifically to lactation. Women in more traditional societies spend most of their reproductive years in lactation amenorrhea, the state in which the hormonal changes required for nursing suppress ovulation and inhibit menstruation. And it is not just that the Dogon bear more children (eight to nine on average); they also nurse each child on demand rather than in scheduled bouts, all through the night as well as the day, and intensely enough that ovulation simply stops for about twenty months per child. Women in industrialized societies typically do not breast-feed as intensely (or at all), and rarely breast-feed each child for as long as the Dogon women do. (The average for American women is four months.)

The Dogon experience with menstruation may be far more typical of the human condition over most of evolutionary history than is the standard menstrual experience in industrialized nations. If so, Strassmann's findings alter some of the most closely held beliefs about female biology. Contrary to what the Western medical establishment might think, it is not particularly "normal" to menstruate each month. The female body, according to Strassmann, is biologically designed to spend much more time in lactation amenorrhea than in menstrual cycling. That in itself suggests that oral contraceptives, which alter hormone levels to suppress ovulation and produce a bleeding, could be forcing a continual state of cycling for which the body is ill-prepared. Women might be better protected against reproductive cancers if their contraceptives mimicked lactation amenorrhea and depressed the female reproductive hormones, rather than forcing the continual ebb and flow of menstrual cycles.

Strassmann's data also call into question a recently popularized idea about menstruation: that regular menstrual cycles might be immunologically beneficial for women. In 1993 the controversial writer Margie Profet, whose ideas about evolutionary and reproductive biology have received vast media attention, proposed in *The Quarterly Review of Biology* that menstruation could have such an adaptive value. She noted that viruses and bacteria regularly enter the female body on the backs of sperm, and she hypothesized that the best way to get them out is to flush them out. Here, then, was a positive, adaptive role for something unpleasant, an evolutionary reason for suffering cramps each month. Menstruation, according to Profet, had evolved to rid the body of pathogens. The "anti-pathogen" theory was an exciting hypothesis, and it

helped win Profet a MacArthur Foundation award. But Strassmann's work soon showed that Profet's ideas could not be supported because of one simple fact: under less-industrialized conditions, women menstruate relatively rarely.

Instead, Strassmann notes, if there is an adaptive value to menstruation, it is ultimately a strategy to conserve the body's resources. She estimates that maintaining the endometrial lining during the second half of the ovarian cycle takes substantial metabolic energy. Once the endometrium is built up and ready to receive a fertilized egg, the tissue requires a sevenfold metabolic increase to remain rich in blood and ready to support a pregnancy. Hence, if no pregnancy is forthcoming, it makes a lot of sense for the body to let part of the endometrium slough off and then regenerate itself, instead of maintaining that rather costly but unneeded tissue. Such energy conservation is common among vertebrates: male rhesus monkeys have shrunken testes during their nonbreeding season, Burmese pythons shrink their guts when they are not digesting, and hibernating animals put their metabolisms on hold.

Strassmann also suggests that periodically ridding oneself of the endometrium could make a difference to a woman's long-term survival. Because female reproductive hormones affect the brain and other tissues, the metabolism of the entire body is involved during cycling. Strassmann estimates that by keeping hormonal low through half the cycle, a woman can save about six days' worth of energy for every four nonconceptive cycles. Such caloric conservation might have proved useful to early hominids who lived by hunting and gathering, and even today it might be helpful for women living in less affluent circumstances than the ones common in the industrialized West.

BUT PERHAPS THE MOST PROVOCATIVE implications of Strassmann's work have to do with women's health. In 1994 a group of physicians and anthropologists pub-

lished a paper, also in *The Quarterly Review of Biology*, suggesting that the reproductive histories and lifestyles of women in industrialized cultures are at odds with women's naturally evolved biology, and that the differences lead to greater risks of reproductive cancers. For example, the investigators estimated that women in affluent cultures may have a hundredfold greater risk of breast cancer than do women who subsist by hunting and gathering. The increased risk is probably caused not only by low levels of exercise and a high-fat diet, but also by a relatively high number of menstrual cycles over a lifetime. Repeated exposure to the hormones of the ovarian cycle—because of early menarche, late menopause, lack of pregnancy and little or no breast-feeding—is implicated in other reproductive cancers as well.

Those of us in industrialized cultures have been running an experiment on ourselves. The body evolved over millions of years to move across the landscape looking for food, to live in small kin-based groups, to make babies at intervals of four years or so and to invest heavily in each child by nursing intensely for years. How many women now follow those traditional patterns? We move little, we rely on others to get our food, and we rarely reproduce or lactate. Those culturally initiated shifts in lifestyles may pose biological risks.

Our task is not to overcome that biology, but to work with it. Now that we have a better idea of how the female body was designed, it may be time to rework our lifestyles and change some of our expectations. It may be time to borrow from our distant past or from our contemporaries in distant cultures, and treat our bodies more as nature intended.

***MEREDITH F. SMALL** is a professor of anthropology at Cornell University in Ithaca, New York. Her latest book,* OUR BABIES, OURSELVES: HOW BIOLOGY AND CULTURE SHAPE THE WAY WE PARENT, *was published in May 1998 [see Laurence A. Marschall's review in Books in Brief, November/December 1998].*

Reprinted by permission of *The Sciences*, January/February 1999, pp. 24–29. © 1999 by the New York Academy of Science. Individual subscriptions are $28 per year. Write to: The Sciences, 2 East 63rd Street, New York, NY 10021.

What About "Female Genital Mutilation"? And Why Understanding Culture Matters in the First Place

Richard A. Shweder

Female genital mutilation (FGM, also known as female circumcision) has been practiced traditionally for centuries in sub-Saharan Africa. Customs, rituals, myths, and taboos have perpetuated the practice even though it has maimed or killed untold numbers of women and girls.... FGM's disastrous health effects, combined with the social injustices it perpetuates, constitute a serious barrier to overall African development.

—Susan Rich and
Stephanie Joyce[1]

On the basis of the vast literature on the harmful effects of genital surgeries, one might have anticipated finding a wealth of studies that document considerable increases in mortality and morbidity. This review could find no incontrovertible evidence on mortality, and the rate of medical complications suggests that they are the exception rather than the rule.

—Carla M. Obermeyer[2]

Early societies in Africa established strong controls over the sexual behavior of their women and devised the brutal means of circumcision to curb female sexual desire and response.

—Olayinka Koso-Thomas[3]

...studies that systematically investigate the sexual feelings of women and men in societies where genital surgeries are found are rare, and the scant information that is available calls into question the assertion that female genital surgeries are fundamentally antithetical to women's sexuality and incompatible with sexual enjoyment.

—Carla M. Obermeyer[4]

Those who practice some of the most controversial of such customs—clitoridectomy, polygamy, the marriage of children or marriages that are otherwise coerced—sometimes explicitly defend them as necessary for controlling women and openly acknowledge that the customs persist at men's insistence.

—Susan M. Okin[5]

It is difficult for me—considering the number of ceremonies I have observed, including my own—to accept that what appear to be expressions of joy and ecstatic celebrations of womanhood in actuality disguise hidden experiences of coercion and subjugation. Indeed, I offer that the bulk of Kono women who uphold these rituals do so because they want to—they relish the supernatural powers of their ritual leaders over against men in society, and they brace the legitimacy of female authority and, particularly,

the authority of their mothers and grandmothers.

—Fuambai Ahmadu[6]

BY RITES A WOMAN: LISTENING TO THE MULTICULTURAL VOICES OF FEMINISM

ON NOVEMBER 18, 1999, FUAMBAI AHmadu, a young African scholar who grew up in the United States, delivered a paper at the American Anthropological Association meeting in Chicago that should be deeply troubling to all liberal freethinking people who value democratic pluralism and the toleration of "differences" and who care about the accuracy of cultural representations in our publicpolicy debates.

Ahmadu began her paper with these words:

I also share with feminist scholars and activists campaigning against the practice [of female circumcision] a concern for women's physical, psychological and sexual well-being, as well as for the implications of these traditional rituals for women's status and power in society. Coming from an ethnic group [the Kono of Eastern Sierra Leone] in which female (and male) initiation and "circumcision" are institutionalized and a central feature of culture and society and having myself undergone this traditional process of becoming a "woman," I find it increasingly challenging to reconcile my own experiences with prevailing global discourses on female "circumcision."[7]

Coming-of-age ceremonies and gender-identity ceremonies involving genital alterations are embraced by, and deeply embedded in the lives of, many African women, not only in Africa but in Europe and the United States as well. Estimates of the number of contemporary African women who participate in these practices vary widely and wildly between eighty million and two hundred million. In general, these women keep their secrets secret. They have not been inclined to expose the most intimate parts of their bodies to public examination and they have not been in the habit of making their case on the op-ed pages of American newspapers, in the halls of Congress, or at academic meetings. So it was an extraordinary event to witness Fuambai Ahmadu, an initiate and an anthropologist, stand up and state that the oft-repeated claims "regarding adverse effects [of female circumcision] on women's sexuality do not tally with the experiences of most Kono women," including her own.[8] Ahmadu was twenty-two years old and sexually experienced when she returned to Sierra Leone to be circumcised, so at least in her own case she knows what she is talking about. Most Kono women uphold the practice of female (and male) circumcision and positively evaluate its consequences for their psychological, social, spiritual, and physical well-being. Ahmadu went on to suggest that Kono girls and women feel empowered by the initiation ceremony (see quotation, above) and she described some of the reasons why.

Ahmadu's ethnographic observations and personal testimony may seem astonishing to readers of *Dædalus*. In the social and intellectual circles in which most Americans travel it has been so "politically correct" to deplore female circumcision that the alarming claims and representations of anti-"FGM" advocacy groups (images of African parents routinely and for hundreds of years disfiguring, maiming, and murdering their female children and depriving them of their capacity for a sexual response)

have not been carefully scrutinized with regard to reliable evidence. Nor have they been cross-examined by freethinking minds through a process of systematic rebuttal. Quite the contrary; the facts on the ground and the correct moral attitude for "good guys" have been taken to be so self-evident that merely posing the rhetorical question "what about FGM?" is presumed to function as an obvious counterargument to cultural pluralism and to define a clear limit to any feelings of tolerance for alternative ways of life. This is unfortunate, because in this case there is good reason to believe that the case is far less one-sided than supposed, that the "bad guys" are not really all that bad, that the values of pluralism should be upheld, and that the "good guys" may have rushed to judgment and gotten an awful lot rather wrong.

Six months before Fuambai Ahmadu publicly expressed her doubts about the prevailing global discourse on female circumcision, readers of the *Medical Anthropology Quarterly* observed an extraordinary event of a similar yet (methodologically) different sort. Carla Obermeyer, a medical anthropologist and epidemiologist at Harvard University, published a comprehensive review of the existing medical literature on female genital surgeries in Africa, in which she concluded that the claims of the anti-"FGM" movement are highly exaggerated and may not match reality.

Obermeyer began her essay by pointing out that "The exhaustive review of the literature on which this article is based was motivated by what appeared as a potential disparity between the mobilization of resources toward activism and the research base that ought to support such efforts."[9] When she took a closer look at that "research base" (a total of 435 articles were reviewed from the medical, demographic, and social science literatures, including every published article available on the topic of "female circumcision" or "female genital mutilation" in the Medline, Popline, and Sociofile databases), she discovered that in most publications in which statements were made about the devastating effects of female circumcision no evidence was presented at all. When she examined research reports actually con-

taining original evidence she discovered numerous methodological flaws (e.g., small or unrepresentative samples, no control groups) and quality-control problems (e.g., vague descriptions of medical complications) in some of the most widely cited documents. She remarks: "Despite their deficiencies, some of the published reports have come to acquire an aura of dependability through repeated and uncritical citations."[10]

In order to draw some realistic, even if tentative, conclusions about the health consequences of female circumcision in Africa, Obermeyer then introduced some standard epidemiological quality-control criteria for evaluating evidence.[11] For example, a research study would be excluded if its sampling methods were not described or if its claims were based on a single case rather than a population sample. On the basis of the relatively small number of available studies that actually passed minimum scientific standards (for example, eight studies on the topic of medical complications), Obermeyer reported that the widely publicized medical complications of African genital operations are the exception, not the rule; that female genital alterations are not incompatible with sexual enjoyment; and that the claim that untold numbers of girls and women have been killed as a result of this "traditional practice" is not well supported by the evidence.[12]

Many anthropologists and other researchers who work on this topic in various field settings in Africa have been aware of discrepancies between the global discourse on female circumcision (with its images of maiming, murder, sexual dysfunction, mutilation, coercion, and oppression) and their own ethnographic experiences with indigenous discourses and physical realities.[13]

Perhaps the first anthropological protest against the global discourse came in 1938 from Jomo Kenyatta, who, prior to becoming the first president of postcolonial Kenya, wrote a Ph.D. thesis in anthropology at the London School of Economics. His thesis was published as a book entitled *Facing Mount Kenya: The Tribal Life of the Gikuyu*, in which he described both the customary premarital sexual practices of the Gikuyu (lots of fondling and rather liberal attitudes toward adolescent petting and sexual arousal) and the practice of female (and male) circumcision.

Kenyatta's words, published in 1938, have an uncanny contemporary ring and relevance. First he informs us that "In 1931 a conference on African children was held in Geneva under the auspices of the Save the Children Fund. In this conference several European delegates urged that the time was ripe when this 'barbarous custom' should be abolished, and that, like all other 'heathen' customs, it should be abolished at once by law."[14]

He goes on to argue that among the Gikuyu a genital alteration, "like Jewish circumcision," is a bodily sign that is regarded "as the *conditio sine qua non* of the whole teaching of tribal law, religion and morality," that no proper Gikuyu man or woman would have sex with or marry someone who was not circumcised, that the practice is an essential step into responsible adulthood for many African girls and boys, and that "there is a strong community of educated Gikuyu opinion in defense of this custom."[15]

Nearly sixty years later echoes of Jomo Kenyatta's message can be found in the writings of Corinne Kratz, who has written a detailed account of female initiation in another ethnic group in Kenya, the Okiek. The Okiek, she tells us, do not talk about circumcision in terms of the dampening of sexual pleasure or desire, but rather speak of it "in terms of cleanliness, beauty and adulthood." According to Kratz, Okiek women and men view genital modification and the bravery and self-control displayed during the operation as constitutive experiences of Okiek personhood."[16]

Many other examples could be cited of discrepancies between the global discourse and the experience of many field researchers in Africa. With regard to the issue of sexual enjoyment, for example, Robert Edgerton remarks that "Kikuyu men and women, like those of several other East African societies that practice female circumcision, assured me in 1961–62 that circumcised women continue to be orgasmic," and similar remarks appear in other field reports.[17]

With regard to the global discourse that represents circumcision as a disfigurement or a "mutilation," Sandra Lane and Robert Rubinstein have offered the following caution:

An important caveat, however, is that many members of societies that practice traditional female genital surgeries do not view the result as mutilation. Among these groups, in fact, the resulting appearance is considered an improvement over female genitalia in their natural state. Indeed, to call a woman uncircumcised, or to call a man the son of an uncircumcised mother, is a terrible insult and non-circumcised adult female genitalia are often considered disgusting. In interviews we conducted in rural and urban Egypt and in studies conducted by faculty of the High Institute of Nursing, Zagazig University, Egypt, the overwhelming majority of circumcised women planned to have the procedure performed on their daughters. In discussions with some fifty women we found only two who resent and are angry at having been circumcised. Even these women do not think that female circumcision is one of the most critical problems facing Egyptian women and girls. In the rural Egyptian hamlet where we have conducted fieldwork some women were not familiar with groups that did not circumcise their girls. When they learned that the female researcher was not circumcised their response was disgust mixed with joking laughter. They wondered how she could have thus gotten married and questioned how her mother could have neglected such an important part of her preparation for womanhood.[18]

These ethnographic reports are noteworthy because they suggest that instead of assuming that our own perceptions of beauty and disfigurement are universal and must be transcendental we might want to consider the possibility that there is a real and astonishing cultural divide around the world in moral, emotional, and aesthetic reactions to female genital surgeries. There is, of course, no doubt that our own personal feelings of disgust and anxiety about this topic are powerful and can be easily aroused and rhetorically manipulated either with pictures (for example, of Third World surgical implements) or with words (for example, labeling the activity "torture" or "mutilation"). But if we want to understand the true character of this cultural divide in sensibilities it may make good sense to bracket our own initial (and automatic) emotional/visceral reactions and to save any powerful conclusive feelings for the end of the argument, rather than have them color or short-circuit all objective analysis. Perhaps, instead of simply deploring the "savages," we might develop a better understanding of the subject by constructing a synoptic account of the inside point of view, from the perspective of those many African women for whom such practices seem both normal and desirable.

MORAL PLURALISM AND THE "MUTUAL YUCK RESPONSE"

People recoil at each other's practices and say "yuck" at each other all over the world. When it comes to female genital alterations, however, the "mutual yuck" response is particularly intense and may even approach a sense of mutual outrage or horror. From a purely descriptive point of view, that particular type of modification of the "natural" body is routine and normal in many ethnic groups. For example, national prevalence rates of 80–98 percent have been reported for Egypt, Ethiopia, the Gambia, Mali, Sierra Leone, Somalia, and the Sudan.[19] In African nations where the overall prevalence rate is lower—for example, 50 percent in Kenya, 43 percent in Cote d'Ivoire, 30 percent in Ghana—this is typically because some ethnic groups in those countries have a tradition of female circumcision while other ethnic groups do not. For example, within Ghana the ethnic groups in the north and the east circumcise girls (and boys), while the ethnic groups in the south have no tradition of female circumcision. In general, for both boys and girls the best predictor of circumcision (versus the absence of it) is ethnicity or cultural group affiliation. For example, circumcision is customary for the Kono of Sierra Leone, but for the

Wolof of Senegal it is not. For women within these groups, one key factor—their cultural affiliation—trumps other predictors of behavior, such as educational level or socioeconomic status. Among the Kono, even women with a secondary-school or college education are circumcised, while Senegalese Wolof women—including the illiterate and unschooled—are not.

There are other notable facts about this cultural practice. For one thing, most African women do not think about circumcision in human-rights terms. Women who endorse female circumcision typically argue that it is an important part of their cultural heritage or their religion, while women who do not endorse the practice typically argue that it is not permitted by their cultural heritage or their religion.[20]

Second, among members of ethnic groups for whom female circumcision is part of their cultural heritage approval ratings for the custom are generally rather high. According to the Sudan Demographic and Health Survey of 1989–1990, which was conducted in northern and central Sudan, out of 3,805 women interviewed 89 percent were circumcised. Of the women who were circumcised, 96 percent said they had circumcised or would circumcise their daughters. When asked whether they favored continuation of the practice, 90 percent of circumcised women said they favored its continuation.[21]

In Sierra Leone the picture is much the same, and the vast majority of women are sympathetic to the practice. Even Olayinka Koso-Thomas, an anti-"FGM" activist, makes note of the high degree of support for genital operations, although she expresses herself with a rather patronizing voice and in imperial tones. "Most African women," Koso-Thomas observes, "still have not developed the sensitivity to feel deprived or to see in many cultural practices a violation of their human rights. The consequence of this is that, in the mid-80s, when most women in Africa have voting rights and can influence political decisions against practices harmful to their health, they continue to uphold the dictates and mores of the communities in which they live; they seem in fact to regard traditional beliefs as inviolate."[22] When it comes to maintaining their coming-of-age and

gender-identity ceremonies, Koso-Thomas does not like the way many African women vote. She thinks she is enlightened about human rights and health and that they remain in the dark. But she does recognize that, despite her censure, most women in Sierra Leone endorse the practice of circumcision.

Third, although ethnic group affiliation is the best predictor of who circumcises and who does not, the timing and form of the operation are not consistent across groups. Thus, there is enormous variability in the age at which the surgery is normally performed (any time from birth to the late teenage years). There is also enormous variability in the traditional style and degree of surgery (from a cut in the prepuce covering the clitoris to the complete "smoothing out" of the genital area by removing all visible parts of the clitoris and most if not all of the labia). In some ethnic groups (for example, in Somalia and the Sudan) the "smoothing out" operation is concluded by stitching closed the vaginal opening, with the aim of enhancing fertility and protecting the womb.[23] The latter procedure, often referred to as "infibulation" or Pharaonic circumcision, is not typical in most circumcising ethnic groups, although it has received a good deal of attention in the anti-"FGM" literature. It is estimated that it occurs in about 15 percent of all African cases.

In places where the practice of female circumcision is popular, including Somalia and the Sudan, it is widely believed by women that these genital alterations improve their bodies and make them more beautiful, more feminine, more civilized, more honorable.

- More beautiful because the body is made smooth and a protrusion or "fleshy encumbrance" is removed that is thought to be ugly and odious to both sight and touch.[24] There is a cultural aesthetics in play among circumcising ethnic groups, an ideal of the human sexual region as smooth, cleansed, and refined, which supports the view that the genitals of both women and men are unsightly, misshapen, and rather unappealing if left in their "natural" state.

- More feminine because unmodified genitals (in both males and females) are seen as sexually ambiguous. From a female's perspective the clitoris is viewed as an unwelcome vestige of the male organ, and its removal is positively associated with several good things: the attainment of full female identity, induction into a social network and support group of powerful adult women, and ultimately marriage and motherhood.[25] Many women who uphold these traditions of female initiation seek to empower themselves by getting rid of what they perceive as an unbidden and dispensable trace of unwanted male anatomy.

- More civilized because a genital alteration is a symbolic action that says something about one's willingness to exercise restraint over feelings of lust and self-control over the antisocial desire for sexual pleasure.

- More honorable because the surgery announces one's commitment to perpetuate the lineage and value the womb as the source of social reproduction.[26]

As hard as it may be for "us" to believe, in places where female circumcision is commonplace it is not only popular but fashionable. As hard as it may be for "us" to believe (and I recognize that for some of "us" this is really hard to believe), many women in places such as Mali, Somalia, Egypt, Kenya, and Chad are repulsed by the idea of unmodified female genitals. They view unmodified genitals as ugly, unrefined, and undignified, and hence not fully human. They associate unmodified genitals with life outside of or at the bottom of civilized society. "Yuck," they think to themselves; "what kind of barbarians are these who don't circumcise their genitals?"

The "yuck" is, of course, mutual. Female genital alterations are not routine and normal for members of mainstream or majority populations in Europe, the United States, China, Japan, and other parts of the world, including South Africa. For members of those cultures the very thought of female genital surgery produces an unpleasant visceral reaction; although it should be noted that for many of us the detailed visualization of any kind of surgery—a bypass operation, an abortion, a sex change operation, a breast implantation, a face lift, or even a decorative eyebrow or tongue piercing-produces an unpleasant visceral reaction. In other words, merely contemplating a surgery, especially on the face or the genitals, can be quite upsetting or revolting, even when the surgery seems fully justified from our own "native point of view."

In the United States and Europe the practice of genital surgery has been disparaged as "mutilation."[27] It has been re-described as rape or torture and associated with the nightmare of some brutal patriarchal male (or perhaps a Victorian gynecologist) grabbing a young woman or girl, pulling her into the back room screaming and kicking, and using a knife or razor blade to deprive her of her sexuality. Various dramatic and disturbing claims have been made about the health hazards and harmful side effects of African genital operations, including the loss of a capacity to experience sexual pleasure.

Saying "yuck" to the practice has become a symbol of opposition to the oppression of women and of one's support for their emancipation around the world. Eliminating the practice has become a high-priority mission for many Western feminists (and for some human-rights activists in Africa, who, understandably enough, often, although not invariably, come from noncircumcising ethnic groups) and for some international health and human-rights organizations (for example, the World Health Organization, Amnesty International, and Equality Now).

Outside of Africa, especially in the United States and Europe, opposition to female circumcision has become so "politically correct" that until very recently most *anti*-anti-"FGM" criticism has been defensive, superficial, or sympathetic. The sympathetic criticisms are mainly critiques of counterproductive "eradication" tactics. They provide advice on how to be more effective as an anti-"FGM" activist.[28]

There have also been occasional complaints that anti-"FGM" campaigns displace attention and divert resources from battles against social injustice in the United States and Europe.[29] And there have been expressions of concern about the anguished state of mind of African children living in the United States who are told by the media and by social-service agencies that their own mother is "mutilated" and that she is potentially dangerous to them too.[30]

But these types of criticisms do not go very deep. In general, the purported facts about female circumcision go unquestioned, the moral implications of the case are thought to be obvious, and the mere query "what about FGM?" is presumed to function in and of itself as a knock-down argument against both cultural pluralism and any inclination toward tolerance.[31]

SO WHAT ABOUT FGM?

So what about "FGM"? I shall treat this as a real question deserving a considered response rather than as a rhetorical query intended to terminate all debate. For starters, the practice of genital alteration is a rather poor example of gender inequality or of society picking on women. Surveying the world, one finds very few cultures, if any, in which genital surgeries are performed on girls but not boys, although there are many cultures in which they are performed only on boys or on both sexes. The male genital alterations often take place in adolescence and they can involve major modifications (including subincision, in which the penis is split along the line of the urethra). Considering the prevalence, timing, and intensity of the relevant initiation rites, and viewing genital alteration on a worldwide scale, one is hard pressed to argue that it is an obvious instance of a gender inequity disfavoring girls. Quite the contrary; social recognition of the ritual transformation of both boys and girls into a more mature status as empowered men and women is not infrequently a major point of the ceremony. In other words, female circumcision, when and where it occurs in Africa, is much more a case of society treating boys and girls equally before the

common law and inducting them into responsible adulthood in parallel ways.

The practice is also a rather poor example of patriarchal domination. Many patriarchal cultures in Europe and Asia do not engage in genital alterations at all or (as in the case of Jews, many non-African Muslims, and many African ethnic groups) exclude girls from participation in this valued practice and do it only to boys. Moreover, the African ethnic groups that circumcise females (and males) are very different from each other in kinship, religion, economy, family life, ceremonial practice, and so forth. Some are Islamic, some are not. Some are patriarchal, some (such as the Kono, a matrilineal society) are not. Some have formal initiations into well-established women's organizations, some do not.[32] Some care a lot about female purity, sexual restraint outside of marriage, and the social regulation of desire, but others (such as the Gikuyu) are more relaxed about premarital sexual play and are not puritanical. And when it comes to female initiation and genital alterations the practice is almost always controlled, performed, and most strongly upheld by women, although male kin often do provide material and moral support. Typically, however, men have rather little to do with these female operations, may not know very much about them, and may feel it is not really their business to interfere or to try to tell their wives, mothers, aunts, and grandmothers what to do. It is the women of the society who are the cultural experts in this intimate feminine domain, and they are not particularly inclined to give up their powers or share their secrets.

In those cases of female genital alteration with which I am most familiar (I have lived and taught in Kenya, where the practice is routine for some ethnic groups), the adolescent girls who undergo the ritual initiation look forward to it.[33] It is an ordeal and it can be painful (especially if done "naturally" without anesthesia), but it is viewed as a test of courage. It is an event organized and controlled by women, who have their own view of the aesthetics of the body—a different view from ours about what is civilized, dignified, and beautiful. The girl's parents are not trying to be cruel to their daughter—African parents love their children too. No one is raped or tortured. There is a celebration surrounding the event.

What about the devastating negative effects on health and sexuality that are vividly portrayed in the anti-"FGM" literature? When it comes to hard-nosed scientific investigations of the consequences of female genital surgeries on sexuality and health, there are relatively few methodologically sound studies. As Obermeyer discovered in her medical review, most of the published literature is "data-free" or else relies on sensational testimonials, secondhand reports, or inadequate samples. Judged against basic epidemiological research standards, much of the published empirical evidence, including some of the most widely cited publications in the anti-"FGM" advocacy literature (including the influential *Hosken Report*[34]), are fatally flawed.[35] Nevertheless, there is some science worth considering in thinking about female circumcision, which leads Obermeyer to conclude that the global discourse about the health and sexual consequences of the practice is not sufficiently supplied with credible evidence.

The anti-"FGM" advocacy literature typically features long lists of short-term and long-term medical complications of circumcision, including blood loss, shock, acute infection, menstrual problems, childbearing difficulties, incontinence, sterility, and death. These lists read like the warning pamphlets that accompany many prescription drugs, which enumerate every claimed negative side effect of the medicine that has ever been reported (no matter how infrequently). They are very scary to read, and they are very misleading. Scary-looking, stomach-churning, anxiety-provoking lists of possible medical complications aside, Obermeyer's comprehensive review of the literature on the actual frequency and risk of medical complications following genital surgery in Africa suggests that medical complications are the exception, not the rule; that African children do not die because they have been circumcised (they die from malnutrition, war, and disease, not because of coming-of-age ceremonies); and that the experience of

sexual pleasure is compatible with the genital aesthetics and related practices of circumcising groups.

Her findings are basically consistent with Robert Edgerton's comments about female circumcision among the Gikuyu in the Kenya of the 1920s and 1930s, when Western missionaries first launched their own version of "FGM eradication programs." As Edgerton remarks, the operation was performed without anesthesia and hence was very painful, "yet most girls bore it bravely and few suffered serious infection or injury as a result. Circumcised women did not lose their ability to enjoy sexual relations, nor was their child-bearing capacity diminished. Nevertheless the practice offended Christian sensibilities."[36]

In other words, the alarmist claims that are a standard feature of the anti-"FGM" advocacy literature that African traditions of circumcision have "maimed or killed untold numbers of women and girls"[37] and deprived them of their sexuality may not be true. Given the most reliable, even if limited, scientific evidence at hand, those claims should be viewed with skepticism and not accepted as fact, no matter how many times they are uncritically recapitulated on the editorial pages of the *New York Times* or poignantly invoked in a journalistic essay on PBS.

If genital alteration in Africa really were a long-standing cultural practice in which parents, oblivious to intolerably high risks, disabled and murdered their preadolescent and adolescent children, there would be good reason to wish for its quick end. Obermeyer's review suggests that this characterization of the practice may be as fanciful as it is nightmarish, or, at the very least, is dubious and misleading. Given the importance of accurate information in public-policy debates about cultural diversity in liberal democracies, it is time for the anti-"FGM" advocacy groups, who seem to have taken the place of yesterday's Christian missionaries, either to revise the "factoids" they distribute to the public, or else to substantiate their claims with rigorously collected data.

The real facts, I would suggest, are quite otherwise. With regard to the consequences of genital surgeries, the

weight of the evidence suggests that the overwhelming majority of youthful female initiates in countries such as Mali, Kenya, and Sierra Leone believe they have been improved (physically, socially, and spiritually) by the ceremonial ordeal and symbolic process (including the pain) associated with initiation. The evidence indicates that most of these youthful initiates manage to be (in their own estimation) "improved" without disastrous or even major short-term or long-term consequences for their health.

This is not to say that we should not worry about the documented 4–16 percent urinary infection rate associated with these surgeries, or the 7–13 percent of cases in which there is excessive bleeding, or the 1 percent rate of septicemia.[38] The reaction of many people to unsafe abortions, however, is not to get rid of abortions. Perhaps some antiabortion groups might be tempted by the argument that because some abortions are unsafe, there should be no abortions at all. However, a far more reasonable reaction to unsafe abortions is to make them safe. Why not the same reaction in the case of female genital alterations? Infections and other medical complications that arise from unsanitary surgical procedures or malpractice can be corrected without depriving "others" of a rite of passage and system of meaning central to their cultural and personal identities and their overall sense of well-being. What I do want to suggest, however, is that the current sense of shock, horror, and righteous "Western" indignation directed against the mothers of Mali, Somalia, Egypt, Sierra Leone, Ethiopia, the Gambia, and the Sudan is misguided, and rather disturbingly misinformed.

CONCLUSION: ON THE VIRTUES OF BEING SLOW TO JUDGE THE UNFAMILIAR AND HAVING A HARD SECOND LOOK

I can think of no better way to conclude this essay than by quoting legal scholar Lawrence Sager, who writes:

> Epistemic concerns and the principle of equal liberty counsel that we be slow to judge the unfamiliar, that we take a hard second look at our own factual beliefs and norma-

tive judgments before we condemn culturally endorsed practices. So, too, they counsel that extant legal categories of excuse and mitigation not be closed to the distinct experience of cultural minorities. And finally, of course, they require that our robust tradition of constitutional liberty— including the rights of speech and belief, the right of parents to guide the development of their children, and the right of people to be free from governmental intrusion into decisions that ought to be theirs alone—be available on full and fair terms to cultural minorities.[39]

In this essay, as a matter of epistemic concern, I have tried to suggest that we should be skeptical of the anti-"FGM" advocacy literature and the global discourse that portrays African mothers as "mutilators," "murderers," or "torturers" of their children. We should be dubious of representations that suggest that African mothers are bad mothers, or that First World mothers have a better idea of what it means to be a good mother. We should be slow to judge the unfamiliar practice of female genital alterations, in part because the horrifying assertions by anti-"FGM" activists concerning the consequences of the practice (claims about mortality, devastating health outcomes, and the loss of a capacity to enjoy sex) are not well supported with credible scientific evidence.

Of course, the anti-"FGM" genre of preemptive overheated claims expressed in moral terms is itself all too familiar. It is the kind of discourse (for example, "you murderer of innocent life") employed by some antiabortion activists, who use it to stigmatize liberal men and women who believe the right to family privacy implies a right to choice in cases of unwanted pregnancy. That is just one more reason to take a second look and hesitate before using the epithet "FGM" to describe the coming-of-age and gender-identity practices embraced by many millions of African women. African women too have rights to personal and family privacy, to guide the development of their children in light of their own ideals of the good life, and to be free of ex-

cessive and unreasonable government intrusion.

Imagine an African mother living in the United States who holds the following convictions. She believes that her daughters as well as her sons should be able to improve their looks and their marriage prospects, enter into a covenant with God, and be honored as adult members of the community via circumcision. Imagine that her proposed surgical procedure (for example, a cut in the prepuce that covers the clitoris) is no more substantial from a medical point of view than the customary American male circumcision operation. Why should we not extend that option to the Kono parents of daughters as well as to the Jewish parents of sons, for example?[40] Principles of gender equity, due process before the law, religious and cultural freedom, and family privacy would seem to support the option.

Or imagine a sixteen-year-old female Somali teenager living in Seattle who believes that a genital alteration would be "something very great." She likes the look of her mother's body and her recently circumcised cousin's body far better than she likes the look of her own. She wants to be a mature and beautiful woman, Somali style. She wants to marry a Somali man or at least a man who appreciates the appearance of an initiated woman's body. She wants to show solidarity with other African women who express their sense of beauty, civility, and feminine dignity in this way, and she shares their sense of aesthetics and seemliness. She reviews the medical literature and discovers that the surgery can be done safely, hygienically, and with no great effect on her capacity to enjoy sex. After consultation with her parents and the full support of other members of her community, she elects to carry on the tradition. What principle of justice demands that her cultural heritage should be "eradicated" and brought to an end?

I have also suggested that merely posing the question "What about FGM?" is not an argument against cultural pluralism. With accurate scientific information and sufficient cultural understanding it is possible to see the (not unreasonable) point of such practices for those for

whom they are meaningful. Seeing the cultural point and getting the scientific facts straight is where tolerance begins. Our cherished ideals of tolerance (including the ideal of being "pro-choice") would not amount to very much if all they amounted to was our willingness to eat each other's foods and to grant each other permission to enter different houses of worship for a couple of hours on the weekend. Tolerance means setting aside our readily aroused and powerfully negative feelings about the practices of immigrant minority groups long enough to get the facts straight and engage the "other" in a serious moral dialogue. It should take far more than overheated rhetoric and offended sensibilities to justify a cultural "eradication" campaign. Needless to say, the question of tolerance versus eradication of other peoples' valued ways of life is not just a women's issue.

The controversy over female circumcision in Africa is not an open-and-shut case. Given the high stakes involved, I believe it is a responsibility of cultural pluralists—both men and women—who are knowledgeable about African circumcision practices to step forward, speak out, and educate the public about this practice. There are many African women who, out of a sense of modesty, privacy, loyalty, or a well-founded sense of fear, may hesitate to speak for themselves. And it is a responsibility of everyone, anti-"FGM" activists and cultural pluralists alike, to insist on even-handedness and the highest standards of reason and evidence in any public policy debate on this topic—or at least to insist that there is a public policy debate, with all sides and voices fully represented.

ACKNOWLEDGMENTS

A longer and far more comprehensive version of this essay will be published in *The Free Exercise of Culture: How Free Is It? How Free Ought It to Be?* ed. Richard A. Shweder, Martha Minow, and Hazel R. Markus (New York: Russell Sage Foundation Press). That essay treats several questions and topics that, because of space limitations, cannot be addressed here, including cultural variations in conceptions of the "normal" body, the lack of a tight link between education and attitudes toward genital surgeries, and the character and implications of "imperial liberalism" and various types of anti-"FGM" "eradication programs." That longer essay also addresses the question of how much toleration of the practice ought to be reasonable in the context of the scientific, medical, legal, and moral traditions of a politically liberal pluralistic democracy such as the United States. It examines the connection between female and male circumcision, and critically evaluates the claim that this particular customary practice of many African ethnic groups should be viewed as a form of "political persecution." Many friends, colleagues, and experts on African initiation ceremonies have generously (and tolerantly) discussed this topic with me and/or critiqued the longer version of this essay. Without in any way holding them responsible for my perspective on this controversial issue I wish to express my deepest gratitude to Fuambai Ahmadu, Margaret Beck, Janice Boddy, David Chambers, Jane Cohen, Elizabeth Dunn, Robert Edgerton, Arthur Eisenberg, Ylva Hernlund, Albrecht Hofheinz, Sudhir Kakar, Jane Kaplan, Frank Kessel, Corinne Kratz, Dennis Krieger, Maivân Lâm, Heather Lindkvist, Hazel Markus, Martha Minow, Carla Obermeyer, Anni Peller, Jane Rabe, Lawrence Sager, Lauren Shweder, Gerd Spittler, and Leti Volpp.

ENDNOTES

1. Susan Rich and Stephanie Joyce, *Eradicating Female Genital Mutilation: Lessons for Donors*, Wallace Global Fund for a Sustainable Future, 1990 M Street, NW, Suite 250, Washington, D.C. 20036, n.d., 1, 3. Susan Rich is an anti-"FGM" activist who developed "FGM eradication programs" in Africa for the Special Projects Fund of Population Action International. Stephanie Joyce is an independent consultant.

2. Carla M. Obermeyer, "Female Genital Surgeries: The Known, the Unknown, and the Unknowable," *Medical Anthropology Quarterly* 13 (1999): 92. Carla Obermeyer is an anthropologist and epidemiologist in the department of population and international health at Harvard University.

3. Olayinka Koso-Thomas, *The Circumcision of Women: A Strategy for Eradication* (London: Zed Books, Ltd., 1987), 37. Olayinka Koso-Thomas is a gynecologist in Sierra Leone and an anti-"FGM" activist.

4. Obermeyer, "Female Genital Surgeries," 95.

5. See Susan Moller Okin with respondents, *Is Multiculturalism Bad for Women?* ed. Joshua Cohen, Matthew Howard, and Martha C. Nussbaum (Princeton, N.J.: Princeton University Press, 1999), 14. Susan Okin is a First World feminist and a political scientist at Stanford University, who contends that multiculturalism is bad for women.

6. Fuambai Ahmadu, "Rites and Wrongs: An Insider/Outsider Reflects on Power and Excision," in Bettina Shell-Duncan and Ylva Hernlund, eds., *Female "Circumcision" in Africa: Culture, Controversy, and Change* (Boulder, Colo.: Lynne Rienner, 2000), 301; also presented in the panel on "Female Genital Cutting: Local Dynamics of a Global Debate," 18 November 1999, 98th Annual Meeting of the American Anthropological Association, Chicago, Illinois. Fuambai Ahmadu is a Kono woman from Sierra Leone. She grew up in the United States and is a Ph.D. candidate in anthropology at the London School of Economics. At the age of twenty-two she returned to Sierra Leone to be initiated into the "women's secret society" and to be circumcised according to the customs of her ethnic group.

7. Ibid., 283.

8. Ibid., 308, 305.

9. Obermeyer, "Female Genital Surgeries," 80.

10. Ibid., 81.

11. Ibid., n. 24.

12. See quotations above; also ibid., 79.

13. See, for example, Janice Boddy, *Wombs and Alien Spirits: Women, Men, and the Zar Cult in Northern Sudan* (Madison: University of Wisconsin Press, 1989); Boddy, "Violence Embodied? Circumcision, Gender Politics, and Cultural Aesthetics," in R. Emerson Dobash and Russell P. Dobash, eds., *Rethinking Violence Against Women* (Thousand Oaks, Calif.: Sage Publications, 1996), 77–110; Ellen Gruenbaum, "The Cultural Debate Over Female Circumcision: The Sudanese Are Arguing This One Out For Themselves," *Medical Anthropology Quarterly* 10 (1996): 455–475; Corinne Kratz, *Affecting Performance: Meaning, Movement, and Experience in Okiek Women's Initiation* (Washington, D.C.: Smithsonian Institution Press, 1994); Kratz, "Contexts, Controversies, Dilemmas: Teaching Circumcision," in Misty Bastian and Jane Parpart, eds., *Teaching Africa: African Studies in the New Millenium* (Boulder, Colo.: Lynne Rienner, 1994, 1999); L. Amede Obiora, "Bridges and Barricades: Rethinking Polemics and Intransigence in the Campaign Against Female Circumcision," *Case Western Reserve Law Review* 47 (1997): 275–378; Melissa Parker, "Rethinking Female Circumcision," *Africa* 65 (1995): 506–524; Shell-Duncan and Hernlund, eds., *Female "Circumcision" in Africa*; Christine J. Walley, "Searching for 'Voices': Feminism, Anthropology, and the Global Debate over Female Genital Operations," *Cultural Anthropology* 12 (1997): 405–438.

14. Jomo Kenyatta, *Facing Mount Kenya: The Tribal Life of the Gikuyu* (London: Secker and Warburg, 1938), 131.

15. Ibid., 133, 132.

16. Krats, *Affecting Performance*, 346.

17. Robert B. Edgerton, *Mau Mau: An African Crucible* (New York: The Free Press, 1989), 254, n. 22; also see Hanny Lightfoot-Klein, "The Sexual and Marital Adjustment of Genitally Circumcised and Infibulated Females in the Sudan," *Journal of Sex Research* 26 (1989): 375–392.

18. Sandra D. Lane and Robert A. Rubinstein, "Judging the Other: Responding to Traditional Female Genital Surgeries," *Hastings Center Report* 26 (1996): 35.

19. Shell-Duncan and Ylva Hernlund, "Female 'Circumcision' in Africa: Dimensions of the Practice and Debates," in Shell-Duncan and Hernlund, eds., *Female "Circumcision" in Africa*.

20. See, e.g., Asma El Dareer, "Epidemiology of Female Circumcision in the Sudan," *Tropical Doctor* 13 (1983): 43.

21. Lindy Williams and Teresa Sobieszyzyk, "Attitudes Surrounding the Continuation of Female Circumcision in the Sudan: Passing the Tradition to the Next Generation," *Journal of Marriage and the Family* 59 (1997): 966–981, Table 1.

22. Koso-Thomas, *The Circumcision of Women*, 2.

23. See Janice Boddy, "Womb as Oasis: The Symbolic Context of Pharaonic Circumcision in Rural Northern Sudan," *American Ethnologist* 9 (1982): 682–698; Boddy, *Wombs and Alien Spirits*; Boddy, "Violence Embodied?"

24. See, for example, Koso-Thomas, *The Circumcision of Women*, 7; Lane and Rubinstein, "Judging the Other," quoted above; Otto Meinardus, "Mythological, Historical, and Sociological Aspects of the Practice of Female Circumcision Among the Egyptians," *Acta Ethnographica: Academiae Scientiarum Hungaricae* 16 (1967): 394; Asma El Dareer, *Woman, Why Do You Weep? Circumcision and Its Consequences* (London: Zed Press, 1982), 73.

25. Ahmadu, "Rites and Wrongs"; Meinardus, "Mythological, Historical and Sociological Aspects of the Practice of Female Circumcision Among the Egyptians," 389.

26. See, for example, Boddy, "Womb as Oasis"; Boddy, *Wombs and Alien Spirits*; Boddy, "Violence Embodied?"

27. Fran P. Hosken, *The Hosken Report: Genital and Sexual Mutilation of Females* (Lexington, Mass.: Women's International Network News, 1993); Abraham M. Rosenthal, "The Possible Dream," *New York Times*, 13 June 1995, A25.

151

28. Rich and Joyce, *Eradicating Female Genital Mutilation: Lessons for Donors*, 4.

29. for example, Yael Tamir, "Hands Off Clitoridectomy," *Boston Review* (October/November 1996).

30. Yewoubdar Beyene, "Body Politics and Moral Advocacy: The Impact on African Families in the U.S.," oral presentation in the panel on "Revisiting Female Circumcision: Beyond Feminism and Current Discourse," 20 November 1999, 98th Annual Meeting of the American Anthropological Association, Chicago.

31. The recent exceptions—essays that are more incisive, ethnographically informed, nondefensive, and/or profoundly skeptical of the current anti-"FGM" global discourse—include Ahmadu, "Rites and Wrongs"; Boddy, "Violence Embodied?"; Doriane L. Coleman, "The Seattle Compromise: Multicultural Sensitivity and Americanization," *Duke Law Review* 47 (1998): 717–783; Sander L. Gilman, "'Barbaric' Rituals," in 0kin, *Is Multiculturalism Bad For Women?*; Ellen Gruenbaum, "Reproductive Ritual and Social Reproduction: Female Circumcision and the Subordination of Women in Sudan," in Norman O'Neill and Jay O'Brian, eds., *Economy and Class in Sudan* (Brookfield, Vt.: Avebury, c1988); Kratz, *Affecting Performance: Meaning, Movement and Experience in Okiek Women's Initiation*; Kratz, "Contexts, Controversies, Dilemmas: Teaching Circumcision"; Obermeyer, "Female Genital Surgeries: The Known, the Unknown, and the Unknowable"; Obiora, "Rethinking Polemics and Intransigence in the Campaign Against Female Circumcision"; Parker, "Rethinking Female Circumcision"; and some of the essays in Shell-Duncan and Hernlund, eds., *Female "Circumcision" in Africa: Culture, Controversy and Change*. For a sample of views and representations concerning female initiation and circumcision, see also Boddy, *Wombs and Alien Spirits*; Mary H. Cooper, "Women and Human Rights," *CQ Researcher* (published by Congressional Quarterly, Inc.) 9 (1999): 353–376; El Dareer, *Woman, Why Do You Weep? Circumcision and Its Consequences*; Gruenbaum, "Reproductive Ritual and Social Reproduction"; Isabelle R. Gunning, "Arrogant Perception, World-Travelling and Multicultural Feminism: The Case of Female Genital Surgeries," *Columbia Human Rights Law Review* 23 (1991–1992): 189–248; Ylva Hernlund, "Cutting Without Ritual and Ritual Without Cutting: Female 'Circumcision' and the Re-Ritualization of Initiation in the Gambia," in Shell-Duncan and Hernlund, eds., *Female "Circumcision" in Africa*; Carol R. Horowitz and Carey Jackson, "Female 'Circumcision': African Women Confront American Medicine," *Journal of General Internal Medicine* 12 (1997): 491–499; Kenyatta, *Facing Mount Kenya*; Lane and Rubinstein, "Judging the Other: Responding to Traditional Female Genital Surgeries"; Meinardus, "Mythological, Historical, and Sociological Aspects of the Practice of Female Circumcision Among the Egyptians"; Alison T. Slack, "Female Circumcision: A Critical Appraisal," *Human Rights Quarterly* 10 (1988): 437–486; Walley, "Searching for 'Voices'"; Williams and Sobieszyzyk, "Attitudes Surrounding the Continuation of Female Circumcision in the Sudan."

32. On the connection between circumcision and entrance into powerful "women's secret societies" in Sierra Leone, see Ahmadu, "Rites and Wrongs."

33. Concerning Kenya also see Kenyatta, *Facing Mount Kenya*; Kratz, *Affecting Performance*; Walley, "Searching for 'Voices.'"

34. See note 27.

35. Obermeyer, "Female Genital Surgeries."

36. Edgerton, *Mau Mau: An African Crucible*, 40.

37. Rich and Joyce, *Eradicating Female Genital Mutilation*, 1.

38. Obermeyer, "Female Genital Surgeries," 93.

39. See Lawrence G. Sager, "The Free Exercise of Culture: Some Doubts and Distinctions," in this issue of *Dædalus*.

40. This is basically what was proposed at the Harborview Medical Center in Seattle, until U.S. Representative Patricia Schroeder objected and raised the possibility of a violation of federal law (see Coleman, "The Seattle Compromise"). The constitutional status of the law in question has yet to be tested.

Richard A. Shweder is professor of human development at the University of Chicago.

This essay is part of a forthcoming volume, The Free Exercise of Culture, *edited by R. Shweder, M. Minow, and H. Markus.* © Russell Sage Foundation. All rights reserved.

From *Daedalus*, Fall 2000, pp. 209-232. © 2000 by Russell Sage Foundation.

Where Fat Is a Mark of Beauty

In a rite of passage, some Nigerian girls spend months gaining weight and learning customs in a special room. "To be called a 'slim princess' is an abuse," says a defender of the practice.

By Ann M. Simmons
TIMES STAFF WRITER

AKPABUYO, Nigeria—Margaret Bassey Ene currently has one mission in life: gaining weight.

The Nigerian teenager has spent every day since early June in a "fattening room" specially set aside in her father's mud-and-thatch house. Most of her waking hours are spent eating bowl after bowl of rice, yams, plantains, beans and *gari*, a porridge-like mixture of dried cassava and water.

After three more months of starchy diet and forced inactivity, Margaret will be ready to reenter society bearing the traditional mark of female beauty among her Efik people: fat.

In contrast to many Western cultures where thin is in, many culture-conscious people in the Efik and other communities in Nigeria's southeastern Cross River state hail a woman's rotundity as a sign of good health, prosperity and allure.

The fattening room is at the center of a centuries-old rite of passage from maidenhood to womanhood. The months spent in pursuit of poundage are supplemented by daily visits from elderly matrons who impart tips on how to be a successful wife and mother. Nowadays, though, girls who are not yet marriage-bound do a tour in the rooms purely as a coming-of-age ceremony. And sometimes, nursing mothers return to the rooms to put on more weight.

"The fattening room is like a kind of school where the girl is taught about motherhood," said Sylvester Odey, director of the Cultural Center Board in Calabar, capital of Cross River state. "Your daily routine is to sleep, eat and grow fat."

Like many traditional African customs, the fattening room is facing relentless pressure from Western influences. Health campaigns linking excess fat to heart disease and other illnesses are changing the eating habits of many Nigerians, and urban dwellers are opting out of the time-consuming process.

Effiong Okon Etim, an Efik village chief in the district of Akpabuyo, said some families cannot afford to constantly feed a daughter for more than a few months. That compares with a stay of up to two years, as was common earlier this century, he said.

But the practice continues partly because "people might laugh at you because you didn't have money to allow your child to pass through the rite of passage," Etim said. What's more, many believe an unfattened girl will be sickly or unable to bear children.

Etim, 65, put his two daughters in a fattening room together when they were 12 and 15 years old, but some girls undergo the process as early as age 7, after undergoing the controversial practice of genital excision.

BIGGER IS BETTER, ACCORDING TO CUSTOM

As for how fat is fat enough, there is no set standard. But the unwritten rule is the bigger the better, said Mkoyo Edet, Etim's sister.

"Beauty is in the weight," said Edet, a woman in her 50s who spent three months in a fattening room when she was 7. "To be called a 'slim princess' is an abuse. The girl is fed constantly whether she likes it or not."

In Margaret's family, there was never any question that she would enter the fattening room.

"We inherited it from our forefathers; it is one of the heritages we must continue," said Edet Essien Okon, 25, Margaret's stepfather and a language and linguistics graduate of the University of Calabar. "It's a good thing to do; it's an initiation rite."

His wife, Nkoyo Effiong, 27, agreed: "As a woman, I feel it is proper for me to put my daughter in there, so she can be educated."

Effiong, a mother of five, spent four months in a fattening room at the age of 10.

Margaret, an attractive girl with a cheerful smile and hair plaited in fluffy bumps, needs only six months in the fattening room because she was already naturally plump, her stepfather said.

During the process, she is treated as a goddess, but the days are monotonous. To amuse herself, Margaret has only an instrument made out of a soda bottle with a hole in it, which she taps on her hand to play traditional tunes.

Still, the 16-year-old says she is enjoying the highly ritualized fattening practice.

"I'm very happy about this," she said, her belly already distended over the waist of her loincloth. "I enjoy the food, except for *gari*."

Day in, day out, Margaret must sit cross-legged on a special stool inside the secluded fattening room. When it is time to eat, she sits on the floor on a large, dried plantain leaf, which also serves as her bed. She washes down the mounds of food with huge pots of water and takes traditional medicine made from leaves and herbs to ensure proper digestion.

As part of the rite, Margaret's face is decorated with a white, claylike chalk.

"You have to prepare the child so that if a man sees her, she will be attractive," Chief Etim said.

Tufts of palm leaf fiber, braided and dyed red, are hung around Margaret's neck and tied like bangles around her wrists and ankles. They are adjusted as she grows.

Typically, Margaret would receive body massages using the white chalk powder mixed with heavy red palm oil. But the teen said her parents believe the skin-softening, blood-stimulating massages might cause her to expand further than necessary.

Margaret is barred from doing her usual chores or any other strenuous physical activities. And she is forbidden to receive visitors, save for the half a dozen matrons who school Margaret in the etiquette of the Efik clan.

They teach her such basics as how to sit, walk and talk in front of her husband. And they impart wisdom about cleaning, sewing, child care and cooking—Efik women are known throughout Nigeria for their chicken pepper soup, pounded yams and other culinary creations.

"They advise me to keep calm and quiet, to eat the *gari*, and not to have many boyfriends so that I avoid unwanted pregnancy," Margaret said of her matron teachers. "They say that unless you have passed through this, you will not be a full-grown woman."

What little exercise Margaret gets comes in dance lessons. The matrons teach her the traditional *ekombi*, which she will be expected to perform before an audience on the day she emerges from seclusion—usually on the girl's wedding day, Etim said.

But Okon said his aim is to prepare his stepdaughter for the future, not to marry her off immediately. Efik girls receive more education than girls in most parts of Nigeria, and Okon hopes Margaret will return to school and embark on a career as a seamstress before getting married.

WEDDINGS ALSO STEEPED IN TRADITION

Once she does wed, Margaret will probably honor southeastern Nigeria's rich marriage tradition. It begins with a letter from the family of the groom to the family of the bride, explaining that "our son has seen a flower, a jewel, or something beautiful in your family, that we are interested in," said Josephine Effah-Chukwuma, program officer for women and children at the Constitutional Rights Project, a law-oriented nongovernmental organization based in the Nigerian commercial capital of Lagos.

If the girl and her family consent, a meeting is arranged. The groom and his

relatives arrive with alcoholic beverages, soft drinks and native brews, and the bride's parents provide the food. The would-be bride's name is never uttered, and the couple are not allowed to speak, but if all goes well, a date is set for handing over the dowry. On that occasion, the bride's parents receive about $30 as a token of appreciation for their care of the young woman. "If you make the groom pay too much, it is like selling your daughter," Effah-Chukwuma said. Then, more drinks are served, and the engagement is official.

On the day of the wedding, the bride sits on a specially built wooden throne, covered by an extravagantly decorated canopy. Maidens surround her as relatives bestow gifts such as pots, pans, brooms, plates, glasses, table covers—everything she will need to start her new home. During the festivities, the bride changes clothes three times.

The high point is the performance of the *ekombi*, in which the bride twists and twirls, shielded by maidens and resisting the advances of her husband. It is his task to break through the ring and claim his bride.

Traditionalists are glad that some wedding customs are thriving despite the onslaught of modernity.

Traditional weddings are much more prevalent in southeastern Nigeria than so-called white weddings, introduced by colonialists and conducted in a church or registry office.

"In order to be considered married, you have to be married in the traditional way," said Maureen Okon, a woman of the Qua ethnic group who wed seven years ago but skipped the fattening room because she did not want to sacrifice the time. "Tradition identifies a people. It is important to keep up a culture. There is quite a bit of beauty in Efik and Qua marriages."

The Initiation of a Maasai Warrior

Tepilit Ole Saitoti

"Tepilit, circumcision means a sharp knife cutting into the skin of the most sensitive part of your body. You must not budge; don't move a muscle or even blink. You can face only one direction until the operation is completed. The slightest movement on your part will mean you are a coward, incompetent and unworthy to be a Maasai man. Ours has always been a proud family, and we would like to keep it that way. We will not tolerate unnecessary embarrassment, so you had better be ready. If you are not, tell us now so that we will not proceed. Imagine yourself alone remaining uncircumcised like the water youth [white people]. I hear they are not circumcised. Such a thing is not known in Maasailand; therefore, circumcision will have to take place even if it means holding you down until it is completed."

My father continued to speak and every one of us kept quiet. "The pain you will feel is symbolic. There is a deeper meaning in all this. Circumcision means a break between childhood and adulthood. For the first time in your life, you are regarded as a grown-up, a complete man or woman. You will be expected to give and not just to receive. To protect the family always, not just to be protected yourself. And your wise judgment will for the first time be taken into consideration. No family affairs will be discussed without your being consulted. If you are ready for all these responsibilities, tell us now. Com-

ing into manhood is not simply a matter of growth and maturity. It is a heavy load on your shoulders and especially a burden on the mind. Too much of this—I am done. I have said all I wanted to say. Fellows, if you have anything to add, go ahead and tell your brother, because I am through. I have spoken."

After a prolonged silence, one of my half-brothers said awkwardly, "Face it, man... it's painful. I won't lie about it, but it is not the end. We all went through it, after all. Only blood will flow, not milk." There was laughter and my father left.

My brother Lellia said, "Men, there are many things we must acquire and preparations we must make before the ceremony, and we will need the cooperation and help of all of you. Ostrich feathers for the crown and wax for the arrows must be collected."

"Are you *orkirekenyi?*" one of my brothers asked. I quickly replied no, and there was laughter. *Orkirekenyi* is a person who has transgressed sexually. For you must not have sexual intercourse with any circumcised woman before you yourself are circumcised. You must wait until you are circumcised. If you have not waited, you will be fined. Your father, mother, and the circumciser will take a cow from you as punishment.

Just before we departed, one of my closest friends said, "If you kick the knife, you will be in trouble." There was laugh-

ter. "By the way, if you have decided to kick the circumciser, do it well. Silence him once and for all." "Do it the way you kick a football in school." "That will fix him," another added, and we all laughed our heads off again as we departed.

The following month was a month of preparation. I and others collected wax, ostrich feathers, honey to be made into honey beer for the elders to drink on the day of circumcision, and all the other required articles.

Three days before the ceremony my head was shaved and I discarded all my belongings, such as my necklaces, garments, spear, and sword. I even had to shave my pubic hair. Circumcision in many ways is similar to Christian baptism. You must put all the sins you have committed during childhood behind and embark as a new person with a different outlook on a new life.

The circumciser came the following day and handed the ritual knives to me. He left drinking a calabash of beer. I stared at the knives uneasily. It was hard to accept that he was going to use them on my organ. I was to sharpen them and protect them from people of ill will who might try to blunt them, thus rendering them inefficient during the ritual and thereby bringing shame on our family. The knives threw a chill down my spine; I was not sure I was sharpening them properly, so I took them to my closest brother for him to check out, and he assured me that the knives were all right. I hid them well and waited.

Tension started building between me and my relatives, most of whom worried that I wouldn't make it through the ceremony valiantly. Some even snarled at me, which was their way of encouraging me. Others threw insults and abusive words my way. My sister Loiyan in particular was more troubled by the whole affair than anyone in the whole family. She had to assume my mother's role during the circumcision. Were I to fail my initiation, she would have to face the consequences. She would be spat upon and even beaten for representing the mother of an unworthy son. The same fate would befall my father, but he seemed unconcerned. He had this weird belief that because I was not particularly handsome, I must be brave. He kept saying, "God is not so bad as to have made him ugly and a coward at the same time."

Failure to be brave during circumcision would have other unfortunate consequences: the herd of cattle belonging to the family still in the compound would be beaten until they stampeded; the slaughtered oxen and honey beer prepared during the month before the ritual would go to waste; the initiate's food would be spat upon and he would have to eat it or else get a severe beating. Everyone would call him Olkasiodoi, the knife kicker.

Kicking the knife of the circumciser would not help you anyway. If you struggle and try to get away during the ritual, you will be held down until the operation is completed. Such failure of nerve would haunt you in the future. For example, no one will choose a person who kicked the knife for a position of leadership. However, there have been instances in which a person who failed to go through circumcision successfully became very brave afterwards because he was filled with anger over the incident; no one dares to scold him or remind him of it. His agemates, particularly the warriors, will act as if nothing had happened.

During the circumcision of a woman, on the other hand, she is allowed to cry as long as she does not hinder the operation. It is common to see a woman crying and kicking during circumcision. Warriors are usually summoned to help hold her down.

For women, circumcision means an end to the company of Maasai warriors. After they recuperate, they soon get married, and often to men twice their age.

The closer it came to the hour of truth, the more I was hated, particularly by those closest to me. I was deeply troubled by the withdrawal of all the support I needed. My annoyance turned into anger and resolve. I decided not to budge or blink, even if I were to see my intestines flowing before me. My resolve was hardened when newly circumcised warriors came to sing for me. Their songs were utterly insulting, intended to annoy me further. They tucked their wax arrows under my crotch and rubbed them on my nose. They repeatedly called me names.

By the end of the singing, I was fuming. Crying would have meant I was a coward. After midnight they left me alone and I went into the house and tried to sleep but could not. I was exhausted and numb but remained awake all night.

At dawn I was summoned once again by the newly circumcised warriors. They piled more and more insults on me. They sang their weird songs with even more vigor and excitement than before. The songs praised warriorhood and encouraged one to achieve it at all costs. The songs continued until the sun shone on the cattle horns clearly. I was summoned to the main cattle gate, in my hand a ritual cowhide from a cow that had been properly slaughtered during my naming ceremony. I went past Loiyan, who was milking a cow, and she muttered something. She was shaking all over. There was so much tension that people could hardly breathe.

I laid the hide down and a boy was ordered to pour ice-cold water, known as *engare entolu* (ax water), over my head. It dripped all over my naked body and I shook furiously. In a matter of seconds I was summoned to sit down. A large crowd of boys and men formed a semicircle in front of me; women are not allowed to watch male circumcision and vice-versa. That was the last thing I saw clearly. As soon as I sat down, the circumciser appeared, his knives at the ready. He spread my legs and said, "One cut," a pronouncement necessary to prevent an initiate from claiming that he had been taken by surprise. He splashed a white liquid, a ceremonial paint called *enturoto*, across my face. Almost immediately I felt a spark of pain under my belly as the knife cut through my penis' foreskin. I happened to choose to look in the direction of the operation. I continued to observe the circumciser's fingers working mechanically. The pain became numbness and my lower body felt heavy, as if I were weighed down by a heavy burden. After fifteen minutes or so, a man who had been supporting from behind pointed at something, as if to assist the circumciser. I came to learn later that the circumciser's eyesight had been failing him and that my brothers had been mad at him because the operation had taken longer than was usually necessary. All the same, I remained pinned down until the operation was over. I heard a call for milk to wash the knives, which signaled the end, and soon the ceremony was over.

With words of praise, I was told to wake up, but I remained seated. I waited for the customary presents in appreciation of my bravery. My father gave me a cow and so did my brother Lillia. The man who had supported my back and my brother-in-law gave me a heifer. In all I had eight animals given to me. I was carried inside the house to my own bed to recuperate as activities intensified to celebrate my bravery.

I laid on my own bed and bled profusely. The blood must be retained within the bed, for according to Maasai tradition, it must not spill to the ground. I was drenched in my own blood. I stopped bleeding after about half an hour but soon was in intolerable pain. I was supposed to squeeze my organ and force blood to flow out of the wound, but no one had told me, so the blood coagulated and caused unbearable pain. The circumciser was brought to my aid and showed me what to do, and soon the pain subsided.

The following morning, I was escorted by a small boy to a nearby valley to walk and relax, allowing my wound to drain. This was common for everyone who had been circumcised, as well as for women who had just given birth. Having lost a lot of blood, I was extremely weak. I walked very slowly, but in spite of my caution I fainted. I tried to hang on to bushes and shrubs, but I fell, irritating my wound. I came out of unconsciousness quickly, and the boy who was escorting me never realized what had happened. I was so scared that I told him to lead me back home. I could have died without there being anyone around who could have helped me. From that day on, I was selective of my company while I was feeble.

In two weeks I was able to walk and was taken to join other newly circumcised boys far away from our settlement. By tradition Maasai initiates are required to decorate their headdresses with all kinds of colorful birds they have killed. On our way to the settlement, we hunted birds and teased girls by shooting them with our wax blunt arrows. We danced and ate and were well treated wherever we went. We were protected from the cold and rain during the healing period. We were not allowed to touch food, as we were regarded as unclean, so whenever we ate we had to use specially prepared sticks instead. We remained in this pampered state until our wounds healed and our headdresses were removed. Our heads were shaved, we discarded our black cloaks and bird headdresses and embarked as newly shaven warriors, Irkeleani.

As long as I live I will never forget the day my head was shaved and I emerged a man, a Maasai warrior. I felt a sense of control over my destiny so great that no words can accurately describe it. I now stood with confidence, pride, and happiness of being, for all around me I was desired and loved by beautiful, sensuous Maasai maidens. I could now interact with women and even have sex with them, which I had not been allowed before. I was now regarded as a responsible person.

In the old days, warriors were like gods, and women and men wanted only to be the parent of a warrior. Everything else would be taken care of as a result. When a poor family had a warrior, they ceased to be poor. The warrior would go on raids and bring cattle back. The warrior would defend the family against all odds. When a society respects the individual and displays confidence in him the way the Maasai do their warriors, the individual can grow to his fullest potential. Whenever there was a task requiring physical strength or bravery, the Maasai would call

upon their warriors. They hardly ever fall short of what is demanded of them and so are characterized by pride, confidence, and an extreme sense of freedom. But there is an old saying in Maasai: "You are never a free man until your father dies." In other words, your father is paramount while he is alive and you are obligated to respect him. My father took advantage of this principle and held a tight grip on all his warriors, including myself. He always wanted to know where we all were at any given time. We fought against his restrictions, but without success. I, being the youngest of my father's five warriors, tried even harder to get loose repeatedly, but each time I was punished severely.

Roaming the plains with other warriors in pursuit of girls and adventure was a warrior's pastime. We would wander from one settlement to another, singing, wrestling, hunting, and just playing. Often I was ready to risk my father's punishment for this wonderful freedom.

One clear day my father sent me to take sick children and one of his wives to the dispensary in the Korongoro Highlands. We rode in the L. S. B. Leakey lorry. We ascended the highlands and were soon attended to in the local hospital. Near the conservation offices I met several acquaintances, and one of them told me of an unusual circumcision that was about to take place in a day or two. All the local warriors and girls were preparing to attend it.

The highlands were a lush green from the seasonal rains and the sky was a purple-blue with no clouds in sight. The land was overflowing with milk, and the warriors felt and looked their best, as they always did when there was plenty to eat and drink. Everyone was at ease. The demands the community usually made on warriors during the dry season when water was scarce and wells had to be dug were now not necessary. Herds and flocks were entrusted to youths to look after. The warriors had all the time for themselves. But my father was so strict that even at times like these he still insisted on overworking us in one way or another. He believed that by keeping us busy, he would keep us out of trouble.

When I heard about the impending ceremony, I decided to remain behind in the Korongoro Highlands and attend it now

that the children had been treated. I knew very well that I would have to make up a story for my father upon my return, but I would worry about that later. I had left my spear at home when I boarded the bus, thinking that I would be coming back that very day. I felt lighter but now regretted having left it behind; I was so used to carrying it wherever I went. In gales of laughter resulting from our continuous teasing of each other, we made our way toward a distant kraal. We walked at a leisurely pace and reveled in the breeze. As usual we talked about the women we desired, among other things.

The following day we were joined by a long line of colorfully dressed girls and warriors from the kraal and the neighborhood where we had spent the night, and we left the highland and headed to Ingorienito to the rolling hills on the lower slopes to attend the circumcision ceremony. From there one could see Oldopai Gorge, where my parents lived, and the Inaapi hills in the middle of the Serengeti Plain.

Three girls and a boy were to be initiated on the same day, an unusual occasion. Four oxen were to be slaughtered, and many people would therefore attend. As we descended, we saw the kraal where the ceremony would take place. All those people dressed in red seemed from a distance like flamingos standing in a lake. We could see lines of other guests heading to the settlements. Warriors made gallant cries of happiness known as *enkiseer*. Our line of warriors and girls responded to their cries even more gallantly.

In serpentine fashion, we entered the gates of the settlement. Holding spears in our left hands, we warriors walked proudly, taking small steps, swaying like palm trees, impressing our girls, who walked parallel to us in another line, and of course the spectators, who gazed at us approvingly.

We stopped in the center of the kraal and waited to be greeted. Women and children welcomed us. We put our hands on the children's heads, which is how children are commonly saluted. After the greetings were completed, we started dancing.

Our singing echoed off the kraal fence and nearby trees. Another line of warriors came up the hill and entered the compound, also singing and moving slowly toward us. Our singing grew in intensity. Both lines of warriors moved parallel to each other, and our feet pounded the ground with style. We stamped vigorously, as if to tell the next line and the spectators that we were the best.

The singing continued until the hot sun was overhead. We recessed and ate food already prepared for us by other warriors. Roasted meat was for those who were to eat meat, and milk for the others. By our tradition, meat and milk must not be consumed at the same time, for this would be a betrayal of the animal. It was regarded as cruel to consume a product of the animal that could be obtained while it was alive, such as milk, and meat, which was only available after the animal had been killed.

After eating we resumed singing, and I spotted a tall, beautiful *esiankiki* (young maiden) of Masiaya whose family was one of the largest and richest in our area. She stood very erect and seemed taller than the rest.

One of her breasts could be seen just above her dress, which was knotted at the shoulder. While I was supposed to dance generally to please all the spectators, I took it upon myself to please her especially. I stared at and flirted with her, and she and I danced in unison at times. We complemented each other very well.

During a break, I introduced myself to the *esiankiki* and told her I would like to see her after the dance. "Won't you need a warrior to escort you home later when the evening threatens?" I said. She replied, "Perhaps, but the evening is still far away."

I waited patiently. When the dance ended, I saw her departing with a group of other women her age. She gave me a sidelong glance, and I took that to mean come later and not now. With so many others around, I would not have been able to confer with her as I would have liked anyway.

With another warrior, I wandered around the kraal killing time until the herds returned from pasture. Before the sun dropped out of sight, we departed. As the kraal of the *esiankiki* was in the lowlands, a place called Enkoloa, we descended leisurely, our spears resting on our shoulders.

We arrived at the woman's kraal and found that cows were now being milked. One could hear the women trying to appease the cows by singing to them. Singing calms cows down, making it easier to milk them. There were no warriors in the whole kraal except for the two of us. Girls went around into warriors' houses as usual and collected milk for us. I was so eager to go and meet my *esiankiki* that I could hardly wait for nightfall. The warriors' girls were trying hard to be sociable, but my mind was not with them. I found them to be childish, loud, bothersome, and boring.

As the only warriors present, we had to keep them company and sing for them, at least for a while, as required by custom. I told the other warrior to sing while I tried to figure out how to approach my *esiankiki*. Still a novice warrior, I was not experienced with women and was in fact still afraid of them. I could flirt from a distance, of course. But sitting down with a woman and trying to seduce her was another matter. I had already tried twice to approach women soon after my circumcision and had failed. I got as far as the door of one woman's house and felt my heart beating like a Congolese drum; breathing became difficult and I had to turn back. Another time I managed to get in the house and succeeded in sitting on the bed, but then I started trembling until the whole bed was shaking, and conversation became difficult. I left the house and the woman, amazed and speechless, and never went back to her again.

Tonight I promised myself I would be brave and would not make any silly, ridiculous moves. "I must be mature and not afraid," I kept reminding myself, as I remembered an incident involving one of my relatives when he was still very young and, like me, afraid of women. He went to a woman's house and sat on a stool for a whole hour; he was afraid to awaken her, as his heart was pounding and he was having difficulty breathing.

When he finally calmed down, he woke her up, and their conversation went something like this:

"Woman, wake up."

"Why should I?"

"To light the fire."

"For what?"

"So you can see me."

"I already know who you are. Why don't *you* light the fire, as you're nearer to it than me?"

"It's your house and it's only proper that you light it yourself."

"I don't feel like it."

"At least wake up so we can talk, as I have something to tell you."

"Say it."

"I need you."

"I do not need one-eyed types like yourself."

"One-eyed people are people too."

"That might be so, but they are not to my taste."

They continued talking for quite some time, and the more they spoke, the braver he became. He did not sleep with her that night, but later on he persisted until he won her over. I doubted whether I was as strong-willed as he, but the fact that he had met with success encouraged me. I told my warrior friend where to find me should he need me, and then I departed.

When I entered the house of my *esiankiki*, I called for the woman of the house, and as luck would have it, my lady responded. She was waiting for me. I felt better, and I proceeded to talk to her like a professional. After much talking back and forth, I joined her in bed.

The night was calm, tender, and loving, like most nights after initiation ceremonies as big as this one. There must have been a lot of courting and lovemaking.

Maasai women can be very hard to deal with sometimes. They can simply reject a man outright and refuse to change their minds. Some play hard to get, but in reality are testing the man to see whether he is worth their while. Once a friend of mine while still young was powerfully attracted to a woman nearly his mother's age. He put a bold move on her. At first the woman could not believe his intention, or rather was amazed by his courage. The name of the warrior was Ngengeiya, or Drizzle.

"Drizzle, what do you want?"

The warrior stared her right in the eye and said, "You."

"For what?"

"To make love to you."

"I am your mother's age."

"The choice was either her or you."

This remark took the woman by surprise. She had underestimated the saying

"There is no such thing as a young warrior." When you are a warrior, you are expected to perform bravely in any situation. Your age and size are immaterial.

"You mean you could really love me like a grown-up man?"

"Try me, woman."

He moved in on her. Soon the woman started moaning with excitement, calling out his name. "Honey Drizzle, Honey Drizzle, you *are* a man." In a breathy, stammering voice, she said, "A real man."

Her attractiveness made Honey Drizzle ignore her relative old age. The Maasai believe that if an older and a younger person have intercourse, it is the older person who stands to gain. For instance, it is believed that an older woman having an affair with a young man starts to appear younger and healthier, while the young man grows older and unhealthy.

The following day when the initiation rites had ended, I decided to return home. I had offended my father by staying away from home without his consent, so I prepared myself for whatever punishment he might inflict on me. I walked home alone.

Originally "My Circumcision" from *The Worlds of a Maasai Warrior* by Tepilit Ole Saitoti, 1986, pp. 66–76. © 1986 by Tepilit Ole Saitoti. Reprinted by permission of Random House, Inc.

UNIT 6
Religion, Belief, and Ritual

Unit Selections

Key Points to Consider

- How can modern medicine be combined with traditional healing to take advantage of the best aspects of both? In what respects do perceptions of disease affect treatment and recovery?

- How do beliefs about the supernatural contribute to a sense of personal security, individual responsibility, and social harmony?

- Why are mortuary practices important to the living?

- How has voodoo become such an important form of social control in rural Haiti?

- In what ways are magic rituals practical and rational?

- How do rituals and taboos get established in the first place?

- How important are ritual and taboo in our modern industrial society?

- What can you tell about a people by watching how they play games?

 **Links: www.dushkin.com/online/**
These sites are annotated in the World Wide Web pages.

Anthropology Resources Page
http://www.usd.edu/anth/

Masks.org
http://www.masks.org

Philosophy of Religion: Magic, Ritual, and Symbolism
http://www.kcmetro.cc.mo.us/longview/socsci/philosophy/religion/magic.htm

Yahoo: Society and Culture: Death
http://dir.yahoo.com/Society_and_Culture/Death_and_Dying/

The anthropological interest in religion, belief, and ritual is not concerned with the scientific validity of such phenomena but rather with the way in which people relate various concepts of the supernatural to their everyday lives. From this practical perspective, some anthropologists have found that traditional spiritual healing is just as helpful in the treatment of illness as is modern medicine, that voodoo is a form of social control (as in "The Secrets of Haiti's Living Dead"), and that the ritual and spiritual preparation for playing the game of baseball can be just as important as spring training (see "Baseball Magic").

Every society is composed of feeling, thinking, and acting human beings who at one time or another are either conforming to or altering the social order into which they were born. Religion is an ideological framework that gives special legitimacy and validity to human experience within any given sociocultural system. In this way, monogamy as a marriage form, or monarchy as a political form, ceases to be simply one of many alternative ways in which a society can be organized, but becomes, for the believer, the only legitimate way. Religion considers certain human values and activities as sacred and inviolable. It is this mythic function that helps to explain the strong ideological attachments that some people have regardless of the scientific merits of their points of view.

While under some conditions religion may in fact be "the opiate of the masses," under other conditions such a belief system may be a rallying point for social and economic protest. A contemporary example of the former might be the "Moonies" (members of the Unification Church founded by Sun Myung Moon), while a good example of the latter is the role of the black church in the American civil rights movement, along with the prominence of such religious figures as Martin Luther King Jr. and Jesse Jackson. A word of caution must be set forth concerning attempts to understand belief systems of other cultures. At times the prevailing attitude seems to be, "What I believe in is religion, and what you believe in is superstition." While anthropologists generally do not subscribe to this view, some tend to explain behavior that seems, on the surface, to be incomprehensible and impractical as some form of religious ritual. The articles in this unit should serve as a strong warning concerning the pitfalls of that approach.

"It Takes a Village Healer" shows how important a person's traditional belief systems, combined with community involvement, can be to the physical and psychological well-being of the

individual. This perspective is so important that the treatment of illness is hindered without it. Thus, beliefs about the supernatural may be subtle, informal, and yet absolutely necessary for social harmony and stability.

Mystical beliefs and ritual are not absent from the modern world. In "Why We Want Their Bodies Back," we learn that funerals have as much to do with affirming the values of the living as they do with memorializing the deceased. "Body Ritual Among the Nacirema" reveals that our daily routines have mystic overtones. "Baseball Magic" examines the need for ritual and taboo in the "great American pastime."

In summary, the writings in this unit show religion, belief, and ritual in relationship to practical human affairs.

It Takes A Village Healer

Anthropologists Believe Traditional Medicine Can Remedy Africa's AIDS Crisis. Are They Right?

By Matthew Steinglass

ON A HOT SUNDAY EVENING, IN A manioc field near the village of Gboto in the small West African nation of Togo, a group of men in city clothes rustle through the brush, periodically stopping to look at bits of uncovered root. At the center of the group stands a stout, gray-haired man in an embroidered African shirt, giving directions. He doesn't seem to be finding what he's looking for. He stops to finger a bush with wide leaves.

"This is called *ahonto*," he says. "It's good for renal problems." But it isn't the plant he needs.

A few dozen yards further on, he pushes into a thicket and motions toward one of his companions, a muscular field hand carrying a machete. The field hand thrusts his machete into the ground, digs until he encounters a root, and then begins to slice away at it. It takes a few minutes of brisk whacking before he comes up with a length of smooth, tan tuber. The man in the embroidered shirt holds it up, examines it, and nods.

"This is *hetsi*," he says with satisfaction.

The man in the embroidered shirt is Dr. Kokou Coco Toudji-Bandje, an African healer who concocts herbal remedies for a variety of ailments. One of these remedies is something he calls Tobacoak's. He believes it is a "natural antiretroviral." More specifically, he says Tobacoak's "destroys HIV in the blood." Over the past ten years, Toudji-Bandje has used Tobacoak's to treat over three thousand AIDS patients. Most of them, he says, have got-

ten better—and some have been completely cured.

Toudji-Bandje is not the only herbal healer in Africa who claims the ability to cure AIDS, but he is one of the best known. Patients fly from as far away as Congo to see him. He has a large air-conditioned villa-cum-office in Togo's capital city, Lomé. He has a Mercedes and a white Toyota van. According to a few other doctors who have looked into his finances, he has tremendous amounts of money. The one thing Toudji-Bandje does not actually have is an M.D., but he doesn't seem to miss it much.

Most members of the Western intellectual community consider people like Toudji-Bandje part of Africa's AIDS problem, not its solution. The dimensions of that problem are by now depressingly familiar: HIV-positive rates in southern Africa run to 20 percent and higher. More than twenty-five million sub-Saharan Africans are already infected, and hundreds of millions more are at risk. No one knows what will happen to the social fabric in these countries when cumulative death rates climb into double digits. Under the circumstances, you might think that anyone who would distract attention from HIV education and prevention efforts by claiming to have cured the disease with an herbal concoction is not the kind of guy international organizations should be working with.

If so, you would have been surprised to see Toudji-Bandje at last December's crucial meeting of the Africa Development Forum, in Addis Ababa, where a

continent-wide AIDS strategy was under development. Toudji-Bandje came with the official Togolese delegation, and the World Health Organization paid his way. He was representing a constituency that the WHO believes should be an integral part of the campaign against AIDS in Africa: traditional healers.

> *Anthropologists used to consider traditional healers were a vanishing breed in need of protection. Today, anyone who talked that way would be laughed out of the lecture hall.*

The WHO's support for collaboration between traditional healers and Western-style public-health systems in Africa actually dates back well before the AIDS epidemic. Public-health experts have advocated such collaboration since the 1970s, drawing on arguments that range from the practical (the crippling lack of M.D.s and trained nurses in the developing world) to the ideological (a refusal to privilege Western biomedical science over alternative systems of medical belief). And some of the most enthusiastic advocates of collaboration with traditional healers have been those Western academics whose job it is to study them: medical anthropologists.

MEDICAL ANTHROPOLOGY'S SLICE of the academic pie consists in studying different cultures' beliefs and practices relating to health and disease. A typical medical anthropologist might spend his time sitting in the homes of Bono healers in north-central Ghana, looking into how they deal with diarrhea: what diseases they associate with the symptom (*ayamtuo, asonkyere*), what they think causes the diseases (unclean substances, contagion), how they treat the diseases (herbal solutions, enemas), and how their disease typologies match up with those of Western medicine (malaria, food poisoning). An anthropologist studying the Manica of Mozambique would find a completely different conception of diarrhea than that of the Bono: The disease might be attributed to a disturbance of a child's "internal snake," to exposure to heat, or to a father touching his still-breastfeeding child after committing adultery and then failing to wash his hands. With its multitude of ethnic groups, who speak more than eight hundred different languages and construct who knows how many startlingly innovative theories of diarrhea, Africa provides medical anthropologists a never-ending supply of thesis fodder.

Back in the 1960s and early 1970s, some medical anthropologists claimed that African traditional healers were a vanishing breed in need of protection from the onslaught of modernity. Today, anyone who talked that way would be laughed out of the lecture hall. Modernity doesn't seem to be doing too well in Africa. Traditional healers, on the other hand, are going strong. There are quite possibly more than two million healers in Africa, and an estimated 80 percent of sub-Saharan Africans consult them. In some countries, these healers outnumber Western-style medical professionals by around forty to one.

If you go into an average village in Togo looking for biomedical health care, you're likely to find an almost empty dispensary, staffed perhaps one or two days a week by a poorly trained community health worker. The same village might have three or four traditional healers within easy walking distance, each ensconced in an attractive compound with flags flying from the roof. And while the community health worker often has a so-cial standing equivalent to that of a cashier at Dairy Queen, traditional healers are generally among the most powerful and respected members of village society.

MEDICAL ANTHROPOLOGISTS TYPically divide healers into two main categories: herbalists and diviner-mediums. The healers' work ranges from administering herbal treatments to eradicating spirit possession to dream interpretation. When it comes to answering the obvious questions—Do the diseases diagnosed by traditional healers actually exist? Do the healers' practices help sick patients?—medical anthropologists are supposed to remain strictly nonjudgmental. And yet, they are typically Westerners, who share a basically biomedical understanding of disease etiology. Medical anthropologists handle this clash of worldviews the same way any of us handle conversations with people whose outlooks differ radically from our own: They finesse the issues. They try not to bring them up. They concentrate on areas of agreement.

The problem is that medical anthropologists' particular area of concentration happens to be one in which certain questions can't be finessed. When children are dying of diarrhea-induced dehydration, and you, as a Westerner, think you know how to save them, you can't sit back and watch a traditional healer apply a treatment you believe to be ineffective. You want to do something.

Starting in the late 1970s, some medical anthropologists began doing more than studying traditional healers—they started working with them. Some saw training traditional healers in Western-style biomedicine as a potential solution to Africa's drastic shortfall of trained health-care personnel. Others thought traditional healers might know things—about medicinal herbs, or about how to deliver care in a spiritually wholesome fashion—that Western doctors didn't. Twenty years later, these same medical anthropologists are spearheading the drive to include traditional healers in AIDS prevention and care. One of the first was Edward C. Green, an independent anthropologist whose 1994 book, *AIDS and STDs in Africa: Bridging the Gap Between Traditional Healing and Modern Medicine*, made the clearest case yet for bringing healers on board in the fight against AIDS.

Green's book drew on his experience in South Africa, where he had established a program that trained traditional healers as educators for AIDS prevention. Such programs, Green was convinced, could be crucial to stopping the spread of HIV. In fact, he wrote in his book, any successful effort to fight AIDS in Africa would have to include "some sort of collaborative action program involving traditional healers."

Traditional healers pervade African societies, Green stressed; instead of ignoring them, doctors and health educators should view them as an untapped resource. His research showed that while Africans rely on doctors and hospitals to treat many illnesses, most believe that traditional healers are better than doctors at curing sexually transmitted diseases. At least part of the reason is that unlike doctors, healers tend to take a "holistic" approach, treating the patient's spiritual and physical well-being together. With a terminal disease like AIDS, the spiritual side becomes very important. In any event, Green reasoned, patients consult traditional healers whether or not the healers have been educated in AIDS prevention. Untrained healers might spread inaccurate information or engage in harmful practices. Moreover, Green asserted, traditional healers are eager to learn about Western medical ideas, and they put what they learn to good use.

Green's controversial ideas largely stemmed from a single core belief: African societies are not a tabula rasa onto which Western biomedicine can simply be imposed. Traditional healers embody the indigenous African medical culture, which cannot be ignored. As Green would later write, "It is Western medicine that is 'alternative' for most Africans."

THESE IDEAS WERE SURPRISINGLY new to the debate on AIDS in Africa, but they weren't new to Green. He had been dealing with them for most of his professional career—a career that neatly parallels the history of medical anthropology's efforts to bring traditional healers into the public-health mainstream.

The WHO first declared itself in favor of increased collaboration with traditional healers in 1977. That same year, Green, then an assistant professor of anthropology at West Virginia University, got an offer from Population Action International to go to West Africa to research population growth in the Sahel region. At some point during the trip, he had "a moment of epiphany," he says. "I was in Niger, I think, and somebody said, 'You know, we have a terrible malnutrition problem among pregnant women, and we have one good source of protein: chicken eggs. But there's a taboo against pregnant women eating eggs. Now, if we could just get an anthropologist in here to figure out a way around that taboo.'" Green laughs. "… I thought, gee whiz, you know, I could be applying what I know to life-and-death issues on a grand scale, instead of teaching anthropology to recalcitrant students who are fulfilling a social-science obligation."

Healers attended the first workshop in disguise. But by the second one, they came "in full regalia, dressed in feathers and beads," says Green. "Out of the closet, as it were."

Green never did get around to tackling the egg problem, but later in the same trip he had a second epiphany. At a cocktail party in Ghana, he ran into Michael Warren, a medical anthropologist from Iowa State. Warren was setting up one of the first serious programs to train traditional healers in Western health-care techniques. Called Primary Health Training for Indigenous Healers Programme (PRHETIH), Warren's project eventually trained hundreds of traditional healers in a few simple biomedical health-care precepts: diagnosing and treating diarrhea, malnutrition, febrile convulsions, and the like.

BY THE EARLY 1980S, GREEN HAD transformed himself into a medical anthropologist, trading in his recalcitrant college students for eager witch doctors. Having completed a study of traditional healers' responses to Swaziland's first cholera outbreak, he worked with the United States Agency for International Development (USAID) to make recommendations for integrating traditional healers into the Swazi public-health-care system. "We did a survey, and we found that something like 99 percent of the healers wanted to learn Western medical techniques," he says. "So I showed these results to the medical association of Swaziland, thinking all these doctors would be so happy that the traditional healers want to learn! And I finished my presentation, and the questions from the doctors were: Why aren't these guys in jail? They're practicing medicine without a license. Why isn't someone arresting them?" Nevertheless, Green and a Swazi colleague, Dr. Lydia Makhubu, managed to set up some workshops. "The first healers came in disguise, dressed as civilians," he says. "By the second or third workshop, they were coming in full regalia, dressed in feathers and beads, and waving their… paraphernalia. Out of the closet, as it were."

Through the rest of the 1980s and into the 1990s, Green worked all over Africa on projects related to traditional medicine—in Nigeria, Liberia, South Africa, and Mozambique. With another USAID grant, Green set up a program in South Africa in 1992 to train thirty healers as trainers-of-trainers in HIV prevention. These healers would each be expected to train thirty other healers, and so on, hopefully reaching twenty-seven thousand healers by the third generation. The training sessions described the etiology of AIDS in terms culturally meaningful to traditional healers. White blood cells were described as healers' apprentices who guard the master healers, T-cells. During sex, the enemy, HIV, sneaks in and kills the master healers, takes their places, and tricks the apprentices into thinking they are still taking orders from their superiors. The enemy orders the apprentices to let in more and more HIV, until finally the enemy takes over the whole body.

When Green evaluated the traditional healers who had completed the program, he found that their knowledge about AIDS had significantly increased. They were willing to recommend and supply condoms to patients. They were eager to counsel patients against sexual promiscuity, which many healers already considered dangerous. And they understood that AIDS could be transmitted by sharing the same razor for ritual scarification, but not by sharing a spoon. By this time, Green was far from the only one running such programs. In 1992, a medical anthropologist named Rachel King, working with Médecins Sans Frontières in Uganda, had started a program called Traditional and Modern Health Practitioners Together Against AIDS (THETA). The program initially trained just seventeen healers, but it did so intensively: fifteen months of training, three days a month. Before the program, according to King, healers were "reluctant to discuss AIDS with their clients, because they feared losing them." After the program, healers promoted and distributed condoms to their clients, counseled them on "positive living," and staged AIDS-education performances using music and theater. Evaluators compared the rate of condom use in areas where THETA had been active with the rate in non-THETA areas. It was 50 percent versus 17 percent.

EIGHT YEARS LATER, THETA IS still going strong, and Uganda is an unparalleled AIDS success story. In 1993, Uganda had an overall HIV-positive rate that reached 14 percent, one of the highest in Africa at the time. As of 2000, Uganda had cut that rate to about 8 percent. It is the only country in the world ever to have fought double-digit HIV-positive rates back down into single digits.

Of course, many things had to go right for that to happen: Uganda's AIDS prevention programs were strong in every sector, involving religious leaders from every major community, including both Christians and Muslims. (In 1989 the mufti of Uganda officially declared a jihad on AIDS.) Community AIDS education projects honeycombed the country, working in every demographic group from market women to bicycle-taxi boys. Uganda had sub-Saharan Africa's first voluntary and anonymous HIV testing program and its first nationwide, multisectoral AIDS prevention coordinating body. Most important, the country's president made a firm political commitment to stopping AIDS. Still, Green feels that THETA served as an invaluable model for other programs in Uganda. "I'm not going to say it's *the* thing that stopped AIDS in Uganda—there is no one thing, there never is," he says. "But I think it was significant."

Throughout the 1990s, local and foreign governments, as well as NGOs, set up collaborative programs with traditional healers in Botswana, Malawi, Mozambique, Tanzania, and Zambia. Medical anthropology's efforts to integrate traditional healers into the fight against AIDS appeared to be succeeding. But there was one problem: None of these other countries had actually managed to stop the spread of HIV. Green's program in South Africa did not prevent infection rates there from zooming up toward the 20 percent mark, and they're still climbing. In Botswana the rate has been estimated as high as 36 percent.

WHAT HAPPENED? IN 1999, ONE OF the grand old men of African demographic research, John C. Caldwell, a professor emeritus at the Australian National University at Canberra, presided over a conference on resistance to sexual behavior change in the face of AIDS. In a paper he delivered at the conference, Caldwell put the problem this way:

There is a mystery at the heart of the African epidemic, which urgently needs explanation.... Much lower HIV seroprevalence levels and AIDS deaths have led elsewhere to marked changes in sexual behaviour and to an early decline in HIV incidence.... In northern Thailand the first evidence of the arrival of the AIDS epidemic led to brothels closing as clients' numbers dwindled, even before government interventions were put in place....

There is now some evidence of the beginning of sexual behaviour change in Uganda and of declining HIV incidence and prevalence. Research elsewhere in sub-Saharan Africa shows no such change.... At first it was thought

possible to explain this lack of change in terms of inadequate information.... Over time, this explanation has become ever less tenable. The Demographic and Health Survey program had shown that among men, 98 percent knew of AIDS in 1991–92 in Tanzania and 99 percent in 1998 in Kenya. For women, levels of knowledge were 93 percent in Tanzania in 1991–92 and 99 percent in Zambia in 1992 and in Kenya in 1998. The great majority knew of the dangers of sexual transmission.

So why didn't they do anything to protect themselves?

ZEIDAN HAMMAD IS AN INTERNAL-medicine specialist at CHU-Tokoin Hospital, the main public hospital in Lomé. The Lebanese-born Hammad was trained in Cuba, and as he walks me through the hospital's rather decrepit white-stucco facilities, he grumbles about the staff's idea of a sterile environment.

"They spread the clean linen out on the ground to dry," he says, waving at multicolored sheets draped across the bushes and dusty grass in the hospital courtyard. "They like that it dries faster that way. You know, in Cuba, there was no money for anything, but they kept things clean!"

The first stop on Hammad's tour is the HIV testing lab, and for this, at least, he has nothing but praise. The lab's two machines, for performing the ELISA and Western Blot tests for HIV, are in perfect, spotless condition, and the staff is efficient and professional. The tests, which cost about three dollars each, are administered in strict privacy, and results are made available to no one but the patient. The lab processes hundreds of results every month.

Next stop on the tour is Ward 4, the long-term-care ward. Only eight of the ward's beds are occupied. That, explains Dr. Hammad, is because the hospital does not treat AIDS patients.

"There's nothing we can do for them here," he says. "If they're rich, they go off to Europe. If they're poor, we send them home to die."

It's not entirely true that the hospital can do nothing. Hammad can treat the opportunistic infections that attack AIDS patients in the early stages of HIV infection, and if their immune systems have not deteriorated too badly, he can prolong their lives. And this is where Hammad's frustration with traditional healers manifests itself.

"I have people come to me with problems that suggest they may be HIV positive, and I tell them, go get tested and then come back," he says. "And then they disappear for six months. I go to the test lab and ask, what happened to this person? And they say, yes, we tested him. Then suddenly six months later the person shows up in my office again, practically on the point of death. And he says, 'Oh, I tested HIV positive, so I went to the traditional healer, but it didn't work. So I went to another healer, but it didn't work either.' So now they're back, and now I can't do anything for them. It's too late. Educated people! And they go to these healers! It's crazy!"

IF HAMMAD AND GREEN WERE TO discuss the value of traditional healers in African health care, they would probably have a hard time keeping their voices down. But sixty years ago, doctors and anthropologists were more united in their frustration with traditional African medical culture. In fact, one of the foundational texts of medical anthropology is E.E. Evans-Pritchard's 1937 classic, *Witchcraft, Oracles and Magic Among the Azande*. The book is essentially a limit case of a culture with which Westerners cannot collaborate. When Habermas or Rorty wants an illustration of a worldview that rests on axioms so different from our own that communication between the two cultures is virtually impossible, they turn to Evans-Pritchard's Azande. According to Evans-Pritchard, the reason the Azande worldview is so inimical to the Western one is that it considers diseases, and other misfortunes, to be caused by sorcery. Whether or not Evans-Pritchard thought the Azande believed *all* diseases to be caused by sorcery has been an ongoing argument in anthropology for sixty years now. Another ongoing argument has been the question of whether Evans-Pritchard's observations about the Azande hold for the rest of Africa as well.

Until fairly recently, most anthropologists felt that they do. G. P. Murdock, whose *Africa: Its Peoples and Their Culture History* is a seminal ethnography of the continent, wrote in 1980 that mystical retribution and sorcery are the main African explanations for disease. George Foster, whose 1976 paper "Disease Etiologies in Non-Western Medical Systems" is another classic of the field, wrote in 1983 that "personalistic" explanations of disease—that is, you get sick because someone, human or demonic, wants you to get sick—predominate in Africa. Most other anthropologists and social scientists, both Western and African, agreed.

Some social-science researchers have blamed the persistence of personalistic theories of disease causation for the failure of Africans to alter their sexual behavior in the face of AIDS. These scholars have hypothesized that Africans' failure to use condoms or limit their number of sexual partners stems partly from the belief that you don't get AIDS unless an enemy wants you to get it. The idea that personalistic ideas about disease are reducing the ability of ordinary Africans to cope with AIDS is even more widespread among doctors like Hammad. Doctors and public-health officials, both Western and African, widely blame the failure of HIV prevention in Africa on local belief in witchcraft, sorcery, and *gris-gris* (black magic).

But they are working with a previous generation's understanding of African traditional medicine. In recent years, anthropologists have reassessed the importance of witchcraft to the African view of disease. In the 1970s, Michael Warren, the founder of the PRHETIH project, began arguing that the Bono of Ghana actually saw most diseases as impersonally caused—that is, caused by environmental factors, whether natural or supernatural, rather than by the malign will of another human being or a deity. Over the years more and more anthropologists have made similar findings with other African ethnic groups.

Anthropologists such as Harriet Ngubane, Mary Douglas, Michael Gelfand, and David Hammond-Tooke reported that ideas of contagion and pollution were actually widespread among many African societies. Some Africans believed that diseases were caused by tiny, invisible insects, or that illness was transmitted by contact with impure substances such as feces or menstrual blood. Shona healers in Zimbabwe practiced variolation, the rubbing of fluid from an infected person's pustule into a cut on a non-infected person, to stimulate an immune response. Practices in other ethnic groups might not have been so obviously biomedically effective, but the important thing was that they were based on *impersonal* theories of disease causation: You contracted a disease because you happened to come into contact with someone or something, not because a person or deity was using magic against you.

The witchcraft question is important because it bears on collaboration. If traditional healers attribute diseases to sorcery, there is not much doctors can do with them.

Green ascribes the overemphasis on witchcraft by earlier anthropologists in part to "xenophilia"—an attraction to the more exotic and flamboyant elements of African medical culture. (*Witchcraft Among the Azande* is a much sexier title than, say, *Pollution Beliefs Among the Azande*.) He also thinks many researchers were not thinking clearly about how to classify beliefs. For example, African survey respondents, asked to explain the causes of certain diseases, may reply, "It's the will of God." This has often been classified by researchers as a "supernatural" or personalistic response. But does it have to be? A Western oncologist might utter the same words when asked why a child contracts leukemia.

There are, undeniably, traditional healers who believe AIDS can be caused by witchcraft. In one oft-cited case in Zambia, a community's devastation by AIDS in the early 1990s led it to consult a "witch finder," who allegedly poisoned some fifteen suspected witches. In a Liberian survey, 13 percent of healers, local leaders, and health workers interviewed named witchcraft as a cause of STDs. But that put witchcraft well behind promiscuity, stepping in urine, or sex with an infected person.

The witchcraft question is important because it bears on the possibility of collaboration. If traditional healers believe that diseases are caused by witchcraft, there is not much you can do with them, from a biomedical perspective. They belong, as one doctor who worked in a district hospital in Africa for thirty-three years put it, to "a system that is irreconcilable with our own." But if traditional healers do not ascribe diseases to sorcery—even if they think illnesses are caused by tiny insects, by imbalances in semimystical forces of heat, by interference with the body's "internal snake," whatever—then you can work with that. You can describe the AIDS virus as a variety of the tiny invisible insects many indigenous medical traditions describe. You can build on many medical traditions' belief that promiscuous or adulterous sex results in pollution. You can collaborate.

More or less. Some medical anthropologists feel that even if traditional healers believe in naturalistic theories of disease causation, working with them is an iffy proposition.

In 1991, Peter Ventevogel, a Dutch medical student working on a master's thesis in medical anthropology, went to Ghana to follow up on Warren's famous PRHETIH project. The project had shut down in 1983, and Ventevogel wanted to find out what the healers had retained from their training. His findings, published in 1996 as *Whiteman's Things: Training and Detraining Healers in Ghana*, were interesting: On the one hand, the healers seemed to retain what they had learned in the workshops to a remarkable extent. On the other hand, they didn't actually seem to be putting that knowledge to use. They had learned that diarrhea could result in dehydration, and often remembered the formula for mixing oral rehydration salts, but almost none of them were actually doing it. They continued to treat diarrhea with herbal enemas, which biomedicine considers actively harmful. "PRHETIH was a powerful force attempting to change healers by training them," Ventevogel wrote. "But the healers formed an intractable counterforce, resisting training by 'detraining' themselves."

"The healers don't write their knowledge down and systematically compare it with each other," explains Ventevogel, now a psychiatrist in Amsterdam, in an interview. "The terms and beliefs differ in every village, in fact even in the same village. Their way of thinking is different from ours. I respect traditional healers, but you can't just mix Western scientific medicine and traditional healers up in a soup and expect to get something that makes any sense."

Unlike Ventevogel, Green thinks traditional medical beliefs are largely consistent within ethnic groups and even across them. But there is one of Ventevogel's critiques with which few people on the front lines would disagree. "Training traditional healers," Ventevogel writes, "is no panacea for a failing Western health care system." And in this belief, Ventevogel is joined by one of the more flamboyant medical anthropologists working on AIDS today: Dr. Paul Farmer.

PAUL FARMER RUNS A FREE CLINIC in A desperately poor region of rural Haiti. He also teaches at the Harvard Medical School and consults on numerous international infectious-disease projects, largely dealing with AIDS and tuberculosis. He made his mark in the AIDS field with a 1992 book called *AIDS and Accusation*, based on his experiences as an anthropologist in Haiti during the 1980s. One of the book's chief arguments was that the spread of AIDS in Haiti had been misattributed to "cultural factors"—particularly the belief in voodoo—when in fact it stemmed from socioeconomic causes: the country's vicious poverty, its lack of an adequate biomedical health-care system, and its exposure to a sex tourism trade that catered to Americans. Farmer did find that local interpretations of AIDS hinged on allegations of sorcery. But he didn't think that belief in sorcery was what was making the villages vulnerable. He thought they were vulnerable because they were poor.

Farmer doesn't think the spread of AIDS in Africa can be blamed on African traditional medical culture. The very notion, in Farmer's view, is merely a smokescreen behind which the rich West can evade responsibility for Africa's AIDS catastrophe. At the same time, he thinks that the newer emphasis on working with traditional healers has also served as an excuse for the West's failure to provide the world's poor with decent scientific medical care. We could stop AIDS in Africa, Farmer is saying—but we don't, because we don't want to spend the money.

This argument has become all the sharper recently, as generic antiretroviral drugs from Brazilian and Indian companies have pushed the cost of treatment ever lower. The recent offer by the Indian pharmaceutical company Cipla to supply Médecins Sans Frontières with an antiretroviral cocktail treatment for $350 per patient per year puts certified antiretrovirals into the same price class as the herbal remedy of Toudji-Bandje, whose six-month course of treatment costs $430. If Farmer is right—if the barriers to stopping AIDS in Africa are about money, not culture—then the cheaper the drugs get, the greater the pressure on the West will be to intervene.

GREEN SPOTS A PROBLEM WITH Farmer's thesis. "The richest countries in Africa have the highest HIV rates," he says emphatically. "And the richest people in each country have the highest HIV rates." This may be an exaggeration, but there does seem to be some positive correlation between HIV rates and a nation's income. Botswana and South Africa are among the countries with the highest HIV-positive rates in southern Africa. The highest rate in West Africa is in Ivory Coast. These are the richest countries in their respective zones.

Early in the epidemic, some studies showed HIV rates rising with markers such as education level and travel. AIDS often seemed to hit the richer, more urban classes first. It struck the men who had the money to employ prostitutes. And, of course, their wives. As the epidemic wore on, these correlations became far less pronounced. After all, some of the poorest nations in sub-Saharan Africa—Zambia and Malawi, for example—also have ex-

traordinarily high rates of infection. Still, most anthropologists agree that many rich, educated Africans continue to use traditional healers, though sometimes in conjunction with bio-medical doctors and often in secret.

Talk of culture can serve as a smokescreen, says Farmer. Africa has an AIDS crisis not because people insist on consulting healers, but because Africa is poor.

Whatever his differences with other anthropologists, Farmer agrees that collaborating with healers can be worthwhile. "I bet I work with them as much as anybody," he remarks. But he doesn't see healers as the repositories of a culture's accumulated medical wisdom. "When they're sick, they don't often go to each other," he says. "They come to see me."

In fact, Farmer doesn't just think traditional healers are ineffective. He thinks they're not really traditional: "It may have been different in Central America, Africa, and Asia in the past, but now you see that most 'traditional' healers use antibiotics, and a weird amalgam of modernity and the products of a globalizing economy."

MANY ANTHROPOLOGISTS HAVE noticed that "traditional" healers in Africa are undergoing a strange process of mutation as the continent modernizes. Lots of them still wear traditional robes, carry staffs with ivory heads, and preside over smoke-filled huts surrounded by mud fetishes. But more and more of them are putting on lab coats, hanging certificates on the wall, selling their products in labeled bottles, or even administering injections. Green has documented the common practice of adding mashed-up ampicillin pills to "traditional" herbal medicines.

A perfect example of this sort of "weird amalgam" is Toudji-Bandje, the inventor of Tobacoak's. Toudji-Bandje, the secretary general of Togo's National Association of Traditional Healers, learned his herbal lore from his aged traditional-healer uncle. He also calls himself "Doctor." He has applied for a patent for Tobacoak's. He sends samples of his patients' blood to a laboratory in France to be tested for viral load. He has a catchy brand name for his product. And he calls it an "antiretroviral." Since when is "antiretroviral" a traditional African medical concept?

Toudji-Bandje's patients don't appear to care whether his theory of disease etiology is autochthonous, import, or creole. If anything, the mixture of North and South enables him to claim authority from both sources. What really matters to his patients is simply that someone is telling them he can cure their illness. And they believe the treatment works. "It completely eliminates my fever," says one patient, who declines to give his name. "When I take the medicine, I can eat. Whether it will cure me completely, I don't know. I haven't been taking it long enough."

"I tested positive in 1992," says a Mr. Kpodar, who claims to have been Toudji-Bandje's second AIDS patient. "I told my wife, and she tested positive too. I begged her to take Toudji-Bandje's medicine, but her family wouldn't let her. She died in 1993. The product saved my life." Toudji-Bandje claims that his remedy is effective in 86 percent of patients. But no third party has examined Toudji-Bandje's data, let alone conducted an independent study of his patients.

IN TOGO, AIDS IS NOT YET COMpletely out of control. But it's about to be. Togo's current rate of infection runs to 5.98 percent of adults aged fifteen to forty-nine, and a UNAIDS official confirms that HIV rates are rising. There have been active AIDS education and prevention programs in Togo since the late 1980s. But they don't seem to have had much effect.

"I've been trying to get traditional healers involved," says Bridget McHenry, a Peace Corps volunteer working in a village called Yometchin, in Togo's southern Maritime Region. "Some refuse. Some are psyched to do it. But most healers don't believe AIDS can't be cured. And they diagnose a lot of AIDS cases as the result of gris-gris."

Peace Corps volunteers in Togo are fairly pessimistic about the possibility of changing local sexual behavior, and they ascribe much of the blame to belief in gris-gris. But few of them know anything about gris-gris. They give the impression of being lost in a culture they don't understand—precisely the situation Green thinks should be avoided. And if you ask them whether they think it would have been useful to have some training in traditional medical ideas before going into villages as AIDS educators, most say no.

"It's different in every village," says Kim Williams, a volunteer in a Plateau Region village called Akpakpakpe. "You have to really listen closely to understand it at all, and they think you're an idiot."

"And they know you're not one of them," adds McHenry. "They know you don't believe it. You'll always be yovo"—a foreigner.

Williams nods in agreement.

Each Peace Corps volunteer is paired with a homologue, or counterpart, from a local Togolese NGO or governmental agency. At a recent meeting, the homologues made it clear they're not interested in collaborating with traditional healers either.

If you try to find out about the Togolese Government's AIDS Prevention Program, you will be directed to a bare, grimy office, where a small old man will deflect your questions repeatedly.

"The healers say they can cure AIDS," says one homologue. "But of course they can't. They deceive people."

"They deny the disease exists," says another. "They say it's an old African sickness traditionally known as dikanaku. It's 'get-thin-and-die' in Ewe."

Although the WHO and UNAIDS are both developing programs directed toward traditional healers in Togo, the country's medical establishment regards traditional practitioners with ambivalence. On the one hand, there are doctors,

like Hammad, who blame traditional healers for preventing Togolese from coming to terms with AIDS. But Messanvi Gbeassor, a biologist at Lomé's Université du Bénin, has good relations with healers. "We even work with their national association," he says. Gbeassor also carried out some tests on Toudji-Bandje's product, with tantalizingly positive results.

As for the Togolese government, its PNLS—Programme National de Lutte contre le SIDA—claims to have an active program for collaboration with traditional healers. If you try to find out more about this program, you will be directed to the PNLS headquarters, a spacious villa in a sleepy residential section of town. The building appears to be devoid of activity, other than the whir of air conditioners and a couple of boys out front listening to the radio. On the first floor, in a bare, grimy office, a small old man will deflect your questions repeatedly, and then, rummaging through the room's single cabinet, will at last come up with a copy of a statement of program goals from 1992, which announces the intention to hold training sessions with traditional healers.

If there is one single reason for Togo's lamentable performance in stopping HIV, it is illustrated in the condition of the PNLS. Unlike Uganda, Togo's government has not made an overwhelming political commitment to the struggle against AIDS. The president, General Gnassingbe Eyadema, has paid lip service to the cause, but he has not committed sufficient resources to it or made it a top priority. "What's lacking here," says Moustapha Sidatt, the WHO's resident representative in Togo, "is political will." Sidatt has an ambitious plan to establish a nationwide association of traditional practitioners, which would inspect their practices to determine that they are not harmful, and would issue membership cards backed by the government and the WHO.

Sidatt would also like to start testing the products of traditional healers who claim to treat AIDS or its associated opportunistic infections. "We're trying to approach them, to gain their confidence," he says. "We have some laboratories here at the university, and virology laboratories abroad, which can test their products.

There are many things we would like to do. But that requires a political decision from the government."

IF YOU DRIVE EAST ON THE HIGH-way from Lomé, toward Aneho and Ouidah, you will see little flags fluttering along the roadside in various colors. The flags are advertisements for traditional healers, and the different colors—white, green, black—symbolize the different practices available: herbal solutions, traditional vaccination (herbs inserted directly into cuts in the skin), sorcery, exorcism. Just a few miles outside of Lomé, you'll come upon the freshly painted clinic of Madame Léocadie Ashorgbor.

Ashorgbor provides herbal remedies. She learned them from her husband, from whom she is now estranged. She does not know where her husband trained, but some of the remedies are probably time-tested elements of Togolese culture. Still, her husband's recipes aren't all Ashorg-bor relies on. "You have to have the gift," she says. "The gift comes from God." Ashorgbor doesn't heal through prayer, but the formulas for some of her herbal remedies come to her in revelations.

What would a medical anthropologist like Green make of Ashorgbor? Well, he would probably find her very interesting, but also a bit confusing. Can Western medicine collaborate with people like her to fight AIDS? If not, why not? "I don't claim working with traditional healers is easy," says Green. "I just think, looking at the public-health benefits, it's a good thing to do."

Ashorgbor agrees. "I think it's a good idea," she says of the WHO's initiative to organize Togo's traditional practitioners. "Depending on how it's done. You know, we traditional therapists are hard people to work with. We get all those herbs up in our heads, and we get a little bit crazy."

Matthew Steinglass is a writer based in Lomé, Togo. His article "Voices Carry: One More Paradigm Shift, and You'll Be Able to Tell Your Computer Everything" appeared in the July/August 2000 LF.

From *Lingua Franca*, April 2001, pp. 29-39. © 2001 by *Lingua Franca*: The Review of Academic Life, published in New York. (www.linguafranca.com).

Why We Want Their Bodies Back

As Humans Have Evolved, They've Learned There Are Good Reasons Not To Bury An Empty Coffin

By Robert Sapolsky

LAST WEEK I GOT A PHONE CALL THAT I'd been waiting for since 1973.

That year I was 16 years old and a student at an alternative high school in New York City. My schoolmates and I were wanna-be hippies, jealous of our older siblings who'd gotten to live the 1960s. That summer there was a rock festival upstate at Watkins Glen that turned out to be one of the biggest ever. Among the 600,000 who made the pilgrimage were two of our friends: Bonnie Bickwit, with her peasant blouse and bandanna, and Mitchell Weiser, with his ponytail. They met up at the summer camp just outside the city where Bonnie was working and hitched to the rock festival. We never saw them again.

Everything we knew about Bonnie and Mitch convinced us they hadn't run away. Something had happened to them. Throughout that fall, we talked to grizzled rural sheriffs and reporters. We spent our weekends posting pictures of Bonnie and Mitch in the East Village in Manhattan, near the buildings of cults that were rumored to kidnap kids. We had nightmares about rape and torture and murder. The loss of these friends was a galvanizing event in my adolescence. Ultimately, it turned out to be the longest unsolved teen disappearance in the nation's history.

Then suddenly the long search ended. Mitch and Bonnie's classmates had gathered for a 25th reunion. A ceremony held in their memory got some news coverage. The right person saw a report on a missing persons show and called the police.

The man told police that a teenage couple he had encountered leaving Watkins Glen had drowned. The couple fit the description of Bonnie and Mitch, and the details of the man's story rang true. The news quickly spread by phone and e-mail among people who now barely remember each other. Amid the muted excitement, we all kept coming back to the same issue: If this man's story is true, the bodies of Bonnie and Mitch should have been found. Show us the bodies, we thought, and the mystery of their disappearance will be resolved once and for all.

THE DESIRE FOR TANGIBLE PROOF OF THE death of someone we know or love is a natural human impulse. But often that desire extends well beyond a purely rational need for certainty. In circumstances where there is not the remotest chance that someone is still alive, we still expend great energy and often put other lives on the line in order to retrieve the dead. Consider, for example, the extreme risks taken by an international team of divers last fall as they worked around the clock for more than two weeks in choppy waters off the coast of Norway to recover corpses from the sunken Russian submarine *Kursk*. In the wake of the terrorist attacks last September 11, the intense emotional longing that is often associated with efforts to recover remains was especially pronounced. As the days and weeks passed following the collapse of the World Trade Center towers, the United States was brought to an awed si-

lence by the nearest thing we've had in generations to a holy national rite: the search for the dead at Ground Zero.

The quest to get the body back is a drama played out in an endless variety of settings. In Chile, for instance, where civilians of the wrong opinion vanished during the murderous reign of Augusto Pinochet decades ago, the now-elderly mothers of the disappeared still gather to demand: "Give us even a single bone of our children." Sometimes the demand for remains crosses national or cultural boundaries and is passed down from generation to generation. Recently Spanish authorities returned the body of a chief to his native Botswana more than a century after it was stolen from its fresh grave by looters and carted off for display in a museum. An even longer-standing dispute was resolved in 1993 when the Japanese made reparations for a 1597 invasion of Korea by returning some grisly spoils of war: 20,000 human noses.

It is tempting to assume that such a widespread obsession with retrieving bodily remains is rooted in a deep-seated human need to ritualistically put the dead to rest in a respectful manner: In the words of an old blues song, "See that my grave's kept clean." But, in fact, death rituals vary dramatically from culture to culture. While most societies traditionally bury or cremate their dead, others such as the Masai in East Africa discard corpses for scavengers. And even among cultures that bury their dead, the sense of a grave as hallowed ground is not necessarily shared. As late as the 19th century in northern Europe, burial was akin to leasing an apartment: Graves were intermittently dug up and the remains discarded to make room for the next tenants. While the Western model of death involves grief and whispered respect, the Nyakyusa in Malawi have ornate funerary rituals of mocking the deceased.

Cultures even differ as to when they decide someone is good and dead. And sometimes individuals who we would consider robustly alive are treated as deceased. In traditional Haitian society, if a person does something deeply taboo, a shaman turns the miscreant into a slave-like zombie; thereafter, the community believes he inhabits the world of the dead. Conversely, some societies continue hearty, active interchanges with people who are no longer alive. In traditional Chinese society in Singapore, younger siblings have to wait their turn to get married, so sometimes an older sibling who dies unwed is betrothed in a "ghost marriage" to someone appropriate and deceased. Even in our own culture and others that are preoccupied with retrieving the dead, with sufficient passage of time (and with the demise of the immediate kin of the deceased) the respectful act becomes just the opposite. Although we consider it a moral imperative to try to recover corpses from the *Kursk*, doing the same to any skeletal remains on the *Titanic* would be seen as inappropriately disturbing the dead.

So why do we go to extraordinary lengths to get the body back?

Until the invention of the modern stethoscope about 185 years ago, determining if someone was dead or just in a coma was often difficult. As a result, all too many people were buried alive

---

The most obvious reason is to make sure the person is really dead. Until the invention of the modern stethoscope about 185 years ago, determining if someone was dead or just in a coma was often difficult. The fact that some people were buried alive gave way to laws in the 17th century mandating a waiting period before burial; aristocrats stipulated in their wills that bodily insults intended to wake the not-dead, such as cutting off toes, were to be inflicted on their corpses. By the 19th century, inventors offered coffins with escape hatches. In German deadhouses, which served as way stations before burial, the fingers of corpses were attached to alarm bells. Just in case.

Many nonhuman primates also take time before literally letting go of their dead. This is something that I have observed in my own studies of baboons. An infant dies, and rather than discarding the body, the mother carries it around for days afterward. Sociobiologists argue that there is an evolutionary reason for such behavior: Females who have the occasional offspring revive from a coma pass on more copies of their genes.

With humans, the desire to get the body back is intertwined with the irrational energy that we put into denial. Beginning with our first toddler encounter with a dead robin in the backyard and our parents' uncomfortable "It's only sleeping," the Western model of death is one of euphemism and denial. As first demonstrated in the landmark work of Elisabeth Kübler-Ross, people in our society tend to react to death or the news of terminal illness with a stereotyped sequence of stages: denial, typically followed by anger, bargaining, depression, and if one is lucky, acceptance. In the context of the euphemistic model of death—Grandpa simply goes to the hospital and does not come back—the process of mourning is viewed as hitting bottom in order to move past the denial stage. Thus the tendency of so many of us to consider it a bracing necessity to take the bull of denial by the horns and ask that the coffin be opened, so that we can look upon our loved one's face. For that, we need the body.

Sometimes we want the body back in order to learn how the person died. This can be a vast source of solace: "It was a painless death; he never knew what was happening." The quest for how involves the ghastly world of forensics, where sequence is everything: "She was already dead by the time X was done." And at times the solace comes from learning something about the deceased by the nature of his death: the heroic act, the sacrifice that affirms a group's values. In his story "A River Runs Through It," Norman MacLean wrote of the youthful murder of his hell-raising brother. He had been beaten to death by thugs unknown, and the autopsy revealed that the small bones in his hands were broken. And thus, "like many Scottish ministers before him, [MacLean's father] had to derive what comfort he could from the faith that his son had died fighting." Similarly, many people were relieved to discover that passengers on the hijacked plane that crashed in Pennsylvania on September 11 had apparently put up a valiant struggle.

The desire to get the body back is also sometimes associated with what we believe to be the spiritual well-being of the dead. The Tlingit of Alaska, for example, believe that a body must be recovered for reincarnation to occur. Among the Nuba of Sudan, men are circumcised only after death, a prerequisite for an afterlife. A top-of-the-line Church of England funeral requires a body that can be blessed and put to eternal rest. Some cultures need not only the body but all of the body. Orthodox Jews save teeth, amputated limbs, and excised appendixes for eventual burial; that is why some Israelis will comb the site of a terrorist bombing for scatterings of shredded flesh.

Another major reason for wanting the body back is for the well-being, spiritual or otherwise, of those in control of the body. In *Grave Matters*, a surprisingly entertaining book on cross-cultural aspects of death, the anthropologist Nigel Barley writes, "The dead do not own their corpses." Funerary ritual, with the body as its centerpiece, is an unmatched opportunity to share, affirm, inculcate, and revitalize group values. A well-scripted funeral for a political martyr can galvanize potential crusaders into a self-sacrificing, homicidal frenzy. On the other hand, Barley argues, few settings match a state funeral as an opportunity for a government to signal power and solidarity. Consider the seemingly odd

SHOW US THE BODY: People who vanish without a trace remain a source of enduring fascination even if they are eventually given up for dead. Amelia Earhart disappeared in 1937 while attempting a round-the-world flight. D. B. Cooper hijacked a Northwest Orient airliner shortly after takeoff from Seattle in 1971, demanded $200,000 in cash, and then parachuted from the rear of the plane, never to be seen again. Joseph Crater, a New York Supreme Court judge with ties to both the Tammany Hall political machine and organized crime, disappeared in 1930 after a meal at Billy Ha's Chop House. Hobbled by frostbitten feet while returning from the South Pole in 1912 with Robert Scott, L. E. G. Oates set out on his own so as not to slow his companions. His last words: "I am just going outside and may be some time." Chandra Levy vanished in Washington, D.C., last year, shortly after finishing an internship with the Federal Bureau of Prisons. John William Anglin was one of three inmates who in 1962 left hand-painted dummies in their bunks at Alcatraz, an island prison in San Francisco Bay, and escaped through air vents dug out with spoons; the case is still open four decades later. Jimmy Hoffa, the mob-connected president of the Teamsters from 1957 to 1971, was last seen in 1975 in the parking lot of a suburban Detroit restaurant where he had gone to meet two associates with Mafia ties. Michael Rockefeller, an heir to the Rockefeller fortune, may have been eaten by cannibals during a 1961 anthropological expedition in New Guinea.

act of the atheist Soviet Union of the 1920s in preserving the body of Lenin in perpetuity like some Slavic saint. The message to the Russian peasantry: "We have crushed and replaced the church."

The group value of a funeral holds even when it is not for the mighty. Consider how we eulogize the dead. The overwhelming pressure is to glorify, exalt, and exaggerate the good acts of the person. This can sometimes involve downright invention if the person was a scoundrel or if the eulogist is a hired gun who didn't actually know the deceased. In our society the good acts are drawn from a list heavily featuring fidelity, devotion to young children and aged parents, religiosity, a robust work ethic, and a fondness for barbecuing. On a certain level, the concrete rituals of a funeral are lessons for the next generation. The values eulogized represent a remarkably effective vehicle of conformity, producing that superego of a whisper in the ears of so many of us: "How do I want to be remembered?"

Thus the pressure at a funeral to make the deceased seem like a saint. And when the funeral is for someone whom that society really does consider a saint, watch out. When Khomeini died in Iran, frenzied crowds of mourners were so eager to touch their beloved ayatollah that they tipped over his coffin and shredded his burial shroud. Nigel Barley tells the story of the death in 1231 of Elisabeth of Thuringia, someone so clearly bound for sainthood that a crowd quickly dismembered her body for holy relics. Even more bizarre is the story of the 11th-century St. Romuald, who in his old age made the mistake of noting plans to move from his Umbrian town; the locals, worried that some other burg would wind up with the holy relics of his body, plotted his murder.

The body can be a vehicle for resolving cultural conflicts. After a small Japanese fishing vessel was accidentally sunk last year by a Navy submarine, the U.S. government mounted a multimillion-dollar effort to recover the dead. A professor of religion advised officials on the culturally sensitive wording to be used in military communiqués about the operation. Corpses were raised to the surface after dusk and, in accordance with Buddhist tradition, placed in body bags feet first.

There is a Maori tale of a man, grievously injured in battle, who begs his comrades to quickly cut off his head and retreat with it so that it won't be appropriated, shrunken, and displayed as a trophy by the enemy

---

By contrast, sometimes a body can be a vehicle for one society to express values that are hostile to another society. There is a Maori tale of a man, grievously injured in battle, who begs his comrades to quickly cut off his head and retreat with it so that it won't be appropriated, shrunken, and displayed as a trophy by the enemy. As a corollary, recall the visceral power of the image of American dead being dragged through the streets by crowds of Somalis. When Zaire's kleptocratic ruler Mobutu was in the final days of his dictatorship, he is believed to have spent his time exhuming the bones of his ancestors so that they would not be desecrated by rebels. Likewise, even though there was no immediate threat of hostility when the United States gave up the Panama Canal, bodies were disinterred from the American cemetery and shipped home along with the microwave ovens and VCRs.

IN THE CASE OF BONNIE AND MITCH, MY schoolmates and I realized years ago that they were never coming home. But because we never got the bodies back, there will always be a measure of uncertainty about what happened to them and about the man who finally made that phone call to the police. Allyn Smith was 24 at the time of the Watkins Glen rock festival. On the way home he hitched a ride in a Volkswagen bus. There was a scrawny young couple riding in the back, also hitching from the festival. Smith and the driver smoked a joint. It was a hot day and there was a river nearby. They stopped, planning to cool off in the water. As Smith crouched to take off his shoes, wondering at the wisdom of going in the rough water, he heard a shout. He turned to see that the girl was in the river. The boy—her companion—leaped in to try to save her. Then they were both swept away, down the rapids, still very much alive.

That is the story Smith told the police. No names were exchanged in the van, but he overheard the two talking about a summer camp where the girl had worked and recalled identifying details about her clothes. It would appear that the couple had been Bonnie and Mitch. Smith is now cooperating with the police, trying to identify the stretch of river where he says they disappeared. "I felt he was credible," says Roy Streever, the investigating detective with the New York State police. Nonetheless, something didn't happen that day. Smith, an athletic Navy vet, didn't try to rescue Bonnie and Mitch. Nor did the driver of the bus. Eventually they drove off. At the next exit, Smith got out and headed in another direction. The driver said he'd make an anonymous phone call to the police from a gas station and report that the two kids had been swept down the river. Police have no record that a call was made.

The parents of Bonnie and Mitch had to cope not only with the loss of their children but also with a burden of horrible uncertainty. One father and one stepfather went to their graves never knowing what had happened. The rest of us finally got the answer to the mystery that plagued us for decades.

Once we were kids who believed enough in our immortality that we would hitch rides with strangers. Now we flaunt the same irrationality by cheating on our low-cholesterol diets. Once we had not yet learned that life brings tragedies beyond control. Now we wonder how we can spare our own children from that knowledge. Once we lost two friends and could only imagine florid, violent sins of commission. Now, instead, we have a doughy, middle-aged lesson about the toxic consequences of quiet sins of omission and indifference.

Sometimes, when you get the body back, or at least find out the whole story, you learn something critical about the nature of the living and of those who knew all along what happened.

From *Discover*, February 2002, pp. 64-69. © 2002 by Robert Sapolsky.

The Secrets of Haiti's Living Dead

A Harvard botanist investigates mystic potions,
voodoo rites, and the making of zombies.

Gino Del Guercio

Five years ago, a man walked into l'Estère, a village in central Haiti, approached a peasant woman named Angelina Narcisse, and identified himself as her brother Clairvius. If he had not introduced himself using a boyhood nickname and mentioned facts only intimate family members knew, she would not have believed him. Because, eighteen years earlier, Angelina had stood in a small cemetery north of her village and watched as her brother Clairvius was buried.

The man told Angelina he remembered that night well. He knew when he was lowered into his grave, because he was fully conscious, although he could not speak or move. As the earth was thrown over his coffin, he felt as if he were floating over the grave. The scar on his right cheek, he said, was caused by a nail driven through his casket.

The night he was buried, he told Angelina, a voodoo priest raised him from the grave. He was beaten with a sisal whip and carried off to a sugar plantation in northern Haiti where, with other zombies, he was forced to work as a slave. Only with the death of the zombie master were they able to escape, and Narcisse eventually returned home.

Legend has it that zombies are the living dead, raised from their graves and animated by malevolent voodoo sorcerers, usually for some evil purpose. Most Haitians believe in zombies, and Narcisse's claim is not unique. At about the

time he reappeared, in 1980, two women turned up in other villages saying they were zombies. In the same year, in northern Haiti, the local peasants claimed to have found a group of zombies wandering aimlessly in the fields.

But Narcisse's case was different in one crucial respect; it was documented. His death had been recorded by doctors at the American-directed Schweitzer Hospital in Deschapelles. On April 30, 1962, hospital records show, Narcisse walked into the hospital's emergency room spitting up blood. He was feverish and full of aches. His doctors could not diagnose his illness, and his symptoms grew steadily worse. Three days after he entered the hospital, according to the records, he died. The attending physicians, an American among them, signed his death certificate. His body was placed in cold storage for twenty hours, and then he was buried. He said he remembered hearing his doctors pronounce him dead while his sister wept at his bedside.

At the Centre de Psychiatrie et Neurologie in Port-au-Prince, Dr. Lamarque Douyon, a Haitian-born, Canadian-trained psychiatrist, has been systematically investigating all reports of zombies since 1961. Though convinced zombies were real, he had been unable to find a scientific explanation for the phenomenon. He did not believe zombies were people raised from the dead, but that did not make them any less interesting. He

speculated that victims were only made to *look* dead, probably by means of a drug that dramatically slowed metabolism. The victim was buried, dug up within a few hours, and somehow reawakened.

The Narcisse case provided Douyon with evidence strong enough to warrant a request for assistance from colleagues in New York. Douyon wanted to find an ethnobotanist, a traditional-medicines expert, who could track down the zombie potion he was sure existed. Aware of the medical potential of a drug that could dramatically lower metabolism, a group organized by the late Dr. Nathan Kline—a New York psychiatrist and pioneer in the field of psychopharmacology—raised the funds necessary to send someone to investigate.

The search for that someone led to the Harvard Botanical Museum, one of the world's foremost institutes of ethnobiology. Its director, Richard Evans Schultes, Jeffrey professor of biology, had spent thirteen years in the tropics studying native medicines. Some of his best-known work is the investigation of curare, the substance used by the nomadic people of the Amazon to poison their darts. Refined into a powerful muscle relaxant called D-tubocurarine, it is now an essential component of the anesthesia used during almost all surgery.

Schultes would have been a natural for the Haitian investigation, but he was too busy. He recommended another Harvard ethnobotanist for the assignment, Wade Davis, a 28-year-old Canadian pursuing a doctorate in biology.

Davis grew up in the tall pine forests of British Columbia and entered Harvard in 1971, influenced by a *Life* magazine story on the student strike of 1969. Before Harvard, the only Americans he had known were draft dodgers, who seemed very exotic. "I used to fight forest fires with them," Davis says. "Like everybody else, I thought America was where it was at. And I wanted to go to Harvard because of that *Life* article. When I got there, I realized it wasn't quite what I had in mind."

Davis took a course from Schultes, and when he decided to go to South America to study plants, he approached his professor for guidance. "He was an extraordinary figure," Davis remembers. "He was a man who had done it all. He had lived alone for years in the Amazon." Schultes sent Davis to the rain forest with two letters of introduction and two pieces of advice: wear a pith helmet and try ayahuasca, a powerful hallucinogenic vine. During that expedition and others, Davis proved himself an "outstanding field man," says his mentor. Now, in early 1982, Schultes called him into his office and asked if he had plans for spring break.

"I always took to Schultes's assignments like a plant takes to water," says Davis, tall and blond, with inquisitive blue eyes. "Whatever Schultes told me to do, I did. His letters of introduction opened up a whole world." This time the world was Haiti.

Davis knew nothing about the Caribbean island—and nothing about African traditions, which serve as Haiti's cultural basis. He certainly did not believe in zombies. "I thought it was a lark," he says now.

Davis landed in Haiti a week after his conversation with Schultes, armed with a hypothesis about how the zombie drug—if it existed—might be made. Setting out to explore, he discovered a country materially impoverished, but rich in culture and mystery. He was impressed by the cohesion of Haitian society; he found none of the crime, social disorder, and rampant drug and alcohol abuse so common in many of the other Caribbean islands. The cultural wealth and cohesion,

he believes, spring from the country's turbulent history.

During the French occupation of the late eighteenth century, 370,000 African-born slaves were imported to Haiti between 1780 and 1790. In 1791, the black population launched one of the few successful slave revolts in history, forming secret societies and overcoming first the French plantation owners and then a detachment of troops from Napoleon's army, sent to quell the revolt. For the next hundred years Haiti was the only independent black republic in the Caribbean, populated by people who did not forget their African heritage. "You can almost argue that Haiti is more African than Africa," Davis says. "When the west coast of Africa was being disrupted by colonialism and the slave trade, Haiti was essentially left alone. The amalgam of beliefs in Haiti is unique, but it's very, very African."

Davis discovered that the vast majority of Haitian peasants practice voodoo, a sophisticated religion with African roots. Says Davis, "It was immediately obvious that the stereotypes of voodoo weren't true. Going around the countryside, I found clues to a whole complex social world." Vodounists believe they communicate directly with, indeed are often possessed by, the many spirits who populate the everyday world. Vodoun society is a system of education, law, and medicine; it embodies a code of ethics that regulates social behavior. In rural areas, secret vodoun societies, much like those found on the west coast of Africa, are as much or more in control of everyday life as the Haitian government.

Although most outsiders dismissed the zombie phenomenon as folklore, some early investigators, convinced of its reality, tried to find a scientific explanation. The few who sought a zombie drug failed. Nathan Kline, who helped finance Davis's expedition, had searched unsuccessfully, as had Lamarque Douyon, the Haitian psychiatrist. Zora Neale Hurston, an American black woman, may have come closest. An anthropological pioneer, she went to Haiti in the Thirties, studied vodoun society, and wrote a book on the subject, *Tell My Horse*, first published in 1938. She knew about the secret societies and was con-

vinced zombies were real, but if a power existed, she too failed to obtain it.

Davis obtained a sample in a few weeks.

He arrived in Haiti with the names of several contacts. A BBC reporter familiar with the Narcisse case had suggested he talk with Marcel Pierre. Pierre owned the Eagle Bar, a bordello in the city of Saint Marc. He was also a voodoo sorcerer and had supplied the BBC with a physiologically active powder of unknown ingredients. Davis found him willing to negotiate. He told Pierre he was a representative of "powerful but anonymous interests in New York," willing to pay generously for the priest's services, provided no questions were asked. Pierre agreed to be helpful for what Davis will only say was a "sizable sum." Davis spent a day watching Pierre gather the ingredients—including human bones—and grind them together with mortar and pestle. However, from his knowledge of poison, Davis knew immediately that nothing in the formula could produce the powerful effects of zombification.

Three weeks later, Davis went back to the Eagle Bar, where he found Pierre sitting with three associates. Davis challenged him. He called him a charlatan. Enraged, the priest gave him a second vial, claiming that this was the real poison. Davis pretended to pour the powder into his palm and rub it into his skin. "You're a dead man," Pierre told him, and he might have been, because this powder proved to be genuine. But, as the substance had not actually touched him, Davis was able to maintain his bravado, and Pierre was impressed. He agreed to make the poison and show Davis how it was done.

The powder, which Davis keeps in a small vial, looks like dry black dirt. It contains parts of toads, sea worms, lizards, tarantulas, and human bones. (To obtain the last ingredient, he and Pierre unearthed a child's grave on a nocturnal trip to the cemetery.) The poison is rubbed into the victim's skin. Within hours he begins to feel nauseated and has difficulty breathing. A pins-and-needles sensation afflicts his arms and legs, then progresses to the whole body. The subject becomes paralyzed; his lips turn blue for lack of oxygen. Quickly—sometimes within six hours—

his metabolism is lowered to a level almost indistinguishable from death.

As Davis discovered, making the poison is an inexact science. Ingredients varied in the five samples he eventually acquired, although the active agents were always the same. And the poison came with no guarantee. Davis speculates that sometimes instead of merely paralyzing the victim, the compound kills him. Sometimes the victim suffocates in the coffin before he can be resurrected. But clearly the potion works well enough often enough to make zombies more than a figment of Haitian imagination.

Analysis of the powder produced another surprise. "When I went down to Haiti originally," says Davis, "my hypothesis was that the formula would contain *concombre zombi*, the 'zombie's cucumber,' which is a *Datura* plant. I thought somehow *Datura* was used in putting people down." *Datura* is a powerful psychoactive plant, found in West Africa as well as other tropical areas and used there in ritual as well as criminal activities. Davis had found *Datura* growing in Haiti. Its popular name suggested the plant was used in creating zombies.

But, says Davis, "there were a lot of problems with the *Datura* hypothesis. Partly it was a question of how the drug was administered. *Datura* would create a stupor in huge doses, but it just wouldn't produce the kind of immobility that was key. These people had to appear dead, and there aren't many drugs that will do that."

One of the ingredients Pierre included in the second formula was a dried fish, a species of puffer or blowfish, common to most parts of the world. It gets its name from its ability to fill itself with water and swell to several times its normal size when threatened by predators. Many of these fish contain a powerful poison known as tetrodotoxin. One of the most powerful nonprotein poisons known to man, tetrodotoxin turned up in every sample of zombie powder that Davis acquired.

Numerous well-documented accounts of puffer fish poisoning exist, but the most famous accounts come from the Orient, where *fugu* fish, a species of puffer, is considered a delicacy. In Japan, special chefs are licensed to prepare *fugu*. The chef removes enough poison to make the fish nonlethal, yet enough re-

mains to create exhilarating physiological effects—tingles up and down the spine, mild prickling of the tongue and lips, euphoria. Several dozen Japanese die each year, having bitten off more than they should have.

"When I got hold of the formula and saw it was the *fugu* fish, that suddenly threw open the whole Japanese literature," says Davis. Case histories of *fugu* poisoning read like accounts of zombification. Victims remain conscious but unable to speak or move. A man who had "died" after eating *fugu* recovered seven days later in the morgue. Several summers ago, another Japanese poisoned by *fugu* revived after he was nailed into his coffin. "Almost all of Narcisse's symptoms correlated. Even strange things such as the fact that he said he was conscious and could hear himself pronounced dead. Stuff that I thought had to be magic, that seemed crazy. But, in fact, that is what people who get *fugu*-fish poisoning experience."

Davis was certain he had solved the mystery. But far from being the end of his investigation, identifying the poison was, in fact, its starting point. "The drug alone didn't make zombies," he ex-

Richard Schultes

His students continue his tradition of pursuing botanical research in the likeliest of unlikely places.

Richard Evans Schultes, Jeffrey professor of biology emeritus, has two homes, and they could not be more different. The first is Cambridge, where he served as director of the Harvard Botanical Museum from 1970 until last year, when he became director emeritus. During his tenure he interested generations of students in the exotic botany of the Amazon rain forest. His impact on the field through his own research is worldwide. The scholarly ethnobotanist with steel-rimmed glasses, bald head, and white lab coat is as much a part of the Botanical Museum as the thousands of plant specimens and botanical texts on the museum shelves.

In his austere office is a picture of a crew-cut, younger man stripped to the waist, his arms decorated with tribal paint. This is Schultes's other persona. Starting in 1941, he spent thirteen years in the rain

forests of South America, living with the Indians and studying the plants they use for medicinal and spiritual purposes.

Schultes is concerned that many of the people he has studied are giving up traditional ways. "The people of so-called primitive societies are becoming civilized and losing all their forefathers' knowledge of plant lore," he says. "We'll be losing the tremendous amounts of knowledge they've gained over thousands of years. We're interested in the practical aspects with the hope that new medicines and other things can be developed for our own civilization."

Schultes's exploits are legendary in the biology department. Once, while gathering South American plant specimens hundreds of miles from civilization, he contracted beri-beri. For forty days he fought creeping paralysis and overwhelming fatigue as he paddled back to a doctor. "It was an extraordinary feat of endurance," says disciple Wade Davis. "He is really one of the last nineteenth-century naturalists."

Hallucinogenic plants are one of Schultes's primary interests. As a Harvard undergraduate in the Thirties, he lived with Oklahoma's Kiowa Indians to observe their use of plants. He participated in their peyote ceremonies and wrote his thesis on the hallucinogenic cactus. He has also studied other hallucinogens, such as morning glory seeds, sacred mushrooms, and ayahuasca, a South American vision vine. Schultes's work has led to the development of anesthetics made from curare and alternative sources of natural rubber.

Schultes's main concern these days is the scientific potential of plants in the rapidly disappearing Amazon jungle. "If chemists are going to get material on 80,000 species and then analyze them, they'll never finish the job before the jungle is gone," he says. "The short cut is to find out what the [native] people have learned about the plant properties during many years of living in the very rich flora."

—G.D.G

plains. "Japanese victims of puffer-fish poisoning don't become zombies, they become poison victims. All the drug could do was set someone up for a whole series of psychological pressures that would be rooted in the culture. I wanted to know why zombification was going on," he says.

He sought a cultural answer, an explanation rooted in the structure and beliefs of Haitian society. Was zombification simply a random criminal activity? He thought not. He had discovered that Clairvius Narcisse and "Ti Femme," a second victim he interviewed, were village pariahs. Ti Femme was regarded as a thief. Narcisse had abandoned his children and deprived his brother of land that was rightfully his. Equally suggestive, Narcisse claimed that his aggrieved brother had sold him to a *bokor*, a voodoo priest who dealt in black magic; he made cryptic reference to having been tried and found guilty by the "masters of the land."

Gathering poisons from various parts of the country, Davis had come into direct contact with the vodoun secret societies. Returning to the anthropological literature on Haiti and pursuing his contacts with informants, Davis came to understand the social matrix within which zombies were created.

Davis's investigations uncovered the importance of the secret societies. These groups trace their origins to the bands of escaped slaves that organized the revolt against the French in the late eighteenth century. Open to both men and women, the societies control specific territories of the country. Their meetings take place at night, and in many rural parts of Haiti the drums and wild celebrations that characterize the gatherings can be heard for miles.

Davis believes the secret societies are responsible for policing their communities, and the threat of zombification is one way they maintain order. Says Davis, "Zombification has a material ba-

sis, but it also has a societal logic." To the uninitiated, the practice may appear a random criminal activity, but in rural vodoun society, it is exactly the opposite—a sanction imposed by recognized authorities, a form of capital punishment. For rural Haitians, zombification is an even more severe punishment than death, because it deprives the subject of his most valued possessions: his free will and independence.

The vodounists believe that when a person dies, his spirit splits into several different parts. If a priest is powerful enough, the spiritual aspect that controls a person's character and individuality, known as *ti bon ange*, the "good little angel," can be captured and the corporeal aspect, deprived of its will, held as a slave.

From studying the medical literature on tetrodotoxin poisoning, Davis discovered that if a victim survives the first few hours of the poisoning, he is likely to recover fully from the ordeal. The subject simply revives spontaneously. But zombies remain without will, in a trance-like state, a condition vodounists attribute to the power of the priest. Davis thinks it possible that the psychological trauma of zombification may be augmented by *Datura* or some other drug; he thinks zombies may be fed a *Datura* paste that accentuates their disorientation. Still, he puts the material basis of zombification in perspective: "Tetrodotoxin and *Datura* are only templates on which cultural forces and beliefs may be amplified a thousand times."

Davis has not been able to discover how prevalent zombification is in Haiti. "How many zombies there are is not the question," he says. He compares it to capital punishment in the United States: "It doesn't really matter how many people are electrocuted, as long as it's a possibility." As a sanction in Haiti, the fear is not of zombies, it's of becoming one.

Davis attributes his success in solving the zombie mystery to his approach. He

went to Haiti with an open mind and immersed himself in the culture. "My intuition unhindered by biases served me well," he says. "I didn't make any judgments." He combined this attitude with what he had learned earlier from his experiences in the Amazon. "Schultes's lesson is to go and live with the Indians as an Indian." Davis was able to participate in the vodoun society to a surprising degree, eventually even penetrating one of the Bizango societies and dancing in their nocturnal rituals. His appreciation of Haitian culture is apparent. "Everybody asks me how did a white person get this information? To ask the question means you don't understand Haitians— they don't judge you by the color of your skin."

As a result of the exotic nature of his discoveries, Davis has gained a certain notoriety. He plans to complete his dissertation soon, but he has already finished writing a popular account of his adventures. To be published in January by Simon and Schuster, it is called *The Serpent and the Rainbow*, after the serpent that vodounists believe created the earth and the rainbow spirit it married. Film rights have already been optioned; in October Davis went back to Haiti with a screenwriter. But Davis takes the notoriety in stride. "All this attention is funny," he says. "For years, not just me, but all Schultes's students have had extraordinary adventures in the line of work. The adventure is not the end point, it's just along the way of getting the data. At the Botanical Museum, Schultes created a world unto itself. We didn't think we were doing anything above the ordinary. I still don't think we do. And you know," he adds, "the Haiti episode does not begin to compare to what others have accomplished—particularly Schultes himself."

Gino Del Guercio is a national science writer for United Press International.

From *Harvard Magazine*, January/February 1986, pp. 31–37. © 1986 by Harvard Magazine, Inc. Reprinted by permission.

Body Ritual Among the Nacirema

Horace Miner
University of Michigan

The anthropologist has become so familiar with the diversity of ways in which different peoples behave in similar situations that he is not apt to be surprised by even the most exotic customs. In fact, if all of the logically possible combinations of behavior have not been found somewhere in the world, he is apt to suspect that they must be present in some yet undescribed tribe. This point has, in fact, been expressed with respect to clan organization by Murdock (1949: 71). In this light, the magical beliefs and practices of the Nacirema present such unusual aspects that it seems desirable to describe them as an example of the extremes to which human behavior can go.

Professor Linton first brought the ritual of the Nacirema to the attention of anthropologists twenty years ago (1936: 326), but the culture of this people is still very poorly understood. They are a North American group living in the territory between the Canadian Cree, the Yaqui and Tarahumare of Mexico, and the Carib and Arawak of the Antilles. Little is known of their origin, though tradition states that they came from the east. According to Nacirema mythology, their nation was originated by a culture hero, Notgnishaw, who is otherwise known for two great feats of strength—the throwing of a piece of wampum across the river Pa-To-Mac and the chopping down of a cherry tree in which the Spirit of Truth resided.

Nacirema culture is characterized by a highly developed market economy which has evolved in a rich natural habitat. While much of the people's time is devoted to economic pursuits, a large part of the fruits of these labors and a considerable portion of the day are spent in ritual activity. The focus of this activity is the human body, the appearance and health of which loom as a dominant concern in the ethos of the people. While such a concern is certainly not unusual, its ceremonial aspects and associated philosophy are unique.

The fundamental belief underlying the whole system appears to be that the human body is ugly and that its natural tendency is to debility and disease. Incarcerated in such a body, man's only hope is to avert these characteristics through the use of the powerful influences of ritual and ceremony. Every household has one or more shrines devoted to this purpose. The more powerful individuals in the society have several shrines in their houses and, in fact, the opulence of a house is often referred to in terms of the number of such ritual centers it possesses. Most houses are of wattle and daub construction, but the shrine rooms of the more wealthy are walled with stone. Poorer families imitate the rich by applying pottery plaques to their shrine walls.

While each family has at least one such shrine, the rituals associated with it are not family ceremonies but are private and secret. The rites are normally only discussed with children, and then only during the period when they are being initiated into these mysteries. I was able, however, to establish sufficient rapport with the natives to examine these shrines and to have the rituals described to me.

The focal point of the shrine is a box or chest which is built into the wall. In this chest are kept the many charms and magical potions without which no native believes he could live. These preparations are secured from a variety of specialized practitioners. The most powerful of these are the medicine men, whose assistance must be rewarded with substantial gifts. However, the medicine men do not provide the curative potions for their clients, but decide what the ingredients should be and then write them down in an ancient and secret language. This writing is understood only by the medicine men and by the herbalists who, for another gift, provide the required charm.

The charm is not disposed of after it has served its purpose, but is placed in the charm-box of the household shrine. As these magical materials are specific for certain ills, and the real or imagined maladies of the people are many, the charm-box is usually full to overflowing. The magical packets are so numerous that people forget what their purposes were and fear to use them again. While the natives are very vague on this point, we can only assume that the idea in retaining all the old magical materials is that their presence in the charm-box, before which the body rituals are conducted, will in some way protect the worshipper.

Beneath the charm-box is a small font. Each day every member of the family, in succession, enters the shrine room, bows his head before the charm-box, mingles different sorts of holy water in the font, and proceeds with a brief rite of ablution.

The holy waters are secured from the Water Temple of the community, where the priests conduct elaborate ceremonies to make the liquid ritually pure.

In the hierarchy of magical practitioners, and below the medicine men in prestige, are specialists whose designation is best translated "holy-mouth-men." The Nacirema have an almost pathological horror and fascination with the mouth, the condition of which is believed to have a supernatural influence on all social relationships. Were it not for the rituals of the mouth, they believe that their teeth would fall out, their gums bleed, their jaws shrink, their friends desert them, and their lovers reject them. (They also believe that a strong relationship exists between oral and moral characteristics. For example, there is a ritual ablution of the mouth for children which is supposed to improve their moral fiber.)

The daily body ritual performed by everyone includes a mouth-rite. Despite the fact that these people are so punctilious about care of the mouth, this rite involves a practice which strikes the uninitiated stranger as revolting. It was reported to me that the ritual consists of inserting a small bundle of hog hairs into the mouth, along with certain magical powders, and then moving the bundle in a highly formalized series of gestures.

In addition to the private mouth-rite, the people seek out a holy-mouth-man once or twice a year. These practitioners have an impressive set of paraphernalia, consisting of a variety of augers, awls, probes, and prods. The use of these objects in the exorcism of the evils of the mouth involves almost unbelievable ritual torture of the client. The holy-mouth-man opens the client's mouth and, using the above mentioned tools, enlarges any holes which decay may have created in the teeth. Magical materials are put into these holes. If there are no naturally occurring holes in the teeth, large sections of one or more teeth are gouged out so that the supernatural substance can be applied. In the client's view, the purpose of these ministrations is to arrest decay and to draw friends. The extremely sacred and traditional character of the rite is evident in the fact that the natives return to the holy-mouth-men year after year, despite the fact that their teeth continue to decay.

It is to be hoped that, when a thorough study of the Nacirema is made, there will be a careful inquiry into the personality structure of these people. One has but to watch the gleam in the eye of a holy-mouth-man, as he jabs an awl into an exposed nerve, to suspect that a certain amount of sadism is involved. If this can be established, a very interesting pattern emerges, for most of the population shows definite masochistic tendencies. It was to these that Professor Linton referred in discussing a distinctive part of the daily body ritual which is performed only by men. This part of the rite involves scraping and lacerating the surface of the face with a sharp instrument. Special women's rites are performed only four times during each lunar month, but what they lack in frequency is made up in barbarity. As part of this ceremony, women bake their heads in small ovens for about an hour. The theoretically interesting point is that what seems to be a preponderantly masochistic people have developed sadistic specialists.

The medicine men have an imposing temple, or *latipso*, in every community of any size. The more elaborate ceremonies required to treat very sick patients can only be performed at this temple. These ceremonies involve not only the thaumaturge but a permanent group of vestal maidens who move sedately about the temple chambers in distinctive costume and headdress.

The *latipso* ceremonies are so harsh that it is phenomenal that a fair proportion of the really sick natives who enter the temple ever recover. Small children whose indoctrination is still incomplete have been known to resist attempts to take them to the temple because "that is where you go to die." Despite this fact, sick adults are not only willing but eager to undergo the protracted ritual purification, if they can afford to do so. No matter how ill the supplicant or how grave the emergency, the guardians of many temples will not admit a client if he cannot give a rich gift to the custodian. Even after one has gained admission and survived the ceremonies, the guardians will not permit the neophyte to leave until he makes still another gift.

The supplicant entering the temple is first stripped of all his or her clothes. In every-day life the Nacirema avoids exposure of his body and its natural functions. Bathing and excretory acts are performed only in the secrecy of the household shrine, where they are ritualized as part of the body-rites. Psychological shock results from the fact that body secrecy is suddenly lost upon entry into the *latipso*. A man, whose own wife has never seen him in an excretory act, suddenly finds himself naked and assisted by a vestal maiden while he performs his natural functions into a sacred vessel. This sort of ceremonial treatment is necessitated by the fact that the excreta are used by a diviner to ascertain the course and nature of the client's sickness. Female clients, on the other hand, find their naked bodies are subjected to the scrutiny, manipulation, and prodding of the medicine men.

Few supplicants in the temple are well enough to do anything but lie on their hard beds. The daily ceremonies, like the rites of the holy-mouth-men, involve discomfort and torture. With ritual precision, the vestals awaken their miserable charges each dawn and roll them about on their beds of pain while performing ablutions, in the formal movements of which the maidens are highly trained. At other times they insert magic wands in the supplicant's mouth or force him to eat substances which are supposed to be healing. From time to time the medicine men come to their clients and jab magically treated needles into their flesh. The fact that these temple ceremonies may not cure, and may even kill the neophyte, in no way decreases the people's faith in the medicine men.

There remains one other kind of practitioner, known as a "listener." This witch-doctor has the power to exorcise the devils that lodge in the heads of people who have been bewitched. The Nacirema believe that parents bewitch their own children. Mothers are particularly suspected of putting a curse on children while teaching them the secret body rituals. The counter-magic of the witch-doctor is unusual in its lack of ritual. The patient simply tells the "listener" all his troubles and fears, beginning with the earliest difficulties he can remember. The memory displayed by the Nacirema in these exorcism sessions is truly remarkable. It is not uncommon for the patient to bemoan the rejection he felt upon being weaned as a babe, and a few individuals even see their troubles going back to the traumatic effects of their own birth.

In conclusion, mention must be made of certain practices which have their base in native esthetics but which depend upon the pervasive aversion to the natural body and its functions. There are ritual fasts to make fat people thin and ceremonial feasts to make thin people fat. Still other rites are used to make women's breasts large if they are small, and smaller if they are large. General dissatisfaction with breast shape is symbolized in the fact that the ideal form is virtually outside the range of human variation. A few women afflicted with almost inhuman hyper-mammary development are so idolized that they make a handsome living by simply going from village to village and permitting the natives to stare at them for a fee.

Reference has already been made to the fact that excretory functions are ritualized, routinized, and relegated to secrecy. Natural reproductive functions are similarly distorted. Intercourse is taboo as a topic and scheduled as an act. Efforts are made to avoid pregnancy by the use of magical materials or by limiting intercourse to certain phases of the moon. Conception is actually very infrequent. When pregnant, women dress so as to hide their condition. Parturition takes place in secret, without friends or relatives to assist, and the majority of women do not nurse their infants.

Our review of the ritual life of the Nacirema has certainly shown them to be a magic-ridden people. It is hard to understand how they have managed to exist so long under the burdens which they have imposed upon themselves. But even such exotic customs as these take on real meaning when they are viewed with the insight provided by Malinowski when he wrote (1948:70):

> Looking from far and above, from our high places of safety in the developed civilization, it is easy to see all the crudity and irrelevance of magic. But without its power and guidance early man could not have mastered his practical difficulties as he has done, nor could man have advanced to the higher stages of civilization.

REFERENCES

Linton, Ralph. 1936. *The Study of Man*. New York, D. Appleton-Century Co.

Malinowski, Bronislaw. 1948. *Magic, Science, and Religion*. Glencoe, The Free Press.

Murdock, George P. 1949. *Social Structure*. New York, The Macmillan Co.

Baseball Magic

George Gmelch

On each pitching day for the first three months of a winning season, Dennis Grossini, a pitcher on a Detroit Tiger farm team, arose from bed at exactly 10:00 a.m. At 1:00 p.m. he went to the nearest restaurant for two glasses of iced tea and a tuna sandwich. Although the afternoon was free, he changed into the sweatshirt and supporter he wore during his last winning game, and, one hour before the game, he chewed a wad of Beech-Nut chewing tobacco. After each pitch during the game he touched the letters on his uniform and straightened his cap after each ball. Before the start of each inning he replaced the pitcher's resin bag next to the spot where it was the inning before. And after every inning in which he gave up a run, he washed his hands.

When asked which part of the ritual was most important, he said, "You can't really tell what's most important so it all becomes important. I'd be afraid to change anything. As long as I'm winning, I do everything the same."

Trobriand Islanders, according to anthropologist Bronislaw Malinowski, felt the same way about their fishing magic. Among the Trobrianders, fishing took two forms: in the *inner lagoon* where fish were plentiful and there was little danger, and on the *open sea* where fishing was dangerous and yields varied widely. Malinowski found that magic was not used in lagoon fishing, where men could rely solely on their knowledge and skill. But when fishing on the open sea, Trobrianders used a great deal of magical ritual to ensure safety and increase their catch.

Baseball, America's national pastime, is an arena in which players behave remarkably like Malinowski's Trobriand fishermen. To professional ballplayers, baseball is more than just a game. It is an occupation. Since their livelihoods depend on how well they perform, many use magic to try to control the chance that is built into baseball. There are three essential activities of the game—pitching, hitting, and fielding. In the first two, chance can play a surprisingly important role. The pitcher is the player least able to control the outcome of his own efforts. He may feel great and have good stuff warming up in the bullpen and then get into the game and not have it. He may make a bad pitch and see the batter miss it for a strike out or see it hit hard but right into the hands of a fielder for an out. His best pitch may be blooped for a base hit. He may limit the opposing team to just a few hits yet lose the game, or he may give up a dozen hits but still win. And the good and bad luck don't always average out over the course of a season. Some pitchers end the season with poor won-loss records but good earned run averages, and vice versa. For instance, this past season Andy Benes gave up over one run per game more than his teammate Omar Daal but had a better won-loss record. Benes went 14–13, while Daal was only 8–12. Both pitched for the same team—the Arizona Diamondbacks—which meant they had the same fielders behind them. Regardless of how well a pitcher performs, on every outing he depends not only on his own skill, but also upon the proficiency of his teammates, the ineptitude of the opposition, and luck.

Hitting, which many observers call the single most difficult task in the world of sports, is also full of risk and uncertainty. Unless it's a home run, no matter how well the batter hits the ball, fate determines whether it will go into a waiting glove, whistle past a fielder's diving stab, or find a gap in the outfield. The uncertainty is compounded by the low success rate of hitting: the average hitter gets only one hit in every four trips to the plate, while the very best hitters average only one hit every three trips. Fielding, as we will return to later, is the one part of baseball where chance does not play much of a role.

How does the risk and uncertainty in pitching and hitting affect players? How do they try to exercise control over the outcomes of their performance? These are questions that I first became interested in many years ago as both a ballplayer and an anthropology student. I'd devoted much of my youth to baseball, and played professionally as first baseman in the Detroit Tigers organization in the 1960s. It was shortly after the end of one baseball season that I took an anthropology course called "Magic, Religion, and Witchcraft." As I listened to my professor describe the magical rituals of the Trobriand Islanders, it occurred to me that what these so-called "primitive" people did wasn't all that different from what my teammates and I did for luck and confidence at the ball park.

ROUTINES AND RITUALS

The most common way players attempt to reduce chance and their feelings of uncertainty is to develop and follow a daily routine, a course of action which is regularly followed. Talking about the routines ballplayers follow, Pirates coach Rich Donnelly said:

> They're like trained animals. They come out here [ballpark] and ev-

erything has to be the same, they don't like anything that knocks them off their routine. Just look at the dugout and you'll see every guy sitting in the same spot every night. It's amazing, everybody in the same spot. And don't you dare take someone's seat. If a guy comes up from the minors and sits here, they'll say, 'Hey, Jim sits here, find another seat.' You watch the pitcher warm up and he'll do the same thing every time. And when you go on the road it's the same way. You've got a routine and you adhere to it and you don't want anybody knocking you off it.

Routines are comforting, they bring order into a world in which players have little control. And sometimes practical elements in routines produce tangible benefits, such as helping the player concentrate. But what players often do goes beyond mere routine. Their actions become what anthropologists define as *ritual*—prescribed behaviors in which there is no empirical connection between the means (e.g., tapping home plate three times) and the desired end (e.g., getting a base hit). Because there is no real connection between the two, rituals are not rational, and sometimes they are actually irrational. Similar to rituals are the non-rational beliefs that form the basis of taboos and fetishes, which players also use to reduce chance and bring luck to their side. But first let's look more closely at rituals.

Most rituals are personal, that is, they're performed by individuals rather than by a team or group. Most are done in an unemotional manner, in much the same way players apply pine tar to their bats to improve the grip or dab eye black on their upper cheeks to reduce the sun's glare. Baseball rituals are infinitely varied. A ballplayer may ritualize any activity—eating, dressing, driving to the ballpark—that he considers important or somehow linked to good performance. For example, Yankee pitcher Denny Neagle goes to a movie on days he is scheduled to start. Pitcher Jason Bere listens to the same song on his Walkman on the days he is to pitch. Jim Ohms puts another penny in the pouch of his supporter after

each win. Clanging against the hard plastic genital cup, the pennies made a noise as he ran the bases toward the end of a winning season. Glenn Davis would chew the same gum every day during hitting streaks, saving it under his cap. Infielder Julio Gotay always played with a cheese sandwich in his back pocket (he had a big appetite, so there might also have been a measure of practicality here). Wade Boggs ate chicken before every game during his career, and that was just one of dozens of elements in his pre and post game routine, which also included leaving his house for the ballpark at precisely the same time each day (1:47 for a 7:05 game). Former Oriole pitcher Dennis Martinez would drink a small cup of water after each inning and then place it under the bench upside down, in a line. His teammates could always tell what inning it was by counting the cups.

Many hitters go through a series of preparatory rituals before stepping into the batter's box. These include tugging on their caps, touching their uniform letters or medallions, crossing themselves, tapping or bouncing the bat on the plate, or swinging the weighted warm-up bat a prescribed number of times. Consider Red Sox Nomar Garciaparra. After each pitch he steps out of the batters box, kicks the dirt with each toe, adjusts his right batting glove, adjusts his left batting glove, and touches his helmet before getting back into the box. Mike Hargrove, former Cleveland Indian first baseman, had so many time consuming elements in his batting ritual that he was known as "the human rain delay." Both players believe their batting rituals helped them regain their concentration after each pitch. But others wonder if they have become prisoners of their own superstitions. Also, players who have too many or particularly bizarre rituals risk being labeled as "flakes," and not just by teammates but by fans and media as well. For example, pitcher Turk Wendell's eccentric rituals, which included wearing a necklace of teeth from animals he had killed, made him a cover story in the *New York Times Sunday Magazine*.

Some players, especially Latin Americans, draw upon rituals from their Roman Catholic religion. Some make the sign of the cross or bless themselves be-

fore every at bat, and a few like the Rangers' Pudge Rodriguez do so before every pitch. Others, like the Detroit Tiger Juan Gonzalez, also visibly wear religious medallions around their necks, while some tuck them discretely inside their undershirts.

One ritual associated with hitting is tagging a base when leaving and returning to the dugout between innings. Some players don't "feel right" unless they tag a specific base on each trip between the dugout and the field. One of my teammates added some complexity to his ritual by tagging third base on his way to the dugout only after the third, sixth, and ninth innings. Asked if he ever purposely failed to step on the bag, he replied, "Never! I wouldn't dare. It would destroy my confidence to hit." Baseball fans observe a lot of this ritual behavior, such as fielders tagging bases, pitchers tugging on their caps or touching the resin bag after each bad pitch, or smoothing the dirt on the mound before each new batter or inning, never realizing the importance of these actions to the player. The one ritual many fans do recognize, largely because it's a favorite of TV cameramen, is the "rally cap"—players in the dugout folding their caps and wearing them bill up in hopes of sparking a rally.

Most rituals grow out of exceptionally good performances. When a player does well, he seldom attributes his success to skill alone. He knows that his skills were essentially the same the night before. He asks himself, "What was different about today which explains my three hits?" He decides to repeat what he did today in an attempt to bring more good luck. And so he attributes his success, in part, to an object, a food he ate, not having shaved, a new shirt he bought that day, or just about any behavior out of the ordinary. By repeating that behavior, he seeks to gain control over his performance. Outfielder John White explained how one of his rituals started:

I was jogging out to centerfield after the national anthem when I picked up a scrap of paper. I got some good hits that night and I guess I decided that the paper had something to do with it. The next night I picked up a gum wrapper and had another good night at the plate… I've been picking up paper every night since.

Outfielder Ron Wright of the Calgary Cannons shaves his arms once a week and plans to continue doing so until he has a bad year. It all began two years before when after an injury he shaved his arm so it could be taped, and proceeded to hit three homers over the next few games. Now he not only has one of the smoothest swings in the minor leagues, but two of the smoothest forearms. Wade Boggs' routine of eating chicken before every game began when he was a rookie in 1982. He noticed a correlation between multiple hit games and poultry plates (his wife has over 40 chicken recipes). One of Montreal Expos farmhand Mike Saccocio's rituals also concerned food, "I got three hits one night after eating at Long John Silver's. After that when we'd pull into town, my first question would be, "Do you have a Long John Silver's?" Unlike Boggs, Saccocio abandoned his ritual and looked for a new one when he stopped hitting well.

When in a slump, most players make a deliberate effort to change their rituals and routines in an attempt to shake off their bad luck. One player tried taking different routes to the ballpark; several players reported trying different combinations of tagging and not tagging particular bases in an attempt to find a successful combination. I had one manager who would rattle the bat bin when the team was not hitting well, as if the bats were in a stupor and could be aroused by a good shaking. Similarly, I have seen hitters rub their hands along the handles of the bats protruding from the bin in hopes of picking up some power or luck from bats that are getting hits for their owners. Some players switch from wearing their contact lenses to glasses. Brett Mandel described his Pioneer League team, the Ogden Raptors, trying to break a losing streak by using a new formation for their pre-game stretching.[1]

TABOO

Taboos are the opposite of rituals. The word taboo comes from a Polynesian term meaning prohibition. Breaking a taboo, players believe, leads to undesirable consequences or bad luck. Most players observe at least a few taboos, such as never stepping on the white foul lines. A few, like the Mets Turk Wendell and Red Sox Nomar Garciaparra, leap over the entire basepath. One teammate of mine would never watch a movie on a game day, despite the fact that we played nearly every day from April to September. Another teammate refused to read anything before a game because he believed it weakened his batting eye.

Many taboos take place off the field, out of public view. On the day a pitcher is scheduled to start, he is likely to avoid activities he believes will sap his strength and detract from his effectiveness. Some pitchers avoid eating certain foods, others will not shave on the day of a game, refusing to shave again as long as they are winning. Early in the 1989 season Oakland's Dave Stewart had six consecutive victories and a beard by the time he lost.

Taboos usually grow out of exceptionally poor performances, which players, in search of a reason, attribute to a particular behavior. During my first season of pro ball I ate pancakes before a game in which I struck out three times. A few weeks later I had another terrible game, again after eating pancakes. The result was a pancake taboo: I never again ate pancakes during the season. Pitcher Jason Bere has a taboo that makes more sense in dietary terms: after eating a meatball sandwich and not pitching well, he swore off them for the rest of the season.

While most taboos are idiosyncratic, there are a few that all ball players hold and that do not develop out of individual experience or misfortune. These form part of the culture of baseball, and are sometimes learned as early as Little League. Mentioning a no-hitter while one is in progress is a well-known example. It is believed that if a pitcher hears the words "no-hitter," the spell accounting for this hard to achieve feat will be broken and the no-hitter lost. This taboo is also observed by many sports broadcasters, who use various linguistic subterfuges to inform their listeners that the pitcher has not given up a hit, never saying "no-hitter."

FETISHES

Fetishes or charms are material objects believed to embody "supernatural" power that can aid or protect the owner. Good luck charms are standard equipment for some ballplayers. These include a wide assortment of objects from coins, chains, and crucifixes to a favorite baseball hat. The fetishized object may be a new possession or something a player found that happens to coincide with the start of a streak and which he holds responsible for his good fortune. While playing in the Pacific Coast League, Alan Foster forgot his baseball shoes on a road trip and borrowed a pair from a teammate. That night he pitched a no-hitter, which he attributed to the shoes. Afterwards he bought them from his teammate and they became a fetish. Expo farmhand Mark LaRosa's rock has a different origin and use:

> I found it on the field in Elmira after I had gotten bombed. It's unusual, perfectly round, and it caught my attention. I keep it to remind me of how important it is to concentrate. When I am going well I look at the rock and remember to keep my focus, the rock reminds me of what can happen when I lose my concentration.

For one season Marge Schott, former owner of the Cincinnati Reds, insisted that her field manager rub her St. Bernard "Schotzie" for good luck before each game. When the Reds were on the road, Schott would sometimes send a bag of the dog's hair to the field manager's hotel room.

During World War II, American soldiers used fetishes in much the same way. Social psychologist Samuel Stouffer and his colleagues found that in the face of great danger and uncertainty, soldiers developed magical practices, particularly the use of protective amulets and good luck charms (crosses, Bibles, rabbits' feet, medals), and jealously guarded articles of clothing they associated with past experiences of escape from danger.[2] Stouffer also found that prebattle preparations were carried out in fixed ritual-like order, similar to ballplayers preparing for a game.

Uniform numbers have special significance for some players who request their lucky number. Since the choice is usually limited, they try to at least get a uniform that contains their lucky number, such as 14, 24, 34, or 44 for the player whose lucky number is four. When Ricky Henderson came to the Blue Jays in 1993 he paid outfielder Turner Ward $25,000 for the right to wear number 24. Oddly enough, there is no consensus about the effect of wearing number 13. Some players will not wear it, others will, and a few request it. Number preferences emerge in different ways. A young player may request the number of a former star, hoping that—through what anthropologists call *imitative* magic—it will bring him the same success. Or he may request a number he associates with good luck. While with the Oakland A's Vida Blue changed his uniform number from 35 to 14, the number he wore as a high-school quarterback. When 14 did not produce better pitching performance, he switched back to 35. Former San Diego Padre first baseman Jack Clark changed his number from 25 to 00, hoping to break out of a slump. That day he got four hits in a double header, but also hurt his back. Then, three days later, he was hit in the cheekbone by a ball thrown in batting practice.

Colorado Rockies Larry Walker's fixation with the number three has become well known to baseball fans. Besides wearing 33, he takes three practice swings before stepping into the box, he showers from the third nozzle, sets his alarm for three minutes past the hour and he was wed on November 3 at 3:33 p.m. Fans in ballparks all across America rise from their seats for the seventh inning stretch before the home club comes to bat because the number seven is lucky, although the origin of this tradition has been lost.

Clothing, both the choice and the order in which they are put on, combine elements of both ritual and fetish. Some players put on their uniform in a ritualized order. Expos farmhand Jim Austin always puts on his left sleeve, left pants leg, and left shoe before the right. Most players, however, single out one or two lucky articles or quirks of dress for ritual elaboration. After hitting two home runs in a

game, for example, ex-Giant infielder Jim Davenport discovered that he had missed a buttonhole while dressing for the game. For the remainder of his career he left the same button undone. For outfielder Brian Hunter the focus is shoes, "I have a pair of high tops and a pair of low tops. Whichever shoes don't get a hit that game, I switch to the other pair." At the time of our interview, he was struggling at the plate and switching shoes almost every day. For Birmingham Baron pitcher Bo Kennedy the arrangement of the different pairs of baseball shoes in his locker is critical:

> I tell the clubies [clubhouse boys] when you hang stuff in my locker don't touch my shoes. If you bump them move them back. I want the Pony's in front, the turfs to the right, and I want them nice and neat with each pair touching each other…. Everyone on the team knows not to mess with my shoes when I pitch.

During streaks—hitting or winning—players may wear the same clothes day after day. Once I changed sweatshirts midway through the game for seven consecutive nights to keep a hitting streak going. Clothing rituals, however, can become impractical. Catcher Matt Allen was wearing a long sleeve turtle neck shirt on a cool evening in the New York-Penn League when he had a three-hit game. "I kept wearing the shirt and had a good week," he explained. "Then the weather got hot as hell, 85 degrees and muggy, but I would not take that shirt off. I wore it for another ten days—catching—and people thought I was crazy." Also taking a ritual to the extreme, Leo Durocher, managing the Brooklyn Dodgers to a pennant in 1941, is said to have spent three and a half weeks in the same gray slacks, blue coat, and knitted blue tie. During a 16-game winning streak, the 1954 New York Giants wore the same clothes in each game and refused to let them be cleaned for fear that their good fortune might be washed away with the dirt. Losing often produces the opposite effect. Several Oakland A's players, for example, went out and bought new street clothes in an attempt to break a fourteen-game losing streak.

Baseball's superstitions, like most everything else, change over time. Many of the rituals and beliefs of early baseball are no longer observed. In the 1920s and 1930s sportswriters reported that a player who tripped en route to the field would often retrace his steps and carefully walk over the stumbling block for "insurance." A century ago players spent time on and off the field intently looking for items that would bring them luck. To find a hairpin on the street, for example, assured a batter of hitting safely in that day's game. Today few women wear hairpins—a good reason the belief has died out. To catch sight of a white horse or a wagon-load of barrels were also good omens. In 1904 the manager of the New York Giants, John McGraw, hired a driver with a team of white horses to drive past the Polo Grounds around the time his players were arriving at the ballpark. He knew that if his players saw white horses, they'd have more confidence and that could only help them during the game. Belief in the power of white horses survived in a few backwaters until the 1960s. A gray haired manager of a team I played for in Drummondville, Quebec, would drive around the countryside before important games and during the playoffs looking for a white horse. When he was successful, he would announce it to everyone in the clubhouse.

One belief that appears to have died out recently is a taboo about crossed bats. Some of my Latino teammates in the 1960s took it seriously. I can still recall one Dominican player becoming agitated when another player tossed a bat from the batting cage and it landed on top of his bat. He believed that the top bat might steal hits from the lower one. In his view, bats contained a finite number of hits, a sort of baseball "image of limited good." It was once commonly believed that when the hits in a bat were used up no amount of good hitting would produce any more. Hall of Famer Honus Wagner believed each bat contained only 100 hits. Regardless of the quality of the bat, he would discard it after its 100th hit. This belief would have little relevance today, in the era of light bats with thin handles—so thin that the typical modern bat is lucky to survive a dozen hits without being broken. Other superstitions about bats do survive, however. Position players on the Class A Asheville Tourists, for example, would not let pitchers touch or swing their bats, not even to warm up. Poor-hitting players, as most pitchers are, were said to pollute or weaken the bats.

UNCERTAINTY AND MAGIC

The best evidence that players turn to rituals, taboos, and fetishes to control chance and uncertainty is found in their uneven application. They are associated mainly with pitching and hitting—the activities with the highest degree of chance—and not fielding. I met only one player who had any ritual in connection with fielding, and he was an error prone shortstop. Unlike hitting and pitching, a fielder has almost complete control over the outcome of his performance. Once a ball has been hit in his direction, no one can intervene and ruin his chances of catching it for an out (except in the unlikely event of two fielders colliding). Compared with the pitcher or the hitter, the fielder has little to worry about. He knows that, in better than 9.7 times out of 10, he will execute his task flawlessly. With odds like that there is little need for ritual.

Clearly, the rituals of American ballplayers are not unlike that of the Trobriand Islanders studied by Malinowski many years ago.[3] In professional baseball, fielding is the equivalent of the inner lagoon while hitting and pitching are like the open sea.

While Malinowski helps us understand how ballplayers respond to chance and uncertainty, behavioral psychologist B. F. Skinner sheds light on why personal rituals get established in the first place.[4] With a few grains of seed Skinner could get pigeons to do anything he wanted. He merely waited for the desired behavior (e.g. pecking) and then rewarded it with some food. Skinner then decided to see what would happen if pigeons were rewarded with food pellets regularly, every fifteen seconds, regardless of what they did. He found that the birds associate the arrival of the food with a particular action, such as tucking their head under a wing or walking in clockwise circles. About ten seconds after the arrival of the last pellet, a bird would begin doing whatever it associated with getting the food and keep doing it until the next pellet arrived. In short, the pigeons behaved as if their actions made the food appear. They learned to associate particular behaviors with the reward of being given seed.

Ballplayers also associate a reward—successful performance—with prior behavior. If a player touches his crucifix and then gets a hit, he may decide the gesture was responsible for his good fortune and touch his crucifix the next time he comes to the plate. If he gets another hit, the chances are good that he will touch his crucifix each time he bats. Unlike pigeons, however, most ballplayers are quicker to change their rituals once they no longer seem to work. Skinner found that once a pigeon associated one of its actions with the arrival of food or water, only sporadic rewards were necessary to keep the ritual going. One pigeon, believing that hopping from side to side brought pellets into its feeding cup, hopped ten thousand times without a pellet before finally giving up. But, then, didn't Wade Boggs eat chicken before every game, through slumps and good times, for seventeen years?

Obviously the rituals and superstitions of baseball do not make a pitch travel faster or a batted ball find the gaps between the fielders, nor do the Trobriand rituals calm the seas or bring fish. What both do, however, is give their practitioners a sense of control, with that added confidence, at no cost. And we all know how important that is. If you really believe eating chicken or hopping over the foul lines will make you a better hitter, it probably will.

BIBLIOGRAPHY

Malinowski, B. *Magic, Science and Religion and Other Essays* (Glencoe, Ill., 1948).

Mandel, Brett. *Minor Players, Major Dreams*. Lincoln, Nebraska: University of Nebraska Press, 1997.

Skinner, B.F. *Behavior of Organisms: An Experimental Analysis* (D. Appleton-Century Co., 1938).

Skinner, B.F. *Science and Human Behavior* (New York: Macmillan, 1953).

Stouffer, Samuel. *The American Soldier*. New York: J. Wiley, 1965.

Torrez, Danielle Gagnon. *High Inside: Memoirs of a Baseball Wife*. New York: G.P. Putnam's Sons, 1983.

NOTES

1. Mandel, *Minor Players, Major Dreams*, 156.
2. Stouffer, *The American Soldier*
3. Malinowski, B. *Magic, Science and Religion and Other Essays*
4. Skinner, B.F. *Behavior of Organisms: An Experimental Analysis*

Department of Anthropology, Union College; e-mail gmelchg@union.edu

UNIT 7

Sociocultural Change: The Impact of the West

Unit Selections

Key Points to Consider

- What is a subsistence system? What have been the effects of colonialism on formerly subsistence-oriented socioeconomic systems?

- How do cash crops inevitably lead to class distinctions and poverty?

- Have ecological disasters in Africa been due to drought or Western-style political and economic institutions? Defend your answer.

- What ethical obligations do you think industrial societies have toward respecting the human rights and cultural diversity of traditional communities?

- What have been the social, economic, and health consequences of the shift from the use of betel and kava to alcohol, tobacco, and marijuana in Oceania?

- What is the "potlatch" and why is it so integral to Northwest Coast cultures?

- What should Americans know about Indians?

 **Links: www.dushkin.com/online/**
These sites are annotated in the World Wide Web pages.

Human Rights and Humanitarian Assistance
http://www.etown.edu/vl/humrts.html

The Indigenous Rights Movement in the Pacific
http://www.inmotionmagazine.com/pacific.html

RomNews Network—Online
http://www.romnews.com/community/index.php

WWW Virtual Library: Indigenous Studies
http://www.cwis.org/wwwvl/indig-vl.html

The origins of academic anthropology lie in the colonial and imperial ventures of the nineteenth and twentieth centuries. During these periods, many people of the world were brought into a relationship with Europe and the United States that was usually exploitative and often socially and culturally disruptive. For almost a century, anthropologists have witnessed this process and the transformations that have taken place in those social and cultural systems brought under the umbrella of a world economic order. Early anthropological studies—even those widely regarded as pure research—directly or indirectly served colonial interests. Many anthropologists certainly believed that they were extending the benefits of Western technology and society while preserving the cultural rights of those people whom they studied. But representatives of poor nations challenge this view and are far less generous in describing the past role of the anthropologist. Most contemporary anthropologists, however, have a deep moral commitment to defending the legal, political, and economic rights of the people with whom they work.

When anthropologists discuss social change, they usually mean change brought about in preindustrial societies through long-standing interaction with the nation-states of the industrialized world. In early anthropology, contact between the West and the remainder of the world was characterized by the terms "acculturation" and "culture contact." These terms were used to describe the diffusion of cultural traits between the developed and the less-developed countries. Often this was analyzed as a one-way process in which cultures of the less developed world were seen, for better or worse, as receptacles for Western cultural traits. Nowadays, many anthropologists believe that the diffusion of cultural traits across social, political, and economic boundaries was emphasized at the expense of the real issues of dominance, subordinance, and dependence that characterized the colonial experience. Just as important, many anthropologists recognize that the present-day forms of cultural, economic, and political interaction between the developed and the so-called underdeveloped world are best characterized as neocolonial.

Most of the authors represented in this unit take the perspective that anthropology should be critical as well as descriptive. They raise questions about cultural contact and subsequent economic and social disruption.

In keeping with the notion that the negative impact of the West on traditional cultures began with colonial domination, this unit opens with "Why Can't People Feed Themselves?" "The Arrow of Disease" and "Drought Follows the Plow." Continuing with "The Price of Progress," we see that "progress" for the West has often meant poverty, hunger, disease, and death for traditional peoples.

The essays that follow emphasize varying aspects of culture affected by the impact of the West. "A Pacific Haze: Alcohol and Drugs in Oceania" illustrates the disruptive social and economic

changes brought about by the recent introduction of psychoactive drugs. "A Plunge Into the Present" chronicles a Pacific island society's transition from a period of serenity and isolation to the same kind of division between the haves and have-nots typical of the modern world. "Underground Potlatch" details the deliberate attempts to destroy a people's ceremonial traditions. Finally, "What Americans Don't Know About Indians" shows how even the images of native peoples' ways can be distorted by the dominant institutions of education and the media.

Of course, traditional peoples are not the only losers in the process of cultural destruction. All of humanity stands to suffer as a vast store of human knowledge—embodied in tribal subsistence practices, language, medicine, and folklore—is obliterated, in a manner not unlike the burning of the library of Alexandria 1,600 years ago. We can only hope that it is not too late to save what is left.

Why Can't People Feed Themselves?

Frances Moore Lappé and Joseph Collins

Question: You have said that the hunger problem is not the result of overpopulation. But you have not yet answered the most basic and simple question of all: Why can't people feed themselves? As Senator Daniel P. Moynihan put it bluntly, when addressing himself to the Third World, "Food growing is the first thing you do when you come down out of the trees. The question is, how come the United States can grow food and you can't?"

Our Response: In the very first speech I, Frances, ever gave after writing *Diet for a Small Planet*, I tried to take my audience along the path that I had taken in attempting to understand why so many are hungry in this world. Here is the gist of that talk that was, in truth, a turning point in my life:

When I started I saw a world divided into two parts: a *minority* of nations that had "taken off" through their agricultural and industrial revolutions to reach a level of unparalleled material abundance and a *majority* that remained behind in a primitive, traditional, undeveloped state. This lagging behind of the majority of the world's peoples must be due, I thought, to some internal deficiency or even to several of them. It seemed obvious that the underdeveloped countries must be deficient in natural resources—particularly good land and climate—and in cultural develop-

ment, including modern attitudes conducive to work and progress.

But when looking for the historical roots of the predicament, I learned that my picture of these two separate worlds was quite false. My two separate worlds were really just different sides of the same coin. One side was on top largely because the other side was on the bottom. Could this be true? How were these separate worlds related?

Colonialism appeared to me to be the link. Colonialism destroyed the cultural patterns of production and exchange by which traditional societies in "underdeveloped" countries previously had met the needs of the people. Many precolonial social structures, while dominated by exploitative elites, had evolved a system of mutual obligations among the classes that helped to ensure at least a minimal diet for all. A friend of mine once said: "Precolonial village existence in subsistence agriculture was a limited life indeed, but it's certainly not Calcutta." The misery of starvation in the streets of Calcutta can only be understood as the end-point of a long historical process—one that has destroyed a traditional social system.

"Underdeveloped," instead of being an adjective that evokes the picture of a static society, became for me a verb (to "underdevelop")

meaning the *process* by which the minority of the world has transformed—indeed often robbed and degraded—the majority.

That was in 1972. I clearly recall my thoughts on my return home. I had stated publicly for the first time a world view that had taken me years of study to grasp. The sense of relief was tremendous. For me the breakthrough lay in realizing that today's "hunger crisis" could not be described in static, descriptive terms. Hunger and underdevelopment must always be thought of as a *process*.

To answer the question "why hunger?" it is counterproductive to simply *describe* the conditions in an underdeveloped country today. For these conditions, whether they be the degree of malnutrition, the levels of agricultural production, or even the country's ecological endowment, are not static factors—they are not "givens." They are rather the *results* of an ongoing historical process. As we dug ever deeper into that historical process for the preparation of this book, we began to discover the existence of scarcity-creating mechanisms that we had only vaguely intuited before.

We have gotten great satisfaction from probing into the past since we recognized it is the only way to approach a solution to hunger today. We have come to see that it is the *force* creating the condition, not the condition itself, that must be the target of change. Otherwise we might change the condition today, only to find tomorrow that it has been recreated—with a vengeance.

Asking the question "Why can't people feed themselves?" carries a sense of bewilderment that there are so many people in the world not able to feed themselves adequately. What astonished us, however, is that there are not *more* people in the world who are hungry—considering the weight of the centuries of effort by the few to undermine the capacity of the majority to feed themselves. No, we are not crying "conspiracy!" If these forces were entirely conspiratorial, they would be easier to detect and many more people would by now have risen up to resist. We are talking about something more subtle and insidious; a heritage of a colonial order in which people with the advantage of considerable power sought their own self-interest, often arrogantly believing they were acting in the interest of the people whose lives they were destroying.

THE COLONIAL MIND

The colonizer viewed agriculture in the subjugated lands as primitive and backward. Yet such a view contrasts sharply with documents from the colonial period now coming to light. For example, A. J. Voelker, a British agricultural scientist assigned to India during the 1890s wrote:

Nowhere would one find better instances of keeping land scrupulously clean from weeds, of ingenuity in device of water-raising appliances, of knowledge of soils and their capabilities, as well as of the exact time to sow and reap, as one would find in Indian agriculture. It is wonderful too, how much is known of rotation, the system of "mixed crops" and of fallowing.... I, at least, have never seen a more perfect picture of cultivation."[1]

None the less, viewing the agriculture of the vanquished as primitive and backward reinforced the colonizer's rationale for destroying it. To the colonizers of Africa, Asia, and Latin America, agriculture became merely a means to extract wealth—much as gold from a mine—on behalf of the colonizing power. Agriculture was no longer seen as a source of food for the local population, nor even as their livelihood. Indeed the English economist John Stuart Mill reasoned that colonies should not be thought of as civilizations or countries at all but as "agricultural establishments" whose sole purpose was to supply the "larger community to which they belong." The colonized society's agriculture was only a subdivision of the agricultural system of the metropolitan country. As Mill acknowledged, "Our West India colonies, for example, cannot be regarded as countries.... The West Indies are the place where England *finds it convenient* to carry on the production of sugar, coffee and a few other tropical commodities."[2]

Prior to European intervention, Africans practiced a diversified agriculture that included the introduction of new food plants of Asian or American origin. But colonial rule simplified this diversified production to single cash crops—often to the exclusion of staple foods —and in the process sowed the seeds of famine.[3] Rice farming once had been common in Gambia. But with colonial rule so much of the best land was taken over by peanuts (grown for the European market) that rice had to be imported to counter the mounting prospect of famine. Northern Ghana, once famous for its yams and other foodstuffs, was forced to concentrate solely on cocoa. Most of the Gold Coast thus became dependent on cocoa. Liberia was turned into a virtual plantation subsidiary of Firestone Tire and Rubber. Food production in Dahomey and southeast Nigeria was all but abandoned in favor of palm oil; Tanganyika (now Tanzania) was forced to focus on sisal and Uganda on cotton.

The same happened in Indochina. About the time of the American Civil War the French decided that the Mekong Delta in Vietnam would be ideal for producing rice for export. Through a production system based on enriching the large landowners, Vietnam became the world's third largest exporter of rice by the 1930s; yet many landless Vietnamese went hungry.[4]

Rather than helping the peasants, colonialism's public works programs only reinforced export crop production. British irrigation works built in nineteenth-century India did help increase production, but the expansion was for spring export crops at the expense of millets and legumes grown in the fall as the basic local food crops.

Because people living on the land do not easily go against their natural and adaptive drive to grow food for themselves, colonial powers had to force the production of cash crops. The first strategy was to use physical or economic force to get the local population to grow cash crops instead of food on their own plots and then turn them over to the colonizer for export. The second strategy was the direct takeover of the land by large-scale plantations growing crops for export.

FORCED PEASANT PRODUCTION

As Walter Rodney recounts in *How Europe Underdeveloped Africa*, cash crops were often grown literally under threat of guns and whips.[5] One visitor to the Sahel commented in 1928: "Cotton is an artificial crop and one the value of which is not entirely clear to the natives..." He wryly noted the "enforced enthusiasm with which the natives... have thrown themselves into... planting cotton."[6] The forced cultivation of cotton was a major grievance leading to the Maji Maji wars in Tanzania (then Tanganyika) and behind the nationalist revolt in Angola as late as 1960.[7]

Although raw force was used, taxation was the preferred colonial technique to force Africans to grow cash crops. The colonial administrations simply levied taxes on cattle, land, houses, and even the people themselves. Since the tax had to be paid in the coin of the realm, the peasants had either to grow crops to sell or to work on the plantations or in the mines of the Europeans.[8] Taxation was both an effective tool to "stimulate" cash cropping and a source of revenue that the colonial bureaucracy needed to enforce the system. To expand their production of export crops to pay the mounting taxes, peasant producers were forced to neglect the farming of food crops. In 1830, the Dutch administration in Java made the peasants an offer they could not refuse; if they would grow government-owned export crops on one fifth of their land, the Dutch would remit their land taxes.[9] If they refused and thus could not pay the taxes, they lost their land.

Marketing boards emerged in Africa in the 1930s as another technique for getting the profit from cash crop production by native producers into the hands of the colonial government and international firms. Purchases by the marketing boards were well below the world market price. Peanuts bought by the boards from peasant cultivators in West Africa were sold in Britain for more than *seven times* what the peasants received.[10]

The marketing board concept was born with the "cocoa hold-up" in the Gold Coast in 1937. Small cocoa farmers refused to sell to the large cocoa concerns like United Africa Company (a subsidiary of the Anglo-Dutch firm, Unilever—which we know as Lever Brothers) and Cadbury until they got a higher price. When the British government stepped in and agreed to buy the cocoa directly in place of the big business concerns, the smallholders must have thought they had scored at least a minor victory. But had they really? The following year the British formally set up the West African Cocoa Control Board. Theoretically, its purpose was to pay the peasants a reasonable price for their crops. In practice, however, the board, as sole purchaser, was able to hold down the prices paid the peasants for their crops when the world prices were rising. Rodney sums up the real "victory":

> None of the benefits went to Africans, but rather to the British government itself and to the private companies.... Big companies like the United African Company and John Holt were given… quotas to fulfill on behalf of the boards. As agents of the government, they were no longer exposed to direct attack, and their profits were secure.[11]

These marketing boards, set up for most export crops, were actually controlled by the companies. The chairman of the Cocoa Board was none other than John Cadbury of Cadbury Brothers (ever had a Cadbury chocolate bar?) who was part of a buying pool exploiting West African cocoa farmers.

The marketing boards funneled part of the profits from the exploitation of peasant producers indirectly into the royal treasury. While the Cocoa Board sold to the British Food Ministry at low prices, the ministry upped the price for British manufacturers, thus netting a profit as high as 11 million pounds in some years.[12]

These marketing boards of Africa were only the institutionalized rendition of what is the essence of colonialism—the extraction of wealth. While profits continued to accrue to foreign interests and local elites, prices received by those actually growing the commodities remained low.

PLANTATIONS

A second approach was direct takeover of the land either by the colonizing government or by private foreign interests. Previously self-provisioning farmers were forced to cultivate the plantation fields through either enslavement or economic coercion.

After the conquest of the Kandyan Kingdom (in present day Sri Lanka), in 1815, the British designated all the vast central part of the island as crown land. When it was determined that coffee, a profitable export crop, could be grown there, the Kandyan lands were sold off to British investors and planters at a mere five shillings per acre, the government even defraying the cost of surveying and road building.[13]

Java is also a prime example of a colonial government seizing territory and then putting it into private foreign hands. In 1870, the Dutch declared all uncultivated land—called waste land—property of the state for lease to Dutch plantation enterprises. In addition, the Agrarian Land Law of 1870 authorized foreign companies to lease village-owned land. The peasants, in chronic need of ready cash for taxes and foreign consumer goods, were only too willing to lease their land to the foreign companies for very modest sums and under terms dictated by the firms. Where land was still held communally, the village headman was tempted by high cash commissions offered by plantation companies. He would lease the village land even more cheaply than would the individual peasant or, as was frequently the case, sell out the entire village to the company.[14]

The introduction of the plantation meant the divorce of agriculture from nourishment, as the notion of food value was lost to the overriding claim of "market value" in international trade. Crops such as sugar, tobacco, and coffee were selected, not on the basis of how well they feed people, but for their high price value relative to their weight and bulk so that profit margins could be maintained even after the costs of shipping to Europe.

SUPPRESSING PEASANT FARMING

The stagnation and impoverishment of the peasant food-producing sector was not the mere by-product of benign neglect, that is, the unintended consequence of an overemphasis on export production. Plantations—just like modern "agro-industrial complexes"—needed an abundant and readily available supply of low-wage agricultural workers. Colonial administrations thus devised a variety of tactics, all to undercut self-provisioning agriculture and thus make rural populations dependent on plantation wages. Government services and even the most minimal infrastructure (access to water, roads, seeds, credit, pest and disease control information, and so on) were systematically denied. Plantations usurped most of the good land, either making much of the rural population landless or pushing them onto marginal soils. (Yet the plantations have often held much of their land idle simply to prevent the peasants from using it—even to this day. Del Monte owns 57,000 acres of Guatemala but plants only 9000. The rest lies idle except for a few thousand head of grazing cattle.)[15]

In some cases a colonial administration would go even further to guarantee itself a labor supply. In at least twelve countries in the eastern and southern parts of Africa the exploitation of mineral wealth (gold, diamonds, and copper) and the establishment of cash-crop plantations demanded a continuous supply of low-cost labor. To assure this labor supply, colonial administrations simply expropriated the land of the African communities by violence and drove the people into small reserves.[16] With neither adequate land for their traditional slash-and-burn methods nor access to the means—tools, water, and fertilizer—to make continuous farming of such limited areas viable, the indigenous population could scarcely meet subsistence needs, much less produce surplus to sell in order to cover the colonial taxes. Hundreds of thousands of Africans were forced to become the cheap labor source so "needed" by the colonial plantations. Only by laboring on plantations and in the mines could they hope to pay the colonial taxes.

The tax scheme to produce reserves of cheap plantation and mining labor was particularly effective when the Great Depression hit and the bottom dropped out of cash crop economies. In 1929 the cotton market collapsed, leaving peasant cotton producers, such as those in Upper Volta, unable to pay their colonial taxes. More and more young people, in some years as many as 80,000, were thus forced to migrate to the Gold Coast to compete with each other for low-wage jobs on cocoa plantations.[17]

The forced migration of Africa's most able-bodied workers—stripping village food farming of needed hands—was a recurring feature of colonialism. As late as 1973 the Portuguese "exported" 400,000 Mozambican peasants to work in South Africa in exchange for gold deposited in the Lisbon treasury.

The many techniques of colonialism to undercut self-provisioning agriculture in order to ensure a cheap labor supply are no better illustrated than by the story of how, in the mid-nineteenth century, sugar plantation owners in British Guiana coped with the double blow of the emancipation of slaves and the crash in the world sugar market. The story is graphically recounted by Alan Adamson in *Sugar without Slaves*.[18]

Would the ex-slaves be allowed to take over the plantation land and grow the food they needed? The planters, many ruined by the sugar slump, were determined they would not. The planter-dominated government devised several schemes for thwarting food self-sufficiency. The price of crown land was kept artificially high, and the purchase of land in parcels smaller than 100 acres was outlawed—two measures guaranteeing that newly organized ex-slave cooperatives could not hope to gain access to much land. The government also prohibited cultivation on as much as 400,000 acres—on the grounds of "uncertain property titles." Moreover, although many planters held part of their land out of sugar production due to the depressed world price, they would not allow any alternative production on them. They feared that once the ex-slaves started growing food it would be difficult to return them to sugar production when world market prices began to recover. In addition, the government taxed peasant production, then turned around and used the funds to subsidize the immigration of laborers from India and Malaysia to replace the freed slaves, thereby making sugar production again profitable for the planters. Finally, the government neglected the infrastructure for subsistence agriculture and denied credit for small farmers.

Perhaps the most insidious tactic to "lure" the peasant away from food production—and the one with profound historical consequences—was a policy of keeping the price of imported food low through the removal of tariffs and subsidies. The policy was double-edged: first, peasants were told they need not grow food because they could always buy it cheaply with their plantation wages; second, cheap food imports destroyed the market for domestic food and thereby impoverished local food producers.

Adamson relates how both the Governor of British Guiana and the Secretary for the Colonies Earl Grey favored low duties on imports in order to erode local food production and thereby release labor for the plantations. In 1851 the governor rushed through a reduction of the duty on cereals in order to "divert" labor to the sugar estates. As Adamson comments, "Without realizing it, he [the governor] had put his finger on the most mordant feature of monoculture:... its convulsive need to destroy any other sector of the economy which might compete for 'its' labor."[19]

Many colonial governments succeeded in establishing dependence on imported foodstuffs. In 1647 an observer in the West Indies wrote to Governor Winthrop of Massachusetts: "Men are so intent upon planting sugar that they had rather buy foode at very dear rates than produce it by labour, so infinite is the profitt of sugar workes...."[20] By 1770, the West Indies were importing most of the continental colonies' exports of dried fish, grain, beans, and vegetables. A dependence on imported food made the West Indian colonies vulnerable to any disruption in supply. This dependence on imported food stuffs spelled disaster when the thirteen continental colonies gained independence and food exports from the continent to the West Indies were interrupted. With no diversified food system to fall back on, 15,000 plantation workers died of famine between 1780 and 1787 in Jamaica alone.[21] The dependence of the West Indies on imported food persists to this day.

SUPPRESSING PEASANT COMPETITION

We have talked about the techniques by which indigenous populations were forced to cultivate cash crops. In some countries with large plantations, however, colonial governments found it necessary to *prevent* peasants from independently growing cash crops not out of concern for their welfare, but so that they would not compete with colonial interests growing the same crop. For peasant farmers, given a modicum of opportunity, proved themselves capable of outproducing the large plantations not only in terms of output per unit of land but, more important, in terms of capital cost per unit produced.

In the Dutch East Indies (Indonesia and Dutch New Guinea) colonial policy in the middle of the nineteenth century forbade the sugar refineries to buy sugar cane from indigenous growers and imposed a discriminatory tax on rubber produced by native smallholders.[22] A recent unpublished United Nations study of agricultural development in Africa concluded that large-scale agricultural operations owned and controlled by foreign commercial interests (such as the rubber plantations of Liberia, the sisal estates of Tanganyika [Tanzania], and the coffee estates of Angola) only survived the competition of peasant producers because "the authorities actively supported them by suppressing indigenous rural development."[23]

The suppression of indigenous agricultural development served the interests of the colonizing powers in two ways. Not only did it prevent direct competition from more efficient native producers of the same crops, but it also guaranteed a labor force to work on the foreign-owned estates. Planters and foreign investors were not unaware that peasants who could survive economically by their own production would be under less pressure to sell their labor cheaply to the large estates.

The answer to the question, then, "Why can't people feed themselves?" must begin with an understanding of how colonialism actively prevented people from doing just that.

COLONIALISM

- forced peasants to replace food crops with cash crops that were then expropriated at very low rates;
- took over the best agricultural land for export crop plantations and then forced the most able-bodied workers to leave the village fields to work as slaves or for very low wages on plantations;
- encouraged a dependence on imported food;
- blocked native peasant cash crop production from competing with cash crops produced by settlers or foreign firms.

These are concrete examples of the development of underdevelopment that we should have perceived as such even as we read our history schoolbooks. Why didn't we? Somehow our schoolbooks always seemed to make the flow of history appear to have its own logic—as if it could not have been any other way. I, Frances, recall, in particular, a grade-school, social studies pamphlet on the idyllic life of Pedro, a nine-year-old boy on a coffee plantation in South America. The drawings of lush vegetation and "exotic" huts made his life seem romantic indeed. Wasn't it natural and proper that South America should have plantations to supply my mother and father with coffee? Isn't that the way it was *meant* to be?

NOTES

1. Radha Sinha, *Food and Poverty* (New York: Holmes and Meier, 1976), p. 26.
2. John Stuart Mill, *Political Economy*, Book 3, Chapter 25 (emphasis added).
3. Peter Feldman and David Lawrence, "Social and Economic Implications of the Large-Scale Introduction of New Varieties of Foodgrains," Africa Report, preliminary draft (Geneva: UNRISD, 1975), pp. 107–108.
4. Edgar Owens, *The Right Side of History*, unpublished manuscript, 1976.
5. Walter Rodney, *How Europe Underdeveloped Africa* (London: Bogle-L'Ouverture Publications, 1972), pp. 171–172.
6. Ferdinand Ossendowski, *Slaves of the Sun* (New York: Dutton, 1928), p. 276.
7. Rodney, *How Europe Underdeveloped Africa*, pp. 171–172.
8. Ibid., p. 181.
9. Clifford Geertz, *Agricultural Involution* (Berkeley and Los Angeles: University of California Press, 1963), pp. 52–53.
10. Rodney, *How Europe Underdeveloped Africa*, p. 185.
11. Ibid., p. 184.
12. Ibid., p. 186.
13. George L. Beckford, *Persistent Poverty: Underdevelopment in Plantation Economies of the Third World* (New York: Oxford University Press, 1972), p. 99.
14. Ibid., p. 99, quoting from Erich Jacoby, *Agrarian Unrest in Southeast Asia* (New York: Asia Publishing House, 1961), p. 66.
15. Pat Flynn and Roger Burbach, North American Congress on Latin America, Berkely, California, recent investigation.
16. Feldman and Lawrence, "Social and Economic Implications," p. 103.
17. Special Sahelian Office Report, Food and Agriculture Organization, March 28, 1974, pp. 88–89.
18. Alan Adamson, *Sugar Without Slaves: The Political Economy of British Guiana, 1838–1904* (New Haven and London: Yale University Press, 1972).
19. Ibid., p. 41.
20. Eric Williams, *Capitalism and Slavery* (New York: Putnam, 1966), p. 110.
21. Ibid., p. 121.
22. Gunnar Myrdal, *Asian Drama*, vol. 1 (New York: Pantheon, 1966), pp. 448–449.
23. Feldman and Lawrence, "Social and Economic Implications," p. 189.

Frances Moore Lappé and Dr. Joseph Collins are founders and directors of the Institute for Food and Development Policy, located in San Francisco and New York.

The Arrow of Disease

When Columbus and his successors invaded the Americas, the most potent weapon they carried was their germs. But why didn't deadly disease flow in the other direction, from the New World to the Old?

Jared Diamond

The three people talking in the hospital room were already stressed out from having to cope with a mysterious illness, and it didn't help at all that they were having trouble communicating. One of them was the patient, a small, timid man, sick with pneumonia caused by an unidentified microbe and with only a limited command of the English language. The second, acting as translator, was his wife, worried about her husband's condition and frightened by the hospital environment. The third person in the trio was an inexperienced young doctor, trying to figure out what might have brought on the strange illness. Under the stress, the doctor was forgetting everything he had been taught about patient confidentiality. He committed the awful blunder of requesting the woman to ask her husband whether he'd had any sexual experiences that might have caused the infection.

As the young doctor watched, the husband turned red, pulled himself together so that he seemed even smaller, tried to disappear under his bed sheets, and stammered in a barely audible voice. His wife suddenly screamed in rage and drew herself up to tower over him. Before the doctor could stop her, she grabbed a heavy metal bottle, slammed it onto her husband's head, and stormed out of the room. It took a while for the doctor to elicit, through the man's broken English, what he had said to so enrage his wife. The answer slowly emerged: he had admitted to repeated intercourse with sheep on a recent visit to the family farm; perhaps that was how he had contracted the mysterious microbe.

This episode, related to me by a physician friend involved in the case, sounds so bizarrely one of a kind as to be of no possible broader significance. But in fact it illustrates a subject of great importance: human diseases of animal origins. Very few of us may love sheep in the carnal sense. But most of us platonically love our pet animals, like our dogs and cats; and as a society, we certainly appear to have an inordinate fondness for sheep and other livestock, to judge from the vast numbers of them that we keep.

Some of us—most often our children—pick up infectious diseases from our pets. Usually these illnesses remain no more than a nuisance, but a few have evolved into far more. The major killers of humanity throughout our recent history—smallpox, flu, tuberculosis, malaria, plague, measles, and cholera—are all infectious diseases that arose from diseases of animals. Until World War II more victims of war died of microbes than of gunshot or sword wounds. All those military histories glorifying Alexander the Great and Napoleon ignore the ego-deflating truth: the winners of past wars were not necessarily those armies with the best generals and weapons, but those bearing the worst germs with which to smite their enemies.

The grimmest example of the role of germs in history is much on our minds this month, as we recall the European conquest of the Americas that began with Columbus's voyage of 1492. Numerous as the Indian victims of the murderous Spanish conquistadores were, they were dwarfed in number by the victims of murderous Spanish microbes. These formidable conquerors killed an estimated 95 percent of the New World's pre-Columbian Indian population.

Why was the exchange of nasty germs between the Americas and Europe so unequal? Why didn't the reverse happen instead, with Indian diseases decimating the Spanish invaders, spreading back across the Atlantic, and causing a 95 percent decline in *Europe's* human population?

Similar questions arise regarding the decimation of many other native peoples by European germs, and regarding the decimation of would-be European conquistadores in the tropics of Africa and Asia.

Naturally, we're disposed to think about diseases from our own point of view: What can we do to save ourselves and to kill the microbes? Let's stamp out the scoundrels, and never mind what *their* motives are!

In life, though, one has to understand the enemy to beat him. So for a moment, let's consider disease from the microbes' point of view. Let's look beyond our anger at their making us sick in bizarre ways, like giving us genital sores or diarrhea, and ask why it is that they do such things. After all, microbes are as much a product of natural selection as we are, and so their actions must have come about because they confer some evolutionary benefit.

Basically, of course, evolution selects those individuals that are most effective at producing babies and at helping those babies find suitable places to live. Microbes are marvels at this latter requirement. They have evolved diverse ways of spreading from one person to another, and from animals to people. Many of our symptoms of disease actually represent ways in which some clever bug modifies our bodies or our behavior such that we become enlisted to spread bugs.

The most effortless way a bug can spread is by just waiting to be transmitted passively to the next victim. That's the strategy practiced by microbes that wait for one host to be eaten by the next—salmonella bacteria, for example, which we contract by eating already-infected eggs or meat; or the worm responsible for trichinosis, which waits for us to kill a pig and eat it without properly cooking it.

As a slight modification of this strategy; some microbes don't wait for the old host to die but instead hitchhike in the saliva of an insect that bites the old host and then flies to a new one. The free ride may be provided by mosquitoes, fleas, lice, or tsetse flies, which spread malaria, plague, typhus, and sleeping sickness, respectively. The dirtiest of all passive-carriage tricks is perpetrated by microbes that pass from a woman to her fetus—microbes such as the ones responsible for syphilis, rubella (German measles), and AIDS. By their cunning these microbes can already be infecting an infant before the moment of its birth.

Other bugs take matters into their own hands, figuratively speaking. They actively modify the anatomy or habits of their host to accelerate their transmission. From our perspective, the open genital sores caused by venereal diseases such as syphilis are a vile indignity. From the microbes' point of view, however, they're just a useful device to enlist a host's help in inoculating the body cavity of another host with microbes. The skin lesions caused by smallpox similarly spread microbes by direct or indirect body contact (occasionally very

indirect, as when U.S. and Australian whites bent on wiping out "belligerent" native peoples sent them gifts of blankets previously used by smallpox patients).

More vigorous yet is the strategy practiced by the influenza, common cold, and pertussis (whooping cough) microbes, which induce the victim to cough or sneeze, thereby broadcasting the bugs toward prospective new hosts. Similarly the cholera bacterium induces a massive diarrhea that spreads bacteria into the water supplies of potential new victims. For modification of a host's behavior, though, nothing matches the rabies virus, which not only gets into the saliva of an infected dog but drives the dog into a frenzy of biting and thereby infects many new victims.

Thus, from our viewpoint, genital sores, diarrhea, and coughing are "symptoms" of disease. From a bug's viewpoint, they're clever evolutionary strategies to broadcast the bug. That's why it's in the bug's interests to make us "sick." But what does it gain by killing us? That seems self-defeating, since a microbe that kills its host kills itself.

Though you may well think it's of little consolation, our death is really just an unintended by-product of host symptoms that promote the efficient transmission of microbes. Yes, an untreated cholera patient may eventually die from producing diarrheal fluid at a rate of several gallons a day. While the patient lasts, though, the cholera bacterium profits from being massively disseminated into the water supplies of its next victims. As long as each victim thereby infects, on average, more than one new victim, the bacteria will spread, even though the first host happens to die.

S o much for the dispassionate examination of the bug's interests. Now let's get back to considering our own selfish interests: to stay alive and healthy, best done by killing the damned bugs. One common response to infection is to develop a fever. Again, we consider fever a "symptom" of disease, as if it developed inevitably without serving any function. But regulation of body temperature is under our genetic control, and a fever doesn't just happen by accident. Because

some microbes are more sensitive to heat than our own bodies are, by raising our body temperature we in effect try to bake the bugs to death before we get baked ourselves.

We and our pathogens are now locked in an escalating evolutionary contest, with the death of one contestant the price of defeat, and with natural selection playing the role of umpire.

Another common response is to mobilize our immune system. White blood cells and other cells actively seek out and kill foreign microbes. The specific antibodies we gradually build up against a particular microbe make us less likely to get reinfected once we are cured. As we all know there are some illnesses, such as flu and the common cold, to which our resistance is only temporary; we can eventually contract the illness again. Against other illnesses, though—including measles, mumps, rubella, pertussis, and the now-defeated menace of smallpox—antibodies stimulated by one infection confer lifelong immunity. That's the principle behind vaccination—to stimulate our antibody production without our having to go through the actual experience of the disease.

Alas, some clever bugs don't just cave in to our immune defenses. Some have learned to trick us by changing their antigens, those molecular pieces of the microbe that our antibodies recognize. The constant evolution or recycling of new strains of flu, with differing antigens, explains why the flu you got two years ago didn't protect you against the different strain that arrived this year. Sleeping sickness is an even more slippery customer in its ability to change its antigens rapidly.

Among the slipperiest of all is the virus that causes AIDS, which evolves new antigens even as it sits within an individual patient, until it eventually overwhelms the immune system.

Our slowest defensive response is through natural selection, which changes the relative frequency with which a gene appears from generation to generation. For almost any disease some people prove to be genetically more resistant than others. In an epidemic, those people with genes for resistance to that particular microbe are more likely to survive than are people lacking such genes. As a result, over the course of history human populations repeatedly exposed to a particular pathogen tend to be made up of individuals with genes that resist the appropriate microbe just because unfortunate individuals without those genes were less likely to survive to pass their genes on to their children.

Fat consolation, you may be thinking. This evolutionary response is not one that does the genetically susceptible dying individual any good. It does mean, though, that a human population as a whole becomes better protected.

In short, many bugs have had to evolve tricks to let them spread among potential victims. We've evolved counter-tricks, to which the bugs have responded by evolving counter-counter-tricks. We and our pathogens are now locked in an escalating evolutionary contest, with the death of one contestant the price of defeat, and with natural selection playing the role of umpire.

The form that this deadly contest takes varies with the pathogens: for some it is like a guerrilla war, while for others it is a blitzkrieg. With certain diseases, like malaria or hookworm, there's a more or less steady trickle of new cases in an affected area, and they will appear in any month of any year. Epidemic diseases, though, are different: they produce no cases for a long time, then a whole wave of cases, then no more cases again for a while.

Among such epidemic diseases, influenza is the most familiar to Americans, this year having been a particularly bad one for us (but a great year for the influenza virus). Cholera epidemics come at longer intervals, the 1991 Peruvian epidemic being the first one to reach the New World during the twentieth century. Frightening as today's influenza and cholera epidemics are, through, they pale beside the far more terrifying epidemics of the past, before the rise of modern medicine. The greatest single epidemic in human history was the influenza wave that killed 21 million people at the end of the First World War. The black death, or bubonic plague, killed one-quarter of Europe's population between 1346 and 1352, with death tolls up to 70 percent in some cities.

The infectious diseases that visit us as epidemics share several characteristics. First, they spread quickly and efficiently from an infected person to nearby healthy people, with the result that the whole population gets exposed within a short time. Second, they're "acute" illnesses: within a short time, you either die or recover completely. Third, the fortunate ones of us who do recover develop antibodies that leave us immune against a recurrence of the disease for a long time, possibly our entire lives. Finally, these diseases tend to be restricted to humans; the bugs causing them tend not to live in the soil or in other animals. All four of these characteristics apply to what Americans think of as the once more-familiar acute epidemic diseases of childhood, including measles, rubella, mumps, pertussis, and smallpox.

It is easy to understand why the combination of those four characteristics tends to make a disease run in epidemics. The rapid spread of microbes and the rapid course of symptoms mean that everybody in a local human population is soon infected, and thereafter either dead or else recovered and immune. No one is left alive who could still be infected. But since the microbe can't survive except in the bodies of living people, the disease dies out until a new crop of babies reaches the susceptible age—and until an infectious person arrives from the outside to start a new epidemic.

A classic illustration of the process is given by the history of measles on the isolated Faeroe Islands in the North Atlantic. A severe epidemic of the disease reached the Faeroes in 1781, then died out, leaving the islands measles-free until an infected carpenter arrived on a ship from Denmark in 1846. Within three months almost the whole Faeroes population—7,782 people—had gotten measles and then either died or recovered, leaving the measles virus to disappear once again until the next epidemic. Studies show that measles is likely to die out in any human population numbering less than half a million people. Only in larger populations can measles shift from one local area to another, thereby persisting until enough babies have been born in the originally infected area to permit the disease's return.

Rubella in Australia provides a similar example, on a much larger scale. As of 1917 Australia's population was still only 5 million, with most people living in scattered rural areas. The sea voyage to Britain took two months, and land transport within Australia itself was slow. In effect, Australia didn't even consist of a population of 5 million, but of hundreds of much smaller populations. As a result, rubella hit Australia only as occasional epidemics, when an infected person happened to arrive from overseas and stayed in a densely populated area. By 1938, though, the city of Sydney alone had a population of over one million, and people moved frequently and quickly by air between London, Sydney, and other Australian cities. Around then, rubella for the first time was able to establish itself permanently in Australia.

What's true for rubella in Australia is true for most familiar acute infectious diseases throughout the world. To sustain themselves, they need a human population that is sufficiently numerous and densely packed that a new crop of susceptible children is available for infection by the time the disease would otherwise be waning. Hence the measles and other such diseases are also known as "crowd diseases."

Crowd diseases could not sustain themselves in small bands of hunter-gatherers and slash-and-burn farmers. As tragic recent experience with Amazonian Indians and Pacific Islanders confirms, almost an entire tribelet may be wiped out by an epidemic brought by an outside visitor, because no one in the tribelet has any antibodies against the microbe. In addition, measles and some other "childhood" diseases are more likely to kill infected adults than children, and all adults in the tribelet are susceptible. Having killed most of the tribelet, the epidemic then disappears. The small population size explains why tribelets can't sustain epidemics introduced from the outside; at the same time it explains why they could never evolve epidemic diseases of their own to give back to the visitors.

That's not to say that small human populations are free from all infectious diseases. Some of their infections are caused by microbes capable of maintaining themselves in animals or in soil, so the disease remains constantly available to infect people. For example, the yellow fever virus is carried by African wild monkeys and is constantly available to infect rural human populations of Africa. It was also available to be carried to New World monkeys and people by the trans-Atlantic slave trade.

Other infections of small human populations are chronic diseases, such as leprosy and yaws, that may take a very long time to kill a victim. The victim thus remains alive as a reservoir of microbes to infect other members of the tribelet. Finally, small human populations are susceptible to nonfatal infections against which we don't develop immunity, with the result that the same person can become reinfected after recovering. That's the case with hookworm and many other parasites.

All these types of diseases, characteristic of small, isolated populations, must be the oldest diseases of humanity. They were the ones that we could evolve and sustain through the early millions of years of our evolutionary history, when the total human population was tiny and fragmented. They are also shared with, or are similar to the diseases of, our closest wild relatives, the African great apes. In contrast, the evolution of our crowd diseases could only have occurred with the buildup of large, dense human populations, first made possible by the rise of agriculture about 10,000 years ago, then by the rise of cities several thousand years ago. Indeed, the first attested dates for many familiar infectious diseases are surprisingly recent: around 1600 B.C. for

smallpox (as deduced from pockmarks on an Egyptian mummy), 400 B.C. for mumps, 1840 for polio, and 1959 for AIDS.

Agriculture sustains much higher human population densities than does hunting and gathering—on average, 10 to 100 times higher. In addition, hunter-gatherers frequently shift camp, leaving behind their piles of feces with their accumulated microbes and worm larvae. But farmers are sedentary and live amid their own sewage, providing microbes with a quick path from one person's body into another person's drinking water. Farmers also become surrounded by disease-transmitting rodents attracted by stored food.

The explosive increase in world travel by Americans, and in immigration to the United States, is turning us into another melting pot—this time of microbes that we'd dismissed as causing disease in far-off countries.

Some human populations make it even easier for their own bacteria and worms to infect new victims, by intentionally gathering their feces and urine and spreading it as fertilizer on the fields where people work. Irrigation agriculture and fish farming provide ideal living conditions for the snails carrying schistosomes, and for other flukes that burrow through our skin as we wade through the feces-laden water.

If the rise of farming was a boon for our microbes, the rise of cities was a veritable bonanza, as still more densely packed human populations festered under even worse sanitation conditions. (Not until the beginning of the twentieth century did urban populations finally become self-sustaining; until then, constant immigration of healthy peasants from the countryside was necessary to make good the constant deaths of city dwellers from crowd diseases.) Another bonanza

was the development of world trade routes, which by late Roman times effectively joined the populations of Europe, Asia, and North Africa into one giant breeding ground for microbes. That's when smallpox finally reached Rome as the "plague of Antonius," which killed millions of Roman citizens between A.D. 165 and 180.

Similarly, bubonic plague first appeared in Europe as the plague of Justinian (A.D. 542–543). But plague didn't begin to hit Europe with full force, as the black death epidemics, until 1346, when new overland trading with China provided rapid transit for flea-infested furs from plague-ridden areas of Central Asia. Today our jet planes have made even the longest intercontinental flights briefer than the duration of any human infectious disease. That's how an Aerolíneas Argentinas airplane, stopping in Lima, Peru, earlier this year, managed to deliver dozens of cholera-infected people the same day to my city of Los Angeles, over 3,000 miles away. The explosive increase in world travel by Americans, and in immigration to the United States, is turning us into another melting pot—this time of microbes that we previously dismissed as just causing exotic diseases in far-off countries.

When the human population became sufficiently large and concentrated, we reached the stage in our history when we could at last sustain crowd diseases confined to our species. But that presents a paradox: such diseases could never have existed before. Instead they had to evolve as new diseases. Where did those new diseases come from?

Evidence emerges from studies of the disease-causing microbes themselves. In many cases molecular biologists have identified the microbe's closest relative. Those relatives also prove to be agents of infectious crowd diseases—but ones confined to various species of domestic animals and pets! Among animals too, epidemic diseases require dense populations, and they're mainly confined to social animals that provide the necessary large populations. Hence when we domesticated social animals such as cows and pigs, they were already afflicted by epidemic diseases just waiting to be transferred to us.

For example, the measles virus is most closely related to the virus causing rinderpest, a nasty epidemic disease of cattle and many wild cud-chewing mammals. Rinderpest doesn't affect humans. Measles, in turn, doesn't affect cattle. The close similarity of the measles and rinderpest viruses suggests that the rinderpest virus transferred from cattle to humans, then became the measles virus by changing its properties to adapt to us. That transfer isn't surprising, considering how closely many peasant farmers live and sleep next to cows and their accompanying feces, urine, breath, sores, and blood. Our intimacy with cattle has been going on for 8,000 years since we domesticated them—ample time for the rinderpest virus to discover us nearby. Other familiar infectious diseases can similarly be traced back to diseases of our animal friends.

Given our proximity to the animals we love, we must constantly be getting bombarded by animal microbes. Those invaders get winnowed by natural selection, and only a few succeed in establishing themselves as human diseases. A quick survey of current diseases lets us trace four stages in the evolution of a specialized human disease from an animal precursor.

In the first stage, we pick up animal-borne microbes that are still at an early stage in their evolution into specialized human pathogens. They don't get transmitted directly from one person to another, and even their transfer from animals to us remains uncommon. There are dozens of diseases like this that we get directly from pets and domestic animals. They include cat scratch fever from cats, leptospirosis from dogs, psittacosis from chickens and parrots, and brucellosis from cattle. We're similarly susceptible to picking up diseases from wild animals, such as the tularemia that hunters occasionally get from skinning wild rabbits.

In the second stage, a former animal pathogen evolves to the point where it does get transmitted directly between people and causes epidemics. However, the epidemic dies out for several reasons—being cured by modern medicine, stopping when everybody has been infected and died, or stopping when everybody has been infected and become immune. For example, a previously unknown disease termed *o'nyong-nyong* fever appeared in East Africa in 1959 and infected several million Africans. It probably arose from a virus of monkeys and was transmitted to humans by mosquitoes. The fact that patients recovered quickly and became immune to further attack helped cause the new disease to die out quickly.

The annals of medicine are full of diseases that sound like no known disease today but that once caused terrifying epidemics before disappearing as mysteriously as they had come. Who alive today remembers the "English sweating sickness" that swept and terrified Europe between 1485 and 1578, or the "Picardy sweats" of eighteenth- and nineteenth-century France?

A third stage in the evolution of our major diseases is represented by former animal pathogens that establish themselves in humans and that do not die out; until they do, the question of whether they will become major killers of humanity remains up for grabs. The future is still very uncertain for Lassa fever, first observed in 1969 in Nigeria and caused by a virus probably derived from rodents. Better established is Lyme disease, caused by a spirochete that we get from the bite of a tick. Although the first known human cases in the United States appeared only as recently as 1962, Lyme disease is already reaching epidemic proportions in the Northeast, on the West Coast, and in the upper Midwest. The future of AIDS, derived from monkey viruses, is even more secure, from the virus's perspective.

The final stage of this evolution is represented by the major, long-established epidemic diseases confined to humans. These diseases must have been the evolutionary survivors of far more pathogens that tried to make the jump to us from animals—and mostly failed.

Diseases represent evolution in progress, as microbes adapt by natural selection to new hosts. Compared with cows' bodies, though, our bodies offer different immune defenses and different chemistry. In that new environment, a microbe must evolve new ways to live and propagate itself.

The best-studied example of microbes evolving these new ways involves myxomatosis, which hit Australian rabbits in 1950. The myxoma virus, native to a wild species of Brazilian rabbit, was known to cause a lethal epidemic in European domestic rabbits, which are a different species. The virus was intentionally introduced to Australia in the hopes of ridding the continent of its plague of European rabbits, foolishly introduced in the nineteenth century. In the first year, myxoma produced a gratifying (to Australian farmers) 99.8 percent mortality in infected rabbits. Fortunately for the rabbits and unfortunately for the farmers, the death rate then dropped in the second year to 90 percent and eventually to 25 percent, frustrating hopes of eradicating rabbits completely from Australia. The problem was that the myxoma virus evolved to serve its own interest, which differed from the farmers' interests and those of the rabbits. The virus changed to kill fewer rabbits and to permit lethally infected ones to live longer before dying. The result was bad for Australian farmers but good for the virus: a less lethal myxoma virus spreads baby viruses to more rabbits than did the original, highly virulent myxoma.

For a similar example in humans, consider the surprising evolution of syphilis. Today we associate syphilis with genital sores and a very slowly developing disease, leading to the death of untreated victims only after many years. However, when syphilis was first definitely recorded in Europe in 1495, its pustules often covered the body from the head to the knees, caused flesh to fall off people's faces, and led to death within a few months. By 1546 syphilis had evolved into the disease with the symptoms known to us today. Apparently, just as with myxomatosis, those syphilis spirochetes evolved to keep their victims alive longer in order to transmit their spirochete offspring into more victims.

How, then, does all this explain the outcome of 1492—that Europeans conquered and depopulated the New World, instead of Native Americans conquering and depopulating Europe?

Part of the answer, of course, goes back to the invaders' technological advantages. European guns and steel swords were more effective weapons than Native American stone axes and wooden clubs. Only Europeans had ships capable of crossing the ocean and horses that could provide a decisive advantage in battle. But that's not the whole answer. Far more Native Americans died in bed than on the battlefield—the victims of germs, not of guns and swords. Those germs undermined Indian resistance by killing most Indians and their leaders and by demoralizing the survivors.

In the century or two following Columbus's arrival in the New World, the Indian population declined by about 95 percent. The main killers were European germs, to which the Indians had never been exposed.

The role of disease in the Spanish conquests of the Aztec and Inca empires is especially well documented. In 1519 Cortés landed on the coast of Mexico with 600 Spaniards to conquer the fiercely militaristic Aztec Empire, which at the time had a population of many millions. That Cortés reached the Aztec capital of Tenochtitlán, escaped with the loss of "only" two-thirds of his force, and managed to fight his way back to the coast demonstrates both Spanish military advantages and the initial naïveté of the Aztecs. But when Cortés's next onslaught came, in 1521, the Aztecs were no longer naïve; they fought street by street with the utmost tenacity.

What gave the Spaniards a decisive advantage this time was smallpox, which reached Mexico in 1520 with the arrival of one infected slave from Spanish Cuba. The resulting epidemic proceeded to kill nearly half the Aztecs. The survivors were demoralized by the mysterious illness that killed Indians and spared Span-

iards, as if advertising the Spaniards' invincibility. By 1618 Mexico's initial population of 20 million had plummeted to about 1.6 million.

Pizarro had similarly grim luck when he landed on the coast of Peru in 1531 with about 200 men to conquer the Inca Empire. Fortunately for Pizarro, and unfortunately for the Incas, smallpox had arrived overland around 1524, killing much of the Inca population, including both Emperor Huayna Capac and his son and designated successor, Ninan Cuyoche. Because of the vacant throne, two other sons of Huayna Capac, Atahuallpa and Huáscar, became embroiled in a civil war that Pizarro exploited to conquer the divided Incas.

When we in the United States think of the most populous New World societies existing in 1492, only the Aztecs and Incas come to mind. We forget that North America also supported populous Indian societies in the Mississippi Valley. Sadly, these societies too would disappear. But in this case conquistadores contributed nothing directly to the societies' destruction; the conquistadores' germs, spreading in advance, did everything. When De Soto marched through the Southeast in 1540, he came across Indian towns abandoned two years previously because nearly all the inhabitants had died in epidemics. However, he was still able to see some of the densely populated towns lining the lower Mississippi. By a century and a half later, though, when French settlers returned to the lower Mississippi, almost all those towns had vanished. Their relics are the great mound sites of the Mississippi Valley. Only recently have we come to realize that the mound-building societies were still largely intact when Columbus arrived, and that they collapsed between 1492 and the systematic European exploration of the Mississippi.

W hen I was a child in school, we were taught that North America had originally been occupied by about one million Indians. That low number helped justify the white conquest of what could then be viewed as an almost empty continent. However, archeological excavations and descriptions left by the first

European explorers on our coasts now suggest an initial number of around 20 million. In the century or two following Columbus's arrival in the New World, the Indian population is estimated to have declined by about 95 percent.

The main killers were European germs, to which the Indians had never been exposed and against which they therefore had neither immunologic nor genetic resistance. Smallpox, measles, influenza, and typhus competed for top rank among the killers. As if those were not enough, pertussis, plague, tuberculosis, diphtheria, mumps, malaria, and yellow fever came close behind. In countless cases Europeans were actually there to witness the decimation that occurred when the germs arrived. For example, in 1837 the Mandan Indian tribe, with one of the most elaborate cultures in the Great Plains, contracted smallpox thanks to a steamboat traveling up the Missouri River from St. Louis. The population of one Mandan village crashed from 2,000 to less than 40 within a few weeks.

The one-sided exchange of lethal germs between the Old and New worlds is among the most striking and consequence-laden facts of recent history. Whereas over a dozen major infectious diseases of Old World origins became established in the New World, not a single major killer reached Europe from the Americas. The sole possible exception is syphilis, whose area of origin still remains controversial.

That one-sidedness is more striking with the knowledge that large, dense human populations are a prerequisite for the evolution of crowd diseases. If recent reappraisals of the pre-Columbian New World population are correct, that population was not far below the contemporaneous population of Eurasia. Some New World cities, like Tenochtitlán, were among the world's most populous cities at the time. Yet Tenochtitlán didn't have awful germs waiting in store for the Spaniards. Why not?

One possible factor is the rise of dense human populations began somewhat later in the New World than in the Old. Another is that the three most populous American centers—the Andes, Mexico, and the Mississippi Valley—

were never connected by regular fast trade into one gigantic breeding ground for microbes, in the way that Europe, North Africa, India, and China became connected in late Roman times.

The main reason becomes clear, however, if we ask a simple question: From what microbes could any crowd diseases of the Americas have evolved? We've seen that Eurasian crowd diseases evolved from diseases of domesticated herd animals. Significantly, there were many such animals in Eurasia. But there were only five animals that became domesticated in the Americas: the turkey in Mexico and parts of North America, the guinea pig and llama/alpaca (probably derived from the same original wild species) in the Andes, and Muscovy duck in tropical South America, and the dog throughout the Americas.

That extreme paucity of New World domestic animals reflects the paucity of wild starting material. About 80 percent of the big wild mammals of the Americas became extinct at the end of the last ice age, around 11,000 years ago, at approximately the same time that the first well-attested wave of Indian hunters spread over the Americas. Among the species that disappeared were ones that would have yielded useful domesticates, such as American horses and camels. Debate still rages as to whether those extinctions were due to climate changes or to the impact of Indian hunters on prey that had never seen humans. Whatever the reason, the extinctions removed most of the

basis for Native American animal domestication—and for crowd diseases.

The few domesticates that remained were not likely sources of such diseases. Muscovy ducks and turkeys don't live in enormous flocks, and they're not naturally endearing species (like young lambs) with which we have much physical contact. Guinea pigs may have contributed a trypanosome infection like Chagas' disease or leishmaniasis to our catalog of woes, but that's uncertain.

Initially the most surprising absence is of any human disease derived from llamas (or alpacas), which are tempting to consider as the Andean equivalent of Eurasian livestock. However, llamas had three strikes against them as a source of human pathogens: their wild relatives don't occur in big herds as do wild sheep, goats, and pigs; their total numbers were never remotely as large as the Eurasian populations of domestic livestock, since llamas never spread beyond the Andes; and llamas aren't as cuddly as piglets and lambs and aren't kept in such close association with people. (You may not think of piglets as cuddly, but human mothers in the New Guinea highlands often nurse them, and they frequently live right in the huts of peasant farmers.)

The importance of animal-derived diseases for human history extends far beyond the Americas. Eurasian germs played a key role in decimating native peoples in many other parts of the world as well, including the Pacific islands, Australia, and southern Africa. Racist Europeans used to attribute those con-

quests to their supposedly better brains. But no evidence for such better brains has been forthcoming. Instead, the conquests were made possible by Europeans nastier germs, and by the technological advances and denser populations that Europeans ultimately acquired by means of their domesticated plants and animals.

So on this 500th anniversary of Columbus's discovery, let's try to regain our sense of perspective about his hotly debated achievements. There's no doubt that Columbus was a great visionary, seaman, and leader. There's also no doubt that he and his successors often behaved as bestial murderers. But those facts alone don't fully explain why it took so few European immigrants to initially conquer and ultimately supplant so much of the native population of the Americas. Without the germs Europeans brought with them—germs that were derived from their animals—such conquests might have been impossible.

Jared Diamond is a contributing editor of DISCOVER, *a professor of physiology at the UCLA School of Medicine, a recipient of a MacArthur genius award, and a research associate in ornithology at the American Museum of Natural History. Expanded versions of many of his* DISCOVER *articles appear in his book* The Third Chimpanzee: The Evolution and Future of the Human Animal, *which won Britain's 1992* COPUS *prize for best science book. Not least among his many accomplishments was his rediscovery in 1981 of the long-lost bowerbird of New Guinea. Diamond wrote about pseudo-hermaphrodites for* DISCOVER'S *special June issue on the science of sex.*

"Drought Follows the Plow"

In spite of the scantiness of the vegetation great herds and flocks were seen and the scrub forest and the grass is burnt, great fires crossing the countryside. Overgrazing and hacking in the forest that is left, annual burning, and sand invasion suggest the question: How long before the desert supervenes?
—E. P. Stebbing, "The Encroaching Sahara... "

I remember watching a group of Bemba men and women in northern Zambia attack their cleared fields with iron-bladed hoes. They had started work early in the day when the sun was low, fanning out in rows over dry and hardened soil thick with weeds and coarse shrubs. *Thunk! Thunk! Thunk!* The hoes struck the obdurate ground again and again, often dozens of times at the same spot. Weeks of backbreaking, unceasing work at the hottest time of year sapped all the farmers' energy. No plows or wheels made the task easier, nor was there any guarantee that the rains would arrive on time. Each family needed about three hectares of cultivated and fallow land to feed itself. The amount of labor required to keep those gardens in production is enormous even in good rainfall years.

Every African subsistence farmer I have ever talked to is philosophical. He knows that at least once in his lifetime he will suffer from drought and malnutrition.

Yet Africans have often triumphed over environmental adversity. They created great kingdoms—Ghana, Mali, Zimbabwe—traded indirectly with the far corners of the earth, and fashioned great art and flamboyant cultures. But many have always lived on the edge. Regions like the southern fringes of the Sahara are so arid and unpredictable that it took remarkable ingenuity and environmental knowledge to survive there. Fam-

ine and disease stalked farmer and herder alike even when population densities were low. In the twentieth century, when colonial governments upset the delicate balance of climate and humanity on a continent that had never supported vast numbers of people or huge urban civilizations, these social disasters have come more frequently....

The Sahara and the Nile Valley occupy about half the entire African continent, an area larger than the United States, including Alaska. The Atlas Mountains of Morocco and the Ethiopian Highlands rise at opposite ends of the desert. In the east, Saharan sand laps the Nile Valley, an oasis for animals and humans since the beginning of the Ice Age. The desert's southern margins pass gradually into stunted grassland, then dry savanna. Each year, the southern frontiers expand and contract as droughts come and go or occasional cycles of higher rainfall allow dry grass to grow a few kilometers farther north.

The Sahara is one of the hottest places on earth. The prevailing wind, a dry, descending northeasterly, raises the temperature above thirty-seven degrees Celsius on more days of the year than anywhere else in the world. The heat causes enormous evaporation loss from surface water and vegetation in an area where the mean rainfall is less than 380 millimeters a year. Vast tracts of the desert have supported no animal or hu-

man life at all for nearly five thousand years.

The Sahara was not always so inhospitable. Long-term climatic changes during the Ice Age brought it higher rainfall. In warmer periods, enormous shallow lakes and semi-arid grassland covered thousands of square kilometers, nourished by seasonal rivers that radiated from the desert mountains. Lake Chad, on the borders of modern-day Chad, Niger, and Nigeria, is a climatological barometer of the ancient Sahara. Today it is minuscule compared with the Lake Chad of 120,000 years ago, which filled a vast basin larger than the Caspian Sea.

Lake Chad's ancient shorelines tell us the desert was very dry during the height of the last glacial period, from about 18,000 to 10,500 B.C. The global warm-up after the end of the Ice Age brought more humid conditions. During these better-watered millennia, the Sahara supported sparse populations of hunters and gatherers, who anchored themselves to lakes and permanent water holes. Not that the Sahara was a paradise. The climate was at best semi-arid, with irregular rainfall.

Around 5000 B.C., some of these tiny nomadic groups either domesticated wild cattle and goats or acquired tame beasts from people living in the Nile Valley or on the desert's northern frontiers. We know cattle herders once lived in the desert because they painted their beasts

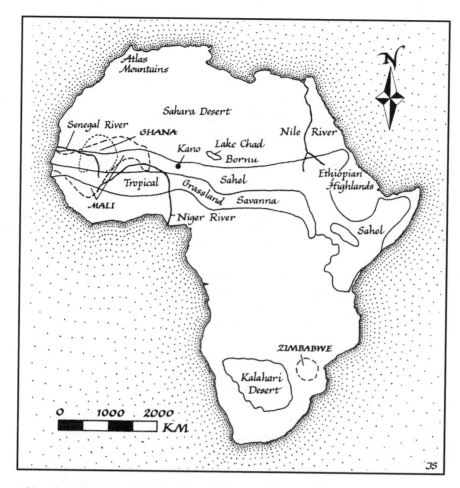

Africa, showing ancient states and the Sahel region.

on cave walls high on the Sahara's central massifs. In 4000 B.C., at least three million square kilometers of the Sahara could have supported herders and, theoretically, as many as twenty-one million head of cattle. Of course, nowhere near that many cattle grazed there, but the pastoralist population of the arid lands grew steadily.

Sometime before 2500 B.C., for reasons that are still not understood, the Sahara began to dry up. A small drop in annual rainfall was sufficient to make the already arid land uninhabitable. As it had done in earlier millennia, the desert acted like a giant pump. During wetter times, it sucked people into its fastnesses to settle by shallow lakes and cool mountain ranges. The same groups migrated out to the desert margins when drier conditions evaporated the lakes and destroyed the grassland. As Ancient Egypt's first pharaohs strove to unify their kingdom, the Sahara's herders moved to the edge of

the Nile Valley and southward into the Sahel, a savanna belt that extends across the continent from West Africa to the Nile River. Their remote descendants still graze their herds there to this day.

The word *Sahel* comes from the Arabic *sahil*, which means "shore," an apt description for a frontier land that borders the largest sea of sand in the world. The Sahel is a gently undulating grassy steppe between two hundred and four hundred kilometers wide, constrained to the north by the Sahara and to the south by a variety of forested terrain. The region just south of the Sahel is also the home of the tsetse fly, fatal to cattle and hazardous to people. Stunted grassland dominates at the margins of the desert, where the rainy season lasts a mere three to five months a year. Farther south, the grass gradually gives way to tree-covered steppe and eventually to more densely vegetated terrain. This inhospitable country, with large areas of sand

dunes and long-dried-up lakes, supported cattle herders when Old Kingdom pharaohs were building the pyramids and when Julius Caesar conquered Gaul. Over many centuries, the herders developed effective strategies for surviving a highly unpredictable environment....

The word *drought* assumes a complex meaning in the Sahel, where there is no such thing as an "average" rainfall, and where rain is highly localized, brief, and often violent. In any given year, as many as half of all modern-day reporting stations experience below-average rainfall. Almost no rain may fall throughout the wet months, or it may fall plentifully for some weeks but then fail completely, leaving young crops and fresh grazing grass to die in the ground. Furthermore, since most rainfall arrives as heavy showers during the hot months, losses from evaporation are enormous, little moisture sinks into the ground, and the potential for plant growth is much reduced.

Drought in the Sahel has both human and environmental dimensions. A single dry year may kill off stock, reduce grazing land, and devastate crops, but improved rainfall the next year will mitigate the impact. However, a succession of arid years may have a cumulative effect on cattle and humans, to the point that an unusually severe drought can deliver a knockout blow to already weakened communities. Sahelian dry cycles can persist for up to fifteen years, as can periods of higher rainfall. The latter lulls everyone into a false sense of security. Cattle herds grow, fields are planted ever farther north into normally arid land, contributing to the disaster if a long dry period arrives without warning. If anything is "normal" in the frontier lands, it is the certainty that severe drought returns. The ancient Sahelian cattle herders planned their lives accordingly.

Before the European powers carved up Africa in the late nineteenth century, the rhythm of cattle herding and agriculture on the Sahel changed little from year to year. The casual observer of a herding community might assume that the constant movements of people and herds were almost haphazard. In fact, the elders discussed every move carefully and acted conservatively. They relied on a remarkably detailed knowledge of the surrounding region, its water supplies and grazing grass, and were constantly in search of information about conditions elsewhere. The people were accustomed to inadequate diets and months of hunger when the rains failed and grazing grass or crops withered in the blistering sun. Over many generations, they had developed effective strategies for minimizing stock losses and surviving arid years. They depended on close family ties and enduring obligations of reciprocity with neighbors near and far to move their beasts, obtain loans of grain, and keep some of their animals safe from rinderpest and other catastrophic diseases.[1]

Groups like the Fulani used to move over large distances, sometimes two hundred kilometers or more. These movements coincided with the seasons. During the wet months from June to October, the herders would move north with the rains, feeding their cattle off fresh grass. As long as the grass ahead looked green, the herds migrated north. In a good year the cattle gained weight and gave ample milk. Nevertheless, the people moved constantly to find the best grass and to keep the cattle away from soggy ground. When the herds reached the northern limits of the rainfall belt, they turned south and consumed the grass crop that had grown up behind them as long as standing water remained.

Back in their dry-season range, the herds found grazing that could tide them over for the next eight months or so. Between November and March, many herds also grazed on farmland, rotating from one village to another, for their manure helped fertilize the soil for the next year's crops and their owners received millet in exchange. By the middle of the dry season, the herders were searching constantly for good grazing range, moving frequently and staying close to river floodplains if they could. The end of the dry season in April and May was the worst time of year. People were lethargic, often hungry, and deeply concerned about the condition of their beasts, who, even in a good rainfall year, might not have enough to eat. Then the first rains fell, green shoots carpeted the landscape, and the entire cycle began anew.

The herders' lifeway remained viable for thousands of years because they used effective strategies for coping with drought. They made best use of seasonal pastures and took great care in planning their moves. They moved their herds constantly to avoid overgrazing valuable range and spreading diseases like rinderpest. At the same time, they saw cattle as wealth on the hoof, so a herder sought to own as many head as possible, both to fulfill marriage gifts and other social obligations and to have as a form of insurance. The more animals he had, the more would survive the next drought.

While each nuclear family owned its own herds, they shared information over a wide area. They minimized risk of disease and drought by farming out the grazing of many of their animals to extended family and kinspeople living a considerable distance away. The Fulani and other herders placed a high premium on reciprocal obligations as a way of coping with unpredictable climate conditions. They suffered but survived.

The twentieth century and the European powers changed everything. The French, who assumed control of most of central Africa from the local inhabitants after 1889, stressed the need for each of their new colonies to become financially self-sufficient, which meant taxing the people to pay for the cost of their government. At the same time, French authorities insisted on the free use of pastoral land by all and abolished the traditional political framework that had maintained control over grazing rights. This draconian policy opened the way for overuse of the best grazing ranges on the edge of the desert. At the same time, new colonial frontiers cut across traditional grazing ranges, further disrupting traditional culture. Sahelian population increased threefold thanks to well digging, improved medical care, and sanitation. National governments restricted mobility, initiated cash-crop planting schemes, and encouraged cattle herders to settle in permanent villages. The colonial economy had arrived on the Sahel. Granaries might bulge with grain, but the stockpile was sold for cash to pay taxes, making it impossible for many communities to feed themselves in lean years. When drought struck, the people had three options: suffer quietly and starve, find alternative food supplies, or move away to find food or earn cash to feed themselves. There was food available, but prices often skyrocketed as much as thirtyfold. Half to two-thirds of the herders were soon reduced to complete penury as they disposed of their animals and possessions under unfavorable terms. One thing never changed: the inexorable demand for scheduled tax payments.

In 1898 a prolonged dry cycle began, culminating in severe droughts in 1911 and 1914–1915. Lake Chad shrank by half, Nile flood levels fell by 35 percent, and thousands of cattle herders died of starvation. The famine remains seared into the memories of the Fulani, Hausa, and others.

Hunger gripped the Sahel with unrelenting severity. In 1914 grain reserves were low, livestock were already weak, and malnutrition was widespread, especially among children. By the time the growing season arrived, many people were too weak to work in the fields. Entire families died at the side of paths as they tried to flee south into better-watered areas. Those who survived did not have the strength to bury the dead. Many mothers abandoned their children in marketplaces, hoping some benefactor would feed them. Hundreds of younger people moved elsewhere to work on groundnut plantations in Gambia and Senegal. Families drove their cattle southward to sell them for gold, establishing a pattern of long-distance trade that persists to this day.

The 1914 famine was the first major challenge faced by British and French colonial administrators in their new Sahelian colonies. A handful of civil servants collected taxes and preserved imperial rule over an enormous area with only a handful of employees and minimal budgets. The Sahel was the obscurest of obscure postings at a time when much of the world was governed by almost forgotten commissioners, governors, and residents far removed from London and Paris. A famine in this part of the world did not cause a ripple of concern in a Europe preoccupied with a bloody world war. When the famine came, a colonial officer could do little except sit and observe the suffering around him. The British resident in Kano, Nigeria, reflected a widespread attitude: "Yes, the mortality was considerable but I hope not so great as the natives allege—we had no remedy at the time and therefore as little was said about it as possible."[2] A scattering of government notebooks, tax records, and tour reports tell a tragic tale. In Nigeria's western Bornu region, ten thousand Fulani had eighty-eight thousand head of cattle in 1913. A year later only fifty-five hundred people remained with a mere twenty-six thousand head. These figures compare well with the drought of 1968, when cattle losses exceeded 80 percent in the lower rainfall areas closer to the desert and between 30 and 60 percent in slightly better watered areas farther south. One administrator's report from Niger in 1913 spoke of "an important exodus to more favorable regions. A great number of cattle have died.... Animal mortality: cattle 1/3, sheep and goats 1/2,

and camels negligible." An official collecting taxes in central Niger reported: "I have walked through 23 villages during this tour.... Last year these villages had a population of 13,495 taxable inhabitants. 3,354 persons have died during the famine."[3] Tax records reveal a 44 percent population decrease in one area of the country between 1910 and 1914. Another region reported a loss of 44,235 tax-paying adults out of a total of 57,626 in August and September 1914. Eventually, at least 80,000 people died in central Niger alone.

The cycles of wetter and drier conditions persisted. Another, less intense drought came in the 1940s. The 1950s and early 1960s saw greater rainfall. By this time every West African country in the Sahel had experienced sharp population growth caused by improved medical care, by a long-term campaign of digging artesian wells, and, above all, by the suppression of debilitating cattle diseases like rinderpest. Fifteen years of good rainfall led naive government planners to rash undertakings. They offered incentives to subsistence farmers to move into drier areas. Many of them were cattle herders who had become cultivators. Dozens of communities moved northward into marginal lands where grazing grass had now sprouted. Carefully rotated livestock could flourish here in good rainfall years, but sustained agriculture without large-scale irrigation was another matter.

As farmers moved in, the nomadic cattle herders shifted even farther north, right to the frontiers of the desert. The nomads were trapped between the Sahara and a rapidly growing farming population, which, in turn, was stripping the natural vegetation off land that could support farming only for short periods of better rainfall. Governments and international agencies both financed well-digging programs, which provided ample water at the local level year-round for large cattle herds. Between 1960 and 1971, the Sahel's cattle population rose to between eighteen million and twenty-five million. According to the World Bank, the optimum is fifteen million.

Then, with the inevitability of a Greek tragedy, the rains failed. Drought first took hold in the north near the desert

margins, then moved southward in subsequent years. By 1968 rainfall in the more marginal areas was less than half that of the 1950s as the drought extended well beyond the Sahel. The dry cycle persisted well into the 1980s, making the twentieth century one of the driest in the past one thousand years.

This time nobody died of thirst, for they could drink from the deep wells. But these same water supplies did not nourish the sparse natural vegetation. The Swedish International Development Agency, studying cattle mortality in the early 1970s, found that most beasts died not of thirst but of hunger, because their forage was gone. Thousands of cows clustered around the wells, then staggered away from the water with bloated stomachs. They would struggle to free themselves from the clinging mud and often keel over from exhaustion. Each well became the center of a little desert of its own, stripped of its vegetation by thousands of cattle converging on the water source from hundreds of kilometers around.

The herders, with their simple technology, had always maintained their herds in a finely tuned balance between natural water supplies and drought-resistant vegetation. Now the balance was gone.

The herders had too many cattle for the land. Overgrazing stripped away the deep-rooted, two-meter-tall perennial grasses that had fed the herds for centuries. Plants with shallower roots replaced them, then gave way to coarse annual grasses. When heavy grazing removed these in turn, next came leguminous plants that dried quickly. Finally, the herds pulverized the bare soil into fine particles that were blown by desert winds to the foot of slopes, where they dried into a hard cement. As the cattle ate the landscape, their owners felled every tree around for firewood. If this was not enough, encroaching farmers set fires to clear the land and killed off at least half the range grass each year.

Within a few years, grazing lands had become desert. At the same time, a rising farming population in the south had taken up just about all the cultivable land. Earlier generations, with plenty of fields to go around, could let much of it lie fallow and regain its strength. By 1968 there was no land to spare, nor did the villagers have fertilizers. Thousands of hectares of farmland yielded ever sparser crops until their owners just walked away, leaving a dustbowl behind them. Thousands of farmers and herders had no option but to flee southward. They descended on villages and cities, many of them ending up in crowded refugee camps.

At the time, may experts believed the expansion of the desert was an inevitable result of natural climatic change. In fact, human activity had degraded the marginal lands in ways unknown in earlier times. Food production declined throughout the Sahel, except on irrigated lands, where governments grew cash crops like groundnuts and grain for export. The drive for export crops pushed groundnuts into areas where drought-resistant millet was once a staple for village farmers. The millet farmers moved onto marginal land, so even more people went hungry. Throughout the crisis, West African governments still exported food while tens of thousands of their citizens subsisted on meager diets from humanitarian aid programs.

This particular drought cycle was unusually persistent. The climatologist Jules Charney believes the drought was reinforced by what he calls "biogeographical feedback": changes in the Sahelian land surface caused by the human impact on the fragile ecosystem of the arid lands. Interestingly, the same drought did not persist in the Sahel's southern equivalent, the Kalahari, where there are no dense herder populations. Numerical models tend to support Charney's hypothesis. They show that changes in the Sahel's land surface could indeed prolong drought. These changes could include a reduction of surface temperature caused by the exposure of soils with a high albedo through stripping of vegetation, by a reduction in surface moisture, and by higher dust levels over the desert, all of which tend to reinforce arid conditions. All these circumstances can result when overuse combines with extreme dryness, as happened in the 1968–1972 drought.

When French newspapers ran stories on the Sahel drought in 1972, the world took notice. Readers saw graphic pictures of emaciated children suffering from malnutrition and arid landscapes stripped by overgrazing and ravaged by years of inadequate rainfall. The governments of Chad, Mali, Niger, and other Sahelian countries were embarrassed by their inability to feed their own populations. Still, foreign governments and United Nations food agencies adhered to a long-standing policy of not interfering in the domestic affairs of member nations. Private famine relief agencies did not have the resources to provide assistance on the scale needed. When food and other supplies did arrive, it was too late for many people. Between 1972 and 1974, 600,000 tons of grain came to the Sahel from the United States alone, but the relief came late, was often unpalatable, and was distributed with great difficulty. The famine cost to foreign governments and private relief agencies was near $100 million. Between 100,000 and 200,000 people perished along with about 1.2 million cattle. Thousands of hectares of marginal land suffered such severe soil erosion from overuse that they became useless for either farmers or herders. The drought could have been predicted, for centuries of experience showed that periods of ample rainfall were followed invariably by dry cycles. Nor was this drought particularly severe by historical standards. But thousands more people were affected.

What had changed was the much larger number of farmers and herders exploiting an already high-risk environment. The imbalance in the equation was the human one. The people in the affected areas lived by a fundamental tenet of the cattle herder. Wealth is cattle, and the more cattle you own the better. At worst, you will lose half your cattle in a drought, but more will survive than if you had not expanded your herds. Said one Fulani elder after the 1968 cataclysm: "Next time I will have two hundred [head]." He believed that one hundred would survive the next drought. However, the carrying capacity of the land is such that he would be lucky to have fifty survivors.

After 1973 the Sahel's farmers enjoyed somewhat better rains and obtained better crop yields. But drought conditions soon returned and endured until the mid-1980s. The 1982–1983 dry cycle, also coming in an El Niño year, was as intense as that of 1972. But international relief agencies had established themselves in the region during the earlier crisis. Severe food shortages developed across the Sahel, but famine gripped only parts of Chad, the Sudan, and Ethiopia, countries engaged in civil wars at the time. As always, war and social disorder aggravated hunger and humanitarian efforts. In 1998 the Dinka and other southern Sudanese people are suffering a major famine only because warring factions prevent adequate rations from reaching the needy.

Are the severe Sahel droughts of the late twentieth century aggravated by human activities? Do they result in part from overexploitation of the land, and in perhaps even larger part from humanly induced global warming? Although everyone agrees that higher Sahel populations are part of the problem, they differ widely on the effects of long- and short-term climatic change. One argument says that as the world gets warmer, arid areas like the Sahel and Kalahari will become even drier, while wet regions become even wetter, than they are today. Another school of thought hypothesizes that climatic zones will shift to make both wet and dry areas more arid. Rising populations and widespread environmental degradation make it hard for climatologists to develop reliable drought and rainfall forecasts.

The West African catastrophe was not caused by unusually severe drought or global warming. It resulted from uncontrolled population growth, careless and naive development planning that took no account of the lessons of history, and people making decisions about their environment in good faith for short-term advantage, without giving thought to the future. In the words of Randall Baker: "When the rains come in the Sahel, and the millet grows again, then the 'problem' will be considered over until next time."[4]

Western-style political and economic institutions have failed dismally in the Sahel. Over the past century they have brought repeated crises and famines, marginalized millions of people, and killed thousands. This failure points up the great achievement of traditional Sahelians in maintaining stable herder societies where modern economies cannot. For thousands of years the herders adapted successfully to their unpredictable and harsh environment. They maintained a detailed knowledge of grazing and water supplies over enormous areas, moved their herds constantly, and adjusted month by month to changing conditions. Their mobility, low population densities, and careful judgments gave them the ability to endure drought, the ravages of cattle disease, and constant uncertainties. The twentieth century and colonial rule brought longer life expectancies and better medical care, but rapid population growth and much larger herd counts followed in their train. The new regime also brought an economic system that fostered cash crops and imposed taxation to support cities and central government. When rainfall was slightly higher and cotton and groundnuts could be grown to feed the cash economy, the farmers and herders lost control of their own production and of their lives. Meanwhile, the same system pushed the herders and their growing herds into marginal areas, abolished their traditional grazing ranges, and made them dependent on the outside world for water and food. As Michael Glantz has aptly noted, "Drought follows the plow."[5]

The Sahel tragedy continues to unfold with dreadful predictability, a replay, on a different scale and in a different place, of the Maya collapse and the Anasazi

dispersals. But this time there is nowhere to go.

NOTES

The literature on the Sahel is enormous, frequently repetitive, and sometimes self-serving, so discerning even a partial consensus is a challenge. John Reader's *Africa: A Biography of the Continent* (New York: Alfred A. Knopf, 1998), is quite simply the best general book on Africa ever written and a wonderful starting point. Michael H. Glantz, ed., *Drought Follows the Plow* (Cambridge: Cambridge University Press, 1994), contains valuable essays on desertification and marginal lands around the world. The same author's edited *Desertification: Environmental Degradation in and Around Arid Lands* (Boulder, Colo.: Westview Press, 1977), focuses mainly on Africa. The National Research Council's *Environmental Change in the West African Sahel* (Washington, D.C., 1984), is an admirable summary for a wide scientific audience. Michael H. Glantz, ed., *The Politics of Natural Disaster* (New York: Praeger, 1974), covers the 1972 famine and its political ramifications, with essays on everything from climatic change to agricultural production and medical care. See also William A. Dando, *The Geography of Famine* (New York: V. H. Winton, 1980), and Ronaldo V. Garcia, *Drought and Man: The 1972 Case History* (Oxford: Pergamon Press, 1981). Robert W. Kates, *Drought Impact in the Sahelian-Sudanic Zone of West Africa: A Comparative Analysis of 1910–1915 and 1968–1974* (Worcester, Mass.: Clark University, 1981), is a much-quoted study. James L. A. Webb Jr., *Desert Frontier: Ecological Change Along the Western Sahel, 1600–1850* (Madison: University of Wisconsin Press, 1995), contains valuable historical background. Earl Scott, ed., *Life Before the Drought* (Boston: Allen and Unwin, 1984), is useful in examining the impact of colonial

governance. J. D. Fage, ed., *The Cambridge History of Africa, vol. 2, c. 500 B.C.–A.D. 1050* (Cambridge: Cambridge University Press, 1978), is a widely available historical work. See also Roland Oliver, *The African Experience* (London: Weidenfeld and Nicholson, 1991).

1. Rinderpest is a contagious viral disease that is almost invariably fatal to cattle. The disease existed in classical times and ravaged Europe and Southwest Asia periodically from a reservoir of infection on the central Asian steppes. The Italian army imported infected cattle from India, Aden, and south Russia into Ethiopia in 1889 to feed their soldiers at Massawa. A fast-moving and virulent rinderpest epidemic swept across the Sahel and the rest of tropical Africa, killing millions of cattle, sheep, and goats, as well as many game populations. Rinderpest wiped out much of Africa's wealth on the hoof almost overnight. Many Fulani wandered distraught, calling imaginary cattle, or committed suicide. In East Africa, the Maasai lost two-thirds of their cattle. Many herders turned to agriculture for the first time but were too weak from hunger to plant and harvest crops.

2. Robert W. Kates, *Drought Impact in the Sahelian-Sudanic Zone of West Africa: A Comparative Analysis of 1910–1915 and 1968–1974* (Worcester, Mass.: Clark University, 1981), 110.

3. Ibid.

4. Randall Baker, "Information, Technology Transfer, and Nomadic Pastoral Societies," quoted in Michael Glantz, "Nine Fallacies of Natural Disaster: The Case of the Sahel," in Michael H. Glantz, ed., *The Politics of Natural Disaster* (New York: Praeger, 1974), 3–24.

5. Michael H. Glantz, ed., *Drought Follows the Plow* (Cambridge: Cambridge University Press, 1994).

The Price of Progress

John Bodley

In aiming at progress... you must let no one suffer by too drastic a measure, nor pay too high a price in upheaval and devastation, for your innovation.

Maunier, 1949: 725

UNTIL RECENTLY, GOVERNMENT planners have always considered economic development and progress beneficial goals that all societies should want to strive toward. The social advantage of progress—as defined in terms of increased incomes, higher standards of living, greater security, and better health—are thought to be positive, *universal* goods, to be obtained at any price. Although one may argue that tribal peoples must sacrifice their traditional cultures to obtain these benefits, government planners generally feel that this is a small price to pay for such obvious advantages.

In earlier chapters [in *Victims of Progress*, 3rd ed.], evidence was presented to demonstrate that autonomous tribal peoples have not *chosen* progress to enjoy its advantages, but that governments have *pushed* progress upon them to obtain tribal resources, not primarily to share with the tribal peoples the benefits of progress. It has also been shown that the price of forcing progress on unwilling recipients has involved the deaths of millions of tribal people, as well as their loss of land, political sovereignty, and the right to follow their own life style. This chapter does not attempt to further summarize that aspect of the cost of progress, but instead analyzes the specific effects of the participation of tribal peoples in the world-market economy. In direct opposition to the usual interpretation, it is argued here that the benefits of progress are often both illusory and detrimental to tribal peoples

when they have not been allowed to control their own resources and define their relationship to the market economy.

PROGRESS AND THE QUALITY OF LIFE

One of the primary difficulties in assessing the benefits of progress and economic development for any culture is that of establishing a meaningful measure of both benefit and detriment. It is widely recognized that *standard of living*, which is the most frequently used measure of progress, is an intrinsically ethnocentric concept relying heavily upon indicators that lack universal cultural relevance. Such factors as GNP, per capita income, capital formation, employment rates, literacy, formal education, consumption of manufactured goods, number of doctors and hospital beds per thousand persons, and the amount of money spent on government welfare and health programs may be irrelevant measures of actual *quality* of life for autonomous or even semiautonomous tribal cultures. In its 1954 report, the Trust Territory government indicated that since the Micronesian population was still largely satisfying its own needs within a cashless subsistence economy, "Money income is not a significant measure of living standards, production, or well-being in this area" (TTR, 1953: 44). Unfortunately, within a short time the government began to rely on an enumeration of certain imported consumer goods as indicators of a higher standard of living in the islands, even though many tradition-oriented islanders felt that these new goods symbolized a lowering of the quality of life.

A more useful measure of the benefits of progress might be based on a formula

for evaluating cultures devised by Goldschmidt (1952: 135). According to these less ethnocentric criteria, the important question to ask is: Does progress or economic development increase or decrease a given culture's ability to satisfy the physical and psychological needs of its population, or its stability? This question is a far more direct measure of quality of life than are the standard economic correlates of development, and it is universally relevant. Specific indication of this *standard* of living could be found for any society in the nutritional status and general physical and mental health of its population, the incidence of crime and delinquency, the demographic structure, family stability, and the society's relationship to its natural resource base. A society with high rates of malnutrition and crime, and one degrading its natural environment to the extent of threatening its continued existence, might be described as at a lower standard of living than is another society where these problems did not exist.

Careful examination of the data, which compare, on these specific points, the former condition of self-sufficient tribal peoples with their condition following their incorporation into the world-market economy, leads to the conclusion that their standard of living is *lowered*, not raised, by economic progress—and often to a dramatic degree. This is perhaps the most outstanding and inescapable fact to emerge from the years of research that anthropologists have devoted to the study of culture change and modernization. Despite the best intentions of those who have promoted change and improvement, all too often the results have been poverty, longer working hours, and much greater physical exertion, poor health, social disorder, discontent, discrimination, overpopulation, and environmental deterioration—combined with the destruction of the traditional culture.

DISEASES OF DEVELOPMENT

Perhaps it would be useful for public health specialists to start talking about a new category of diseases.... Such diseases could be called the "diseases of development" and would consist of those pathological conditions which are based on the usually unanticipated consequences of the implementation of developmental schemes.

Hughes & Hunter, 1972: 93

Economic development increases the disease rate of affected peoples in at least three ways. First, to the extent that development is successful, it makes developed populations suddenly become vulnerable to all of the diseases suffered almost exclusively by "advanced" peoples. Among these are diabetes, obesity, hypertension, and a variety of circulatory problems. Second, development disturbs traditional environmental balances and may dramatically increase certain bacterial and parasite diseases. Finally, when development goals prove unattainable, an assortment of poverty diseases may appear in association with the crowded conditions of urban slums and the general breakdown in traditional socioeconomic systems.

Outstanding examples of the first situation can be seen in the Pacific, where some of the most successfully developed native peoples are found. In Micronesia, where development has progressed more rapidly than perhaps anywhere else, between 1958 and 1972 the population doubled, but the number of patients treated for heart disease in the local hospitals nearly tripled, mental disorder increased eightfold, and by 1972 hypertension and nutritional deficiencies began to make significant appearances for the first time (TTR, 1959, 1973, statistical tables).

Although some critics argue that the Micronesian figures simply represent better health monitoring due to economic progress, rigorously controlled data from Polynesia show a similar trend. The progressive acquisition of modern degenerative diseases was documented by an eight-member team of New Zealand medical specialists, anthropologists, and nutritionists, whose research was funded by the Medical Research Council of New Zealand and the World Health Organization. These researchers investigated the health status of a genetically related population at various points along a continuum of increasing cash income, modernizing diet, and urbanization. The extremes on this acculturation continuum were represented by the relatively traditional Pukapukans of the Cook Islands and the essentially Europeanized New Zealand Maori, while the busily developing Rarotongans, also of the Cook Islands, occupied the intermediate position. In 1971, after eight years of work, the team's preliminary findings were summarized by Dr. Ian Prior, cardiologist and leader of the research, as follows:

We are beginning to observe that the more an islander takes on the ways of the West, the more prone he is to succumb to our degenerative diseases. In fact, it does not seem too much to say our evidence now shows that the farther the Pacific natives move from the quiet, carefree life of their ancestors, the closer they come to gout, diabetes, atherosclerosis, obesity, and hypertension.

Prior, 1971: 2

In Pukapuka, where progress was limited by the island's small size and its isolated location some 480 kilometers from the nearest port, the annual per capita income was only about thirty-six dollars and the economy remained essentially at a subsistence level. Resources were limited and the area was visited by trading ships only three or four times a year; thus, there was little opportunity for intensive economic development. Predictably, the population of Pukapuka was characterized by relatively low levels of imported sugar and salt intake, and a presumably related low level of heart disease, high blood pressure, and diabetes. In Rarotonga, where economic success was introducing town life, imported food, and motorcycles, sugar and salt intakes nearly tripled, high blood pressure increased approximately ninefold, diabetes two- to threefold, and heart disease doubled for men and more than quadrupled for women, while the number of grossly obese women increased more than tenfold. Among the New Zealand Maori, sugar intake was nearly eight times that of the Pukapukans, gout in men was nearly double its rate on Pukapuka, and diabetes in men was more than fivefold higher, while heart disease in women had increased more than sixfold. The Maori were, in fact, dying of "European" diseases at a greater rate than was the average New Zealand European.

Government development policies designed to bring about changes in local hydrology, vegetation, and settlement patterns and to increase population mobility, and even programs aimed at reducing certain diseases, have frequently led to dramatic increases in disease rates because of the unforeseen effects of disturbing the preexisting order. Hughes and Hunter (1972) published an excellent survey of cases in which development led directly to increased disease rates in Africa. They concluded that hasty development intervention in relatively balanced local cultures and environments resulted in "a drastic deterioration in the social and economic conditions of life."

Traditional populations in general have presumably learned to live with the endemic pathogens of their environments, and in some cases they have evolved genetic adaptations to specific diseases, such as the sickle-cell trait, which provided an immunity to malaria. Unfortunately, however, outside intervention has entirely changed this picture. In the late 1960s, sleeping sickness suddenly increased in many areas of Africa and even spread to areas where it did not formerly occur, due to the building of new roads and migratory labor, both of which caused increased population movement. Large-scale relocation schemes, such as the Zande Scheme, had disastrous results when natives were moved from their traditional disease-free refuges into infected areas. Dams and irrigation developments inadvertently created ideal conditions for the rapid proliferation of snails carrying schistosomiasis (a liver fluke disease), and major epidemics suddenly occurred in areas where this disease had never before been a problem. DDT spraying programs have been temporarily successful in controlling malaria, but there is often a rebound effect that increases the problem when spraying is discontinued, and the malarial mosquitoes are continually evolving resistant strains.

Urbanization is one of the prime measures of development, but it is a mixed blessing for most former tribal peoples. Urban health standards are abysmally poor and generally worse than in rural areas for the detribalized individuals who have crowded into the towns and cities throughout Africa, Asia, and Latin America seeking wage employment out of new economic necessity. Infectious diseases related to crowding and poor sanitation are rampant in urban centers, while greatly increased stress and poor nutrition aggravate a variety of other health problems. Malnutrition and other diet-related conditions are, in fact, one of the characteristic hazards of progress faced by tribal peoples and are discussed in the following sections.

The Hazards of Dietary Change

The traditional diets of tribal peoples are admirably adapted to their nutritional needs and available food resources. Even though these diets may seem bizarre, absurd, and unpalatable to outsiders, they are unlikely to be improved by drastic modifications. Given the delicate balances and complexities involved in any subsistence system, change always involves risks, but for tribal people the effects of dietary change have been catastrophic.

Under normal conditions, food habits are remarkably resistant to change, and indeed people are unlikely to abandon their traditional diets voluntarily in favor of dependence on difficult-to-obtain exotic imports. In some cases it is true that imported foods may be identified with powerful outsiders and are therefore sought as symbols of greater prestige.

This may lead to such absurdities as Amazonian Indians choosing to consume imported canned tunafish when abundant high-quality fish is available in their own rivers. Another example of this situation occurs in tribes where mothers prefer to feed their infants expensive nutritionally inadequate canned milk from unsanitary, but *high status*, baby bottles. The high status of these items is often promoted by clever traders and clever advertising campaigns.

Aside from these apparently voluntary changes, it appears that more often dietary changes are forced upon unwilling tribal peoples by circumstances beyond their control. In some areas, new food crops have been introduced by government decree, or as a consequence of forced relocation or other policies designed to end hunting, pastoralism, or shifting cultivation. Food habits have also been modified by massive disruption of the natural environment by outsiders—as when sheepherders transformed the Australian Aborigines' foraging territory or when European invaders destroyed the bison herds that were the primary element in the Plains Indians' subsistence patterns. Perhaps the most frequent cause of diet change occurs when formerly self-sufficient peoples find that wage labor, cash cropping, and other economic development activities that feed tribal resources into the world-market economy must inevitably divert time and energy away from the production of subsistence foods. Many developing peoples suddenly discover that, like it or not, they are unable to secure traditional foods and must spend their newly acquired cash on costly, and often nutritionally inferior, manufactured foods.

Overall, the available data seem to indicate that the dietary changes that are linked to involvement in the world-market economy have tended to *lower* rather than raise the nutritional levels of the affected tribal peoples. Specifically, the vitamin, mineral, and protein components of their diets are often drastically reduced and replaced by enormous increases in starch and carbohydrates, often in the form of white flour and refined sugar.

Any deterioration in the quality of a given population's diet is almost certain

to be reflected in an increase in deficiency diseases and a general decline in health status. Indeed, as tribal peoples have shifted to a diet based on imported manufactured or processed foods, there has been a dramatic rise in malnutrition, a massive increase in dental problems, and a variety of other nutritional-related disorders. Nutritional physiology is so complex that even well-meaning dietary changes have had tragic consequences. In many areas of Southeast Asia, government-sponsored protein supplementation programs supplying milk to protein-deficient populations caused unexpected health problems and increased mortality. Officials failed to anticipate that in cultures where adults do not normally drink milk, the enzymes needed to digest it are no longer produced and milk *intolerance* results (Davis & Bolin, 1972). In Brazil, a similar milk distribution program caused an epidemic of permanent blindness by aggravating a preexisting vitamin A deficiency (Bunce, 1972).

Teeth and Progress

There is nothing new in the observation that savages, or peoples living under primitive conditions, have, in general, excellent teeth.... Nor is it news that most civilized populations possess wretched teeth which begin to decay almost before they have erupted completely, and that dental caries is likely to be accompanied by periodontal disease with further reaching complications.

Hooton, 1945: xviii

Anthropologists have long recognized that undisturbed tribal peoples are often in excellent physical condition. And it has often been noted specifically that dental caries and the other dental abnormalities that plague industrialized societies are absent or rare among tribal peoples who have retained their traditional diets. The fact that tribal food habits may contribute to the development of sound teeth, whereas modernized diets may do just the opposite, was illustrated as long ago as 1894 in an article in the *Journal of the Royal Anthropological Institute* that described the results of a comparison between the teeth of ten Sioux Indians were examined when they came to London as members of Buffalo Bill's Wild West Show and were found to be completely free of caries and in possession of all their teeth, even though half of the group were over thirty-nine years of age. Londoners' teeth were conspicuous for both their caries and their steady reduction in number with advancing age. The difference was attributed primarily to the wear and polishing caused by the traditional Indian diet of coarse food and the fact that they chewed their food longer, encouraged by the absence of tableware.

One of the most remarkable studies of the dental conditions of tribal peoples and the impact of dietary change was conducted in the 1930s by Weston Price (1945), an American dentist who was interested in determining what caused normal, healthy teeth. Between 1931 and 1936, Price systematically explored tribal areas throughout the world to locate and examine the most isolated peoples who were still living on traditional foods. His fieldwork covered Alaska, the Canadian Yukon, Hudson Bay, Vancouver Island, Florida, the Andes, the Amazon, Samoa, Tahiti, New Zealand, Australia, New Caledonia, Fiji, the Torres Strait, East Africa, and the Nile. The study demonstrated both the superior quality of aboriginal dentition and the devastation that occurs as modern diets are adopted. In nearly every area where traditional foods were still being eaten, Price found perfect teeth with normal dental arches and virtually no decay, whereas caries and abnormalities increased steadily as new diets were adopted. In many cases the change was sudden and striking. Among Eskimo groups subsisting entirely on traditional food he found caries totally absent, whereas in groups eating a considerable quantity of store-bought food approximately 20 percent of their teeth were decayed. This figure rose to more than 30 percent with Eskimo groups subsisting almost exclusively on purchased or government-supplied food, and reached an incredible 48 percent among the Vancouver Island Indians. Unfortunately for many of these people, modern dental treatment did not accompany the new

food, and their suffering was appalling. The loss of teeth was, of course, bad enough in itself, and it certainly undermined the population's resistance to many new diseases, including tuberculosis. But new foods were also accompanied by crowded, misplaced teeth, gum diseases, distortion of the face, and pinching of the nasal cavity. Abnormalities in the dental arch appeared in the new generation following the change in diet, while caries appeared almost immediately even in adults.

Price reported that in many areas the affected peoples were conscious of their own physical deterioration. At a mission school in Africa, the principal asked him to explain to the native schoolchildren why they were not physically as strong as children who had had no contact with schools. On an island in the Torres Strait the natives knew exactly what was causing their problems and resisted—almost to the point of bloodshed—government efforts to establish a store that would make imported food available. The government prevailed, however, and Price was able to establish a relationship between the length of time the government store had been established and the increasing incidence of caries among a population that showed an almost 100 percent immunity to them before the store had been opened.

In New Zealand, the Maori, who in their aboriginal state are often considered to have been among the healthiest, most perfectly developed of people, were found to have "advanced" the furthest. According to Price:

Their modernization was demonstrated not only by the high incidence of dental caries but also by the fact that 90 percent of the adults and 100 percent of the children had abnormalities of the dental arches.

Price, 1945: 206

Malnutrition

Malnutrition, particularly in the form of protein deficiency, has become a critical problem for tribal peoples who must adopt new economic patterns. Population pressures, cash cropping, and gov-

ernment programs all have tended to encourage the replacement of traditional crops and other food sources that were rich in protein with substitutes, high in calories but low in protein. In Africa, for example, protein-rich staples such as millet and sorghum are being replaced systematically by high-yielding manioc and plantains, which have insignificant amounts of protein. The problem is increased for cash croppers and wage laborers whose earnings are too low and unpredictable to allow purchase of adequate amounts of protein. In some rural areas, agricultural laborers have been forced systematically to deprive nonproductive members (principally children) of their households of their minimal nutritional requirements to satisfy the need of the productive members. This process has been documented in northeastern Brazil following the introduction of large-scale sisal plantations (Gross & Underwood, 1971). In urban centers the difficulties of obtaining nutritionally adequate diets are even more serious for tribal immigrants, because costs are higher and poor quality foods are more tempting.

One of the most tragic, and largely overlooked, aspects of chronic malnutrition is that it can lead to abnormally undersized brain development and apparently irreversible brain damage; it has been associated with various forms of mental impairment or retardation. Malnutrition has been linked clinically with mental retardation in both Africa and Latin America (see, for example, Mönckeberg, 1968), and this appears to be a worldwide phenomenon with serious implications (Montagu, 1972).

Optimistic supporters of progress will surely say that all of these new health problems are being overstressed and that the introduction of hospitals, clinics, and the other modern health institutions will overcome or at least compensate for all of these difficulties. However, it appears that uncontrolled population growth and economic impoverishment probably will keep most of these benefits out of reach for many tribal peoples, and the intervention of modern medicine has at least partly contributed to the problem in the first place.

The generalization that civilization frequently has a broad negative impact on tribal health has found broad empirical support (see especially Kroeger & Barbira-Freedman [1982] on Amazonia; Reinhard [1976] on the Arctic; and Wirsing [1985] globally), but these conclusions have not gone unchallenged. Some critics argue that tribal health was often poor before modernization, and they point specifically to tribals' low life expectancy and high infant mortality rates. Demographic statistics on tribal populations are often problematic because precise data are scarce, but they do show a less favorable profile than that enjoyed by many industrial societies. However, it should be remembered that our present life expectancy is a recent phenomenon that has been very costly in terms of medical research and technological advances. Furthermore, the benefits of our health system are not enjoyed equally by all members of our society. High infant mortality could be viewed as a relatively inexpensive and egalitarian tribal public health program that offered the reasonable expectation of a healthy and productive life for those surviving to age fifteen.

Some critics also suggest that certain tribal populations, such as the New Guinea highlanders, were "stunted" by nutritional deficiencies created by tribal culture and are "improved" by "acculturation" and cash cropping (Dennett & Connell, 1988). Although this argument does suggest that the health question requires careful evaluation, it does not invalidate the empirical generalizations already established. Nutritional deficiencies undoubtedly occurred in densely populated zones in the central New Guinea highlands. However, the specific case cited above may not be widely representative of other tribal groups even in New Guinea, and it does not address the facts of outside intrusion or the inequities inherent in the contemporary development process.

ECOCIDE

"How is it," asked a herdsman... "how is it that these hills can no longer give pasture to my cattle? In my father's day they were green and cattle thrived there; today there is no grass and my cattle starve." As one looked one saw that what had once been a green hill had become a raw red rock.

Jones, 1934

Progress not only brings new threats to the health of tribal peoples, but it also imposes new strains on the ecosystems upon which they must depend for their ultimate survival. The introduction of new technology, increased consumption, lowered mortality, and the eradication of all traditional controls have combined to replace what for most tribal peoples was a relatively stable balance between population and natural resources, with a new system that is imbalanced. Economic development is forcing *ecocide* on peoples who were once careful stewards of their resources. There is already a trend toward widespread environmental deterioration in tribal areas, involving resource depletion, erosion, plant and animal extinction, and a disturbing series of other previously unforeseen changes.

After the initial depopulation suffered by most tribal peoples during their engulfment by frontiers of national expansion, most tribal populations began to experience rapid growth. Authorities generally attribute this growth to the introduction of modern medicine and new health measures and the termination of intertribal warfare, which lowered morality rates, as well as to new technology, which increased food production. Certainly all of these factors played a part, but merely lowering mortality rates would not have produced the rapid population growth that most tribal areas have experienced if traditional birth-spacing mechanisms had not been eliminated at the same time. Regardless of which factors were most important, it is clear that all of the natural and cultural checks on population growth have suddenly been pushed aside by culture change, while tribal lands have been steadily reduced and consumption levels have risen. In many tribal areas, environmental deterioration due to overuse of resources has set in, and in other areas such deterioration is imminent as resources continue to dwindle relative to the expanding population and increased

use. Of course, population expansion by tribal peoples may have positive political consequences, because where tribals can retain or regain their status as local majorities they may be in a more favorable position to defend their resources against intruders.

Swidden systems and pastoralism, both highly successful economic systems under traditional conditions, have proved particularly vulnerable to increased population pressures and outside efforts to raise productivity beyond its natural limits. Research in Amazonia demonstrates that population pressures and related resource depletion can be created indirectly by official policies that restrict swidden peoples to smaller territories. Resource depletion itself can then become a powerful means of forcing tribal people into participating in the world-market economy—thus leading to further resource depletion. For example, Bodley and Benson (1979) showed how the Shipibo Indians in Peru were forced to further deplete their forest resources by cash cropping in the forest area to replace the resources that had been destroyed earlier by the intensive cash cropping necessitated by the narrow confines of their reserve. In this case, certain species of palm trees that had provided critical housing materials were destroyed by forest clearing and had to be replaced by costly purchased materials. Research by Gross (1979) and other showed similar processes at work among four tribal groups in central Brazil and demonstrated that the degree of market involvement increases directly with increases in resource depletion.

The settling of nomadic herders and the removal of prior controls on herd size have often led to serious overgrazing and erosion problems where these had not previously occurred. There are indications that the desertification problem in the Sahel region of Africa was aggravated by programs designed to settle nomads. The first sign of imbalance in a swidden system appears when the planting cycles are shortened to the point that garden plots are reused before sufficient forest regrowth can occur. If reclearing and planting continue in the same area, the natural patterns of forest succession may be disturbed irreversibly and the soil can be impaired permanently. An extensive tract of tropical rainforest in the lower Amazon of Brazil was reduced to a semiarid desert in just fifty years through such a process (Ackermann, 1964). The soils in the Azande area are also now seriously threatened with laterization and other problems as a result of the government-promoted cotton development scheme (McNeil, 1972).

The dangers of overdevelopment and the vulnerability of local resource systems have long been recognized by both anthropologists and tribal peoples themselves. But the pressures for change have been overwhelming. In 1948 the Maya villagers of Chan Kom complained to Redfield (1962) about the shortening of their swidden cycles, which they correctly attributed to increasing population pressures. Redfield told them, however, that they had no choice but to go "forward with technology" (Redfield, 1962: 178). In Assam, swidden cycles were shortened from an average of twelve years to only two or three within just twenty years, and anthropologists warned that the limits of swiddening would soon be reached (Burling, 1963: 311–312). In the Pacific, anthropologists warned of population pressures on limited resources as early as the 1930s (Keesing, 1941: 64–65). These warnings seemed fully justified, considering the fact that the crowded Tikopians were prompted by population pressures on their tiny island to suggest that infanticide be legalized. The warnings have been dramatically reinforced since then by the doubling of Micronesia's population in just the fourteen years between 1958 and 1972, from 70,600 to 114,645, while consumption levels have soared. By 1985 Micronesia's population had reached 162,321.

The environmental hazards of economic development and rapid population growth have become generally recognized only since worldwide concerns over environmental issues began in the early 1970s. Unfortunately, there is as yet little indication that the leaders of the new developing nations are sufficiently concerned with environmental limitations. On the contrary, governments are forcing tribal peoples into a self-reinforcing spiral of population growth and intensified resource exploitation, which may be stopped only by environmental disaster or the total impoverishment of the tribals.

The reality of ecocide certainly focuses attention on the fundamental contrasts between tribal and industrial systems in their use of natural resources, who controls them, and how they are managed. Tribal peoples are victimized because they control resources that outsiders demand. The resources exist because tribals managed them conservatively. However, as with the issue of the health consequences of detribalization, some anthropologists minimize the adaptive achievements of tribal groups and seem unwilling to concede that ecocide might be a consequence of cultural change. Critics attack an exaggerated "noble savage" image of tribals living in perfect harmony with nature and having no visible impact on their surroundings. They then show that tribals do in fact modify the environment, and they conclude that there is no significant difference between how tribals and industrial societies treat their environments. For example, Charles Wagley declared that Brazilian Indians such as the Tapirape

are not "natural men." They have human vices just as we do…. They do not live "in tune" with nature any more than I do; in fact, they can often be as destructive of their environment, within their limitations, as some civilized men. The Tapirape are not innocent or childlike in any way.

Wagley, 1977: 302

Anthropologist Terry Rambo demonstrated that the Semang of the Malaysian rain forests have a measurable impact on their environment. In his monograph *Primitive Polluters*, Rambo (1985) reported that the Semang live in smoke-filled houses. They sneeze and spread germs, breathe, and thus emit carbon dioxide. They clear small gardens, contributing "particulate matter" to the air and disturbing the local climate because cleared areas proved measurably warmer and drier than the shady forest. Rambo concluded that his research "demonstrates the essential functional similarity of the environmental interactions of primitive and civilized societies" (1985: 78) in contrast to a "noble savage" view (Bodley, 1983) which, according to Rambo (1985: 2), mistakenly "claims that traditional peoples almost always live in essential harmony with their environment."

This is surely a false issue. To stress, as I do, that tribals tend to manage their resources for sustained yield within relatively self-sufficient subsistence economies is not to make them either innocent children or natural men. Nor is it to deny that tribals "disrupt" their environment and may never be in absolute "balance" with nature.

The ecocide issue is perhaps most dramatically illustrated by two sets of satellite photos taken over the Brazilian rain forests of Rôndonia (Allard & McIntyre, 1988: 780–781). Photos taken in 1973, when Rôndonia was still a tribal domain, show virtually unbroken rain forest. The 1987 satellite photos, taken after just fifteen years of highway construction and "development" by outsiders, show more than 20 percent of the forest destroyed. The surviving Indians were being concentrated by FUNAI (Brazil's national Indian foundation) into what would soon become mere islands of forest in a ravaged landscape. It is irrelevant to quibble about whether tribals are noble, childlike, or innocent, or about the precise meaning of balance with nature, carrying capacity, or adaptation, to recognize that for the past 200 years rapid environmental deterioration on an unprecedented global scale has followed the wresting of control of vast areas of the world from tribal groups by resource-hungry industrial societies.

DEPRIVATION AND DISCRIMINATION

Contact with European culture has given them a knowledge of great wealth, opportunity and privilege, but only very limited avenues by which to acquire these things.

Crocombe, 1968

Unwittingly, tribal peoples have had the burden of perpetual relative deprivation thrust upon them by acceptance—either by themselves or by the governments administering them—of the standards of socioeconomic progress set for them by industrial civilizations. By comparison with the material wealth of industrial societies, tribal societies become, by definition, impoverished. They are then forced to transform their cultures and work to achieve what many economists now acknowledge to be unattainable goals. Even though in many cases the modest GNP goals set by development planners for the developing nations during the "development decade" of the 1960s were often met, the results were hardly noticeable for most of the tribal people involved. Population growth, environmental limitations, inequitable distribution of wealth, and the continued rapid growth of the industrialized nations have all meant that both the absolute and the relative gap between the rich and poor in the world is steadily widening. The prospect that tribal peoples will actually be able to attain the levels of resource consumption to which they are being encouraged to aspire is remote indeed except for those few groups who have retained effective control over strategic mineral resources.

Tribal peoples feel deprivation not only when the economic goals they have been encouraged to seek fail to materialize, but also when they discover that they are powerless, second-class citizens who are discriminated against and exploited by the dominant society. At the same time, they are denied the satisfactions of their traditional cultures, because these have been sacrificed in the process of modernization. Under the impact of major economic change family life is disrupted, traditional social controls are often lost, and many indicators of social anomie such as alcoholism, crime, delinquency, suicide, emotional disorders, and despair may increase. The inevitable frustration resulting from this continual deprivation finds expression in the cargo cults, revitalization movements, and a variety of other political and religious movements that have been widespread among tribal peoples following their disruption by industrial civilization.

A Pacific Haze:
Alcohol and Drugs in Oceania

Mac Marshall
University of Iowa

All over the world people eat, drink, smoke, or blow substances up their noses in the perennial quest to alter and expand human consciousness. Most of these substances come from psychoactive plants native to different regions—coca, tobacco, and peyote, in the New World; khat, coffee, and marijuana in North Africa and the Middle East; betel and opium in Asia. Some people use hallucinogens from mushrooms or tree bark; others consume more exotic drugs. Produced by fermentation, brewing, or distillation of a remarkable variety of raw materials—ranging from fruits and grains to milk and honey—traditional alcoholic beverages were found almost everywhere before the Age of Exploration.

As European explorers trekked and sailed about the globe between 1500 and 1900, they carried many of these traditional drugs back to their homelands. Different exotic drugs became popular at different times in Europe as the explorers shared their experiences. In this manner, tea, tobacco, coffee, marijuana, and opium gained avid followers in European countries. Today, this worldwide process of drug diffusion continues at a rapid pace, with changes in attitudes toward different drugs and the introduction of new laws governing their use varying accordingly.

Oceanic peoples were no exception to the widespread quest to expand the human mind. From ancient times they used drugs to defuse tense interpersonal or intergroup relations, relax socially, and commune with the spirit world. Betel and kava were far and away the most common traditional drugs used in the Pacific Islands. The geographical distribution of these two drugs was uneven across the islands, and, in a few places (for example, Chuuk [Truk]), no drugs were used at all before the arrival of foreigners. Kava and betel were not only differentially distributed geographically, but they were also differently distributed socially. Every society had rules governing who might take them (and under what circumstances) that limited their consumption, often only to adult men.

In the four-and-a-half centuries since foreign exploration of the Pacific world began, the islanders have been introduced to several new drugs, most notably alcoholic beverages, tobacco, and marijuana. This chapter discusses substance use in the contemporary Pacific Islands by examining the history and patterns of use of the five major drugs found in the islands today: alcohol, betel, kava, marijuana, and tobacco. To the extent that reliable information exists, such recently introduced drugs as cocaine and heroin are also discussed. The primary concern of the chapter is with the negative social, economic, and health consequences that result from consumption of alcohol, tobacco, and marijuana in the contemporary Pacific Islands.

BETEL AND KAVA

"Betel" is a convenient linguistic gloss for a preparation consisting of at least three distinct substances, two of which are pharmacologically active: the nut of the *Areca catechu* palm, the leaves, stems, or catkins of the *Piper betle* vine, and slaked lime from ground seashells or coral. These substances usually are combined into a quid and chewed. In some societies, people swallow the resultant profuse saliva, while in others they spit out the blood red juice. Kava is drunk as a water-based infusion made from the pounded, grated, or chewed root of a shrub, *Piper methysticum*. Whereas betel ingredients can easily be carried on the person and quickly prepared, kava makings are not as portable, and its preparation calls for a more involved procedure. Betel is often chewed individually with little or no ceremony; kava is usually drunk communally, and frequently accompanied by elaborate ceremonial procedures.

Betel chewing appears to have originated long ago in Island Southeast Asia and to have spread into the islands of the Western Pacific from there. While betel use is widespread in Melanesia (including the New Guinea Highlands where it has recently been introduced), it is absent from the Polynesian Triangle, and it is found only on the westernmost Micronesian islands of Palau, Yap, and the Marianas (Marshall 1987a).

In most parts of the Pacific Islands where betel is chewed, its use occupies a social position akin to coffee or tea drinking in Western societies. For example, Iamo (1987) writes that betel is chewed to stimulate social activity, suppress boredom, enhance work, and increase personal enjoyment among the Keakalo people of the south coast of Papua New Guinea. Similarly, Lepowsky (1982) comments that for the people of Vanatinai Island in Papua New Guinea, shared betel symbolizes friendly and peaceful social relations. Iamo notes that betel consumption "is rampant among children, young people, and adults" in Keakalo; that is, it has few social constraints on its use, except in times of scarcity (1987:146). Similarly, "Vanatinai people chew betel many times a day," and they also begin chewing betel early in childhood: "By the age of eight to ten, boys and girls chew whenever they can find the ingredients" (Lepowsky 1982:335).

In those parts of Papua New Guinea where the betel ingredients can be produced in abundance, such as Keakalo and Vanatinai, they figure importantly as items of exchange or for sale as "exports" to surrounding peoples. The enterprising Biwat of East Sepik Province are remarkable in this regard. They trade *Areca* nut, *Piper betle*, and locally grown tobacco with other peoples in the vicinity, carry these products by canoe to the regional market town of Angoram (98 miles away), and occasionally even charter a small airplane to sell as far away as Mount Hagen in the Western Highlands Province (Watson 1987).

Traditionally, kava was drunk only in Oceania, the world region to which the plant appears native. Kava drinking occurred throughout the high islands of Polynesia (except Easter Island, New Zealand, and Rapa), on the two easternmost high islands of Micronesia (Pohnpei and Kosrae), and in various parts of Melanesia, particularly Fiji, Vanuatu, and New Guinea proper. Kava and betel were often in complementary distribution, although there were some societies where both were routinely consumed.

Whereas betel is chewed by males and females, old and young, kava is different. In most Pacific Islands societies, at least traditionally, kava drinking was restricted to men, and often to "fully adult" or high-status men. Although its consumption was thus restricted, young,

uninitiated or untitled men, or young women, usually prepared it. These distinctions were notably marked in the elaborate kava ceremonies of Fiji, Tonga, and Samoa. Wherever it was used, however, kava played important parts in pre-Christian religion, political deliberations, ethnomedical systems, and general quiet social interaction among a community's adult men.

On the island of Tanna, Vanuatu, for example, Lindstrom (1987) argues that getting drunk on and exchanging kava links man to man, separates man from woman, establishes a contextual interpersonal equality among men, and determines and maintains relations of inequality between men and women. Kava is drunk every evening on Tanna at a special kava-drinking ground, separated from the village, and from which women and girls are excluded. Lindstrom argues that kava (which is grown by women) is both itself an important exchange item and symbolically represents male appropriation and control over women and their productive and reproductive capacities. Tannese men fear that women intoxicated on kava would become "crazed" and usurp men's control over them, become sexually wanton, and cease to cook. Lindstrom concludes, "Gender asymmetry in Tannese drunken practice maintains and reproduces social relations of production and exchange" (1987:116).

Among the Gebusi of Papua New Guinea's Western Province, the men of a longhouse community force their male visitors to drink several bowls of kava in rapid succession, usually to the point of nausea. This is done to prevent the chief antagonists at ritual fights or funeral feasts "from disputing or taking retaliatory action against their hosts during a particularly tense moment in the proceedings" (Knauft 1987:85). Forced smoking of home-grown tobacco is used in an analogous manner "to forestall escalation of hostilities" among a people for whom homicide tied to sorcery accusations is a leading cause of male mortality. As on Tanna, Gebusi women never drink kava. Both peoples link kava to sexuality: Lindstrom (1987:112–113) describes a Tannese-origin myth of kava that he calls "kava as dildo"; Knauft

(1987:85–88) notes that kava often serves as a metaphor for semen in jokes about heterosexual relations or the ritual homosexuality practiced by the Gebusi.

As is typically the case in human affairs, these long-known and highly valued drug substances were deeply rooted in cultural traditions and patterns of social interaction. Pacific Islands peoples had developed culturally controlled ways of using betel and kava that usually precluded abuse.[1] Users also were unlikely to develop problems because of the relatively benign physiological effects of these two substances and because neither drug by itself seems to produce serious harmful disease states when consumed in a traditional manner.

Kava drinking leads to a variety of physical effects, perhaps the most pronounced of which are analgesia, muscle relaxation, and a sense of quiet well-being. In addition to its ceremonial and recreational uses, kava is a common drug in Oceanic ethnomedicine, and kava extracts also are employed in Western biomedicine. Of the various drugs discovered by human beings around the world, kava seems to be one of the least problematic. Its physiological effects induce a state of peaceful contemplation and euphoria, with the mental faculties left clear, and it produces no serious pathology unless taken (as by some Australian Aborigines since 1980) at doses far in excess of those consumed by Pacific Islanders. The most prominent effects of prolonged heavy kava consumption among Oceanic peoples are a dry scaly skin, bloodshot eyes, possible constipation and intestinal obstruction, and occasional weight loss (Lemert 1967). Even excessive kava use does not produce withdrawal symptoms, and all of the above conditions are reversible if drinking is discontinued.

The situation with betel is somewhat more complex. The main physical effect obtained by betel chewers is central nervous system stimulation and arousal producing a sense of general well-being (Burton-Bradley 1980). Arecoline, the primary active ingredient in betel, also stimulates various glands, leading to profuse sweating and salivation, among other things. Beginners typically experience such unpleasant symptoms as

"Driving Under the Influence" Accident, Weno Island, Chuuk, Federated States of Micronesia (1985).

nausea, diarrhea, and dizziness, and prolonged use leads to physiological addiction. There is some preliminary experimental evidence that arecoline enhances memory and learning, and it is being explored as a possible medicine for patients suffering from Alzheimer's disease (Gilbert 1986).

Considerable controversy surrounds the health risks of betel chewing, particularly as regards its possible role in the development of oral cancer (MacLennan et al. 1985). This debate has been confounded by the fact that many betel chewers in Southeast and South Asia (where most of the clinical data have been collected) add other ingredients to the betel chew, most commonly, and notably, tobacco. A summary of the epidemiological evidence available to date leads to the conclusion that chewing betel using traditional ingredients without the addition of tobacco probably does not carry any significant risk for oral cancer (Gupta et al. 1982).[2] Occasionally, a betel chewer develops what Burton-Bradley (1966) calls "betel nut psychosis," following a period of abstinence and in response to a heavy dose of the drug. This acute reversible toxic psychosis is characterized by delusions and hallucinations in predisposed individuals, but it must be emphasized that its occurrence is rare. There is thus no conclusive evidence that regular betel chewing without the addition of tobacco results in physical or mental health problems for most people. Like kava, betel

appears to produce a relatively harmless "high."

As usually taken in Oceania, not only do kava and betel consumption pose few—if any—health risks, but neither drug leads to intoxicated behavior that is socially disruptive (indeed, quite the contrary). The plants from which these substances are derived are locally grown and quite readily available, and the processes for making and taking these two traditional drugs do not require commercial manufacture. In the past twenty years, some cash marketing of both drugs has developed, but this is primarily by smallholders or local concerns, and neither substance is handled by multinational corporations. Thus, kava and betel do not have negative social and economic consequences for the Pacific Islands societies where they are used.

ALCOHOLIC BEVERAGES

Pacific Islanders, like most North American Indians, had no alcoholic beverages until Europeans brought them early in the contact period. Initially, most islanders found alcohol distasteful and spat it out, but eventually they acquired a fondness for what sometimes was called "white man's kava." During the late eighteenth and first half of the nineteenth century, whalers, beachcombers, missionaries, and traders arrived in the islands in growing numbers. Many of them were drinkers and provided models of drunken behavior for the islanders to

copy. Some of them established saloons in the port towns, and alcohol was widely used as an item of trade with the islanders. By at least the 1840s, missionaries to the islands, reflecting temperance politics in the United States and Great Britain, began to speak out forcefully against "the evils of drink" (Marshall and Marshall 1976).

As the European and American powers of the day consolidated colonial control over Oceania in the nineteenth century, they passed laws prohibiting islanders from consuming beverage alcohol. While such laws usually had strong missionary backing, they were also intended to maintain order, protect colonists from the possible "drunken depredations of savages," and serve what were deemed to be the islanders' own best interests. Despite prohibition, production of home brews continued in some areas, theft provided an occasional source of liquor, and the drinking of methylated spirits offered a potentially deadly alcohol alternative in some parts of the Pacific (Marshall 1988:579–582).

Colonially imposed prohibition laws remained in place until the 1950s and 1960s, when they were set aside one after another in the era of decolonization. Since then, the establishment of new Pacific nations has fostered a maze of legal regulations surrounding alcohol use, and it has also led to the encouragement of alcohol production and marketing. In many different parts of the Pacific Islands, problems have accompanied the relaxation of controls and the expansion of availability.

It is generally true around the world that more men drink alcoholic beverages than women, and that men drink greater quantities than women, but these gender differences are particularly pronounced in most of Oceania. In many of the islands, there are strong social pressures against women drinking, reinforced by church teachings, that effectively keep most women from even tasting alcoholic beverages. With a few exceptions, it is usually only Westernized women in the towns who drink on any sort of a regular basis. Boys below age fourteen or fifteen seldom, if ever, drink, but by the time they are in their late teens or early twenties, nearly all of them partake of alcohol. So much is this the case that in Chuuk (Truk) drinking and drunkenness is called "young men's work" (Marshall 1987b).

These gender differences have resulted in profoundly different attitudes toward alcohol by men and women that sometimes have resulted in outspoken social opposition by women to men's drinking and its attendant social problems (see Marshall and Marshall 1990). Weekend binge drinking by groups of young men—especially in towns—frequently leads to social disruption and confrontations that have been labeled "weekend warfare" in one Micronesian society (Marshall 1979).

For many Pacific Islanders, alcoholic beverages have come to symbolize "the good life" and active participation in a modern, sophisticated lifestyle. Beer is usually the beverage of choice in Oceania, and, in some places, it has been incorporated into ceremonial exchanges surrounding such events as bride price payments, weddings, and funerals. In the Papua New Guinea Highlands' Chuave area, beer is treated as an item of wealth and "has assumed a central role in inter- and intraclan prestations" (Warry 1982:84). Cartons of beer have been endowed with a number of social and symbolic qualities in common with pork, the most highly esteemed traditional valuable. For example, the success of a ceremony is judged, increasingly, by the amount of beer, as well as pork, available for display and distribution; beer in car-

tons has a known value and the twenty-four bottles are easily divisible; like pigs, the stacked cartons of beer (sometimes as many as 240!) are appropriate items for display; alcohol is a social facilitator in these sometimes tense feast situations; beer—like pork and other foodstuffs—is consumable; and, like pork, beer is used at feasts both as a tool to create relationships and as a weapon to slight rivals (Warry 1982).

The chief problems associated with alcohol use in Oceania are social ones, although it is difficult to divorce these from the interrelated public health and economic costs. Among the more prominent and widespread social problems are domestic strife, particularly wife beating; community fighting and disruption, often with attendant trauma and occasional fatalities; crime, and drunk-driving accidents.

In the post–World War II era, these alcohol-related problems have been a continuing concern of community-based and government agencies in Pacific Islands countries. For example, a seminar was held in 1977 on "Alcohol Problems with the Young People of Fiji" (Fiji National Youth Council 1977), and, in 1986, Catholic youth in the Highlands of Papua New Guinea rallied to oppose alcohol abuse (*The Times of Papua New Guinea 1986a*). Other examples of community-based concerns are church women's groups who championed a legal prohibition against alcohol on Weno, Chuuk (Moen Island, Truk) (Marshall and Marshall 1990), and an ecumenical Christian training center in Papua New Guinea (the Melanesian Institute) that has given voice to village peoples' concerns over abuse of alcohol for many years. Within a decade after it became legal for Papua New Guineans to drink, the government felt it necessary to sponsor an official Commission of Inquiry in 1971 to assess the widely perceived problems that had ensued. Less than ten years later, another investigation of alcohol use and abuse under national government auspices was launched in Papua New Guinea through its Institute for Applied Social and Economic Research (IASER). Such government commissions and groups of concerned citizens usually produce recommendations for

action; however, serious and effective alcohol control policies are rarely forthcoming.

Although they have received less attention in the literature, primarily because of the absence of adequate hospital records and autopsy reports for Pacific Islands countries, the physical and mental illnesses linked to either prolonged heavy ethanol intake or binge drinking appear to be considerable. Among these are alcoholic cirrhosis, cancers of the upper respiratory and upper digestive tracts, death from ethanol overdose, alcoholic psychoses, and suicide while under the influence of alcohol.

In recent years, researchers have focused on non-insulin-dependent diabetes mellitus (NIDDM), which has increased in urbanized and migrant Pacific Islands populations (for example, Baker et al. 1986; King et al. 1984). With changes from traditional diets to "modern" diets of refined foods and higher intakes of fats, sugar, sodium, and alcoholic beverages, some Micronesian and Polynesian populations have shown what is thought to be a hereditary susceptibility to NIDDM, which apparently is only expressed with a change from the traditional rural lifestyle. Urban and migrant islanders typically engage in less physical activity and have higher levels of obesity than their rural nonmigrant counterparts. Given that individuals with diabetes are more vulnerable to the hypoglycemic effects of alcohol because alcohol interferes with hepatic gluconeogenesis (Franz 1983:149; see also Madsen 1974:52–53), heavy drinking that may produce complications for diabetics poses an added health risk.

TOBACCO

Although the Spanish and Portuguese introduced tobacco into the East Indies from the New World in the late sixteenth and early seventeenth centuries, and although this new drug spread rather quickly to the island of New Guinea via traditional trade routes, *Nicotiana tabacum* did not reach most Pacific Islands until the nineteenth century. It became a basic item of trade and even served as a kind of currency during the heyday of European exploration and colonization of Oceania. The first German plantations on the north coast of New Guinea near Madang were tobacco plantations, and the crop continues to be grown commercially in Fiji and Papua New Guinea. In the 1800s, pipe and homemade cigar smoking were quite popular; today manufactured cigarettes dominate the market in most parts of the Pacific Islands. The prevalence of tobacco smoking by both men and women in Pacific Islands populations is much higher than in the developed countries of Australia, New Zealand, and the United States, and higher than in most developing nations elsewhere in the world (Marshall 1991). In some isolated rural parts of Oceania, nearly everyone in a community smokes—including children as young as eight or ten years of age.

With the decline in tobacco use in the developed nations of the West, the multinational corporations that control global production and marketing of this drug have shifted their emphasis to the huge and rapidly growing market in the Third World. Developing countries offer few restrictions to tobacco companies: most such countries have no maximum tar and nicotine levels, no laws restricting sales to minors, no advertising limits, no required health warnings, and no general public awareness of the serious health risks associated with smoking (Stebbins 1990). As a result, tobacco consumption has grown steadily in Third World countries, leading public health experts to predict and document the beginning of a major epidemic of diseases known to be linked to chronic tobacco use. During the 1980s, numerous studies have been published by health care professionals and other concerned individuals noting these alarming trends and calling for action. Studies documenting these problems exist for Africa, Latin America, and Asia, and researchers have begun to chronicle the same sad story for Oceania (Marshall 1991).

As with the upsurge in alcohol use and its aggressive marketing by multinational corporations in Pacific Islands countries, so it is, too, with the production and sale of commercial tobacco products, particularly cigarettes. Almost any store one enters in Oceania today displays tobacco advertisements promi-

nently inside and out, and has numerous tobacco products readily available for sale. Among the many ploys used to push their brands, the tobacco companies sponsor sweepstakes contests with large cash prizes which can be entered by writing one's name and address on an empty cigarette pack and dropping it into a special box for a drawing. Tobacco firms also routinely sponsor sporting events, with trophies and prizes in cash and in kind. In other promotions, those who present fifteen empty packs of the pertinent brands are given "free" T-shirts emblazoned with the cigarette brand name.

PHOTO BY M. MARSHALL

Cigarette advertisements on the outside of a store, Goroka, Eastern Highlands Province, Papua New Guinea (1980).

The association of tobacco smoking with serious cardiovascular and respiratory diseases—lung cancer, chronic bronchitis, and emphysema—is by now well known. These diseases are particularly linked to the smoking of flue-cured commercial cigarettes, which now have been readily available in Oceania for about thirty years. As the Pacific Islanders who have smoked such cigarettes for many years develop health problems, more suffer from these smoking-related illnesses (Marshall 1991). One New Zealand study shows that those Maori women who smoke heavily during pregnancy produce infants of a lower average birth weight than those of Europeans or other Pacific Islanders in New Zealand (Hay and Foster 1981). Another study shows Maori women to have a lung can-

cer rate that is among the world's highest (Stanhope and Prior 1982).

As yet, there have been few efforts to gain control over the smoking epidemic in Pacific Islands countries. In one, the Fiji Medical Association announced a campaign to ban cigarette advertising following a directive from the Fiji Ministry of Health to stop smoking in all patient areas in government hospitals (*Pacific Islands Monthly* 1986). But the most encouraging program has been mounted in Papua New Guinea. In the early 1980s, an antismoking council was established there by members of the medical profession (Smith 1983), and, following several years of public debate, Parliament passed the Tobacco Products (Health Control) Act in November 1987. This law mandates various controls on tobacco advertising, requires health warning labels on cigarette packs and cigarette advertisements, and provides the authority to declare various public places as nonsmoking areas. As of March 1990, these included all national and provincial government offices, the offices and buildings of all educational institutions (other than staff quarters), all hospitals, health centers, clinics and aid posts, cinemas and theatres, public motor vehicles (PMVs), and all domestic flights on scheduled airlines. While there are some enforcement problems, the Department of Health has mounted an aggressive antismoking campaign (tied to the anti-betel-chewing campaign), and this is likely to have a positive impact over the next few years.

Despite the encouraging signs in Papua New Guinea, public-health-oriented antismoking campaigns have met with relatively small success to date in the face of the large sums of money devoted to advertising by the tobacco multinationals. Much more effort is needed in community and public health education if this preventable epidemic is to be brought under control in Oceania.

MARIJUANA

Unlike the use of alcohol, betel, kava, and tobacco, marijuana smoking is uniformly illegal in Oceania. Nonetheless, the plant is now grown quite widely in the islands and has a substantial number

PHOTO BY M. MARSHALL

Wall Painting (by Robert Suine), Kuglame Taverne, Simbu Province, Papua New Guinea (1980).

of devotees. In part because its cultivation and use is against the law, fewer data are available on marijuana smoking than on the other four common Pacific drugs.

Native to central Asia, marijuana diffused to Oceania much more recently than alcohol or tobacco. While it doubtless was present in such places as Hawaii and New Zealand well before World War II, in other island areas like Micronesia or the New Guinea highlands, it appears to have been introduced only during the 1960s and 1970s.

While considerable controversy surrounds the long-term health effects of marijuana smoking, certain things are by now well known and give cause for concern. Marijuana induces an increased cardiovascular work load, thus posing a potential threat to individuals with hypertension and coronary atherosclerosis. Both of these health problems have been on the rise in Pacific Islands populations, especially in urban areas (Baker et al. 1986; Patrick et al. 1983; Salmond et al. 1985), and both can only be worsened by marijuana use.

Marijuana smoke is unfiltered and contains about 50 percent more cancer-causing hydrocarbons than tobacco smoke (Maugh 1982). Recent research has shown that "marijuana delivers more particulate matter to the smoker than to-bacco cigarettes and with a net four-times greater burden on the respiratory system" (Addiction Research Foundation 1989:3). This same work revealed significant structural changes in the lungs of marijuana smokers, with a higher rate among those who also smoked tobacco. These changes are associated with chronic obstructive lung disease and with lung cancer. Another study has found significant short-term memory impairment in cannabis-dependent individuals that lingers for at least six weeks after use of the drug is stopped (Schwartz et al. 1989). As was discussed above for tobacco, the limited amount of research that has been done shows respiratory illnesses to be major serious diseases in Oceania. Clearly, smoking marijuana will simply raise the incidence of health problems that were already significant in the Pacific Islands even before marijuana gained popularity.

In the Pacific Islands, as in the United States, marijuana growing is attractive because it yields a higher cash return per unit of time per unit of land than other agricultural crops. Even though marijuana is grown as a cash crop and often sold by the "joint," the plant is easy to grow, requires little attention, and thrives in most island environments. As a result, most marijuana consumed in the Pacific Islands, like betel and kava, is locally grown and not imported by drug cartels or multinationals. Even so, marijuana grown in the islands is sometimes exported to larger and more lucrative markets (Nero 1985). This has become the subject of major police concern in Papua New Guinea, where there are some indications that organized crime may be involved in the purchase of marijuana grown in the highlands to be sent overseas (for example, *Niugini Nius* 1990). It will be well nigh impossible to uproot marijuana from Oceania today, but much more could be done to educate islanders about the health risks associated with its use.

OTHER DRUGS

As of 1989, hard drugs such as cocaine and heroin have made little headway in Pacific Islands communities. The most dramatic example of a place where such penetration has begun is Palau, where heroin first showed up in the early 1970s (Nero 1985:20–23). By 1985, cocaine was being used in Palau as well, and, by then, a number of Palauan heroin addicts had been sent to Honolulu for detoxification and treatment (Polloi 1985).

Although the Palauan case is somewhat unusual for the Pacific Islands at present, there are increased reports of hard drugs being shipped *through* the islands from Asia for metropolitan markets in Australia, New Zealand, and North America. Clearly, given the ease of air travel and relatively lax security and customs checks, more hard drugs will appear in the islands in the coming years.

CONCLUSIONS

Oceania's traditional drugs—betel and kava—create few if any social problems and pose minimal health risks to users. Moreover, these drugs are locally produced, and even when they are sold in the market the profits remain in islanders' hands and enrich the local economy. From an economic perspective, the cropping and selling of marijuana in most of the Pacific Islands operates in much the same way: small growers cultivate the plant for their own use or to sell in local markets. The major differences between marijuana and betel and kava are that marijuana is illegal and that smoking marijuana poses significant health risks. Oceania's other two major drug substances are produced and distributed in a very different manner and pose much more serious social and public health problems.

Over the past decade, an accumulation of studies has shown that alcoholic beverage and tobacco multinational corporations have increasingly targeted developing countries as prime markets for their products (for example, Cavanaugh and Clairmonte 1985; Muller 1978; Stebbins 1990; Wickström 1979). This marketing involves aggressive advertising, often aimed especially at young people and women. Frequently, it takes the form of joint ventures with host governments, on the grounds that large profits can be shared (which ignores the significant health and social costs involved).

The multinationals also have become infamous for inducing governments (for example, the United States) to threaten trade embargoes against countries that balk at the unrestrained marketing of alcohol and tobacco products within their borders (*The Nation's Health* 1989).

The developing countries of Oceania have been subject to this "legal pushing" of harmful substances, even though their populations are small and transport poses certain logistical problems. Breweries, ultimately owned by huge overseas corporations, operate in French Polynesia, Western Samoa, Tonga, Fiji, Vanuatu, and Papua New Guinea, and there are distilled beverage producers in Fiji and Papua New Guinea.

For example, domestic production of hard liquor began in Papua New Guinea in 1985 by Fairdeal Liquors Pty. Ltd. Fairdeal imports raw materials (concentrates and ethanol) from its parent corporation based in Malaysia and from other overseas sources. The company then mixes and bottles both its own brands and selected internationally known brands on franchise (for example, Gilbey's gin, Jim Beam whiskey) in its factory in the Port Moresby suburb of Gordons. Initially, Fairdeal was able to market its own product ("Gold Cup") in small, clear plastic sachets for around 35 cents (U.S.) each. These were a marketing success but a social disaster because irresponsible storekeepers sold them to children as well as adults, and because many men drank them to excess. The ensuing public outcry led the Prime Minister to ask the company to withdraw the sachets from the market two months after they were introduced. Following the outcry from concerned citizens, especially in the highlands (*The Times of Papua New Guinea* 1986), Fairdeal briefly closed its Port Moresby factory in December 1986 because the national government also imposed a 1,200 percent increase in the import tax on the concentrate used to produce liquor (*The Times of Papua New Guinea* 1986). But even with this momentary setback, Fairdeal continues to market its own brands in bottles for half the price of comparable imports. This is possible because by bottling locally the company still avoids paying as much excise duty as that paid by importers of alcoholic beverages that are bottled abroad.

It was announced in mid-1989 that new breweries would be built in Papua New Guinea and Western Samoa (*Pacific Islands Monthly* 1989). The Papua New Guinea venture, which since has fallen through, was to be constructed at Kerowagi in Simbu Province, and represented a proposed joint venture among Danbrew Consult of Denmark and the five highlands provincial governments. At least two highlands provincial premiers had to be cajoled into committing their provinces to participation in this scheme, and the highly controversial project was opposed by women's organizations and church groups. Papua New Guinea's major brewery—South Pacific—itself a subsidiary of the Heineken Group, bought out its sole competitor (San Miguel, PNG) early in 1983. San Miguel (PNG) was a subsidiary of "the most successful conglomerate group in the Philippines," a group that held overseas interests in mining, brewing, fishing, finance, and development in nine different countries in Asia and Europe (Krinks 1987).

In 1978, War on Want published a slender volume entitled, *Tobacco and the Third World: Tomorrow's Epidemic?* Just over a decade later, the *question* in that book's title has been answered—a smoking epidemic has swept the Third World, and the Pacific Islands have not been immune to this global trend. While cigarettes and stick tobacco are locally produced in Papua New Guinea and Fiji by subsidiaries of the giant British Tobacco Company, the overwhelming majority of tobacco products sold in Oceania today are commercial cigarettes imported from the developed countries, principally Australia, New Zealand, and the United States. Promotional campaigns continue to have few, if any, restrictions placed upon them, and the costs of sweepstakes and raffle giveaways is small compared to the substantial profits to be earned once new consumers are "hooked."

A haze hangs over the Pacific Islands today, a result of widespread alcohol and tobacco abuse and of the smokescreens put up by multinationals to buy off politicians under the guise that production and marketing of these legal drugs contributes to economic development. In fact, the public health costs of alcohol and tobacco use and the social disruption surrounding alcohol abuse *undermine* economic and social development over the long run. If Pacific Islands governments do not develop more effective systems to prevent and control the aggressive marketing of alcohol and tobacco by multinationals, then the haze in the air and the glazed looks on the faces of island citizens will increase. The resultant social and health costs can only weaken Oceanic communities and make more difficult their dream of building prosperous, healthy, modern societies.

Acknowledgment: I am grateful to Linda A. Bennett for useful comments on an earlier version of this chapter.

NOTES

1. This statement remains true for Pacific Islanders; however, Australian Aborigines, to whom kava was introduced in the 1980s, and who consume it in quantities far in excess of those taken by Pacific Islanders, have developed such clinical side effects as weight loss, liver and kidney dysfunction, blood abnormalities, and possible pulmonary hypertension (Mathews et al. 1988; Riley and Mathews 1989).

2. Recently, in Papua New Guinea, and possibly elsewhere in the Pacific Islands, lime manufactured by commercial chemical firms has been substituted for lime produced in the traditional manner from ground seashells or coral. There is some evidence to suggest that the industrially manufactured lime is much more caustic than that traditionally used by Pacific betel chewers, and that this may increase the risk of oral cancer. Although controlled studies to demonstrate this have yet to be done, the Papua New Guinea Department of Health has mounted an active public health campaign advising people that if they chew betel, they run a risk of developing oral cancer.

A Plunge into the Present

Twenty-five years ago, the Ibatan lived in near total isolation from the world. Now they have running water, Christianity, satellite TV—and their own variation on the global divide between haves and have-nots.

By Ron Suskind

Ruben Dican adjusts the television, as everyone waits. A picture comes into focus. It's Bryant Gumbel. There's a shot of United Flight 175 ramming the south tower. Then it's run again. And again.

It is Sept. 12, and 22 men, women and children sit, rapt, at the end of the earth. They've never actually seen a skyscraper. Or a Bryant Gumbel. Or a plane, other than the tiny ones that infrequently alight on a grassy strip near the volcano.

Yet they watch. An older man peers out from behind a door. Children, past their bedtime, sit on the floor in a daze. Their parents study the flickering images, perplexed. *Are those people living in the same world as we are?*

Twenty-five years ago, the inhabitants of Babuyan Claro, a tiny, unapproachable island that lies a hundred miles of churning Pacific north of the Philippine mainland, were animistic and without written language. Called the Ibatan, they lived in almost total isolation for much of the 19th and 20th centuries, a quirk of ocean currents, geography and

fate. In just over two decades, since the arrival of a pair of headstrong, freewheeling missionaries, they have raced up man's 5,000-year developmental arc, embracing monotheism, free enterprise and CNN. They have evaluated each step with the fresh, appraising eyes of the arriviste.

Familiar accouterments have lately fallen into place: knockoffs of Fila shorts and Nike T-shirts (worn lovingly into faded crepe) have been acquired from passing fishing boats; new babies are being called Joe and Russell, Americanizing the mostly Iberian names that spread across native populations when the Spanish colonized this region in the 1600's; the metallic light of the television flickers tonight across a rare, upstairs room in the island's nicest home, a simple two-story box with carved mahogany trellises, cement floors and running water from faucets.

Since the 40-year-old Ruben Dican, the wealthiest man on the four-mile wide atoll, got a satellite dish a few weeks ago, his house has become the local mega-

plex. A quietly cheerful man who has grown portly on an island where life's rigors keep almost everyone slim, Ruben is one of the few English speakers here. Since most of the 54-channel selection is from the United States, he must also act as a translator of strange words and even stranger images.

"It feels like we are rushing forward, trying to decide what to keep of the modern world and what to throw away, while not losing hold of what has given us life and happiness for all time," he says, softly, in his halting, precise English, before his attention is drawn away by Lisa Beamer, who is talking about the last call from her husband, Todd, before he fought the hijackers. Everyone watches.

"It seems so real, the pictures," Ruben murmurs, "sometimes more real than our own lives."

It was nothing more than a coincidence that I was on my way to Babuyan to examine the accelerated development of its society on the very day that the United States was attacked. Later, when I returned home, I learned that the shock and bewilderment the Ibatan registered was not so different from what was felt in a lot of other places. I also came to understand that what I found on the island, away from the television set, was a kind of microcosm of what the world was suddenly fighting over—not simply West versus East or Judeo-Christian versus Islam, but the very idea of modernity and what constitutes human progress.

Many on Babuyan still remember the "before time," when there was a settled egalitarianism rather than every-man-for-himself enterprise, when no one here knew that the Ibatan were poor in a world of vast wealth. Within their tiny civilization of 1,400 people, you can see so clearly the effects of modernity and measure what is gained against what has been lost. And in the person of Ruben Dican, the richest and most modernized figure on the island, you can see the struggle to manage a problem that is new to them, but quite familiar to the rest of the world: the divide between haves and have-nots.

T he story of the Ibatan starts in the late 1860's, when a nameless, Malay-Polynesian tribe was swept off course in a typhoon and steered their outrigger toward a single point of hope, a 4,000-foot volcano poking up from the horizon. They discovered an island enveloped by treacherous rocks. It's a place you wreck onto, which is what they did, seven of them, demolishing their vessel and becoming castaways. Exploring the dense jungles, with wild pigs, pythons, monitor lizards and strange, large-footed chickens, they found remnants of ancient structures and burial urns, with bones and artifacts.

From these relics, the Ibatan would develop their own brand of mysticism: the island, they came to believe, was occupied by a community of "invisibles," wise, unseen inhabitants who were custodians of the flora and fauna, the winds and tides. From this vision grew a theology, replete with ritual offerings, shamanic cures and burial rites, all directed toward the ideal of *machitonos*, the Ibatan word for "balance" or "harmony."

A few other shipwrecks in the late 19th and early 20th centuries added hybrid vigor to the gene pool, and a discrete language evolved, with several names for each of six winds, shaded terms for hundreds of varieties of plants and no words for war, envy, jealousy, property, buy, sell or own.

The Ibatan passed the decades in a kind of serenity. Though they did dispense with a few unlucky visitors, they were otherwise peaceful. They wore clothes of pounded bark and found herbal remedies in python gallbladders. Their world evolved with a gentle, premodern rhythm—until the day, in 1977, when a 29-year-old missionary named Rundell Maree slipped off a boat into the water, carrying his shortwave radio overhead, and scraped his way across the rocks toward shore.

Rundell had come to advance the mandate of the Wycliffe Bible Translators, also known as SIL International (derived from its original name, Summer Institute of Linguistics). The organization sends missionaries trained in linguistics to the most remote corners of the world, places that do not yet have written language, a concept first developed by the Sumerians more than 5,000 years ago. Their mission is to construct a written language from an ancient spoken tongue, teach the indigenous population to read, translate the entire New Testament (and portions of the Old) into the people's "mother tongue" and then give copies to one and all. They say this is the best way to spread God's word.

But that was a long way off for Rundell. First, he had to just coexist with the Ibatan, a task he approached with characteristic Western confidence. He fancied himself a survivor and citizen of the world, having moved through childhood from his birthplace in Rhodesia, to England, Canada, then Bible college and a graduate theology degree in California, before catching the itinerant crosswind of a missionary's life.

He was the only Caucasian most islanders had ever seen, and in his first two years on the island, he was run ragged, poisoned, almost killed by malaria and made a "plaything" by the Ibatan. As he tried to learn the language—using an elegant system developed by SIL's founders—the Ibatan, now numbering about 600, joyously substituted common words with the names of body parts. Trying to find a lost hammer, for instance, Rundell would ask if anyone had seen his penis, that he'd lost it somewhere. Ibatan would roll on the ground in hysterics, ask him, "How big is it?" and then add new words. The subtext, though, was all too serious: some elders saw him as a threat and wanted him dead.

At the moment Rundell was ready to abandon the project and his sanity, he caught a 10-year-old boy trying to scam him out of pads and pencils. Under interrogation, the boy explained how the Ibatan had made a fool of him.

Rundell broke down, a moment he remembers vividly even after the passage of two decades. "I'm not a fool," he said to the boy. "There are things I can teach you, amazing things, about a world beyond your imagination, about a God that will love you no matter what. But you must help me. We must be friends. Do you understand?"

That boy, whose name was Frank Simon, did understand. "I can teach you what you need to know to survive here," the boy said. But there was one condition: "Someday, I want to go over the horizon in a boat. You'll help me do that, right?" "Yes," Rundell said, seeing a first glimpse of his future. "Yes, I will."

IT WAS A BARGAIN, and each would hold up his end: Rundell learned the ways of the Ibatan; Frank, a youngster with endless questions, learned much about the world and heard the story of Christ. A period of heady optimism and activity unfurled, as, year by year, the cornerstones of the "developed" world were laid on Babuyan. Rundell was joined on the island by his wife, Judi, a Chinese-American, and their baby daughter. (A second daughter was born on the island.) The family settled into a hut made of rattan and split palms. Curious Ibatan, mostly teenagers, nosed in, many of them soon learning to read and write the Roman alphabet that had now been woven into a representation of their native language.

The arrival of written language, scholars say, creates an architecture for a civilization to become "sticky," making it possible to transmit knowledge more effectively, in greater volume and detail, and to build on advances. Rundell and Judi began their own vanity press with titles like "Stories Concerning Us Here on Babuyan"—a collection of folk tales—and "Atlas Book," with drawings and text that showed where the island sat in relation to the Philippines, the wider Pacific, the world... and where earth sits within the solar system. Judi created a cookbook, which, along with recipes for preparing indigenous crops and grains, described the uses of flour, something never seen on the island. Soon enough, one of the women had sent her husband out to barter with a passing Taiwanese fishing junk; the next day, a sack of white powder appeared on the Marees' doorstep.

Rundell, meanwhile, had two-man handsaws delivered by a plane so that the men could more effectively cut the island's precious nara trees and make boards. A school was built, and sturdier houses began to appear, one of which belonged to the Marees. In their own dwelling, they set up a medical clinic, which consisted of Rundell using the text "Where There Is No Doctor" and whatever medicines he could scrounge on infrequent trips to the mainland.

Three boys emerged as a kind of "bridge generation." There was Frank, the young Ruben Dican and his young uncle Orlando Thomas. Together they helped Rundell on one of his first and most significant transformational projects: the building of a water system. At that time, the island was still what anthropologists call a "spring culture," where everyone gathered at a few large springs to fill buckets and discuss everything each day. So the building of a rudimentary system of sisterns and pipes—a baby step toward modernity—represented a significant disruption of traditional Ibatan culture.

Indeed, as the water flowed, Christianity began to take root. In the early 1980's, Rundell took a few Ibatan for short stints to a rural SIL center in the northern province of the Philippines, where they helped with translation of the New Testament. They tended to be young, in their late teens or early 20's, and this group, including a core trio of Frank, Ruben and Orlando, were among the first "believers."

This new nondenominational Christian faith, based on an intimate, humanized deity who would love each believer unconditionally, appealed to converts as an alternative to the mystical, earth-bound complexities of the "invisibles." Being worthy of this God's love seemed to offer a new sensation of self-worth. People were suffused with the Judeo-Christian octane of individual destiny, a perfect fit with the new ideas about education, business and personal behavior that Rundell and Judi were also introducing.

Ruben and Orlando, and their soon-to-be wives, Miriam and Nancy, were sent to college on the mainland by the Marees. The missionaries, for their part, were supported by a far-flung group of about 75 regular contributors, who wrote checks from kitchen tables, church pews and offices around the world. These contributions averaged about $32,000 a year, and the couple, with their two growing daughters, spent modestly on themselves and gave away the rest.

Frank, however, would take nothing from Rundell, neither compensation for Bible translating nor grants for education. "He always looked at me as a peer, an equal," Rundell says. "He said he didn't want money to be part of our relationship."

Rather than go off to school, Frank became the island's innovator and explorer, its Magellan. When nearly all the houses on the island were destroyed in a typhoon in 1987, it was Frank who decided they needed to build a great boat. The island's fleet of outriggers was limited in size by what could be lifted over the rocks and brought to safety inland. But Frank went ahead and designed a 50-foot ship; he and Rundell built it; and then they sailed it 210 miles to the mainland and back with cement, wood and other supplies. Hundreds of Ibatan men carried the vessel to an inland lagoon as another storm approached. Soon, a separate medical clinic was built, and the Marees were living in the island's first cement house; a cement church followed, as well as the squat, solid A-frame of a new school.

In 1992, Frank sailed off in his outrigger and pantomimed his way onto a Taiwanese fishing junk. He spent six months as a fisherman, then six months in jail once the boat docked and he was found to have no immigration papers. When he returned to Babuyan a year later, two things occurred; his mildly felonious sojourn became a career path for other young men; and using the Taiwanese he learned in prison, he negotiated deals on a shortwave with passing junks, offering fresh water, fruit and fish that the Ibatan were specialists in catching. Soon, 40 Ibatan outriggers fanned out to fill orders on the fly.

By the mid-90's, a modern beat was becoming audible: frenzied daytime hustling matched, on evenings and weekends, with repentant prayer. The population grew fast (as it will in places where there is no electricity), and by 1995, there were 1,000 Ibatan, 400 of whom were devout Christians, a community of fervent Puritan ethicists that would make Max Weber take notice.

And Marx too. With growing disparities in income, possessions and the sizes of homes came class division: an upper class, living around a town center by the water, anchored by a small cooperative store; and the rest, mostly living in the mountain jungles, feeling their first tug of envy and resentment.

At the uppermost strata were a dozen or so Ibatan whose education the Marees underwrote, led by Ruben and his wife, Miriam. By the 90's, both had become emblems of what de Tocqueville called bourgeoisie virtue, studying furiously for their teaching certification exams, tirelessly educating the island's children, ever resourceful and frugal. Here, in what teachers everywhere would consider a perfect world, they became the highest-paid people on the island, earning a combined 20,000 pesos a month (about $400) from the Philippine Department of Education. On Babuyan, this is a fortune, and it enabled Ruben and Miriam to build their grand, fenced two-story house, with the island's first indoor kitchen.

While Frank provided the bursts of ingenuity, Ruben, supported by his government salary, established the kind of sustained, patient enterprises upon which economies are built. After Judi taught Miriam accounting skills, she and Ruben effectively ran the island's main cooperative, a 15-foot-square cement box with basic dry goods and packaged foods. Ruben became the island's banker, lending money for all needs; the head of its power company, stringing wire from his diesel-powered generator to lighthouses; its ice company, selling ice from his diesel-powered freezer; and its communications system, checking radio reports for the weather and making emergency calls. Step by step, he became a civic man and contributor to the community, a centrist, a moderate, in all things, but with an eye always on a kind of enlightened self-interest wherein people's needs and wants could be served… at an attractive margin.

Meanwhile, the sensitive Orlando, who from his youth assisted Rundell in the medical clinic, became a teacher as well. But from the start, Orlando asked hard questions, often from the sidelines, about what was suitable and what was not, for the Ibatan. With his educational advantages, he moved into the realm of service, ministering to the sick on weekends, as well as helping Rundell and Judi in their translation of the Bible and the creation of an Ibatan dictionary. In his spare time, he wrote songs and poems. He poked fun at Ruben's growing portliness—"Yes, yes, there goes a wealthy man"; and Frank's yearning: "My friend will only rest when he has no choice…"

Like Ruben's, Orlando's role on the island represented the arrival of specialization, a crucial step in human development—it took hold in the Fertile Crescent 7,000 years ago—in which a few elites are paid by society for their unique skills, freeing them from physical labor. It's a principle upon which diversified, developed economies surely rest. Though the Philippine government had dropped a few teachers on the island in the 1960's, they were mostly there on what seemed like extended vacations, occasionally drilling some children in perfunctory recitations of Tagalog, the national language. None had ever bothered to learn the local tongue. Ruben and Orlando, local boys who got credentials and came home, became the first genuine elites, wearing hats, it often seemed, for an entire professional class.

Frank, for his part, pushed forward without a formal education. Despite his brilliance and grasp of several regional languages, he chose to remain on a lower rung of the ladder with most of the Ibatan. Each day, he struggled to support his young family with a patchwork of subsistence farming and grand schemes, always at the pitiless whims of weather and tides.

Orlando worries that television images 'will make us feel dissatisfied with our life here. This will be very bad and wrong. But it's so hard to turn away.'

By 1996, the beginning of the new Babuyan was nearly at an end. Rundell and Judi drew close to finishing the Ibatan Bible, a 1,000-page translation of the New Testament, plus Genesis, into Ibatan. The project had stretched across 20 years and was now ready for final proofreading. When it was done, there was great fanfare. Rundell and Judi's extended families, friends and supporters arrived from the United States and Canada, along with SIL leaders and Philippine officials, for the dedication of the completed book. There were 350 copies passed out to the Ibatan. The parties and prayers lasted a week.

With their daughters now off to college and their specific SIL mission completed, Rundell and Judi prepared to leave for their next project. Everyone gathered on the landing strip to see them off. A daily conversation across time and cultures, lasting 20 years, was about to end. Songs were sung, and Orlando, Ruben and all the others hugged Rundell and Judi amid tears. And Frank, fighting back a sensation of being left behind,

watched the plane vanish through a point in the sky, far above the horizon.

IT IS NEARLY FIVE YEARS LATER. Ruben rides the island's only bike down the dirt main street. He parks it near a banyan tree where burial urns were found more than 130 years ago, an ancient, twisted presence long thought to be the home of "invisibles."

The tree, its trunk recently burned out by vandals, now overlooks the cooperative store that Ruben helps run. It has become the town's gathering place. Supplies for the store are transported from the mainland by a boat he owns, the island's largest. His mercantile energies are visible everywhere: a man planing wood in the town square, cradling his portable electric planer like a newborn baby, says that Ruben bought it for him, and he's paying it off, bit by bit.

Ruben says he is expecting a new, diesel-powered five-kilowatt generator, meaning more houses will soon have light. "It helps make the days longer, the nights shorter and less boring than just sitting in the dark telling stories," he says. He steps back to let a man on a water buffalo pass. "Yes, my bike is better," he says, shaking his head at the beast. "No question, this is progress." He pats the handlebars and smiles. "Eventually, everyone will agree."

I am here with Rundell and Judi, on one of their longest visits since their mission was formally completed. Judi, a woman of tireless precision, is gathering data for a book on the geneaology of the island, dating to 1860. Rundell, who now helps oversee the Philippine region for SIL, is mostly on a sightseeing mission, comparing the "then" with the "now." The islanders had long anticipated our arrival; they had even heard about me, a Jewish reporter from the United States, and they joyously greeted us at the airfield and accompanied us into the village.

Ruben has "become like Santa Claus, with one new thing after another," says Rundell, unpacking suitcases in the bedroom of their old house, which has since been converted into a library. "Even Orlando is being sucked in."

Ruben's electricity has carried a growing current of visual images. He first got a television, a small one, three years ago, and attached it to a VCR. There are now four VCR's on the island, with some of his competitors charging guests to view bootleg tapes procured from passing boats.

As a church elder, Ruben has tried to exert quality control over what is shown. A recent hit at his house was "Ben-Hur," the 1959 classic with Charlton Heston as a he-man Jewish slave and chariot champion during the time of Christ. "We thought the Jews were the world's toughest people," Ruben tells me that evening, as he switches away from CNN to a station from Manila. "Everyone thought you'd be bigger."

> **'Written language** gave us a way to capture our history and compare ourselves to people everywhere,' Frank says. 'Now that we have a past, I find that I think only of the future. I always feel a clock ticking and time rushing by.'

A weekly, hourlong Philippine drama begins. After a car chase and some shooting, the protagonists, a handsome pair, end up in bed. The Ibatan men snicker, then, taking their cue from the women, quickly hush. Everyone slips into a kind of group trance, sitting absolutely still, as the couple roll beneath the sheets and the music swells.

Orlando is here, sitting a few feet away with his appraising look. He says

he worries that these images "will make us feel dissatisfied with our life here. This will be very bad and wrong. But it's so hard to turn away."

Ruben, seeking a midcourse of enlightened self-interest, shrugs. "Maybe it will make people strive more. To get to this life they see. Maybe that won't be so bad."

The next morning, Rundell, Judi and I go for a walk in the jungle with Frank, who brings along his 18-month-old son, Joe. We are in search of the oldest people on the island so that Judi can interview them for her book. Along the way, Frank tells us how the children, learning about the larger world, are growing away from adults. Once, he says, "you could leave money out and not worry about it. Now the teenagers steal it to buy what they can, to watch videos at someone's house or buy cigarettes or liquor." The island's second liquor store was recently opened across from the school by a Filipino teacher who got his posting on the island as a political favor. The first one is run by Frank's older brother.

After walking an hour in the midmorning heat, we come across Joaquin, an ancient, loinclothed man in a tiny hut, chewing on areca nut, a local narcotic. Judi, after a few questions, determines Joaquin was born in 1917, probably in May. The man, it turns out, is Frank's great-uncle, his grandmother's brother. This is not too surprising—almost everyone on the island is related. Frank, holding his son, gently eases under the grassy eaves of the hut's doorway, and with her digital camera, Judi takes a picture of the three of them, crossing four generations, for the book.

It is striking how far their paths have diverged in such a short period. Frank spends his days worrying about the yield of his rice crop, businesses he might start and how he'll ever manage to send his son to college. Joaquin is concerned about feeling in harmony with the "invisibles" and spearing wild pigs. After the photo is taken, they chat briefly about relatives. The old man, squatting on the floor of his hut, looks quizzically at Frank, who is dressed in a polo shirt, and says, "It does not look like we are related."

After we leave Joaquin, Frank seems reflective. Rundell pokes at him to get a sense of why. "Written language gave us a way to capture our history and compare ourselves to people everywhere," Frank says after a moment. "Now that we have a past, I find that I think only of the future. I always feel a clock ticking and time rushing by. But Joaquin, he lives always in the present. He hears no clock. Once, that's the way we all were."

A FEW MORNINGS LATER, an exhausted Orlando, up too late watching television, studies the sky. He takes in a wisp of cloud passing low, and raises an eyebrow: "Usually, monsoon doesn't come this early, but that wind… it is the wind that brings it."

Ruben arrives, and together they analyze the breeze, its altitude, speed and precedents for monsoon season—five months of almost nonstop rain and wind—to start this early. At moments like this, they are most visibly "a bridge generation," at the very forefront of change, yet still employing the skills of "the before time." They will be the last generation of islanders, most likely, to know all six Ibatan names of the wind.

The rain begins to arrive in large drops. Children crack off shiny leaves of elephant cabbage from the jungle foliage and disappear under a laughing green canopy that twists up the mountain. Orlando possesses a precious luxury, an umbrella, and he and I crowd under it as the full, humbling ferocity of nature pours down.

"If we stick together, work together, we can get all that we need right here," Orlando says. "This is what I tell people. If we stay close, the umbrella is big enough for us all to stay dry."

As it turns out, monsoon season is not arriving. All we have is a typhoon, with 100-mile-an-hour winds. As the storm approaches, the Ibatan go into a frenzy, tying down boats and securing the foundations of huts. Since early morning, Frank has been furiously racing through his rice terraces, trying to harvest whatever he can. Men and women scramble madly in fields on all sides of him. Despite his creativity and sense of personal destiny, Frank is still bound to moments of profound helplessness and humility.

The timing of the typhoon is inauspicious: the rice needs a few more weeks to ripen.

Ruben is not worried about rice, and he retreats to the front porch of his safe, solid house, in a cluster of nara trees just across from the school. He talks about the struggle with nature, about the amazing resourcefulness of the old Ibatan to survive here during typhoons and volcanic eruptions. Then, smiling brightly at me, he says, "If you have nothing better to do, why don't we go watch TV?" He turns on the generator, saunters across the tiled porch floor, past a tiny plastic chirping bird, with motion sensor, that you might find in a souvenir shop on Sunset Boulevard, and upstairs to the TV.

George Bush's address before Congress is just coming on, and we watch intently, listening to the speech and the thunderous applause. "That's what it is always about, deep down," Ruben says. "About the haves and the have-nots. Whether they will admit it or not, bin Laden's followers are jealous of America." He pauses. "It is not easy having a lot when others have so little. I know."

Ruben's view on how a wealthy man, like a wealthy country, avoids ill will, is pragmatic: he charges next to nothing for ice and electricity—and nothing for watching his satellite TV—offers modest terms for people who owe him money and contributes heavily to the common projects. When his boat fortunately arrived at dawn this morning, loaded with enough supplies to fill his cooperative through monsoon, Ruben made sure, as is his custom, to dive into the surf for the hardest job: dragging the small skiff out and back between the rocky shore and the boat to haul the goods to shore. An hour later, after 60 men had helped lift the 40-foot outrigger from the water, Ruben, wet and exhausted, murmured, "It's important that I do the worst work and the hardest, so they know I'm not different from any of them."

But, with each day, class exerts its divisions. Ruben's education and use of capital have freed him from the shared burdens of the Ibatan and from the shared purpose that flows from it. Safe and warm, he flips from Bush's speech to the National Geographic channel, a fa-

vorite of his, as the typhoon begins to roar.

For five straight days, everyone is trapped indoors, until the rain and winds recede and the Ibatan emerge to take stock. The banana trees have been decapitated, but most of the coconut trees have held. Quite a few grass huts and some wooden houses will need repair. The island is awash in mudslides.

Ruben, with Orlando at his side, ventures over to Frank's house, near the shoreline. Like most of the Ibatan, he has lost his rice crop, which means he will have to sell the nine pigs he has acquired over the past few years, essentially his life savings, so that his family has enough to eat through the monsoon season.

His latest idea—an ice-making cooperative to freeze fish and sell ice to the growing number of large fishing boats in the nearby waters—is now out of reach. He was planning to sell the excess of his rice crop and a few pigs for seed capital. This is hard for Frank, the eternal optimist, to swallow. "Again, for me it's about survival," he says, forcing a smile as his wife looks on.

The next morning everyone gathers at church, the crowd flowing out the doorway and standing in a light Sunday mist. Rundell, naturally, is the guest preacher this morning, and he dives confidently into Matthew 25, called "the Parable of Talents." He summons a little girl, a teenage boy and a man to the stage and has them try to lift different-size rocks. Eventually, after much laughter, each picks up a rock suited to his or her strength, allowing Rundell to intone about how "God does not judge us based on how many talents each of us have, but what you do with whatever talents you are given." The service closes with Frank on guitar and Ruben playing a portable organ he just bought, as the Ibatan let loose with a thunderous rendering of an old Baptist chant, "Stand Up, Stand Up for Jesus."

A few days later, when the landing strip is dry enough for a plane to land, Rundell radios the mainland for a pickup the following morning. As darkness falls, he invites Frank, Ruben and Or-

lando to his house, and we gather at the table. They talk easily, chiding, laughing, challenging one another's sense of what's needed and what's possible. Rundell leaps up to the blackboard and starts scribbling notes, assessing, first, the progress that has been made; the church is vibrant, the education up to sixth grade is strong. (After that, if parents want their children to continue their education, they have to be sent off the island to boarding academies, which are too expensive for most Ibatan.) Commerce is growing, if slowly. More than half the houses have running water, and electricity is spreading.

Then the conversation shifts to the thing most needed, and Rundell starts drawing the outlines of a high school. For half an hour, they talk fast, imagining it, free form, until the drawing has a gym, a science lab, a home-economics center, a library, "with more books than we have chickens on this island," Orlando says. Looking wistfully at the chalk marks, they smile and fall silent.

One trap for the Ibatan, as for so many across a world connected by sound and image, is becoming overwhelmed with yearning. In the bracing first months of a new globalism, one thing seems plain: people need to feel some sense of forward motion, or hope collapses. It is dangerous to dream of things that are so far out of reach, and the school they have just conjured on the chalkboard is precisely that—a fantasy.

"What about the bridge?" Frank pipes up. Everyone knows about the bridge, and Rundell erases the school and starts drawing horizontal lines. The problem: a dry bed running from high on Mount Babuyan to the ocean turns into a swift river during monsoon. The children from half the island have to cross a rickety wooden bridge to get to school. It's hazardous. Parents have complained. Some kids have stopped attending.

Everyone, including Rundell, is a self-taught engineer—they've had to be—and there's rapid, purposeful talk of how to build a cement bridge, another first for the island.

Orlando stops the proceedings. "The long metal rods inside the cement. There's no boat big enough on the island to transport them here." He's right. Hiring a large boat for the long trip to Babuyan Claro would be too expensive.

"There's one way," Frank finally says, and out it flows: after the typhoon, many people will be selling their pigs or cows to buy rice, and the livestock brokers, with the largest boats that ever come near here, are probably preparing a visit. Their boats are not only big; they have flat bottoms that allow them to get very close to the shore, making it easier to load and unload unwieldy cargo. "We need to come together, so everyone selling livestock can negotiate as one" and stipulate that the boats bring the rods on their way out, he says. "This way, we can also get a better overall price for our livestock and contribute the extra to whatever modest transportation costs there'll be for the rods."

Orlando, the voice of careful consideration, nods a few times. "It just might work," he says. Ruben quickly sketches out a swift plan for implementation and negotiating position.

Frank just smiles. He has taken his woe and found, at its dark core, a kernel of possibility. A plan. A way for everyone to move forward, to taste a bit of sweet progress in its purest form. And, for an instant, I was certain that on this windy night a guy named Frank saved the world.

Even if it was just one bridge.

Ron Suskind is a Pulitzer Prize-winning journalist and the author of "A Hope in the Unseen."

Underground Potlatch

How the Kwakiutl kept the faith

by Douglas Cole

DURING CHRISTMASTIDE 1921 DAN Cranmer, a Nimkish Kwakiutl from Alert Bay on the coast of British Columbia, hosted a five-day ceremony of dances and gift giving. Part of his accumulated wealth consisted of property and family prerogatives his wife's family had transferred to him as part of the traditional "repurchase" of the bride. Now the 300 or so assembled guests witnessed Cranmer's giving away of all the property he had received, as well as more from his own and his family's resources.

Among the first items given away were twenty-four canoes, pool tables for two chiefs, four gasoline boats, and another pool table. Blankets, gaslights, violins and guitars, kitchen utensils and sewing machines, gramophones, bedsteads and bureaus, and 300 oak trunks followed. Dresses, shawls, and bracelets were given to women; sweaters and shirts to young people. Change was thrown up for the children to collect. On the fifth and last day of the ceremony came hundreds of sacks of flour, each worth three dollars. This was Cranmer's famous potlatch, one of the largest ever recorded among his people.

Dan Cranmer's potlatch became famous not only because of the volume of the gifts that changed hands over those December days but also because it brought criminal charges against fifty-one of those who attended. Twenty-two went to prison for two months, and the rest were given suspended sentences on the condition that they "voluntarily surrender" their dance masks, ceremonial whistles, plaques of beaten copper, and other potlatch paraphernalia. The potlatch, the ceremony that Cranmer celebrated with his relatives and friends, was illegal under Canada's Indian Act of 1885.

The potlatch had been a custom widespread among the Indians of the Northwest Coast, from Alaska to Oregon (the word derives from the Nootka *patshatl;* the Kwakiutl term was *P!Esa'*). It was the ceremony in which one person bestowed traditional names, ranks, and privileges upon another, a public event that gave the transfer general validation. The occasions included the naming of a child, marriage and the redemption of a bridal payment, and death (when a relative would assume the name and position of the deceased). The distribution of property was meant as payment to the guests, who served as witnesses and, in turn, had their own status confirmed by their presence and the size of the gifts they received.

Much like the ball that marks a debutante's coming out into society or the bar mitzvah that heralds a Jewish boy's elevation to manhood, the potlatch celebrated a change of rank or status with dancing, feasting, and gifts. Like many other societies, those of the Northwest Coast associated prestige with wealth, and the potlatcher gained prestige according to the liberality of his giving. A true chief "always died poor" because he had potlatched his wealth, but he died rich in the rank and honor that he had accumulated for himself through giving and that he would pass on to his family, heirs, and descendants.

This social system, based on the distribution of wealth, was alien to European society and everywhere came under attack by missionaries and government officials. The accumulation of goods merely for giving away seemed to them to produce indigence and thriftlessness, "habits inconsistent with all progress." "It is not possible," wrote an early commentator, "that the Indian can acquire property, or can become industrious with any good result, while under the influence of this mania." It was, agreed a leading legislator, and "insane exuberance of generosity." Such reasoning led the Canadian government to ban the ceremony.

At the same time, legislators also outlawed what they called tamananawas, secret society rituals that included ceremonial cannibalism. These rituals were practiced along portions of the coast. Most notable was the *hamatsa* of the Kwakiutl, in which an initiate possessed by a cannibal spirit devoured human flesh (or pretended to) until the powerful forces within him were tamed. Such practices actually expressed repugnance at inhuman behavior but were acted out in a way that horrified white Canadian society.

Passing laws in Ottawa was easy, although even there skeptical lawmakers warned of the difficulty of enforcement in British Columbia. Prospects of preventing the potlatch were not very favorable, since Indians living in the province were widely scattered in areas remote from police, magistrates, and the few agents appointed to supervise them. In the first attempt at enforcement, Indian resistance forced a hasty retreat; in the second, the case was thrown out of court when an unsympathetic judge insisted on a clear definition of what was outlawed. Most white residents opposed enforcement, seeing little harm in the ceremony and wishing no unnecessary provocation to threaten the generally friendly relations with the Indians.

Nevertheless, under the influence of missionaries, most of the province's Indians gradually began to give up the potlatch or modify it to accommodate European ways. This was not true of the Kwakiutl, however. Among these people, who lived along the inland coast of Vancouver Island and the adjacent mainland, the potlatch went on, perhaps even increased in the decades after the passage of the antipotlatch law. Their "incorrigibility" probably had something to do with the hazy gradation of rank within Kwakiutl society and the ability to obtain new rank through marriage, even multiple marriages, and the attendant potlatches. A defiant attitude toward the white man's law may have contributed. For whatever reasons, the Kwakiutl stood out as inveterate potlatchers. As Indian agent William Halliday reported in 1912, "There is no decrease in the number of potlatches held nor is its influence apparently less."

The federal government in Ottawa, in the person of the civil servant responsible for Indian affairs, Deputy Superintendent General D. C. Scott, decided to enforce the law. According to the 1911 census, Indians made up only 5 percent of the province's population. Railways or steamships penetrated almost all the coastal channels and rivers, and gasoline boats were available to most police detachments and agents. Reduced in numbers, loyal and law abiding (if sometimes law avoiding), and often intimidated by the power and paternalism of white authority, British Columbia's native population was not something to be feared. Indians, although they might resist pas-

sively, were impotent. Initially, local judges and jurors refused to convict or impose sentences, but soon a number of prison terms were given to potlatchers. The first convictions were in 1919; the first prison terms in 1920. Others followed the next year, culminating in the mass trials of the Cranmer potlatch participants in February and April of 1922. Swift and thorough, the prosecutions seemed to have worked, and agent Halliday declared the potlatch dead.

The Kwakiutl were loath to see so sudden an end to a ceremony they regarded as "one of our oldest and best customs." "We don't see any fault in it," they wrote; it was "a good thing for us all." They sent a delegation to Ottawa, hired lawyers, petitioned the government and sought the support of their local member of Parliament. Most of all they asked for an impartial investigation. Convinced that nothing was wrong with their ceremony, they were confident that a commission, perhaps just "a good straight man," would conclude that the whole law was an unjust mistake. But petitions, lawyers, and appeals had no effect on Deputy Superintendent General Scott, who was convinced that the potlatch stood in the way of Indian progress and hampered their assimilation into Canadian civilization. Unable to secure even an investigation, the Kwakiutl fell back upon their own resourcefulness.

Within a few years the Indians established a pattern of evasion. They did not hold potlatches openly at Alert Bay, the home ground of agents and police, but transferred them to distant or inaccessible villages. The most notable was Gwayi at Kingcome Inlet, a village located two miles up a shallow, snag-ridden river that froze over in winter. It was sixty miles away from Alert Bay, and the only regular route to it was by steamer from Vancouver and then by gas boat upriver. Surprise was impossible: Gwayi was so situated that any approach, day or night, could be seen. The village's security was irksome to agents. They proposed to break it by disguise, by stationing a policeman there, even by using seaplanes, but all such proposals proved impractical or too expensive. The Gwayi fortress remained unbreached.

Other villages, isolated in winter, were also used. In the early 1930s, frequent potlatches were held at Village Island, only fifteen miles from Alert Bay, with fishing boats carrying the goods from Alert Bay. Turnour Island, Fort Rupert, and Cape Mudge were also scenes of clandestine potlatches. "If there is nobody to watch," reported anthropologist Franz Boas, "they do whatever they like."

While such uncompromising potlatches increased after 1927, some Indians sought a means to potlatch more conveniently and closer to home. When Jane Nowell married Arthur Shaughnessy, the groom's payment was given privately, with only the chiefs present. A church wedding was followed by a feast and dance "in the white man's way," but Charlie Nowell, the bride's father, announced that everyone could go to the movies free on Saturday night, and he bought candy, cakes, and fruit to distribute there. Later, when one of the young couple's daughters died, men were sent around the village with $300 to give away.

House-to-house visits satisfied obligations but took away much of the potlatch's significance. Songs and dances, vital components of the ceremony, could not be presented on a doorstep. So the Indians, with the advice of Vancouver lawyer W. R. Vaughan, invented the "disjointed potlatch." Separating the ceremonies from the gift giving, the Kwakiutl thwarted the Indian Act's specification that the giving-away must form part of an Indian ceremony. Authorities had great difficulty proving that gifts given on one day formed part of a dance held six months before.

The first disjointed potlatch that came to the attention of the Department of Indian Affairs was at Village Island, where 1,500 sacks of flour were given away but no dance or ceremony took place. On a second occasion, at Kolokwis village, Henry Speck held a large dance with all the old ceremony but gave nothing away—yet he recorded all his guests' names in a book and assured them he would give things away in six months. Agent Halliday saw a dance at Fort Rupert but had no evidence "that even a five cent piece had been given away." The flour distributions were particularly irritating. The man who delivered 1,500 sacks to Village Island left them with the remark, "Here is some flour I have brought to help you over the hard winter." And when Charlie Nowell landed 900 sacks at Fort Rupert, he brazenly told police that it was nothing more than "an act of Christian charity for the benefit of poor people."

There were other expedients. Feasts blended into Christmas dinners, and potlatch gifts were wrapped as holiday presents. In Alert Bay in December 1934, Moses Alfred simply tagged each item within a great heap of goods with the name of the person for whom it was intended and walked away. Such evasions depended upon the solidarity of the Kwakiutl. No one turned witness; the authorities could obtain no evidence. "Everywhere," wrote a police constable, "I find myself up against a stone wall." In 1934 an official reported, "We are about as far away from doing anything really effective toward the suppression of the potlatch system as we were when actions against the Indians were started years ago." By the 1930s it was the Indian agent, not his wards, who felt frustrated and thwarted. "My position in relation to the Potlatch is becoming intolerable," wrote the Kwakiutl agent in 1936.

That year the Department of Indian Affairs put forward an amendment aimed at circumventing Kwakiutl strategies. It would have allowed agents or police to seize any property deemed excessive for an Indian's needs. The proposal ran into objections from the House of Commons, where members strongly opposed it on the grounds that it was unreasonable, unjust, and un-British. The amendment was withdrawn, and the department resigned itself to leaving the matter to the influence of church, school, and the "good sense of the Indians themselves." The potlatch had, in fact, begun to fall on hard times. Christianity was taking stronger root among the Kwakiutl, and young people were losing interest in long rituals and arranged marriages. Resources were also becoming limited: as early as the 1920s the Indians suffered from competition with white Canadian and Japanese Canadian fishing boats, and then the whole economy was devastated by the depression of the 1930s.

Although better times returned in the 1940s, the potlatch remained in decline. Members of the younger generation were more concerned with issues of contemporary social justice: obtaining equality in pensions, veterans' benefits, and child allowances; more hospitals and better health care; the right to vote; better education; and an end to federal taxes on fishery earnings outside the reserves. In the hearings leading up to the 1951 revision of the Indian Act, the issue of the potlatch went unnoticed. Even the proposals submitted by the Native Brotherhood, led by the high-ranking Kwakiutl Bill Scow, made no mention of the prohibition.

The revised Indian Act, reflecting the parliamentary committee's recommendation that it be purged of its many "anachronisms, anomalies, contradictions and divergences," simply discarded the antipotlatch provision. A new consciousness of their heritage and rights soon arose among all Northwest Coast Indians. Within the Kwakiutl and other Indian communities there was a renaissance of artistic work, a resurgence of potlatching, and an increase in political activity, which was centered on the issues of land and self-government.

The potlatch of the 1990s is part of that renewed pride and identity. While it differs in some ways from ceremonies of the nineteenth century, the occasions do not depart significantly from tradition. The same phases of the life cycle—birth, naming, puberty, marriage, death—are marked by feasts, dances, and gifts to witnesses. The same regard for rank and descent, the same concern for recognition of guests according to station, and the same spirit of free and unconcerned generosity prevail.

The antipotlatch law, and particularly the prosecutions and imprisonments of the 1920s, remain indelible in the memory of the Kwakiutl, symbols of persecution of their identity and way of life. But at least the masks and coppers that they had to surrender have now been returned to Alert Bay and Cape Mudge and placed in Kwakiutl museums and cultural centers, where they serve as visible evidence of the continuity of a people and of their ceremonial and artistic traditions.

What Americans Don't Know about Indians

Jerry Mander

In 1981, when my sons Yari and Kai were attending San Francisco's Lowell High School, they complained to me that their American History class began with the arrival of whites on this continent and omitted any mention of the people who were already here. The class was taught that Columbus "discovered" America and that American "history" was what came afterward.

That same year, Ronald Reagan gave his first inaugural speech, in which he praised the "brave pioneers who tamed the empty wilderness." Still, I was surprised to hear that the wilderness was also empty for the faculty at Lowell High, a school usually considered among the top public high schools in this country.

The American History teacher asked my kids why they were so keen on the subject of Indians, leading them to mention the book I was planning to write. This in turn led to an invitation for me to speak to the class. As a result, I got some insight about the level of Indian awareness among a group of high-school kids.

The youngsters I met had never been offered one course, or even an extended segment of a course, about the Indian nations of this continent, about Indian-Anglo interactions (except for references to the Pilgrims and the Indian wars), or about contemporary Indian problems in the U.S. or elsewhere. These teenagers knew as little as I did at their age, and as little as their teacher knew at their age—or now, as he regretfully acknowledged to me. The American educational curriculum is almost

bereft of information about Indians, making it difficult for young non-Indian Americans to understand or care about present-day Indian issues. European schools actually teach more about American Indians. In Germany, for example, every child reads a set of books that sensitizes them to Indian values and causes. It is not surprising therefore, that the European press carries many more stories about American Indians than does the American press....

THE MEDIA: INDIANS ARE NON-NEWS

That the Lowell High students should know nothing about Indians is not their fault. It is one of many indicators that this country's institutions do not inform people about Indians of either present or past. Indians are non-history, which also makes them non-news. Not taught in schools, not part of American consciousness, their present-day activities and struggles are rarely reported in newspapers or on television.

On the rare occasions when the media do relate to Indians, the reports tend to follow very narrow guidelines based on pre-existing stereotypes of Indians; they become what is known in the trade as "formula stories."

My friend Dagmar Thorpe, a Sac-and-Fox Indian who, until 1990, was Executive Director of the Seventh Generation Fund, once asked a network producer known to be friendly to the Indian cause about the reasons for the lack of in-depth, accurate reporting on Indian sto-

ries. According to Dagmar, the producer gave three reasons. The first reason was guilt. It is not considered good programming to make your audience feel bad. Americans don't want to see shows that remind them of historical events that American institutions have systematically avoided discussing.

Secondly, there is the "what's-in-it-for-me?" factor. Americans in general do not see how anything to do with Indians has anything to do with them. As a culture, we are now so trained to "look out for number one" that there has been a near total loss of altruism. (Of course American life itself—so speedy and so removed from nature—makes identifying with the Indians terribly difficult; and we don't see that we might have something to learn from them.)

The third factor is that Indian demands seem preposterous to Americans. What most Indians want is simply that their land should be returned, and that treaties should be honored. Americans tend to view the treaties as "ancient," though many were made less than a century ago—more recently, for example, than many well-established laws and land deals among whites. Americans, like their government and the media, view treaties with Indian nations differently than treaties with anyone else.

In fairness to the media, there are some mitigating factors. Just like the rest of us, reporters and producers have been raised without knowledge of Indian history or Indian struggles. Perhaps most important, media people have had little personal contact with Indians, since Indians live mostly in parts of the country, and the world, where the media isn't. Indians live in non-urban regions, in the deserts and mountains and tundras that have been impacted least by Western society, at least until recently. They live in the places that we didn't want. They are not part of the mainstream and have not tried to become part.

When our society *does* extend its tentacles to make contact—usually when corporations are seeking land or minerals, or military forces are seeking control—there is little media present to observe and report on what transpires. Even in the United States, virtually all Indian struggles take place far away from media: in the central Arizona desert, in the rugged Black Hills, the mountains of the Northwest, or else on tiny Pacific islands, or in the icy vastness of the far north of Alaska. The *New York Times* has no bureau in those places; neither does CBS. Nor do they have bureaus in the Australian desert or the jungles of Brazil, Guatemala, or Borneo.

As a result, some of the most terrible assaults upon native people today never get reported. If reports do emerge, the sources are the corporate or military public relations arms of the Western intruders, which present biased perspectives.

When reporters are flown in to someplace where Indians are making news, they are usually ill prepared and unknowledgeable about the local situation. They do not speak the language and are hard pressed to grasp the Indian perception, even if they can find Indians to speak with. In addition, these reporters often grew up in that same bubble of no contact/no education/no news about Indians.

To make matters even more difficult, as I explained at length in my TV book, it is also in the nature of modern media to distort the Indian message, which is far too subtle, sensory, complex, spiritual, and ephemeral to fit the gross guidelines of mass-media reporting, which emphasizes conflict and easily grasped imagery. A reporter would have to spend a great deal of time with the Indians to understand why digging up the earth for minerals is a sacrilege, or why diverting a stream can destroy a culture, or why

cutting a forest deprives people of their religious and human rights, or why moving Indians off desert land to a wonderful new community of private homes will effectively kill them. Even if the reporter does understand, to successfully translate that understanding through the medium, and through the editors and the commercial sponsor—all of whom are looking for action—is nearly impossible.

So most reporters have little alternative but to accept official handouts, or else to patch together, from scanty reports, stories that are designed for a world predisposed to view Indian struggles as anomalies in today's technological world: formula stories, using stereotyped imagery.

PREVALENT STEREOTYPES AND FORMULAS

The dominant image of Indians in the media used to be of savages, of John Wayne leading the U.S. Cavalry against the Indians. Today the stereotype has shifted to *noble savage*, which portrays Indians as part of a once-great but now-dying culture; a culture that could talk to the trees and the animals and that protected nature. But sadly, a losing culture, which has not kept up with out dynamic times.

We see this stereotype now in many commercials. The Indian is on a horse, gazing nobly over the land he protects. Then there's a quick cut to today: to oil company workers walking alongside the hot-oil pipeline in Alaska. The company workers are there to protect against leaks and to preserve the environment for the animals. We see quick cuts of caribou and wolves, which imply that the oil company accepts the responsibility that the Indians once had.

The problem here is that the corporate sponsor is lying. It does not feel much responsibility toward nature; if it did, it would not need expensive commercials to say so, because the truth would be apparent from its behavior. More important, however, is that treating Indians this way in commercials does terrible harm to their cause. It makes Indians into conceptual relics; artifacts. Worse, they are confirmed as existing only in the past, which hurts their present efforts.

Another stereotype we see in commercials these days is the *Indian-as-guru*. A recent TV spot depicted a shaman making rain for this people. He is then hired by some corporate farmers to make rain for them. He is shown with his power objects, saying prayers, holding his hands toward the heavens. The rains come. Handshakes from the businessmen. Finally the wise old Indian is shown with a satisfied smile on his flight home via United Airlines.

Among the more insidious formula stories is the one about how Indians are always fighting each other over disputed lands. This formula fits the Western paradigm about non-industrial people's inability to govern themselves; that they live in some kind of despotism or anarchy. For example, in the Hopi-Navajo "dispute," ... the truth of the matter is that U.S. intervention in the activities and governments of both tribes eventually led to American-style puppet governments battling each other for development rights that the traditional leadership of each tribe does not want. But the historical reality of that case, and most Indian cases, is unknown to the mass media and therefore left unreported.

Another very popular formula story is the one with the headline INDIANS STAND IN THE WAY OF DEVELOPMENT, as, for example, in New Guinea or Borneo or in the Amazon Basin. These stories concern Indian resistance to roads, or dams, or the cutting of forests, and their desire for their lands to be left inviolate.

The problem with these formula stories is not that they are inaccurate—Indian peoples around the world most certainly are resisting on hundreds of fronts and do indeed stand in the way of development—but that the style of reporting carries a sense of foregone conclusion. The reporters tend to emphasize the poignancy of the situation: "stone-age" peoples fighting in vain to forestall the inevitable march of progress. In their view, it is only a matter of time before the Indians lose, and the forests *are* cut down, and the land *is* settled by outsiders. However tragic the invasion, however righteous the cause of the Indians, however illegal the acts being perpetrated against them, however admirable the Indian ways, reporters will invariably adopt the stance that the cause is lost, and that no reversal is possible. This attitude surely harms the Indians more than if the story had not been reported at all.

Finally, and perhaps most outrageous, is the *rich Indian* formula story. Despite the fact that the average per-capita income of Indians is lower than any other racial or ethnic group in the United States, and that they suffer the highest disease rates in many categories, and have the least access to health care, the press loves to focus on the rare instance where some Indian hits it big. Sometimes the story is about an oil well found on some Indian's land, or someone getting rich on bingo, but often the stories emphasize someone's corruption, e.g., Peter MacDonald, the former chairman of the Navajo Nation. This formula story has a twofold purpose: it manages to confirm the greatness of America—where *anyone* can get rich, even an Indian—and at the same time manages to confirm Indian leaders as corrupt and despotic.

A corollary to this story is how certain Indian tribes have gotten wealthy through land claims cases, as, for example, the Alaska natives via the Alaska Native Claims Settlement Act. As we will see, a little digging into the story— if reporters only would—exposes that settlement as a fraud that actually deprived the Alaska natives of land *and* money.

The press's failure to pursue and report the full picture of American Indian poverty, while splashing occasional stories about how some are hitting it big, creates a public impression that is the opposite of the truth. The situation is exacerbated when national leaders repeat the misconceptions. Ronald Reagan told the Moscow press in 1987 that there was no discrimination against Indians in this country and the proof of that was that so many Indians, like those outside Palm Springs (oil wells), have become wealthy.

INDIANS AND THE NEW AGE

While most of our society manages to avoid Indians, there is one group that does not, though its interest is very measured.

I was reminded of this recently during my first visit to a dentist in Marin County, an affluent area north of San Francisco. The dentist, a friendly, trendy young man wearing a moustache, looked as if he'd stepped out of a Michelob ad. While poking my gums, he made pleasant conversation, inquiring about my work. When he pulled his tools from my mouth, I told him I was writing about Indians, which got him very excited. "Indians! Great! I love Indians. Indians are my hobby. I have Indian posters all over the house, and Indian rugs. And hey, I've lately been taking lessons in 'tracking' from this really neat Indian guide. I've learned how to read the tiniest changes in the terrain, details I'd never even noticed before."

In this expression of enthusiasm, this young man was like thousands of other people, particularly in places like Marin or Beverly Hills, or wherever there is sufficient leisure to engage in inner explorations. Among this group, which tends to identify with the "New Age," or the "human potential movement," there has been a renaissance of awareness about Indian practices that aid inner spiritual awakening.

A typical expression of this interest may be that a well-off young professional couple will invite friends to a lawn party to meet the couple's personal Indian medicine person. The shaman will lead the guests through a series of rituals designed to awaken aspects of themselves. These events may culminate in a sweat ceremony, or even a "firewalk." There was a period in the seventies when you could scarcely show up at a friend's house without having to decide whether or not to walk on hot coals, guided by a medicine man from the South Pacific.

Those who graduate from sweat ceremonies or firewalks, as my dentist had, might proceed to the now popular "vision quests." You may feel as you read this that I am ridiculing these "human potential" explorers. Actually, I find something admirable in them. Breaking out of the strictures of our contemporary lifestyles is clearly beneficial, in my opinion, but there is also a serious problem. For although the New Age gleans the ancient wisdoms and practices, it has assiduously avoided directly engaging in the actual lives and political struggles of the millions of descendants who carry on those ancient traditions, who are still alive on the planet today, and who want to continue living in a traditional manner....

Jerry Mander is senior fellow at the Public Media Center in San Francisco and director of the Berkeley ecological think tank, the Elmwood Institute.

Index

Index

Test Your Knowledge Form

We encourage you to photocopy and use this page as a tool to assess how the articles in *Annual Editions* expand on the information in your textbook. By reflecting on the articles you will gain enhanced text information. You can also access this useful form on a product's book support Web site at *http://www.dushkin.com/online/*.

NAME: DATE:
_____

TITLE AND NUMBER OF ARTICLE:
_____

BRIEFLY STATE THE MAIN IDEA OF THIS ARTICLE:

_____

LIST THREE IMPORTANT FACTS THAT THE AUTHOR USES TO SUPPORT THE MAIN IDEA:

_____

WHAT INFORMATION OR IDEAS DISCUSSED IN THIS ARTICLE ARE ALSO DISCUSSED IN YOUR TEXTBOOK OR OTHER READINGS THAT YOU HAVE DONE? LIST THE TEXTBOOK CHAPTERS AND PAGE NUMBERS:

_____

LIST ANY EXAMPLES OF BIAS OR FAULTY REASONING THAT YOU FOUND IN THE ARTICLE:

_____

LIST ANY NEW TERMS/CONCEPTS THAT WERE DISCUSSED IN THE ARTICLE, AND WRITE A SHORT DEFINITION:

We Want Your Advice

ANNUAL EDITIONS revisions depend on two major opinion sources: one is our Advisory Board, listed in the front of this volume, which works with us in scanning the thousands of articles published in the public press each year; the other is you—the person actually using the book. Please help us and the users of the next edition by completing the prepaid article rating form on this page and returning it to us. Thank you for your help!

ANNUAL EDITIONS: Anthropology 03/04

ARTICLE RATING FORM

Here is an opportunity for you to have direct input into the next revision of this volume.
We would like you to rate each of the articles listed below, using the following scale:

1. Excellent: should definitely be retained
2. Above average: should probably be retained
3. Below average: should probably be deleted
4. Poor: should definitely be deleted

Your ratings will play a vital part in the next revision.
Please mail this prepaid form to us as soon as possible.
Thanks for your help!

RATING	ARTICLE	RATING	ARTICLE
	1. Doing Fieldwork Among the Yanomamö		36. The Price of Progress
	2. Spin-Doctoring the Yanomamö		37. A Pacific Haze: Alcohol and Drugs in Oceania
	3. Doctor, Lawyer, Indian Chief		38. A Plunge Into the Present
	4. Eating Christmas in the Kalahari		39. Underground Potlatch
	5. Battle of the Bones		40. What Americans Don't Know About Indians
	6. Language, Appearance, and Reality: Doublespeak in 1984		
	7. Why Don't You Say What You Mean?		
	8. "I Can't Even Open My Mouth"		
	9. Shakespeare in the Bush		
	10. Understanding Eskimo Science		
	11. Mystique of the Masai		
	12. Too Many Bananas, Not Enough Pineapples, and No Watermelon at All: Three Object Lessons in Living With Reciprocity		
	13. Life Without Chiefs		
	14. When Brothers Share a Wife		
	15. The Visit		
	16. Death Without Weeping		
	17. Our Babies, Ourselves		
	18. Parallel Brides		
	19. Arranging a Marriage in India		
	20. Dowry Deaths in India: 'Let Only Your Corpse Come Out of That House'		
	21. Who Needs Love! In Japan, Many Couples Don't		
	22. Society and Sex Roles		
	23. The Berdache Tradition		
	24. A Woman's Curse?		
	25. What About "Female Genital Mutilation"?		
	26. Where Fat Is a Mark of Beauty		
	27. The Initiation of a Maasai Warrior		
	28. It Takes a Village Healer		
	29. Why We Want Their Bodies Back		
	30. The Secrets of Haiti's Living Dead		
	31. Body Ritual Among the Nacirema		
	32. Baseball Magic		
	33. Why Can't People Feed Themselves?		
	34. The Arrow of Disease		
	35. "Drought Follows the Plow"		

(Continued on next page)

BUSINESS REPLY MAIL
FIRST-CLASS MAIL PERMIT NO. 84 GUILFORD CT

POSTAGE WILL BE PAID BY ADDRESSEE

McGraw-Hill/Dushkin
530 Old Whitfield Street
Guilford, Ct 06437-9989

ABOUT YOU

Name   Date

Are you a teacher? ❑   A student? ❑
Your school's name

Department

Address   City   State   Zip

School telephone #

YOUR COMMENTS ARE IMPORTANT TO US!

Please fill in the following information:
For which course did you use this book?

Did you use a text with this ANNUAL EDITION?   ❑   yes ❑   no
What was the title of the text?

What are your general reactions to the *Annual Editions* concept?

Have you read any pertinent articles recently that you think should be included in the next edition? Explain.

Are there any articles that you feel should be replaced in the next edition? Why?

Are there any World Wide Web sites that you feel should be included in the next edition? Please annotate.

May we contact you for editorial input?   ❑   yes ❑   no
May we quote your comments? ❑   yes ❑   no